BRIEF CONTENTS

PREFACE   XI

Part One: The Musical Child   1

1 The Multiple Meanings of Music for Children   2

2 From Theory to Practice in Teaching Music to Children   17

3 Methods of Teaching Music to Children   47

4 The Singing Child   71

5 Pitch and the Child   111

6 The Moving Child   128

7 Rhythm and the Child   165

8 The Playing Child   208

9 The Listening Child   239

10 The Creating Child   264

Part Two: The Facilitating Teacher   287

11 Motivation and Management   288

12 Curriculum Design   315

13 Assessment and Evaluation   340

14 Music in an Integrated Curriculum   356

15 Music, Children, and Cultural Diversity   381

16 Music for Exceptional Children   404

Appendix   431
     The School Music Program: A New Vision   431

References and Resources   439

Index   449

CONTENTS

PREFACE   XI

Part One: The Musical Child   1

1 The Multiple Meanings of Music for Children   2

Musical Learning to Engage Children   3
Music's Many Functions   3
Music at the Curricular Core   7
Children's Musical Capacities   8
Music's Historical Role in the Curriculum   10
Music for Children in a Changing Society   12
A Musical Future   13
   Review / Critical Thinking   15
   Projects   16

2 From Theory to Practice in Teaching Music to Children   17

Stage and Phase Theories   18
Social Systems and Scapes   22
Theories of Musical Play and Socialization   23
A Constructivist Theory of Meaning Making   24
Social Learning and Reinforcement Theories   26
Neuroscience and Music Learning   28
Learning Style Theories   29
Theories of Instruction   34
Relating Theory to Practice   36
   THE CLASSROOM ENVIRONMENT   37
      What Should the Music Classroom Look Like?   37
      What Should the Music Classroom Feel Like?   37

What Other Resources Can Enhance
   A Music Classroom's Potential for Effective
   Instruction?   37
What Print, Audio, Video, and Web-Based
   Materials Should a Teacher Have Available
   for Music Instruction?   37
A CHILD-CENTERED CURRICULUM   38
   Know the Children   38
   Begin Where the Children Are   38
   Allow Time for Musical Play and Exploration   38
   Integrate Music into the Other Parts of
      a Child's Life   39
THE TEACHER AS TRANSMITTER   39
   Know the Subject Matter   39
   Model the Musical Behaviors   39
   Present with Energy and Enthusiasm   39
INSTRUCTIONAL STRATEGIES   41
   Starting the Class   41
   Ending the Class   41
   Supplying Feedback: The TST   41
   Stimulating Aural Learning   42
   Providing for Repetition and Rehearsal   42
Informed Teaching   44
   Review / Critical Thinking / Projects   46

3 Methods of Teaching Music to Children   47

Dalcroze: Movement with a Mission   48
Kodály: Inner Hearing and Music Literacy   52
Orff: Expression Through Musical Experience   56
Other Approaches to Music Learning   60
   COMPREHENSIVE MUSICIANSHIP   60
   GORDON'S MUSIC LEARNING THEORY   61
   MANHATTANVILLE MUSIC CURRICULUM
      PROJECT   62

MUSIC IN EDUCATION   63
EDUCATION THROUGH MUSIC   64
WEIKERT'S MOVEMENT SEQUENCE   65
A Comparison of Methods and Techniques   66
A Personal Method   66
    Review / Critical Thinking / Projects   70

4 The Singing Child   71

The Developing Child Voice   72
Physical Training for the Child Voice   76
Toward Accurate Singing   81
The Vocal Model   87
Selecting and Teaching Songs   94
How to Teach Singing in Parts   99
Children's Choirs   105
Assessment of Singing   107
    FORMATIVE EVALUATION   108
    SUMMATIVE EVALUATION   108
Reasons to Sing   108
    Review / Critical Thinking / Projects   110

5 Pitch and the Child   111

Growth in Understanding of Linear Pitch
   Structures   112
Discrimination and Contour Awareness   113
Pitch Relations and Melodic Motion   117
Advanced Pitch Concepts   119
Growth in Understanding of Vertical Pitch
   Structures   122
Assessment   124
Helping Children to Think Musically   125
    Review / Critical Thinking / Projects   126

6 The Moving Child   128

Movement and Child Development   130
    ACTION SONGS AND SINGING GAMES   130
    EURHYTHMICS   132
    CREATIVE MOVEMENT   132
    DANCE   132
Precepts and Principles of Movement   133
Prelude to Movement-Based
   Musical Experiences   135

ACTION SONGS AND SINGING GAMES   136
Dalcroze Eurhythmics   145
Creative Movement   149
Dance   153
Assessment of Moving   159
    FORMATIVE EVALUATION   160
    SUMMATIVE EVALUATION   161
Movement for Musical Development   161
    Review / Critical Thinking / Projects   164

7 Rhythm and the Child   165

Rhythm and Child Development   166
Rhythm in Speech   168
Rhythm in Movement   172
The Pulse   174
Meter   175
Durations and Their Patterns   178
Rhythm Mnemonics   193
Notation for Writing and
   Reading Rhythms   196
Syncopations   199
Polyrhythms   201
From Natural Rhythms to Rhythmic Training:
   Rhythmicking Well!   203
    FORMATIVE ASSESSMENT   204
    SUMMATIVE ASSESSMENT   204
    Review / Critical Thinking   206
    Projects   207

8 The Playing Child   208

Developmental Sequence   209
The Body as a Percussion Instrument   211
Nonpitched Percussion Instruments   215
    GOURDS   215
     Maracas   215
    WOODS   216
     Sticks   216
     Claves   216
     Woodblock   216
     Temple Blocks   216
     Sandblocks   216

Slit Log Drum	216
Guiro	217
SKINS (DRUMS)	217
Hand Drum	217
Bongo Drums	217
Conga Drum	217
Djembe Drum	217
Goblet Drum	218
Timpani	218
METALS	218
Cymbals	218
Finger Cymbals	218
Triangle	218
Tambourine	218
Jingle Bells	218
Gong	218
Cowbell	219
Double Iron Agogo Bells	219
Pitched Instruments	221
Barred Instruments of the Orff Approach	221
THE RECORDER	226
Harmony Instruments	228
THE AUTOHARP	228
THE GUITAR	229
KEYBOARDS	231
Assessment of Playing Instruments	234
FORMATIVE EVALUATIONS	234
SUMMATIVE EVALUATIONS	235
THE BENEFITS OF INSTRUMENTAL STUDY	235
Review / Critical Thinking / Projects	237

9 The Listening Child — 239

The Centrality of Listening	239
Growth in Listening	240
THE DEVELOPMENT OF PERCEPTIVE LISTENING	240
THE DEVELOPMENT OF ATTITUDES TOWARD MUSIC	240
Active Involvement in Listening	242
PRINCIPLES IN TEACHING MUSIC LISTENING	242
LISTENING IN EARLY CHILDHOOD SETTINGS	242
BUILDING SKILLS OF AURAL PERCEPTION	245
DEEP-LISTENING	250
STUDENT CONSTRUCTION OF LISTENING EXPERIENCES	251

BUILDING AN AURAL REPERTOIRE	253
LISTENING SEQUENCE	254
Assessment of Listening	258
FORMATIVE EVALUATIONS	258
SUMMATIVE EVALUATIONS	261
Keys to Listening	261
Review	262
Critical Thinking / Projects	263

10 The Creating Child — 264

The Importance of Creativity	264
Developmental Sequence	265
Creative Thinking	265
Creative Processes	266
EXPLORATION AND DISCOVERY	266
IMPROVISATION	268
COMPOSITION	271
Structure and Context	271
Aural Plans	274
Notational Systems	275
Inventing Songs	277
Individualized Plan	280
Assessment	282
FORMATIVE EVALUATIONS	282
SUMMATIVE EVALUATIONS	283
The Rewards of Nurturing Creativity in Music	283
Review / Critical Thinking / Projects	285

Part Two: The Facilitating Teacher — 287

11 Motivation and Management — 288

What Is Motivation and Where Does It Come From? A Short Review of Education Psychology	290
THREE SOURCES OF MOTIVATION	290
DRIVE REDUCTION THEORY OF MOTIVATION	292
BEHAVIORISM: OPERANT CONDITIONING	292
COMPETITION AS A MOTIVATOR	294
Foundations of Understanding and Managing Student Behaviors	295
UNDERSTANDING THE ROLE OF PERSONAL TRAITS AND THE EDUCATIONAL ENVIRONMENT	295
UNDERSTANDING SELF AND OTHERS THROUGH ENNEAGRAMS	295

UNDERSTANDING SELF AND OTHERS
    THROUGH TRANSACTIONAL ANALYSIS   295
LOGICAL CONSEQUENCES   298

Setting Up Your Classroom to Nurture Positive
Social and Academic Learning   299

ORGANIZING CLASSES INTO COOPERATIVE
    LEARNING GROUPS   299
ORGANIZING THE CLASSROOM AND
    RECORD KEEPING   300
LEARNING AND REMEMBERING STUDENTS'
    NAMES   301
GUIDELINES FOR MOTIVATING AND
    MANAGING STUDENTS   302
TOKEN PRIZES   302
SPECIAL PERSON   303
OTHER EXTERNAL MOTIVATORS   304

Strategies for Confronting Inappropriate
Behavior   304

ESTABLISHING EXPECTATIONS AND
    PROCEDURES   305
JUDICIOUS DISCIPLINE   307
DISCIPLINE WITH LOVE AND LOGIC   308
BEHAVIOR EXPECTATION FORMS   308
BEHAVIOR CONTRACTS   308
THE INTERVENTION THERMOMETER   310
    Review / Critical Thinking / Projects   313

12 Curriculum Design   315

Program Vignettes   315
The Nature of Curriculum   316
Types and Sources of Curriculum   317

NATIONAL STANDARDS   317
STATE AND LOCAL STANDARDS   318
OTHER SOURCES OF CURRICULUM   318

Planning a Curriculum   319

GENERAL CURRICULUM CONTENT   319
EARLY CHILDHOOD PLANNING   322
K–6 PLANNING   322

Implementing a Curriculum   325

LESSON PLANNING   325
    The Three-Legged Model   326
    The Problem-Solving Approach   328
    The Quadrant Approach   329
    The Immersed Approach   331
THEMATIC AND UNIT PLANNING   333
    Curriculum Connections   334
    Topics Within Music   335

Distilling the Essence of Curriculum   337
    Review / Critical Thinking / Projects   338

13 Assessment and Evaluation   340

Evaluation   340

FORMATIVE AND SUMMATIVE EVALUATION   341
TEACHER EVALUATION   342

Testing and Measurement   342
Assessment   343

TEACHER ASSESSMENT OF CHILDREN   343
    Overt and Covert Behaviors   344
    Questioning   345
    Rubrics   346
STUDENT SELF-ASSESSMENT   348
PEER ASSESSMENT   348
TEACHER SELF-ASSESSMENT   349

Tracking Student Growth   350

RECORD KEEPING   350
PORTFOLIOS   351

Reporting to Parents   352
Distilling the Essence of Assessment
    and Evaluation   353
    Review / Critical Thinking / Projects   355

**14 Music in an Integrated
Curriculum**   356

Vignettes of Artistically Rich Music Classrooms   356
The Invitation to Arts Integration   358
The Challenges of Arts Integration   359
Integrating Other Arts into the
    Music Curriculum   360

INTERDISCIPLINARY CURRICULUM IN
    THE ARTS   362
SHARED CURRICULUM IN THE ARTS   363
    Creative Movement and Dance   363
    Visual Arts   364
    Literature and Poetry   366
    Creative Drama and Theater   367

Models of Integration   368

THE THEMATIC WEB DESIGN   368
THE THREADED CURRICULUM   369
THE IMMERSED CURRICULUM   370

Creating Valid Connections 370

INTEGRATING THE ARTS PROCESS 371
THE ARTS IN SOCIAL STUDIES 372
THE ARTS IN SCIENCE AND MATH 375
THE ARTS AND LANGUAGE ARTS 376
Assessing 378
Reflections on the Integrated Curriculum 378
Review / Critical Thinking / Projects 380

15 Music, Children, and Cultural Diversity 381

Definitions 382
Uncertainties in Teaching New Musical Styles 385
The Musically Competent Teacher 386
New Repertoire for Familiar Pedagogies 388
The Aural-Oral Transmission Process 392
Curricular Redesign 394
Many Musical Worlds 401
Review / Critical Thinking / Projects 403

16 Music for Exceptional Children 404

Who Are Exceptional Children? 405

PUBLIC LAWS 406
PERSON FIRST LANGUAGE 406
CHILDREN AT RISK 407
Educating Exceptional Children 407
Inclusion and the Music Classroom 408

IEP in Music 409
Inclusion in Music Instruction 411
The Music Classroom and Exceptional Children 411

INTELLECTUAL AND DEVELOPMENTAL DISABILITIES 412
SPECIFIC LEARNING DISABILITIES 414
ATTENTION DEFICIT HYPERACTIVITY DISORDER (ADHD) 416
EMOTIONAL OR BEHAVIORAL DISORDERS 418
AUTISM SPECTRUM DISORDERS 419
SENSORY DISORDERS 420
Hearing Impairments 420
Vision Impaired 422
PHYSICAL DISABILITIES 422
Adapting for Movement 423
Adapting Instruments and Materials 424
ENGLISH LANGUAGE LEARNERS (ELL) 425
GIFTED AND TALENTED 426
The Joys of Reaching All Children 427
Review 428
Critical Thinking / Projects 429

Appendix 431
The School Music Program: A New Vision 431

References and Resources 439

Index 449

PREFACE

OF ALL THE beautiful things in this world, few surpass the images of music in childhood. Our own earliest memories are rich with music: soft lullabies on a parent's lap; patty-cake rhymes in the nursery; parade music played by brass bands; seasonal songs at the dinner table, at the piano, or around the campfire; chants for jumping rope and clapping hands; and the music played with friends on homemade instruments. Music played a prominent role in our childhood then, as it still does for children today.

Music emerges magically from children, as they search for and find ways to represent their world. Intuitively and naturally, young children respond to music as they communicate through it. Music is part of their process of enculturation, of their acquisition of cultural values and behaviors. They develop as members of their family, their neighborhood community, and their religious and ethnic groups through music. Parents are the first music teachers, transmitting to children the songs they remember and filling their children's ears with the music they love. Children learn a musical system—its tuning, timbres, predominant pitch and rhythmic patterns, textures, and formal structures—as surely as they learn other aspects of their family and then their community cultures. They are socialized into these groups through music and are deeply rooted in this first musical system early in childhood.

As children begin their formal schooling, in preschool or in kindergarten, they are ready to begin their formal musical education as well. With their intuitive learning embedded, children can develop musical literacy and the conceptual understanding of music as one among many disciplines featured within a school curriculum. The musical competence to sing in tune and step in time, to listen perceptively, to perform from notation, and to create a personal music that is as musically logical as it is expressive are all skills taught in a music curriculum. Unlike intuitive musical responses, however, these competencies do not appear magically. They are the outcomes of a musical education, with an expert musician-teacher as guide. If children are to become competent and even masterful musicians, a formal musical education is necessary.

Music teachers continue the musical development that began with children's early enculturation. They are the principal players in the spiraling development of children's listening, performance, literacy, and creative expressive skills. Music teachers are the catalysts that stimulate children's musical intelligence and the guides to the pathways through which children can channel their ideas. Music teachers tap the beauty that is within children.

The benefits of a musical education are many. Musically trained children are able to add layer upon layer of musical knowledge to their earliest experiences. This early training can inspire children to continue musical activities into their adult years: singing a Bach chorale after supper; reading recorder music with friends on a Sunday afternoon; becoming wholly engaged while listening to the sounds of a Beethoven sonata or, Turkish makam, a jazz session; folk dancing in time and in a musical way to the tunes of a string band; creating spontaneous harmonies vocally or on an instrument; and composing music for personal expression or to share with others. These are the sophisticated behaviors of musically educated people who were brought beyond the playful musical experiences of their childhood by teachers who taught them repertoire and notational literacy and who developed the skills for performing, responding to, and creating music. When people mature musically, and when they maintain musical interactions that remain meaningful to them as adults, the benefits of a musical education are apparent. The beauty of music in childhood becomes more than mere memory: It is the seed that takes root and is nourished through training.

A commitment to raising more musical children requires information. We trust that the information we have provided within these pages can be translated from words to actions both by teachers who are musicians and by musicians who are teachers. With an accumulated one-hundred and twenty years of teaching music to children, teachers, and teachers-to-be between us, we offer ideas garnered from our experiences that have been evaluated, revised, and tested again, in many settings, with many students. The commitment we have to a substantive and meaningful musical education for all children is both the impetus and the desired outcome of the volume.

While we have made choices in the selection of materials and methods that fill the pages of this book, we also recognize that for information to be truly relevant, it will take the user's personal exploration and evaluation of suggested ideas to make them relevant and real. We open the chapters with a stream of questions as "Things to Think About," and we close chapters with recommendations for converting philosophical principles to action and shifting activities into points of reflection. While the book may at first appear as a daunting compilation of "everything one needs to know about music and children," it is only preparatory to the realities of children and classrooms (or perhaps interim reading for the more experienced teachers who may wish further resources and instructional advisories). We uphold and applaud the thoughtful and inventive ways of good teachers, and know full well that these pages will prove useful launches to the teachers' own selection of ideas on teaching music to children.

The following chapters delineate music and instructional approaches suited to the perceptual-cognitive, physical, and affective development of children in early and middle childhood. The various ways in which children manifest their musicality form the basis of a number of chapters: "Rhythm and the Child," "Pitch and the Child," "The Singing Child," "The Listening Child," "The Moving Child," "The Playing Child," and "The Creating Child." We have noted the natural and incipient musical behaviors associated with child development, and they become the backdrop to recommendations for teacher-informed musical experiences and educational sequences.

We have attempted to present music as a developmental process in the intellectual and affective lives of children, one that is accelerated, enriched, and deepened through the guidance of the expert musician-teacher. We offer a sampling of musical experiences that can be presented by teachers to children in graduated fashion and in increasingly complex matrices that continue to challenge preschool and school-age children through the sixth grade. We will discuss how to

- structure a classroom for maximum learning
- preserve children's natural motivation for experiencing and knowing music
- plan lessons and long-term goals
- measure, grade, and report musical competencies of children to them, their parents, and administrators

We present models, samples, and graphs to illustrate techniques and systematic methods for teaching musical concepts and for developing musical skills in children. Scenarios, Review questions, Critical Thinking questions, and Projects are found at the conclusion of each chapter, for purposes of reviewing, extending, and putting into practice the information given. References appear at the end of the book.

In addition to practical information, we provide the conceptual frameworks that initiate and stimulate thinking on issues of music, teaching, and children. We have not intended this as a collection of recipe-like lessons, although examples of partial and complete lessons can be found scattered throughout the book. Instead, we present a broad array of concept-associated musical experiences in each chapter as the best way for teachers to develop lessons for children. We believe that successful lessons can spring from either the selection of a concept, embedded in a song or musical piece, which is then reinforced and expanded through a variety of instructional strategies or from providing children with a challenge and a context to solve musical problems appropriate to their developmental stage. The full flowering of a lesson is best left to the perceptive and imaginative teacher, who can match the musical concept, repertoire, and teaching and learning strategies to the classroom context with a thorough knowledge of what children are capable of doing and understanding.

Chapter 3 addresses method—the classic techniques and systems of Dalcroze, Kodály, and Orff; the recently emerging pedagogies; and the personal methods that evolve through experience. We believe that teachers will combine techniques from various philosophies to develop a personal pedagogy that suits them, their students, and the instructional content.

At a time of cultural diversity informed by the need for social justice, we have attempted to thread its themes throughout the book, while concentrating on curricular trends and issues in Chapter 15. Likewise, while we believe that each child is individual and special in his or her approach to the musical experience, and have maintained this position as central to the volume, Chapter 16 presents perspectives relevant to children who may have challenges in learning music and who require a teacher's sensitivity to meet special needs.

There is much that's new in this fourth edition. Every chapter is updated with contemporary ideas on musical content and method. There are new model lessons, illustrations of experiences in conceptual understanding, exercises for skill development. Featured in many of the chapters are suggestions for the integration of ideas for adapting instruction for children with various needs, and recommendations for the meeting of the national standards in music. Over one hundred songs, chants, and rhythms (including many new songs) have been integrated through the pages of the book, and for which recordings are available. Ideas on the use of technology in the classroom are available online at the text's Premium Website, with additional links to important technological resources that will enhance both teaching and learning. The text's Premium Website is a unique, password-protected website that provides material that will supplement your Music Education course, including video segments featuring students and teachers in classroom settings and audio tracks for many of the pieces discussed within the text.

Along with the developmental approach and contemporary issues we have emphasized, we hope that the reader senses the joy, the musical stimulation, and the intellectual challenge that come from teaching music to children. We have known these sensations often, and we are restored and invigorated by them. *Music in Childhood* provides a channel for teachers to develop musically and pedagogically in ways relevant to children's growth from musical intuition to musical mastery. The ultimate result of its reading—and application—may be a more musical world, through the bonding of children, music, and teachers.

Acknowledgments

We wish to thank our mentors and colleagues who have stimulated our thinking and encouraged our growth as musicians and teachers, our students who have helped to shape our ideas even as they work with them and who bring fresh perspectives to the realm of music for children, and the children themselves, who have given much more than they know to the sharpening of our understanding of human musical development and its nurturance through instruction. Thanks to Rita Klinger and Patti Casey for their tuneful suggestions (and many late-night talks on music, children, and schooling in general); Karen Howard and Matt Swanson for their very musical renditions of children's traditional songs; Dalcroze teachers Anne Farber, Herb Henke, Annabelle Joseph, Virginia Mead, Lisa Parker, Marta Sanchez, and Julia Schnebly-Black, whose ideas have "begotten" some of our ideas; Barbara Lundquist for her continuing influence on our thinking of music alongside culture; James Carlsen for his expertise in musical thinking and growth; and Shirley McRae, Jean Sinor, and Sandra Stauffer for their insightful comments along the way. We also thank Nadine Santo Pietro at Echo Lake Elementary in the Shoreline Schools. Thanks to Jerry Gay for his photographs as well as to Jo Daly and the teachers at the B. F. Day School in Seattle, and to Ann Palmason and teachers at the Bush School of Seattle—and their children—for helping us to fill our book with images of joyous music making. We also thank Kelly Foster Griffin, Bethel Santos, and the students at Moorlands Elementary School in Kenmore, WA; Christopher Roberts, Rick Boyle, and the students at St. Joseph School in Seattle; Deborah Stone, Bob Jones, and the students at Shelton View Elementary School in Bothell, WA; Patty Bourne and the students at Canyon Park Elementary School in Bothell, WA; Patti Casey and the students at Oak Heights Elementary School in Edmonds WA for helping us to provide our readers with video footage from elementary music classrooms for the MindTap. We are enormously grateful to Kirk Kassner for writing Chapter 11 ("Motivation and Management") and the various sections throughout the text and on the MindTap on integrating technology within the classroom. His varied experiences as a classroom music teacher offer a world of suggestions on motivating children to learn (and managing a classroom setting that is conducive to learning), and his wealth of knowledge of technology spans the continuum from the highly theoretical issues relevant to instruction to the details of technological systems and the most feasible and user-friendly classroom applications. Further, he has directed the production of the recordings that accompany this volume, and the children of Panther Lake Elementary on the recording, and arrangements of his own making contribute immeasurably to this fourth edition effort. Kirk's continuous stream of on-the-ground and in-the-field suggestions and his ever-present good humor have been invaluable. Thanks also to Charlie Campbell for his patience with the late-night madness of our networking sessions to put into print what we truly believe. We would also like to thank the following reviewers for the valuable feedback on the writing of this text and the development of this edition:

Sarah Bartolome, Louisiana State University

Melissa Berke, University of Nebraska at Omaha

Abby Butler, Wayne State University

Marian Dura, Lebanon Valley College

Bill Fordice, Luther College

David Gonzol, Shepherd University

Lisa Gruenhagen, Bowling Green State University

Janette Harriott, University of Nebraska, Kearney

Kathryn Marsh, University of Sydney

June Miller, Trinity Christian College

Diane Persellin, Trinity University

Sheila Woodward, Eastern Washington University

About the Authors

PATRICIA SHEHAN CAMPBELL is Donald E. Peterson Professor of Music at the University of Washington. She is a certified teacher of the Dalcroze eurhythmics and has lectured and published widely on music, children, and pedagogy. Author of *Songs in Their Heads, Teaching Music Globally, Musician and Teacher, Tunes and Grooves in Music Education*, and *Lessons from the World*, she is also coeditor of the *Global Music Series* and the *Oxford Handbook of Children's Musical Cultures*. Her work in world music pedagogy keeps her active in the curricular development of source recordings from the archives of Smithsonian Folkways and the Alan Lomax Association for Cultural Equity.

CAROL SCOTT-KASSNER is a writer and consultant in music education and former professor of music education. An expert in the musical growth of young children, she has written and spoken extensively on that topic. Carol was cofounder and chair of the Early Childhood Commission of the International Society of Music Education and chaired both the Society for Research in Music Education and the Society for General Music in MENC. She is coauthor of three textbook series by Silver Burdett Ginn and has contributed chapters in both editions of the *Handbook of Research in Music Teaching and Learning*. Carol currently works as a spiritual director and in the field of the spirituality of aging.

PART 1

The Musical Child

WELCOME TO THE MUSICAL world of children and to their various musically expressive ways of being. They are singers, players, dancers, listeners, and creators, developing from infancy and toddlerhood into their preschool and full-fledged elementary school experiences, all the while growing in their music-making capacities. They are filling out their musical potential alone, together, within families, and among friends, and under the careful watch of skilled teachers with musical knowledge and training. Children are naturally musical, but features of pitch and rhythm, of what their voices and bodies can do, and of how to think in more fully developed musical ways are revealed to them through a rich program of instruction designed and delivered to them on a regular basis.

Each of the chapters in Part One, The Musical Child, brings you more greatly in touch with children's music, their musically evolving selves, and the ways and means by which a musical education can stretch them to their maximal capacity as young performers, composers and improvisers, and musical thinkers. Both classic and contemporary scholarship direct the discourse on developmentally appropriate strategies for raising musical children from their earliest ages to the onset of adolescence and lead the way to recommendations for effective education in and through music.

The Multiple Meanings of Music for Children

IN THIS CHAPTER

- Musical Learning to Engage Children
- Music's Many Functions
- Music at the Curricular Core
- Children's Musical Capacities
- Music's Historical Role in the Curriculum
- Music for Children in a Changing Society
- A Musical Future

"I like music. I can't explain it: Sometimes it makes me happy, sometimes sad, but all the times it's there like a friend, and I need it."

—FIRST-GRADE CHILD

"I want my child to know what I never was privileged to learn, and that includes learning how to sing, dance, and draw artistically."

—PARENT OF SECOND-GRADE CHILD

"I've found enjoyable ways to achieve the curricular goals of literacy and numeracy through music, from chanting rhymes and singing songs to counting rhythms and moving in geometric patterns across the floor."

—THIRD-GRADE TEACHER

"I enjoyed the winter concert, and am especially impressed with how, as they sang and played, music seemed to bring a coalescence to a crowd of what I know to be some pretty ornery and unsettled kids."

—PARENT OF FOURTH-GRADE CHILD

"You should see what's happened to kids' interests since we added music to our classes on American history and culture. Overnight success!"

—FIFTH-GRADE TEACHER

"I think I might be making as important an impact in the musical world teaching kids to sing and play and read music, maybe as much as I might have as a world-class concert pianist. Who knows what musical minds I may tap?"

—ELEMENTARY SCHOOL MUSIC TEACHER

"Schools are reconsidering earlier educational plans that underscored the basics: We now see that guiding children's holistic development, to include experiences in the expressive arts of language, music, and the visual arts, is basic to their more complete and evolving intellectual, emotional, and physical well-being."

—ELEMENTARY SCHOOL PRINCIPAL

"I don't know everything about music yet, but I guess it just grabs me the right way."

—SIXTH-GRADE CHILD

THINGS TO THINK ABOUT

- How do you use music in your life?

- What musical activities and interests did you have as a child?

- Have you observed children at musical play?

- Are there some musical skills that you feel you can teach more easily to children than others?

- What do you think all children should be able to do, musically, as a result of a musical education?

Musical Learning to Engage Children

MUSIC IS IMPORTANT TO children. Some wish to listen to it alone through headphones, while others are inclined to sing, hum, whistle, or chant it. Some want to play it on a musical instrument—solo or with friends. Others enjoy dancing to it, and thus music gives rise to physical responses. Some wish to create "brand new music" and poems, plays, and dances to go with it. Whether listening, singing, playing, moving, or creating music, musical experiences are prominent in the lives of children. They, themselves, as well as their spokespersons—parents, guardians, and teachers—attest to this fact (Campbell, 2010).

Music's Many Functions

Music's powerful role offers compelling reasons for its inclusion in the schools. The numerous ways in which children engage in music underscore its appeal for them and highlight the many dimensions of their beings that can be met by the musical experiences they have. Given that music is embraced by people everywhere for its unique qualities, to deny it a solid place in curricular studies would be a terrible mistake. Music is too powerful to be excluded from children's lives, whether in school or out.

The uses of music by children (and adults) of all ages and cultures are evidence of its staying power. Music has maintained its prominence among people over time and distance. Anthropologist Alan P. Merriam (1964) presented what has become a classic outline of music's many functions across cultures. These functions are relevant to children's own musical involvement—within their culture, their world—for a number of reasons.

With Laughter and Singing (Germany)

1. Sing the song for the children, asking for responses to these questions:

   • Can you keep a steady pulse while listening to the song?

   • What is the song about? What makes it sound so cheerful?

   • Which phrase contains the highest pitches?

2. Sing the song through multiple times, inviting children to join in as they can.

3. "Draw" the rise and fall of the melody in the air, on the board, or on paper.

4. Sing the song on "loo," but sing the tonic home tone on "do."

5. Conduct the song in twos (down on "1," up on "2") while singing.

6. Sing the song while stepping the pulse. At a slower speed, pat (and then step) the rhythm of the melody.

7. Dance the song in a circle. Holding hands, step "1-2-3-4" to the right (phrase 1), step "1-2-3-4" to the left (phrase 2), step "1-2-3-4" to the middle (phase 3), arms raised.

8. Sing the song as a three-part round.

9. Create an instrumental accompaniment, with emphasis on the tonic and dominant pitches within bourdons and repeated ostinato patterns.

10. Sing, dance, and play the song in performance for others (another class, members of the staff, parents).

Alabama Gal (United States, African American)

3. I showed you how, how, *(3 times)*
   Alabama Gal.

4. Ain't I rock candy, *(3 times)*
   Alabama Gal.

1. Sing the song for the children, asking for responses to these questions:

   - Can you pat the strong beat and clap the weak beat? Pat (1) Clap (2)
   - Listen to this melody (m-s-m-r-d). What words are sung on this phrase?
   - What do you think this song is about?

2. Sing the song through multiple times, inviting children to join in as they can.

3. "Draw" the rise and fall of the melody in the air, on the board, or on paper.

4. Sing the song on "loo," but sing the tonic home tone on "do."

5. Conduct the song in twos (down on "1," up on "2") while singing.

6. Sing the song while stepping the pulse. At a slower speed, clap the rhythm of the melody while stepping the pulse.

7. Form a circle, face center, hold hands, and step the pulse to the right while singing the song. Play the singing game, in which a center-circle person is selected who tries to leave the circle through a "'weak link"—a window of possible passage formed by the held hands of two side-by-side players. If the center-circle person passes through, then both players join in the center-circle to try their skill in passing under a window. This continues until the circle becomes too small to accommodate center-circle players, and then the game starts over. (Note: there can only be one window-passing action per verse.)

8. Create a harmonic instrumental accompaniment on xylophones and metal-lophones, in which all pitches of the pentatonic scale are fair game. Rules may include these: "Play just on the strong beat (once every two beats)" or "Play on every strong and weak beat (every 1-2 beats, of every measure)" and "Choose two pitches of the pentaton and play them alternately (such as "g" and "b")" or "Choose to play any and all pitches of the pentaton in the same order (such as "d," "e," "g," "a," "b")."

9. Play the melody on recorders, keyboards, or other melody instruments. Add in the harmonic accompaniment. Then, switch between instruments and voices as melody-carriers to the instrumental harmonies.

1. *Emotional expression*: The releasing of emotions and the expression of feelings. Children may release sadness in their singing or joy in their dancing.

2. *Aesthetic enjoyment*: The use of music for deep emotional and intellectual enjoyment, for experiencing artistic and nonverbal expressions of life's beauty. The music that children listen to or perform touches them in profound ways that are not easily expressed through the words they know.

3. *Entertainment*: The use of music as diversion and amusement. Children enjoy the musical diversions presented by the media, from the current pop genres to the background music for videos, films, and television shows. Media music is effortless "easy listening" for them and greatly entertaining.

4. *Communication*: The conveying of feelings and emotions that are understood by people within a particular culture. Children receive and can be led to the musical expression of ideas and feelings in styles that are meaningful to them within their family, community, and societal cultures.

5. *Symbolic representation*: The expression of symbols exists in the texts of songs and in the cultural meaning of the musical sounds. Overlapping the communication function, children find the sounds of certain musical modes and meters more meaningful than others through their conditioning within the musical cultures of their families, communities, and society at large.

6. *Physical response*: The use of music for dancing and other physical activity. Children are greatly affected in physical ways by the music they hear or perform and may be drawn to dance, hop, skip, or sway to the sounds. They may also be soothed to sleep by the qualities of sedative music.

7. *Enforcement of conformity to social norms*: The use of music to provide instructions or warnings. Children, especially young children, are often taught the rules of social etiquette by adults (say "please" and "thank you," wash your hands before meals) through chanted rhymes and songs.

8. *Validation of social institutions and religious rituals*: The use of music in religious services and state occasions. Children frequently build music into the rituals of their play, including chants and songs to accompany games or to select team members ("eeny meeny miney mo"). They also validate their civic and religious affiliations through the patriotic, sacred, and seasonal songs they sing.

9. *Contribution to the continuity and stability of culture*: Music as an expression of cultural values. Few other cultural elements are such complete vehicles for the transmission of history, literature, and social mores as is music, offering children an understanding of the long life and stability of their culture.

10. *Contribution to the integration of society*: The use of music to bring people together. Children are socialized through music and recognize their membership within a group through music that is shared among its members. For example, singing games increase children's integration within a group, just as a school song offers children a common bond with other children.

Music is a human phenomenon, with its uses by children as widespread as they are for adults. Music is much more than an addendum in the lives of children. It is part and parcel of their development as individuals and as members of social groups of family, neighbors, and friends. While it exists "for its own sake" (as in the aesthetic principle of "art for art's sake"), music also functions as a vehicle for teaching children ways of living their lives according to the fundamental values of a culture. Countless communities of people hold music in high esteem for its functional life-guiding and life-giving properties. If music is thus understood to be at the core of human thought and behavior in so many communities, then it logically follows that it must be placed at the core of learning provided for children in the schools. Musical training can supply components critical to children's holistic development, including their intellectual, emotional, physical, and spiritual selves.

Music at the Curricular Core

In recent years, considerable attention has been given to identifying subjects as part of an "elite core" of "basic knowledge" to be mastered by all children. Music and the arts have been marginalized by many in American schools and society, and they are viewed as less central for development than linguistic and mathematical knowledge and skills. As articulated by Arne Duncan (2010), however, the arts play an important role in a basic and balanced education for children and youth: "The arts can help students become tenacious, team-oriented problem-solvers who are confident and able to think creatively." Moreover, a basic curriculum would seem to encompass a musical education, in which consequential ideas, experiences, and traditions common to all within a civil society could be studied and experienced. John Goodlad (2004) postulated that school programs be about the development of *civitas*, or human goodness, where a set of common human principles and values could be agreed upon by teachers and brought thoroughly into children's daily lives. Communities rely on schools as institutions that can inculcate desired moral and social behaviors, provide training in civility, and provide fundamental understanding as well as the capacity to reason, interpret, and transfer ideas and processes, thereby facilitating the independent acquisition of new knowledge (Gardner, 2000, 2007). Music is basic because it is a critical component of American and international societies as well as a repository of historical traditions and contemporary ideas.

Furthermore, music is a comprehensive subject for study. Music is a means of knowing, through perceptive listening, performance, and the creative processes of composition and improvisation, the "self" and the "other"—the world and its component parts. Samuel Hope, former director of the National Association of Schools of Music, observed that "the intellectual functions of art, science, history, and philosophy come together with the knowledge, skills, subject matters and purposes of dance, music, theatre and the visual arts" (2000, p. 83). The major modes of human thought and action are experienced through inquiry in these disciplines, including music.

Music deserves a rightful place at the core of a preschool through elementary school curriculum. All children have equal rights to knowledge of their cultural heritage, including music; to the development of their aural, artistic, expressive, and musical sensibilities; and to familiarity with music beyond the commercially available and currently popular. *What Every Young American Should Know and Be Able to Do in the Arts: National Standards for Arts Education* (MENC, 1994) stipulated that children should know and be able through training to communicate through the arts, develop and present basic analyses of works of art, and have an informed acquaintance with exemplary works of art from a variety of cultures and historical periods. These standards permeate the practices of music teachers, and curriculum has been carefully crafted to meet the challenges of these standards and benchmarks (Reimer, 2000; Lindeman, 2003). In considering what a curriculum should contain, music and the arts at large provide avenues of artistic, personal, and communal expression that all children deserve and which cannot be found in study of other curricular subjects.

Estelle Jorgensen called for an awareness of the persistent connection between education and culture, and of music as a means of socializing children into the sensibilities of the culture, of enculturating them into the social mores and values of a group of people (1997). Furthering this stance, she advocated that education at large and music education in particular be directed at preparing the young to grow into their roles as informed and compassionate citizens of the world (2003). Schools that seek to enrich children's lives through knowledge and skill development cannot afford to relegate music to the curricular periphery but should instead place music alongside language arts, mathematics, and other basic subjects.

Children's Musical Capacities

All children are musical. Anthropologist John Blacking observed the musical nature of children of the Venda people of South Africa and then developed his position on the musical capacities of all children. He observed that music is innately there for children in the body, waiting to be brought out and developed (1995) by those who can facilitate their musical development. Cognitive psychologist Howard Gardner (1983, 2004) suggested in his theory of multiple intelligences that, while children may demonstrate greater strength in one of the seven intelligences, all children possess musical abilities that can be nurtured through instruction. Christopher Small (1998), a sociologist concerned with the manner in which humans participate in the musical process, coined the term "musicking" to embrace children and adults in the acts of singing, playing, and moving to music, noting that all are capable of more than some societies allow.

In various forms and degrees, children possess the capacity to become more musical than they may currently demonstrate. Children quite naturally listen, sing, dance, play, and express themselves musically, with little or no previous training. When learning experiences are tailored to develop their musical abilities, the complete musicians inside them begin to emerge. Certainly, because differences exist in children's individual

One-year-old child in music class

Patricia Shehan Campbell

8

interests and aptitudes, some variance is evident among children regarding the extent to which a particular musical intelligence, or specific musical talent, can be developed. Some may prefer to sing rather than to play, and some may be driven toward creating original musical expressions.

Children are capable of careful and attentive listening, so they are able to perceive and understand the musical language they will create or re-create. Some children will need greater help in focusing their listening and may require the removal of aural and visual distracters so that they might tune in to the components of a song or musical work. Through directed listening, children will learn a vocabulary of recurring melodic and rhythmic phrases that represent a given musical style or culture and that may reappear in music they perform or in their original improvisations and compositions. Because most children possess the physical capability to hear sounds, they can then be led to listening intelligently to the manner in which these sounds are organized as music.

Nearly all children possess the ability to sing accurately in tune, although vocal qualities may vary slightly from lighter to darker, whispery-soft to fuller in tone, and with minor differences in range. Good singers develop through frequent listening and then by replicating the sound of the singing model. Even the more powerful and resonant young singers are likely to have developed their abilities through practice, singing regularly because they enjoy it. Adults who sing regularly, in tune, for and with children, make ideal models for emulation. The capacity to sing sweetly in tune is well within the reach of children, awaiting discovery and development.

Children can respond to music through movement in controlled and expressive ways. The following of the musical pulse is just one of the initial milestones in movement development; this skill is directly related to attentive listening. Movement can demonstrate the extent to which children are focused on rhythmic durations and patterns, the rising and falling contours of melodies, or the different phrases in a musical composition. While children may need to be taught gestures, steps, and sequences, nothing can replace their careful listening so that the movement—or the dance—will be musically rendered.

Musical performance on an instrument is viewed by some as a more sophisticated musical activity than other modes of musical skills, and thus it may be deemed to suit only those who show great musical talent. However, all children who are good listeners, and who have the interest and discipline to take daily time to build both physical and musical skills, will make good players. Children may begin with musical toys in their earliest years, progress to nonpitched percussion instruments, and then to xylophones, recorders, and keyboards. String, wind, and brass instruments of the orchestral and band variety are likely to be introduced to children in the intermediate grades. Given strong musical experiences in their early years, all children are thus capable of further musical growth through instrumental study.

Children are refreshingly creative when given the chance. With guidance, they can project both logic and expressiveness in their musical inventions, improvisations, and compositions. Their musical expressions are influenced by the music they know, and the choices they make as musical creators are greatly expanded through their listening experiences. Given opportunities to create, some children may require frameworks. Pitch, rhythm, and even the length of the work are some of the "game rules" they may need to guide their musical inventions. Children may also look to adults for inspiration, as well as to stories, poems, photographs, or illustrations. However, children primarily come to realize their musical creativity through an understanding of musical structure and how the components of music have been manipulated by other composers or performers before them. This understanding is attained best through instruction.

> "There is never a single, culturally dominant conception of music; rather, we see a whole spectrum of conceptions."
> Jean-Jacques Nattiez, 1990

Clearly, if all children are inherently musical, then musical training should not be reserved for the hypothetical talented few. The myth that few children are musically endowed is a dangerous one that threatens the right of all to a musical education, and it may even endanger a musical culture. The work of Charles Keil and Steven Feld (1994) cries out for recognition of the human attraction to involvement in music as an integrative mind-body experience and as a means for communicating in ways that only the human species can. "Children are born with the sensory means for dancing and drumming, for singing and deep-listening potential, and they need only be nurtured to develop their sensibilities to their maximal capacity." (Keil and Campbell, 2017.)

Music's Historical Role in the Curriculum

Since the earliest conceptions of schools and schooling in the Western world, music has been considered a basic subject. The ancient Greek philosophers, and later the Romans, claimed music and the arts to be key to children's moral development. Through the centuries, Europeans regarded the study of music as part science, in its theoretical analysis, and part art, in its performance practice. Musical training was considered one of the high marks of refinement in the Middle Ages, from the twelfth through the fifteenth centuries. A musical education was central to those seeking to fulfill humanistic goals or striving to become "Renaissance men" (and women). Journal accounts document the significance of vocal and instrumental instruction for children not only of the nobility but also of the rising middle class. By the time of the Enlightenment in the eighteenth century, the artistic-expressive needs of children were as likely to be addressed through schooling as their intellectual-logical needs were. Music instruction was more than window dressing in European schools; it was viewed as basic to the education of all children.

Formalized musical training in the United States began with the establishment of singing schools in the late seventeenth and eighteenth centuries. People in towns and rural or frontier settlements were visited for a week or two at a time by singing masters who offered instruction in singing and note-reading. At the close of the day's labors, adults and children would gather to be instructed in the use of tunebooks, which featured notational exercises and hymns. Communities were well served by singing schools, and the congregational singing at church services greatly improved as a result.

Music was included in the curricular programs of private academies in colonial America, and music of the Baroque (ca. 1600–1750) and then of the Viennese Classical (ca. 1750–1820) periods was spread through the efforts of European-trained masters. While European arts and culture were a class privilege for the Southern gentry, New England progressively looked toward providing all children with cultural knowledge through education in common schools (Mark and Gary, 2007). Growing support for public education, along with the expansion of cultural societies dedicated to choral (and less frequently, instrumental) music, set the scene for the introduction of music into the curriculum of the elementary school by Lowell Mason in Boston in 1838.

The Boston schools, persuaded by Mason to test the inclusion of music in the curriculum, stipulated that children be given vocal training and music reading lessons twice weekly. Soon, children presented public concerts that demonstrated their considerable musical progress, much to the delight (and surprise) of school officials, parents, and community members. Mason's method of instruction emphasized pragmatic learning-by-doing techniques, beginning with focused listening and rote repetition of vocal music that advanced children toward music literacy. Swiss educator Heinrich Pestalozzi (1746–1827) was undeniably influential in Mason's approach, particularly as evidenced by the application of the principles of Anschauung (literally, "sense intuition"), or learning through the senses. The earliest methods used in public school music instruction thus were based on the logic of "sound before sight" and "practice before theory"; listening and singing experiences led to an understanding of notation and theory.

The emergence of music as a curricular subject in the elementary schools unfolded gradually through the nineteenth and twentieth centuries. Vocal music was praised for its contribution to children's moral culture and for its functional means of cultivating the speaking voice, of developing correct expression and diction, and of providing concentration at the start and close of the day. Music listening and note-reading developed in tandem, as children were directed by the music masters to attend to the intervals between pitches, to associate solfège syllables with the melodies they sang, and to sight-read songs and exercises.

Not until schools had access to recordings and radio, however, did a more global form of music listening begin to emerge. Music appreciation classes for children were developed as early as the 1920s. The infusion of rhythmic movement and dance into children's music classes began to flourish in the opening decades of the twentieth century, when movement was recognized as offering an avenue for musical expression as well as for physical, social, and cultural growth. The eurhythmics of Émile Jaques-Dalcroze (1865–1950) first intrigued and then guided teachers toward the development of children's greater musical sensitivity through whole-body movement. John Dewey's (1859–1952) advocacy for music, movement, and the arts in a child-centered curriculum helped to stabilize music as a part of school instruction, even through the troubled economic and political times of the Great Depression of the 1930s and World War II.

Music for children was sparked by numerous innovations in the second half of the twentieth century. From Hungary came the philosophy and practices of Zoltán Kodály (1882–1967) and his associates, with their emphasis on music literacy through rigorous ear-training and vocal exercises. The early experiments in music for children by German composer Carl Orff (1895–1982), first with dancer Dorothee Gunther and then with colleague Gunild Keetman, evolved into practices that merge music with children's play and with dance and the dramatic arts. Over several decades, both Kodály's and Orff's approaches have been embraced by music educators and given American perspectives.

Various professional gatherings of teachers at conferences and in projects have had a further impact on music instruction for children. In the 1960s, the Yale Seminar, the Manhattanville Music Curriculum Project, and the Tanglewood Symposium made recommendations for (1) a broader and more representative music repertoire for listening and performance, including music of all Western historical periods; world cultures; and popular, avant-garde, and American styles; (2) greater opportunities for musical expression and creativity, through composition and improvisation experiences; and (3) more extensive use of technology and the media to aid instruction. The challenges have continued into the twenty-first century, as teachers confront ways to balance experiences in European art music with the musical interests and learning styles of

© Patricia Shehan Campbell

an increasingly diverse population of children and as they consider computers, interactive videos, and multitasking iPhones as user-friendly enhancements—not threats—to children's musical education.

Music takes its rightful place in the school curriculum today, resting on the long history of its acceptance in children's education. Through the ages, music instruction has provided children with skills for their musical expressions and knowledge of their cultural heritage(s). Despite societal changes, the need for a musical education continues. Through a musical education, children may learn the many facets of the uniquely aural art that allows them an opening through which to channel their many personal expressions.

> *"Musical training is a more potent instrument than any other, because rhythm and harmony find their way into the inward places of the soul, on which they mightily fasten, imparting grace. . . ."*
>
> **Plato**

Music for Children in a Changing Society

How quickly the world has changed and is changing still. Could grandparents have envisioned a world of slim-line wallet-size phones that text, email, take photographs, and provide an "amusement library" of listening, video, and gaming possibilities? Could parents have imagined the rise of popular music from its cultlike appeal to teenagers (only) to its pervasive presence, streaming through laptops and even, occasionally, embedded in the music of serious composers? Could they have fathomed that a world of knowledge could be had via website infobytes that flow across small screens at the flickering of fingers on tiny computer keyboards? Could we ourselves have guessed when we were children that a global village would emerge and that the world's peoples and their cultural expressions could become so present (and so vital) in today's schools? The changes are riveting, their pace rapid and relentless, and their impact on musical culture profound.

Children of the twenty-first century face challenges very different from those just a generation ago. They grow up within family units of various sorts, including single-parent families, working-parent families, and extended families of aunts, uncles, and cousins. They know about substance abuse and sexual abuse, some from firsthand experience. They are bombarded with media images offering examples of deviant behavior and hear dialogue on television and radio that was considered inappropriate for previous generations. They worry about the environment, about people living in poverty both at home and abroad, about wars, and about the spread of diseases that threaten lives, with no certain remedies in sight. Today's world can overwhelm children with challenges.

Enter music into this world of changes and challenges. Music is, for children, a port in the storm, a resting spot, a retreat from the madding crowd and their hectic lives. It is their safety valve, an appropriate release of energy at those times when no other channel seems possible. As music is transformed by technology and by the blending of cultural traditions from near and far, children are offered a wide array of expressions from which to choose for listening and performing. Their out-of-school musical experiences are greatly enriched by in-school instruction, so that the meaning of multiple musical expressions is deepened for them by music teacher specialists with the support of classroom teachers, parents, and other responsible adults.

> *"Music is too important to be left to the musicians [alone]. . . ."*
> **Christopher Small, 1998**

> *"You wouldn't starve without music. But it makes my life worth more?"*
> **Tuyen, 11-year-old girl;**
> **(Patricia Shehan Campbell, 2010)**

A Musical Future

With an understanding of the functions and meanings of music, along with sensitivity to children's musical capacities and modes of musical experiences, teachers can develop their own personal method for stimulating the musical development of their students. Children will be guaranteed a musical future when the design of a curriculum takes into account the comprehensive goals of a musical education and the sequence for its attainment. Children have their first musical experiences in the home, under the tutelage of their mothers and fathers, but teachers are entrusted with the responsibility for building on these experiences. The transmission of musical culture is in their hands.

Music transmission cannot be haphazard if it is to be especially meaningful. Throughout their schooling, children need musical nurturing by trained music specialists, so that the experiences they know are musical as well as thoughtfully presented. The music teacher possesses knowledge and skills honed through many years of solo and ensemble performance experience and the study of music history, theory, and cultures. The music teacher also brings a sense of sequence, and a delivery style that appeals to children, based on an understanding of child development and pedagogical methods. Through long and specialized training, the music teacher can ensure that quality music instruction is provided.

The musical future of children rests on careful selection of music and instructional techniques to maximize the sometimes minimal curricular time explicitly assigned to music. It rests on the imaginative ways in which creative teachers infuse music into the school days, weaving music into lessons in the language arts, social studies, mathematics, and the sciences. It rests on the belief that today's tremendous cultural diversity and technological advances will enhance, embellish, enlighten, and expand the musical experiences of children.

Most important, the musical future of children rests on the teacher's confidence that he or she is first and foremost a musician, one with a lifetime of music to share. Live music making led by the teacher's own performance, along with opportunities for guided listening to performances and recordings of other professional musicians, makes music meaningful to children. While there are many effective instructional techniques, probably no certain method exists for teaching music to children, any more than there is just one way to climb a mountain or to fall in love. The comprehensive and most effective method through which children become musically educated is to be found within the teacher's own training and interests. The possession of musical knowledge and skills, coupled with a love and understanding of children, will pave the way for a combination of techniques from various philosophical approaches into a personal pedagogy that suits the teacher, the children, and the music.

Scenario

JESSICA WHITEMAN WAS FEELING a nervous energy simmering inside her as she arrived to the Monday afternoon staff meeting at Emily Dickenson Elementary School. She knew that the agenda would include "a conversation" about possible cuts to music and the other "specials" for the following year. It was March, and the principal, Ms. Ascenzi, had already met with Jessica, the art teacher, the librarian, and the PE teacher about possible reductions of their schedules come September. Ms. Ascenzi had noted that budget cuts looming ahead were requiring her to make "some hard decisions," and that she was meeting with teachers about their needs for additional resources and materials for the math and language arts curriculum. Jessica had spoken to her specialist colleagues, and they were responding variously to the news, from seeking endorsement in general classroom teaching, to retraining in another field, to considering (very) early retirement. Jessica was not defeated yet, however, and had been working out the details of a personal campaign that would clarify why music needed to remain a regular part of the school curriculum.

Jessica asked Ms. Acsenzi for some time at the staff meeting and was given a slot of ten minutes to present her points. As she stood and walked to the front to face her colleagues, Jessica felt the butterflies in her stomach. She heard herself, in a weak and almost apologetic voice, thank them in advance for listening to her, and then took a deep breath. She sang out "Sorida," the Shona-language greeting song of Zimbabwe, and asked her colleagues to join in while she gestured a clapping pattern and circular motions with her hands. They began to sing and clap, first softly but with increasing enthusiasm as Jessica repeated the song several times. She moved to her laptop and flicked on a rousing tune by Cesario Evora, Cape Verdean musician, called her colleagues to a standing position, and modeled a few steps—first to the right, then to the left, out to the front, down to the back. They were with her, she was adding her arms in an ascending clap-and-wave gesture, and she heard hoots, laughter, and "You go, girl."

Immediately, in the midst of the phrase, she pressed stop, gestured that they sit down, and began her pitch. "Stop the music?" she asked. "Why stop the music? Why deny our children the chance to express themselves in song and dance, and on instruments? Why deny them opportunities to know the artistic and cultural expressions of others in the world? Is school all about the intellectual and academic? What about the social-emotional well-being of our children? What about the ways in which music is an intellectual and academic pursuit, and then some? It's deep, rich, historic, contemporary, cultural, multicultural, private, collective, and vital to the holistic education of our children. We need to find a way to prevent ourselves from stripping the expressive needs of children right out of the curriculum." And on she went, now in a strong and dynamic voice, and her butterflies were gone. When Ms. Ascenzi rose, her teacher-friends were clapping for Jessica. One colleague, a second-grade teacher, spoke up: "Move over, math, we need some music time." The principal thanked Jessica, and before moving to the next agenda item, remarked, "Let's talk, Jessica. I've got some time on Friday morning." Before the end of the academic year, Ms. Ascenzi had made a decision to preserve music (and Jessica's job), although the other "specials" were reduced, and the decision had been made to cut visual art and turn it over to the classroom teachers. Jessica's campaign was short yet very sweet, and Ms. Ascenzi had found her pitch to be persuasive enough to seek out support for music in exchange for Jessica's record-keeping reports of explicit ways in which the children at Emily Dickenson Elementary School were benefiting from music.

Questions

1. What appeared to work in Jessica's pitch to her colleagues on music's place in the elementary school curriculum at Emily Dickenson?

2. What other techniques or strategies might Jessica have added or substituted to persuade colleagues outside of music and the arts of the importance of music for children?

3. What might be developed further (daily, weekly, or otherwise regularly) as means of following up as reminders to the Emily Dickenson Elementary School teachers of the important role that music plays in the school?

REVIEW

1. List the ten functions and uses of music. Are some more prominent in your life, and in the lives of children, than others?

2. How do children demonstrate their musical capacities?

3. How has music been placed historically within the curriculum?

4. What recommendations for changes in the music curriculum emerged (and are emerging still) from various sociopolitical events, both historic and recent?

CRITICAL THINKING

1. Nature or nurture? Discuss your stance on children's musical abilities as natural or learned, biological or entrained. Find support for either stance.

2. In the age of iPhones, and technologically wired classrooms, is the Pestalozzian concept of Anschauung relevant? Explain.

PROJECTS

1. Conduct a series of interviews to determine the meaning of music to people, both currently and from their memories. Ask open-ended questions not only of children but also of friends, family members, colleagues, and teachers. Analyze the responses according to the Merriam chart of musical uses and functions. Compare the current musical involvement of adults with their childhood memories of musical experiences.

2. Prepare a three-minute speech to be given to the board of education elucidating the benefits of music instruction for children. Present it to the class, and be prepared to respond to questions regarding your position.

3. Stage a scenario: a music teacher's consultation with a concerned parent who wonders whether her child is musical or musically talented.

4. How can in-school instruction in music expand on the musical interests and experiences that children have outside the classroom? Suggest three outside musical experiences that merit deeper exploration through the guidance of a music teacher.

MINDTAP Visit **MindTap** to access classroom videos, audio, and more!

2

From Theory to Practice in Teaching Music to Children

IN THIS CHAPTER

- Stage and Phase Theories
- Social Systems and Scapes
- Theories of Musical Play and Socialization
- A Constructivist Theory of Meaning Making
- Social Learning and Reinforcement Theories
- Neuroscience and Music Learning
- Learning Style Theories
- Theories of Instruction
- Relating Theory to Practice
  - The Classroom Environment
  - A Child-Centered Curriculum
  - The Teacher as Transmitter
  - Instructional Strategies
- Informed Teaching

THEORIES OF LEARNING, TEACHING, and instruction are embedded in nearly every musical experience. Jeremy and Bryan playfully explore the music-making possibilities of spoons, cups, pots, and pans; Bruner (1966, 1996), Vygotsky (1978; Daniels, Cole, and Wertsch, 2007), and Jonassen (2011) have developed theories to explain this behavior. Annmarie works best alone at a listening station, while Rosa grows musically when in a socially interactive group; theories on field dependence and independence explain some of the differences. Inga follows the teacher's modeling of a musical phrase and imitates it a bit better with each successive trial; both Skinner (1953; Chiesa, 2004) and Bandura (1977, 1997) offer theoretical explanations. Rob acquires and retains music aurally; Tony through symbols, graphs, and notes on staffs; and Charissa through associated movements and gestures; these learning modalities are theorized, analyzed, and classified in the literature on learning styles. When Donny does not attend to a listening lesson, Ausubel (1968, 2000) suggests "advance organizers" (or building a foundation of familiar ideas for the new learning situation), Gagné (1993, 2004) recommends ways of gaining attention, and Skinner offers behavioral techniques for bringing him to task.

Theories about how children learn and how teachers can help maximize this learning are at the heart of every practical musical experience that teachers provide for children. Instead of being dull, dry, and remotely related to the real-life challenges of teaching music to children, theories can illuminate for the teacher how children gain musical knowledge, skills, and values. Theories of instruction are based on effective techniques used by teachers and on scientific observation of and experimentation in how children learn. By understanding theory as the fruit of multiple lifetimes spent explaining how children acquire, retain, and then

- What theories of music learning and instruction do you know through study and actual experience?

- Describe your preferred way of learning. How has it changed since your childhood?

- What did you musically know, and what could you musically do, as a result of home enculturation experiences? How were these experiences enriched and deepened through training?

- What sorts of teacher-directed and child-centered learning have you observed?

- Recall what your music classroom looked and felt like as a child. How was it conducive to learning and what would have made it more so?

- How do effective teachers you have known start and end music classes?

"Theory links the teacher to the child learner, as it relates teaching events to learning processes and demonstrated learning outcomes."

rework musical knowledge into their personal expressions, teachers can become more efficient at guiding this musical development. Theory is wedded to practice, in that it emanates from practical teaching and learning experiences as it also informs these practices. Teachers who think about what they do, and are informed by theory, are deeply committed to leading children to their maximal musical development.

A theory of music instruction can describe factors related to the teacher, the children, their family, social and cultural influences, and the classroom environment. A theory of music instruction comprises three components: (1) instruction, a set of events provided by the teacher; (2) learning processes of the child learner, including attention, perception, memory, rehearsal, and recognition and recall; and (3) learning outcomes in the form of a child's demonstration of verbal information, intellectual skills, motor skills, cognitive strategies, and attitudes. Thus, theory directs the teacher in providing sequential experiences for understanding a rhythmic pattern or for gaining techniques necessary for playing a musical instrument. It describes the child's need for initial attention to the learning task and the progression through which the child learns and remembers that task, and it suggests the means by which the child demonstrates such learning.

Teachers—and parents—concerned with enhancing the musical development of children will be well served by the brief introduction to theories of instruction and learning that follows. Selected research and recommendations by theorists in psychology, sociology, anthropology, and education are noted, as well as the ways in which these theories can inform the practice of music instruction. Table 2.1 sketches selected theories that are relevant to teaching music to children.

Stage and Phase Theories

A number of theories refer to stages, phases, or levels through which children or adult learners proceed in gaining knowledge. Some of these multileveled theories stem from developmental psychology and are called "stage dependent," referring to the intellectual stages that children pass through as they mature. Others are not governed by maturation but nonetheless feature earlier stages of learning that provide the foundation for later, more complex learning. Whatever the emphasis, multileveled theories establish that children do not learn all at once, but bit by bit, and in increasingly complex ways over time.

The stage-dependent theory of Swiss biologist Jean Piaget (1952), a key twentieth-century conceptualization of childhood, still provides an important model of cognitive development in its combination of the child's biological growth with an increasingly mature intellectual grasp of concepts. Through longitudinal observations of children from birth through late adolescence, Piaget evolved a theory that has greatly influenced views on child development. He observed that children progress through four stages of thinking: (1) sensorimotor (ages zero to two), learning through direct sensory experience; (2) preoperational (ages two to seven), learning through the manipulation of objects—noting the consequences and internalizing them for the future, thus transforming stimuli to symbols; (3) concrete operations (ages seven to eleven), viewing objects in concrete, tangible, and systematic ways but not abstractly; and (4) formal operations (ages eleven through adulthood), learning abstractly using logic and deductive reasoning.

TABLE 2.1 Summary of Selected Theories Informing Music

THEORIST	THEORY	PRINCIPAL FEATURES
STAGE AND PHASE THEORIES		
Jean Piaget	Stage-dependent theory	Children progress through four stages of intellectual development: sensorimotor, preoperational, concrete operations, and formal operations
Jerome Bruner	Modes of representation	Learners progress through three ways of representing meaning or understanding, related to, but not dependent on, maturation: enactive, iconic, and symbolic
Lauren Sosniak	Developmental stages of the pianist or performer	Student musicians progress through three phases: tinkering, technical, and masterful music making
Gregory Bateson; Catherine Ellis	Learning I, II, III	Learners progress through three phases: enculturation, acquisition of skills or competence, and personal and aesthetic expression
SOCIAL SYSTEMS AND SCAPES		
Uri Bronfenbrenner	Ecological systems	Nested systems that contribute to learning and education: microsystem (family or classroom), exosystem (external environments), mesosystem (microsystem-exosystem interactions), macrosystem (sociocultural context)
Arjun Appadurai	Global cultural flow	A realization of cultural activity as globally shaped by the flow and influence of immigrants and travelers (ethnoscape), media (mediascape), technology (technoscape), trade and finance (finanscapes), and ideas (ideascape).
MUSICAL PLAY AND SOCIALIZATION THEORIES		
G. Stanley Hall	Musical play	Children train for adulthood through games; musical play leads to musical understanding
Lev Vygotsky	Socialization	Children are socialized through adult intervention and guidance; socialization leads to acquisition of cultural knowledge
CONSTRUCTIVIST THEORY		
David Jonassen	Constructivism	Children develop their understanding through the meaning they make from their experiences
REINFORCEMENT AND SOCIAL LEARNING THEORIES		
B. F. Skinner; Robert Thorndike	Reinforcement	Learning can be shaped through the process of positive or negative reinforcement; appropriate behaviors are shaped through successive approximation techniques
Albert Bandura	Social learning	Children observe and emulate their adult models
NEUROSCIENCE AND MUSIC LEARNING		
Richard Restak	Cerebral dominance	Learners are dominated by left-hemispheric (linear) or right-hemispheric (holistic) processing
Gordon Shaw	General and spatial intelligence	Neural firing patterns triggered by singing and playing music lead to higher brain function, some of which transfers to academic subjects like math
Anders Ericsson	Deliberate practice	Expertise in music and other realms requires 10,000 hours of deliberate and thoughtful practice
Daniel Levitin	Neuromusical matrix	Network of brain regions engaged in emotion, timing, perception, and production of sequences in music performance and listening

(Continued)

TABLE 2.1 *(Continued)*

THEORIST	THEORY	PRINCIPAL FEATURES
LEARNING STYLE THEORIES		
Howard Gardner	Multiple intelligences	Learners possess one or more types of intelligence or ways of being intelligent
Walter Barbe; Raymond Swassing	Learning modalities	Learners process information through a preferred sensory channel: visual, auditory, or kinesthetic
Rita Dunn and Kenneth Dunn	Learning style model	A variety of factors influence learning: environmental, emotional, social, and physical
Harold Witkin	Field dependence and field independence	Learners may be content bound, experiencing concepts as embedded within their environment; or content independent, experiencing concepts as discrete entities removed from their background
Isabel Myers; Peter B. Briggs	Myers Briggs Type indicator	Learners may demonstrate one or several of eight Myers-Briggs personality types that influence the way they approach the learning task: extroversion/introversion, sensing/intuitive, thinking/feeling, and judging/perceiving
INSTRUCTIONAL THEORIES		
David Ausubel	Meaningful reception	Students acquire information most effectively when teachers package lessons well and prepare students through "advance organizers"
Jerome Bruner	Discovery learning; spiral curriculum	Students learn through exploration and problem solving; subject matter can be taught to children through age-appropriate experiences and can be embellished through repeated exposure
Robert Gagné	Events of instruction	Learners progress through eight instructional events, from awareness and attention through concept formation and transfer
Edwin Gordon	Music learning theory	Students progress through an eight-stage process that begins with aural and oral experiences with music and ends with theoretical understanding; audiation is the goal

These four classic stages suggest that younger children in particular be given many opportunities to listen, sing, play, and move to music (Piaget and Inhelder, 1969). The introduction of staff notation should occur only after preliminary experiences. Piagetian theory implies that music instruction follows a sound-before-symbol approach. Other notable applications of Piaget's principles to music learning indicate that age eight is a watershed year in a child's cognitive development. At this time, children are capable of identifying timbres, discriminating among random melodies, and perceiving structure in simple melodies, although they are less successful in perceiving the sound of more than one simultaneous musical line (or harmony). As they progress into the stage of concrete operations, children also begin to conserve, or to realize the invariance of one musical element when another is altered. In other words, they begin to recognize a melody when it has been sung in a minor instead of a major modality or in triple instead of duple time. By the time they complete fifth grade, many children are capable of thinking in the abstract about music and are able to manipulate musical structures through improvisation and composition experiences.

In his modes of representation, Jerome Bruner (1966, 1996) suggests a type of stage progression that is somewhat dependent on maturation but can be applied to all ages and intellectual stages. He proposed three teaching and learning strategies: enactive, learning through a set of actions; iconic, learning through images and graphs; and

© Billie Judy/Reel Life Productions

symbolic, learning by going beyond what is immediately perceptible in the environment. For example, learning to read notation can be broken into three stages corresponding to Bruner's model. Instruction may begin with arm and body movement to represent melodic contours (enactive), followed by line graphs that trace these contours (iconic), and ending with the reading and writing of notation itself on the staff (symbolic). These modes of representation are useful in providing increasingly sophisticated instructional sequences for any concept.

In a longitudinal study of concert pianists, Lauren Sosniak (1985) developed a theory also involving three phases of learning. During the initial phase, the young musician tinkers at the piano in playful exploration and is encouraged and supported by her or his parents to do so. The teacher is positive, gentle, and thus motivating for the learner. The second phase emphasizes a more systematic and technical approach to instruction. The development of playing technique brings a need for greater repetition and more careful listening to and emulating of the model, the teacher. The playfulness of the first phase is replaced by a more concentrated and serious attention to detail. In the third phase, mastery emerges in the young pianist's performance of targeted pieces. Gone is the positive and playful instructional approach as the teacher becomes more critical of smaller flaws in an attempt to develop a near-perfect performance. The instructional mission changes, as do the student's goals, over the three phases. While the theory is hardly one of cognitive development in the Piagetian sense, progressive maturation nonetheless occurs over the time of five or ten years (or more) of lessons. A parallel can be drawn for children's study of any instrument or voice.

Anthropologist Gregory Bateson (1978; Bateson and Donaldson, 1991) defined three broad dimensions of learning similar to Sosniak's three-phase model. These types were related to music learning by Catherine Ellis (1986). Learning I occurs without effort, as music within the environment is absorbed by the learner. Such informal encounters with music are part of the enculturation process by which children come to know the components of their society. In Learning II, thinking is combined with experience when the child learner strives to become a competent performer through lessons or classroom instruction. In this phase, the child becomes more seriously interested in music and engages in practice that develops coordination, strength, agility, and speed

FIGURE 2.1

Three Phases of Musical Learning

Mature: Musical mastery
Refinement and perfection
Music as personal expression
and aesthetic experience

Middle: Conscious attention
to performance technique
Commitment to practice
Concentration for competence

Early: Musical enculturation
Playful exploration of music
Informal encounters with music
in the environment

> "To instruct someone . . . is not a matter of getting him to commit results to mind. Rather, it is to teach him to participate in the process that makes possible the establishment of this knowledge."
>
> **Jerome Bruner, 1960**

on a given instrument or voice. The final phase, which Ellis contends is attained only rarely, takes the performer past technical skills to music as a personal expression of joy and even religious faith.

Children who study instruments may make their way through the phases proposed by Sosniak and by Bateson and Ellis (see Figure 2.1). Certainly, children everywhere have an initial enculturation experience. Musically, this may manifest in their development as perceivers and performers of simple songs and instrumental pieces in their musical "mother tongue." The second phase in both theories indicates a commitment to practice in order to develop technique and build a performance repertoire. The ultimate phase is reached when performance skills are refined and the goal of music as an aesthetic expression can be attained. Few children realize this goal, although many are well on their way. The greatest focus of music instruction for children through the sixth grade is on the second phase, the skill-building stage.

Social Systems and Scapes

Children's learning happens in schools and on the far outside of schools, in formal and informal experiences that they know. While teachers, parents, and caregivers provide them with content and circumstances for learning academic and everyday knowledge and skills, they are also influenced by social systems that surround them in their lives at home, in school, and in every nook and cranny of their experience. These influences are local, national, and international, and may be more indirect than direct. They are multiple rather than singular influences, and they function in a webbed, nested, and interactive social system. They shape the environment in which children learn music, and all other knowledge and skills valued by the society in which they live.

As a scholar of child development, Uri Bronfenbrenner (1979, 2004) posed an ecological systems theory that has been widely welcomed as a means of understanding the social network of children's learning. He described a nested system that consists of four types of influences: the microsystem of the family or individual classroom; the exosystem of indirect, external influence such as parental occupations that include the workplace; the mesosystem of interactions between microsystems and exosystems (as in the case of family and parental occupations); and the macrosystem of the larger sociocultural system of society as it interacts with government policy and civic institutions. Recognition of an ecological complex of influences is helpful in understanding how children are nurtured by the roles and rules of each nested environment, from the most intimate to the broadest-reaching. This social system thus helps to explain the music that children grow to know, and which encompasses various facets of their environmental experiences.

In a time of increasing globalization, in which nations and cultures are connecting through continuous exposure to (and interactions with) one another on various levels, a steady stream of influences is crossing communities and shaping children's experience in powerful ways. The cultural anthropologist Arjun Appadurai (1996, 2001) described contemporary society as rapidly evolving by means of a global cultural flow of ideas that moves from one place to the next, creating imagined and virtual communities while also reorienting people in the real communities in which they live. Children, as well as adults, are affected by global cultural flow consisting of the impact of immigrants and travelers (ethnoscape), the media (mediascape), technology (technoscape), trade and finance (finanscape), and ideas (ideoscape) from everywhere in the world. Their cultural knowledge, including artistic practices and musical expressions, is influenced by who and what enters into their surroundings. The social system that envelops them is a result of the processes and products of a global cultural flow. And the media, technology, and changing demographics of neighborhoods are important components of the music that children enjoy and value.

Theories of Musical Play and Socialization

When children play with other children and socialize with adults, they are learning as well. Contrary to the word's connotation, "play" can thus be serious business for children. Socialization, a type of play in which children engage in social interactions with adult guides, can be a weighty endeavor for children, with serious implications for their cognitive development. Musical play and socialization through music (and for the sake of music learning) can be bona fide means for children to gain information about the world around them.

Various schools of child psychology have supported play as a natural process and a part of child development. Historic figures in the field, G. Stanley Hall and Sigmund Freud were in agreement that young children are in training for adulthood through the games they play. Musical play should be nurtured in nursery school and continued through the primary grades, according to the pedagogies of Zoltán Kodály, Émile Jaques-Dalcroze, and Carl Orff. Singing games, newly invented songs by children, musical improvisations, and compositions that are practiced, preserved, and performed repeatedly are examples of musical play at its best.

Musical play deserves a prominent place in the education of children—at least through the primary grades—with improvisation occurring throughout the elementary grades. The key to successful music learning may be at least partly linked to the songs children know, invent, and transmit to each other while at play and to the music they create on instruments during free-play time. Certainly, a teacher's goals and well-planned lessons are necessary in the educational process, as is an open mind to the music that children know and spontaneously create. Children's musical play can be the means by which a conceptual understanding of music is more fully developed in the classroom.

The teacher's role as guide, not solely as leader, can foster learning and the development of favorable attitudes toward music that will long endure.

The Russian social psychologist Lev Vygotsky (1978; Daniels, Cole, and Wertsch, 2007) established that the adult, primarily the parent and teacher, is the primary influence on a child's socialization process. The adult not only transmits music to a child, but also participates in the child's discovery and manipulation of the music to be acquired. During musical play, the teacher or parent delivers to the child cultural signs—such as verbal comments, facial expressions, or indicatory gestures—that direct the child's attention to specific elements of an experience and that activate appropriate learning behaviors. According to Vygotsky, these signs provide the means for drawing children into knowing their culture (in this case, musical culture) while also shaping and coloring their perceptions and eventual understanding of the cultural object (the music). As the teacher interacts musically with children, for example, while singing, the children come to know the song and to progress toward singing it independently. They grow in ownership of the song and become more familiar as well with elements of that musical tradition. Their musical interactions with the adult while singing, moving, listening, and playing musical instruments are vital to their musical independence and to their coming into the musical culture itself.

A Constructivist Theory of Meaning Making

Every child has real-world experiences, and ideas become meaningful as a result of the events that happen in particular ways to each individual. Consistent with a belief in the child as an active player in the shaping of knowledge, the constructivist theory of learning explains knowledge as a result of the process by which the child creates meaning from his or her experiences. Like a carpenter or a builder of houses, learning proceeds in active instead of passive ways as the child builds up knowledge piece by experiential piece until a meaningful whole forms—and then some, for every experience to follow has also the potential of broadening as well as deepening his or her understanding. The child is the key player in this constructivist process, building a conceptualization of self, other, and outer world through each progressive experience, encounter, and interaction that comes along. Reflecting an earlier humanistic perspective, constructivism holds to the premise that children who initiate and direct their learning will find that learning lasts longer and is relevant to their lives (Rogers, 1969).

David Jonassen's constructivism is associated with mental constructs or principles—the germinal units that comprise knowledge—and how they are developed (Jonassen, 1991, 2011). The reconstruction of principles by new learners of a subject is of key interest, and the shaping of experiences into new information and new interpretations is integral to the learning process. Within the instructional process, the accent shifts from the teacher to the child, from the view of teacher-as-absolute and the font of all knowledge to the child as active seeker of ideas from multiple sources. Those teachers who profess a constructivist approach to instruction become facilitators, instead of dictatorial leaders, of children. Their responsibilities are to set up an environment that is conducive to learning and to allow the setting to support the engagement of children in experiences that lead to the acquisition of principles, skills, and understandings.

Within the realm of music in a child's life, constructivism brings with it certain images; for example, a child playing at the keyboard, trying this key and then that key while creating her own tune, and figuring out a motif or gesture that is followed by its repetition and development. In such a case, the teacher is there to provide the instrument, the space (in terms of both time and physical distance from the child's need for experimentation), and occasional prompts, feedback, and encouraging and motivating remarks. Another image of the constructivist approach is the gathering of children who are working collaboratively on a project—a collective composition in which all are contributing members to the final product, a listening analysis in which children together discuss (according to preset guidelines) the presence and meaning of certain sonic events, or a sectional rehearsal in which children take responsibility for learning (by way of teaching, reviewing, and revising component parts) an assigned piece. In all cases, the teacher's work is in the advance planning and design of circumstances in which children can explore, experiment, accomplish general goals, and acquire understanding.

The quality of construction depends on the range of information available to the child-constructor, and while all constructions must be considered meaningful, some are incomplete or simplistic. Learning is not a complete free-for-all in which anything goes, all outcomes are equal, and no one is in danger of misinterpreting. Instead, mental constructs have been held as accurate and appropriate within societies and cultures for millenia, and they form the basis of fundamental human understanding. This then becomes the challenge of constructivism to teachers: determining how to balance personal, flexible, or even free processes of knowledge acquisition by children with the initial setup of the learning environment and guideposts along the way by teachers, so that the result is the acquisition of shared knowledge that can also be individually interpreted. Those professed constructivist teachers swear by the theory, and their children revel in what appears to be a less restrictive and more personally meaningful means of learning than that espoused by other theories (see Lesson 2.1).

LESSON 2.1 Constructivist-Styled Learning

1. *Children listen and find pulse, meter, melodic and rhythmic patterns, "expressive dimensions," and general impressions in repeated listenings to a recorded Trinidadian soca song.*
   Teacher has selected a recording that illustrates musical components, accepts all children's discussion points by listing them on the board, suggests some possibilities when children struggle with descriptive words, plays the recording again so that children might review their thoughts and impressions, and prompts for ideas about song words and their musical setting.

2. *Children learn to sing "Viva la musica" in canon.*
   Teacher leads children in singing the song in unison, provides for children to conduct the group with their choices of tempo and dynamic level, allows for children's evaluation of their singing, sets children into practice teams of three—each with rotating conductors—and then brings them back together to sing in canon.

3. *Children create percussion piece on season theme.*
   Teacher has set up five groupings of two xylophones, two metallophones, a drum, and a woodblock in the center and corners of the room; plays several examples of composed "seasonal music" pieces on recordings; notes parameters of "fifteen minutes to create 'seasonal music' (winter, spring, summer, autumn)"; circulates to answer questions of children; and organizes the groups for class performances, discussion, and evaluation.

Social Learning and Reinforcement Theories

Two theories from the fields of sociology and psychology, both highly relevant to teaching and learning, are linked by their examination of environmental agents that promote and influence learning. Neither is technically an instructional theory, although each targets behaviors that frequently appear in classrooms. Social learning theory explains the significance of environmental models for learning, while reinforcement theory describes the manner in which persons in the environment shape and increase learning behaviors.

Albert Bandura's (1977, 1997) social learning theory is a provocative view of the power of persons within an environment to serve as models of behavior that are later replicated by the observer. Children choose to watch and listen to their parents and teachers, whose behaviors they later emulate. Their observations of these models are mentally organized, memorized, and recalled when similar situations for thinking and acting arise in their lives. The process of environmental influences and social learning are played out as the student recalls the visual or aural codes of earlier observations and practices the behaviors first demonstrated by the models. Social learning theory is prominent in musical settings, because modeling is critical to the student's watching, listening, and then performing the music in the manner and style of the teacher. Children learn to sing and play instruments, as well as how to listen, by doing as their models do.

Table 2.2 shows how social learning theory can be adapted to a learning sequence that integrates the act of listening in the development of performance skills, in this case, singing. A song is learned in three stages. First, it is introduced by the teacher; second, an intermediate stage is reached after several run-throughs or even weeks later; and third, a final stage of refinement is achieved some time after that. The teacher as model is central to the development of listening and performance skills. The children imitate the model and evaluate their attempts to re-create it, showing increasing ability to match the model's performance, even as they offer personal expression in their rendering of

Teacher-as-model singing with children

TABLE 2.2

Applications of Social Learning Theory to Music Instruction

EARLY	The model (teacher) sings/children listen Can you sing the final tone? What is the meter? How many phrases are there? Are there any repeated patterns?
MIDDLE	The model sings/children listen; children sing What pitches are to be accented? Have you lowered/raised the pitch? Are you sustaining for the complete duration? Can you achieve the rhythmic swing or flow?
LATE	Children sing; the model sings/children listen; children sing How closely can you approximate the model? How might you vary the model's rendering? Where are the peak expressive points? What are the overlaps and distinctions between you and the model?

the song. Questions by the teacher direct children to listen carefully in order to develop their ability to sing accurately and expressively. This sequence could also be contained within a single lesson; thus, it becomes a lesson plan for teaching a song.

The reinforcement theory of the behavioral school of psychology has been embraced by teachers and parents, having long provided suggestions for effective means of shaping children's behaviors toward those considered acceptable and appropriate. B. F. Skinner's (1953, 1987; Chiesa, 2004) classic theory of operant conditioning is at the heart of behavioral change, including learning. Operant conditioning is a three-part instructional "kernel," or process, comprised of a stimulus that is presented to the learner, a response that is elicited by the learner as a consequence of the stimulus, followed by the presentation of another stimulus that reinforces the response. Stimuli operating in the environment, including the verbal and nonverbal approval of a teacher, have an impact on children's learning behaviors. Skinner's reinforcement theory holds that when a child's behavior—singing in tune or playing rhythms accurately—is positively reinforced by the teacher's smile, nod, or positive comment, that behavior will be maintained or increased.

The Skinnerian technique of successive approximation, or the shaping of behavior by reinforcing each progressive step toward an ideal, is one of the most common used by teachers. Shaping requires teachers to break songs, pieces, or musical passages into small parts; to offer approving remarks for musical behaviors that are similar to, or that approximate, the desired performance behaviors ("Yes, now you've got the right rhythm!"); and to use clear feedback to state what needs to change in moving learners toward the ideal ("No, you need to sing it a half-step higher."). The teacher reinforces less perfect musical behaviors in the hopes of directing children to more perfect ones. The teacher's reinforcing comments are eventually diminished as children begin to evaluate their own musical behaviors as approximating the model or ideal sound. Reinforcement theory is recognized by behaviorists as a premier influence on learning, with the teacher acting as environmental agent, dispenser of feedback, and model of appropriate behavior.

Reinforcement theory is also the basis of the system of classroom management called behavior modification, in which children are given external reinforcement for appropriate social or academic behaviors. In its classic form, children receive rewards contingent on or following good behavior; these rewards have included M&M candies, tokens to be applied to prizes, free time, and field trips. This system is well known for keeping children on task, or focused on goals of cooperative and nondisruptive behavior and on the completion of projects and assignments.

The work of Clifford K. Madsen and his associates (C. H. Madsen and Madsen, 1981; C. K. Madsen and Kuhn, 1994) on the application of reinforcement theory to musical settings has inspired a host of music research studies and teaching practices. Madsen and colleagues have developed four observational research principles: pinpointing a trouble behavior, observing and recording the frequency of the behavior, applying a teaching strategy to reduce the behavior, and evaluating the effect of the strategy by observing the frequency of the behavior. In countless studies, inappropriate behaviors are reduced while appropriate behaviors emerge. The key appears to be viewing the trouble behaviors one at a time and applying teaching strategies that work.

> "Of the many cues that influence behavior, at any point in time, none is more common than the actions of others."
>
> **Albert Bandura, 1986**

Neuroscience and Music Learning

In recent decades, neuroscientists have been instrumental in piecing together explanations of how the mind works, and studies of human cognition are revealing thinking processes and ways in which information is perceived, learned, and retained. Brain research reveal developmental processes that are linked to the growth of children's skills and understandings, and to their moods and social dispositions. Relative to their musical development, children's active involvement in music-making activity appears to be associated with not only skill-building but also the evolution of their language discrimination, mathematical ability, and problem-solving skills. A consensus is emerging that not only is music a biological fact of human life, but that children who participate in music can enhance the rapid physical development of their brains. Further, brain research has provided data that clarifies music's role in enhancing how children think, reason, and create.

Research has shed considerable light on the different but complementary tasks of the brain's right and left hemispheres. When the corpus callosum, the bundle of nerves connecting the two hemispheres, is severed, the left hemisphere responds better to verbal, sequential, and linear processing, while the right hemisphere is inclined toward nonverbal, spatial-visual, and simultaneous processing. This has led cognitive psychologists to develop a theory of cerebral dominance, which suggests that some individuals are "left-brain convergent" thinkers while others are "right-brain divergent" thinkers (Restak, 1979; Geschwind and Galaburda, 1988). Depending on the task and on the level of learning already attained, people use both sides of the brain with facility, and communication between the hemispheres is rapid and complex. Some educators have taken steps past the conceptual theory to the design of instructional strategies that reach both "brains." The notions of left-brain/right-brain processing continues as common parlance in educational circles to describe students' propensities for sequential and simultaneous thinking.

Neuroscientists have found neural firing patterns that suggest that music may be a pathway to higher brain function (Shaw, 2000). Young children who take music lessons score higher on tests of "general and spatial intelligence," the same cognitive abilities that are foundational for competence in math and engineering. Children who play a musical instrument are strengthening their eye-hand coordination and fine motor skills, as they also develop discipline through regular practice that focuses their attention on required discrete tasks. Their practice leads to musical accomplishment, too, as they learn that there are rewards for hard work, that 10,000 hours of attentive "deliberate practice" lead to high-level performance skills (Ericsson, Charness, Feltovich, and Hoffman, 2006). Further, there appears to be a relationship between making music and getting along with others, such that children who make music together—working to make something beautiful in the company of others learn to regulate their emotions and to become aware of other people's feelings. Music plays an important role in childhood, undergirding the growth of children's thought processes and social interactions.

Research on music and the brain has indicated that both music-making and music listening are sophisticated neural processes, and that specific areas of the brain are involved in emotion, timing, perception, and the production of sequences (Levitin, 2006)—all components of the complex "neuromusical matrix" that comprises a musician's skill-set. Musical ability is more likely a set of abilities, rather than just a singular component, that include aural acuity, tonal and rhythmic memory, the capacity to detect patterns, eye-hand coordination, and the intelligence to integrate sensory information into the individual's web of knowledge and to imbue meaning to it. Studies of human evolution have contributed theories as to why humans developed music, including music as an evolutionary accident, with humans exploiting and extending language to invent music as sonic pleasure, and a Darwinian theory that suggests that music was selected early in human evolution because it signals certain kinds of intellectual, physical, and sexual fitness to a potential mate. Still another theory of music's evolution in human life is that it supported cognitive development: Because of music's complex activity, music has assisted our early ancestors in the development of speech communication.

Learning Style Theories

Several learning style theories have been inspired by research on the functioning of the human brain and on the complexities of the human personality. While these are not instructional theories per se, they underscore the individual differences among children's learning styles, for which an array of instructional strategies may be necessary.

Stemming partly from his observations of brain-damaged individuals who demonstrated specific types of intelligence even though they showed an intellectual deficiency, Howard Gardner (1983/2004) proposed a theory of multiple intelligences. He suggested that there may be eight intelligences, one or several of which are dominant in the learner's processing of the world. Gardner was concerned that the definition of intelligence was too limited and that a person may be intelligent in more than one domain or especially strong in one area while only moderately so in another. The eight intelligences of Gardner's theory are linguistic, logical-mathematical, spatial, interpersonal, intrapersonal, musical, bodily-kinesthetic, and naturalistic; he has also considered two additional domains, that of moral and existential intelligence. His recent work has probed the nature of a teacher's illumination for students of the nature of truth, beauty, and morality through carefully crafted lessons on a theory of evolution, the Holocaust, and the music of Mozart (Gardner, 2000, 2007). While seemingly emerging from his earlier theory, the many dimensions of intelligence emerge in his description of the teacher's craft.

Clearly, Gardner's theory stands on its own, but if each intelligence is more centered in one hemisphere or the other, then his theory can be related to research in cerebral dominance. Left-hemisphere processes are emphasized in linguistic and logical-mathematical intelligences, while spatial intelligence reflects right-hemisphere excellence. Interpersonal and intrapersonal intelligences emanate from right-hemisphere functions. Musical intelligence is balanced by processes of both hemispheres, for it allows sequential (left-brain) processing through its perception of durational and pitch patterns and phrases, and simultaneous (right-brain) processing through its perception of various polyphonic textures, including harmony. The bodily-kinesthetic intelligence is the only emphasis that appears to stem more from the motor and sensory parts of the cortex than from either hemisphere in particular. Each intelligence is like a learning style that calls for specific instructional strategies.

Along with its reference to brain-based research, Gardner's theory of multiple intelligences suggests that there is more than one intellect and that nonverbal forms of learning merit greater attention than is currently given to them by educators. If it can be accepted that the two hemispheres have specialized yet complementary functions, then it would seem critical to pay greater attention to teaching to the somewhat neglected right hemisphere. The exercise of children's subjective, affective, and divergent qualities can be greatly served through lessons in music and the arts. While music can be analyzed linearly by the left hemisphere, it can also be nonverbally experienced and creatively expressed by the right hemisphere. The nature of music instruction allows children occasions for activating the best of both brains.

A theory of learning modalities first proposed by Walter Barbe and Raymond S. Swassing (1979) has remained relevant in contemporary educational practice, as it submits that a learner processes information most efficiently through one of three

Listening, looking, doing:
The multiple modalities
at play

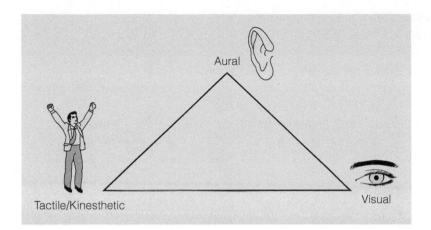

FIGURE 2.2

Learning Modalities: Independent Yet Able to Be Integrated

sensory channels: visual, auditory, or tactile/kinesthetic. The visual learner absorbs information by seeing, reading, and observing demonstrations by others. The auditory learner benefits from verbal instructions and from oral examples presented by the teacher, another student, or recordings. The kinesthetic learner develops knowledge and skills by touching, moving, and physically acting on his or her environment. Learning modalities are thought to be relatively stable over time, but evidence also shows that very young children tend to be kinesthetically oriented, primary-grade children more inclined toward auditory learning, with adolescents shifting toward the visual modality. Figure 2.2 illustrates the modalities; their configuration within a single closed shape suggests the three modalities should all be included in lessons.

Learning modalities can be applied to music instructional approaches. While music classroom environments must be rich in stimulation for all the senses, knowing the modality strengths of individual students would be helpful. The best teaching involves the stimulation of all modalities. This is particularly easy to do in music, which is multimodal by nature. Lesson 2.2 offers a sample lesson that utilizes the three modalities in developing an understanding of pitch and duration within the traditional song "Charlie over the Ocean."

Environmental, emotional, sociological, physical, and psychological issues affecting learning are addressed by Rita Dunn and Kenneth Dunn's (1992) learning style model. Not to be confused with the social systems and surrounds theories, the Dunns' model is directly concerned with the conditions in the classroom and among the students who are found within it. The environmental set of factors is perhaps the most unique aspect of the model, because it includes sound, light, temperature, and classroom design—all of which can be adjusted by the teacher. Some children are negatively affected by loud and noisy environments, while others require some ambient sound to think. Some children's quality of thinking is diminished by learning spaces that are too bright or too dull (dim). If children are too hot or too cold, they may not attain their learning potential. A fourth environmental factor involves the design of a room, which may appear too crowded, overstimulating, and distracting for some.

Field dependence or field independence is postulated by numerous psychologists, including Harold Witkin (1977; Kirton, 2003). Field dependence is defined as content bound, experiencing concepts as embedded within their environment, whereas field independence is content independent, experiencing concepts as discrete entities removed from their background. The field-dependent learner learns best from other people in a social setting and through class discussions and teacher-directed activities. The field-independent learner prefers learning alone and in an autonomous manner and is most comfortable setting his or her own goals and working at his or her own

Charlie over the Ocean (United States, African-American)

Grade Level	One–two
Focus	d–r–m, m–r–d, d–s

⁶⁄₈ rhythm: ♩♪; ♫♫; ♩.

Objectives Children will be able to:

1. Sing and chant pitch and rhythm patterns noted above, in isolation and in the context of the song "Charlie over the Ocean" (a).

2. Map the pitch and rhythm patterns as they are sounded in the song, in the air, on paper, and on the blackboard (v, k).

3. Identify pitch and rhythm patterns as they are sounded vocally or on instruments (a).

4. Walk the pulse while patting rhythm patterns (k).

5. Show pitch levels of patterns through gestures while singing (k, v).

6. Notate the song on music staff (v).

Sequence

1. Children pat the pulse, while teacher chants ⁶⁄₈ rhythms in various patterns:

   ♩♪ (ta-ti); ♫♫ (ti-ti-ti); ♩. (ta-i) (a).

2. Teacher chants ⁶⁄₈ rhythms of song in one- and two-measure phrases. Children pat the pulse while listening and then chanting in imitation (a).

3. Children pat the pulse, while teacher sings pitch patterns:

   d–r–m, m–r–d, d–s (a).

4. Teacher sings song in one- and two-measure phrases, using tonic solfa (solfège) patterns. Children pat the pulse while listening and singing in imitation (a).

5. Teacher sings song with words in full, and then in two-measure phrases, to be imitated by children (a).

6. Children sing the song, mapping in the air, on paper, and on the blackboard the pitch levels of the melody and their durations (v, k).

Melody:

Rhythm: 1   2
-- - -- -- --   -- - -- - --

3   4
-- - - -- - -- -- -- --

7. When the song is learned, teacher isolates several rhythm patterns to clap or play on drum. Children chant back using rhythm syllables (see No. 1). Example:

T (claps): ♩ ♪ ♫♫

C (chant): ta ti ti ti ti

T (claps): ♪♩. ♩. ♩.

C (chant): ti ta-i ta-i ta-i

8. Teacher isolates several pitch patterns to sing on "loo" or to play on the recorder. Children sing back using tonic solfa or words. Example:

T (sings or plays): ♩ ♪ ♫♫ ♩.

C (sings with solfa): d d d d d s₁

C (sings words) Char-lie o-ver the sea

9. Teacher plays the pulse on drum. Children walk the pulse. On cue, they pat the rhythms of the song (on their tummies, shoulders, and head) while walking (k).

10. While singing the song, children use hand levels to show pitch. Then they use Curwen-Kodály hand signs associated with individual pitches (k, v).

11. Measure by measure, children chant the rhythm as teacher notates it above the staff (v, a).

12. Measure by measure, children sing the pitches (with solfa or words) as teacher notates it on the staff (v, a).

13. Teacher adjusts pitches for appropriate rhythms (v).

Note: a = aural; v = visual; k = kinesthetic.

pace. In a musical setting, field-dependent learners may thrive on singing games, group improvisation, and ensemble performance. Field-independent learners may more easily gain knowledge through computer-assisted programs of instruction, solo practice, and individual composition. The astute observer, teacher, or parent soon distinguishes among these learners and makes allowances for them.

A related theory by Isabel Myers, Peter B. Briggs, M. H. McCaulley, and R. Most (1985) postulates that four types of personality factors inform learning: (1) extroversion/introversion, (2) sensing/intuitive, (3) thinking/feeling, and (4) judging/perceiving. They are measured through the Myers-Briggs Type indicator. Extroverted learners are more socially directed to the external world, thinking aloud to process ideas, while introverted learners require silent internal processing time to figure out what they have observed or experienced. Sensing learners rely heavily on their sensory channels to give them information, while intuitive types invent and reason new information from previous experiences. Thinking learners make decisions based on objective rational analyses, and feeling learners rely on subjective personal values as the basis of decisions. Finally, judging learners make decisions easily and promptly, while perceivers are tentative, choosing to delay decisions while gathering further information. These varied personalities challenge the teacher to carefully gauge the personalities of their students and to creatively develop ways to enhance their learning.

Theories of Instruction

Over the past several decades, instructional psychologists have developed many theories about the effects of interactions between teachers and learners. Only a small selection of the more significant theories to music instruction for children is described here.

David Ausubel (1968, 2000) maintained that a person's existing cognitive structure is the foremost factor governing whether new material is potentially meaningful as well as how readily it can be acquired and retained. In his theory of meaningful reception, the role of the learner is to receive ideas and information, with the teacher being the lecturer or explainer. Critical to the learner's meaningful reception of new information is the provision of "advance organizers" by the teacher, the structuring of a foundation of familiar ideas on which new information can be laid. The teacher who outlines the material to be covered and goals to be met is also organizing for children in advance the learning that will occur. Children must listen intently and actively seek to reorganize their existing knowledge in view of the teacher's ideas, so that they can then formulate new ways of looking at the world.

Jerome Bruner (1966, 1996) is the major proponent of the "discovery method." The discovery method is a type of learning that involves problem solving, requiring the learner to manipulate materials and to cope with incongruities from which information is derived. Discovery learning encourages taking risks, guessing, and exploring student-initiated hypotheses. Exploratory experiences and occasional nonconformity are indicators of creative thinking, which is the ultimate goal of all learning. Improvisation and composition experiences are the most obvious examples of musical exploration and experimentation, but any musical experience that challenges children to think while listening, performing, or creating can exemplify discovery learning. Musical concepts can be most effectively taught via the discovery method. By experiencing a concept (such as pulse, meter, a three-pitch melody, or binary form) without initially labeling it, children can explore and be guided toward an understanding of that concept and then learn its official name.

Brunerian ideas were influential in the development of curriculum and instruction in music, most notably the highly innovative Manhattanville Music Curriculum Project, or MMCP, that, while no longer intact, may still influence music education programs here and there. In addition to directing musical experiences for children to include musical exploration, improvisation, and composition, Bruner's concept of a spiral curriculum that allows children to learn music through age-appropriate experiences was put to its test through MMCP. The spiral curriculum recommended that "any subject could be taught to any child at any age," so long as it is set in lessons suitable for the intellectual level of the child. Thus, the components of music for example, melody and rhythm—can be taught to preschool and secondary school students, just as the music of Mozart and Messiaen, and that from Bali and Bulgaria, can be experienced earlier and later in a child's school career.

Robert Gagné's descriptive studies of cognitive processes a half century ago led to his development (with his colleagues) of eight "events of instruction" or "conditions of learning" (1993, 2004). The events or conditions include a progression of sensory information from perception to concept formation. These events embrace the need for preparing children for new information, offering occasions for their responses to and practice of new information, and supporting the transfer of information gained to the greater acquisition of knowledge. The teacher's role in engaging children's interest is an important first step for knowledge acquisition; that role becomes increasingly prominent later, when he or she introduces the more complex process of problem solving. More than most theories, Gagné's events of instruction are clear-cut steps that can be readily applied to music. See Box 2.1 for an application of Gagné's eight events to music for children. These steps may apply to a complete lesson or to single activities within a lesson.

Edwin E. Gordon's (1997) music learning theory appears to be at least partially influenced by some of Gagné's early theoretical work. Gordon's earlier work was nearly a direct application of Gagné's events to music. Like the events of instruction, Gordon's theory is hierarchical in nature, progressing through eight levels that begin with aural or oral reception and transmission and lead to generalization, improvisation, and finally music theory—the whys and hows of musical pitch and rhythm functions. Gordon compares learning music with mastering a spoken language, as a progression from first simply perceiving and responding to sounds to the advanced levels of problem solving and conceptual understanding. Gordon also addresses the sequential nature of acquiring basic discrimination and music literacy skills, and the use and transfer of these skills to bring about more sophisticated possibilities for music learning.

Gordon's music learning theory is a comprehensive model of skill development, founded on the principle of audiation, or inner hearing: the ability to "hear" notation and to notate what one hears. Gordon's recommendations for music instruction begin with musical sound and vocalized patterns, proceeding gradually to the notational symbols of pitch and rhythm. His music learning sequence is a prescribed succession of music skills (or performance behaviors), music content, and tonal and rhythm patterns, and it is intended to develop musical audiation and understanding. See Chapter 3 for further explanation of the method that Gordon developed from his theory.

BOX 2.1 Gagné's Events of Instruction: Applications to Music for Children

1. Gaining and maintaining attention
   - Ask a probing question to pique curiosity
   - Present a startling statement
   - Tell a short story
   - Sing a favorite familiar song with children
   - Clap a rhythm children can imitate
   - Play a recording that encourages children's movement responses
   - Engage children in immediate participation

2. Preparing learners for instruction
   - Repeat #1, but with relevance to the new music to be learned
   - Share with children the goals and expectations of the lesson or activity
   - Present fragments and phrases of the new music to be learned as teasers for children's imitation

3. Presenting the material
   - Present the lesson's music in live or recorded form
   - Present small sections or chunks of the new music that can be linked together to form the whole

4. Prompting and guiding learning
   - Illustrate problem melodic and rhythmic phrases through mnemonics
   - Call attention to repeated patterns and unusual musical features
   - Allow time to rehearse individually, in small or large groups

5. Providing conditions for response
   - Offer occasions for active participation and performance by all
   - Switch from playing to singing a piece; from singing to moving to its rhythm or pulse

6. Providing feedback for response
   - Remind children of learning goals and expectation of the lesson or activity
   - Offer specific comments when possible
   - Allow children opportunities to change and to perfect their performance

7. Promoting and measuring retention
   - Critique children's performance
   - Allow children to evaluate their performance
   - Provide opportunities for children to develop the musical ideas of the piece through improvisation

8. Enhancing transfer of learning to new tasks or information
   - Transfer concepts and skills to performance of unfamiliar piece
   - Transfer concepts and skills to listening of unfamiliar piece

Relating Theory to Practice

Five components of guidelines based on the theories of teaching and learning provide for the effective delivery of instruction by teachers to children in preschool and the elementary grades: the classroom environment, the child-centered curriculum, the teacher as transmitter, instructional strategies, and motivation and management. Chapter 11 offers considerable discussion of this last topic.

The Classroom Environment

WHAT SHOULD THE MUSIC CLASSROOM LOOK LIKE? Theories of child development, musical play, and learning styles inform the physical setting of the music classroom. Most important, furniture in the music room must be minimal so that a great variety of musical play and performance experiences can occur. A piano is always useful, whether acoustic or electric, and preferably one with wheels for easy maneuvering. Various types of xylophones and percussion instruments can be laid on tables for easy access by children. Larger drums and bass xylophones can be laid across the floor or kept in storage until needed. Computers for independent and small-group projects can be set up in one corner of the room, and various programs and packages are available for children's opportunities to composing, listening, and learning notation. Even in a medium-sized room, a small keyboard lab of four to six pianos can be placed at one end.

For seated activities, floor space is still preferable to desks. Children can pick up three-foot carpet squares (usually available as remnants from a carpet store) when they enter the classroom, or they can situate themselves on the periphery of a circle of masking tape laid out on the floor. Choral risers can make for useful seating or standing arrangements, especially for the upper grades. These should be located against a wall so that open space remains in the center for movement activities.

Various audiovisual resources are vital for teaching and can be kept on wheel carts for greater portability. A high-quality sound system, typically a laptop with the capacity to play audio and video downloads, is basic to any successful music instruction. A simple screen or SMART board interactive whiteboard should be strategically placed such that it is easily visible to all. A table with chairs, on which basic laptop or cellphone listening centers with headphones can be set, can make for an ideal independent listening and ear-training lab. A teacher's desk, a personal computer, files, and storage cabinets complete the list of necessary furniture.

WHAT SHOULD THE MUSIC CLASSROOM FEEL LIKE? Teachers need to be aware of factors that create an environment conducive to music listening, performing, and creating. The music room should be well ventilated, with plenty of windows for fresh air and light. It should be low on ambient sound and moderate in temperature, ventilation, and light. Cafeterias, with the noise of cookware clanging together, are not ideal for use as music rooms. Gyms are built for sports and games, but they are not appropriate for developing musical sensitivity, performance techniques, and aural skills because of their poor acoustics.

WHAT OTHER RESOURCES CAN ENHANCE A MUSIC CLASSROOM'S POTENTIAL FOR EFFECTIVE INSTRUCTION? Visual appeal can motivate children to want to come to music and to learn. A SMART board or whiteboard, preferably with staff lines, is the sine qua non of the music room, especially by the time notation is introduced. Felt boards and bulletin boards can be places for attractive posters and color photographs of performers, composers, dancers, instruments, maps, and timely announcements. Notational symbols make pleasant borders, and colorful lists of terms can be pinned to these boards. Instruments should be labeled in bold letters so that their names are known. Sheets of butcher paper (available from art supply or butcher's shops) are useful for writing and posting song words and key concepts of a lesson.

WHAT PRINT, AUDIO, VIDEO, AND WEB-BASED MATERIALS SHOULD A TEACHER HAVE AVAILABLE FOR MUSIC INSTRUCTION? A personal collection of audio and video files and favorite websites (bookmarked and ready to use) is of tremendous value to a teacher, and CD recordings, DVDs, the old standard basal series textbooks, story books, and supplemental books can stimulate the design of successful lessons. An annotated listing of the contents of such a collection can trigger the memory and serve as a guide for lesson plans. Updated basal series music textbook offer ready-made online lessons, and a rich array of web-based materials. Sources for beginning to build a personal library of music education materials and methods are listed at the end of each chapter. While websites come and go, some of the long-lasting treasuries of music fit for use with children are available on sites of Smithsonian Folkways <www.folkways.si.edu/>, the Association for Cultural Equity <www.culturalequity.org/>, and the Library of Congress <www.loc.gov/index.html>. A teacher's personal storehouse of instructional materials may be a balance of electronic and physical sources, and the key is the teacher's careful review, organization, and planning for ways of best use.

When fundamental materials, such as a sound system and musical instruments, are not available, small educational grants or gifts can be obtained to provide for them.

A Child-Centered Curriculum

A child-centered curriculum offers instruction that is relevant to the child's experiences and abilities, needs, and interests. This curriculum is more playful and more integrated than other curriculums, and it is more likely to be led by the responses of children than by the whims of the teacher. What are the realities of a child-centered curriculum in music? Several key issues merit consideration in the design of a music program.

KNOW THE CHILDREN. What musical skills and knowledge do children possess? What music interests and moves them? What are their learning styles? What subject strengths do they possess? Where are they developmentally? What are their cultural and familial backgrounds? What, if any, are the musical and educational expectations of their parents? Do they have musical goals and dreams they hope to attain? Generalizing about children leads to surefire foiled experiences that fail to reach them. By talking to teachers and parents, reviewing school files, and asking questions of the children themselves, teachers can offer far more relevant musical experiences and training.

BEGIN WHERE THE CHILDREN ARE. While many specific questions may be asked for which answers should be sought, universal concepts must be considered when designing music instruction for children. These include (1) providing lessons that lead children from the familiar to the unfamiliar—that is, teaching ♩♫ after they know ♫♫ and teaching $\frac{7}{8}$ after they understand two- and three-beat meters; (2) giving children many occasions for active instead of passive experiences (most children achieve their greatest learning when they have actively participated through manipulation of a concept or through performance); and (3) offering children lessons with variety (various approaches to a concept, various musical examples, and various musical pieces and styles).

ALLOW TIME FOR MUSICAL PLAY AND EXPLORATION. For young children, musical sound is a discovery of how loud and how soft, how choppy and how smooth, how long and how short, how fast and how slow, how high and how low a set of pots and pans, the teeth of a comb, or two pencils can sound. Given a drum, sandblocks, or a xylophone, how many different sounds can a young child play? For older children, the music curriculum can be linked to solving musical problems creatively through experimentation: Choose the pitches for a rhythmic pattern and create a new song; or write a poem and perform it rhythmically and with dynamic expression. Time must be allotted as well for experimentation and personal expression through music.

INTEGRATE MUSIC INTO THE OTHER PARTS OF A CHILD'S LIFE. Songs blend with stories, music listening mixes with movement, and a study of musical instruments is also a lesson in the science of acoustics. Like the whole language approach in other subject areas, music is not to be treated as a separate entity but can be coupled with the learning of concepts in social studies, language arts, mathematics, and the sciences. A musical experience can be enhanced by experiences in the visual arts, stories, poetry, theater, and movement and dance.

The Teacher as Transmitter

Teachers are transmitters of culture. How they package and present information to children is critical to whether the transmission process is completed; that is, whether the information is received and assimilated by children. Theories of instruction, reinforcement, socialization, and social learning underscore the powerful impact that a teacher can have on children's learning and development. Of the many qualities that good music teachers possess, several are most prominent.

KNOW THE SUBJECT MATTER. The effective music teacher knows well the music, concept, or technique to be taught. Knowing the music requires preparation; without it, the lesson will fail. A Russian folk song cannot be taught before the teacher has practiced the song's words, melody, and rhythm. A xylophone arrangement cannot be masterfully taught if the teacher has not worked out the parts: by reading and rereading, chanting, patting, singing, or even playing them. The teacher should be able to sing, play, or move to the music selected for lessons with ease and refinement. As the teacher transmits the music, his or her enjoyment and love for it is also passed on to the children. Music concepts must be clearly understood in terms of their critical perceptual qualities so activities can be chosen to highlight those qualities.

MODEL THE MUSICAL BEHAVIORS. The effective music teacher serves as the live model for the music to be learned. Performance skills are learned by children who imitate or are otherwise influenced by the behavior and comments of their teacher. Verbal explanations are far less effective than demonstration. How can children be told in words alone how to sing staccato, to sustain a sound, or (initially) to play a bourdon (bass drone) or xylophone? As the adage goes, a teacher's "actions speak louder than words." Many children will know no other musicians who can sing well and perform proficiently on musical instruments. For them, the teacher who performs is critical to their musical well-being. While absolute mimicry by children is not the goal of a teacher's musical demonstrations, model musicianship can be observed, absorbed, and reinterpreted by children in their own performance.

PRESENT WITH ENERGY AND ENTHUSIASM. The effective music teacher is enthusiastic about music and children, and he or she presents lessons that are charged with energy. Enthusiasm is conveyed in many ways: a broad spectrum of vocal inflections and facial expressions, steady eye contact, varied gestures and demonstrative movements of the body, and descriptive vocabulary. The teaching pace needs to at least occasionally match that of television programs to which children are accustomed, with quick changes of experiences and approaches to a musical concept. High energy and vitality most successfully convey ideas. While enthusiasm

"Teachers are transmitters of culture."

Methodological Suggestions for Early Childhood

- **For class-starters,** consider singing a story to young children (with a response that they can sing back periodically through the story), or performing a very loud and fast (or very soft and slow) song or instrumental selection played "live," or engaging in a musical question-and-response sequence or imitation of them via chanting, singing, patting, clapping, stamping, and the like.

- **For class-closers,** consider leading young children in singing a familiar song in a sitting circle, or quietly telling a musical story (of a music-making family, a famous drummer, dancer, pianist, guitarist), or clapping rhythms around the circle one at a time within the frame of four beats each, or taking answers to the question "What did we learn today?"

- **Give young children plenty of time for musical discovery** by providing them with genuine musical instruments (drums, rattles, pennywhistles and recorders, home-made monochords, harmonicas, small xylophones), sound-making objects (boxes, pots, pans, dowels), and unrestricted periods for their exploration alone and together.

- **Teach young children through example** as you model what you would have them do. Actions speak louder than words to them; by doing first they will understand the words and symbols that stand for the experience.

- **Reward young children for their musical accomplishments** (for learning a song, playing bourdons or ostinati) with smiles, verbal praise, and special privileges (free-choice music time, for example). Let them know that you notice their growth as the young musicians that they are, and that their music making is special to all those who hear them.

comes naturally for some teachers, others can learn by reviewing teaching behaviors via videotaped recordings and then making a conscientious effort to increase their eye contact or to vary their facial expressions. No doubt, a teacher's enthusiasm is also related to job satisfaction as well as his or her interest in the music selected for the lesson.

Children's choir in the setting of the music classroom

Instructional Strategies

The clearest way to understand instructional theories is to apply them to your teaching. What are some of the recent instructional strategies that promote learning and develop strong and lasting interactions between teacher and children? Some strategies are governed by children's age, stage, or phase of development, while others relate to their individual learning styles and personalities.

STARTING THE CLASS. The manner in which a class begins can entice and motivate children to learn or can turn their attentions away from the subject for the remainder of the period. Gaining children's attention may proceed in many ways. Play live or recorded music as children enter. Ask a question ("How might a composer portray the sound of a train?" leading to playing Honneger's "Pacific 231"). Tell a story ("Beauty and the Beast," leading to Ravel's piece of the same title). Make a bold and startling statement ("People in Mozambique do not sit still at concerts," leading to a lesson incorporating song, story, dance, and xylophone performance). Clap a rhythm to be imitated by children. Give a silent gesture that, over time, means to come to attention, a signal that something important is about to happen. As a musician-teacher, sing a song or play a piece. Perform a familiar song with the class. Show a photograph or illustration, in silence or with a leading question. Depending on the lesson, any number of these strategies will direct children's attention toward class.

ENDING THE CLASS. The music and the learning will linger longer when the class ends in a memorable or stimulating fashion. There are many possibilities. Sing or play a familiar song. Play or snap, clap, pat, and stamp a rhythmic piece or passage. Ask a question to be answered in the next music class ("What could we do to make this song more interesting texturally?"). Tease by previewing the next class ("And if you want to know how to play an Afro-Cuban rhythm on the conga drum, you'll have to come back next _____!"). Rapidly review the main points of the lesson. Play live or recorded music as children exit.

SUPPLYING FEEDBACK: THE TST. The interactive instructional kernel of the teaching and learning process is a three-step sequence that involves the (T)eacher's presentation of information, the (S)tudents' response to that information, and the (T)eacher's specific feedback to the response. Based on operant conditioning, the TST is the Skinnerian stimulus-response-stimulus sequence that makes for effective instruction. There are multiple TST kernels in a lesson, because the teacher's feedback in the third step progresses to the next TST. An example of three TSTs in a row is this interchange at the beginning of a recorder lesson:

> T: Let's learn the playing position of the recorder. Hold the recorder in your left hand.
>
> S: (Children hold their recorders in their left hands.)
>
> T: Good. Now relax. It should feel easy, almost natural.
>
> T: Now, let's blow air out gently, as if into a straw.
>
> S: (Children blow air.)
>
> T: Not too hard. Gently. Pretend you're blowing small bubbles.
>
> T: Let's try this out on the recorder. Ready, blow.
>
> S: (Children blow air into recorder.)
>
> T: Not bad. You're on your way.

Clearly, the lack of any steps in these three TSTs means that the instruction is not complete. There must be information from the teacher, followed by a response from the children, concluding with the teacher's evaluation of their response. From one TST to the next, the teacher is interacting with students through information given and gained.

STIMULATING AURAL LEARNING. Understanding and skill building in music require careful listening. Music literacy is advanced through aural learning, which includes the use of modeling, imitative devices, and strategies for strengthening the memory. The instructional approaches of Kodály, Dalcroze, and Orff suggest that melodic and rhythmic ideas, phrasing and form, expressive elements, and performance techniques can initially be taught aurally. The aural acquisition of music may even facilitate music literacy; it is a necessary phase toward that development. Recorded music for aural learning can be supplemented by live performances given by the teacher, older and more experienced students, visiting artists, and amateur musicians from the community. Musical patterns, fragments, phrases, and pieces can help to build in children a functional musical vocabulary for their later listening and performance. Learning by listening is a logical procedure, bringing children directly into the sound of the music.

PROVIDING FOR REPETITION AND REHEARSAL. The acquisition of performance and listening skills takes time and effort, and children can show considerable progress through repeated attempts to achieve them. Learning to sing four phrases of a traditional song such as "Charlie over the Ocean" is a complex endeavor for very young children. The words, rhythm, melodic patterns, and tonality may take many listenings, and even more occasions for singing it, before the components begin to fall in place. Listening to Stravinsky's "Greeting Prelude" or to Bach's "Little Fugue in G Minor" is challenging to older children, when the object is to listen analytically for the formal organization of melodic and rhythmic ideas. Preference for, or at least tolerance of, a musical piece may require a bare minimum of ten listenings, and probably more. Fleeting experiences do not guarantee learning; repetition can.

Various instructional strategies are played out in this sketch of a lesson (Box 2.2) for children that features musical openers and closers, two grade-level songs, a

BOX 2.2 Instructional Strategies in a Full-Fledged Lesson

RECORDED (OR LIVE) MUSIC AS CHILDREN ENTER

INTRODUCTIONS/GREETING/(AIMS) (~1 MINUTE)

OPENER (~3 MINUTES); EXAMPLES:

Opener 1: Body percussion imitation: 5–10 rhythms using stamps, pats, claps, snaps

Opener 2: Chant imitation: 5–10 vocalized rhythms on "ba," "chee," "taw," "sss"

Opener 3: Sung imitation: 5–10 vocalized patterns using phrases from songs and/or simple phrases like "hel-lo" (s-m), "how are you?" (l-s-m)

GRADE LEVEL SONG 1 (~5 MINUTES)
If initial/introductory experience (first lesson):

Introduction: Three questions/Three sings/Three answers (See Chapter 1 model)
Then, set pitch/tempo and sing together (three times)

(Continued)

BOX 2.2 *(Continued)*

In subsequent returns to the song (second, third, fourth lessons):

1. Ask: Do you remember this song? (T sing with enthusiasm and energy!)
2. Ask: Can you sing the song with me/us? (T set pitch/tempo, sing)
3. Ask: Can you sing the song silently while I/we sing aloud?
4. Ask: Let's sing it out loud again. (T set pitch/tempo, sing)
5. Ask: Can you supply the missing phrase? (T sing the song, drop one phrase)
6. Ask: Can you tap/pat/clap on two fingers the rhythm of the song melody?
     (First time—sing aloud; Second time—sing silently.)
7. Sing the song and do-something-special. (Game, action/gestures, dance)

And then: Practice-Practice-Practice! Via Immersion/Whole-Song Method Culminating Activity (Instrumental Play, Game, Dance, Challenge)

RHYTHMICKING ACTIVITY (~7–8 MINUTES)
Choose a two-line poem and set it to rhythm, including vocalization and body percussion

1. Rhythmically chant the proverb (or partial) poem
2. Pat the steady pulse, rhythmically chant again
3. Repeat (2)
4. Clap the rhythm of the words while rhythmically chanting aloud
5. Clap the rhythm of the words while rhythmically thinking them
6. Play a body percussion rhythm to/with the word-rhythms
     (use stamps, pats, claps, snaps, slaps, etc.)
7. Repeat (6)
8. Play a body percussion rhythm while rhythmically thinking the word-rhythms
9. Repeat (6)

GRADE LEVEL SONG 2 (~5 MINUTES)

Repeat song-teaching sequence, using a grade-level song

Follow sequence of Grade Level Song 1

CHOICE ACTIVITY (~5 MINUTES)

Rhythmic movement (to recorded/live music)

Story/poem (to present together in a musical way)

Instrumental experience (related to or separated from grade-level song)

Improvisation or composition (on instruments or vocally, in large- or small groups)

MUSICAL CLOSERS (~3 MINUTES)

Closer 1:   Sing a string of familiar melodies on neutral syllables

Closer 2:   Sing, pat/clap, chant in imitation

Closer 3:   Take answers to the question, "What did we learn today?"

Closer 4:   Softly chant a poem in rhythm while children soft pat on laps

Closer 5:   Story-Tell "your musical life": Give them a taste of the life of a professional musician!

RECORDED (OR LIVE) MUSIC AS CHILDREN DEPART

rhythmicking activity (rhythm participation experience), and a "choice activity" that may allow for listening, movement, the integration of a story or poem, experiences in playing instruments, or improvisation or composition. While this is a large order of multiple activities for a single thirty- or forty-five-minute lesson, organized teachers can make much happen in short time frames that will keep children stimulated and growing their musical knowledge and skills from one lesson to the next.

Informed Teaching

All practices are guided by theory; music teaching and learning are no exception. Several disciplines offer theories for framing music instruction for children—developmental and stage and phase theories, musical play and socialization theories, social learning and reinforcement theories, learning style theories, and the blossoming field of instructional psychology.

Teachers engaged in the design of curriculum and instruction in music for children would do well to compare the ideas of others with their own practical perspectives. A theory can be an academic endeavor, evolved by those who once taught and later thought. It can also be a personal effort, a marriage of ideas by insightful teachers who think as they do. By knowing the literature on instructional theory and connecting it to their own practice, teachers can have a significant impact on the music instruction that children receive.

TECHNOLOGY *for* TEACHING: FROM THEORY *to* PRACTICE *in* TEACHING MUSIC *to* CHILDREN

Technology often can be integrated with other methods, approaches, and strategies for teaching music in a whole-class setting, and in addition, technology can offer special benefits that a teacher in a classroom simply doesn't have the time or attention for. Just a few of these special benefits are:

1. provide differentiated instruction to individuals or small groups,

2. reteach as many times as it takes for some students to achieve mastery,

3. give students huge amounts of carefully sequenced musical challenges and individual specific feedback,

4. allow each student to proceed at his or her own pace,

5. provide remedial instruction and advanced instruction to different individuals or groups simultaneously,

6. expand student learning into hours beyond the music class time, using software and the Internet at home, libraries, and other classrooms,

7. provide formative and summative measurements of students' musical achievement without taking away from valuable instruction time.

To learn more about what and how technology can augment other methods, approaches, and strategies for teaching music, visit the Technology Resource links in the MindTap.

MINDTAP

Scenario

FROM THE VANTAGE POINT of eight years of experience as the music teacher at Hillside Elementary School, Kristin reflected on her initial years just "out-the-gate" and into a professional teaching experience. She had only a few minutes between her third- and fifth-grade music classes, but could take a few questions, she said, and began with a response to a question on her first year of teaching. "If I do say so myself, I managed pretty well to work children through a curriculum that blended who I was as a musician with who they were as young learners. Our lessons were a mix of what I learned in my methods classes, what I gained from my student teaching practicum, and even what I learned as a child myself in a very fine elementary school program."

Kristin ticked off the things she did in her first year: "We sang a ton of songs, solfeged them, had lots of rhythmicking experiences—you know, vocal chants of short poems, connected to body percussion (clapping, patting, snapping, stamping), some note-reading (especially rhythm reading for the primary grades and more pitch reading when we got to recorders in the third grade and after that). Oh, and composing units, improvising opportunities, listening—listening at the start and end of classes, and listening lessons that combined movement. You know, the usual curriculum for elementary school music. Come to think of it, what I did that first year of teaching is foundational to all that I've done since. I worked it out pretty well, but I really worked hard that first year."

And what about theory? Did Kirsten find it useful to know the theories behind her practice? "Oh, don't get me started. You've got to know something about child development, about brain theory, learning styles, and phases, stages, levels of how they learn in order to know how to teach them. You can't teach like a spacehead, and some of these theories are useful and interesting, both. Teachers don't have time on their hands to learn theory when they're teaching, but they're at a serious disadvantage if they didn't get their Piaget, their Vygotsky, their multiple intelligences, and some kind of understanding about how kids learn informally. We get too busy once we're teaching to study theory, but if we come in with some understanding of how kids learn, it makes the lesson-planning and on-the-spot decision-making much easier." An illustration, perhaps? "So, I would expect much less of my kids in what they can understand and do if I didn't have some idea as to how their brains develop, what they have the capacity for, how there are some important learnings (you know, academic-intellectual and social) that happen when they play, and how the media influences what they know. Then there's the modalities, how some are more prone to visual, or auditory, or kinesthetic learning, and watching out for which kids learn what ways. And on and on."

Kirsten continued, clearly on a roll and wanting to get to some closure on the matter of thoughtful, theory-based music teaching. "Plus, I want my staff and my parents to know that I'm an educated musician who is connecting the dots of children, to music, to learning and development, to culture and society. I'm more than just a musician in the schools. I care about children's meta-development, overall, and how music fits into their thinking process. I'm part of the team of teachers, and I take my work as an educator seriously. Theory helps me to think and articulate what I do."

The fifth-grade students were arriving, she greeted them as she closed the conversation, turned on a Bobby McFerrin performance of Fauré's Pavane, and began to model a conducting pattern that rose and fell with the movement of the graceful melody.

Questions

1. Which theories did Kirsten describe as important for music teachers to know? Clarify the contributions of these theories and theorists to an understanding of learning and instruction in music.

2. In her listing of her first year's teaching, discuss theories that would readily inform the various components.

3. About the start into the lesson on Fauré's Pavane (and how the lesson could potentially evolve), what theories are useful for Kirsten in making this an effective and appealing learning experience?

REVIEW

1. Why do teachers need theory for teaching music to children?

2. How are stage-dependent and phase theories related?

3. What theories support the following statements: (1) Good teachers are models for children to emulate. (2) Children should be allowed to learn through their own experimentation. (3) The interaction of teachers with children leads to learning. (4) Children may respond to one form of presentation more favorably than another.

4. What implications do brain and personality theories hold for instruction?

5. Are the theories of Ausubel and Bruner mutually exclusive? Why or why not?

6. Which theories govern children's motivation to learn as well as the teacher's management of their behaviors?

CRITICAL THINKING

1. Which theories can help to guide the design of a child-centered curriculum? How might such a curriculum manifest itself in the behaviors of teachers and children?

2. How is it that musical play can be a child's work—a means for their development intellectually, physically, socially, and emotionally. Give examples of musical play and its effects on children's development.

PROJECTS

1. In small groups, choose a theory, articulate its principal features, and prepare for demonstration a lesson segment that illustrates the theory in action. As an alternative activity, prepare a lesson to teach and then discuss what theories are illustrated within it.

2. Observe a music class for children, and draw relationships between the instructional procedures and theories.

3. Observe the individual responses of children in music classes, and discuss learning style theories as they relate to these responses.

4. Design and teach a lesson based on Gagné's eight events of instruction.

5. Enumerate a set of behavioral rules that you will use as guidelines to ensure an effective learning environment for children.

MINDTAP Visit **MindTap** to access classroom videos, audio, and more!

3

Methods of Teaching Music to Children

IN THIS CHAPTER

- Dalcroze: Movement with a Mission
- Kodály: Inner Hearing and Music Literacy
- Orff: Expression through Musical Experience
- Other Approaches to Music Learning
  - Comprehensive Musicianship
  - Gordon's Music Learning Theory
  - Manhattanville Music Curriculum Project
  - Music in Education
  - Education through Music
  - Weikert's Movement Sequence
- A Comparison of Methods and Techniques
- A Personal Method

THERE MAY BE AS many methods of teaching music as there are music teachers. Still, certain images conjure up some of the best-known instructional approaches. Julia's bourdon playing with felt-covered mallets on metallophones recalls the Orff-Schulwerk approach, as does the rhythmic chanting of the poem that Jimmie and Aaron set to temple blocks and kettle drums. Donna and Soo Mee add hand signals to the melodies of traditional singing games they know, putting the Kodály philosophy to practice. As Jorge skips to a $\frac{6}{8}$ melody, changing directions at the change of phrases, two facets of Dalcroze eurhythmics are clearly evident. Carmen's free exploration of sounds on bottles, boxes, and plastic balls brings to mind the Manhattanville Music Curriculum Project (MMCP). Lisa and her classmates study a Mozart minuet in the multiple ways espoused by proponents of Comprehensive Musicianship. Denny's chanting of rhythms in imitation of his teacher's presentation underscores Gordon's initial aural and oral stage, while Fatin and Katelin learn folk dances through Weikert's sequence of saying-while-doing.

Of the numerous instructional approaches used in music classes for children, some are familiar and, couched in tradition, have stood the test of time and experience. Other approaches have been developed more recently through changes in societal values, patterns of living, and technology. Some teachers hold steadfastly to a single method, while others merge techniques from many methods to convey even a single aspect of music. In the end, every teacher finds his or her own pathway to a personal teaching method that works effectively in guiding children toward the development of musical skills and understanding. This personal teaching method depends on the teacher's training and experience, the instructional goals, the classroom setting, and the musical (and extramusical) needs and interests of the children to be taught. The manner in which musicality is defined also provides for the variety of techniques used.

THINGS TO THINK ABOUT

- How did you learn music?

- Which teachers were able to facilitate the development of your singing voice, your ability to play an instrument, your deeper listening, your ability to move expressively to the musical sound, your musical creativity?

- How did your teachers teach so that you might learn?

- What ways of teaching come naturally to you?

- Which teaching strategies do you want to learn? Why?

Some classic and contemporary methods of music instruction, many of them familiar to experienced teachers, are described here according to their principal goals and techniques. Sample experiences are presented for three of the best-known pedagogies: Dalcroze, Kodály, and Orff. Their instructional techniques are also delineated throughout the book. A comparison of the methods and further discussion of the development of a personal method conclude the chapter.

Dalcroze: Movement with a Mission

"MOVEMENT WITH A MISSION" is one description of the Dalcroze approach to music instruction. Dalcroze eurhythmics has been inaccurately described as dance—the stereotypical image of a Dalcroze lesson featuring young dancers in black leotards leaping to the rhythms of improvised piano music is not complete. The Dalcroze approach is three-pronged, including not only a unique form of rhythmic movement called eurhythmics but also ear training (solfège and solfège-rhythmique) and improvisation. The key qualities that link accomplishment in each of these elements are imagination, a keen listening sense, and an immediacy of response to the musical stimulus.

The founder of the Dalcroze approach was Émile Jaques-Dalcroze (1865–1950), a Swiss musician who served as professor of solfège, harmony, and composition at the Geneva Conservatory. His pedagogy originated early in the twentieth century as he experimented with approaches to ear training. He astutely recognized that, despite the advanced stages of technical proficiency that his students demonstrated through the playing of their instruments, notable gaps were evident in their musical abilities. Simple rhythms were wrongly rendered, and flaws in pitch and intonation were frequent. Students were demonstrating mechanical, not musical, understanding.

Beginning with rhythmic gymnastics that activated the diaphragm, lungs, and articulatory functions of the mouth and tongue, the students of Professor Jaques-Dalcroze were soon singing scales in dichord (d-r, r-m, m-f, and so on) and trichord (d-r-m, r-m-f, m-f-s, and so on) arrangements, in canon with the teacher, at double and half the speed of the original statement, and alternating silent internal singing and singing aloud on cue. As his eurhythmics approach evolved, students developed the muscular rhythms and nervous sensibilities that would allow them to discriminate among even slight gradations of duration, time, intensity, and phrasing. Jaques-Dalcroze believed that people were musical when they came to possess an ensemble of physical and spiritual resources and capacities comprising the ear, brain, and body. Eurhythmics became the core of his approach and the foundation for raising each person's musical sensitivity to its fullest potential.

For experienced performers and children alike, the Dalcroze techniques lay the foundation for a thorough musicianship. The achievement of proficient eurhythmic movement requires a repertory of complex kinesthetic reactions. Children's eurhythmic movement will include any number of possibilities in space and place as well as locomotor and nonlocomotor movement—isolated gestures using the hands, arms, head, shoulders, or a combination of body parts. Their movement is a personal and immediate response to the music played on the piano, on percussion instruments, or (more rarely) on recordings or performed vocally. Children become proficient as they follow the tempo, rhythm, and meter of music with their bodies, learning to react quickly to changes in any aspect of the music, for example changes in meter, rhythm patterns, dynamics, or phrase length.

Ear training, including solfège and solfège-rhythmique, is a second critical component in a Dalcroze education. Children are taught to understand tones and semitones and their relationships in scales, songs, and musical passages. The fixed-do system is advocated

© Jerry Gay

by most Dalcroze teachers, in which C is the starting note of the scale regardless of the tonic. For example, when the fixed-do system is used, a G Major scale begins on C and contains an F#.

Jaques-Dalcroze reasoned that children develop absolute pitch as the sense of C is impressed on the ear, the muscles, and the mind. He believed that the interrelationship of the scales would become clear, with children able to aurally determine the order of tones and semitones that constitute each scale. Singing via the Dalcroze approach is accompanied by hand gestures that show the position of the pitch in space or by movement of the fingers on the arm as an imaginary keyboard. Children are led to hearing and responding through movement to harmonic progressions: facing center for tonic, turning right for dominant, and moving left for subdominant chords.

The third Dalcroze component, improvisation, opens children to a freedom of expression through movement, in rhythmic speech, with instruments, or at the keyboard. Beginning with precise imitation of the teacher's or a partner's melodies, rhythms, and movements, children eventually acquire a repertory of movement and musical ideas from which they can draw for improvisation. Both eurhythmics and solfège offer a base of musical knowledge for improvisation. See Lesson 3.1 for some sample experiences using Dalcroze components.

Dalcroze techniques have permeated the teaching of music to children, even though few teachers in the United States are trained in the pedagogy. This may be due to the widespread recognition of movement as an important channel of musical response for children, as well as the method's longtime presence in the United States, albeit in isolated instances, since the 1920s. The training for certification in the method is challenging because of its reliance on piano as the principal medium for providing music for eurhythmic response. The certification test calls for mastery of piano improvisation that demonstrates a variety of rhythmic qualities for movement, in various keys, rendered in musically expressive ways. For further reading on the Dalcroze techniques, see the classic work by Jaques-Dalcroze (1921; Sadler, 2007) and the writings of Mead (1994) and Schnebly-Black and Moore (2003, 2004) for practical applications of eurhythmics with children.

Eurhythmics
- To teacher's drum tap, children walk the pulse. When the teacher strikes the drum rim, children stand in place and clap the pulse. Alternate between walking and clapping.
- To teacher's improvised piano music, children walk the pulse, clapping on beat one. On cue (a high piano cluster, for example), children change clap to beat two, three, or four. Extend by suggesting that children clap on several pulses (one and three, two and three) or bend the knees on one while clapping on two, three, and four.
- With masking tape across the classroom's floor to demarcate two sides of the room, children walk to the teacher's improvised piano music, stepping the slow pulse on one half of the room and stepping twice-as-fast on crossing to the other half of the room. Children themselves determine which side of the room to walk in, and how often they may wish to change sides.
- Children step the pulse of the teacher's improvised piano melodies lower than middle C, and clap the pulse of piano melodies higher than middle C. When a lower and higher melody are played simultaneously, children clap and step the pulse.
- With drums in hand, or wood blocks, claves, and cow-bells, children listen for the recurring ostinato phrase played by the teacher on the piano and play its rhythm—without and eventually while stepping the pulse.
- Children move expressively to the teacher's piano music, realizing the meter, rhythmic phrases, dynamic changes, phrasing, and articulation through movement.
- While listening repeatedly to a small segment of recorded music (of Bach, Mozart, Shumann, Bartók, Steve Reich, Pat Metheny, Balinese gamelan, Egyptian maqam), children move to express rhythmic durations, melodic phrases, formal sections, and dynamics. In small groups, they design a movement piece that, as a result of trying out and layering in movement responses to various music features, becomes a choreographed movement piece that looks like the music (whether the music is sounding or not).

Solfège
- While conducting a $\frac{4}{4}$ meter, teacher and children chant the solfège syllables (do, re, mi, fa, so, la, ti, do), one per beat, forward (up) and backward (down), repeating the do at either end (similar to the solfeggio exercises of Italian conservatories).
- Teacher and children sing the ascending and descending scales on solfège syllables while conducting. On cue, the syllables are sung twice as fast or twice as slow.
- Children sing ascending and descending scales, playing the imaginary keys on their forearms. Using the fixed-do system, sing the C Major, G Major, and F Major scales from C to c (differentiating pitch and playing movement) for F, F#, and B, B♭).
- Using a wide-open hand in front of them to indicate whole tones and a half-closed hand to indicate semitones, children sing ascending and descending scales (including C Major, G Major, and F Major), supported by teacher's scale-chording.
- While singing ascending and descending scales, children step with their feet—wide for whole steps and narrow for half-step intervals. They can essentially leap for whole tones and short-step for semitones, as they sing to the teacher's scale-chording.
- In groups of eight children, arrange bodies in a row. Designating each child on a particular pitch, sing a scale, with children stepping forward and out of the row on the sound of their designated pitches. Experiment similarly with simple songs that are moved in and out of the row, such as "Rain, Rain Go Away" and "Sing Together."
- Children sing familiar songs to solfège syllables while conducting the meter, clapping and patting the meter's pulse per measure (for example, a $\frac{3}{4}$ song might be accompanied by a clap-pat-pat gesture), playing the melodic pitches on their forearms, moving wide and narrow steps to indicate intervals between the melodic pitches.

Improvisation
- On cue (set by teacher or designated student), children play their pitched and nonpitched percussion instruments. There is no set meter, rhythmic framework, or pitch-set, as the exercise is exploratory only and with the intent of responding to stop and start cues.

- Given just three pitches, do, re, and sol, children sing these pitches in imitation of various orderings as performed by their teacher in four-beat (or eight-beat) phrases. After sufficient exposure to these pitches, set a four-beat conducting pattern to be gestured by the children and invite children to come up with short do-re-sol improvisations of four or eight beats that are imitated by the large group.
- Standing in the center of a circle, the teacher taps his or her drum for four beats (or eight beats) and requests that children respond immediately with an improvised phrase of the same length on their drums or other nonpitched percussion instruments.
- In a circle, the first child plays an eight-beat question phrase on his or her xylophone, ending the question on sol or pitch 5. All immediately imitate the phrase, and the second child plays an eight-beat answer-phrase, ending on do or pitch 1, which is immediately imitated by all. The third child gives the next question, and the fourth child the next answer, each of whom is immediately imitated.
- On keyboards, partner one plays a question in an antecedent phrase, to which partner two plays an improvised consequent phrase of equal length. Parameters can be set, such as only in $\frac{6}{8}$ meter, use of just black keys, no Cs allowed, or use of D-E-F keys.
- With the teacher or a child as the conductor, the class group creates a collaborative piece. The conductor comes up with a subject theme; sets the pitch restrictions; and conducts the tempo, meter, dynamics, and entrance and exit of instruments.
- After listening numerous times to a recording of a musical selection (a medieval dance tune, a Guatemalan marimba ensemble, a Dominican merengue), discussing its component parts, and then moving to some aspect(s) of it in another listening, children gather into small groups to create something on classroom instruments in the style of the studied piece. For comparison later, play the recorded selection (and move to it), followed by movement participation in the children's pieces.

A Dalcroze-Inspired Musical Experience

Trotting Horses (P. S. Campbell)

Trot - ting lit - tle hors - es, Trot - ting hap - py hors - es,
Trot - ting through the fields of grass and back to the barn to rest.

Galloping Horses (P. S. Campbell)

Gal - lop - ing hap - pi - ly Free - dom they feel when they
Gal - lop as on - ly good hors - es can do. [Watch them]

(Continued)

1. Sing the songs, "Trotting Horses" and "Galloping Horses" (while the teacher plays them with simple harmonization at the piano). Notice their distinctive rhythmic qualities.
2. Pat the pulse of the two songs while singing them to the piano's accompaniment.
3. Pat the strong pulses and clap the weak pulses to the piano's accompaniment.
4. Step the rhythm of songs while singing them with the piano.
5. Play the strong pulses on hand drums and the weak pulses on wood blocks, with piano accompaniment.

Kodály: Inner Hearing and Music Literacy

"Music must not be approached from its intellectual, rational side, nor should it be conveyed as a system of algebraic symbols, or as the secret writing of a language with which he has no connection. The way should be paved for direct intuition."

Zoltán Kodály, 1974

If there is a single underlying philosophy of the Kodály approach to music instruction, it is that "music belongs to everyone." Zoltán Kodály and his Hungarian associates who first evolved the method maintained that music is the right of not only the talented few but all children, who can and should develop performance, listening, and literacy skills. With music instruction beginning in early childhood, children discover folk and art music through a sequence that begins with singing and leads to the development of musically independent individuals who can read and write with ease. Kodály proponents believe that the content and sequence of the curriculum should be derived from children's musical development and from their musical literature. While hand signs and rhythm syllables are closely associated with this approach, it is far more comprehensive than these techniques suggest, with systematic training that results in musical and musically literate children at an early age.

Zoltán Kodály (1882–1967) was a composer, ethnomusicologist, and advocate of music education for children. He and Béla Bartók collected songs in Hungary, Romania, and other parts of southeastern Europe. Kodály's PhD dissertation was on the stanzaic structure of Hungarian folk song. He lectured on composition, harmony, counterpoint, and orchestration at the Academy of Music in Budapest from 1907 to 1940. His best-known works, including the *Háry János Suite*, *Dances of Marosszék*, *Dances of Galanta*, and *Summer Evening*, feature folk song and folklike melodies for orchestral instruments. As a vocally oriented composer, his many choruses and eleven books of folk song arrangements demonstrate the characteristic features of his cultural heritage to Hungarians and to the world.

By the early 1920s, he was writing singing and reading exercises and composing group vocal works that revived the Hungarian choral movement. Kodály started a singing movement for young people in the 1930s that soon brought about a radical change in the manner in which children were musically educated in elementary schools. Although he never taught in a primary or secondary school, Kodály's ideas on pedagogy challenged generations of musicians and teachers to raise the musical potential of their students. His educational ideas on singing, solmization, reading, and folk song material crystallized into what has become known as the Kodály method. The method was elaborated by students and colleagues, including Jenö Ádám, Lajos Bárdos, Katalin Forrai, Gyorgy Kerenyi, Benjamin Rajeczky, and Erzsébet Szönyi. Kodály traveled throughout Hungary, giving encouragement to group singing as the basis for a broad musical culture. In his later years, the Hungarian government was persuaded to give financial support to strong school music instruction.

The Kodály pedagogy in Hungary stipulated four to six weekly periods of music from kindergarten through secondary levels and a sequence of musical experiences that progressed from rhythm training through singing to instrumental lessons. American-style Kodály retains the use of pentatonic folk songs; the Tonic Sol-fa approach to sight-reading, with its hand signs; a rhythmic system of mnemonic syllables; and an emphasis on unaccompanied song. As part of the focus on music reading and writing, a preparatory period of ear training emphasizes rhythmic and melodic patterns that are encountered in songs and later in visual form. The development of inner hearing—the capacity to think musical sounds without hearing or necessarily voicing them—is important to Kodály training.

Relative or movable do is used for solfège exercises, where the tonic of the scale moves: C is do in C Major, D is do in D Major, and so on. Such a system is seen as an efficient means of understanding the function of individual scale degrees in various keys, by allowing the tonic of the key to provide an aural anchor for dominant, subdominant, and other tonal functions. An adaptation of the French Chevé system of rhythmic mnemonics is also a critical technique, particularly for younger children, in learning rhythmic values and their relationships in a pattern. The chanting of "ta ti-ti's" is well known as a technique to be used by students of every level for mastering difficult rhythms. The sequence by which rhythmic and melodic phrases and fragments are taught is also specified by the Kodály approach (see Chapters 4 and 7).

The most basic of Kodály's ideas, that the use of good music is vital to the life of every person, is a challenging one for American teachers. Kodály recognized art music of the European tradition and its folk or traditional origins as good. He especially favored the beautiful pentatonic melodies of the Hungarians, and he greatly admired the a cappella vocal music of the Renaissance. For American teachers, not only Western European art music but also the many coexisting musical cultures of American society present rich resources of good music for use with children. Some popular music is equally vibrant, with beautiful melodies, exciting rhythms, and resonant timbres. Lesson 3.2 presents some sample experiences in the Kodály method.

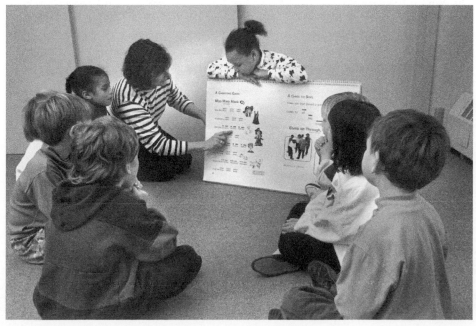

Kodály's literacy thrust: Primary-level children reading large-chart notation

Inner Hearing
- Sing the major scale with solfège syllables and Kodály-Curwen hand signs, in different keys and ranges, increasing to an octave and a fifth, or two octaves. Gradually increase the tempo. On cue, sing the scale silently, up and down, until cued again to sing aloud. Shift the exercises to the harmonic minor scale, sounding the tonic on "la" and singing "si" for the raised seventh degree.
- Recall the melody of an art-music selection or folk song, and sing it on a neutral syllable, then with solfège syllables. Later, sing with hand signs.
- After singing a familiar melody, play the rhythm of the melody by tapping it on the lap, desk or table top, or floor. Chant the melody's rhythm using the French Chevé system of "ta's" and "ti's" (see Chapter 7).
- Chant aloud the rhythms of favorite songs, then sing the song with the rhythm syllables.
- Sing a familiar song. On cue, continue to sing it silently. On another cue, sing it aloud.
- Extract and isolate a phrase from a song that works as a melodic ostinato, and divide a group of singers into melody and ostinato parts in performing it. Sing the song while patting or clapping an extracted phrase as a rhythmic ostinato.
- Find pentatonic songs (for example, "Alabama Gal" and "Little Johnny Brown") and sing them in unison on solfège, then on rhythm syllables, then with words. Finally, sing the song in canon, with a second group of singers following eight beats behind the first group.

Literacy
- Following study of isolated rhythmic and melodic patterns—their sounds and notational symbols—sight-read a new song that includes these patterns.
- Mix the order of measures of rhythm and or pitch notation for an unfamiliar song or melody. Sing or play it and challenge children to place the measure in correct order.
- Select a rhythm pattern (♩♩♫♩♩, ♩♩.♪) or a melodic pattern (l-s-m, s-l-t-d) and find songs and recorded selections that include it.
- Take dictation on familiar, and later not-so-familiar, songs and musical selections. Allow the use of invented notation, then stick notation for rhythm, and finally staff notation for melodies.
- Using neutral syllables, sing a measure of melody or chant or clap a measure of rhythm from a song, asking children to determine from the notation which measure is being featured. Once identified, the measure can be sung with solfège or chanted with Chevé syllables.
- Challenge children to compose a short melody that contains particular rhythm and pitch patterns. Student composers can conduct the class in performing the notated melody vocally or on instruments.

Works by Choksy (1999a, 1999b), Szönyi (1974–1979), Forrai (1988), and Houlahan and Tacka (2008) provide information on materials and sequence espoused by Kodály. Kodály's philosophical position on music instruction, and a history of the early years of the movement, are set down in his collected writings (1974).

A Kodály-Inspired Musical Experience

Going on the Bus (P. S. Campbell)

Go - ing on the bus for to see my friend, sing - in' hey ho and I'm as

hap - py as a clam. We'll be best of friends un - til the ve - ry hap - py end, sing - in'

(Continued)

hey   ho and feel - ing   free is who I am.   It's a   Sat - ur - day and it's a

free   day,   too,   and my   friend and I will choose what we   want   to   do,   sing - in'

hey   ho   and thank   you   sir   and thank   you   ma'am.

1. Chant and clap the following rhythm, using rhythm syllables. ♫♫♩
2. As the teacher sings the song, ask children to count the number of times the rhythm appears.
3. Repeat 1, asking children to clap the rhythm pattern as the teacher sings the song.
4. Sing the following melodic phrase, using solfège and hand signs.

    ♩   ♫   ♫   ♫   ♫   ♩   ‹
    s---   mm   m m   r d   r m   d   -

5. As the teacher sings the song, ask children to count the number of times the melodic pattern appears.
6. Repeat 4, asking children to sing solfège and use hand signs as the teacher sings the song.
7. Invite children to sing the song, repeatedly, until they know it.
8. Add a hand-clapping pattern between partners, following this ostinato rhythm.

    ♩   ♩   ♩   ♩   ♩   ♩   ♩   ♫
  clap   R pat   clap   L pat   clap   B pat   clap   B pat   B pat

- clap—clap one's own hands together
- pat—clap the hand of one's partner; R= Right hand, L=Left hand, B= Both hands

Children gathered in schoolyard singing and clapping hands

Orff: Expression through Musical Experience

The influence of the Orff approach on the teaching of music to children has been explosive since its introduction to North America in the 1960s. The natural behaviors of childhood—singing, saying, dancing, playing, along with improvisation and creative movement—form the basis of the Orff-Schulwerk (literally, "school work") approach. Frequently referred to as elemental music making, the pedagogy is closely linked to the child's world of play and fantasy, of games, chants, and songs. In its original form, elemental music was preintellectual and exploratory, with music, movement, and speech interrelated and overlapping. While the prevalence of special-model Orff xylophones of wood and metal is testimony to its popularity, the Orff approach is far richer and more varied in its musical experiences than initial exposure to the pedagogy may suggest.

The Schulwerk grew from the ideas of German composer Carl Orff (1895–1982), whose experimentation with musicians and dancers in the 1920s planted the seeds for his method's association of music with dance and theater. Together with dancer Dorothee Gunther, Carl Orff established an experimental school in Munich, the Guntherschule, for the integration of the performing arts. A Guntherschule ensemble of dancers, players, and singers, many of them preparing to be teachers, performed at educational conferences throughout Europe.

With the destruction of the Guntherschule during World War II, Orff set out with a young musician-teacher named Gunild Keetman to restore the spirit of integrated music and movement through radio broadcasts, focusing on children instead of adults. Orff believed children to be naturally musical, uninhibited in their expressive movement, and more receptive to his brand of musical training than adults. The collaborative efforts of Orff and Keetman resulted in the establishment of the Schulwerk method and the publication of five volumes of chants, songs, and instrumental pieces called *Musik für Kinder* (*Music for Children*). Canadian and then American adaptations of Orff and Keetman's work in the 1960s helped to spread their pedagogy across the world.

Principal components of the Schulwerk as conceived and practiced in Europe are the imitation and exploration of music and its components, with opportunities to improvise original pieces as learners become more musically skilled. As adapted in the United States, the process is extended to four stages: imitation, exploration, literacy, and improvisation. Imitation may be simultaneous, or it may be canonic—either echolike in the form of an interrupted canon (leader claps, then the group) or overlapping in a continuous canon. Imitation may occur through song, movement, or performance on pitched or nonpitched percussion instruments. Exploration challenges children's imaginations to find new ways to apply learned information, for example, "Now that we know the rhythm (♩.♩.♫♫♩.), can you play it (faster or slower, louder or softer, on a different instrument, on two alternating pitches)?" Literacy, or competence in reading and writing music, is a development of children's earlier musical experiences and progresses toward the skillful use of both graphic and conventional staff notation. The Schulwerk advocates extensive musical experience before literacy can become a truly musical, instead of mechanical, tool and a means for children to preserve the music they create. Rhythmic notation for quarter notes and eighth notes may be introduced in kindergarten and first grade, with melodic notation beginning with limited pitches (sol-mi and mi-re-do) in the first grade, proceeding to the pentatonic scale by second and third grade, and extending to the reading and writing of the diatonic scale by the fifth grade.

Improvisation is the ultimate stage of the Orff process, allowing musical invention that emanates from earlier learning. It is conceivable for improvisation to occur in preliterate stages as well, but the abilities to read and write music provide children with greater knowledge of musical structures for the original works they create. In this sense, improvisation is the culminating experience that demonstrates extensive musical knowledge and creative expression. The earlier stage of growth (exploration) involves changing one component within a familiar rhythm, chant, song, movement, or instrumental piece, while improvisation is the combination of skills and understanding into new and original forms. In this way, improvisation becomes the ultimate aim of Comprehensive Musicianship for children through the American-style Orff approach. Because of the extent of improvisational qualities in many of the world's musical cultures, the Orff process provides a natural opening into an understanding of these cultures. In particular, the improvised drumming traditions of Ghana, xylophone music of Zimbabwe, and percussion music of China can be learned by children in a manner of expressive creativity outlined by the Orff-Schulwerk.

The Orff process is complemented by the use of such musical features as folk and folk-like songs in the pentatonic mode; ostinato patterns that are spoken, sung, played, and moved; tonic drones or pedal tones; and static and moving bourdon accompaniments on xylophones and various other percussion instruments. These are the more prominent facets of the Schulwerk; the modes of music making in the four-step process are its pedagogy. Lesson 3.3 offers some suggestions for incorporating the Orff approach into classes.

> *"Music educators need to break out of the little boxes of restrictive thought and practice and reach across the real and imagined borders of narrow and rigid concepts, classifications, theories, and paradigms to embrace a broad and inclusive view of diverse music educational perspectives and practices."*
>
> **Estelle Jorgensen, 2003**

Integrating musical experiences via the Orff approach: Children singing, moving, and playing

© Jerry Gay

IMITATION

- Invite children to listen to a four-beat rhythm on a wood block or drum and then to clap in imitation of it. Challenge them to perform a continuous canon, in which the leader plays a four-beat rhythm and children imitate it while the leader is playing the next four-beat rhythm without a break.

- Vocally imitate short melodic patterns of four or eight beats played on a melodic instrument such as a piano, violin, or clarinet.

- Imitate eight-beat body-percussion rhythms by having one child offer a rhythm followed by the group.

- Imitate a partner's eight-beat body-percussion piece. Turn the piece into a movement piece, again with one partner following the movement immediately after its performance by the other partner.

- Imitate the rhythms of body-percussion gestures on nonpitched instruments. For example, finger snaps can be played on a triangle, claps on wood blocks, and stamps on drums.

EXPLORATION

- Experiment with different ways of rendering a familiar folk song, altering just one musical element at a time (for example, dynamics, tempo, mode, meter, accompaniment).

- Sing a familiar major-key melody in minor.

- Sing a familiar song in a different meter, as in turning a 2/4 song into a 3/4 song.

- Choose a lullaby and a sea chantey to sing in expressive ways characteristic of the genre and then in an opposite manner, sampling soft vs. loud and smooth vs. choppy qualities.

- Play a variety of accompaniments on percussion instruments (with combinations that produce varied textures).

LITERACY

- Compose an eight-beat piece that can be notated graphically. Choose colors and shapes that represent melodic phrases, rhythmic motifs, and/or timbres (voices, instruments, body percussion).

- Compose a short piece for pitched and nonpitched instruments. Write it as closely as possible to its intended sound, using staff notation. Pass the piece to a friend or a new group to perform.

- Choose two phrases from a set of short melodic phrases of four or eight beats. Read them, play them on pitched and nonpitched instruments, and determine

- Realize the shapes and contours of contemporary artwork in music (see, for example, the work of Juan Miro or Salvador Dali), assigning a conductor to clarify which component should inspire the musical expression. (Allow scientific graphs to be read as musical direction.)

- Play a simple song's melody. Develop variations of the melody and accompaniment. Notate these.

IMPROVISATION

- Select a simple rhythm and see what permutations a group of singers and players can create. Do the same with a melody.

- Choose a poem. Chant it rhythmically, and then add a nonpitched percussion accompaniment. Turn it into a three-pitch song with pitched accompaniment and movement to express its form.

- Listen to a recording (for example, of a Tallis canon, an Anglo-American hymn, a Puerto Rican salsa, or a Chinese percussion piece)—repeatedly, so as to become immersed in the style. Using classroom instruments, improvise music in the style of the recording (similar tempo, meter, rhythms, pitches, timbres, for example).

- Find a painting or photograph. Study its colors, shadings and shadows, textures, and composition of figures and shapes, and note the emotions that appear to be communicated. Consider the structural elements and the mood that is conveyed, and develop an improvisation that responds to the sum of these parts.

- Select a story and figure ways of musically enhancing the story through the provision of a soundscape, musical responses to the story, other musical insertions, interludes, introduction, and closing music.

Among the most thorough accounts of the Orff-Schulwerk are the volumes by Frazee (1987, 2007), Steen (1992), and Warner (1991). Keetman (1970; Frazee, 1999) presents important perspectives on the Schulwerk as it was conceived and developed, and Goodkin (2002) introduces the principles in contemporary North American practice. The classic Schulwerk contained within Orff and Keetman's *Musik für Kinder* (1950– 1954) and the English-language version by Hall (1956) are particularly valuable to those wishing to pursue the historical foundations of the approach.

An Orff-Inspired Musical Experience

A Pocket of Miracles (P. S. Campbell)

1. While the teacher sings the song, sway right to left and pat and clap the strong and soft pulses.

2. Continue to sway and pat while the teacher chants the spoken verse.

3. Step a ♩ ♫ (quarter-eighth note) pattern while singing the song, swinging their hands in a downbeat-upbeat conducting pattern. At the spoken verse, stop in one place and chant while playing a basic body percussion to this rhythm pattern:

   ♩   ♫   ♫   ♩

   pat   clap   slap   clap

   Pat (pat lap), clap (clap hands together), slap (slap right hand to chest)

4. Sing and chant, with suggested movement, until the melody, rhythm, and words are synced together.

5. Play a simple accompaniment on pitched and nonpitched percussion instruments. Note that when chanting begins, only the nonpitched instruments play, to be joined again by pitched instruments when the singing resumes.

6. Gather students in a double ring of children, the outer ring facing right and the inner ring facing left. As children sing they step forward, swinging their arms in a downbeat-upbeat conducting pattern. At the spoken verse, they stop and face a partner, chanting while performing the body percussion pattern. On the second clap of every pattern, they clap each other's hands.

Methodological Suggestions for Early Childhood

- **Emphasize the experiential aural and kinesthetic potential** of music as it is heard and responded to through movement.

- **Discover musical sounds** in toys; kitchen, office, and garden tools; and other objects at home and in school.

- **Add musically meaningful movement to singing activities** by gesturing high and low pitches (or phrase contours) and patting not only pulses but particular rhythms.

- **Imitate sounds** in the environment through the use of voice and body percussion.

- **Fill the lesson** (and the day) with live musical chants, rhythms, and songs: for openings into circle time, at lunch and snack times, during transitions between activities, at the close of each day.

- **Play recordings** of a variety of musical styles as children play freely.

Other Approaches to Music Learning
Comprehensive Musicianship

The interdisciplinary study of music is the thrust of the approach called Comprehensive Musicianship, which advocates the integration of performance, theory, history and literature, and composition into the music curriculum—all in a single lesson. The Ford Foundation funded the Contemporary Music Project (CMP) in 1963 in order to reshape school music programs to give greater emphasis to creative composition and contemporary music, to bring composers into contact with children, and to reduce the compartmentalization of the music profession into separate subdisciplines.

Two years later, the CMP sponsored a seminar on Comprehensive Musicianship. This seminar changed the direction of CMP from providing contemporary music in the schools to the broad-based teaching of all musical styles through the development of performance, listening and analysis, and compositional and improvisational competencies. A series of regional institutes brought these ideas on curriculum revision to collegiate, secondary, and elementary teachers.

While Comprehensive Musicianship was intended to influence all levels of music instruction, it appears to have naturally found a home in music classes for children. One of its major thrusts is the common elements approach to music, in which music of any style can be studied through its sound properties of frequency (pitch), duration (rhythm), intensity (loudness), and timbre. These elements make for convenient organizers of listening lessons, suggesting questions on high and low pitches; short and long rhythmic values; loud and soft volumes; and the quality of instrumental, vocal, and other sounds. They are related to the six elements made popular by the basal music textbook series: melody, rhythm, texture, form, dynamics, and timbre.

Children who are taught with the goals of Comprehensive Musicianship in mind are actively involved in listening to and performing representative music of many cultures and time periods. Few lessons are devoted completely to singing or playing instruments without some opportunity to experience the real thing on recordings, as performed by trained musicians. Children are led to understand music by listening analytically to a piece, performing it when possible (or sampling fragments of it, such as a recurring rhythmic pattern or melody), and taking what they know and transferring it creatively to new compositions and improvisations they invent. Fuller explanations of Comprehensive Musicianship can be found in Choksy, Abramson, Gillespie, Woods, and York (2000).

Gordon's Music Learning Theory

American music educator Edwin E. Gordon began to develop a sequence for music instruction in the 1970s, culminating in the formulation of his Music Learning Theory. He coined the term *audiation* to refer to the goal of music instruction: inner hearing (or hearing music in the mind when it is not physically present). Similar to the classic European pedagogies, Gordon's theory of music learning supports the sound-before-symbol approach to music instruction. As in the development of language, children listen to tonal and rhythm patterns, imitate them, and then read and write them. Audiation occurs when children have had ample listening experiences, so that they can see a notated rhythm or melody and make musical sense of it, hearing it even if it is not sounded aloud.

Gordon's theory suggests a hierarchy of musical skill-building that begins with aural perception and discriminative listening and progresses through the development of music reading and writing, improvisation, and a theoretical understanding of music. The eight-step hierarchy of his learning sequence is as follows:

Discrimination learning

1. Aural and oral
2. Verbal association
3. Partial synthesis
4. Symbolic association
5. Composite synthesis

Inference learning

6. Generalization

7. Creativity and improvisation

8. Theoretical understanding

Discrimination learning begins with listening and imitating small patterns of sound, often on a neutral syllable. These tonal and rhythmic patterns are then given verbal associations by way of solfège syllables and a set of rhythmic mnemonic syllables (for example, ♩♫ = du du-de or ♩ ♫♫ = du du-ta-de-ta). Partial synthesis is the testing of children to determine how well they are able to aurally recognize and discriminate tonal and rhythm patterns that have been taught. Their success in this stage prepares them for symbolic association, the introduction of the written symbols for the solfège and rhythmic mnemonic syllables they have listened to, imitated, and aurally identified. There is no discussion, for example, of quarter notes and eighth notes at this level, but instead the shift of what they hear to how it is symbolized—and vice versa—is considered. A composite synthesis is achieved when isolated notational patterns can be grouped in a series (in a song's notation) and read with ease. Likewise, children should be able to notate an aurally dictated melody or rhythm that uses familiar patterns that have been previously sounded and symbolized.

Inference learning is a higher-order learning, largely of unfamiliar stimuli. It begins with generalization, a test of whether children can transfer familiar tonal and rhythmic patterns to new pieces, to be read or written. Improvisation and composition encourage the use of learned patterns in new and personally creative ways, with opportunities for children to notate what they have invented. The final stage, theoretical understanding, allows for the acquisition of knowledge about why music is what it is, as well as what meter and key signatures mean, how lines and spaces of a staff are lettered, what relationships a series of pitches may have, and what the mathematical values of rhythms are. Theory is last in the sequence, following all opportunities to know music aurally, orally, and symbolically.

Gordon's sequence is further revealed through materials listed at The Gordon Institute for Music Learning <www.giml.org>, including the textbook series *Jump Right In! The Music Curriculum* (2003), and in the assessments of music learning, *Primary Measures of Music Audiation and Intermediate Measures of Music Audiation*. Exercises and songs that reinforce tonal and rhythmic patterns are included for children from kindergarten through middle school. The theoretical framework for the series is found in Gordon (2012), and various exercises and songs that reinforce tonal and rhythmic patterns are available for use with children across age levels.

Manhattanville Music Curriculum Project

During the review and redesign of music instruction programs in the 1960s, the Manhattanville Music Curriculum Project (MMCP) emerged as one of the most progressive and influential programs. Funded by the U. S. Office of Education and named for Manhattanville College, where it originated, it was as intensive as it was extensive. The project resulted in a comprehensive curriculum for grades three to twelve that was derived from children's perspectives instead of the teacher's, providing a sequence of basic musical concepts to be learned through exploratory yet teacher-guided experiences. MMCP connected learning from one grade level to the next via a spiral of progressively more sophisticated aspects of the musical elements, in a variety of musical styles.

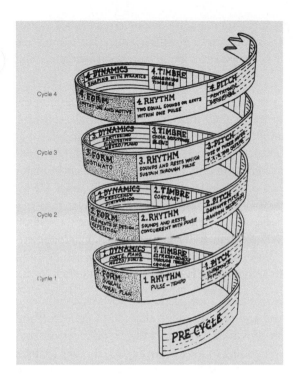

MMCP is strongly anchored in the tradition of perceiving by exploring and of understanding by creating, improvising, and composing. Children are encouraged to experience music and to sample their own sound world by making sounds with their bodies: snapping, clapping, patting, stamping, whistling, tapping, shuffling, moaning, and various vocalizations. They are stimulated to produce found sounds through objects they gather and new instruments they can build. They develop concepts of pitch (melody and texture), rhythm, form, dynamics, and timbre by creating their own musical expressions, and eventually notating them. These concepts become increasingly more sophisticated as children mature (see Figure 3.1).

MMCP includes seven types of experiences: MMCP strategies (composing, performing, evaluating, conducting, listening), student recitals, listening to recordings, research and oral reports, guest recitals, skill development, and group singing. Children's musical expressions are stimulated through new ideas in the music selections they hear. Composed pieces are approached holistically, so that children not only listen to them but also conduct them, perform them, invent variations, and then create entirely new compositions inspired by them. MMCP supports the development of aural, dexterous (performing and conducting), and translative (notational) skills—with emphasis on graphic forms invented by children.

MMCP has fostered an attitude that some of the most meaningful music learning occurs when the environment is informal and relaxed and when the teacher's approach is flexible enough to accommodate children's unique learning styles. Effective music instruction incorporates alternative sound sources for making music, the room and space for movement and for gathering in groups of performers and composers, and enough time to work through musical problems.

Music in Education

Technology assisted music instruction entered the realm of the music classroom several decades ago, providing a transformation of the way skills and knowledge can be acquired by children. The Yamaha Corporation developed an interest in children's conceptual learning of music through the computer and computerized keyboard programs. Its Music in Education (MIE) <usa.yamaha.com/music_education/> approach suggests that children supplied with keyboards can build aural, performance, and notational skills in an integrative way.

The MIE goals are to develop intelligent listeners who can describe and discuss the music they hear, make, and create. The curriculum includes print materials, software, and hardware, integrated with one another and divided into learning modules that focus on specific elemental areas and musical concepts—from beat and meter to tonality and atonality, and from ostinato accompaniments to chord progressions in major and minor keys. The curriculum offers a repertoire that includes folk songs ("New River Train"), patriotic songs ("America"), pop songs, songs from popular musicals ("My Favorite Things"), and classical selections ("Eine Kleine Nachtmusik"). Children progress at their own pace through exercises in melodic and rhythmic dictation, composition, and keyboard performance. Ensemble and independent performances, and class and independent study, are possible through MIE.

Critical to the MIE program is a classroom of state-of-the-art keyboards, allowing children access to instruction, rehearsal and review, and evaluation of their skill and knowledge attainment. It is central in providing children with experiences on keyboards in performing, creating, and responding to music. Through MIE, they become active participants in music-making, and the technology and cooperative group-instructional strategies allow them to learn concepts, skills, and repertoire. Yamaha continues to shape and evolve Music in Education to stand up to its goals of achieving a comprehensive music education that is reflective of the realities of becoming a skillful and thoughtful young musician, step-by-small-sequential step.

Education through Music

As the sound of its title indicates, Education through Music (ETM) is a holistic approach to music instruction. It is a historic movement begun by American music educator Mary Helen Richards some fifty years ago to examine ways in which the ideals of Kodály's Hungarian pedagogy could be adapted to the needs of children and teachers in the United States. Following extensive correspondence with Zoltán Kodály and observations in Hungarian schools, she began her adaptation of the Kodály principles to English-language songs and American curricula emphases. Richards first published her songs and instructional sequence in *Threshold to Music*, a series of books and charts that were a prelude to ETM. She used Kodály's suggestions in finding folk songs from the North American continent to introduce to children, and she became fascinated with the relationship between the ways songs and language were acquired through pattern recognition.

The ETM spirit is alive and well in the curricular approaches of Peggy Bennett (1997, 2010), who pays tribute to the work of Mary Helen Richards, directly and through her acknowledgments to Richards in the various publications. The first- and second-level goals of ETM are to bring children comfort and self-esteem, as well as cooperation with others, within the context of group music-making. These are followed and supported by the goals of aural skill acquisition and an understanding of the melodic and rhythmic patterns of the musical language. The ETM approach makes use of folk songs and singing games of the United States and British Isles. Many of the songs are selected because they involve children in both singing and kinesthetic experiences (actions, circle games, line and partner dances, and so forth). Movement is viewed as a necessary technique for leading children in their discovery of melodic and rhythmic patterns and repeated words and word-phrases. The pattern recognition touted by ETM prepares children for sight-reading. With literacy accomplished, the relationship of ETM to the Hungarian approach is undeniable—and so as Kodály inspired Richards, so do they both inspire methods and materials in current use.

Weikert's Movement Sequence

The growth of interest in movement as a component of music instruction led to the acceptance of the work of Phyllis Weikert. In her work in physical education and recreational folk dance, Weikert observed that people struggle with basic movement because they cannot maintain a steady beat. She devised a sequence for teaching folk and choreographed dance that takes into account the relationship between language and movement and that underscores the development of beat competence through movement and dance. That four-step process has been found to be effective by music teachers who incorporate structured movement in their music classes, particularly folk dance, and who view the development of the feeling for steady beat as a primary instructional objective. Weikert's process is as follows:

Step 1. Say "Step-hop, step-hop, side-close"

Step 2. Say and do "Step-hop, step-hop, side-close"

Step 3. Whisper and do "Step-hop, step-hop, side-close"

Step 4. Do (think and do) "Step-hop, step-hop, side-close"

Weikert's sequence is straightforward and can be used by classroom teachers and physical education instructors with limited musical training. Its chief contribution in music education is as a technique for teaching steady beat, not as a comprehensive method. It may best be used in remedial ways or as a supplement to more musical pedagogies such as Dalcroze eurhythmics or Orff-Schulwerk. Weikert (2003) published several volumes of folk-dance instructions that are accompanied by recordings of arranged dance music.

Children's kinesthetic engagement in performing a singing game.

Billie Jucy/Reel Life Productions

TABLE 3.1 A Comparison of Methods for Teaching Music to Children

METHOD	FOUNDER	GOAL	MUSICAL MATERIAL
Dalcroze, or Dalcroze eurhythmics	Émile Jaques-Dalcroze, theorist and composer	Natural rhythmic movement of the body to improve aural skills	Improvised music on the piano
Kodály; the Hungarian method	Zoltán Kodály, composer and ethnomusicologist	Musical literacy and inner hearing	Traditional folk music and art music (in Hungary, Hungarian music first)
Orff-Schulwerk	Carl Orff, composer	Musical experience, expression through music	Folk songs and children's melodies
Comprehensive Musicianship	Norman Dello Joio, composer (Contemporary Music Project); Robert Werner, music educator; and others	Descriptive, performing, and creative competence	Composed music, including contemporary, traditional, and world music
Gordon; Music Learning Theory	Edwin E. Gordon, music educator	Audiation (hearing music in the mind)	Tonal and rhythmic patterns; folk and composed songs in *Jump Right In!*
Manhattanville Music Curriculum Project (MMCP)	Ronald Thomas, music educator, and others	Improvement of musicianship through experimentation and exploration	Contemporary and other composed music; children's sound pieces
Music in Education (MIE)	Yamaha Corporation	Keyboard, aural, and notational skills	Keyboard arrangements of folk, patriotic, popular, and classical works
Education through Music (ETM)	Mary Helen Richards, music educator	Musical literacy and inner hearing	Traditional folk music of the United States and British Isles
Weikert	Phyllis Weikert, physical education specialist	Development of feeling for steady beat	Recorded arrangements of folk-dance music

A Comparison of Methods and Techniques

Table 3.1 offers a comparison of the various pedagogical approaches, focusing on several categories: goals, recommended musical material, principal experiences, aural skills and ear-training techniques, approaches to literacy and notation, and instructional structure. Because of the necessary brevity of the chart, prominent factors are highlighted instead of all aspects of the pedagogy.

A Personal Method

Despite the myriad of techniques intended to advance the musical development of children, each teacher in the end chooses to incorporate those pedagogical aspects that are harmonious with his or her personal goals and definitions of music education.

> *"We sing good songs, we learn to read music, we play some instruments, we listen to good stuff, and she can play piano really well and sing well, too."*
>
> **Jonathan's description of his music teacher, in Campbell, 2010**

PRINCIPAL EXPERIENCES	AURAL SKILLS	NOTATION	INSTRUCTIONAL SEQUENCE
Eurhythmies, solfège, improvisation	Fixed do, dichords, tri-chords, solfège combined with conducting and movement	Phrases are mapped; single- and double-line staves lead to full staff	Germinal, building from rhythmic phrase to a complete piece
Singing (a cappella), directed listening, folk songs, singing games, folk dance	Movable do and rhythmic mnemonics	Song patterns are heard, then sung or chanted, then notated	Sequential development of melodic and rhythmic vocabulary
Speech chants, movement, singing, instrumental performance, improvisation	Imitation and exploration of rhythmic and melodic patterns	*In its original form:* No prescribed system, preliterate experiences. *In its American adaptation:* Experience precedes notation symbols	From imitation to exploration (to notational literacy) to improvisation
Relating theory and history to performance and composition; common elements	Listening and performing large works and discrete patterns	Representational icons leading to conventional notation	Sequence stemming from working curriculum
Listening, reading, writing discrete tonal and rhythmic patterns	Aural and oral rote learning to movable do and rhythmic mnemonics	Easy, moderate, and difficult patterns to hear, read, and write	Eight-step process in two phases: discrimination and inference learning
Exploring, creating, performing	Listening to environmental sounds and composed pieces	Emphasis on invented icons and graphs	Stemming from children's needs and interests; seven guides
Keyboard experiences	Melodic and rhythmic dictation exercises at the keyboard	Staff notation and terminology through keyboard performance	Designated through 145 instructional modules
Singing, directed listening, games and dances	Movable do and rhythmic mnemonics	Song patterns are heard, sung, and chanted, then notated	Sequential development of melodic and rhythmic vocabulary
Folk dancing	Not addressed	Not addressed	Four-step sequence for folk-dance instruction; books with recordings

Often, those goals are based on the teacher's own musical strengths and personal preferences in music and instruction. Singers may be inclined to sing more than to move or to play, pianists may be more prone to utilize a keyboard laboratory or to accompany songs and movement on the piano, and kinesthetically oriented teachers may center their music instruction on assorted movement experiences. There is no one correct way to teach musical understanding, skills, and values, nor is there only one of ten standard ways to approach these goals.

"We teach as we have been taught" is an adage relevant to the philosophy that guides instruction and to the techniques selected and blended into each teacher's personal pedagogy. Undergraduate programs leading to degrees and teaching certification in music provide teachers with extensive preparation in applied music, aural and keyboard skills, ensemble performance, conducting, theory, and history and culture, with occasional courses in improvisation and composition. This training, when coupled with methods courses that emphasize musical materials and techniques proven to be effective in teaching children, holds the potential for producing independent and successful musician educators.

Instruction is further shaped through additional training in music. A postgraduate course in conducting may direct a teacher's attention toward potential movement and expressive gestures that children may learn to use as they listen and perform a song. A clinic in improvisation may inspire lessons in creative musical thinking and doing. A string of workshops in technology-oriented instruction or in the music of world cultures will provide a teacher not only with new musical materials but also with innovative instructional techniques. A graduate course in ear training, theory, or analysis will hone a teacher's listening skills, while also providing approaches for training children's ears. The development of musicianship is an ongoing process. To use colloquial expressions, when we don't (continue to) train, we don't gain, and when we don't use it (the musical skills we may have earlier developed), we lose it.

Training in classic and contemporary methods of music instruction for children can greatly enhance the development of a personal teaching method. Summer courses in Kodály, Dalcroze, and Orff are provided at universities throughout North America and abroad, with certification available following extensive coursework and demonstration of selected proficiencies in music, teaching, and planning. Also, summer courses are available on the approaches espoused by Gordon, Weikert, Education through Music, and Music in Education. Training in these methods leads to the adaptation of aspects of their philosophies, goals, and techniques, for these all are logical pathways that have been tested with children. In the end, however, the teacher's interests, strengths, and classroom needs emerge again to bring about the blend of a newly acquired layer of skills with those that the teacher has used for some time.

A personal method of music instruction does not preclude the opportunity to find affinities with certain established methods. More than likely, the teacher who strives for greater musicianship will seek out the set of techniques that appeal to his or her personal interests. But does the provision of movement experiences classify her as a follower of Dalcroze? Does an emphasis on folk song and the great art music make him a Kodály teacher? Does the rhythmic chanting of poetry brand them followers of Orff? Or is there variation among the practices of teachers who have been influenced by the pedagogical emphases of Dalcroze, Kodály, or Orff? How are culturally based pedagogies blended with standard instructional methods when teaching a Zulu song or a Brazilian samba? All teachers make choices in the techniques and musical materials they select for use with children, and most might conceivably be judged as showing an inclination toward one or another known method. Still, the personalization of these techniques and methods following training is the true test of the teacher's independent musicianship and ability to lead children in their own musical development.

Scenario

AS A FINAL-SEMESTER MUSIC education major attending her first regional meeting of professional music teachers, Carly Thompson was intrigued by the conversation she was hearing. She had entered a workshop session early, had found herself a seat about midway in the room, and was opening her iPad for some note-taking ahead when she overheard a conversation behind her between two teachers. It was an animated one. The first teacher's remarks were introductory: "I'm looking forward to this session. What about you: Are you Orff, Kodály, or Dalcroze?" The second teacher replied, "Orff, absolutely. That's why I'm at this session. This guy's great. I had him in my Orff training, and he does just what I believe we should do as teachers—music and movement, with singing, chanting, body percussion, the instruments. It's all about the integration of so many music-making ways. My kids stay focused with Orff. What about you?" She heard this reply: "I have my Level I Kodály training, and that's been a blessing. I learned so much about kids' singing voices, and the songs that fit their voices. And kids love the singing games that are so Kodály. Since I'd been a clarinet major and not a singer, I really needed to up-the-ante on singing, so this was it for me."

Carly wondered why it seemed that they were "one-method-only teachers" and not involved in a mixed-methods way of teaching. She had every reason to respect any experienced teacher who would know more than she did about any method, but there had just been a lecture-discussion in her methods class this week about the importance of a "personal method" that was not to be tied to any one school of thought. She turned around, smiled, and politely introduced herself. She raised her voice while speaking to get their approval before asking the real questions on her mind. "Hi. I'm finishing my music education degree this year? And I overheard you talking about your Orff and Kodály expertise?" She pressed on. "So, do you think Orff and Kodály are equally valid? Is one better for certain circumstances than others? What about the other methods, like Dalcroze and all?" There was a grand pause as the two experienced teachers smiled back at her and (knowingly) at one another. "Well . . . " began the Orff teacher. "It all depends." The Kodály teacher nodded, and continued, "Really. It does. The method you take on is really you. I don't teach the same way the next Kodály teacher teaches. We have our own interpretations of Kodály teaching." The Orff teacher added, ". . . and of Orff teaching. You teach the way it feels right for your kids and for yourself. I'm not pure Orff, and she isn't pure Kodály. I'm glad I took some Orff workshops, because they offered me specific materials and ways of teaching them that I never learned in college."

Carly was following them now. "So, do either of you teach any parts of the other method?" Both teachers were nodding as affirmative, as the Orff teacher clarified: "I'd say that we do what other teachers do: We teach using whatever works, and that is usually a combination of our training, a lot of sharing among our teacher friends, and some of the interests and needs we figure out that are specific to our students and the school and community settings." The Kodály teacher pitched in: "Some of what we teach goes back to our college methods classes, too. So," she shook her finger, "Pay attention! You know what, the methods are not so far apart from each other, either, so I may be calling myself a Kodály person, and she's an Orff-er, but in reality we're probably not so different from each other. We sing, we dance, we play." Carly laughed, thanked the teachers, and turned around to face the clinician, who was just starting into a session that was promising "singing, playing, moving, listening, and creating, all with the aim of teaching children musical skills, understandings, and values."

Questions

1. Did Carly have reason to be concerned about the dialogue between the teachers? Were they "one-method-only teachers"?

2. How did the teachers develop their particular pedagogical approaches?

3. What shapes the method that a teacher employs?

REVIEW

1. Which pedagogies stress the use of movement as an instructional technique? To what extent does movement advance musical understanding in these pedagogies?

2. What is the relationship of inner hearing to audiation? Which methods espouse these goals?

3. Which approaches are American-made? In what ways? Are the European methods suitable for adaptation in American settings? How?

CRITICAL THINKING

1. What are the relationships among the three classic European methods (Dalcroze, Kodály, Orff) regarding the development of aural skills, musical literacy, and creative musical expression?

2. What aspects of these notated pedagogies for children can be continued into the realm of music instruction for adolescents? Adults? In choral settings? Instrumental settings?

3. Experiment with the samples of the Dalcroze, Kodály, and Orff pedagogies. Design and implement original examples of the principles.

PROJECTS

1. Identify and observe the teaching of those trained in the techniques of a specific pedagogy. Discuss with them their philosophy and goals, and note their use of specific techniques and media.

2. Select a musical concept: $\frac{3}{4}$ meter, m-r-d, ♩♪♩♩, or binary form. Design three (or more) ways of teaching the concept, using the distinctive techniques and materials of three (or more) methods.

3. Interview teachers regarding their personal goals of music experience and instruction for children, their preferred techniques, and their professional activity and advanced training and certification. Later, note any overlap of goals and techniques.

4. In a letter to the principal, describe your personal method of instruction. Include a statement of goals and experiences you have and musical materials and techniques you use.

MINDTAP Visit **MindTap** to access classroom videos, audio, and more!

4

The Singing Child

IN THIS CHAPTER

- The Developing Child Voice
- Physical Training for the Child Voice
- Toward Accurate Singing
- The Vocal Model
- Selecting and Teaching Songs
- How to Teach Singing in Parts
- Children's Choirs
- Adapting Instruction for Various Needs (Sensory Needs, Behavioral Needs,
- Accomplishing Multiple Music Standards through Singing
- Assessment of Singing
  - Formative Evaluations
  - Summative Evaluations
- Reasons to Sing
- Scenario
- Questions

FOR THE CHILD, to sing is to turn interests, experiences, and feelings into a personal musical expression. Kimberly sings about flowers, and Tony about lions, bears, dogs, and dragons. Michelle chants with Rosalita and Katie the songs of their hand-clapping games. Robert and Charoen trade songs they learned at church and in the temple, making up new words and tunes as they sing them. Lonnie sings before sleep, while Tuyen invents new tunes in the morning. Wayne mixes singing with lip-syncing all the latest tunes on MTV. Heather eagerly awaits her weekly choir rehearsals, while Marla sings her solos like the singing star she dreams of being.

The sounds of singing children can bring joy to those who listen, for these sounds emanate from their childlike thoughts and experiences. The quality of children's voices reflects a combined innocence, playfulness, and energy that befits them. Children sing alone and together, with and without the accompaniment of instruments or the electronic media of tapes, television, and radio. They sing spontaneously and often without knowing it—at meals, while walking to school, and in the middle of an independent school project. As they imitate and personalize the songs they have heard, children bring joy to themselves as well as to those who listen.

In today's high-tech societies, some may say that the singing child is an anachronism—a symbol of days gone by. Some may believe that "children would rather be entertained than entertain" themselves and others by singing, that "boys beyond grade two do not sing," and that "folk-song singing has been replaced by pop-song shouting." This gloom-and-doom perspective can discourage teachers and parents who recall their own active childhoods as singers and who wish to incorporate songs within the learning experiences of children.

Are children singing less (and less well) in the contemporary world of high-tech media? While the media may appear to pacify children as they entertain them, children begin to sing at or before the stage at which they acquire speech—at a time before they may even be attracted to the media. It follows that children will continue singing when given opportunities to do so. Away from their iPods, iPads, and laptops, they sing a great deal. Teachers and parents can provide occasions for singing—before classes

- Are you comfortable with your singing voice?

- Recall your earliest singing experiences. What did you sing? With whom and for whom? What did you sound like?

- How would you describe your singing voice today in terms of range, tessitura, and quality?

- What songs would you include in a list of "songs all children should know?"

- Describe any observations of, or direct experiences with, children's choirs.

"'Having a song in one's heart' means to rejoice, to remember, and to bring solitude to our souls. Songs are one of the essential needs of our being...."

**Brycene A. Neaman,
Yakama Indian, 1999**

and assemblies, at the start and close of the school day, after dinner, before bedtime, or while camping, walking, or riding in the car or on the bus. These are the times for singing favorite songs as well as for learning new ones. As for the media, rather than reducing children's singing, radio, recordings, and television may be stimulating their songfulness as well as adding to their repertoire (Campbell, 2010).

Singing is primary content in a sequential program of musical study for children in schools (MENC, 1994). Children can develop the skills to sing independently and together, on pitch and in rhythm, with appropriate timbre, diction, and posture. Children in the elementary grades can learn to sing expressively, with regard to the appropriate use of dynamics, phrasing, and interpretation. Further, children should sing a varied repertoire of songs representing genres and styles from diverse cultures, and they should progress from singing melodies with simple ostinatos to rounds and canons. These goals are attainable by children when led by trained music teachers in programs with instruction that is thorough and consistent.

Singing is a phenomenon for all ages, times, and cultures, but it begins and is nurtured in childhood. Children's vocal development can be greatly enhanced through training. The teacher who understands the physiology and capabilities of the young voice will select an appropriate repertoire and instructional techniques for children from preschool through the elementary grades. Contrary to the myth that singing lessons should begin in or after adolescence, vocal technique can be taught from the earliest ages by knowledgeable teachers.

The Developing Child Voice

AS EARLY AS INFANCY, as children begin to discover their vocal capabilities, they are making musical sounds. Playfully, they explore sounds with the vowels and consonants that they have heard before, extending their duration, repeating them rhythmically and in rising and falling pitch passages. Like the babbling that precedes speech, musical babbling is the vocalization that precedes the performance of melodies (Dissanayake, 2001; Trehub, 2006). As they toddle toward two years, children progress in their vocalizations, producing increasingly longer melodic phrases spontaneously. While young children may seldom use words in their spontaneous songs, they string nonsense syllables together in small intervals of seconds and thirds. By the age of three, children begin to develop the periodic accents of regular rhythmic patterns in their spontaneous songs, and slightly larger intervals may occur. Besides their own invented songs, children reproduce the short songs of nursery rhymes and childhood chants at this age, including the simple movements associated with them. An outline of children's vocal development can be found in Table 4.1. See also Music Example 4.1.

Children four and five years of age begin to discover the difference between their singing and speaking voices. Their singing may shift from a light, airy sound to a playground yell for lively songs. While their spontaneous singing may span nearly two octaves, the range at which they can sing accurately in tune may extend only five pitches, from d to a. As children learn new songs, they progress through five stages, reproducing the words, the rhythm of the words, a general but inaccurate sense of the melody's contour, a more accurate sense of individual pitches within the melody, and the tonality of the song across all its phrases. They learn songs through imitation of a model and require the teacher's step-by-step guidance toward more accurate reproduction.

TABLE 4.1 Children's Vocal Development

AGE	DEVELOPMENTAL ACTIVITY
LESS THAN ONE	Vocalizes (babbles) vowels and consonants
ONE TO TWO	Babbles in irregular rhythmic patterns Imitates the contour of songs' melodic phrases, but not discrete pitches
TWO	Babbles in extended melodic phrases Babbles in small intervals of seconds, thirds Imitates occasional discrete pitches of songs
THREE	Invents spontaneous songs with discrete pitches and recurring rhythmic and melodic patterns Reproduces nursery rhymes and childhood chants
FOUR TO FIVE **(KINDERGARTEN)**	Discovers differences between speaking and singing voices Shifts song qualities from light and airy to the playground yell for lively songs Sings spontaneous songs spanning two octaves Sings in tune within range of five pitches, d to a
SIX TO SEVEN **(GRADE ONE)**	Sings in tune in range of C to b, with smaller tessitura Can begin to develop head voice, with guidance Begins to have expressive control of voice
SEVEN TO EIGHT **(GRADE TWO)**	Sings in tune in range of octave, about C to c´ or d to d´, with smaller tessitura
EIGHT TO NINE **(GRADE THREE)**	Sings in tune in range of B¨ to e¨´, with smaller tessitura Can perform fundamental harmony songs such as melody over vocal ostinato or sustained pitch
NINE TO TEN **(GRADE FOUR)**	Sings in tune in range of A¨ to e´, with smaller tessitura Sings with increasing resonance (grades four, five, and six) May experience first vocal change (boys, beginning age ten) Can perform canons, rounds, descants, countermelodies Can sing with appropriate phrasing, with guidance
TEN TO ELEVEN **(GRADE FIVE)**	Sings in tune in range of A¨ to f´, with C to c´ octave tessitura Is increasingly selective of song repertoire Prefers songs in middle range Prefers songs without sentimental or babyish texts Can perform two-part songs
ELEVEN TO TWELVE **(GRADE SIX)**	Sings in tune in range of G to g´, with C to c´ octave tessitura Can perform three-part songs

Note: c = middle c; c´ = one octave higher; C = one octave lower than middle c.

First grade; ages six to seven

Second grade; ages seven to eight

Third grade; ages eight to nine

Fourth grade; ages nine to ten

Fifth grade; ages ten to eleven

Sixth grade; ages eleven to twelve

As children learn to sing a repertoire of songs, they also acquire rhythmic and melodic fragments that spill into their own musical play and invented songs. In many Western cultures, children through the elementary grades may incorporate in their invented songs the descending minor third often accompanied by a fourth.

"Rain, Rain Go Away," "Little Sally Walker," and "Bluebird" are examples of Western traditional children's songs that feature this common melodic pattern. However, it may be premature to suggest that, despite its frequent presence, the minor third is the first or most frequent interval to emerge in children's vocalizations, especially before systematic study of children in other world cultures has been undertaken. As children in the West gain exposure to popular music, the songs they strive to sing and create anew may contain the syncopated rhythms and the melodic patterns characteristic of the popular sound. Similarly, children's extended experience with any other musical style is likely to influence their accumulated repertoire and to flavor their musical expressions.

Children in the primary grades are more apt to sing in tune than younger children. Their singing range widens from C to b for six-year-olds; to about an octave by second grade, from C to d′; and from about B′ to e′ by third grade. Their tessitura, or the average range in which most pitches of a song lie, is somewhat smaller. So although children are capable of a larger vocal range, songs that linger on the lowest to highest pitches should be avoided. Children may continue to sing as they do at play, in their lower chest range, unless their head voice is developed—particularly through pitch-matching exercises. The use of a pure neutral syllable such as "loo" will assist children in concentrating on appropriate vocal production through their ranges.

At eight years (or by second grade), children are likely to be able to maintain the same tonality throughout a song. As their musical memory increases, they are able to learn longer and more complex songs. By the age of nine, children may succeed at performing fundamental harmony songs—those with a recurring vocal ostinato, or sustained sounds overlapped by moving melodies. Their need for socialization with friends may nurture their interest in singing with others, while at the same time their perceptual development offers them greater awareness of blending their voices with the ensemble of singers.

In the intermediate grades, when children are showing signs of rapid physical development, their voices are also affected by the maturation process. Their singing quality is fuller and more resonant in the fourth, fifth, and sixth grades than in the primary grades, although some children may feel more self-conscious about singing (especially solos) and thus may sound softer and lighter than their full-volumed capacity. The range of children's voices before the first changes that accompany adolescence typically spans from A to e′ for fourth graders, from A¨ to f′ for fifth graders, and from G to g′ for sixth graders. The tessitura for children ten through twelve years may be limited to about one octave. Some boys will experience a first vocal change by age ten or eleven, although others will sing well into early adolescence with a robust yet pure quality unmatched by children at any other age.

Children begin to manifest signs of physiological and psychological changes typical of adolescence by the close of their elementary years. Unless they are accustomed to singing, they may lose interest and resist any occasion to sing. While in some societies singing is an act of great pride that brings on admiration by members of the opposite sex, in American schools it is not unusual to find girls who are embarrassed to sing in front of boys and boys who view singing as a feminine or at least a less virile activity. To many children on the brink of adolescence, singing is no longer cool. Maintaining children's interest in singing requires a careful selection of songs with texts that are meaningful to them (and not too sentimental or babyish), with melodic ranges well within the safety of their tessitura.

The changing male voice is a symptom of the hormonal changes that begin to occur at the onset of puberty. When boys show a sudden growth spurt and a physical awkwardness, they may also demonstrate a heavier quality as they speak and sing. Their voices may occasionally crack as they reach beyond their middle range. While experts vary somewhat in their approaches to boys' changing voices, most recommend singing within the middle and most comfortable section of their range and avoiding register extremes.

As children come to understand the vocal mechanism, they are better able to use their voices productively. Children in the intermediate grades are also capable of performing with appropriate phrasing, diction, and intonation—all important facets of choral singing. Because they can perceive more than one simultaneously occurring musical line at a time, and because their voices are stronger and more independent than earlier, they can sing in harmony the rounds, partner songs, and part songs that comprise the repertoire of children's choirs. As they mature, children are able to sing expressively and to evaluate their own musical and vocal performance in terms of accuracy and appropriate tone, blend, and style.

© Billie Judy/Reel Life Productions

Methodological Suggestions for Early Childhood

- **Sing songs with young children**, guiding them to raise and lower their arms to the rise and fall of the melody while singing.
- **In a circle of young children**, encourage one child at a time to step into the middle, improvising a story in song.
- **Grow a list of familiar songs** that young children can sing together, and add to the list when both melody and words of a new song are learned.
- **So that young children can learn of topics through song**, sing songs of animals, people, weather, and modes of transportation.
- **Lead young children** in swaying, swinging, nodding, and patting as they sing.

Physical Training for the Child Voice

Beyond the natural development that occurs from preschool through the elementary grades, children's voices can be greatly enhanced through training. This is not to say that private singing lessons are advisable for children; lessons may best be reserved for the later years of adolescence and adulthood, when vocal development is complete. The astute teacher, however, who knows and provides occasions for exercising children's voices through songs, vocal games, and drills, will quicken the pace of development and extend the capacity for musical expression. Daily or even twice-weekly "group sings" will undoubtedly create more musical singers at an earlier age.

Perfect singing posture, or PSP, is a prerequisite to gaining good breath control, producing a beautiful tone, and phrasing a set of tones expressively (see Box 4.1). Although they are physically active and seldom sedentary, children require regular coordination, conditioning, and postural-development exercises. Imagery and exercise (instead of verbal explanations) can lead to the correct stance (or sitting position) for singing.

BOX 4.1 Perfect Singing Posture

Perfect singing posture (PSP) involves bottom-to-top body parts. Here are some suggestions for how to achieve the correct position.

1. Feet should be flat on the floor, about six inches apart, with one foot slightly ahead of the other. The weight is on the balls (not the heels) of the feet. Practice in shifting the weight from heels to toes will bring about an awareness of where the weight should be.

2. Knees need to be relaxed and not locked. A light bouncing in place, one knee alternating with the other, and then both knees, can eliminate tightness and tension.

3. The spine is to be lifted up and away from the hips. It should be straight but not stiff. Leading with the arms extended, and hands clasped backward, a spinal stretch can extend down to the toes; outward from the chest to the front, right, and left sides; and then high above the head. A return back to center will move the spine gently into place.

4. The chest should be slightly raised. Movement of the arms in a circular breast-stroke gesture from the middle of the chest to above the head and down to the side can loosen yet also coordinate the musculature of the chest, rib cage, lungs, and sternum.

5. Shoulders are held back slightly and down. Shoulder rolls are helpful: Rotation of the shoulders forward, down, and up will decrease tension; the reverse movement (backward, down, and up again) can also be helpful.

6. The head is held high as it rises up out of the spine and neck and rests level and well aligned. Head rolls achieve this position, by dropping the head to the chest and rolling it to one side and then the other.

7. Arms and hands should hang easily down at the sides. This can be achieved at the end of the spinal stretch or breast-stroke gesture, although attention may need to be called to the position of the arms and hands.

Reproduced with permission from *Teaching Kids to Sing* by Kenneth H. Phillips, Schirmer Books, 1992.

One of the most complete means for attaining appropriate alignment of the body parts for PSP is the image and imitation of a marionette puppet. Children begin this exercise by standing tall and imagining that there are two strings attached to them—from the ceiling to the bottom of their back and to the top of their head. An invisible puppeteer loosens the string, and the children drop from their waist, with head and arms hanging down past their knees, to the floor. In that position, they gently bounce. When the puppeteer begins to pull at the strings, the marionette children slowly rise and realign themselves: chest, shoulders, neck, head, and arms fall relaxedly into place.

PSP can be achieved in a sitting, as well as standing, position. The alignment of the middle and upper body transfers from standing to sitting positions. Children on chairs should sit on the front half of the seats with their feet flat on the floor. For those whose feet do not touch the floor, they should sit further back on the seats while hooking their feet on the front rung of the chair. Children who sit on the floor can be coaxed to cross their legs, raise themselves out of their hips, and lean slightly forward. No one position should be maintained for too long a time; standing and sitting positions can be taken alternately throughout a singing session.

Breathing for singing is similar to breathing for high-endurance sports such as swimming and long-distance running. Children are intrigued when they discover the physicality of good singing and the parallel of singing to athletic endeavors. With perfect singing posture, their bodies are readied for the deep breathing that must

"If you can talk, you can sing, and if you can walk, you can dance."

Traditional proverb, Macedonia

initiate and sustain the vocal sound. The image of filling the feet, the knees, the stomach, and the diaphragm (and the lungs) with air shows how complete and all-encompassing the breathing must be. Children can come to understand that as they fill themselves with the air of a very deep breath, their lower rib cage expands along with their lungs. Like a balloon or a bagpipe, they have air within them that can be moved up the windpipe and across the vocal cords, causing vibration to occur and sound to be produced.

Breathing exercises should precede singing activity. Children can take in air as they would sip soda through a straw: With puckered lips, they slowly sip the air in a manner similar to drinking. Because sipping is an easy and gentle action, there should be no tension in the exercise. Taking the image of the balloon, children can compare the expansion of their own lungs to the fullness of a blown balloon. They can imitate the roundness of a balloon as they breathe in through their mouths, their arms curved in front of them, fingers touching. The more air they inhale, the wider the balloon becomes; their arms move out more widely so that their fingers can no longer touch. As air in a balloon is slowly released, they can slowly release air without producing a vocal sound, and their fingers touch again. The inhaling and exhaling process can challenge children physically, especially when the appropriate vocal sound to which the exercises lead is demonstrated.

Vocal exercises that combine the inhaling, sustaining, and releasing of air develop control essential to good singing. Lesson 4.1 provides several suggestions for warming up the voice with attention to the breathing mechanism.

Marionette strategy for attaining PSP

© Jerry Gay

LESSON 4.1 Vocal Exercises That Develop Breath Control

The Ha-Ha

Imitate the quick, deep breathing of a dog panting at the end of a long and energetic run. Place the hands just under the rib cage at the diaphragm, take a deep breath, and exhale in short "ha-ha's." Breathe again, and while exhaling, sing the "ha-ha's" on one pitch. A third variation is to sing the "ha-ha's" stepwise from do to sol and back again, and then on a triadic do-mi-sol-mi-do.

harmony: I   I   I   V(6)   I

The Cool "OO"

Because the *u* vowel, as sounded in *new*, resonates well and is a relaxed sound for children to produce, it is commonly used in warm-ups and for tuning voices to one another. Using a descending stepwise pattern that ends in a skip of a fifth up and down, sing an "oo" sound with the letter *l* interspersed. Care should be taken not to form the lips too tightly. A relaxed and slightly dropped jaw will allow maximal air flow without changing the vowel sound.

harmony: V   V   I   V(7)   I

The "No-ah's Ark"

The pure *o* as in *cold* requires the jaw to drop more than in the *u*. It should also have little of the "vanishing oo" sound of "no"; that is, "no-oo." The *a* of *father* is sounded by dropping the jaw to a space long enough to allow the insertion of two fingers vertically. A slight smile contributes to a brighter *a*, not the "uh" sound. By singing "No-ah's Ark," children exercise two distinctive positions of the mouth and thus two separate vowel and vocal sounds. A smaller- and larger-ranged version of ascending and successive thirds is appropriate for children in the primary and intermediate grades.

harmony: I   V   I   IV   iii   IV   V7   I

(Continued)

The "Mmmmm" on the Vowels

Using the "m" sound to lead easily to vowel sounds, sing on one pitch the vowels *i* sounded as "ee," *e* sounded as "ay," *a*, *o*, and *u*. The *i* is like the sound in "green" and is produced with the lips slightly puckered so that the sound does not spread too widely. The *e* is a diphthong similar to the sound in "play," with an emphasis on "eh" that closes on "ee." In this exercise, five vowels are sounded on a single pitch. The transition from the consonant *m* to each vowel and back to the consonant again should be smooth, connected, and all on one sustained breath. The exercise can be accompanied by I, IV, I, V⁷, I.

The Echo

The modeling of pitches and pitch patterns by a leader is then imitated by the children. In leader-follower fashion, sing patterns and phrases from familiar songs as well as those yet to be learned. Use neutral syllables such as "loo," "noo," "la," and "bee" for tuning voices, and solfège syllables for building understanding of pitches and their relationships.

Toward Accurate Singing

Children who can hear and perceive melody are well equipped for singing accurately. The ability to hear is a physical endowment, but to perceive the melody of a song well enough to sing it requires focused and attentive listening.

The percentage of problem singers is greater now than ever before, and some children will need care and consistent instruction to become proficient singers. In order from having less to more singing skill, presingers do not sing but chant the song text, speaking-range singers sustain tones within the speaking voice range only, limited-range singers typically sing only from d to f, initial-range singers sing within a range of d to a, and full-fledged singers can sing in a range beyond the minimal register (B–d). Individual and small-group instruction via games and activities that combine singing with socializing experiences can camouflage the disciplined exercise that needs to occur to develop children's voices. Patience is key, however, because an entire academic year may be necessary for more effective singing to break through and remain consistent.

Children need the teacher's direction to attend to the pitches, phrases, and contours of a melody, as well as its rhythm, text, and formal organization. Some learn best through repeated listenings alone, others learn well when visual means (including color-coded shapes, numbers, pictures, and graphs; staff notation; and printed song words) are applied, and still others require the use of their bodies to feel the melody. One means of focusing children's listening is the use of direct questions, such as "Does the melody move mostly upward or downward?" or "Which word sounds the highest pitch of the song?"

Children can draw the melody's movement with their fingers, hands, arms, or even torso. This graphing of the melody's rise and fall is sometimes referred to as mapping. Such mapping can be broad and involve the entire body, or it can be contained within a very small space. Mapping may consist of a line drawing that moves each phrase from left to right with a finger in the air, on chalkboards with chalk, or on large pieces of paper with crayon.

Another means of directing children's attention to individual pitches and their relationships is through the use of a hand sign system first developed by Sarah Glover and John Curwen in England in the middle of the nineteenth century. The system was later popularized by proponents of the Kodály approach, and it is often referred to as Kodály hand signs (see Figure 4.1). In this system, each pitch of the diatonic scale is associated

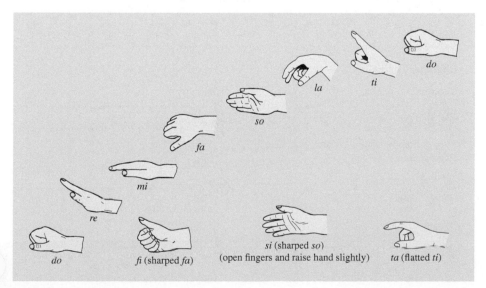

FIGURE 4.1

Kodály-Curwen Hand Signs

with a hand sign. Additional signs are used to indicate chromatic pitches, or accidentals outside of the song's key signature. Children can be taught the hand signs with relative ease as they sing the pitch names of the diatonic scale or as they learn the melodic fragments and tonal phrases of the songs they know. The hand sign system is effective as a technique for teaching melodic direction and shape, and it is enjoyed by children as a game that challenges their listening, critical thinking, moving, and singing skills.

Children are more likely to sing accurately when they can discriminate among higher or lower pitches and when they are presented with occasions for reproducing short melodic phrases. Pitch matching requires not only listening perception and short-term memory skills, but also the skills of vocal production. Through a series of echo-chants built on neutral syllables, solfège syllables, or word-phrases, children can match the pitches of short melodic phrases that are sung to them. These phrases may be embedded in familiar songs, or in songs they will eventually learn to sing, or in a familiar music repertoire. These melodic phrases may also be built into conversational or dialogue phrases, in which the same pitches used for a question may be used by children in their response.

Lesson 4.2 presents a sampling of musical fragments for pitch matching, proceeding from simple to more complex content. When such phrases are accompanied by appropriate gestures to indicate pitch direction and pitch relationships, children may sing them with even greater accuracy.

LESSON 4.2 Pitch-Matching Samples

Assorted Phrases

Dialogue Chants

These and other melodic phrases and fragments can be found intact, too, embedded in songs and instrumental selections. Proponents of the Kodály method offer a sequence for the teaching of melodic patterns that derive logically from traditional songs that children sing. A songful sequence of pitch patterns for songs found within this book is shown in Box 4.2, as demonstration of an approach to organizing songs to sing according to their increasingly sophisticated melodic content. The sequence begins with songs with just s-m, and graduates to songs with tritonic, tetratonic, pentatonic, and finally diatonic pitch content. Information on Kodály-inspired sequences for teaching melody may be found in works by Szönyi (1971-74) and Choksy (1999a, 1999b).

As children develop the abilities to discriminate pitches and to sing in tune, they should also be developing tonal memory. The teacher can guide children in strengthening their tonal memory by playing "name that tune," in which they identify the title of a familiar song that is sung by the teacher or selected leader without words on a neutral syllable. Another playful approach to strengthening the memory is to lead children in singing a song, and on a prearranged cue (such as a tap on the drum) to sing silently, only to return to singing aloud when given the cue again. Children must retain a sense of pulse, tempo, and pitch while silently performing the melody so that they can join in together again when the cue is given. Tonal memory, like rhythmic memory, requires children's utmost concentration. With it, their musicianship—and their repertoire of songs—can grow.

How ma-ny bro-thers do you have? I have one bro-ther, yes I do.

Do you like straw-ber-ries? Yes, I like straw-ber-ries

Do you like the zoo? Yes, I like the zoo.

Melodic Direction Chants

Ascending — We can sing high. Descending — We can sing low.

Ascending — Let's climb to a hill-top. Descending — Let's climb right back down a-gain.

BOX 4.2 A Songful Sequence of Pitch Patterns

PITCH SET	SONG	LOCATION
s-m	Rain, Rain, Go Away	Pg. '80
s-m, d-s	Vista	Pg. 88
l-s-m	Bounce High	Pg. 180
s-l-s-m	Bluebird	Pg. 88
s-l-s-m, m-d-l-s	Hill an' Gully Rider	Pg. 89
l-s-m-s	Liza Jane	Pg. 186
l-s-m	Little Sally Walker	Pg. 181
l-s-m-d	Teddy Bear	Pg. 137
s-m-l-s-m	Ring around the Rosy	Pg. 140
s-m-d	Mos'! Mos'!	Pg. 399
s-m-d	Sorida	Pg. 399
m-s	Tideo	Pg. 188
m-d-s	Looby Loo	Pg. 89
m-d	Weevily Wheat	Pg. 184
d-m	Just from the Kitchen	Pg. 90
l-s-m-d	Rocky Mountain	Pg. 90
d-m-s-m-r-d	Michael Finnigan	Pg. 187
d-s	Leila	Pg. 186
s-l-s-m-d	Bow Wow Wow	Pg. 142
d-s-m-s-d	The Noble Duke of York	Pg. 144
m-r-d	Suogan	Pg. 136
m-r-d	Hop Old Squirrel	Pg. 90
d-r-m, m-r-d	Long Legged Sailor	Pg. 94
m-r-d	How Many Miles to Babylon?	Pg. 142
d-r-m, m-r-d	All Round the Brickyard	Pg. 183
m-r-m-s	Dance Josey	Pg. 188
d-r-m-s	Let Us Chase the Squirrel	Pg. 90
d-r-m-d	Hashewie	Pg. 390
s-m-r-d	Singabahambayo	Pg. 186
d-m-s; r-m-r-d	Johnny Works with One Hammer	Pg. 137
d-r-m-s-l-s	Little David	Pg. 91
m-r-d-s'	A la Rueda de San Miguel	Pg. 189
d-l	All Around the Kitchen	Pg. 182
d-l	Shortnin' Bread	Pg. 91
d-l-s	Charlie's Neat	Pg. 191
l-m	Ala De'lona	Pg. 390
l-d-m	Loop de Loo	Pg. 92
l-d-r-m	Little Johnny Brown	Pg. 185
d-l-d-m	Alabama Gal	Pg. 5

(Continued)

BOX 4.2 (Continued)

PITCH SET	SONG	LOCATION
d-m-r-d-l-s	This Train	Pg. 92
m-r-d-l'	I Got a Letter This Morning	Pg. 184
m-r-d-l,-s,	Hey, Betty Martin	Pg. 181
d-r-m-r-d-s	Bucket of Water	Pg. 200
s-l-s-d	Lak Gei Moli	Pg. 396
s-s-m-r-d	Feng Yang Song	Pg. 397
s-f-m	Old Joe Clarke	Pg. 183
m-f-r-d	Las Mañanitas	Pg. 190
s-f-m-r-d	Kye Kye Kule	Pg. 200
l-s-f-m-r-d	Knick-Knack Paddy Whack	Pg. 181
f-m-r-d	Oh, How Lovely Is the Evening	Pg. 192
d-r-m-f-m-r-d	Kaeru No Uta	Pg. 101
s-f-m-f-s	London Bridge Is Falling Down	Pg. 140
m-f-s-l-s-f-m	Gerakina	Pg. 158
s-m-f-s	San Sereni	Pg. 143
s-l-t-d, d-l-s-d	I Went to California	Pg. 93
s-l-t-d	Music Alone Shall Live	Pg. 102
s-l-t-d	Punchinella	Pg. 141
s-f-m-r-d-t'-l'	Ah, Poor Bird	Pg. 100
t-l-t-d	Rig-a-jig-jig	Pg. 137
d-t-l	Rise Up, O Flame	Pg. 103
s-d-t-l-s	With Laughter and Singing	Pg. 4
s-d-t-l, f-t-l-s	Tinga Layo	Pg. 182
d-l-t-d-l-s	Kookaburra	Pg. 96, 187
d-t-l-s, f-m-r-d	Sansa Kroma	Pg. 200
s-f-m-r-d-t-d-t	Viva la Musica	Pg. 102
s-t-s-t-s-t	La Raspa	Pg. 156
s-f-m-r-d	Come, Let's Dance	Pg. 101
f-m-r-d-r-d	Hava Nashira	Pg. 102

For every phrase or song that is sung, the pitch and tempo must be set by the teacher. Children need to know on just what pitch they are to begin their singing, or all attempts at accurate singing are foiled. Familiar songs can begin with the teacher's sounding of the tonic, or home tone, of the song and then the 1-3-5-3-1 (d-m-s-m-d) of the key. A piano, xylophone, guitar, or other pitched instrument may be more helpful to the teacher than to the children, who may need to hear the vocally produced pitch to match it. Even in teaching individual song phrases by rote, the teacher should make a practice of sounding the first pitch, vocally, on a neutral syllable such as "loo" or "la," and then signaling the children to sing that pitch on that syllable before repeating the phrase. The pitch and tempo for familiar and new songs can be set together by conducting the meter while singing an initial phrase on the first pitch of the song. One example for pitch and tempo setting at the same time is shown in Music Example 4.2.

Here we go, read-y, sing: This old man He played one...

Here we go now, read-y sing: This old man He played one...

As children listen to song phrases and fragments, they must also strive to learn and retain their components to sing them accurately. They learn the words, rhythm, and melody of a song through repeated listening, and then by imitating the singer who serves as a model for them. Young singers require far more repetition of songs and song segments than they typically receive to grasp all of the musical details. For example, an eight-measure melody such as "Hey, Betty Martin" may require six or eight repetitions before a group of seven-year-olds can retain and reproduce the song with the words, melody, rhythm, and tonality intact. The teacher can sing alone while the children listen, or the children can sing while following the teacher's lead. A longer and more complex song such as "Tinga Layo" may necessitate as many (or more) repetitions for a group of ten-year-olds to learn it.

Not all children sing accurately in tune, although the great majority of children are capable of it. Children who sing daily at home or in school develop in-tune singing by the end of the second grade. For those in environments without regular opportunities to listen to music and to sing, vocal troubles may require attention. Instead of labeling the uncertain singers as monotones or nonsingers, teachers may need to devise remedial exercises within class and help sessions before school, after school, or at recess. Some children need coaxing to find their singing voice, and they may need to sing close to the pitch of their speaking voice. Others need to know that it is safe to sing aloud (and possibly solo). This will entail discussing with the group the rules of etiquette while singing alone, so that all children can be helped to become a part of their singing team. A series of sirenlike sound effects can be modeled and then imitated to extend the range of children who drone on one or two pitches or who sing below the appropriate pitch (see Music Example 4.3).

The sound of a ghost is another aural image that can assist children in hearing and feeling how their voices can reach registers not usually associated with their own speaking ranges. Likewise, children can imitate the sound of "yoo-hoo" or a train whistle.

These experiences can lead to pitch-matching exercises and to songs with simple rhythms and small melodic ranges. Unless children have physiological conditions (such as damaged vocal cords or severe hearing deficits) or the rare condition known as amusia, they can learn to sing accurately. The patient teacher's knowledgeable and inventive remedies can ensure success.

siren   ghost   call   train

aah   oo   Yoo-hoo Yoo-hoo   Woo-Woo

The Vocal Model

Children tend to sing a song in the manner and style in which it was presented to them. Thus, the presence of an accurate vocal model is critical to the instructional process. Whether the teacher, parent, or other adult seeks to teach a song, attention must be paid to musical style and voice quality as well as to the components of the song itself. If children are to sing in a light head tone, then the song must be sung by the model in that way. If a song is to be sung with vigor at high volume, then that model should be presented. If a song is suited for a softer and slower performance, then children must hear it that way. Children will sing a song presented in legato style in that manner, just as they are likely to sing a song in as many phrases (with as many breaths) and as many accents and dynamic nuances as they hear from the model.

The teacher or other singer who models for children should assume a singer's posture: straight and well aligned, but not stiff. Children need to see and hear what is expected of them. They need to see a singer's facial expression and gestures reflecting the mood and text of the song and hear the singer's energy and enthusiasm for the song, because the singer's performance can convince them that they should learn the song. Most important, the singer who models for children should sing the song musically—in tune, in its correct rhythm, and according to its stylistic nuances.

If the voice quality of the model is in many cases imitated by children, then what can be said about the male singer intent on teaching children to sing? Until the fourth grade, even children who sing regularly may have difficulty matching pitches when they hear the male voice sounding an octave below their own register. Some children attempt to sing at the lower octave, while others target a set of pitches somewhere between the model's pitch and that of the higher octave. Male singers working with young children or with children inexperienced in singing make more effective models for children when they sing using a falsetto quality. This falsetto sound should not be forced or at the full volume of a countertenor. Instead, the sound should be light and somewhat softer than the full dynamic intensity of the real voice. As children are able to transfer the sound of a male voice to their own register, often by fourth grade, they can begin to reap the benefit of hearing the male voice in its characteristic register.

> "...The singer who models for children should sing the song musically—in tune, in its correct rhythm, and according to its stylistic nuances."

Male singer with children—from light falsetto to characteristic register

© Jerry Gay

Although much of the singing children do can be led by the teacher without the aid of other accompaniment, the use of instruments may enhance the vocal sound. A tasteful accompaniment for recorder, xylophone ensemble, guitar, or piano can add musical interest, particularly for public performance (for the parents' club meeting or a school assembly, for example). A recorder descant played by a small group of children can provide a light contrapuntal line to the voice melody. The percussive quality of xylophone bourdons and ostinatos can provide striking contrast to smooth and well-supported singing. By strumming or plucking a guitar, the teacher can move closer to the children to hear and to help them with singing problems. The piano can provide an excellent support to singing, although it must be played with sensitivity to the vocal balance. However, because school music classrooms are often outfitted with a piano, it is tempting to overuse it in the early stages of learning a song so that children cannot listen to the teacher's (or their own) voice.

Should recordings be used in teaching children to sing? This is an irresistible proposition, and when instruments beyond those of the classroom appear on a recording, there may be greater musical intrigue and possibly greater motivation for children to sing. Some recordings have the advantage of demonstrating to children the ideal aural image of how their own young voices should sound. A recording can make a most acceptable model of a perfected sound and can be used to introduce a song, or to later reinforce it. Still, it may be largely the task of the teacher to start and stop the song, and to raise and lower the pitch, tempo, and volume of the song, according to the vocal abilities and musical needs of the children. No recording or other electronic apparatus can do this with such ease and immediacy.

MUSIC EXAMPLE 4.4

Sampling of Group Songs

Vista (s-m, d-s) (United States, As sung by Karen Howard)

Vi - sta, Vi - sta, cu-ma-la cu-ma-la cu - ma - la vi - sta Oh no no no

—— no la vi - sta ee - nie mee - nee sa - la - mee - nee oo - wa - ka - ma - na - mee - nee

Eek bee - del - lee o - kee - do - kee bo - bo skee aw - tn - daw - tn

*Solo voice, first time; Group response, second time

Bluebird (s-l-s-m) (United States)

Here comes a Blue-bird, through my - Win - dow Hey, did - dle-dum doo dah day.

Hill an' Gully Rider (s-l-s-m, m-d-l-s) (Jamaica)

Hill an' gul-ly ri - der, hill an' gul-ly.

Hill an' gul-ly ri - der, hill an' gul-ly, but my

horse come down and hill an' gul-ly, but my horse come stum-ble down.

Hill an' gul-ly, And the night come tumb-lin' down, hill an' gul-ly.

Looby Loo (m-d-s) (United States)

Chorus:

Here we go Loo - by Loo, Here we go Loo - by Light,

Here we go Loo - by Loo, All on a Sat-ur-day night._____

Verse 1:

You put your right foot in,_____ You put your right foot out,_____

You give your right foot a shake, shake, shake, And turn your-self a - bout.

2. You put your left foot in . . .

3. You put your right hand in . . .

4. You put your left hand in . . .

5. You put your whole self in . . .

Just from the Kitchen (d-m) (United States, As sung by Bessie Jones)

Just from the kit - chen, Shoo - lie - loo, with a hand - ful of bis - cuits, Shoo - lie - loo, Oh.

Miss Ma - ry, Shoo - lie - loo, Fly a - way o - ver yon - der, Shoo - lie - loo.

Rocky Mountain (l-s-m-d) (United States)

Rock - y moun - tain, rock - y moun - tain, rock - y moun - tain high.

When you're on that rock - y moun - tain hang your head and cry.

Hop Old Squirrel (m-r-d) (United States)

Hop old squirrel eid - le - dum eid - le dum Hop old squirrel eid - le - dum dum.

Hop old squirrel eid - le dum eid - le - dum Hop old squirrel eid - le - dum day.

Let Us Chase the Squirrel (d-r-m-s) (United States)

Let us chase the squir - rel. Up the hick - 'ry down the hick - 'ry.

Let us chase the squir - rel up the hick - 'ry tree.

Little David (d-r-m-s-l-s) (United States, African American)

1. Lit-tle Dav - id, play on your harp, Hal - le - lu, Hal - le - lu,
2. Se - re - na, dance up your dance,

Lit - tle Dav - id, play on your harp, Hal - le - lu.
Se - re - na, dance up your dance,

Lit - tle Dav - id, play 2, 3, 4, 5, 6, go!
Se - re - na, play dance,

Lit - tle Dav - id, play, 2, 3, 4, 5.
Se - re - na, dance,

Shortnin' Bread (d-l) (United States, African American)

Refrain: Call: Reponse: Call: Reponse: Call:
I do love__ short - nin' bread. I do love__ short - nin' bread. Ma - ma loves

Reponse: Call: Reponse: Call: Reponse: Fine
2nd time to Verse 2
short - nin' bread. Pa - pa loves short - nin' bread. Ev - 'ry - bod - y loves short - nin' bread.

Verse 1: To Refrain
Two lit - tle ba - bies lay - in' in the bed; one play sick and the oth - er play dead I

Old la - dy Di - nah's sick in the bed; Called the doc - tor, the

To Refrain

doc - tor said, "Oh,_____ she needs some short - nin' bread!" I

Loop de Loo (l-d-m) (United States, African American)

Here_____ we go loop de loo._____ Here_____ we go loop de loo._____ Here

_____ we go loop de loo all on a Sat - ur - day night. I put my *right hand in, I

put my right hand out. I give my right hand a shake shake shake and turn my bo - dy a - bout.

*1. right hand
2. left hand
3. right leg
4. left leg
5. big head
6. whole self

This Train (d-m-r-d-l-s) (United States, African American)

1. This train is bound for glo - ry, this train.__
2. This train don't pull no sleep - ers, this train.__
3. This train don't take your mon - ey, this train.__

This train is bound for glo - ry, this train.
This train don't pull no sleep - ers, this train.
This train don't take your mon - ey this train.

This train is bound for glo - ry, don't car - ry none but the good and ho - ly.
This train don't pull no sleep-ers, Don't pull nothing' but the right - eous peo - ple.
This train don't take your mon - ey, Pay your way with milk and hon - ey.

This train is bound for glo - ry, this train.
This train is bound for glo - ry, this. train.
This train is bound for glo - ry, this train.

I Went to California (s-l-t-d, d-l-s-d) (United States)

I went to Cal - i - for - nia far, far a - way; I met a sen - or - i - ta with

flow - ers in her hair, Oh! shake it, shake it, shake it,

shake it if you can, and if you can not shake it, you

do the best you can, Oh! shake it to the bot - tom

shake it to the top and turn a - round and turn a - round,

till you make a stop.

Long-Legged Sailor (d-r-m, m-r-d) (United States)

Have you ev - er ev - er ev - er in your long leg - ged life seen a long leg - ged sai - lor with a long leg - ged wife?

Selecting and Teaching Songs

Processes for teaching songs to children range from rote to note, or combinations of the two. Teaching a song by rote is transmitting the song orally, while teaching by note clearly involves children's ability to read music. The process depends on the teacher's perspective, the lesson objectives, and the children's skill levels. Yet even before the teaching process begins, initial steps can be taken to ensure children's successful singing. The critical first step is selecting songs that are musically, textually, and developmentally appropriate. Guidelines for song selection are noted in Box 4.3, along with other preparatory issues.

Song collections are plentiful, with songs of every genre—traditional, patriotic, art and classical, composed, popular, and even songs transmitted and preserved by children. The collections of Erdei and Komlos (1974), Campbell (2008), and Fowke (1969, 1977) contain songs from North America, as do the online archives of Smithsonian Folkways and the Association for Cultural Equity. A rich collection of rounds suitable for children has been compiled by Finckel (1993), and a set of British traditional songs is

BOX 4.3 Song Selection and Preparation

1. Select a song that is age-appropriate. Check the song's range.

   Check the song's tessitura.
   Check the text:
   - Is it too babyish?
   - Is it too grown-up or lovey-dovey?
   - Will the subject matter interest children?
   - Does it contain offensive language (perhaps unintended)?
   - If in a foreign language, can you pronounce it?

2. Select a song in a style that you can sing.

   Check the style: If it is outside your training and experience, can you learn to sing it in its appropriate style?

3. Review the song for its musical and textual highlights.

   Check the melody: Are there tonal phrases to sing in isolation?
   Check the rhythm: Are there rhythmic phrases to chant in isolation?
   Check the text: Are there ideas that relate to a story, poem, or discussion of a historical or cultural issue?

the result of research by Langstaff, Swanson, and Emlen (1999). Songs and chants for young children are found in numerous collections by Feierabend (1999) and Kleiner (1996). For examples of children's songs from other world cultures, there are the ageless collections by Adzinyah, Maraire, and Tucker (1996); Campbell, McCullough-Brabson, and Tucker (1994); Campbell with Frega (2001); Kwami (1998); Lavendar (1998); Lew and Campbell (2006); Nguyen and Campbell (1992); and Campbell, Williamson, and Perron (1996); all accompanied by recordings. The basal music series, online and in textbook-and-recording collections, contain a wide variety of songs appropriate for use with children from kindergarten through the eighth grade.

One of the most popular ways for the teacher to present a song is through oral and aural means, or by rote. In the rote approach, children are given numerous opportunities to listen to the complete song. Fragments of the song are then presented sequentially to the children (oral) in small phrases or chunks; children listen (aural) and then echo these fragments. These chunks are sung repeatedly until accuracy is achieved, and then the chunks are combined with other chunks until the whole song is learned. The children's imitation of the model is a necessary strategy in the rote approach, which can nearly guarantee the development of a large repertoire of songs. A sequence for teaching a song through oral-aural means can be found in Lesson 4.3. The song is introduced, then practiced, and a culminating activity embraces the use of instruments or sometimes movement and games. The entire song-based lesson runs about 13 minutes (the numbers in parentheses are estimates for time expenditures by minute).

LESSON 4.3 Teaching a Song via Oral-Aural Means

Mos'! Mos'!

See page 399 in Chapter 15 for notation.
(<1/2 min.) "Greetings"/Introduction/Share-the-Plan.

Introduction

1. "This song is about a cat. What in the world do you think is going on in this 'cat' song?" (Teacher sings the song for the first time.)
   (It is a Hopi song about a bobcat stealing a sheep (skin). Listen for the 'nya-nya' at the end of the song?)

2. "Listen for ♩♩♩♩ ♩ [ti-ti-ta]. Count many times you hear this rhythm." (Teacher sings the song for the second time.)
   (Four times is the correct answer)

3. "When you hear me sing these pitches [s-d-m], raise your hand." (Teacher sings the song for the third time.)
   (Good listening, especially if you raised your hand four times.)

Practice

1. Children sing the song with minimal Teacher assistance
   ("How much of this song can you sing with me?")

2. Children sing the song with minimal Teacher assistance.
   ("Let's try it again. Remember to sing the 'nya-nya' at the end, from high to low.")

3. Other ways of singing the song (with minimal-to-no Teacher assistance)
   "Sing in two groups, 1 and 2, following my cue"
   "Sing outside and inside, on cue."
   "Sing strong and soft, on cue."
   "Sing without me."

(Continued)

Culminating Activity

Culminating Activity Instruction/Demonstration
Sticks on rhythm of phrases 1 and 2, rattles on phrase 3.

1. Song with Culminating Activity.
   Sticks and rattles

2. Song with Culminating Activity, repeated.
   Sticks and rattles

3. Song with Culminating Activity, one more time (!).
   Sticks and rattles
   (<1/2 min.) Reinforcement/Evaluation/"Farewell"

Another approach to teaching a song involves children in reading notation. A selected song may contain melodic and rhythmic patterns that were sung, chanted, and played in earlier lessons. Given the great array of songs in series textbooks and in song collections, children can be challenged to seek familiar notated patterns within the new song and to perform them. Rhythms can be chanted according to the preferred system, and melodic patterns can be sung on neutral syllables or with solfège syllables. While there may be unfamiliar patterns to be learned by rote, by trial and error, or by putting to practice the logical and analytical skills required of reading words or notes, children can connect the familiar to the new patterns in learning the song. The teacher may eventually sing the entire song to provide them with a coherent image of the song. Children can feel accomplished in having the ability to decode the notation themselves. Lesson 4.4 presents both rote and note approaches to teaching "Kookaburra."

Rote and note are two approaches, although combinations of these approaches are also possible. The immersion process is another means for learning a song, in which children hear the song sung by the teacher, parent, or another child to the extent

LESSON 4.4 Rote and Note Approaches to Teaching *"Kookaburra"*

Kookaburra (Australia)

Kook-a-bur-ra sits on an old gum tree, __ Mer-ry, mer-ry king of the bush is he. __

Laugh, kook-a-bur-ra, laugh, kook- a-bur-ra, Glad your life must be.

BY ROTE

1. "Can you keep the steady pulse?" Teacher sings the song while children accompany by patting and clapping.

2. "Can you draw the melody's rises and falls?" Teacher sings the song again while children draw in space the melodic contour.

3. "What word is sung on the highest pitch of the song?" Teacher sings the song again, followed by children's answer.

4. "Listen and then sing after me: 'Kookaburra sits on an old gum tree.'" Teacher sings first phrase; children imitate.

5. Repeat first phrase as necessary.

6. "Listen and then sing after me: 'Merry, merry king of the bush is he.'" Teacher sings second phrase; children imitate.

7. Repeat second phrase as necessary.

8. "Listen and then sing after me: 'Laugh, Kookaburra, laugh, Kookaburra.'" Teacher sings third phrase; children imitate.

9. Repeat third phrase as necessary.

10. "Listen and then sing after me: 'Glad your life must be.'" Teacher sings final phrase; children imitate.

11. Repeat final phrase as necessary.

12. "Let's sing the first two phrases, first me and then you." Teacher sings phrase one and two; children imitate.

BY NOTE

1. Teacher presents notated rhythm patterns: ♫♫ ♫ ♩ ♫ ♩ "Take a minute to practice. Silently chant and clap the familiar patterns."

2. "Let's chant and clap as I point to the individual patterns." Teacher and children perform them, using favored chant system (for example, ti-ri-ti-ri, ti-ti-ri, ti-ti ti-ti).

3. Repeat as necessary.

4. "Sing with me": ♫♫ ♫ ♩ ♫ ♩
   s s s s l   l l s   m   s m
   Teacher and children sing together.

5. Repeat as necessary.

6. "Now, what would happen if we sang that phrase beginning on mi? Shall we try it?" ♫♫ ♫ ♩ ♫ ♩.
   m m m m f   f f m   d   m d
   Teacher and children sing together.

7. "Let's try singing these phrases with our hand signals and our musical syllables." Teacher and children sing and signal the two phrases.

8. "Look at two new rhythm patterns": ♩ ♫♫ ♫ ♫ ♩ "Let's clap and chant them." Teacher and children clap and rhythmically chant.

9. "What if we added pitches to those rhythms? Could you sing them?" Teacher presents notation for last two phrases.

10. "What's the highest pitch?" (Do.) Listen and follow with your hand signs: ♩ ♫♫ ♩ ♫♫ ♫ ♫
    d l t d l s   s l s f m d d d

11. "Now sing with me." Teacher and children sing last two phrases with syllables and hand signals.

12. Repeat as necessary.

(Continued)

13. Repeat as necessary.

14. "Let's sing the last two phrases, first me and then you." Teacher sings phrases three and four; children imitate.

15. Repeat as necessary.

16. "Now we're ready to sing the whole song." Teacher and children sing together.

17. "Can you sing the song without me? I'll get you started." Teacher sets pitch and tempo; children sing.

13. Teacher presents the notated song. "Can you clap and chant the whole song?" Teacher and children clap and chant together.

14. "Can you, slowly, sing the melody with our musical syllables and hand signals? Watch me when you get lost." Teacher and children sing and signal together.

15. Repeat as necessary.

16. "Let's read the words to this song in rhythm."

17. "Let's sing the song with the words."

18. Repeat as necessary.

19. "Can you sing the song without me? I'll get you started." Teacher sets pitch and tempo; children sing.

Adapting Instruction for Various Needs

Behavioral Needs

- *Externalizing Behaviors.* Spend some time (at morning arrival, recess, lunch) building a rapport with a child who acts out and working together on a contract that will help the monitoring of distracting and distracted behaviors; build in rewards that are ideally suited to the child's interests (i.e., "we will sing your song if we also sing our songs"). In class, surround him/her with enthusiastic singers who are motivated and will sing with energy.

- *Internalizing Behaviors.* Allow the withdrawn child to be positioned around children he/she trusts, and to sing together rather than solo.

Autism Spectrum

- For a low functioning child with autistic behaviors, allow quiet observation of activity so that engagement can gradually evolve. Move to that area while singing/conducting, inviting the child to sing (verbally, with gestures, or eye contact).

Mobility Impairment

- Model and describe the importance of taking a deep breath for singing every phrase, no matter whether standing or sitting. For songs with gestures and movement, model modified movements.

Gifted

- Challenge children to sing songs with wider ranges, to sing while playing simple accompaniments, to sing a song in several styles (following the model of recorded versions).

they individually require before joining in. When a song is learned, children can then be led to related activities, including playing body percussion on ♩, ♫, and ♫♫; creating a dance to reflect its phrases and form; accompanying the song with ostinati on classroom instruments; improvising a variation on recorder; or including it in a performance of other songs and chanted poems on similar subjects. However, any possibilities to extend their capabilities for singing expressively require their full knowledge and skills in performing the song. With this accomplished and with the vocal production capacity in good working order, children can then be taught to sing musically.

How to Teach Singing in Parts

When children have developed the perceptual and productive skills that come with singing in tune, the next natural stage is to sing in harmony. Children in the third grade can be successful in singing songs in two-part arrangements: melodies with drones and ostinati. Fourth-grade children perform canons (or rounds), descants, partner songs, and countermelodies well in two independent groups; three-part canons can be reserved for children in fifth and sixth grades. When music instruction has been consistent and strong, bona fide two-part choral pieces can be read, rehearsed, and perfected for performance in the last years of elementary school.

In testing children's ability to sing in independent groups, songs such as "Old Texas," with active melodies sung over the sustained pitch of a second group, can be selected (see Music Example 4.5). The teacher can lead the singing, sustaining as children sing in imitation. Eventually, two groups can perform this fundamental form of part-singing.

Among the first attempts at singing in parts is the use of a repeated melodic pattern, or ostinato, to accompany the melody, as in "Hey, Ho, Nobody Home" or "Ah, Poor

Melody over Sustained Pitch

Old Texas (United States)

Hey, Ho, Nobody Home (England)

Ah, Poor Bird (England)

Bird" (see Music Examples 4.6 and 4.7). Ostinato parts are created by examining the melody for its harmonic possibilities and sampling on a pitched instrument one- or two-measure segments that jell harmonically with each measure of the song. While seconds or sevenths occasionally may sound together in passing, so long as they are resolved to thirds, fourths, or fifths on the strong beats, the ostinato will probably be satisfying.

Canons and rounds comprise some of the most fulfilling musical experiences for children in their elementary years. Critical to that fulfillment, however, is the process by which they are taught. First, the teacher should be certain that the children are secure in singing the song's melody as a larger group, and then in smaller groups. Second, the teacher can cue the class to begin singing and then can begin softly singing the second part at the canon. The number 2 on the scores signifies the point at which the group must be when the teacher begins singing. Third, a small group of children can be selected to sing with the teacher at the canon. Finally, the class can be divided equally, so that the two groups can maintain their independent parts while performing. (see Music Example 4.8).

A descant is an independent melody that can be added above a first and usually more familiar melody. It is higher in pitch than the main melody. Conversely, a countermelody can be added below a familiar main melody. Using some of the procedures for teaching a round, children can sing the melody while the teacher softly adds a descant or countermelody; the class can gradually be divided into two groups.

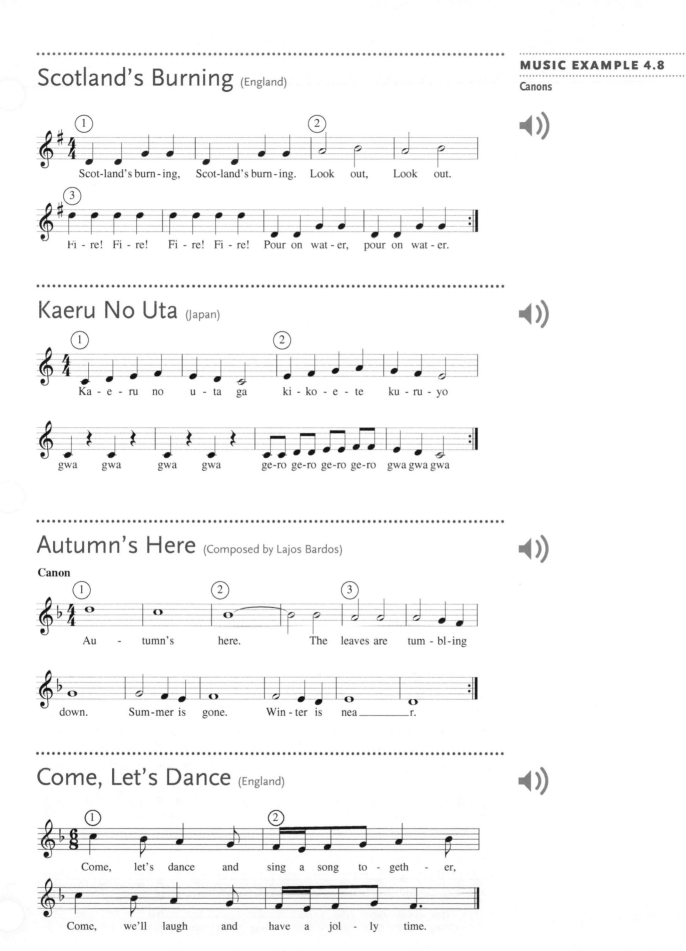

Scotland's Burning (England)

Scot-land's burn-ing, Scot-land's burn-ing. Look out, Look out.

Fi-re! Fi-re! Fi-re! Fi-re! Pour on wat-er, pour on wat-er.

Kaeru No Uta (Japan)

Ka-e-ru no u-ta ga ki-ko-e-te ku-ru-yo

gwa gwa gwa gwa ge-ro ge-ro ge-ro ge-ro gwa gwa gwa

Autumn's Here (Composed by Lajos Bardos)

Canon

Au-tumn's here. The leaves are tum-bl-ing

down. Sum-mer is gone. Win-ter is nea_____r.

Come, Let's Dance (England)

Come, let's dance and sing a song to-geth-er,

Come, we'll laugh and have a jol-ly time.

Music Alone Shall Live (Germany)

All things shall per - ish from un - der the sky.

Mus - ic a - lone shall live, Mus - ic a - lone shall live,

Mus - ic a - lone shall live nev - er to die.

Viva la Musica (Germany)

Canon

Vi - va vi - va la mu - si - ca, Vi - va vi - va la

mu - si - ca, Vi - va la mu - si - ca.

Hava Nashira (Israel)

Canon

Hah - vah nah - she - rah she - rah lay - loo - yah.
Sing and be joy - ful. sing ah lay - loo - yah.

Hah - vah nah - she - rah she - rah lay - loo - yah.
Sing and be joy - ful. sing ah lay - loo - yah.

Hah - vah nah - she - rah she - rah lay - loo - yah.
Sing and be joy - ful. sing ah lay - loo - yah.

Rise Up, O Flame (United States)

① ②

Rise up, O flame, _____ by __ thy __ light glow _____ ing.

③ ④

Bring to us beau _____ ty, __ vi __ sion, __ and joy.

The songs "Skye Boat Song" and "Yo Mamana, Yo!" illustrate the use of the counter-melody and descant (see Music Examples 4.9 and 4.10).

Some musical traditions of the world are best sung in unison if a culturally authentic sound is to be rendered. Still, harmony is an important feature of many songs from Anglo-American and African American traditions, as well as from parts of sub-Saharan Africa, the Pacific Islands, and much of the Hispanic world. Excerpts from two pieces appear in Music Example 4.11: "Savalivalah," from Samoa, and "Mbube," from South Africa.

Skye Boat Song (Scotland)

MUSIC EXAMPLE 4.9

Countermelody

Countermelody

melody: Speed, bon-ny boat, like a bird on a wing, On-ward the sail-ors

countermelody:

cry. Car-ry the lad that's born to be king o-ver the sea to

Fine

Skye. Loud the winds howl! Loud the waves roar! Thun-der clouds rend the air! Baf-fled, our foes stand on the shore. Fol-low they will not dare.

D.C

Yo Mamana, Yo! (Mozambique)

Descant

descant: Yo ma - ma - na, yo! Yo ma - ma - na, yo!

melody: Yo ma - ma - na, yo! Yo ma - ma - na, yo!

Un - ga fun - ba u - ni si - ya, U - ni si - ya la vu si-wa-na

Un - ga fun - ba u - ni si - ya, U - ni si - ya la vu si-wa-na

Source: As sung by Salamao Manhica. From *Roots and Branches*. © 1994 World Music Press.
Used by permission.

Savalivalah (Samoa)

Three-Part Song

"Sa - va - li - va - lah" means "Go for a walk." "Tau - ta - la - ta - la" means

"Sa - va - li - va -lah" means "Go for a walk." "Tau - ta - la - ta - la" means

"Sa - va - li - va -lah" means "Go for a walk." "Tau - ta - la - ta - la" means

"Too much talk." "A - lo - fa iā te oe" means

"Too much talk." "A - lo - fa iā te oe" means

"Too much talk." "A - lo - fa iā te oe" means

"I love you." "Take it ea - sy," Fai Fai - le - mu.

"I love you." "Take it ea - sy," Fai Fai - le - mu.

"I love you." "Take it ea - sy," Fai Fai - le - mu.

Mbube (South Africa)

Four-Part Song

(1) In the jun - gle the qui - et jun - gle the li - on sleeps to - night.
(2) In the jun - gle the might - y jun - gle the li - on sleeps to - night.

M-bu-be m - bu-be m-bu-be m - bu-be m - bu-be m - bu-be m - bu-be m - bu-be

M-bu-be m - bu-be m-bu-be m - bu-be m - bu-be m - bu-be m - bu-be m - bu-be

M-bu-be m - bu-be m-bu-be m - bu-be m - bu-be m - bu-be m - bu-be m - bu-be

Two- and three-part songs for children in the intermediate grades are increasingly available from publishing companies that specialize in choral music. Children's ability to sing in tune, to sing in harmony, and to render songs with musical sensitivity makes singing a pleasure for them as well as for their listeners.

Children's Choirs

When children have been raised to enjoy singing, they may be eager for the additional musical experiences that membership in a choir provides. Children's choirs in schools, churches, and communities are a growing phenomenon. When viewed as an educational entity as much as a performance one, the choir can extend the musical goals as well as the vocal development of children. Aural skills can be refined, pitch matching can be improved, and children can become exposed to a variety of the historical and cultural repertoire. Within the framework of the school curriculum, a twice-weekly choir meeting of forty-five minutes to an hour can greatly enhance children's vocal and musical development.

School choirs often open membership to children of mixed ages beginning in the third or fourth grade, although two or three choirs can be formed according to age and experience. A public performance for parents or at a school assembly may be one of

Accomplishing Multiple Music Standards through Singing

1. *Singing*: All of the ideas in this chapter connect to listening.

2. *Playing*: Children can sing their instrumental music. For example, they can sing melodies they play on recorders or on beginning strings and band instruments. As well, they can play the songs they sing, taking them to their recorders, violins, clarinets, and trumpets. Using chord instruments such as guitar and keyboard, they can sing their songs to the basic accompaniments they learn to play.

3. *Improvising*: For the songs they know very well, challenge them to sing the last phrase "a little differently," improvising an ending. In a four-phrase song like "Skip to My Lou" or "Kookaburra," have children change the second phrase one time, and the third phrase another time, improvising a new melody on the same words (or improvising melody and words, both).

4. *Composing and Arranging*: Create an accompaniment on xylophones and metallophones for selected songs. Then, create new instrumental music in between known songs. For example, once children learn to sing "Long-Legged Sailor" and "Little David," assign them to creating (a) accompaniments of ostinati and bourdons and (b) "in-between" eight-measure musical transitions.

5. *Reading and Notation*: Allow children to sight-read the songs they are learning, or to read melodic and rhythmic motifs and then find them in the songs they are learning.

6. *Listening*: Together, have children listen to recordings of adults and children singing familiar, learned songs, in various styles, with various accompaniments.

7. *Analyzing and Evaluating*: Record class efforts to sing songs, and listen to them in order to evaluate musical accuracy, expression, and stylistic nuances. Compare to other recorded renditions of the songs.

8. *Connecting to Other Arts and Curricular Areas*: Sing with expression befitting a storytelling event or an on-stage dramatic performance, complete with gestures and proper body posture and position. Perform the song with careful attention to the movements of an associated dance, as in the case of "Rig-a-jig-jig" and "How Many Miles to Babylon?"

9. *Connecting to Culture and History*: Discover the historical and cultural details of songs like "The Noble Duke of York," "Old Texas," "Hava Nashira," or "Jubilee!"

the choir's targeted goals, so that children can know the joy of performing for others. Seasonal, holiday, and graduation programs that feature children from all classes and grade levels can be capped off with a set of songs performed by the school choir. Citywide or districtwide festivals of elementary school choirs are other occasions for sharing with an audience the results of children's efforts in their rehearsals.

An audition is useful if only to emphasize the commitment of children to singing in a choir, and so that there is an understanding that each child's voice is important in its contribution to the group sound. This is not to say that the choir should be exclusive in its acceptance of only the most talented children. All children who express interest in singing in a school choir should be given a fair chance to become a member of the singing team. An audition allows the director to know the vocal quality and musicianship of each child and helps to guide the type of vocal exercises and repertoire to be used in rehearsal. Children who need remedial work can also be identified through the audition process.

Auditions can take place before or after school or at recess, but preferably not during the music class. To determine range and pitch accuracy, each child can be asked to sing a familiar song such as "America" or "Are You Sleeping?" first in a comfortable middle-range key, and then in higher and lower keys. Vocal quality and range can also be assessed by singing a descending major scale on a neutral syllable, starting first at c′ (c above middle C), then at d′, e′, and so forth. Another test of pitch accuracy is having each child sing a set of short melodic patterns that are first sung or played by the teacher. Tonal memory can be tested by lengthening the melodic patterns to be imitated from four to six to eight beats. Finally, vocal independence can be evaluated by asking the student to sing a familiar song ("Are You Sleeping?" "Row Your Boat," "Music Alone Shall Live") while the teacher sings it in canon. These tasks offer the information teachers require in selecting and arranging music for the choir, while they challenge children musically and vocally.

A choir rehearsal may progress in several stages, beginning with physical warm-ups and vocal exercises. To maintain attention, a rehearsal should contain a variety of musical selections and approaches to them. One rule of thumb is to efficiently rehearse each song, or song section, for a maximum of seven minutes before proceeding to a new piece. In the case of a part song, those who are not singing should be silently following their part, which they may be directed to sing on cue at any given moment. When children show signs of distraction or inattention, a physical exercise or rhythmic pattern can be introduced to restore focus and energy. All rehearsals, regardless of how soon a performance may be, should close with a familiar song that is guaranteed to send children on their way with good sounds and feelings about themselves and their membership in the choir. For further advice on organizing a children's choir, see McRae (1991) and Bartle (2003).

Children singing in a choir

Billie Judy/Reel Life Productions

Assessment of Singing

Children's singing skills grow through use and the concentrated effort it takes to develop (1) musical (tonal and rhythmic) accuracy, (2) the physical capacity to support a clear and focused vocal quality, and (3) the expressive nuance that flows from understanding the intent of the composer, the poet, and the cultural tradition. The teacher's own vocal training provides not only a model for children to emulate in their process of learning to sing, but also the musical intelligence to be able to distinguish when children's vocal skills are keeping pace with their potential at given ages and stages. Children can also be drawn into understanding what is, and is not, musical, vocally balanced, and expressive singing. Just as a listening ear is vital to the growth of singing skills, listening is key in children's assessment of their own vocal development.

Formative Evaluation

The following questions are useful to have at hand as children sing alone or together, and as they listen to themselves in the act of singing or as they play back a recording of their singing for later critique.

1. Was the singing in tune? Was it flat or sharp? (Could you have filled yourself with deeper breaths and greater energy to support your singing?)

2. Was the singing in time? Was it rhythmically alive? (Could you have been more aware of the music and text ahead of you, and more prepared to sing each pitch, word and syllable, and phrase?)

3. Was the singing relaxed and open, or tense and tight? (Could you have stood taller and with better alignment of your feet, spine, chest, shoulders, and head? Could you have opened yourself up to fuller breaths?)

4. Was the singing expressive of the text? (Could you have put more into making the song meaningful, to charge the listener and give him or her goose bumps in receiving the musical message?)

Clearly, assessment of children's singing can occur naturally in the daily process of a class singing activity, when a teacher may ask children in rapid-fire succession to sing a phrase or a song segment in small groups, duos, and even individually. He or she is in effect providing assessment at every step of the instructional process.

Summative Evaluation

As children practice singing and hear good singers perform live and on recordings, they will naturally be drawn into grasping the components of singing well. They will come to recognize different vocal styles and the spectrum of expressive qualities of which the voice is capable for conveying various meanings. The teacher may wish to record children's singing progress by arranging for periodic recording sessions of students on a given song or exercise. Such a procedure can happen at the end of a scholastic term, or following a study unit or a concert program, or on a bimonthly basis, when children can file one by one to a closet or out to the hall to sing a song or several phrases into a tape recorder. Such recordings can become a part of student portfolios, tracing the development of children's vocal range and tessitura, vocal strength, musical accuracy, and expressivity. Children can be given these recordings at the end of the year as documentation of their growth as young singers, to be shared with their families.

Reasons to Sing

Children are still singing despite rumors that the media-rich world in which they live has turned them to passive listeners and lip-syncers. The voice is the one musical instrument that all possess and for which no rental fee or elaborate arrangement for private instruction is necessary. For many children, singing is the path that they will choose to experience as participants and performers the great joy of music. Teachers who enjoy singing will further kindle the interests of children, because enjoyment is irresistible; it is contagious.

Scenario

IT IS SEPTEMBER, AND Ms. Patterson has begun the school year with a plan for her fourth-grade children at Thompson Elementary School: to learn to sing in parts. Her students arrive, settling in at the outer rim of a large braided carpet of many colors, three girls here, a couple of girls there, and the eleven boys packed in shoulder to shoulder within about one-third of the rim. Ms. Patterson stands by the piano, just outside the circle, plays a few chords to bring children to attention, and announces the plan: "Because you have all had four years of experience in our music program, and your voices have developed such strength, we will be learning to sing harmony this year—in parts." She shares the sequence of the day's lesson with them: "We'll begin with some vocal warm-ups, and then we'll be ready to learn our first real part song, 'Old Texas.'" With a flourish of several more chords to set the key, she directs them to sing a major scale on a neutral syllable and then on solfège syllables, accompanying them chordally on each pitch they sing. Most of the girls are with her, and a few of the boys, while others are chanting and half-shouting the syllables (but in a very rhythmic manner). She proceeds to pitch-matching exercises, playing a brief melodic phrase at the piano to which they respond in imitation on a neutral syllable. "Pretty good," she says, in part to balance her remarks to a group of both in-tune singers and others who seem uncertain, uninterested, or unable to match pitches.

As promised, Ms. Patterson proceeds to introduce the children to "Old Texas." She steps into the middle of the circle and sings the melody to the children in a light voice. To connect to the children, she moves from child to child, making eye contact as she sings the song four times through. Most of the children are attentive, and two or three children are already singing along with her. Having introduced the song, she then breaks the song into two-measure phrases, singing and then cueing the children to sing after her. There is a sequence: first she (and then the children) sings the phrase with the song's words, then on neutral syllables, and lastly with solfège syllables. Phrase by phrase, most of the children are coming to grips with the song's melody (five or six of the boys are singing with a cowboy twang and swaying left to right, but Ms. Patterson finds their performance otherwise acceptable—and amusing).

Ms. Patterson directs the children to sing the song in unison from start to finish, and they do so with gusto, so she announces that they will now sing in parts. "I'll sing first, and then you follow, on cue, in imitation of what I just sang. Listen to me, watch, and sing when I signal you." She sings with her strong and clear voice, and as she sustains the pitch, she cues the children, who stagger in after her. She acknowledges their efforts, and they try it again. About half of the class is entering on cue, while the others are rapidly losing interest. Ms. Patterson continues to walk around the circle, trying to make eye contact as she sings, and then signaling the children in. She then divides the class into the girls as leaders and the boys as followers, and she directs the two groups in their performance of "Old Texas" four times through. The attempt is a shaky one, as the girls outsing the boys by twice as much strength, and the girls are singing head tones while the boys continue to twang. "It's a start, and you're on your way to singing in harmony," Ms. Patterson concludes in a cheerful voice, knowing that they will take up the song again in the next class.

Questions

1. Were Ms. Patterson's exercises appropriate in warming up the young singers? Why or why not?

2. How was Ms. Patterson effective in her teaching of the melody of the song and the elementary part-singing? What might she have added or deleted to make for a more effective lesson?

3. How might Ms. Patterson extend and develop this beginning lesson in part-singing in the next class?

REVIEW

1. Trace the development of children's voices from early childhood through the intermediate grades, with special attention to changes in range and quality.

2. What is PSP? How is it attained?

3. What is a developmental sequence for children's part-song singing?

4. What are the components of an audition for membership in a children's choir?

CRITICAL THINKING

1. Cite evidence to support the view of singing as a physical as well as mental endeavor.

2. Choose a traditional song and write a vocal ostinato for it that suits second graders and fourth graders.

PROJECTS

1. Prepare a song to teach by rote and by note. How do the approaches differ? How might aspects of each be combined over several lessons?

2. Collect ten songs that you feel all children in preschool or elementary school should know. Analyze the songs for their melodic and rhythmic content, order them from less to more complex, and determine the grade level at which you would teach these songs.

3. Visit a music store specializing in choral scores, and begin a card file of the song title, composer and arranger, publisher, and range and tessitura for songs and part songs useful in music class and in the school choir. Select a set of songs that could conceivably comprise an autumn, winter, or spring program.

MINDTAP Visit **MindTap** to access classroom videos, audio, and more!

5

Pitch and the Child

IN THIS CHAPTER

- Growth in Understanding of Linear Pitch Structures

- Discrimination and Contour Awareness

- Pitch Relations and Melodic Motion

- Advanced Pitch Concepts

- Growth in Understanding of Vertical Pitch Structures

- Assessment

- Helping Children to Think Musically

"A melody is like taking a pitch for a walk."

R. Murray Schafer, 1976

JEFFREY LISTENS DREAMILY TO the rise and fall of his parents' voices as he plays with his toys. Later, he is rocked to sleep by the soothing sounds of a lullaby. Mindy hums a self-made song to her doll as she dresses it. Katie laughs with the surprise of recognition as her music teacher introduces a song based on the melodies of some of her favorite television jingles. Melody, the linear shaping of pitches combined with rhythm, comes to children in many places and forms, sometimes through listening and sometimes through performing. These experiences create a foundation for building conscious understanding of melodic concepts.

Eventually, children also become aware of harmony, the simultaneous sounding of pitches. Ian's Dad plays a guitar as they sing together. Esther hears people sing in harmony in her church, and she eagerly joins in. Rashad's class is learning to play the Autoharp to accompany some of their songs. As children experience different harmonies, feeling the tension and release that results from chordal motion, they build the concrete basis for understanding harmony's theoretical structures.

The word *melody* comes from the Greek words *melos*, meaning "song," and *aeidein*, meaning "to sing." In the Greek sense, melody is inextricably bound with the idea of song. For children, song is undoubtedly the most immediate experience they have of melody. The ability of children to master the production of melodies and to sing in harmony is addressed in Chapter 4.

The focus in Chapter 5 is on the ways teachers and parents can enhance children's perception and understanding of different aspects of melody and harmony. Numerous techniques for developing sensitivity to pitch and pitch patterns will be provided. The activities that follow are important in helping children to

1. Think about music

2. Discuss what they notice happening in musical events—eventually using musical terms

3. Use these ideas creatively

These techniques can be incorporated into lessons as a part of ongoing work on pitch development.

THINGS TO THINK ABOUT

- What are the concepts that you associate with pitch and pitch structures?

- At what age did you acquire each concept?

- How do you use these concepts now in your musical performing and listening?

"Like adults, infants can recognize a previously heard melody when they hear it in a different key or tempo."

Sandra Trehub, 2005

Growth in Understanding of Linear Pitch Structures

Many challenges face children as they grow in their ability to perceive and understand the pitch-related aspects of melody. Yet, infants appear to come into this world biologically ready to perceive and respond to subtle differences in pitches, scales, and melodies as well as to remember familiar tunes (see Trehub, Chapter 4 in Flohr, 2005). At about six months, children develop a sense of their own culture's ways of constructing melodies, probably in the same way that they develop a sense of the syntax of their native language. Sensitivities to pitch emerge gradually and are retained through adulthood, regardless of training in music. A knowledge of when these perceptual sensitivities emerge can help the parent or teacher plan developmentally appropriate activities.

The following tasks constitute a kind of *taxonomy*, or ordering, of pitch percepts and concepts from simple or basic to more difficult or complex.

- At the most basic level is the task of discrimination—Are two pitches, patterns, or melodies the same or different?

- At the next level is recognition of shape or contour—What is the overall curve of a melody?

- These abilities, along with the ability of children to form aural images of songs, result in recognition—Is the melody familiar?

Next comes a focus on more discrete aspects of melody.

- Pitch register—Are pitches relatively high or low?

- Pitch direction—Is the melody moving upward or downward?

- Pitch motion—Are the pitches moving by steps, leaps, or repeats?

- Interval size—Are the leaps large, medium, or small?

Later children become aware of

- Tonality—What is the focal point of the melody?

- Melodic phrase—What constitutes a complete idea melodically?

- Scale—What is the underlying pattern of tones for the melody?

Eventually, children become aware of additional concepts such as major modes, minor modes, and melodic sequence.

The teacher or parent can help children move from *percept* (the ability to notice these various qualities of melody) to *concept* (the ability to identify or describe how these qualities function in a variety of settings and permutations). Adults need, however, to be conscious of the readiness of children for a particular level of thinking. For example, a child may perceive that some pitches are high and some are low but may not be able to group the highest and the lowest ones in separate categories. In addition, the child may or may not be ready to explain his or her thinking in familiar terms such as high and low or upward and downward.

Table 5.1 presents an appropriate sequence for teacher activity during children's melodic development. As the table shows, rapid growth in pitch perception occurs in the early childhood years, birth through age eight. Percepts and concepts stabilize and refine after

TABLE 5.1 Children's Melodic Development and Teachers' Guidance

AGE	PERCEPT AND CONCEPT	TEACHER ACTIONS
LESS THAN SIX MONTHS	Responds to differences in pitch. Can match vocally sustained pitches and begins to imitate sounds.	Sing with words or neutral syllables such as "loo." Sustain pitches in middle register. Imitate sounds. Generate new ideas.
SIX TO EIGHTEEN MONTHS	Differentiates between pitch contours. Sensitive to phrase endings and intervals.	Continue vocal play. Sing nursery songs and other simple songs from child's culture. Play recorded music.
EIGHTEEN MONTHS TO FOUR YEARS	Able to recognize familiar phrases and songs based on contour and rhythm. Increased ability to replicate familiar material. More attention to absolute value of pitches than to relative value. Sensitivity to phrase, shown through movement.	Sing many songs with children. Engage in vocal play, extending the range upward and downward. Add words to vocal play upward and downward and high and low to match pitch patterns. Experiment with keyboards and computer programs that reinforce contour and pattern discrimination skills. Show contour and phrase with bodies.
FOUR TO EIGHT YEARS (KINDERGARTEN TO GRADE THREE)	Beginning to conceptualize aspects of pitch and melody such as high and low, upward and downward. Able to demonstrate this knowledge first (age four to five) through showing and later (age five to six) through telling. Sensitivity to intervals and to tonality emerges. Continued development of phrase as unit.	Provide many opportunities through singing, movement, use of bells, and use of computer programs to demonstrate pitch concepts and contours. Have children vocally supply endings to familiar songs. Help them add musical vocabulary to describe melodic events. Respond to phrase endings.
EIGHT TO TWELVE YEARS (GRADES THREE TO SIX)	Can identify discrete aspects of pitch motion such as steps, leaps, and repeated tones. Perceives patterns moving downward most easily—later moving upward. Recognition of melodic sequence. Can build concepts of scale and mode around age ten to eleven.	Continue to build experience with melodies through singing, shaping through movement, and playing instruments. Add reading of contours and patterns using precise notation.

that. The development of individual children can vary. Some musically experienced children may have clear, foundational pitch concepts at the age of four. Most children seem to develop these concepts around the ages of six to eight, in the primary grades.

Discrimination and Contour Awareness

Although infants are capable of noticing the difference between two pitches or two melodic contours, the task for older children is to begin to describe what they notice. At first, they may say "same" or "different" in response to patterns, or "I know that song!" or "I don't know it" in response to questions regarding the familiarity of various songs.

Preschool-aged children usually show their recognition of familiar songs simply by singing along. Around the age of three, children may recognize that the contours of familiar songs are the same, for example, "The Alphabet Song," "Baa, Baa Black Sheep," and "Twinkle, Twinkle Little Star." And, as children between ages four and seven develop relational concepts such as high and low, they can begin to describe the movement of contours and the relationship among different pitches such as the repeated tones in Music Example 5.1.

The activities in Box 5.1 are designed to increase children's sensitivity to pitch differences and melodic contour through active experimentation and discovery. Although these are being presented in separate categories of singing, moving, playing, listening, reading, and creating, most children will benefit from *multiple* approaches. Because reading is an abstraction of concrete experiences of music, it is best to have the reading come out of numerous experiences of singing, moving, and playing music. These percepts are basic to the formation of other pitch understandings and need to be developed regardless of the age of the child.

The following early childhood (ages three to four) strategies enhance discrimination and contour awareness:

- Use the words *same* or *different* to describe repeated or contrasting melodic patterns.
- Play the same/different game in *Making Music I* by Morton Subotnik.

MUSIC EXAMPLE 5.1

Finding Repeated Patterns in Songs

Old John the Rabbit (African American Singing Game)

Reproduced with permission from World of Music, Grade 1 (Parsippany, NJ: Silver Burdett Ginn, 1992).

114

BOX 5.1 Age-Appropriate Activities in Pitch Discrimination and Contour

MODE	AGES FIVE TO EIGHT	AGES NINE TO TWELVE
Singing	Learn songs to use as images of shapes and patterns. Echo different shapes with voice or kazoo. Find and sing repeated patterns in songs such as "Old John the Rabbit" (Music Example 5.1).	Sing many songs. Signal when all voices match pitch. Sing familiar songs or patterns on "loo" and identify them from their contours.
Moving	Shape contour with hands or bodies as children listen or sing—add flashlight for variety. Learn Kodály-Curwen hand signs; practice and identify patterns from hand signs.	Take aural dictation of different melodic shapes by listening, then moving using either levels or Kodály-Curwen hand signs; discover those patterns in songs.
Playing	Have children generate contour at keyboard that teacher imitates—label *same*; then teacher plays contrast—label *different*. Play single pitch, and see if child can match it on another instrument; expand to two, three, and four pitches.	Echo—play individual pitches or melodic contours by ear on keyed percussion instruments or soprano recorders or both.
Listening	Play two pitches or contours. Children show palms down if same and palms sideways if different.	Listen to melodies on recordings. Shape with body or hand signs or trace on paper.
Reading	Present children with various visuals of melodic curves. Have them sing or play. Have several children hold a long rope with both hands and shape a melody by raising or lowering hands. Use computer software programs that connect sight and sound: *Music Ace I*; *Making Music I*; *Thinkin' Things I and II*.	Give children tracing paper to place over melodies in books. Have them connect the notes in a dot-to-dot fashion. Discuss contours. Place melodies of familiar songs on bulletin board or overhead—see how quickly children can name the tune from the contour. Use software programs that connect sight and sound: *Music Ace I and II*; *Making Music II*; *Carry-A-Tune*.
Creating	Improvise a short piece on keyed percussion, taking melodic contours and displacing them. Compose using the software program *Making Music I*.	Compose a piece using contrasting contours jagged or smooth. Compose a piece using a skyline of a city or mountain for a contour.

- Shape contours of melodies in the air while singing and have children imitate.
- Draw various continuous lines on board or paper and have children trace the lines using their voices on "oo" to swoop upward, downward, or across.
- Dance with scarves to recorded music, moving them upward and downward with the rise and fall of melodies.

© Jerry Gay

Adapting Instruction for Various Needs

Most children regardless of their needs will be able to perform the tasks listed in this chapter. The following adaptations may need to be made, however.

MOBILITY IMPAIRMENTS:

• Invite children to respond to pitch motion using whatever part of their body still moves: eyelids, mouth, tongue, head, arms, upper torso.

• Use some of the techniques for adapting equipment suggested in Chapter 16 so that children who have trouble grasping mallets can still respond playing instruments.

• Even if a child is a wheelchair user, be sure to include him or her in any pitch related games, finding ways to have that child move his/her chair appropriately or have others assist.

AUDITORY IMPAIRMENTS:

• Invite children who are hard of hearing or deaf to place a hand on the sounding board of a piano or large xylophone to sense the changes in vibration of pitch patterns. Then encourage them to trace those shapes with their body. Have them play patterns on keyed percussion—especially low sounding instruments.

• Children with Auditory Processing Disorder (APD) may not be able to perceive speech directions clearly or perceive musical patterns accurately. Speak to them using clear simple directions. Have them sit in the front of the room. Eliminate surrounding noises as much as possible. Use multiple modalities for them to experience pitch motion, including touch and whole body movement as well as playing instruments.

Pitch Relations and Melodic Motion

Around the age of four, most children begin to demonstrate the ability to categorize specific aspects of pitch as being relatively the same. For example, they might group three relatively high pitches together and two relatively low pitches together. Or, they might recognize that two melodic contours are the same even though they use different pitches to shape them. Often it is easier for them to demonstrate their understandings through pointing, grouping, or playing than through telling.

The words *high* and *low* or *up* and *down*, when applied to pitch, are confusing to young children. Because pitches are not high or low acoustically and because most keyboards are presented to children on a horizontal plane, children are understandably confused by the vocabulary used to discuss pitch. In addition, the words up and down are often used to talk about volume as well as pitch; for example, "Turn down the TV; it's too loud!" Finally, pitch notation is an arbitrary system that is often confusing for learners, because it places pitches in a two-dimensional visual plane that does not match the acoustic sense perceivers have of pitch.

Teachers and parents wishing to help children apply terminology correctly should use words such as *upward* or *downward* and *moving higher* or *lower* to describe pitch motion. Other strategies, using step bells, slide whistles, movement, and vertically oriented xylophones, may also help. Ultimately, because music is more than pitches in isolation, it is desirable to present children with patterns taken from melodies of familiar songs and instrumental works to build their sense of pitch relations.

Box 5.2 gives strategies and age-appropriate activities designed to help children form concepts about discrete aspects of pitch relations such as high and low; upward and downward; stepwise, leaping, or repeating motion; and small, medium, or large intervals. Singing, moving, and playing instruments provide the most concrete means of experiencing pitch relations. Listening and reading involve greater intellectual abstraction, and creating allows children to synthesize the new understandings they have developed.

Children with step bells and vertical glockenspiel

© Jerry Gay

BOX 5.2 Age-Appropriate Activities in Pitch Register, Motion, and Interval Size

MODE	AGES FIVE TO EIGHT	AGES NINE TO TWELVE
Singing	Have children imitate high and low sounds—sing songs with exaggerated differences of high and low. Sing scale songs and describe upward and downward motion. (Music Example 5.2) Develop a sense of interval size and melodic motion through use of Kodály-Curwen hand signs	Sing upward-moving passages of a familiar song out loud and downward-moving passages internally. Use words *upward* and *downward* and *high* and *low* to describe passages in songs. Sing songs with various kinds of motion. Discuss effect of size of leaps, steps, and repeated tones.
Moving	Make high or low motions in response to individual pitches or pitches embedded in songs. Move gradually upward and downward to glissandi and scale songs.	Walk forward if melody moves upward, backward if melody moves downward, and step in place when it repeats. Refine by stepping if melody steps and leaping if melody leaps.
Playing	Place "lower <—> higher" on body of keyed instruments. Have children play high, medium, and low sounds in response to cues. Suspend a small xylophone vertically on pegboard, high pitches on top; connect with staff notation. Use step bells to reinforce sense of upward and downward movement. Play various kinds of patterns—stepping, leaping, repeating—to accompany songs.	Experiment with tuning bottles in a stepwise tuning. Color cold water and use to accompany various patterns in songs or to play ear tunes. Notate using colors. As children are preparing to play various ostinati, bourdons, and other accompaniment patterns, discuss the movement of the patterns and the relative size of the intervals.
Listening	Show upward motion by pointing upward; downward by pointing downward; and repeated tones with palm flat, facing floor. Circle iconic patterns on response sheets that represent different kinds of melodic motion: 	Learn to identify melodic patterns within recorded works; read and play or sing them first, then identify them. Select patterns on response sheet as numbers are called while listening to:
Reading	Make a score out of dots at various levels in different patterns; have children play on keyboard: Show pitch motion and intervals on a hand staff (palm facing chest) or by placing buttons on a paper staff.	Work with software programs to practice the various concepts (see Chapter 14). Notate or highlight various repeated-note, stepping, and leaping patterns. Play on keyed percussion instrument. Begin to associate staff locations and pitch names.
Creating	Create a high- and low-contrast piece; record it and add movement to it. Experiment with how to create glissandi on various instruments. Create a piece for glissandi using various tone colors.	Have children notate a melody as if on a walk, incorporating steps, leaps, and repeats. (Notation could resemble a map.) Perform pieces on pitched instruments.

Alle Meine Entchen (Germany)

Al - le mei - ne Ent - chen schwim-men auf dem See,
All the lit - tle duck - lings swim - ming here and there.

Kopf - chen in das Was - ser, Schwanz-chen in die Hoh.
Heads down in the wat - er, tails up in the air.

The following are early childhood strategies for pitch relations and melodic motion:

- Sing using ascending and descending scale passages as children take a walk up or down a hill or stairs or slide on a slide. (For example, "We are climbing up the hill now," "We are sliding down.")

- Stretch high and low in response to songs or recordings with pitches that use wide intervals.

- Experiment with high, medium, and low sounds on piano or keyed percussion instruments to tell stories such as "Goldilocks and the Three Bears." Have the pitched sounds in different registers represent the different characters in the story. Encourage children to do the same.

- Play a high/low game where you invite children to crouch down or jump up high to pitches that are a wide distance apart. Gradually narrow the distance to see if children are perceiving the differences.

- Grow taller or shorter in response to glissandi played on a slide whistle.

Advanced Pitch Concepts

Around the age of six or seven, children begin to develop a clear sense of tonality, or that a piece of music is centered within a logical system and moves within that system to a final point of resolution or rest. They bring to this an already developing sense of melodic phrase (music is expressed in a series of ideas that have a sense of completeness). These percepts can be developed into concepts during the primary grades. Then, in combination with concepts of melodic motion, they can be refined into more specific concepts regarding pitch organization during the intermediate years. These concepts include:

1. Scale—the underlying set of tones for a melody. Scale is from the Latin word *scala*, which means ladder or stairs. Scales use specific intervals as they rise and fall. The size of those intervals varies with the type of scale and the tuning systems used in the culture in which the scale occurs.

2. Major and Minor Modes—the two most commonly used modes in the Western tradition. They are distinguished by a difference in the treatment of the third and

sixth tones of the scale. Each is used for different musical effects. The major scale consists of stepwise intervals in the pattern of:

The natural minor scale pattern is:

3. Melodic Sequence—a short melodic pattern repeated at different pitch levels. It is used as a forming device for building melodies.

The activities in Box 5.3 suggest concrete ways of involving children with these ideas. Because many of these activities are dependent on understanding of and experience with foundational concepts, the preponderance of the activities are geared toward the

BOX 5.3 Age-Appropriate Activities in Tonality, Phrase, Scale, and Sequence

MODE	AGES FIVE TO EIGHT	AGES NINE TO TWELVE
Singing	Ask children to supply the final note of both familiar and unfamiliar songs; label that as the home tone; note the strength of the home tone in scale songs.	Learn to shape phrases expressively; discuss various effects.
		Using familiar songs, notice differences between strong and weak phrase endings.
		Sing a given song in a major key and then a minor key; discuss differences. Sing songs in other scales: pentatonic, whole tone, chromatic.
	Have groups of children sing alternating phrases in a song; identify as phrases	Discover sequences in melodic patterns; assign singing of each to different groups.
Moving	Move around the room to a melody, coming to rest at the final point.	Choreograph various phrases in recorded music; if phrase repeats, repeat movements.
	Use arms, scarves, or streamers to shape phrases in the air.	Learn Kodály-Curwen hand signs for scales; note relationship of minor half step to other tones; discover whole and half-step differences in major and minor scales.
	Move in style to song, changing direction at end of phrases.	Move to major and minor scales through room, taking full step on whole step and smaller step on half step; sing or play scales while moving.
		Move sequential patterns with body in space; alternate with a partner.
Playing	In songs with equal phrase length, play finger cymbals to highlight end of each phrase.	Highlight phrases by playing contrasting rhythm instruments on beat or melodic rhythm.
	Give each child a set of diatonic octave bells; have them play the tonal center in tonic-oriented songs.	Learn to play major and minor scale patterns on piano, chromatic bells, or synthesizer.
	Have children play the final phrase of songs on keyed instruments; relate sense of close to tonal center.	Begin with C Major and A natural minor; transpose patterns to other starting points improvise within those scales.
		Play handbell or tone bell to highlight beginning of each occurrence of a melodic sequence.

(Continued)

BOX 5.3 *(Continued)*

Listening	Trace phrases on paper while listening to recorded works; compare lengths.	Using randomly ordered pitches from the C Major scale, give one tone bell and mallet to each of eight children.
		Line them up and have them play.
		Encourage other children to place them in correct order to form a human scale; play scale song.
		Use human scale to add black keys, and discover whole- and half-step relationships for both major and minor scales.
Reading	Find beginning and ending pitches in songs that end on do; develop understanding that most songs move toward tonal center at ending though they may not begin there.	Take melodic dictation for phrases using Kodály techniques.
		Help children associate different tonal centers with different scales and different keys.
	Discover repeating and contrasting phrases in songs by looking at notation; listen to confirm perception.	Give pairs of children a familiar melody and some staff paper; extract the various pitches from the melody and notate them; discover whether the melody uses all of the pitches of the scale on which it was based.
		Highlight melodic sequences on the score.
Creating	Once children become aware of tonal center, challenge them to end vocal or instrumental improvisations on Do.	Improvise using various scales structured on Orff instruments.
		Using a chromatic instrument, invent a scale and compose a four-measure melody using it.
	Improvise in call-and-response form across an eight-beat phrase.	Compose a piece using melodic sequences as a structural device; try inverting them for variety.

older elementary child. Many of the activities listed here for children aged four to eight could be adapted for older children if necessary.

The following early childhood strategies for enhancing perception of advanced pitch concepts:

- Learn to sing scale songs such as Music Example 5.2, "Alle Meine Entchen." Dramatize them but also move upward and downward in small intervals to the melodic line. Play scale songs by ear on bells.
- Sing a range of songs in both major and minor modes.

Singing a melody while shaping it with string

Growth in Understanding of Vertical Pitch Structures

Musically perceptive listeners are not only aware of what is occurring melodically in music. They are also aware that sounds occur simultaneously and that these vertical arrangements of sound result in something called harmony. Harmony can be created by a combination of independent melodic lines (polyphonic texture) or a stacking of pitches (homophonic texture). The progression of harmonies through a piece of music and the choice of harmonic colors create various feelings of tension and release in the listener.

Once again, this awareness builds gradually and is influenced by the cultural and stylistic norms for what constitutes agreeable and disagreeable combinations of sounds and sequences of those combinations. Table 5.2 describes the course of that growth based on current research (see Colwell, 1992; Hargreaves, 1986; Peery, Peery, and Draper, 1987; and Serafine, 1988). Box 5.4 suggests a range of ideas for the development of percepts and concepts related to harmony and texture. As in Box 5.2, the majority of the activities are aimed at older children. Many of the activities for younger children can be adapted and used with older children as necessary. The following early childhood strategies promote harmonic awareness:

- Play a range of recorded music *through* which children are exposed to a rich variety of harmonies, from jazz to classical to rock/pop and from sung harmonies to instrumental music.
- Add a guitar, piano, or Autoharp accompaniment to songs you sing with children, so that they can hear the harmonic.
- Use the I–V^7 sequence on the Autoharp to signal children to stand up after group time or the V^7–I sequence to signal them to sit down.
- Sing songs in major and minor tonalities with accompaniment.

TABLE 5.2 Children's Harmonic Development and Teachers' Guidance

AGE	PERCEPT AND CONCEPT	TEACHER ACTIONS
FIVE TO SEVEN (KINDERGARTEN TO GRADE ONE)	Developing sensitivity to relation between melody and harmony—harmonic fit. Small number of children beginning to notice separate vertical events. May perceptually combine two pitches into one.	Help children distinguish between accompanied and nonaccompanied music. Ask children to indicate when chords need to change as accompaniment to a melody.
EIGHT TO TEN (GRADES TWO TO FOUR)	Stronger ability to notice numbers of vertical events. Beginning to sense closed or strong and open or weak cadences.	Build triads and add to songs. Sing songs with combined lines such as ostinatos and rounds. Add Autoharp accompaniments to songs.
ELEVEN TO TWELVE (GRADES FIVE TO SIX)	Able to correctly identify number of simultaneous events. Clear sense of strong and weak cadence. Can harmonize accurately by ear.	Keep refining perception of simultaneous sounds through listening. Have children use simultaneous sounds and cadences creatively. Give students melodies to harmonize with basic chords.

BOX 5.4 Age-Appropriate Activities in Harmony and Texture

MODE	AGES FIVE TO EIGHT	AGES NINE TO TWELVE
Singing	Sing songs with and without Autoharp or guitar accompaniment; discuss differences. Age seven and beyond: sing vocal ostinati to accompany songs; keep track of lines.	Sing two- and three-chord songs, indicating chord changes with I, IV, or V fingers or root of chord with hand sign. Sing songs that alternate strong and weak cadences; discuss differences. Sing rounds in two, three, and four parts; tape and listen to differences in texture. Add vocal chording on I, IV, and V chords to accompany songs.
Moving	With a two-chord song, move through general space, changing direction when the chords change.	Make up different movements, alone or with a partner, to show I, IV, and V chords; move in response to music. Choreograph the melody of a round with simple movements; perform the song and movements in a round; note layers. Learn to lead two-part singing with Kodály-Curwen hand signs.
Playing	Have children accompany songs with Autoharp, bell chords, or automatic chords on a synthesizer; begin with one-chord songs and move to two-chord songs in which they identify changes by ear. Accompany melodies with ostinati, bourdons, or descants; discuss texture and harmony.	Accompany songs using chords on Autoharps, bells, or keyboards by ear and then by sight. Play two-, three-, and four-part rounds on recorders or pitched percussion; discuss textures created. Build triads on every pitch of the diatonic scale; identify them as major or minor. Learn the chord progression for a favorite pop tune or twelve-bar blues, play to accompany songs. Learn to perform various African rhythm complexes with rhythmic percussion instruments such as those from Ghana or on xylophones such as the Mandinka would play; discuss textures created by layers.
Listening	Age six or seven on: listen as teacher sings a song with a harmonic accompaniment; raise hands to indicate when chords need to change.	While listening, mark beats to a song with pens, changing colors when the chords change, or hold up different color cards as chords change (that is, red = tonic, blue = dominant, yellow = subdominant). In a small group, develop a listening map to show the overlapping lines of a polyphonic work; check the map against the music.
Reading	Age seven and up; learn to track chord changes in music while playing an accompaniment.	Follow the relationship of lines in a two-line polyphonic piece on a listening map, and later with music. Learn to build root-position triads using buttons on a paper staff.
Creating	Improvise an accompaniment to a pentatonic melody on an Orff-keyed percussion instrument.	Improvise an accompaniment using broken chords. Using the pentatonic scale, compose a piece for three different melodies that are layered to create various textures. Compose a piece for chords, experimenting with different progressions and rhythms; use different instruments for variety; start with root-position triads, later add seventh, ninths, or elevenths.

Accomplishing Multiple Standards through Pitch Activities

The following ideas repeat and extend ideas presented throughout this chapter.

1. *Singing*: Draw various pitch patterns using lines or dots and have children replicate those vocally. Have children sing short melodic patterns using solfège. Then have them show the patterns using Kodály-Curwen hand signs.

2. *Playing*: Play various pitch patterns on pitched instruments, following the visual representation of those patterns through invented or discrete notation. Show an

(Continued)

understanding of scales and scale patterns in various keys using resonator bells or other keyboards. Add chords on keyboards.

3. *Improvising*: Improvise pitch patterns using a neutral syllable. Improvise pitch patterns using scat syllables, staying within a given key.

4. *Composing and Arranging*: Compose a melody aurally using either the voice or keyed instruments. Compose a melody visually through devised or discrete notation, then play the melody. Revise it as needed. Take a given melody and alter it, playing it in a different style or adding embellishments.

5. *Reading and Notating*: Over time, build children's reading skills from two-note patterns to entire melodies using solfège. Invite them to look for repeated melodic patterns or phrases to enhance their reading skills. Use aural dictation to have children notate simple patterns. Invite children to invent their own ways of notating pitch motion in music they compose.

6. *Listening*: Learn the themes of various works via notation and singing. Identify them when they occur in the recorded work. Listen to music of various styles and periods. Respond to the pitch motion including range and contour in those works through movement and drawing. Note the similarities and differences between the styles and periods.

7. *Analyzing and Evaluating*: Record songs performed by your class. Listen to the recording and evaluate the pitch accuracy and melodic phrasing of the singing.

8. *Connect to Other Arts and Curricular Areas*: Study the relationship of pitch to frequency and loudness in the science of sound. Learn the frequency of particular pitches on the keyboard, such as A = 440. Learn the importance of that pitch in tuning an orchestra. Build a simple stringed instrument and determine various ways you can change the pitch of the strings through changing tension or length of the string.

9. *Connect to Culture and History*: Older children learn various scales that are traditionally used in various parts of Africa; in Japan; in India. Compare them to the Western scale. Try replicating those scales. Learn the difference between monophonic, polyphonic, and homophonic structures in music and listen to examples of those from the various periods they were primarily used. Listen to the music of key composers who used these various pitch-based techniques.

Assessment

Formative evaluations of pitch perception and conception happen as you develop the various strategies listed in this chapter. Monitor children's responses as they move to shape pitch motion; as they take aural dictation; as they play instruments responding to notation; as they identify patterns within listening experiences; and as they use pitch creatively. If children are having problems or show confusion, then you need to reteach that concept or show them more examples of that idea until they can demonstrate that they understand.

Summative evaluations of pitch concepts can come in having children generate their own examples of a concept such as a scale, describe why it is a scale, and use that creatively within a composition. Applying a concept at the highest level of creativity and evaluation provides a teacher with solid evidence that a concept has been mastered.

Remember that having children sing something to show you their understanding of pitch concepts is not a valid assessment tool. Children may indeed be able to perceive pitch motion and understand various pitch-related concepts but not have the vocal accuracy to reproduce what they already understand. Use techniques of describing, drawing, naming, showing new examples, and/or creating to measure children's understandings. At the same time, singing in response to pitch motion and pattern is a solid way to experience pitch and it will help children to internalize some of the ideas you are trying to develop.

Helping Children to Think Musically

Research in pitch perception clearly shows that people develop sensitivities to pitch and pitch structures as a natural part of responding cognitively to the music that surrounds them. The challenge for the teacher is to build on these percepts and expand them into conscious concepts that can be applied through a lifetime of musical experiences.

As teachers strive to make musical learning meaningful, they need to be selective, choosing activities that will stimulate musical growth. However, any activity, done in isolation, runs the risk of simply filling time in interesting or not-so-interesting ways. A well-developed series of strategies involves a variety of modes: singing, moving, playing, listening, reading, and creating. Discussion and reflection will also be a regular part of the process of learning. Strategies carefully selected, ordered, and implemented across time, at levels appropriate to a child's development, have a much greater likelihood of expanding the ability of children to think about music.

TECHNOLOGY *for* **TEACHING** *and* **LEARNING MUSIC:**
PITCH *and the* **CHILD**

A large array of excellent buy-and-run software programs exist, which teach basic structural hearing concepts, such as higher/lower, same/different phrases and melodies, melody shape or contour, pitch register, pitch direction, pitch motion (moving by steps, leaps, or repeats), and interval size. Once children are familiar with these concepts, other programs teach more advanced structural listening, such as tonality, modes and scales, and harmony. Some uses of technology are already suggested in this chapter. To learn more, visit the Technology Resources links in the MindTap.

MINDTAP

Scenario

MRS. BEVLEN HAS TRIED a number of pitch-related strategies with her second graders in music. Most of the children showed their ability to perceive the patterns accurately and respond to them in a variety of ways through singing, playing instruments, and moving. One child named Brian, didn't seem to understand what Mrs. Bevlen was asking him to do. Even when she tried to show him the connection between the visual pattern and what she was asking him to play, he seemed confused. Aural dictation was impossible for him. She became more and more frustrated. She wondered if it was an attention problem, but she knew Brian did not have ADHD. She was really puzzled as to how to reach Brian. Mrs. Bevlen talked with Brian's classroom teacher and found that Brian did have some problems following spoken directions in class. The classroom teacher was at a loss to determine how to help Brian too. He was not being served by the special education system at this point and did not have an IEP that would help either of them to understand how to meet Brian's needs. His struggles with perception seemed to be most apparent in music classes, where work with pitch was a regular part of the content of the curriculum. Brian was clearly of normal intelligence and enjoyed much of school. Both teachers were puzzled about what to do.

Questions

1. Whom else might Mrs. Bevlen talk with to get more information about what is happening with Brian?

2. What other strategies might she use in working with him?

3. How might the speech therapist be of help in Brian's case?

REVIEW

1. What is the difference between a percept and a concept? How are the two related?

2. At what point are children developmentally ready to explore ideas related to tonality? What are some ways to reinforce that perception?

3. At what point can children accurately perceive the number of simultaneous sounds in a piece of music? What kinds of tasks might you create to test that ability?

CRITICAL THINKING

1. If children automatically gain perceptions of pitch and pitch structures as a result of growing up in a musically rich environment, why should parents and teachers devote time to expanding those perceptions? List three reasons.

2. Why is it important to have a developmental perspective, beginning from the early childhood years, regarding what children are capable of perceiving? What meaning might that have for an elementary general music specialist?

PROJECTS

1. Create music manipulatives such as a dowel staff or magnet board that you can use with children to reinforce various musical concepts.

2. Using the model of moving from concrete activities of singing, moving, and playing instruments to more abstract experiences of listening, reading, and creating, plan a series of activities to teach and extend the concept of upward and downward pitch motion to second-grade children. Work in a team to plan the activities. Use music

series texts as basic resources. Feel free to go beyond those sources as needed.

3. Select a perceptual task that children should be able to perform at the age indicated in this chapter. Work with another person to devise a way to test whether children have that percept or concept. Implement this test with at least five children to determine where they are developmentally. Bring your results back to class and present your discoveries.

4. Select an activity or a series of activities from this chapter designed to expand understanding of pitch and implement them with children. Modify them as necessary to fit the unique needs of the children involved.

5. Review some of the musical activities suggested in Anderson and Campbell (2010). Select two that could be used to develop pitch-related concepts. List what those concepts are.

6. In one of the books on musical creativity listed in the references, find a strategy related to pitch development and implement it with children.

MINDTAP Visit MindTap to access classroom videos, audio, and more!

6

The Moving Child

IN THIS CHAPTER

- Movement and Child Development
  - Action Songs and Singing Games
  - Eurhythmics
  - Creative Movement
  - Dance
- Precepts and Principles of Movement
- Prelude to Movement-Based Musical Experiences
  - Action Songs and Singing Games
- Dalcroze Eurhythmics
- Creative Movement
- Dance
- Assessment of Moving
  - Formative Evaluations
  - Summative Evaluations
- Movement for Musical Development
- Scenario

IN THE WORLD OF children, music and movement are nearly inseparable from one another. Clear the room, set the rules, start the music, and watch the movement begin: Rochelle pirouettes like a ballerina to the light and whirling music of the flute. Ally glides like a swan to the cello's melody. Nicolas jumps with two feet and then hops on one foot to the dialogue of the clarinet and bassoon. With the entrance of the brass instruments, Sally marches with her knees high and her toes pointed. Sean, Li, and Tommy strut forward with long legs overlapping, arms stretched across each other's shoulders. Jimmie jogs with an imaginary basketball to the pulse of the percussion section. Consuela and Trina find the pulse and clap hands, forward, backward, and upside down. Anna stands at the center of it all, conducting.

Children love to move. With the sound of music, they release their bundles of boundless energy. Heads nod; toes tap; bodies rock; arms swing. Even without music, while children play, they often move in some semblance of a musical rhythm. Moving children skip, hop, walk, run, slide, gallop, jump, twist, and turn. Movement—of all kinds—is one of their favorite things to do.

The foundation of music for children is ultimately and intimately entwined with their physical selves. Music, the aural art, is also music, the kinesthetic art. Children develop their musical abilities through a combination of what they experience through their ears, eyes, and bodies. As children listen, sing, or play instruments—even as they read music—their aural, visual, and kinesthetic senses are activated. Movement is thus vital to their musical development and basic to all that they do.

Music classes for children in elementary schools and in early childhood settings are animated affairs. The teacher's task is to harness, shape, and direct the spontaneous and natural movements of children toward an understanding of rhythm, melody, phrasing, texture, dynamics, and form. Under a teacher's guidance, children combine their movement with body sounds: stepping, clapping, patting, or snapping. They sing songs with associated actions or games. They practice the preparatory movements that ease them toward the playing of musical instruments. They move creatively to express what they hear and feel. They learn the structured steps of a dance. For all of these experiences, the teacher uses logic and creativity to steer children through their movement toward musical understanding.

Movement helps children internalize musical concepts. While there is no explicit content for movement within the National Standards for music (MENC, 1994), teachers with years of successful experience assume that movement is the means for leading children to singing and playing instruments more musically, to composing and improvising in meaningful ways, and to showing evidence of listening with a clear understanding of music's structures and sonic flow. The National Standards in dance (MENC, 1994) prescribe content standards in the elements and skills of moving with artistic purpose, but the use of movement in the musical education of children presumes no artistic end. Instead, movement is a means for learning musical ideas and for expressing how the music sounds by way of pulse, rhythm, melodic shape, phrasing, and various qualities: loud-soft, fast-slow, and choppy-smooth. It is also used by teachers to allow children to let off steam and to change the classroom pace from a sit-down activity to a move-around exercise that rewards children for hard work well done. Movement gives opportunities for socialization and cooperation through singing games and dances. It offers children a means for understanding other cultures through folk dances. It stimulates thinking, including musical thinking. It is an important way by which children can express themselves. Movement balances the academically passive parts of the school day with the children's characteristically active nature. Movement can successfully merge children's energies, attitudes, and ideas.

Movement responses to music may be instinctive and natural, but children's instincts can be further developed and refined through instruction. When children are receptive to musical sound, the rhythm or melody will inspire them to actively participate in the music through the movement they imitate or invent. They are capable of responding to music with motion and emotion; it evokes in them both kinesthetic and aesthetic reactions. Children's natural movements can be used as avenues to music learning when lessons are designed by teachers to match movement to musical concepts.

THINGS TO THINK ABOUT

• What musical experiences do you associate with movement?

• Were you a kinesthetic learner, most apt to learn via physical experience that required your moving (and touching) in order to understand?

• What concepts are likely to be learned through movement?

• Describe what you have noticed of children's movement at play in terms of its quality, speed, energy, and use of space.

• How might you go about developing your own movement ability to be able to provide possible models?

Partnered up and mirroring movement patterns

© Jerry Gay

Movement and Child Development

FROM INFANCY, CHILDREN LISTEN attentively to music and respond by moving to its rhythm. By the age of six months, when infants are increasingly able to coordinate the actions of their sense organs, they move their whole body in a generalized—albeit not synchronized—manner (Zentner and Eerola, 2010). If infants move their heads, arms, chest, and legs, they move them rhythmically, whether sucking or kicking (Pouthas, 1996). By two years, toddling children are seen rocking from side to side, bouncing up and down, and waving their arms in conducting patterns. As children begin to listen more attentively to music at the age of three to four, the variety of their movements declines and they enter into a period of practicing and perfecting the movements they already know. Their physical coordination improves as they enter kindergarten, when four- to six-year-olds are able to move more often than not to the pulse of the music (Keil and Campbell, 2012).

Children develop their capacity to use the large muscles necessary for such locomotor activities as walking, running, and hopping before they can control the small muscles they need for writing, drawing, or playing instruments such as the recorder or keyboard. By the time they are in kindergarten, children have usually developed the coordination that enables them to hop, gallop, skip, and jump rope. They enjoy physical activity and move successfully to singing games, action songs, and simple folk dances. They also seize opportunities to respond freely to recorded and live music. They enjoy creating movements to music in individually expressive ways.

Movement ability and the psychomotor skills necessary for performance improve with advancing age. By third grade most children can accurately maintain a steady beat through tapping their fingers in time to the music. Developmental patterns are apparent, in that when children in the primary grades are asked to reproduce rhythms, they do so most accurately by chanting the rhythms, moderately so by clapping, and least accurately when stepping them. Children show a gradual but marked increase in accuracy through the first three grades in these types of rhythmic movement, with girls generally outperforming boys, who may lag about a year behind. While children's larger muscles develop earlier than their small muscles, the extent to which they can fine-tune coordination of the torso, the arms, and the legs to express themselves musically improves gradually through the age of ten or eleven years. This complex perceptual-motor coordination is vital to reading and performing music. See Table 6.1 for a summary of children's movement development.

Through the primary grades, as children develop strength, agility, and flexibility, they increase their ability to play with some control percussion instruments such as the drum, tambourine, claves, and maracas. They can play simple accompaniments on xylophones and bells, including sustained bourdons and simple ostinato patterns. Preparatory movements performed initially without the instruments will provide children with the motor patterns necessary to play them with rhythmic accuracy and fluency of movement. The motor coordination necessary for the performance of wind, brass, stringed, and keyboard instruments is usually not well developed before the age of eight or nine years. However, those children presented with opportunities to play these instruments will develop the necessary muscles to do so, should they be motivated to heed the adage that "practice makes perfect."

Action Songs and Singing Games

From the perspective of child development, movement is more than just the motor coordination necessary for the performance of a musical instrument. It is the essence

> "The infant is born into a temporally organized world. Furthermore, he or she is endowed with a host of biological rhythms and motor rhythms whose range or frequency is very wide...."
>
> **Viviane Pouthas, 1996**

TABLE 6.1 Children's Movement Development

AGE	DEVELOPMENTAL SKILL
LESS THAN SIX MONTHS	Responds to music through generalized body movement; movement not yet synchronized to rhythm
TWO YEARS	Responds by rocking, bouncing, waving arms to rhythm Develops walking and running skills Attempts to imitate clapping and patty-cake movements
THREE TO FOUR	Practices known movements by repeating them Invents and imitates new movements Begins to develop large muscle coordination for jumping, hopping Can perform simple action songs and game songs
FIVE TO SIX (KINDERGARTEN)	Begins to develop rhythmic clapping and patting Begins to develop skills for galloping (one-sided skip) and jumping rope Can perform simple folk dances in circles and lines Begins to develop small muscle coordination for drawing and printing (writing)
SIX TO SEVEN (GRADES ONE AND TWO)	Begins to develop skipping skills Responds (frequently) to music through hand clapping; achievement of beat competence Can follow the pulse and dynamics of music and respond to gradual changes through movement Can perform beat on drum, rhythm sticks; can play sustained bourdons on xylophone (but requires preparatory movement to precede performance)
EIGHT TO NINE (GRADE THREE)	Can maintain a steady beat while tapping, patting, clapping Can accurately reproduce rhythms by chanting, tapping, patting, clapping, or stepping Can perform ostinatos on xylophones (but requires preparatory movement to precede performance) Develops small muscle coordination for playing recorder, keyboard Can respond quickly and accurately to musical changes (in tempo, rhythmic patterns, texture) through movement; can have quick reactions Can perform more complex folk dances in circles, lines, squares, and partners Can conduct meters with rhythmic accuracy
TEN TO TWELVE (GRADES FOUR TO SIX)	Girls begin to show early signs of physical maturation Develops small muscle coordination (and dual coordination of breathing and fingers) for performing wind and brass instruments Enjoys active physical involvement; may prefer sports to dance Can perform rhythmic canons by moving to music that is previously sounded (four beats earlier) while listening to other music Can respond to two distinctive features of music through simultaneous movement (stepping the rhythm while conducting the pulse)

of children's play and the manner through which they come to know their world. From early childhood, children move playfully as they sing songs associated with games, actions, and dances. The melodies of action songs and singing games draw from children the movements they have naturally encountered in their free play. These movements are recalled and organized by children to express the song's rhythmic and expressive qualities. Even in the upper elementary grades, carefully selected songs to appeal to the interests of older children can provide the orderly release of physical energy that the music requires.

© Jerry Gay

Eurhythmics

Eurhythmic activities, in which children are encouraged to "do what the music tells you to do," can be designed to be in step developmentally with children's physical capacities. Children from preschool through the sixth grade can be motivated to use their bodies to illustrate music's salient features. By stepping the pulse, conducting the meter, tapping the melody's repeated rhythmic pattern, or drawing the melodic contour or shaping the phrase length in the air, children can demonstrate without words their understanding of musical concepts. Through eurhythmics, the body becomes a personal instrument for realizing the music from the simplest to the more challenging exercises.

Creative Movement

While the development of feeling for a steady beat may be one among many musical goals, it may not always be necessary that children synchronize their movement with others or to a unifying pulse. In creative movement, children may be guided to develop their own repertoire of movements to express loud or soft, slow or fast, high or low, or choppy or smooth. They may explore a single movement, repeating it and expanding it, or take the movement modeled for them and vary it. By imitating the teacher or another student, children build their movement vocabulary for later recall and use. Music supplies the impetus for children to assemble new and familiar movements in ways that are personally expressive.

Dance

The structured movements of dance require the basic skill of keeping time with the music. Even in the primary grades, children are frequently able to perform simple folk dances in a synchronized manner, although this is partly dependent on their physical development. The synchronicity required for perfecting the structured steps and formations of circle, square, partner, and line dances should not necessarily delay the teaching of these dances. The practice of doing the dances will provide children with the exercise for developing their sense of rhythm and time.

Precepts and Principles of Movement

In designing lessons and experiences for children that unite music with movement, the teacher will want to include musical concepts and genres of movement that children can potentially develop. The teacher with musical training will recognize the musical concepts as fundamental to children's understanding of "what makes music tick." The teacher who has observed children at play will recognize that the movement genres describe the natural inclinations of children toward physical activity (see Table 6.2). The challenge is how to match musical concepts with movement genres. How can these repertoires be merged? How does movement teach a musical concept? How does a musical concept motivate movement?

Movement and music are both concerned with time, so the concepts of pulse, duration, accent, and tempo figure prominently in each. Of all the possible combinations of movement with music, then, the most obvious is the way in which these rhythmic (pulse, duration, accent) and expressive (tempo) concepts might be expressed through

TABLE 6.2 Musical Concepts and Their Related Movement Genres

MUSICAL CONCEPTS	MOVEMENT GENRES
Rhythm	Nonlocomotor (in place)
Pulse (beat)	Stretch
Duration	Bend
Accent	Swing
Meter	Twist
Patterns	Bounce
	Shake
Melody	Push
Pitch: high and low	Pull
Contour	Sway
Repeat, step, skip	Rise
	Collapse
Timbre	
Musical sound and nonmusical sound	Locomotor (across space)
Voices (type)	Walk
Instruments (type)	Run
Alone	Jump
In groups	Hop
	Gallop
	Skip
Form	Slide
Repetition	Leap
Variation	Lunge
Contrast	Strut
	Movement variations
Texture	Space
One line	Shape (round, angular, bodily designs)
Multiple lines: simultaneous	Size (large, small)
Multiple lines: independent	Level (high, middle, low)
	Place (in place, through space)
Expressive qualities	Direction (forward, backward, sideways, turning)
Tempo: fast and slow	Pathway (straight, curving)
Tempo: changing	
Dynamics: loud and soft	
Dynamics: changing	*(Continued)*

TABLE 6.2 *(Continued)*

MUSICAL CONCEPTS	MOVEMENT GENRES
Time	
Pulse (beat)	
Duration (long, short)	
Accent (force)	
Tempo (fast, slow)	
Energy	
Attack (sharp, smooth)	
Weight (light, heavy)	
Flow (bound, free)	
Strength (tight, loose)	

movement. But melody, timbre, form, and texture can also be expressed physically by children through various locomotor and nonlocomotor movement styles and through variations in space, time, and energy. The action songs, singing games, eurhythmics, creative movement, and dance lessons suggested below will illustrate how.

For movement-based musical experiences to be educationally sound, the teacher also needs to consider a set of precepts and physical arrangements to ensure the success of these exercises with children. The following items are intended to guide the teacher in the planning of music-and-movement lessons for children (see also Box 6.1 and Box 6.2).

BOX 6.1 **Preparation for Music-and-Movement Experiences**

1. Observe children at play during recess. Notice their energy, speed, direction, levels, and various locomotor and nonlocomotor genres of their movements. Note the distinctions in the movement of boys and girls and among children of various age groups.

2. Consider ways in which the movement qualities of athletic activities, sports, and playground games can be brought into lessons that explore musical concepts.

3. Be prepared to model a variety of movement possibilities for children's imitation and eventual variation and personal interpretation. Also, take note of children who move with ease and flair and can serve as models of movement for their peers.

4. Encourage children to explore the variety of ways in which the various body parts can be moved, including experiments with energy, speed, directions, and levels in space.

BOX 6.2 **Arranging for Music-and-Movement Experiences**

1. Make room for movement. Move chairs and desks to the side of the room, go outdoors in good weather, and use cafeterias, gyms (although acoustics can be a problem), lobbies, and hallways.

2. Explore possibilities for movement in tight spaces, in chairs, and at desks. Some of the most fulfilling movement can be done sitting down and snapping, clapping, patting, stamping, and conducting.

3. While allowing children the freedom to express musical ideas through movement, set movement rules (move without touching anyone, listen before moving) that will organize what might otherwise prove chaotic to the classroom.

4. Choose live music (on piano, for example) and recorded music in a variety of styles that will motivate children to want to move in various expressive ways.

Prelude to Movement-Based Musical Experiences

In beginning to develop a sensitivity to music through movement, children need to be aware of (1) the potential of their bodies to move in place (nonlocomotor) and across space (locomotor); (2) the relationship of their bodies to people and objects in the room; and (3) the related qualities of space, time, and energy found in both music and movement. Exploratory movement ideas suggested in Table 6.3, act as a prelude to movement-based musical experiences and can be performed with and without musical accompaniment.

Exploratory movement experiences can be initiated or further developed by the classroom teacher or physical education instructor. Nonetheless, the music teacher may use these suggestions for movement as a means of warming up children's physical selves in preparation for musical exercises that require agility, grace, flexibility, and the coordination of thinking with doing. Children enjoy discovering the capacity of their bodies to move as suggested and to act on command; such exercises are inherently motivating. Children can be led toward problem solving, presented as questions or creative imagery, as they offer solutions through the most personal of entities: their bodies. For the music teacher, however, the end product of all movement experiences is the development of children's musical understanding, skills, and values.

TABLE 6.3 Exploratory Movement with and without Music

GOAL	EXPLORATORY TASKS
BODY AWARENESS	Find different ways of moving your fingers, hands, arms, elbows, shoulders, feet, legs, head, and hips
BODY RELATIONSHIP	Walk your own path without touching anyone; walk around every chair, block, or hoop placed on the floor Touch two fingers to the two fingers of your neighbors as you pass them Follow teacher across the floor in exactly the same way (but after teacher has completed movement)
TIME (SPEED)	Move a body part: fast, faster, slow, slower, gradually faster or slower
SPACE (DIRECTION)	Walk forward, backward, sideways, toward the door, toward the windows
SPACE (LEVELS)	Walk high, low, medium; alternately high and low
ENERGY (WEIGHT)	Make yourself heavy, light, strong, limp
ENERGY (FLOW)	Walk without stopping; stop suddenly or gradually
NONLOCOMOTOR MOVEMENT	Draw with your hands, elbows, head, or feet a straight line, a curved line, a zigzag, a loop; shape your body into a box, a triangle, a *T*, a *V*; move from one shape to the next within four beats or seven beats
LOCOMOTOR MOVEMENT	Walk, leap, lunge, run, jump, hop, gallop, skip, strut, slide

Playing singing games on the grassy school grounds

Billie Judy/Reel Life Productions

Action Songs and Singing Games

For young children from the toddling stages through the primary grades, action songs and singing games help develop coordination, synchronized rhythmic movement, and the singing voice. Many children's songs that are performed in schoolyards during recess are oriented toward actions and games. The movements of these songs offer a release for pent-up energy and may serve as a memory cue for learning the words of the songs. The songs provide avenues for channeling children's energies toward meaningful movement.

Action songs are those to which rhythmic gestures are added, often to coincide with the meaning of the song text (see Lesson 6.1). These songs can usually be performed

LESSON 6.1 Action Songs

Suogan (Wales)

Su - o - gan, do not weep, Su - o - gan, go to sleep,

Su - o - gan, Moth-er's near, Su - o - gan, have no fear.

Song	"Suogan"
Level	Early childhood through grade one
Movement	Cradle the baby in the arms, rocking it back and forth to the musical pulse.

Johnny Works with One Hammer (United States)

John - ny works with one ham-mer, one ham-mer, one ham-mer.

John - ny works with one ham-mer, then he works with two.

2. two hammers, then he works with three.
3. three hammers, then he works with four.
4. four hammers, then he works with five.
5. five hammers, then he goes to sleep.

Song   "Johnny Works with One Hammer"

Level   Early childhood through grade one

Movement   Verse 1, pound one fist on knee. Verse 2, pound two fists on knees. Verse 3, pound two fists and one foot. Verse 4, pound two fists and two feet. Verse 5, pound two fists, two feet, and nod head. On "then he goes to sleep," rest head on hands.

Teddy Bear (United States)

Ted - dy bear, ted - dy bear, turn a - round,_____
                                 tie your shoe,_____
                                 go up - stairs,_____
                                 turn out the light,_____

Ted - dy bear, ted - dy bear, touch the ground.
                                 that will do.
                                 say your prayers.
                                 say good - night.

Song   "Teddy Bear"

Level   Early childhood through grade one

Movement   Act out the words of the text.

Rig-a-jig-jig (United States)

As I was walk - ing down the street, down the street, down the street,

(Continued)

A pret-ty girl I chanced to meet, Heigh - ho, heigh-ho,___ heigh - ho!

Rig - a - jig - jig and a - way we go, way we go, way we go,

Rig - a - jig - jig and a - way we go, Heigh - o, heigh-o,___ heigh - o!___

Song	"Rig-a-jig-jig"
Level	Kindergarten through grade two
Movement	Follow the metric rhythm and text in the two sections:

A: Walk individually

B: On heigh-ho, find a partner, join hands (skater's position), and skip

Pleeng Chaang (Thailand)

Chaang, chaang, chaang, naung koey hen chaang rüü plaao? Chaang
El - e - phant! Oh, see the el - e - phant? He

man tua too mai___ bao. Ca muuk yaao
is a big an - i - mal. His nose is

yaao riak waa___ nguang. Mii khieo___ taai___
long, and called __ (trunk). See un - der 'neath his

nguang riak waa ___ ngaa. Mii huu___ mii taa haang___ yaao.
trunk are strong teeth. See ears, eyes, long skin - ny tail.

Song	"Pleeng Chaang"
Level	Grades two through four
Movement	Act out the words of the text:

Phrase 1 (Chaang…): Step heavily from side to side

Phrase 2 (Ca muuk yaao…): Wave arm from nose like a trunk

Phrase 3 (Mii Khieo taai…): Move fingers in front of mouth like long teeth/tusks

Phrase 4 (Mii huu mii…): Quickly point to or show ears, eyes, and tail

with little previous training and without movement exercises preceding them. As a lullaby, "Suogan" suggests the rocking of a baby to sleep, while the texts of "Johnny Works with One Hammer" and "Teddy Bear" tell the young singers to hammer with one or more hammers and to turn around and touch the ground, respectively. "Pleeng Chaang" entices children to move like elephants, swinging their trunk and then pointing to their own corresponding ears, eyes, and mouth. "Rig-a-jig-jig" invites children to walk and then to skip as the meter shifts between simple and compound meter. Beyond the traditional action songs, children may enjoy inventing gestures for familiar songs.

Many children's traditional songs incorporate games (see Lesson 6.2). Singing games may have survived many generations because of the joy they bring to children. The games typically require children to gather in circles, lines, small groups, or with partners, and the movement they perform is often matched to the pulse or melodic rhythm of the song. Counting songs and hand-clapping songs are singing games as well, and children enjoy the excitement of songs that have a game goal in mind. "Ring around the Rosy" and "London Bridge" are well-known singing games in English-speaking countries. From Spain, "San Serení" invites children to imitate the work of a shoemaker (and other occupations). Cambodia's "Leak Kanseng" involves a scarf and a chase around the circle. "Guru Ndiani" is a children's singing game from Zimbabwe. From the northern city of York, England, comes "The Noble Duke of York," a double-lined contra dance. North American singings include "Punchinella," "Bow Wow Wow," and "How Many Miles to Babylon?" As with action songs, the children's own singing provides the necessary accompaniment to the movement and the game.

There are historical collections of action songs stemming from the late nineteenth century as well as a wide variety of Kodály- and Orff-based published materials. Collections by Forrai with Sinor (1988), Campbell (2008), and John Feierabend (2002a, 2002b) are useful for children from preschool through the elementary school years, as are archived recordings available from Smithsonian Folkways Recordings (www.folkways.si.edu) and the Alan Lomax materials of the Association for Cultural Equity (www.culturalequity.org).

Ring around the Rosy (England)

Ring a-round the Ro - sy, a pock-et full of po - sies,

Ash - es, Ash - es, we all fall down.

Song	"Ring around the Rosy"
Level	Early childhood through grade one
Singing game	Children hold hands while walking in a circle. At "ashes, ashes," they clap their hands twice. On "down," they all jump down. The last one to go down must sit in the middle.

London Bridge Is Falling Down (England)

1. Lon - don bridge is fall - ing down, fall - ing down, fall - ing down.

Lon - don bridge is fall - ing down, my fair la - dy

2. Build it up with sticks and stones
3. Sticks and stones we do not have
4. Build it up with iron bars
5. Iron bars we do not have
6. Build it up with silver and gold

7. London Bridge is all built up
8. Through the chopper you must go
9. Off to prison you must go
10. Take the key and lock her up

Song	"London Bridge Is Falling Down"
Level	Early childhood through grade one
Singing game	Two children form a bridge by raising their hands high so that other children can walk under it. On "all built up," only one hand of each child is raised. On "through the chopper," the bridge is brought up and down on the backs of children passing. On "off to prison," one child is caught and taken away. On "take the key," the child is pushed back and forth between the set of arms.

Punchinella (United States; African American)

(1) Look who is here, Pun - chi - nel - la, Pun - chi - nel - la.

Look who is here, Pun - chi - nel - la fol - low me.
(2) What can you do? Pun - chi - nel - la fol - low me.
(3) I'll do it, too, Pun - chi - nel - la fol - low me.

Song	"Punchinella"
Level	Early childhood through grade two
Singing game	Children form a circle, holding hands, with one child at the center acting the part of "Punchinella."

Verse 1: Children move to the right, stepping the pulse
Verse 2: Children stop, face forward, as center child performs a movement
Verse 3: Children imitate the movement of the center child
(At the end of verse 3, a new "Punchinella" is selected)

Leak Kanseng (Cambodia)

Leak kan - seng chma khaim keng oh leng oh long

Leak kan - seng chma khaim keng oh leng oh long

Song	"Leak Kanseng"
Level	Early childhood through grade two
Singing game	In an open space, children gather to sit in a circle and place their hands on their knees. One child holds a scarf as he or she walks on the outside of the circle while all repeatedly chant. After two or three trips around the circle, the child places the scarf behind the back of one sitting child. If the sitting child is aware of the scarf placed behind her or him, she or he picks it up and chases the scarf-hiding child around the circle. The scarf-hiding child takes the space of the former sitting child, and the game begins anew.

Source: "Leak Kanseng" as sung by Sam-Ang Sam. From *Silent Temples, Songful Hearts: Traditional Music of Cambodia.*
© 1991 World Music Press. Used by permission.

(Continued)

Guru Ndiani (Zimbabwe)

Gu - ru   ndi - an - i   jong - we.

Ha   jong - we   Gu - ru.

Gu - ru ndi - an - i jong - we.

Ha jong - we Gu - ru.

Song	"Guru Ndiani"
Level	Early childhood through grade two
Singing game	In the center of a circle, two children hop on one leg, hands behind their backs, trying to bump the other onto two legs. The winner chooses a new child to challenge him or her. The circle of children is divided into two halves to sing the two interlocking parts.

Bow, Wow, Wow (United States)

Bow, wow, wow,   whose dog are thou?   Lit-tle Tom - my Tuck - er's dog.   Bow, wow, wow,

Song	Bow, Wow, Wow
Level	Grades one and two
Singing game	Children form two circles, one inside and one outside, with partners facing one another

There is one movement for each four-beat phrase:

Phrase 1 Stamp right, left, right

Phrase 2 Clap hands, point forefinger up in the air

Phrase 3 Hold hands with partner and turn quickly in full circle

Phrase 4 Outer circle moves right to face new inner circle partner

How Many Miles to Babylon? (United States)

How   man - y miles   to   Ba - by - lon?   Three   score   and   ten.

Will we be there by can - dle - light? Yes, and back a - gain.

O - pen the gates and let us through. Not with - out a beck and bow.

Here's your beck, here's your bow! O - pen the gates and let us through.

Song	"How Many Miles to Babylon?"
Level	Grades two through four
Singing Game	Children form two lines, shaking hands with the partner across from them.

Line one sings the questions (mm 1, 3) and line two sings the answers (mm 2, 4)

    Mm 5–6 Children clap 4 times, then stamp 4 times

    Mm 7 Line one gestures line two to "come," and then bows to them

    Mm 8 Line one forms arches and line two runs through the arches

Now the lines have switched places and in another go-round, they switch roles.

....

San Serení (Spain)

San Se - re - ní de la bue - na, bue - na vi - da,

ha - cen a - sí, a - sí los za - pa - te - ros, a -

sí, a - sí, a - sí, a - sí me gus - ta a mí!

Song	"San Serení"
	Translation: San Sereni, a place for the good life. See how they work. The shoemaker makes shoes. I like this!
Level	Grades two through four

(Continued)

Singing game Children hold hands, surrounding one child in the middle, the shoemaker, who is pantomiming the act of making shoes. They walk to their left at a steady pulse, gently swinging their arms. At "así," children imitate the working movement of the shoemaker, who immediately chooses a new shoemaker to model the movement for the others. Add other occupations that the children may choose to emulate, such as carpenteros (carpenters), camareros (waiters), or bailadores (dancers).

The Noble Duke of York (England)

Oh, the no-ble___ Duke of___ York, he had ten___ thou-sand___ men; he
Now, when they were up they were up; and when they were down, they were down; and

marched them___ up to the top of the hill and he marched them down a - gain.
when they were on-ly___ half___ way up, they were nei - ther up nor down.

Oh! A - hun-ting we will go,_____ a - hunt-ing we will go;_____ we'll

catch a fox and put him in a box, and then we'll let him go.

Song	"The Noble Duke of York"
Level	Grades three through five
Singing game	In contra-dance formation of two lines of partners facing one another, children move within and on the outside of the lines. The top couple takes hands and steps quickly down between the lines, turning on the word "men" and returning to the original place. Then they skip around the outside, down to the bottom of the lines and form an arch. All other couples join hands and step together under the arch, and then move back to their places. The old head couple is left at the bottom of the lines, and a new head couple starts up the dance again.

Dalcroze Eurhythmics

Principles developed by Swiss musician Émile Jaques-Dalcroze provide the single most complete system of rhythmic training to appear in the twentieth century. He recognized movement as the foundation of a thorough musicianship and thus developed a means of communication linking the ear, the brain, and the body. He established eurhythmics (good rhythm) as an alternative to dance and gymnastics, developing in his students a fuller musical consciousness through directed and improvised physical responses to music. Eurhythmic experiences can be integrated within music classes for children using drums, keyboard improvisations, or prerecorded music as the impetus for movement.

Eurhythmics has been misinterpreted frequently as physical conditioning exercises, creative movement, or dance; it is none of these. Still, eurhythmics requires children to be limber, quick, and controlled. It requires them to express the music they hear through a creative reorganizing of the movements they already know. It sets their bodies to dance (in a figurative sense) to the musical sounds they perceive.

Elements of music, including basic sound awareness, pulse (beat), tempo, articulation, style, dynamics, accent, meter, melody, phrases, anacrusis (upbeat), duration, proportional relationships, and timbre, can be taught through Dalcroze eurhythmics. Little is needed to bring children into contact with music through eurhythmics: a large space, a drum, a piano, a stereo, and rules for boundaries and acceptable behavior that all children understand. Lesson 6.3 presents a sampling of suggestions for eurhythmics experiences. The creative teacher will use these as springboards for further development into ten-minute experiences, full lessons, and experiences that extend for days, weeks, or months.

At times, recorded music can be used to stimulate movement, but the live and partly spontaneous music played by the teacher on piano or percussion instrument is best. Children learn at different paces. Some need to hear a musical idea many times, and with the teacher's access to an instrument, the music can be easily slowed down,

Engaging in Dalcroze eurhythmics

© Jerry Gay

LESSON 6.3 Sample Experiences in Dalcroze Eurhythmics

Musical Concept	Experience
Sound versus silence	Children move when music is heard and freeze during silences.
Pulse (tempo)	Children step to the pulse of one child (no music). As teacher calls out the name of another child, children step the tempo and quality of that child's walk.
Pulse (tempo, timbre)	Children step to the beat of the drum. When the drum stops, children stop. When teacher taps the rim of the drum, children change the direction of their walking. (Variation: Children continue walking to the same beat even when the drum has stopped, testing their internalization of its sound.)
Articulation	Children hop or jump to choppy, staccato music, and glide, slide, or sway to legato, smooth music.
Dynamics	Children improvise strong movements for loud (forte) music and quiet, subtle movements for soft (piano) music. As music crescendos, children gradually enlarge their movements, diminishing them for diminuendo parts.
Style (tempo, dynamics, articulation)	Children clap, step, or follow teacher's improvisation on piano or xylophone. They should be encouraged to use as much variety of space, time, and energy as is necessary to kinesthetically realize the music.
Tempo	The room is divided into two parts: a slow half and a fast half. Without music, children move from one side to the other using the designated tempo of each half. When teacher plays music, children resolve their movement to that new tempo. Teacher demonstrates a movement that children imitate. Then, as music in various tempos is played, children perform the movement slower or faster.
Accent	Children walk, run, or skip through the forest. On accent, they jump behind a tree to hide from a bear.

repeated, or given more emphasis. Whatever the instrument, the teacher should feel comfortable with it. Basic rhythms, melodies, and harmonies can stimulate sensitive movement when they are played musically.

Short composed piano pieces also provide the impetus for teaching musical concepts through movement. In planning a lesson that emanates from a composed piece, the teacher should thoroughly analyze its rhythmic and melodic nuances, phrasing, and

Phrase	Children move in response to musical phrases. After several listenings, they use the same movements for the repeated phrases and change the movement for contrasting phrases.
Timbre	As teacher plays piano in various registers, children clap the high melodies and step the low melodies. Challenge them to coordinate the two when both treble and bass parts are sounding.
Meter	Children walk the pulse and clap on the first beat of each measure to teacher's improvised music in twos, threes, fours, fives, sixes, sevens, and so on. Choose a number, and while teacher plays music, children clap, pat, step, and rest for that number of beats. Challenge children to respond to the call of other numbers with the same sequence of movements. (For example, on four, children clap, pat, step, and rest for four beats each, and on seven, children clap, pat, step, and rest for seven beats each.)
Meter	In partners or a circle of children, choose a way to demonstrate a meter of two, three, four, five, six, seven, and so on, by rolling, tossing, or passing a ball. (For example, in a $\frac{2}{4}$ meter, partners might bounce and catch the ball. In a $\frac{3}{4}$ meter, a circle of children might bounce, hold, and pass the ball.)
Melody	As ascending music plays, children rise like the sun. They fall slowly like the sun setting on the horizon with the sound of descending music.
	Children move forward to ascending melodies, backward to descending music, and stand in place for melodies of static and unchanging pitch.
Anacrusis	Children step the pulse and conduct the meter. On music with an upbeat, or anacrusis, they step counterclockwise, and on music with a downbeat, or crusis, they step clockwise.
Duration	Children walk the quarter notes of teacher's improvised music on drum or piano, and stop and clap when eighth notes are played.
	Children sit in a circle. As the teacher improvises music on piano or drum, children walk the quarter notes by patting their laps, run the eighth notes by clapping, pat the half notes on their head, and tap the whole notes on the floor in front of them.
Proportional relationships	Children step the pulse of the music. When a verbal or musical clue is given, they step twice as fast or twice as slow.

overall formal organization, as well as the expressive markings that indicate tempo, dynamics, and articulation. The piece may require concentrated practice in preparation for the lesson, so that the composer's musical intentions are artfully presented to the children. When the teacher has reached a level of familiarity and confidence that will allow him or her to occasionally glance away from the instrument so as to be able to evaluate the movement responses of the children, then that piece is probably ready for teaching. Lesson 6.4 presents a

Schumann: "The Wild Horseman"
(measures one to eight)

Musical Concepts

Pulse; tempo; style
(Gallop like a horse) ♩ ♪ ♩ ♪

Triplet figure of melody
(Clap the continuous trotting sound) ♫

Two-measure accompaniment figure
("Hop, hop – – step, hop, hop") ♪ 𝄾 𝄾 ♪ 𝄾 𝄾 | ♩ ♪ ♪ 𝄾 𝄾 |

Melody and accompaniment
(Group one trots, while group two hops)
(Group one plays on woodblock, while group two plays on drum)

Beethoven: "Ecossaise in G"
(measures one to eight)

Musical Concepts

Steady eighth-note accompaniment pattern ♩ ♫ ♩
(Lightly step the steady accompaniment pattern)

Two similar four-measure phrases: A A′
(Change direction at the end of each phrase, but retain same quality
ifthe phrase is the same)

Two-measure crescendo, two-measure decrescendo <>
(Enlarge movements for crescendo, and decrease size and space for
decrescendo)

Anacrusis ♫ | ♩ ♩
(Make a movement that leans into the first pulse of measure one and
five)

Staccato and legato ♫ ♩ ♩ ♫♫
(Glide on legato and give a slight hop to the staccato sounds)

Accent
(On measures two and six, hop and land on the accented pitch e′)

Rhythmic pattern in treble ♫ ♩ ♩ ♫♫ ♩ ♪ ♩
(Step the rhythmic pattern, with attention to articulation, accent,
dynamics, and anacrusis)

Schumann: "Soldier's (March"
(measures one to sixteen)

Musical Concepts

Pulse; tempo; style
(March like a soldier)
♫ ♪ pattern, measures one, five, nine, and thirteen
("Skip-ty, step" [binary] or "step-hop, step")

Four-measure phrases: A B A B
(Change direction at the end of each phrase, and move at distinct
levels for A and B phrases)
(In partners, create movements for A and B)

sampling of technically easy, and commonly found, piano pieces along with suggestions for musical concepts that can be highlighted through eurhythmics.

The teacher who incorporates Dalcroze eurhythmics in music lessons will find that children become astute listeners for musical elements in order to meet the challenges of these movement games. While specialized Dalcroze training will shape the teacher's ability to improvise at the piano, a good musician who takes time out for practice will be capable of facilitating fundamental eurhythmics experiences into classes. Further information on eurhythmics can be found in the writings of Abramson (1973, 2003), Schnebly-Black and Moore (2003, 2004), and Mead (1994).

Methodological Suggestions for Early Childhood

- Rather than only leading young children to move to your music, improvise music that fits their own natural movement—at their precise speeds.
- In silence, lead young children to imitate movements that make use of various body parts, in a variety of directions, levels, and speeds.
- Suggest to young children that they "dance" their favorite stuffed animal, doll, or action figure to the music they hear.
- Build movement and music into the stories you tell, and invite young children to sing and dance their own stories.
- Play recordings that stimulate free and creative movement, and be receptive to the stories that may be told through young children's creative imagination as they develop actions and gestures to the music.

Creative Movement

Creative movement is a form of dance that is personal, interpretive, and expressive. It can be used to socialize children, provide entertainment to an audience of parents, and communicate ideas and feelings more directly or deeply than words. Unlike most dance forms, creative movement lacks authoritarian structure. There is no one right way of doing things, and there are no specific steps to learn. It is inspired by verbal and musical imagery, and it is an extension of exploratory movement experiences. It primes the kinesthetic impulses for responding to a stimulus. It may spring from a musical source, but it is not as closely united to specific musical concepts as required by eurhythmics. Creative movement links children's emotional and inventive selves with the kinesthetic skills of their bodies to utilize space, time, and energy in a unique dance.

The concepts to be taught should be presented as questions and challenges that inspire individual solutions. The Socratic method should be used prominently as the teacher guides children's movement through such questions as the following: "How do squirrels scamper?" "What parts of the squirrel's body move?" "Can you swing like a puppet blowing in the wind?" "Can you swing high or low?" "Can you swing while you walk, run, or skip?" "Can you swing in an even rhythm or uneven rhythm?" Children should be encouraged to explore and discover the concepts of breath, body parts, sounds, shapes, accents, levels, and pathways instead of being told or shown what to do. The teacher may lead children in preparatory movement experiences; select and present the stimulus for creative movement; direct attention to the concept through imagery that may be verbal, visual, or musical; and shape the final form of the experience through suggestion and approval. The learning, however, emanates from the child's own willingness to discover the expressive potential of his or her body.

Creative movement can be inspired by a word, a picture, a poem, a story, a song's melody, a rhythmic pattern, or a symphonic work. Teachers who strive for the development of musical understanding through creative movement may begin with any of these stimuli, but should be certain to reinforce a selected concept as an aid to the children's realization of an image or to incorporate music at the culmination of the exercise. To ensure learning, the teacher must ensure that the lesson is based on a preset goal; that children are informed of the goal; that they are presented with a variety of questions, problems, and stimuli; and that they are encouraged to achieve the lesson goal (if they do) through particular attention to the strengths of individual children as well as the group as a whole.

Suggestions for experiences in creative movement are found in Lesson 6.5. Some will encompass complete lesson periods, others can be included as short segments within a lesson, and still others may require several periods and much practice to fulfill. The creative teacher will likely extend, vary, and develop these experiences to suit the needs of children.

> *"Nobody should have to sit still when there's music. It moves, and it makes you move."*
>
> Jonathan, in Campbell, 2010

LESSON 6.5 Experiences in Creative Movement

Goal	Experience
To portray words in movement and sound	In partners or small groups, present children with words to be turned into movement and sound pieces: yawn, tramp, spin, shuffle, ooze, flutter, drip, explode, crack, spurt, swish, ripple, crunch, stir, sprinkle, plunge, slither. In a presentation to the class, these pieces may be moved silently and then presented with vocal, body, and instrumental accompaniment.
To portray musical terms in movement	Assign groups of children various musical terms and ask that they express them through movement: legato, staccato, forte, marcato, sforzando, cantabile, piano, piacere, lento, allegro, appassionato, doloroso. (First they must learn the meanings of these terms as applied to music.) They may later invent a melody to express the term and to coincide with the movement.
To express music and forms in movement	Play a recording of Camille Saint-Saëns's "The Lion" from *Carnival of the Animals*. Direct children's attention to pitch register and direction in the lion's growl. Through repeated listenings, ask that they move like a lion (large, strong, forceful), stopping to growl at the appropriate time. Ask children to listen to a recording of Aaron Copland's *Fanfare for the Common Man*, to note the sounds and the silences, and to identify the long and sustained sounds, the instruments, the melodic leaps, and the changes in dynamics. Play the opening forty-five seconds of the recording repeatedly, giving children the task of finding their own individual movements to personify the piece.

To create a movement-and-music version of a visual image	Show children a copy of a painting or a photograph. In small groups (depending on the number of figures), encourage them to make the visual image come to life. They will need to discuss what the people are doing, where they are going, and how they are moving. Their tableau should begin as a still image and can proceed through a movement piece that communicates without words. Vocal, body, and instrumental music may be improvised by another group of children to accompany the tableau. Paintings such as George Caleb Bingham's *Raftsmen Playing Cards*, Frederic Remington's *Howl of the Weather*, or John Stuart Curry's *The Mississippi* may inspire movement.
To create a movement piece from a collection of individual movements	Gather children into groups of four to eight. Ask that each child invent a movement to be included in a movement collection; each group should have as many movements as there are children. As a group, they practice their collective movements until one flows easily to the next. As an extension, they can choose to allow each movement one, two, or four pulses, or repeat some or all of the movements. Children can develop different levels of energy and space for these movements, should they wish to express them as tired, intimidated, angry, or gentle. Musical accompaniment can be suggested, selected, or created.
To express a poem through movement	A poem paints a visual image that can be realized through movement. Children can choose to follow the rhythm of the words or move more freely to the images that strike them.

The Puzzled Centipede (Anon.)

A cen' tipede' was hap' py quite,'
Until' a frog,' in fun,'
Said, "Pray/ which leg' comes af' ter which'?"
This raised' her mind' to such' a pitch,'
She lay' distract' ed in the ditch'
Consid' ering how' to run.'

The Animal Dance (P. S. Campbell)

The owl,' the skunk,'
The bull,' and the bear'
Went dan' cing one eve' ning.
They let' down their hair.'

The owl' did wad' dle.
The skunk' gave a twirl.'
The bull' hopped on two' feet.
The bear' took a whirl.'

Closing in' on a cir' cle,
They turned' to their right.'
Holding paws,' hoofs, and feath' ers,
They took' off in flight.'

The skunk' set the speed'
For all three' of his friends.'
Fast. Fas' ter. They cir' cled
And spun' to the end.'

(Continued)

LESSON 6.5 *(Continued)*

Goal	Experience
	Centri' fugal force,' As they laughed' and they screamed,' "We're the an' imal danc' ers! We dance' in your dreams'!"
To express a story through movement	Action stories inspire movement. Collections such as Joanna Cole's *Best-Loved Folktales of the World* provide many examples for dramatization. One story, with potential for both movement and musical accompaniment, is "A Crocodile's Tale," from the Philippines.

A Crocodile's Tale

A little boy named Juan saves the life of a crocodile by untying a rope around his neck. But instead of thanking him, the crocodile sweeps little Juan up with his tail and wraps it around him. He wants to eat the boy. While the crocodile catches fish from the river as "appetizers," Juan cries for help. He is heard by a monkey sitting in a tree on the bank of the river. The monkey shouts to the crocodile, "What are you doing with Juan?" To which the crocodile replies, "I'm going to eat him." The clever monkey shouts "Can't hear you! What did you say? Come a little closer." The crocodile swims to the middle of the river, with his tail wrapped around Juan. "I'm going to eat him, and maybe you, too." Again the monkey shouts "Can't hear you! Come a little closer." The crocodile swims to the bank and shows his teeth to the monkey in the tree. In an instant, the monkey lunges down with a rope to tie the crocodile's snout tightly shut, and Juan frees himself from the tail and jumps to safety. The monkey and Juan celebrate by joyfully dancing the Tinikling, a traditional dance of the Philippines (see Lesson 6.7 on how to perform the Tinikling dance.)

Creative movement generates enthusiasm among children. It gives them permission to explore and express freely and playfully the ideas that are brought to mind by poems, pictures, music, and stories. It gives them freedom to experiment with their own space, time, and energy, leading them to a discovery of the language of movement. The use of music as a stimulus for movement, as part of the learning process or as a component of the final product, provides a more fulfilling and integrative experience for children. In this manner, children learn music as they also learn to speak through their bodies. For additional ideas on creative movement, see Fraser (2000) and Bloom and Shreeves (1998).

Billie Judy/Reel Life Productions

Dance

Dance is purposeful, choreographed, and much-rehearsed movement to music. Dance knows many forms: classical ballet; modern dance as inspired by Martha Graham or Katherine Dunham; classical court dances of Southeast Asia; theater dances of China and Japan; martial arts–inspired dances of Latin America; dances that involve entire communities in sub-Saharan Africa or Native American pow-wows; and ballroom, hip-hop, and a grand variety of folk dances. To dance these forms well involves physical training that is dependent on technique, knowledge, and experience. Unlike other types of movement for children, dance is an art. It is structured and premeditated movement that demands concentration in learning the postures, positions, and steps and that requires practice to keep the specific movements in the memory.

For children through the elementary grades, folk dance is one of the best avenues for experiencing music, cultures, and movement all at once. The first dances attempted should be those with simple and repetitive footwork set to music with a clearly defined pulse. Line and circle dances are often easier for beginners than partner dances because children can focus on the steps instead of their relationships to their partners. In fact, some of the singing games so prominent in music classrooms are technically folk dances, too (see especially "Bow Wow Wow," "How Many Miles to Babylon?", and "The Noble Duke of York"). Emphasizing physical education goals, Weikert (2003) suggests a progression for learning folk dances. However, the sequence shown in Lesson 6.6 is more effective as an approach for musically educating children, in which the accent is on musical learning through movement.

Lesson 6.7 presents instructions for a selection of folk dances, along with their associated melodies and references to accessible recordings. Melodies played on classroom instruments by children can provide the culminating performance for programs and for children's own pleasure. As well, these well-known songs (and dance music

LESSON 6.6 An Effective Sequence for Teaching Folk Dances

Listen

As an introduction to the musical style of the dance, the teacher should guide children to listen carefully to the music. Children can attend to musical details. What instruments are playing? Which are the melody instruments? Do they hear repeated rhythmic patterns? Can they chant, clap, or write them? Is the melody wide or narrow in range? Can they sing the melody? Is the texture of the combined instruments chordal, unison, or heterophonic (simultaneous variations played by several melody instruments)? Concentrated and repeated listenings will create a more comfortable dance experience, and the music will be better understood and appreciated.

Respond

The teacher should direct children to listen to the recording (or to the song as it is sung or played), and respond to the underlying rhythm in the bass line, the chordal accompaniment, or the percussion instruments. By patting the accented beats on their laps, children are responding to the dance rhythm. When teaching a dance to a song, instead of a recorded musical piece, the teacher can nonetheless present the steps as a clapped or patted ostinato rhythm for all to follow.

Chant and Pat

Ask children to chant descriptive words to indicate the motion of the dance. By chanting "step," "hop," "pause," "left," "right," and the like, children will more easily perform the necessary rhythmic movement of the feet. The words are spoken in the rhythm of the steps, which are danced with the hands on the lap.

Chant and Step

The transfer of movement from the hands to the feet occurs next. The repeated rhythmic chant should continue, so that the children match the steps to the descriptive words. This speech-action activity is initially more successful without the music, which may confuse some students who will be distracted by other musical aspects such as timbre and melody.

Step and Internalize

In the final stage, the music returns to accompany the movement. Children begin to internalize the rhythmic chant, thinking and doing the steps. As a result of earlier stages in the sequence, children develop an inner hearing for the rhythm and a kinesthetic ease in performing the movement.

selections) are available online as instrumental and/or vocal pieces, via iTunes, YouTube, and other sources.

The movements of folk dance are natural and unaffected, stylized but not stilted, offering a means of socialization, enrichment of school programs, and exposure to the folkways of world cultures. As a movement-based musical experience, folk dance makes

Skip to My Lou (United States)

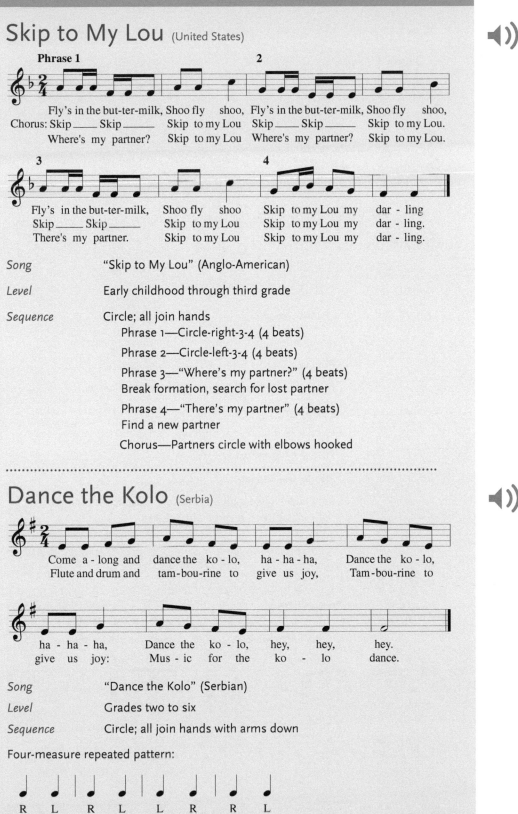

Phrase 1 **2**

Fly's in the but-ter-milk, Shoo fly   shoo, Fly's in the but-ter-milk, Shoo fly   shoo,
Chorus: Skip ___ Skip ___   Skip to my Lou Skip ___ Skip ___   Skip to my Lou.
Where's my partner?   Skip to my Lou Where's my partner?   Skip to my Lou.

3 **4**

Fly's in the but-ter-milk,   Shoo fly   shoo Skip to my Lou my   dar - ling
Skip ___ Skip ___   Skip to my Lou Skip to my Lou my   dar - ling.
There's my partner.   Skip to my Lou Skip to my Lou my   dar - ling.

Song   "Skip to My Lou" (Anglo-American)

Level   Early childhood through third grade

Sequence   Circle; all join hands
                    Phrase 1—Circle-right-3-4 (4 beats)
                    Phrase 2—Circle-left-3-4 (4 beats)
                    Phrase 3—"Where's my partner?" (4 beats)
                    Break formation, search for lost partner
                    Phrase 4—"There's my partner" (4 beats)
                    Find a new partner
                    Chorus—Partners circle with elbows hooked

Dance the Kolo (Serbia)

Come a - long and   dance the ko - lo,   ha - ha - ha,   Dance the ko - lo,
Flute and drum and   tam-bou-rine to   give us joy,   Tam-bou-rine to

ha - ha - ha,   Dance the   ko - lo,   hey,   hey,   hey.
give us joy: Mus - ic   for the   ko - lo   dance.

Song   "Dance the Kolo" (Serbian)
Level   Grades two to six
Sequence   Circle; all join hands with arms down

Four-measure repeated pattern:

R   L   R   L   L   R   R   L
"Walk Walk Walk Touch Walk Touch Walk Touch"

(Continued)

Sakura (Japan)

Song	"Sakura" (Japan)
Level	Grades two to six
Sequence	Independent, in lines or circle (phrase = 4 beats)

Phrase 1—Arms extended, nod right, nod left

Phrase 2—Make right arm circle, left arm circle

Phrase 3—Move right arm side-front, left arm side-front

Phrase 4—Hands pat right lap, hands pat left lap

Phrase 5—Repeat 3

Phrase 6—Repeat 1

Phrase 7—Raise right arm, fingers skyward, left hand below right elbow, then reverse with left arm

La Raspa (Mexico)

Song	"La Raspa" (Mexico)
Level	Grades three to five
Sequence	Partners, facing each other, hands on hips
	Phrases 1–8

R	L	R			L	R	L		
"Step	Step	Step	Clap	Clap	Step	Step	Step	Clap	Clap"

Measures 9–10—Link right elbows, skip once around

Measures 11–12—Link left elbows, skip once around

Tinikling (Philippines)

Level	Grades three to six
Sequence	Two poles of six to ten feet on the floor
	Child holds two poles at each end

Pole movement: Count 1—Strike poles together

Count 2—Poles apart, strike floor

Count 3—Poles apart, strike floor

Dance movement: Count 1—Jump out, spreading feet apart

Count 2—Jump in, with feet together

Count 3—Jump in, with feet together

Schottische (Sweden)

(Continued)

Song   "Schottische" (Sweden)

Level   Grades four to six

Sequence   Partners side by side, in circle facing right, inside hands linked

Phrase 1—Move apart

R	R	L	L	R	R	L	Pause
"Step	Hop	Step	Hop	Step	Hop	Step	Hop"

Phrase 2—Move together

R	R	L	L	R	R	L	Pause
"Step	Hop	Step	Hop	Step	Hop	Step	Hop"

Gerakina (Greece)

Ger - a - ki-na's at the fair,   Ger - a - ki-na with her gol-den ban-gles on,

There's mu-sic ev-'ry - where.   Ring, pret-ty gol-den   ban-gles, jin-gle, jin-gle,

jan - gle. Sing in the   air, Ger-a-ki - na   danc-ing at the   fair. All the vil-lage

boys will come to the   square For the jin-gle   jan - gle dance at the   fair

Song   "Gerakina" (Greece)

Level   Grades four to six

Sequence   Line, all join hands
Shoulder hold
Two-measure repeated pattern

R	R	L	R	L	—
"Step	Step	Step	Step	Behind	Pause"

Alternate repeated pattern

R	L	R	L	R	R
"Step	Behind	Step	Step	Toe-in	Toe-out"

a meaningful contribution to the musical development of children. Folk dance collections by Longden, Longden, and Derfler (2006) and Longden and Weikert (2003), with their accompanying recordings of dance arrangements, are useful for teachers, who can modify the instructional sequence to suit their musical goals.

Adapting Instruction for Various Needs

SENSORY NEEDS

- *Blind or visually impaired*: Clarify movements through particular visual images rather than general statements, such as "Open and close the door" rather than "Open and together." Gently shape the body to new movement, and then when the muscle memory is there, give the movement a name like "Move A" or "the Door."

- *Deaf or hearing impaired*: Counting on residual hearing, dancing to live piano on wood floors, or to music especially rich in bass tones, or to amplified music, can aid musically expressive movement among the hearing impaired. It is useful to count visually and to communicate through signs.

BEHAVIORAL NEEDS

- *Externalizing behaviors*: Review rules for movement, and encourage acting-out children to achieve control of their bodies for success in stopping, starting, and staying with the music.

- *Internalizing behaviors*: Locate the withdrawn child with children he/she trusts, and encourage steady (if somewhat delayed and hesitant) progress toward full movement engagement.

MOBILITY IMPAIRMENT

- For children in wheelchairs and on crutches, movement is possible in modified ways. Exploratory sessions are useful out of class time, and children (and their teachers, parents, and aides) can work through physically integrated movement exercises that can help to strengthen their bodies and develop their coordination.

AUTISTIC SPECTRUM

- Facing children, explore small and large movement that links directly to the tempi, pulse, rhythms, dynamics, articulations, and phrasing of music played on drum, piano, or recording.

Assessment of Moving

If movement is a pedagogical tool for achieving musical understanding and a means for demonstrating musical perception and cognition, it can also be an artistic end product of instruction for children, who learn to connect their ears, minds, and bodies in expressive ways. The teacher needs to consider what place movement will hold in a curricular program—whether it is part of the instructional process that leads, for example, to more perceptive listening, or whether the product and programmatic result of a lesson are intended to complement and elaborate on a sung song or instrumental piece. For some, the choice may be one or the other, while for others it will seem natural to expect children to grow musically through movement possibilities as well as to move in an expressive manner approaching the art of dance. In any case, movement with musical intent will be more than free and unbridled motor energy; it will be an entity that can be assessed.

Formative Evaluation

Assessment questions that the teacher can ask and that can comprise a guide to children in their attempts to engage in movement with a musical focus include the following:

1. In the case of action songs and singing games, are you rhythmically on time with your gestures, steps, and other means of physical movement? Or are you performing out of sync with the song, the game, and fellow players?

2. In the case of eurhythmics, are you able to capture the musical feature (pulse, meter, rhythmic pattern, melodic contour, form) in your movement? Or are you drawn to some other musical feature than the one prescribed? Why?

3. In the case of creative movement, are you able to move in a way that feels good to you, with thought given to the use of space, time, and energy in your own personal way? Or are you simply following someone else's ideas?

4. In the case of dance, are you following the sequence of movements required of the dance, in proper order, in rhythmically accurate time, and within the expressive style associated with the dance?

Movement can easily go awry with children, in that it can be filler (and a time killer) within a class and a cute and clever addition to a program, with no merit or real contribution to musical understanding. It can be so much more than that, however, and a view toward how children might be assessed in their movement development can ensure that musical goals surround and steer its use in music instruction. Along with considering the above questions, which can be posed to children as a framework for their more thoughtful movement, children can increase their understanding of both the commonalities and the differences between movement for recreation (sports and other playful endeavor) and movement as an expressive extension of the self, incited and supported by music. These questions can be considered by children in group discussion, on paper (as in short journal-like accounts), or in silent ways that nonetheless direct their careful attention to how their bodies respond to the music that propels them.

Summative Evaluation

By the close of a year's worth of experiencing music through movement, children should in fact be developing an integration of ear, body, and brain in their growth of musical understanding and skills. A comparison of video footage from September to May would likely show, if a conscious attention was given to the use of the body as a musically responsive "instrument," development in the speed and accuracy of the body to pulse, rhythm, and phrasing. Experiences in the use of gesture and full-body movement with songs, instrumental pieces, and recorded music result in "body-smart" behaviors. A portfolio of before-and-after experiences with the same music might tell the story of children who listen-and-move (and then also understand musical components), and who know the full routines and rules of safe and expressive movement.

Movement for Musical Development

Teachers are sometimes hesitant to initiate movement experiences. What if the music room is too small? Explore the school building and schoolyard for alternative spaces. Modify the size and scope of some of the movement experiences. What if the children do not know their left from their right? Most action songs, singing games, eurhythmics, and creative-movement experiences do not require a knowledge of left and right. In learning folk dances, children can tie a ribbon around their left (or right) wrists. What if the children are not getting a musical concept? Focus their attention. Repeat the melody, the rhythm, the chant, and the directions. Model the movement. Sequence the activity, breaking it into smaller segments. Give them time to practice. What if they get rowdy? Set the rules at the start, remind children of the penalties for broken rules, and follow through on them. What should the rules be? That depends on the activity, the goals, the space, and the age of the children. Keep the rules simple and straightforward; sometimes no-touch and stop-when-the-music-stops rules are enough. What if the children will not move? Determine whether the movement is age-appropriate. For older children, opportunities for teaching each other and working in small groups may be more readily received than too many teacher-directed lessons.

Movement is more than an occasional experience. It is an integral part of children's musical education. Children develop musical sensitivity when their natural movements are channeled toward the discovery or reinforcement of musical features and components. The musically trained teacher who recognizes children's movement capacities is critical to advancing their musical knowledge, skills, and sensitivities.

Scenario

THE LATE-AFTERNOON CLASS of third-grade children is lively, even for them, on one Tuesday afternoon in February, and Mr. Robinson is convinced that they are one of his more kinesthetically prone classes that will do well to spend much of their music time in movement. His classroom, a 1970s-style portable building of aluminum exterior siding set at the far end of the parking lot, is conducive to movement, too. There are no desks or chairs, no clutter of books or instruments on the floor, and the tile floor stretches over a space as large as a standard school cafeteria.

The children have taken their places in a standing circle, and although most are either laughing, or talking loudly, or twirling, or even stamping in place, Mr. Robinson moves quickly to the middle of the circle with a colorful Ghanaian-style djembe drum hung from his shoulder. Without a word of instruction, he slaps his hand on the head of the drum, and the deep-sounding "thud" signals the children to turn to their right, tune their ears to the beat, and walk. Mr. Robinson's third-grade music class has begun.

For nearly two minutes, the children walk when the drum sounds and freeze when the drum rests. They match the tempo of the $\frac{6}{8}$ drum beat, from moderately fast, to medium, to slow, and to a gradually increasing speed that turns around again to become so slow as to finally stop. Mr. Robinson then sets his drum down and without words signals the children with his arms to slowly sit down. "You're tuned in," he compliments the children. "Your energy is going into all the right moves, and your ears are leading the way. Good job!" He asks the children to remember the rules for moving in music class, and they raise their hands to tick off two: "Use your ears to move" and "Move safely." Mr. Robinson has made his way to the piano just outside the circle and asks the children to follow his beat with hands on the floor. They bend over to the floor, and as he plays a jiglike melody at the piano (with a left-handed drone accompaniment), the children pat their palms onto the floor. They are not together, however, and some children are patting eighth notes while others have found the dotted-quarter note to pat.

"Listen to the low sounds, and pat softly," he calls out to them, and then he drops the melody out and gives accent to the drones. The children are soon patting together. He brings the melody back, and most (but not all) of the children are able to retain the dotted-quarter pat. A cluster of high pitches signals the children to stop.

"Jimmy, Jacob, Kelly, Sean, take a stack of hand drums and pass them out." Mr. Robinson plays Schumann's "The Wild Horseman" as the drums are distributed. Children are playing various $\frac{6}{8}$ rhythms, from ♪♪♪ to ♩♪, and also ♩., most of them a little faster than the piano's tempo.

"Shhh," Mr. Robinson reminds them, and the children lighten their drum taps, but then play a tad slower as well.

"Two fingers," he cautions, and the drum taps become even lighter. "Bounce lightly," he suggests, and they begin to get more of the character that Schumann had intended. This continues through several repetitions of the piece, and it seems that Mr. Robinson's goal is to allow the children to keep a steady rhythm going—any rhythm that fits within the piece.

He asks the children to stand with their hand drums and tells them that the entire classroom is their space; they can go wherever they wish, but they must walk the beat when they hear high-pitched music and play the beat on their drums, standing still in one place, when they hear low-pitched music. Beginning with the "The Wild Horseman" again, Mr. Robinson plays first the left hand's low pitches and then the right hand's high pitches, one section at a time. He plays again, alternating between high and low pitches, phrase by phrase. The children have the gist of the game, responding to the highs and lows by playing or walking, but they are tuned to the rhythm of the pitches they hear (as they had been in the previous activity)—not to the beat.

Mr. Robinson calls the children back to the circle and directs them to sit with their drums in their laps. He sits himself between two of the liveliest boys. "Here's a poem for you. If you can find the beat, you can tap it on your drum—with one finger only."

He chants "The Animal Dance" with a $\frac{6}{8}$ metric feeling, and three children are immediately on the beat with him. Others join in a scattershot kind of sound. He stops and starts to sway, subtly, from the right to the left, and soon the children are with him, swaying and tapping their drums. "Keep it slow, keep it steady," he cautions them in a $\frac{6}{8}$ rhythm, and begins the poem again. The children are more able to keep the dotted-quarter-note beat, and they continue to sway as they do so.

"Which words are 'moving words'?" he asks, and the children call out "dancing," "waddle," "twirl," "hop," and "turn." Mr. Robinson challenges them to a waddle, grabs his djembe drum to play a waddle rhythm, and the children are up on their haunches, falling over, colliding, laughing; about half the class is in total confusion. He runs for the light switch and flicks it off until the children settle down.

"Is that moving safely? No, so watch yourselves, or you'll lose your privileges." The children are better at following the turning, hopping, and twirling rhythms that Mr. Robinson plays, and they use the floor space well to get into the flow of the drum's sounds. Mr. Robinson calls the children back to the circle, compliments them on "what was mostly a very good class," and informs them that they have begun to get a sense of $\frac{6}{8}$ meter.

Questions

1. What was the theme of Mr. Robinson's class? In what ways was it demonstrated?

2. What factors made for successful movement experiences? What adjustments might be made to the class setting and plan to ensure greater success?

3. Should any of these activities be repeated in another class session or extended? How?

REVIEW

1. Discuss the musical and social outcomes of including movement in a music lesson for children.

2. Define the movement components of space, time, and energy.

3. At what age would action songs be appropriate for use with children? Singing games?

4. List musical goals for teaching folk dance to children. How would they differ from the goals of a physical education instructor who teaches folk dancing?

CRITICAL THINKING

1. How are eurhythmics and creative movement related? How are they different?

2. Why would movement as employed by music teachers not be likely to meet the achievement expectations outlined in the National Standards in dance?

PROJECTS

1. Visit a school or park playground to observe the movement of children at play. What games do they play that include songs and movement? What movements can older children perform for which younger children have not yet mastered the coordination? Make a list of your observations regarding children's use of space, time, and energy.

2. Begin a collection of songs, including game, dance, and action songs, that require or suggest movement. Organize the songs chronologically according to the level of kinesthetic development necessary to enable children to successfully perform them.

3. Choose a musical concept and prepare a set of movement experiences appropriate for children in kindergarten, grade three, and grade six.

4. Select a sample experience in Dalcroze eurhythmics, and prepare a ten-minute lesson to teach in class. Develop that same idea into a thirty-minute lesson.

5. Listen to recordings of music from various historical periods and cultures. Select one or more musical concepts from each, and consider ways in which movement can be applied as a vehicle for developing children's understanding of the concept(s).

6. Write a letter to your principal to explain how the movement experiences he or she observed in your music class were educationally justified. Include an explanation of which specific musical concepts were learned by children through the movement demonstration.

7. Develop a "Mini-Musicking" Activity. (a) Choose a recorded musical selection, featuring an excerpt of thirty seconds; (b) Design a "Listen and Do" Mini-Musicking experience that consists of three experiences in responding through movement to musical qualities; (c) Feature movement experiences in pulse, subdivisions, rhythmic patterns, melodic contour, phrase, timbre(s), texture, "expressive dimensions"; (d) Facilitate the "Mini-Musicking" Activity using music but no words.

MINDTAP Visit MindTap to access classroom videos, audio, and more!

7

Rhythm and the Child

IN THIS CHAPTER

- Rhythm and Child Development
- Rhythm in Speech
- Rhythm in Movement
- The Pulse
- Meter
- Durations and Their Patterns
- Rhythm Mnemonics
- Notation for Writing and Reading Rhythms
- Syncopations
- Polyrhythms
- From Natural Rhythms to Rhythmic Training: Rhythmicking Well!
  - Formative Evaluations
  - Summative Evaluations

RHYTHM IS EVERYWHERE IN the lives of children. When children speak, their words tumble and flow in regular streams of sounds, in starts and stops, with emphasis or not on particular syllables. When they move, they step at a self-regulated pace; they run, hop, jump, and skip in rhythms of their own. The rhythms they experience extend beyond speech and movement: Maria hears the rhythm of her mother's heartbeat, soft and steady, and is soothed by it. Aaron can feel the throbbing of his own pulse as he holds his wrist, feeling it gradually decrease in speed as he settles down after hopping around the playground. When Lamont recites a favorite poem, he gives accent and rhythm to the rhyming words, shaping them into units of loudness and softness, and faster and slower sounds. Jacqueline pours her own rhythm into the teddy bear, dancing him in time to the tune she hums. When the grind of a homework assignment presses him, Robby raps as he rhythmically reads aloud his weekly list of spelling words. With surprising frequency, rhythm emerges in the things that children do.

Children at play or at work show their natural attraction to and fascination with rhythm. The word comes from the Greek verb *rhein*, meaning "to flow." Children flow eagerly through rhythmic experiences that engage them in listening, speaking, or moving. They develop greater rhythmic facility naturally and easily while singing and when rhythm is embedded in language and movement. The counting of beats can be experienced later as a higher level of musical knowing, but children's first experience with rhythms is through their daily speech and movement.

Children learn to understand concepts of rhythm in music through their teachers and musically sensitive parents. In school music classes as well as through private instrumental instruction, children learn by participating in the activity of a sequenced curriculum. Children chant, sing, listen, play, read, and write their way to a thorough knowledge of pulse (or beat), subdivisions and extensions of the pulse (for example ♫ and ♩), other durations and patterns of rhythm (and their related rests), accents, meter, syncopation, and polyrhythms. Children's natural affinity for rhythm is more fully realized through training, which takes them from the experiences of listening and responding to rhythms to reading and writing the notes that symbolize them; that is, music literacy.

- What are the concepts and terms you associate with rhythm?

- At what age did you acquire an understanding of long/short, fast/slow, faster/slower?

- How do these concepts surface in your performance and listening?

- Have you observed the rhythms of children's speech, song, and movement when they play?

- Describe the characteristics of rhythm in some of your favorite music.

Rhythm and Child Development

THE MOTHER'S HEARTBEAT, INITIALLY experienced in the prenatal environment, may be the earliest rhythmic experience of all. In early infancy, children add the rhythmicity of sounds in their environment—the rocking movements and rhythmic cooings made by their parents, the pulse of music emanating from televisions and stereos, and the often regular loud-soft and fast-slow gradations of speech in conversations that surround them. Well within their first year, children respond rhythmically to music as they sway, rock, and bounce. Toddlers may show their perception of rhythm through the rhythmic dancelike movements they perform, first with others and then by themselves. Young children experience rhythm by feeling, hearing, and moving to it. Table 7.1 summarizes aspects of children's developmental stages of rhythmic perception and understanding.

TABLE 7.1 Children's Rhythmic Development

AGE	DEVELOPMENTAL SKILL
LESS THAN ONE	Demonstrates rhythmic swaying, rocking, bouncing
ONE TO TWO	Demonstrates babbling in irregular rhythmic patterns Performs dancelike rhythmic movements
TWO	Sings spontaneous songs framed around regular rhythmic pulses and patterns
THREE	Sings spontaneous songs with some feeling for meter and with regularly recurring rhythmic patterns Imitates short rhythmic patterns
FOUR TO FIVE (KINDERGARTEN)	Taps in time to a regular set pulse Begins to develop rhythmic clapping and patting Replicates short rhythmic patterns on instruments
SIX TO SEVEN (GRADES ONE AND TWO)	Distinguishes fast and slow, long and short Can perform songs faster and slower Can PRW* quarter-, eighth-, and half-note rhythms
EIGHT TO NINE (GRADE THREE)	Can PRW dotted-quarter and eighth notes (♩. ♪), and syncopated quarter- and eighth-note rhythms (♪♩♪) Can recognize and conduct music in $\frac{2}{4}$, $\frac{4}{4}$, $\frac{6}{8}$, and $\frac{3}{4}$ meter
NINE TO TEN (GRADE FOUR)	Can PRW sixteenth-note patterns (♫♫ ♫♪ ♪♫) Can recognize and conduct music in cut time and compound meters ($\frac{9}{8}$, $\frac{12}{8}$)
TEN TO TWELVE (GRADES FIVE AND SIX)	Can PRW dotted eighth- and sixteenth-note patterns (♫♩ ♫♩.) Can recognize and conduct music in asymmetric meters ($\frac{5}{8}$, $\frac{7}{8}$)

*Note: PRW = perform, read, and write; children are singing, playing, moving these rhythms sooner than they learn to read and write them.

The spontaneous songs children sing become increasingly rhythmic with age. Progressing from musical babbling at one year to eighteen months, when their singing is often a string of pitches with occasional and often irregular pauses for breaths to occur, children at two years may already be framing their melodies around steady beats within and between phrases. By three years of age, children's songs may take on rhythmic structures that include strong metric tendencies and recurring patterns. With increasing exposure to standard nursery rhymes, chants, and songs, as well as to folk and popular songs, preschool children are often integrating rather sophisticated rhythmic patterns into their spontaneous songs. Their attempts to reproduce songs presented to them also become more accurate in both rhythmic and melodic elements as they approach school age.

From a very early age, children's spontaneous sounds are regular in pulse but unaccented. Keeping a steady pulse appears to be developmental. While few three-year-old children can tap, clap, or pat in time to a set regular pulse, most six-year-olds accomplish this task with great accuracy. Beat competence is widely evident by first grade, yet some children still require training, or at least reinforcement of the skill, to maintain a steady beat. The accurate replication of short rhythmic patterns by young children reveals a similar developmental progression from toddler through kindergarten age. Not only does rhythmic perception develop early, but also the abilities to perform (or produce) pulse and to reproduce patterns emerge even before most children begin formal schooling.

With increasing musical exposure, children in the elementary grades evolve a sophisticated understanding of how music is organized rhythmically. Primary-grade children demonstrate their readiness for learning about tempo, durations, and metric groupings through their rhythmic chants and through the rhythmic recitation of numbers, letters, words, and word-phrases. They learn to use the regular rhythmic pulses and patterns of spoken language, and to use expressively the accents, flow, and shadings of language in ways that parallel musical expression. Long before they learn to read and write rhythmic notation, they are involved in singing, playing, and dancing rhythms of considerable sophistication—including syncopations and even polyrhythmic patterns.

In first grade, children can typically discern fast from slow and long from short. This prepares them for experiences in performing songs faster and slower, and for recognizing the sounds of quarter notes and their eighth-note subdivisions. By second grade, they are usually capable of reading and writing various rhythmic patterns based first on quarter and eighth notes, and then with the addition of half notes. Third-grade children (who have had sufficient practice with earlier durations) are ready for directed listening and the performance of music with dotted quarter notes and syncopated patterns that mix quarter and eighth notes (♪♩♪) and can develop the skills to read and write patterns with these durations. During this period, children become capable of discerning the metric grouping of pulses in simple duple ($\frac{2}{4}$ and $\frac{4}{4}$), compound duple, ($\frac{6}{8}$) and triple ($\frac{3}{4}$) time, showing their knowledge through conducting patterns and various other movements.

With a solid foundation of rhythmic understanding, and the development of skills for performing, reading, and writing, children in the intermediate grades can progress easily into experiences with rhythms of greater complexity. Sixteenth notes, along with patterns combining sixteenth and eighth notes (♫♪ and ♪♫), can be introduced to fourth-grade children, dotted eighth- and sixteenth-note patterns (♫ and ♫.) to fifth-grade children, and triplets to children in the sixth grade. With an understanding of music in $\frac{2}{4}$, $\frac{4}{4}$, $\frac{6}{8}$, and $\frac{3}{4}$ under way, children can then explore other compound meters ($\frac{9}{8}$, $\frac{12}{8}$), cut time or alla breve ($\frac{2}{2}$) as symbolized by ¢ as opposed to common time ($\frac{4}{4}$), and irregular or asymmetric meters ($\frac{5}{8}$ and $\frac{7}{8}$ for example). Many of the more sophisticated rhythmic concepts targeted for learning at the intermediate level are nonetheless inherent in popular music and children's listening preferences, and thus were experienced at younger ages.

The logic of a rhythm learning sequence must be set by teachers with a comprehensive knowledge of music and children's developmental levels. A large part of children's rhythmic perception develops without training, but the capacity to perform it, code it through notation, and decode it by reading the notation is dependent on instruction and long experience hearing these rhythms. A refined ability to discern the rhythmic nuances of music is also greatly enhanced through the directed listening that teachers provide.

Rhythm in Speech

The rhythm of spoken language is the natural gateway to musical rhythm. Words and word-phrases provide children with every component of rhythm—from the basic pulse to the multilayered complexity of polyrhythm.

Words become musical when:

1. They are spoken over the foundation of a set pulse.
2. Their sounds are transformed into chants of longer and shorter musical durations.
3. Some words in a group are emphasized over others.

From the discovery of language in early childhood through the sophisticated wordplay of preadolescence, children develop musical understanding in their rhythmic chants.

Children can be made aware of musical rhythm through experiences that engage language as a tool for learning duration, accent, and temporal units. Because speech is oral, children learn its rhythmic patterns through enculturation. The media present universal patterns of the rhythmic flow and stress of language, a homogenized pronunciation of words and phrases. Children are not likely to intentionally distort or perform inaccurately the spoken language they have learned orally and are thus readied for learning concepts of musical rhythm by the very nature of their extensive listening to and speaking of language.

The Orff approach adheres to the development of rhythmic understanding through chant. Words of one, two, and three syllables form the building blocks of music, because they provide the substance for the recitation of longer and shorter durations equivalent to quarter, eighth, half, whole, and sixteenth notes, as well as triplets. Typically, children's names, or names of colors, fruits, or animals, provide occasions for chanting to a steady pulse. From single words, children can explore word-phrases, sentences, and paragraphs that equate to half-phrases of two measures, full phrases of four measures, and musical forms such as binary, ternary, and rondo. Greetings and farewells, colloquialisms, proverbs, rhymes, famous quotations, and poems are rich with potential for musical rhythm. As children recite these bits of speech and language, they come into contact with rhythmic values and nuances.

The pedagogy of Orff-Schulwerk provides experiences not only for rhythmic chanting, but also for the abstraction and accompaniment of speech rhythms by clapping, tapping, snapping, and stamping. While Carl Orff did not specify the transfer of rhythmic speech to the reading and writing of rhythmic notation, American proponents of the approach have successfully developed music literacy by following the extensive rhythmic experience with wordplay that they provide for their children.

See Lessons 7.1 through 7.8 for examples of rhythm embedded in spoken phrases that can be incorporated within a lesson on pulse, durations, and durational patterns.

Because language is so fundamental to children's daily lives, they comfortably and easily express rhythmically its phonemes (sounds, including syllables) and phrases. While rhythmic chant is a musical realization of language, the challenge is to eventually perform the rhythms of the words while silencing the words themselves, to achieve a more complete musical understanding of the rhythmic components. After chanting, patting, clapping, tapping, stamping, and stepping the rhythm, can children fade away the words and maintain the integrity of the rhythm itself? After internalizing the rhythmic phrase, can they graph it—through dots, dashes, lines, and shapes? Can they notate it? Can they hear the rhythm of the word-phrase in a new musical context—a song or recorded piece? Can they recognize the rhythm and read it when it occurs in notated music? These are sophisticated skills in the development of rhythmic understanding. It all begins with an awareness of the rhythm of speech. The work of Frazee (1987, 1999, 2007), Keetman (1974), and Steen (1992) provide many examples of Orff practices of rhythmic speech, as do works by Goodkin (1998, 1999, 2002).

LESSON 7.1 Rhythmic Duration through Name Chants

Patting the pulse, chanting the words:

LESSON 7.2 Rhythmic Chants: Colors

Patting the pulse, clapping the off-beats, chanting the words:

LESSON 7.3 Rhythmic Chants: Animals

Patting the pulse, clapping the off-beats, chanting the words:

Li - ons, ti - gers, dogs, and a cat,

El - e - phants, rhi - nos, how a - bout that?

LESSON 7.4 Rhythmic Chants: Fruits

Chanting with body rhythms:

Snap

pear. where.

Clap

peach - es, fruits from

Pat

pine-ap-ple, ev' - ry

Stamp

Man - go, Tas - ty

Pulse: ① ② ③ ④ ⑤ ⑥ ⑦ ⑧

LESSON 7.5 A Half Phrase of Rhythm

Patting the pulse, chanting the words:

In a feeling of twos (2)

Birds of a fea - ther

In a feeling of threes (3)

Birds   of   a   fea - ther

LESSON 7.6   A Full Phrase of Rhythm

Patting the pulse, chanting the words:

In a feeling of twos (2)

Red   sky   at   morn - ing,

sail - ors   take   warn - ing.

In a feeling of threes (3)

Red   sky   at   morn - ing,

sail - ors   take   warn - ing.

LESSON 7.7   A Musical Form: Rondo

Chanting the words, choosing the body rhythms:

A: Pit - ter,   pat - ter,   sprin - kle,   splat - ter

Rain - drops   fall.   What   does   it   mat - ter?

B: Rain,   rain,   go   a - way

Come   a - gain   a - noth - er   day

A: Pit - ter, pat - ter, sprin - kle, splat - ter

Rain - drops fall. What does it mat - ter?

C: (It's) rain - ing, it's pour - ing

The old man is snor - ing

A: Pit - ter, pat - ter, sprin - kle, splat - ter

Rain - drops fall. What does it mat - ter?

D: (It) rained a mist, a mist, a mist,

The flow - ers by the rain were kissed.

A: Pit - ter, pat - ter, sprin - kle, splat - ter

Rain - drops fall, What does it mat - ter?

Rhythm in Movement

Children of all ages enjoy physical activity. Together with speech, movement is a natural means by which children can develop an understanding of rhythm. Their movement to an underlying pulse, to subdivisions of the beat, and to rhythmic patterns almost guarantees their understanding of these musical elements. Once their ears receive and bodies respond to rhythm, children internalize the sound and feeling, leading to conceptualization. They come to know quarter notes, because they have walked them, and a pattern such as ♩♪ because they have skipped it. No mathematical analysis or counting-out procedure is necessary. No notation is meaningful to children until they have sensed through movement its rhythmic essence.

Chant the words, create a body percussion sequence (of patting, clapping, snapping), and add an ostinato chant:

Doctor Foster (England)

Doc - tor Fos - ter went to Glou - cester In a sho - wer of rain. He

stepped in a pud - dle right up to his mid - dle and he ne - ver went there a - gain.

Vocal Ostinato:

In a sho - wer of rain. Oh my!

When children are provided with occasions for moving rhythmically to music, they develop conceptual understanding relative to their natural developmental stage. Rhythmic movement may require their coordinated use of larger muscles in such locomotor activities as walking, running, skipping, galloping, hopping, jumping, or swaying, and in kinesthetic activities such as swinging the arms and conducting. Movement can also complement speech chants when children engage in patting, clapping, snapping, and stamping. Whether moving in place or across space, children grow in their understanding of rhythm when they can kinesthetically respond to what they hear.

The classic music pedagogies underscore the importance of movement as a tool for enhancing rhythmic development. The techniques of Dalcroze eurhythmics are based on the belief that rhythm is the fundamental element of music, whose source is the natural locomotor rhythms of the human body. Dalcroze eurhythmics includes exercises in conducting, stepping the beat, and changing movement qualities of speed, direction, and weight, all in an effort to reflect the rhythm of the music through movement. Carl Orff's elemental approach is based on the premise that rhythmic movement is inseparable from music itself, as it is also critical to the child's natural responses to his or her world. Rhythmic movement is not as central to the broader-based Schulwerk as it is to Dalcroze eurhythmics, but it nonetheless is an important avenue through which children can learn to sense rhythms more fully through basic body rhythms (patting, clapping, snapping, and stamping) and

> "To be completely musical, a child should possess an ensemble of physical and spiritual resources and capacities, comprising, on the one hand, ear, voice, and consciousness of sound, and on the other, the whole body (bone, muscle, and nervous systems), and the consciousness of bodily rhythm."
>
> **Émile Jaques-Dalcroze, 1921**

locomotor activities. The sequential teaching of proponents of the Kodály method maintains the use of folk dances as well as songs, and it recommends the curricular infusion of dances that demonstrate rhythmic concepts such as pulse, pattern, and metric unit. The logic of teaching rhythm through movement is undeniable and is woven throughout these and other pedagogies. See Chapter 6 for sample experiences in rhythmic movement for children.

The Pulse

Of the fundamental elements of rhythm, none is more basic in the Western world (and perhaps universally) than the pulse, or beat. Its presence is heard or felt in almost all music. It regulates music, because it is a recurring and steady stress underlying a variety of other rhythms, melodies, and textures. Regardless of whatever else is sounding within the music, "the beat [usually] goes on."

Children may demonstrate a sensitivity to the pulse as toddlers, rocking steadily to recorded music. Other children are still coming to terms with a feeling of pulse in the intermediate grades. While sensitivity varies, most children can maintain a steady clapping pulse by the age of eight. For comprehensive rhythmic development to occur, children must first be able to follow the pulse present in the music. Lesson 7.9 can be expanded to a complete lesson, offering experiences that serve to establish sensitivity to musical pulse.

"The beat [usually] goes on."

LESSON 7.9   Establishing Sensitivity to Musical Pulse

1. Play a recording of a Sousa march or a rock song. Ask children to clap the pulse. Model the clapping of the beat in correct time. Pat the beat on the shoulder of those who are having difficulty or place your hands on theirs to direct their clapping.

2. Ask children to show the pulse by patting their knees. On the cue word *change*, children show the pulse elsewhere (clapping hands, patting shoulders or head, snapping fingers).

3. Write the one-syllable names of children in the group horizontally across the board. Ask children to pat a steady pulse on their knees and then to chant:

   Juan   Anne   Jim   Jane   Pat   Tom   Mike   Lynn

4. Ask children to pat the pulse on their knees as they sing familiar songs such as "Knick-Knack Paddy Whack," "Frère Jacques," or "Old Joe Clark."

5. Play a steady pulse on a drum or a melody with a steady pulse on piano or xylophone. Ask children to sit facing a partner and to roll balls or pass bean bags to each other on every pulse.

6. Ask children to form small groups and to create a chant of one-syllable and two-syllable words in a single category: colors, animals, insects, flowers, and cars. Ask them to determine a way of sounding a steady beat as they prepare their chant pieces for performance.

© Patricia Shehan Campbell

Meter

In most music, the steady and regular pulse, or beat, is defined by accent, or emphasis that is given to some but not all pulses. The recurring pattern of stronger and weaker pulses is called meter. More than independent pulses, an understanding of meter enables the listener to perceive the flow of musical ideas.

Time signatures at the beginning of a notated piece are indications of meter, or the number of pulses in a musical unit or measure. Bar lines separate one measure from another. In general, the top number shows the number of pulses, while the bottom number signifies the value of the note that receives one pulse. For example, in $\frac{2}{4}$ meter, there are two pulses per measure, and the pulse is notated as a quarter note (♩). In a compound meter such as $\frac{6}{8}$ or $\frac{7}{8}$, there are six or seven pulses per measure, and the pulse is notated as an eighth note (♪). An exception to this rule is when the tempo quickens: The six eighth notes in $\frac{6}{8}$ are heard and felt in two groups of three instead of as six separate pulses (♪♪♩ ♪♪♩). For children, the feeling of a quick $\frac{6}{8}$ in a song such as "Oh Dear, What Can the Matter Be?" or "The Farmer in the Dell" is easily felt; it is only the explanation that appears complex.

Children come to understand meter through attentive listening and through kinesthetic responses that follow the musical flow of stronger and weaker sounds. As early as age three or four, children listen and respond to music in two or four beats (duple meter), three beats (triple meter), and a quick-paced compound meter. Some children respond naturally by rocking, swinging, swaying, chanting rhymes, and singing, but

1. Play a selection of recordings in various meters. Ask children to pat their knees on the strong beats and to hold on the weak beats. Play the recordings again, asking children to continue to pat their knees on the strong beats and to find another movement (clap, snap, or pat floor) for each of the weak beats.

2. Lead children in chanting the following phrases while patting the strong beats and clapping the weak beats (p = pat, c = clap).

most require a model to lead them to sensing the appropriate loud-and-soft metrical pulses. Children in the intermediate grades who are skilled in identifying these basic meters can be challenged to combine 2 + 3 pulses or 3 + 2 + 2 pulses in asymmetric meters such as $\frac{5}{4}, \frac{5}{8}, \frac{7}{4}$, or $\frac{7}{8}$, or to alternate meters such as $\frac{4}{4}$ and $\frac{3}{4}$ in mixed meter.

Various approaches lead children to an understanding of meter, some requiring movement. Speech rhythms accompanied by rhythmic ostinati involving body movements such as patting, clapping, snapping, and stamping reinforce the concept of meter. Conducting is another primary means of sensing the strong and weak pulses: The strong pulse of each measure is shown by a vertical downbeat, while all other pulses are indicated somewhat horizontally. Children are frequently adept at learning conducting patterns for some of the commonly found meters. The experiences in Lesson 7.10 are useful in developing a sense of meter; they are techniques and strategies to be used in lessons of various levels. Taken collectively, they are the substance of a lesson on meter.

(Slow 6)
(Fast 6)

Skip-ping feels good when you do it as one, but

(Slow 6)
(Fast 6)

Skip-ping with friends is for - ev - er more fun.

3. Draw basic conducting patterns on the board. Lead children in drawing the conducting patterns in the air. Chant aloud the words *strong* for the first down-beat and *weak* for all other pulses. As children learn the conducting patterns, sing or hum familiar songs in the appropriate meter.

4. Ask children to play improvised melodies on the piano or xylophone. Other children can listen, step the pulse, and identify the meter by conducting.

5. Sing a familiar song such as "Row Your Boat" or "Yankee Doodle" in a different meter while patting and clapping or conducting.

6. In small groups, create a recurring movement pattern that can be repeatedly performed to a predetermined song or recording.

Conducting the meter

© Jerry Gay

- Guide young children in using the words *same* and *different* to describe repeated or contrasting rhythm patterns.
- Play the rhythms of a familiar song on a drum, asking young children to imitate those rhythms on their own instruments.
- As young children listen to recordings, encourage them to keep the steady pulse of the music by patting, clapping, or stepping.
- Rhythmically chant a poem with young children, encouraging them to stress the metric accents.
- Develop rhythmic dialogues with young children in which they individually play a rhythm the length of four pulses, to be repeated by the group.

Durations and Their Patterns

As the fundamental pulse, or beat, and then the accented and unaccented pulses of meter are understood, children gradually become aware that chants, songs, and recorded musical works contain other rhythmic elements as well. While keeping the pulse, children may be rhythmically chanting two words or three syllables. They may be singing songs that appear to have faster rhythms, for example, with more rhythmic durations and pitches than they are conducting. In fact, the rhythms are more accurately viewed as shorter rather than faster (and also longer rather than slower) than the pulse. As they listen to a recording, children may find more rhythmic diversity than the meter beats they have been asked to identify. Rhythm is fundamental to music in its underlying pulse, but it also decorates and energizes music through its many durations that are longer and shorter, and faster and slower, than the pulse.

Durational values may be viewed as subdivisions or extensions, for example, elongations, of the basic pulse. If the pulse is symbolized by ♩, then its subdivision is ♫ or two eighth notes. Twice the length of the quarter-note pulse is ♩, and four times the pulse is 𝅝. While these durational values can be analyzed mathematically, this is not the manner by which rhythm is perceived by children—or adults. Instead, music is commonly perceived as patterns of durations and pitches, not as single isolated sounds. These patterns often occur more than once in a song or musical composition, offering coherence, tying musical ideas together, and giving the work a sense of a unified whole. Thus, children learn rhythmic durations with relative ease when sounds are linked together in patterns instead of when single sounds are treated mathematically.

When rhythmic patterns are associated with the chants and songs children have performed, their learning is accelerated. Once children have had opportunities to perform rhythmic patterns within the music, these patterns and even individual durations can be extracted, chanted, played on pitched and nonpitched percussion instruments, and used as a basis for improvisation. Further rhythmic development can occur as children are challenged to identify these patterns in new songs, to create chants and songs that incorporate them, and ultimately to read and write them.

Proponents of the Kodály method offer a sequence for the teaching of rhythmic patterns that derive logically from traditional songs that children sing. The sequence begins with quarter- and eighth-note patterns and is followed by the introduction of the half note, sixteenth notes, syncopated patterns, and patterns of compound meters such as $\frac{6}{8}$, $\frac{9}{8}$, $\frac{5}{8}$, or $\frac{7}{8}$. The first patterns of quarter and eighth notes are usually four pulses long, but those patterns with other durations may be briefer than that. Box 7.1 provides a logical order for the presentation of rhythmic patterns to children, along with familiar children's songs in which the patterns are found. Information on Kodály-inspired sequences for teaching rhythm may be found in works by Szönyi (1974–1979) and Choksy (1999a, 1999b).

Many other permutations of single rhythmic durations are possible; in fact, the possible combinations of durations are nearly infinite. Likewise, most songs probably contain more

BOX 7.1 A Sequence of Rhythmic Patterns

Meter	Rhythmic Pattern	Song
Duple Meter:	$\frac{2}{4}$ ♩ ♩ / ♩ ♩	Bounce High
	$\frac{2}{4}$ ♩ ♩ / ♫ ♩	Rain, Rain, Go Away
	$\frac{2}{4}$ ♩ ♫ / ♩ ♩	Hey, Betty Martin
	$\frac{2}{4}$ ♫ ♫ / ♩ ♩	Little Sally Walker
	$\frac{2}{4}$ ♫ ♩ / ♫ ♩	Knick-Knack Paddy Whack
	$\frac{2}{4}$ ♩ / ♩ (half notes)	Tinga Layo
	$\frac{4}{4}$ ♩. ♪ ♩	Mighty Pretty Motion
Duple Meter:	$\frac{2}{4}$ ♩. ♪	All Around the Kitchen
	$\frac{2}{4}$ ♪. ♬	Old Joe Clarke
	$\frac{2}{4}$ ♩, ♪. ♬	All Round the Brickyard
Duple Meter:	$\frac{2}{4}$ ♪ ♩ ♩	Weevily Wheat
Duple Meter:	$\frac{4}{4}$ ♪, ♩. ♩ ♩ + ♩ ♪ ♪ ♩.	Little Johnny Brown
Duple Meter:	$\frac{2}{4}$ ♪ ♩ ♩	Liza Jane
	$\frac{2}{4}$ ♪ ♩ ♩	Leila
Duple Meter:	$\frac{4}{4}$ ♪ ♩ ♪	I Got a Letter This Morning
Duple Meter:	$\frac{4}{4}$ ♪ ♪ ♩ ♪ ♪	Singabahambayo
Duple Meter:	$\frac{2}{4}$ ♬♬ ; also ♩ ♬	Kookaburra
Duple Meter:	$\frac{2}{4}$ ♫ ♪ , ♬♬	Michael Finnigan
	$\frac{2}{4}$ ♬♬♪ , ♩ ♫	Dance Josey

(Continued)

BOX 7.1 (Continued)

Hey, Betty Martin (United States)

Hey, Bet-ty Mar-tin, tip-toe, tip-toe, Hey, Bet-ty

Mar-tin, tip-toe fine, Hey, Bet-ty Mar-tin, tip-toe,

tip-toe, Hey, Bet-ty Mar-tin, please be mine.

Little Sally Walker (United States)

Lit-tle Sal-ly Wal-ker sit-ting in a sau-cer,

Rise Sal-ly, rise, Sal-ly, wipe a-way your tears, Sal-ly,

turn to the east, Saly-ly, turn to the west, Sal-ly,

turn to the one that you love the best, Sal-ly.

Knick-Knack Paddy Whack (United States)

This old man, he played one, He played Knick-Knack on my thumb, With a

Knick-Knack pad-dy whack, give the dog a bone, This old man comes rol-ling home.

(Continued)

BOX 7.1 (*Continued*)

stop right still, Cock - y doo - dle doo - dle doo, Put your
hand on your hip, Cock - y doo - dle doo - dle doo, Let your
right foot slip, Cock - y doo - dle doo - dle doo, Then
do like this, Cock - y doo - dle doo - dle doo, Then
do like this, Cock - y doo - dle doo - dle doo.__

Old Joe Clarke (United States)

Round and round, old Joe Clarke, Round and round, I say,

Fine

Round and round, old Joe Clarke, I ain't got long to stay.

Old Joe Clarke he had a house, Six - teen sto - ries high,

D.C. al fine

Ev' - ry sto - ry in that house Was full of chick - en pie.

All 'Round the Brickyard (United States)

All 'round the brick - yard, re - mem ber me, I'm gon - na

(Continued)

BOX 7.1 (Continued)

I Got a Letter This Morning (United States, African-American)

I got a let-ter this morn-in', Oh, yes,

I got a let-ter this morn-in', Oh, Oh, yes.

Weevily Wheat (United States)

Don't want your wee-vil-y wheat, Don't want your bar-ley,

Take some flour in half an hour and bake a cake for Char-lie.

Five times five is twen-ty-five, Five times six is thir-ty,

Five times sev'n is thir-ty-five, Five times eight is for-ty.

BOX 7.1 (*Continued*)

Liza Jane (United States)

I've got a house in Bal - ti - more, li'l Li - za Jane.

Street car runs right by my door, li'l Li - za Jane.

Oh E - li - za, li'l Li - za Jane,

Oh E - li - za, li'l Li - za Jane.

Leila (United States)

Lei - la, that's shoe my love. Lei - la, that's shoe my love.

Turn me in a hur - ry now. Shoe ba - by, shoe my love.

Singabahambayo (South Africa)

Sin - ga - ba - ham - ba - yo thi - na, ku - lom - hla - ba. __
Oh, we are march - ing for free - dom, we're go - ing home. _

Ke - pha si - ne - kha - ya,___ e - Zul - wi - ni.___
Our hearts are filled with joy.___ Sing girl and boy!_

Ha - le - lu - ya!___ Ha - le - lu - ya!___

Ha - le - lu - ya! Ha - le - lu - ya! Ha - le - lu - ya!___

Kookaburra (Australia)

Kook-a-bur-ra sits on an old gum tree, _ Mer-ry, mer-ry king of the bush is he. _

Laugh, Kook-a - bur-ra, Laugh, Kook-a - bur-ra, good your life must be.

Michael Finnigan (United States)

1. There was an old man named Mi - chael Fin - ni - gan,
2. There was an old man named Mi - chael Fin - ni - gan,
3. There was an old man named Mi - chael Fin - ni - gan,

He had whis - kers on his chin - ni - gan, The
He went fish - ing with a pin - ni - gan, He
Climbed a tree and barked his thin - ni - gan, He

(Continued)

BOX 7.1 (Continued)

wind came up and blew them in a - gain,
caught a fish but dropped it in a - gain,
lost a - bout a yard of skin - ni - gan,

Poor old Mi - chael Fin - ni - gan, Be - gin a - gain.

4. There was an old man named Michael Finnigan,
He grew fat and then grew thinnigan,
Then he died and had to begin again,
Poor old Michael Finnigan, Begin again,

Dance Josey (United States)

Chick-en on the fence post, can't dance Jo - sey, Chick-en on the fence post, can't dance Jo - sey.

Chick-en on the fence post, can't dance Jo - sey, Hel - lo Su - san Brown - i - oh!

Tideo (United States)

Pass one win - dow Ti - de - o, pass two win - dows Ti - de - o.

Pass three win - dows Ti - de - o. Jing - le at the win - dow Ti - de - o.

Zum Gali Gali (Israel)

Zum ga-li ga-li, ga-li, Zum ga-li ga - li, Zum ga-li ga-li, ga-li, Zum ga-li ga - li.

1. Pi - o-neer work hard on the land; ___ Men and wom-en work hand in hand.
2. As they la - bor all day ___ long, ___ They ___ lift their voice in ___ song.

Skip to My Lou (United States)

Fly's in the but-ter-milk, Shoo fly shoo, Fly's in the but-ter-milk, Shoo fly shoo,

Fly's in the but-ter-milk, Shoo fly shoo Skip to my Lou my dar - ling.

A la Rueda de San Miguel (Mexico)

1. A la rue - da la rue - da de San Mi - guel,
2. Rea - dy here we go danc-ing for San Mi - guel,

(Continued)

BOX 7.1 (*Continued*)

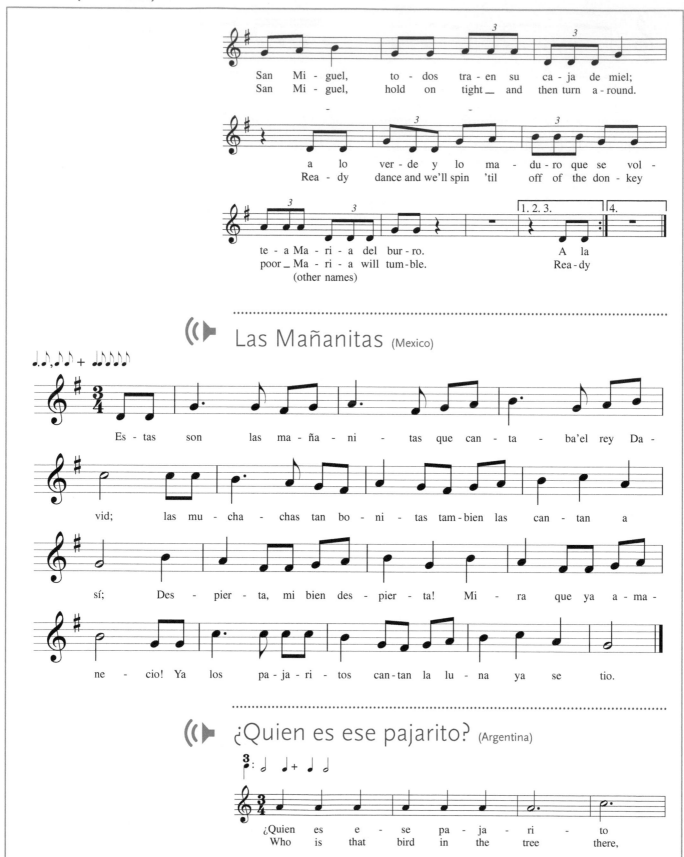

San Mi - guel, to - dos tra - en su ca - ja de miel;
San Mi - guel, hold on tight __ and then turn a - round.

a lo ver - de y lo ma - du - ro que se vol -
Rea - dy dance and we'll spin 'til off of the don - key

te - a Ma - ri - a del bur - ro.
poor __ Ma - ri - a will tum - ble.
(other names)

1. 2. 3. A la
4. Rea - dy

Las Mañanitas (Mexico)

Es - tas son las ma - ña - ni - tas que can - ta - ba'el rey Da -

vid; las mu - cha - chas tan bo - ni - tas tam - bien las can - tan a

sí; Des - pier - ta, mi bien des - pier - ta! Mi - ra que ya a - ma -

ne - cio! Ya los pa - ja - ri - tos can - tan la lu - na ya se tio.

¿Quien es ese pajarito? (Argentina)

¿Quien es e - se pa - ja - ri - to
Who is that bird in the tree there,

que can - ta   so - bre_el li - mon? _____   An - da y
sing - ing   on   lem - on tree   limb? _____   Go   and

di - le _____   que no can - te _____   que me
tell   him _____   to stop   sing - ing _____   as he

ro - ba_el   co - ra - zon. _____
ste - als   my   heart   a - way. _____

Charlie's Neat (Scotland)

Char - lie's neat   and   Char - lie's sweet   and   Char - lie   he's   a   dan - dy.   Char - lie   is   the

ve - ry   lad   that   stole   my   su - gar   can - dy.   O - ver   the   ri - ver   to

feed   my   sheep.   Ov - er   the   ri - ver   to   Char - lie.   O - ver   the   ri - ver   to

feed   my   sheep   and   mea - sure   up   my   bar - ley.

Sing Together (United States)

Sing,   sing   to - geth - er,   Mer - ri - ly   mer - ri - ly   sing.

(Continued)

BOX 7.1 (Continued)

Sing, sing to - geth - er. Mer - ri - ly mer - ri - ly sing.

Sing.   Sing.   Sing.   Sing.

Oh, How Lovely Is the Evening (England)

Oh, how love - ly is the eve - ning is the eve - ning.

When the bells are sweet - ly sing - ing sweet - ly sing - ing.

Ding Dong Ding Dong Ding Dong.

Billy Boy (England)

Where have ye been all the day?
Is she fit to be your wife? Bil - ly Boy, Bil - ly Boy,
Can she cook an I - rish stew?

Where have ye been all the day?
Is she fit to be your wife me Bil - ly Boy?
Can she cook an I - rish stew?

I've been walk - in' all the day with me char - min' Nan - cy Gray.
She's a fit to be me wife as the fork is to ___ the knife and me
She can cook an I - rish stew eye and sing in Hin - nies too,

Nan - cy Kit - tle - me - fan - cy. Oh, me char - min' Bil - ly Boy. ___

The Ship's Carpenteer (England)

'Twas in Lis-burgh of late a — fair dam-sel did dwell; Her

wit and her beau-ty — no one could e'er tell. She — was

loved by a fair one — who called her his dear And

he by his trade was — a ship's car-pen-teer.

Mountain Climbing (Bulgaria)

Climb-ing up the moun-tains see the pret-ty sights be - low.
Lead the way up to the moun-tain, sing-ing as we go.

See the vil-lage hous-es scat-tered by the riv-er - side.
At the top we'll dance to-geth - er cel - e-bra-ting time.

than one pattern that can be highlighted and extracted for chanting, clapping, stepping, and playing experiences. The pedagogical mission is to lead children to a more complete and lasting understanding of rhythm when it is experienced in the songs that they sing.

Rhythm Mnemonics

Because music is an aural phenomenon, it is logical to assume that rhythm can be learned by listening—at least at first. In many cultures, rhythms are transmitted by master musicians and teachers to their students without the assistance of notation, graphs, or other visual aids (Campbell, 1991). While literacy is an important goal of school music instruction, it cannot be fully developed without children first internalizing the sound of the rhythm. As in many oral cultures, rhythm is thus effectively taught to children through

> "Because music is an aural phenomenon, it is logical to assume that rhythm can be learned by listening—at least at first."

rhythm syllables called mnemonics (pronounced "neh-mon-iks"). These mnemonics have no semantic meaning and are associated with specific rhythmic durations.

Several mnemonics systems have proven successful in introducing rhythms to children, have developed their inner hearing of these rhythms, and have led to their reading and writing of rhythms. These systems include the word-chant system similar to the speech rhythms of Orff-Schulwerk and to Kodály and Gordon syllables. There are also notable historical systems, counting systems, culture-specific systems, and systems that combine duration and drum syllable strokes. Those systems most commonly and effectively used in teaching rhythm to children in American schools will now be described.

In that speech rhythms are fundamental to the Orff-Schulwerk, the fixed word-chant system may have been derived from that approach. In the word-chant system, each rhythmic duration is assigned a specific word, often at the discretion of the teacher. These words may be chosen from one category or another. For example, if "fruit" is the selected category, then a quarter note may be chanted as "pear" whenever it occurs in a pattern, eighth notes as "ap-ple," sixteenth notes as "boy-sen-ber-ry," and so on. Any word combination is possible in a longer phrase, and because these words designate specific durations, they serve as mnemonics for internalizing the rhythms and patterns.

One well-known tool of the Kodály method is its rhythm duration syllables. The syllables are related to the French Chevé system of mnemonics, which dates to the early nineteenth century and was practiced in conservatories throughout Europe, before being popularized by the Hungarians in their musical education of children. The crisp dental "t" sound begins most syllables, and the more sustained syllables are sounded as "ah" for each pulse. Like the Orff-inspired word-chant, the Kodály syllables can be combined in as many ways as there are rhythmic patterns and phrases. The chanting of these syllables is known to lead successfully to the reading and writing of notation.

Edwin E. Gordon proposed another mnemonics system, based on the rhythm syllables first suggested by McHose and Tibbs in the 1940s. Similar to the word-chant and Kodály systems, syllables are learned orally so that audiation, or inner hearing, can be developed before the introduction of notation. Similar to the Kodály syllables, there is a crispness to the "d's" and "t's" that initiate them. In the Gordon system, "du" is used whenever the melodic rhythm pattern coincides with the underlying macro beat feeling. For example, in $\frac{4}{4}$ where four macro beats are felt in a measure, a series of eight eighth notes would be "du-de-du-de-du-de-du-de," and if only two macro beats were felt in the measure, the syllables would be "du-ta-de-ta-du-ta-de-ta." While Kodály syllables are always associated with the same written note value regardless of the rhythmic feeling or meter, Gordon syllables are associated with the sound of the rhythm patterns as they relate to the feeling of the underlying macro and micro beats that constitute the meter.

Box 7.2 offers a comparison of the word-chant, Kodály, and Gordon syllable systems, featuring rhythmic durations and patterns that can be offered intact or adapted to suit the musical needs of children. In all three systems, rests are taught as beats of silence. They may be chanted in hushed tones, or their durational words and syllables may be merely thought and felt instead of voiced.

The use of a mnemonics system is an important part of children's music learning, and it is most effective when used consistently and without overlap into other systems. Rhythm syllables allow children to build an extensive vocabulary of rhythmic patterns and to discriminate between individual durations, their patterns, and the characteristic meters in which they are set. Children who have internalized rhythms through chant are thus prepared to read and write the notation that symbolizes their sounds.

"While in many cultures music is thought of as a pattern of sounds, in fact, the durations, pauses, rests, or empty spaces which surround the sound are also a vital element in delineating patterns in our perception."

Robert Garfias, 2004

BOX 7.2 Rhythm Mnemonics

DURATION	WORD-CHANT	KODALY		GORDON
♩	pear	ta		du
♫	ap - ple	ti - ti	4/4	du - de
♪	date	ti		du, de, or ta
♬♬	boy - sen - ber - ry	ti - ri - ti - ri	2/4	du - ta - de - ta
(triplet)	pine - ap - ple	tri - o - la	2/4	du - da - di
♩.	peach	ta - i		du –
♩.♫♩	co - co - nut	tim - ri - ta	4/4	du - ta du
♩	plum	ta - ah		du du –

Phrase

SENSORY NEEDS

- *Blind or visually impaired*: Because rhythm is aurally discernible, the visually impaired may actually "best" their sighted classmates in the extent of their listening acuity. Braille notation is available, too, and there are technological means for darkening and enlarging notation.

- *Deaf or hearing impaired*: It is certainly possible to feel rhythm through the vibrations on a drum, on a wood floor, or on a raised wooden platform. Visual cues can help, too, directing children to the durations as they are sounding live or on recordings, and hand gestures and full-body movement can enhance the rhythmic flow (and specific rhythms) of the music.

BEHAVIORAL NEEDS

- *Externalizing behaviors*: Remind an acting-out child of the appropriate behaviors necessary for staying in the activities for listening, playing, singing, moving, and reading/writing rhythms, and of the consequences for not staying in control of his/her behaviors. Spend a few minutes prior to or following class, or at recess, in review of expectations for music class.

- *Internalizing behaviors*: The withdrawn child may light up for those rhythmicking activities that do not put him/her on the spot, and a teacher's occasional nod, smile, or friendly pat on the back may encourage participation.

MOBILITY IMPAIRMENT

- Many experiences in rhythm trigger movement responses, and a teacher's modeling of modified movement can be useful. For vocalized rhythms (chanting syllables, for example), slow the tempo a bit and build in additional repetitions so that through practice children with mobility impairments can develop their skills.

AUTISM SPECTRUM

- Given the manner in which the act of making music can be a communal and collective enterprise that fosters communication, rhythmicking in call-and-response dialogue can be a successful means of connecting drummers and/or players of woodblocks, bells, and shakers. Children learn that the object of even basic rhythmicking is in connecting to the lead player who responds with a rhythm that imitates (or complements) the call their friend or classmate offered.

Notation for Writing and Reading Rhythms

All avenues of musical experience lead eventually to notational literacy, so that children may attain a comprehensive musicianship. While sensitivity to music's rhythm—its pulse, meter, and durations—is developed through chants, songs, and movement, a child's musical education is more encompassing when he or she becomes musically literate. Music literacy is the ability (1) to see symbols and to think or reproduce the sound, and (2) to hear the sound and to think or write the symbols. Just as the reading of words can be systematically learned by children following their experience in the spoken language, music notation can be learned when its teaching is systematically addressed.

The adage "sounds before symbols" serves as a slogan for the teaching of rhythmic notation to children. A rhythmic pattern sounded by the teacher on piano, xylophone, or hand drum is often understood by children through movement. When children coordinate their bodies to step, clap, or realize this pattern through a combination of body rhythms, they are prepared for the Dalcrozian "dash-a-note" challenge. Children can draw horizontal dashes from left to right on a chalkboard to represent what they hear and feel: the longer the sound, the longer the dash. The dashes are eventually converted into notes, with vertical stems and noteheads drawn. Dash-a-note maps can be drawn in the air or on paper, but the rhythmic patterns require ample large-muscle movement experience before they can be drawn accurately. Before and after the advent of literacy, this technique can solidify the relationship of rhythmic sound to symbol.

One of the tools of the Kodály practice involves the initial use of note stems for rhythm reading. All stem notes (except half notes) are notated without the body of the note (for example, $|$ = ♩ and ⊓ = ♫). This releases children from the time-consuming act of coloring in the noteheads, so that dictation can envelop a greater number of rhythms per class period. Rhythmic patterns are heard and quickly depicted by writing only the stems. Variations of this technique include the use by younger children of Popsicle sticks, rhythm sticks, and dowels to represent patterns.

If children can learn to read and write letters, words, and sentences, they can also decipher, interpret, and write rhythmic notation. Through the kindergarten year, rhythmic learning should be experiential, while children are discovering the sounds of their environment and playing with them. By first grade, children are ready to match

Showing notation as cue for clapping rhythms

rhythms to circles or discs, squares, diamonds, hearts, stick people, or vertical lines. These images represent the rhythms of familiar songs children have previously sung. As children hear the various combinations of quarter notes and eighth notes, they can follow the images that represent the pulse and its subdivision, pointing to the sounds that are ordered from left to right on the blackboard, feltboard, or floor. If children have sung "Knick-Knack Paddy Whack," for example, and have chanted the syllables for some of its patterns, they are ready to read the images that represent the rhythm and to write them out using selected shapes or sticks. Such a lesson appears in Lesson 7.11 and is suitable for children in grades one and two.

LESSON 7.11 Reading and Writing Music

1. Pat the pulse while singing "Knick-Knack Paddy Whack."

2. Ask children to listen to the clapped pattern while they pat the pulse:

3. Identify the words for the pattern:

"This   old   man,   he   played   one"

4. Chant mnemonics for the pattern:

ti - ti   ta   ti - ti   ta

5. Draw the pattern in the air and on the blackboard:

—— —— —— ——

6. Follow images on blackboard or feltboard while chanting and clapping:

ap - ple   pear   ap - ple   pear
ti - ti   ta   ti - ti   ta
du - de   du   du - de   du

7. Construct the rhythmic pattern by laying sticks on the floor:

8. Point to sticks or blackboard images while singing "Knick-Knack Paddy Whack."

9. At a later time, children can be evaluated for their ability to (1) aurally identify the sounded pattern, (2) read and perform its notation, and (3) notate its aurally presented sound.

The process for learning to read and write other patterns continues similarly as children mature, using rhythms that are increasingly complex. When they have developed their ability to print legibly (no later than second grade), children are also ready to take rhythmic dictation with paper and pencil. They no longer require the iconic visual images. Sticks and shapes are replaced by stem notation, and eventually children gain the facility to quickly attach noteheads to the stems. With practice, this can occur by the fourth grade. Central to the process of reading and writing, however, are singing, chanting, and movement experiences that must come first. The rhythm patterns presented above provide a logical progression for not only the performance experience in assorted rhythms, but also the development of notational literacy.

Syncopations

Some of the most exciting music that children can know consists of syncopation—rhythms that have displaced accents, in which unaccented rhythms are given emphasis while normally accented pulses are deemphasized. Popular, rock and roll, sub-Saharan African, African American, and Latin American music are replete with syncopated rhythms. While syncopation in its notated form is seldom introduced before the intermediate grades, children have listened to off-the-beat rhythms for many years. The concept of syncopation can be taught at an earlier stage through experience, analysis, and more experience. Lesson 7.12 provides a sampling of these experiences that can be partly or fully incorporated into lessons appropriate for use in grades three and four.

LESSON 7.12
Syncopation Experiences for Grades Three and Four

1. Clap or pat even pulses, accenting the first of every two.

2. On the cue word *change*, syncopate by accenting the second of every two pulses.

3. In two on-beat and off-beat groups, accent the first or second of every two pulses by patting the accent and clapping the unaccented pulse.

   Group I: on-beat

   Group II: off-beat

(Continued)

4. Practice chanting rhythm syllables and applying body rhythms for syncopated patterns.

date	pear	date	date	pear	date
ti	ta	ti	ti	ta	ti
du	de	de	du	de	de

5. Seek out the syncopated patterns in these songs, chanting and clapping them while tapping the steady pulse or conducting the meter.

Bucket of Water (Jamaica)

Draw me a buck-et of wa - ter for my old - est daugh - ter,

none in the bunch, no none in the bunch you go un - der sis-ter Sal - ly.

Sansa Kroma (Ghana)

San - sa kro - ma Ne nay woo ah chay chay ko - ko - ma.

San - sa kro - ma Ne nay woo ah chay chay ko - ko - ma.

Kye Kye Kule (Ghana)

Kye kye ku - le Kye kye ku - le Kye kye ko-fee - sah
(Chay chay koo - lay)

Kye kye ko-fee - sah ko-fee - sah lang - a ko-fee sah lang - a

Ko-ko - shi-lang - a ko-ko - shi-lang - a kum a-den - de
(day)

kum a-den - de kum a-den - de Hey!
(day) (day)

Polyrhythms

Rhythms can occur one after another (sequentially) or they can occur simultaneously. In the polyphonic music from the European Renaissance and in much of the music of sub-Saharan Africa and the Caribbean, and African-influenced music of both North and South America, two or more rhythmic layers that sound simultaneously provide the striking rhythmic feature known as polyrhythm. When children are capable of keeping a steady pulse and of chanting, clapping, and playing rhythmic patterns that last eight or more pulses, they have achieved the musicianship required to perform one rhythm as other rhythms are sounding. By the third grade, most children possess the rhythmic stability necessary to perform polyrhythmic pieces. It will take the teacher's careful sequencing of lessons, however, for children to perform them cleanly, steadily, and independently yet cooperatively, as is the nature of polyrhythm. Lessons 7.13 through 7.15 suggest three sets of experiences that easily comprise three single lessons to develop an understanding of the intricacies of polyrhythm.

Playing polyrhythms on African- and Latin-inspired classroom instruments

© Jerry Gay

LESSON 7.13 The Eight-Count Polyrhythm

1. Learn to perform the eight-count polyrhythm.
   (a) Chant the two rhythmic patterns separately.
   (b) Clap and chant the patterns separately.
   (c) Clap and (silently) chant the patterns separately.

(Continued)

(d) Divide into two groups; clap the patterns separately.

(e) In two groups, clap the patterns together (four or more times).

(f) For greater rhythmic clarity, choose different body sounds on which each group plays its rhythm: hand-clap, lap-pat, foot-stamp, finger-snap, vocalizations.

(1)

1 — 3 4 — 6 7 —

(2)

1 2 — — 5 6 — 8

LESSON 7.14 A Four-Part Polyrhythm

2. Follow the same sequence as above, but increase the number of groups to clap this four-part polyrhythm. Transfer to different body rhythms and instruments.

(a) (clap, woodblock)

1 — 3 4 — 6 7 — 9 10 — 12

(b) (snap, rattle)

1 2 3 4 5 6 7 8 9 10 — —

(c) (pat, iron bell, tone bell)

1 — — — 5 6 — 8 9 — 11 12

(d) (stamp, drum)

1 2 3 — 5 6 — 8 — 10 — 12

LESSON 7.15 Creating Polyrhythms

3. Challenge children to perform a personal polyrhythm in their bodies.

(a) Clap and chant the following rhythm:

1 — 3 — 5 6 7 —

(b) Step and chant the following rhythm:

(c) Combine the stepping and clapping patterns.

(d) Create new eight-beat patterns that interlock with (a) and (b), to be snapped and patted.

Accomplishing Multiple Music Standards through Listening

1. *Singing*: Sing songs with rhythm syllables, using ta's and ti-ti's (and other appropriate syllables) through the song. Chanting rhythms of songs is a standard vocalization effort as well.

2. *Playing*: Play on nonpitched percussion instruments the beat of a song while singing, or the rhythm of the melody, or just specific highlighted rhythms.

3. *Improvising*: Given a four-beat (or eight-beat) rhythm, challenge children to find four different ways to play it on pitched percussion instruments, varying the pitch but holding firm on the rhythm.

4. *Composing and Arranging*: Assign groups of children a four-beat (or eight-beat) rhythm for building a eight (or sixteen-) measure piece. Suggest that the rhythm should sound at least twice, on various pitched or nonpitched instruments, and that the invention of a contrasting rhythm will offer variety to the composition.

5. *Reading and Notating*: Practice reading the notation of familiar and new music, with special attention to seeking out familiar rhythm patterns.

6. *Listening*: As various recordings are playing of orchestral music and chamber music, popular and rock songs, and music of the world's cultures, listen for rhythms that repeat. Pat or clap them, then notate them.

7. *Analyzing and Evaluating*: As the class sings, plays, and creates rhythms, have children listen with a keen ear for rhythmic accuracy to include steady tempo, beat, meter, and particular patterns.

8. *Connecting to Other Arts and Curricular Areas*: Use the body in dancelike movements to show pulse, meter, and rhythm. Notice the rhythms of the spoken word in film, and the repeated patterns of color, shape, and texture that offer a sense of the visual rhythm of paintings and photographs.

9. *Connecting to Culture and History*: Rhythm is (almost) always present in music, and by listening to music of Bulgaria, Brazil, Tanzania, Thailand, Schubert, and Schoenberg, children can grow an appreciation of people's valuing of a diversity of rhythms.

From Natural Rhythms to Rhythmic Training: Rhythmicking Well!

Children demonstrate their natural rhythms in nearly all that they do, but primarily through speech and movement. The challenge for teachers is to channel these natural rhythms into an understanding of one of music's most elemental parts. The challenge becomes greater when teachers recognize the need to season instruction with the playfulness with which children have perceived and explored rhythm from their earliest years. Some of the most powerful musical experiences children can know may be the discovery of how their own physical energy can be ordered, regularized, and combined with others in rhythmic chant, song, and movement. Rhythm may be the magical dynamism that attracts and maintains the interest of children in music, both in school and out.

Teachers and parents can explore with children the rhythmic components of language and the manner in which rhythmic movement can add to their enjoyment of singing a song or listening to music. Children's conceptual understanding of rhythm—its pulse, meter, and durations—can be developed further through experiences that associate listening with speech and movement, leading to inner hearing. There is a logical sequence in the introduction of rhythm patterns, from pulses and their subdivisions to sixteenth notes and syncopations, and from rhythms in duple meter to those in triple and compound meters. There is a logical learning order as well in the progression from sound to symbol, as teachers guide children through listen-and-response experiences in rhythm, to chanting their mnemonic syllables, to reading the rhythms that are notated, to notating the rhythms that are heard. This is the musical foundation that can be formed in the elementary grades and from which more sophisticated musical understanding can proceed.

Formative Assessment

For every song that is sung, beat-keeping can be assessed through the patting and clapping that children do. Their ability to stay in time (tempo) and to give accent to some pulses over others (meter) can be readily seen and heard, as children respond through movement to listening examples, songs they sing, and little musical pieces they play on instruments. Teachers often find that regular assessments of durational patterns and rhythmic phrases can be inserted into lessons as five-minute spots, in which children clap and chant short 4-beat or 8-beat phrases from laminated cards, or on a screen. Problem patterns are repeated, and may later emerge in full-bodied eurhythmic lessons where children respond to a teacher's playing of the pattern on piano or drum while children step it across the floor; later, the pattern is revisited in vocalizations and body percussion.

Summative Assessment

By the close of a unit, a semester's set of lessons, or a full year of musical instruction, a thoughtful sequence will lead children to the development of their capacity to listen for and discern aspects of rhythm, and to express rhythmic patterns vocally, in body percussion, and on instruments. For every age and grade level, there are rhythmic patterns that are embedded in songs they sing and that they eventually can read. Individual and small-group assessments can be done in class, and can even be exciting to children who enjoy a little competition or an opportunity to show their competence on a skill. There is very reason to believe that a regular program of instruction will lead to children's rhythmic development, particularly when the teacher keeps a close watch on regularly occurring experiences in rhythm.

TECHNOLOGY *for* **TEACHING** *and* **LEARNING**
MUSIC: RHYTHM *and the* **CHILD**

Several software programs are available to help children learn about music rhythm. To learn more, visit the Technology Resources links in the MindTap.

MINDTAP

Scenario

MR. KIM KEEPS A CLOSE watch on rhythm as an important component of his class lessons, and he exudes rhythm in every interaction he has with his children. He greets them in rhythmic salutations ("Hel-lo there and how-do-you-do? I'm pleased to be mak-ing mu-sic with you!"), has a drum as he pulses them into their places in their seating arrangement on the carpeted floor, and then moves to the smartboard to show them "the rhythm of the day." The fourth grade children see the sixteenth notes, and on cue they chant "ti-ki-ti-ki" until he signals them to stop, accenting the first of the four syllables with a clap. Mr. Kim asks the children to pat the rhythm on their laps while he plays it on the piano, and then he instructs six children at a time to play the rhythm on the conga drums that sit in the front of the room. He keeps them together (and keeps the music interesting) by improvising melodies at the piano, consistently providing a chord on the first of the four durations in the pattern. The children are tuned to the rhythm of the day, and Mr. Kim keeps the focus as he then joins to sing "Kookaburra" while he plays the melody on the piano and they pat the rhythm of the melody on their laps. He challenges them further in several revolutions of the song, asking them to pat only the "ti-ki-ti-ki" rhythm while staying silent on the rest of the song, and then to sing aloud the entire song while tapping the sixteenth notes.

The children then hear the melody of an unfamiliar song as Mr. Kim asks them to find "the rhythm of the day" and to pat it. In answer to his question, "How many times did you hear 'ti-ki-ti-ki'?," the children respond correctly. Mr. Kim then sings this new song in full, "Michael Finnigan," asking them to check their answer. He sings the song again, challenging the children to find a rhythm that is not-quite the rhythm of the day. He is searching for their listening identification of two-sixteenths and an eighth-note, "ti-ki-ti—" and several children raise their hands in recognition. Mr. Kim proceeds to a conga drum and sings while playing the new "not-quite-rhythm" along with "the rhythm of the day." He then plays the two-sixteenths and eighth-note rhythm while chanting, and invites the children to pat and chant along with him. By now, "Michael Finnigan" is sounding familiar to the children and they sing it all the way through with Mr. Kim playing the two sixteenth-note patterns as they occur. He asks the children whether they would know how to write the rhythm for "Fin-ni-gan" and "in-a-gain," and one boy near the front says "Easy: ti-ki-ti—" two-sixteenths and an eighth-note." Mr. Kim smiles, projects the whole song onto the screen, and the children sing through the song with their teacher chording at the piano, lead-singing, and the children patting the sixteenth notes. He invites one child up to play the pulse on a cowbell, another to play eighth-notes on the claves, and six drummers to play the two sixteenth-note patterns. Every child gets a chance to play as he rotates through the class.

The rhythm of the day is built into a short poem that Mr. Kim proceeds to recite:

"Com-ing-and-a- go-ing-and-I'm

mov-ing-might-y fast. I

may-not-be-the first-but-I-will

nev-er-be-the last."

He follows a sequence of changing, patting, clapping, and body percussion that his children are clearly familiar with.

Sequence

1. Rhythmically chant the rhyme or poem
2. Pat the steady pulse, rhythmically chant again
3. Repeat (2)
4. Clap the rhythm of the words while rhythmically chanting aloud
5. Clap the rhythm of the words while rhythmically thinking them
6. Play a body percussion rhythm to/with the word-rhythms
   (use stamps, pats, claps, snaps, slaps, etc.)
7. Repeat (6)
8. Play a body percussion rhythm while rhythmically thinking the word-rhythms
9. Repeat (6)

The children are stamping and patting in precision, and are delighted with what they are accomplishing in their rhythmic ways. The class comes to a close with a listening selection of Irish traditional fiddles and a bodhran drum beating away sixteenth notes, as Mr. Kim lightly plays the conga and the children pat along. Mr. Kim sends them off with a challenge: "I expect you to come back ready to sing Michael Finnigan and Kookaburra, to play the sixteenth-notes, and to be ready to add another 'ti-ki-ti-ki' song to the mix!"

Questions

1. Was the rhythm of Mr. Kim's lesson appropriate for the age/grade level of his children? Were the instructional strategies geared to their experience level?
2. What segments of the lesson have the potential to invite chaos or confusion? How might a teacher like Mr. Kim keep the children focused and on-task?
3. In the sequence of rhythmic engagement, create a body percussion rhythm (#6).

REVIEW

1. Differentiate between speech and rhythmic speech. In what ways does language offer a means by which rhythmic understanding can be developed?
2. In what order should these rhythmic concepts be presented to children and at what ages or grade levels: accents, duration and durational patterns, syncopation, pulse, meter, polyrhythms?
3. Why is $\frac{6}{8}$ called a compound meter? How does the definition apply to $\frac{12}{8}$, $\frac{5}{8}$, or $\frac{7}{8}$?
4. Discuss the function of mnemonics, and compare the grammar of the more frequently found systems. What other systems are in use?

CRITICAL THINKING

5. How does the achievement of music literacy contribute to the comprehensiveness of children's musical sensitivity and understanding?
6. To what extent might rhythm be the featured activity in learning to sing a song? For example, discuss multiple ways to underscore rhythmic components in "Zum Gali Gali" and how these strategies enhance song learning.

PROJECTS

1. Listen to recordings of musical works of various styles. Compile a list of ten works that can be used to teach concepts of rhythm to children. For each work, determine its meter and prominent rhythmic patterns.

2. Choose five colloquialisms, proverbs, or famous quotations. Recite them aloud, listening for accents and durations. Notate their rhythms in duple and triple meter.

3. Select a rhythmic pattern, and prepare a ten-minute lesson that incorporates rhythmic speech chant and body rhythms.

4. Analyze the rhythmic content of ten traditional children's songs. Arrange them in order of complexity, noting the repeated rhythmic patterns that might be highlighted in a lesson for children. Recommend the grade level at which the song's rhythms would be suitable for learning.

MINDTAP Visit **MindTap** to access classroom videos, audio, and more!

8

The Playing Child

IN THIS CHAPTER

- Developmental Sequence
- The Body as a Percussion Instrument
- Nonpitched Percussion Instruments
  - Gourds
  - Woods
  - Skins (Drums)
  - Metals
- Pitched Instruments
  - Barred Instruments of the Orff Approach
  - The Recorder
- Harmony Instruments
  - The Autoharp
  - The Guitar
  - Keyboards
- Assessment of Playing Instruments
  - Formative Evaluations
  - Summative Evaluations
- The Benefits of Instrumental Study
- Scenario
- Questions

STRIKE UP THE BAND, and the child is captivated by the colorful sounds of musical instruments. As the instruments thump, soar, chime, rattle, slide, shimmer, ring, bellow, and shake, the various timbres are as stimulating to children as they are spell-binding. And when children are given the chance to play, they do so with great pleasure. Janie beats the drum at a snappy and spirited speed. Andrew and Jorge hammer out melodies together on wooden xylophones. Shannon sings a song she knows while pushing chord keys on an Autoharp. Marcus practices two guitar chords over and over, creating new rhythmic strums as he goes. Rex and Evan are at the keyboard, playing a blues progression that matches a popular song's harmonies.

Children of all ages are players of musical instruments, or they would like to be. Infants shake rattles, toddlers bang on cardboard boxes, tables, chairs, or pots and pans. Toy pianos, flutes, and guitarlike instruments make popular birthday gifts for preschoolers. In early childhood centers, the highlight of any day is music making—especially when it includes the playing of drums, jingle bells, wooden sticks, and tambourines.

As children mature, pitched instruments available at home and in their elementary school classrooms can offer them challenging and gratifying musical experiences. Some instruments, such as the xylophone, recorder, and tone bells, are for playing melodies; some, such as the Autoharp and guitar, primarily produce harmonies or chords. Ensembles of xylophones or recorders provide both melody and harmonic accompaniment. Keyboard instruments such as piano, organ, MIDI (Musical Instrument Digital Interface) synthesizers, small tabletop or lap pianos, and piano apps for laptops and iPhones provide musical challenges to older children. Children continue to be fascinated by nonpitched rhythm instruments through the elementary years, particularly by drums of all sizes and shapes—kettle, bongo, conga, and hand drums. Whether they play alone, in small groups, or in full ensemble, children will play to be heard and to hear themselves play.

Because of their natural attraction to the sounds of musical instruments, it is well within the realm of reason for children to achieve the skills set by the National Standards in Music for their age and grade levels. They are capable of playing at least one instrument—be it recorder, keyboard, xylophone, guitar, or one of a wide selection of percussion instruments, band and orchestral instruments, or instruments of the steel drum (pan), mariachi, gamelan, Zimbabwean-style marimbas, and other heritage ensembles—accurately and independently, alone and in ensemble, with appropriate playing techniques. Given the opportunity, children will perform the music of diverse genres and cultures with expression and technical accuracy. With their curiosity for instruments piqued early in their development, children are able to produce instrumental sounds by ear and to read the music that corresponds to a selected instrument. In a curricular program that allows for exploratory experiences and regular, sequential instruction, children can become proficient on nearly any instrument they choose.

Beyond the solo performance of an instrument, or its performance in a standard ensemble, instrument playing is often the icing on the cake in the performance of sung music in a class lesson. Songs such as "Little Johnny Brown," "This Train," "I Got a Letter This Morning," "San Sereni," "Skye Boat Song," and "Sansa Kroma" can be enhanced through accompaniments on pitched and nonpitched percussion instruments, by the addition of a countermelody on recorder, or by chordal harmonies on keyboard or guitar. Children can learn just enough on classroom instruments to provide ostinati for songs like these, for interludes, and for introductions and codas. They can also grow to a greater level of accomplishment and provide more intricate, polyphonic textures for a vocal line. They can create new musical expressions through the instruments they play, working individually and in partners and small groups to come up with fresh new pieces that fit the structural parameters of a particular style, genre, or teacher-prescribed activity. Along with their use in singing and creating experiences, instruments can underscore and reinforce concepts that are the focus of a listening lesson and even be used as accompaniment to any number of folk dances. From preschool explorations with instruments, children can be guided to grow their instrumental skills to a level that will serve them in many musical ways.

Developmental Sequence

CHILDREN'S ABILITIES TO PLAY musical instruments are closely related to their physical development. An example of this relationship might be seen in the playing of maracas or gourd rattles found in much African and Latin American music. Infants in their fourth and fifth months master the task of grasping toys and other objects, including their own baby rattles, and are already on their way to making music. By the time children are three years old, they have usually developed the muscle control that goes with playing and silencing the rattle at will. Primary-grade children have the coordination as well as the perceptiveness to keep the musical pulse and to play basic rhythmic patterns. Children in the intermediate grades can become adept at playing a host of rhythms on maracas, due to their physical maturation, musical perception, and cognitive understanding of the characteristics of the music they are making.

While rhythmic skills are usually the first to emerge—as early as the first year of life— the muscular coordination essential to playing musical instruments may develop much later. The early rhythmic rocking of an infant leads later to the swinging of the arms (about age three), which progresses to the alternation of one hand and then the other for playing two mallets on a drum (about age five or six). The more sophisticated eye-hand coordination skills begin to be refined from the age of seven onward, becoming more perfect through practice. For example, eye-hand coordination allows the child's visual sense to signal and set his or her neurophysical system in gear in the complex operation of striking a xylophone key. Something so seemingly simple as playing a melody on piano requires motoric machinery that involves the eyes, ears, and multiple muscles of the finger, hand, and forearm. Add to that the coordination of the breathing apparatus in the playing of wind instruments, and it is no wonder that recorders are only introduced to children in the third or fourth grade, with instruction on orchestral wind and brass instruments initiated at the close of the elementary school years, in fifth or sixth grade.

The pedagogy of Shinichi Suzuki has been widely recognized for the manner in which it develops listening skills and performance techniques at an early age. While the image of pint-sized violins comes to mind, it is the philosophy and practices of the Suzuki approach that attracts parents and their children. Suzuki called the method "Talent Education" and based it on the premise that all children are born musical. The tenet that children learn musical instruments in the same way they learn to speak is reflected through seven principles of Suzuki's method: (1) begin early, with listening at birth and lessons from about two-and-a-half years onward; (2) delay music reading until musical skills and performance techniques have developed; (3) involve parents in lessons and home practice; (4) use excellent music literature that is developmentally appropriate; (5) balance private lessons (for attention to technical skills) with group lessons (for motivation and socialization); (6) repeat, review, and reinforce the performance of previously learned music; and (7) accentuate self-development while deemphasizing competition. The Suzuki method maintains that children will develop musically through their instrument when they are given occasion to develop the motor abilities necessary for performance on violin (or cello, piano, flute, and numerous other instruments).

But because motoric development progresses naturally and is largely unassisted by such specialized instruction as Suzuki, children learn best when presented with experiences playing musical instruments that match their developmental abilities. This is not to say that the exploration of assorted sounds that musical instruments can produce cannot be initiated in earlier stages; such discovery learning should be encouraged at every age. Still, children are likely to cultivate performance techniques on an instrument when they are physically ready to do so, thus the importance of matching motoric development to instruments. Table 8.1 provides a sequence for the formal introduction of musical instruments into children's performance experiences. Playing techniques introduced at a given age will require practice for refinement.

"The goal of instruction is to develop students who depend upon the sound of a piece rather than upon a musical score."

Shinichi Suzuki, 1963

TABLE 8.1 Developmental Sequence for Playing Instruments

AGE	MUSICAL-MOTORIC DEVELOPMENT	INSTRUMENTS; INSTRUMENTAL TECHNIQUES
LESS THAN TWO YEARS	Rocking, nodding, swaying Capacity to grip and grasp	Rattles (shaking) Jingle bells (shaking)
TWO TO THREE	Short periods of rhythmic regularity	Hand drum (hand tapping) Sticks (striking)
THREE TO FOUR	Longer periods of rhythmic regularity Sensitivity to pulse Swaying of arms	Claves (striking) Sticks (rubbing) Woodblock (mallet striking, rubbing) Sandblocks (rubbing)

		Tambourine (shaking, striking)
		Guiro (rubbing)
		Maracas (shaking)
		Gong (mallet striking)
		Cowbell (mallet striking)
FIVE TO SIX (KINDERGARTEN TO GRADE ONE)	Maintenance of pulse Alternation of hands Basic eye-hand coordination	Finger cymbals (striking rim to rim) Bongo drums (hand striking) Timpani (mallet striking) Cymbals (striking) Triangle (mallet striking) Keyboard (one hand)
SEVEN TO NINE (GRADES TWO TO THREE)	Eye-hand coordination	Finger cymbals (striking; attached) Slit log drum (mallet striking) Temple blocks (mallet striking) Conga drum (hand striking) Goblet drum (hand striking) Double iron agogo bells (mallet striking) Tone bells (mallet striking) Xylophone (simple drone, bourdon, ostinato; two mallets striking) Keyboard (both hands, melody with chords) Recorder (g-d') Autoharp (chording)
TEN TO TWELVE (GRADES FOUR TO SIX)	Increased facility of eye-hand coordination Finger flexibility Control of breathing apparatus	Xylophone (moving drone, ostinato, melody; two mallets striking) Keyboard (both hands, two moving parts) Recorder (c-g') Guitar (chording) Orchestral wind and brass

The Body as a Percussion Instrument

The body can be viewed as a musical instrument. Clapping, slapping, tapping, snapping, stamping, and patting the shoulders, head, elbows, knees, and stomach produce various sounds that delight children everywhere. In some cultures, the body is considered one of the primary sources of musical sound. For example, African American sacred songs, particularly folk spirituals and gospel, often feature clapping, just as African American folk songs frequently include hand jives of slaps, claps, and snaps. The potential for timbral variety through corpophones, the body's sound producers, has gone unnoticed in some cultures but nonetheless can be successfully brought into the culture of the classroom.

Children at play often create their own original body-percussion pieces. They can also learn through imitation body-percussion sounds that can enhance their rhythm skills, increasing their vocabulary of internalized rhythms. With guidance, children can be

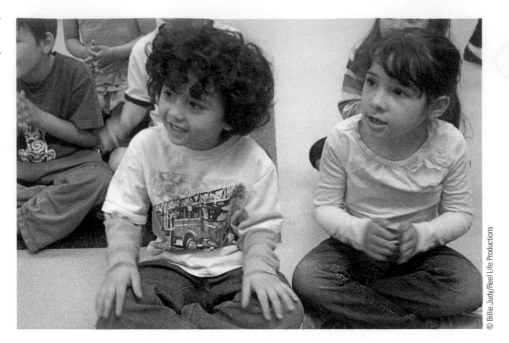

© Billie Judy/Reel Life Productions

led to perform ensemble pieces that feature the rhythms of body percussion, one pattern layered on another. Body percussion makes for an exciting performance piece for audiences of parents, other children, and people in the community.

Body-percussion exercises can also be used to prepare children to perform on non-pitched rhythm and barred instruments. By patting the rhythm of an ostinato on their laps, children are better able to play the pattern on a drum, a woodblock, or a xylophone. Even guitar and Autoharp strums can be played first in the air, while fingers can play imaginary recorders and piano keyboards on the arm, the floor, or a tabletop. A reward for initially working out the rhythm through a body-percussion exercise is the opportunity to play it on the instrument itself. Examples of body-percussion pieces and exercises that can stand on their own, or be transferred to instruments, are found in Lesson 8.1.

LESSON 8.1 Experiences in Body Percussion

1. Teach the rhythms through measure-by-measure imitation, with the intention of engaging all children in performing all parts in body percussion.

2. Transfer rhythms to instruments, to be performed by four groups of children.

3. Transfer these complete rhythm phrases to xylophones to be played on any keys of the pentaton according to children's personal choices.

4. Teach the following rhythms through imitation. Practice to perform the parts in three groups that gradually combine, overlap, repeat, increase in volume, and conclude on cue.

(Continued)

Possible Performance Plan: Arrange children in three groups of equal numbers, to be placed in three circles, one long line, or an open-ended, three-sided square. The director may wish to use claves to keep a constant pulse and to aurally signal changes, additions, or deletions of groups in some preplanned way. Group one begins performing its rhythm, continuing as group two enters, followed by the entrance of group three. A previous form can be determined, so that groups perform, wait out several cycles, and return again; one such form is given on the next page. The director can cue louder and softer cycles, while the pulse remains the same throughout. Basic movements (such as changing the direction the children face) may be added for visual impact, although the major objective is the performance of polyrhythms through body percussion.

Suggested Form: Numbers stand for group, one complete rhythm cycle per number.

Sequence of Groups in Rhythm Performance, with Dynamics

Group 1 1	1	1	1		1	1	1	1		1	1	1	1		1	1	1	1
Group 2	2	2			2	2		2	2		2	2		2	2		2	2
Group 3			3	3	3		3	3	3		3	3	3		3	3	3	

$$p < mf > p \quad f > p \quad f \quad mf \qquad p \quad f \quad mf < \quad f \quad p \quad f$$

Alternative Plan: All parts are combined into a six-measure pattern and learned. The six-measure rhythm is then performed in canon, with group two entering one measure after group one, and so forth.

Methodological Suggestions for Early Childhood

- **Guide young children to an awareness** of their own bodies as sources of sound by hand clapping; finger snapping; patting laps, chests, and heads; tongue clicking; foot stamping; whistling; growling; cooing; and howling.

- **Allow young children discovery time** with various percussion, stringed, wind, and keyboard instruments, so that they might tap, click, pluck, bow, blow, shake, and press keys on instruments for the sounds they can offer.

- **Encourage the use of instruments** by young children to embellish and dramatize stories you read or tell to them, using instruments for individual characters and events.

- **Provide young children with the opportunity to create** their own "shows" of instrumental music mixed with story, song, and movement.

- **Arrange for young children to hear** up-front and in personal ways the instruments of visiting musicians as they are performed, demonstrated, and described.

Nonpitched Percussion Instruments

Also known as rhythm instruments, nonpitched percussion instruments are found nearly everywhere that children are gathered—from preschools to public schools, from child care centers to churches and temples. Rhythm instruments can be played alone or in groups, with or without pitched instruments such as xylophones or keyboards, to accompany songs, chants, poems, or stories. They can accent and interpret narratives, and they provide leitmotif-like sounds to represent story characters. They provide colorful timbres in improvisations and pieces composed by small groups of children. When played together in polyrhythmic fashion, they provide a fascinating complex of sound. Nonpitched percussion instruments may be classified as membranophones (various sizes and shapes of drums that produce sound through a vibrating skin or membrane) or idiophones (instruments of wood, metal, and gourd that are struck, shaken, scraped, or tapped). They may also be categorized according to the material from which they are made: woods, skins, metals, and gourds.

Children enjoy exploring the possible sounds that rhythm instruments can produce, either informally and independently or as stimulated by words of a poem or story. They should also be led by demonstration to learning the traditional ways of holding and playing the instruments to obtain the greatest resonance from them.

The musical quality of commercially available instruments varies somewhat, but many of them produce pleasant and resonant sounds that are attractive to children through their elementary years. A set of classroom instruments typically includes sticks, flat and notched woodblocks, cymbals, triangles, tambourines, jingle bells, and sandblocks. Additional rhythm instruments in these sets frequently include gongs, finger cymbals, cowbell, and claves. Of the many varieties of drums, those most typically found in well-stocked classrooms include hand drums, bongo drums, conga and goblet drums, and timpani. Still other nonpitched percussion instruments, including those from various world cultures, are the Latin American guiro, claves, and maracas; West African double iron agogo bells and djembe drum; East Asian temple blocks; and the slit log drum, commonly found in West and Central Africa. Some of these instruments can be made by a teacher or parent, or by children as an art project, although their musical quality may be questionable. A number of nonpitched percussion instruments are described on the following pages, along with techniques for playing them. A vast array of the world's percussion instruments are documented in a wide variety of on-line sources such as www.themim.org.

> "[In Africa] the mental and emotional aspects of drum performance, whether it involves individual members or the whole ensemble… call for a full exercise of musical talent, which most players believe is manifest from early childhood."
>
> **Andrew Tracey and Joshua Uzoigwe, 2003**

Gourds

MARACAS (also rattle, shekere, hosho, cabasa). Found throughout Latin America, maracas are pairs of dried gourds with seeds inside, which are shaken like rattles. Those played in Mexico, the Caribbean, and South American countries are related to the rattles of Native American and West African cultures. The shekere, hosho, or cabasa, found throughout much of sub-Saharan Africa, is covered with a beaded netting that is moved by the hand, providing a scraped, rattling sound. Maracas are surprisingly difficult to play correctly, as the beads move around before and following the shaking motion. Thus, when rhythmic accuracy is important, they are best left to older children who are physically coordinated and have a strong sense of rhythm.

Woods

STICKS. Played in pairs, one stick is struck against the other. Ridged sticks rubbed against each other produce an alternative sound. Young children can learn to play the pulse accurately with sticks, and older children can find it stimulating to imitate interesting rhythms in group exercises.

CLAVES. Typically made of rosewood, claves are thick sticks about one inch in diameter. They are played by holding one clave in the cup of one hand and striking it with the other—a position that may take practice and some physical maturation to play correctly. Of the many rhythms, one of the best known Latino rhythms is this clave pattern: |♩.♩.♩|♩♩♩|

WOODBLOCK. A partially hollowed block of wood, the woodblock produces its most resonant sound when struck with a wooden mallet over the slot on the wide surface. The tone block is a variant of the woodblock, with ridges around its hollowed cylindrical shape. It can be struck or rubbed with a mallet. Children enjoy discovering that so simple an instrument can produce an impressive variety of timbres.

TEMPLE BLOCKS. Similar to woodblocks, colorful temple blocks of about four or five sizes are positioned horizontally on a stand at about waist level. When struck by a wooden mallet, they produce sounds that are nearly (but not quite) pitched. These East Asian instruments can be used to accent songs from China, Taiwan, Japan, Korea, and Vietnam. While the tones may not match the pitches of a song, the temple blocks nonetheless provide the flavor of differentiated pitches, which children find attractive and enticing.

SANDBLOCKS. The friction of rubbing together two blocks of wood that are covered with sandpaper produces the swishing sound of sandblocks. Sandblocks can effectively instill in preschool- and primary-grade children the feel and sound of pulse and meter, and have a special appeal to kinesthetic learners of all ages.

SLIT LOG DRUM. Often just larger than a shoe box, the classroom version of the sub-Saharan African slit log drum consists of slits cut into the flat top side of a hollowed log or block of wood. The longer and shorter wooden slits are played with mallets, producing lower and higher sounds. Not really a drum at all, the slit log provides a set of colorful timbres in an improvisation or composition. Younger and older children alike are intrigued by the resonant quality of the varied pitches, and may select it out for sound-pieces of their own creation.

Wood, metal, skin, and rattle: Hand percussion instruments

© Jerry Gay

216

GUIRO. Pronounced "gwee-do," the ridged surface of this wooden instrument is scraped with a stick. Much of Latin America's music features its sound. Older children with a developed sense of rhythm and physical coordination are more likely than younger children to play it well and at a lively tempo.

Skins (Drums)

HAND DRUM. Named because it is held at the rim by the hand, the hand drum is played by striking its head with the other hand or with a mallet. On some, the skin can be tightened or loosened by adjusting the screws at the rim. The hand drum is useful for keeping the pulse and for playing rhythm patterns. Young children may play it on their laps, but the best sound comes from holding it with the hand or between the legs so as to open up the drum to fullest resonance.

BONGO DRUMS. Bongo drums are a pair of drums, usually connected by a wooden crosspiece, held on the lap or between the knees. Bongos are played with the finger-tips, the palm, and the thumbs. They play an important rhythm role in music from the Caribbean. These drums are found less often in classrooms than other drums, and unless proper playing techniques are applied, their full timbral advantage will not be known.

CONGA DRUM. A long upright drum in the shape of a narrow barrel with a skin head stretched across one end, the conga drum produces a variety of resonant timbres when the player strikes its center, edge, or wooden side with the palm and heel of the hand, the flat and cup of the hand, the fingertips, or even with sticks (at the side). Sounds reminiscent of Latin American and sub-Saharan African cultures emanate from the conga drum. It may be played alone or in pairs. For starters, older children may differentiate between tapping and slapping the drum heads, and then gradually be moved into one or more of the standard playing patterns.

DJEMBE DRUM. An instrument common to Ghana, the djembe drum is wide at the head and narrow at the base, standing about three feet from the floor. It is played with fingers and palms, often in groups, and personifies for many classrooms the West African sound. Children are attracted to its visual appeal (particularly the colorful commercial model), as well as to the resonant sound it produces.

Drumming sideways in a third grade music class

© Billie Judy/Reel Life Productions

GOBLET DRUM. An important Middle Eastern instrument, the goblet drum is wide at the head and narrow at the base, about eighteen inches high. It is played with fingertips and the palm of the hand at the center and edge of the head. It is also known as "dombek," "tombek," "darabukka," and "derbeki." Children of all ages can learn to tap out its differentiated center and side sounds.

TIMPANI. Similar to the symphonic timpani in function, the children's version can be tuned to the tonic, dominant, subdominant, or other prominent pitch of a musical piece by adjusting the screws at the rim. Timpani sit at about waist level on stands with metal legs, and they are played with padded mallets. They come in various sizes, so that several pitches in a piece can be sounded as a percussive bass line. Following individual instruction, older children are capable of producing ostinati with considerable accuracy.

Metals

CYMBALS. Two concave, metal disks (with knobs for holding), cymbals can be struck or rubbed together. They can also be played separately with a mallet or wire brush. Young children respond variously to this instrument, some enjoying the crashing sound and others finding it too voluminous.

FINGER CYMBALS. Finger cymbals are smaller versions of hand held cymbals. Elastic loops are used to attach the cymbals to the middle finger and thumb of the same hand. Finger cymbals produce ringing and muted sounds, and they are commonly heard in the performance of Middle Eastern music. They can also be played without attachment to the fingers, by touching the rim of one to the rim of the other. Because it takes time to adjust the elastic loops to the finger and thumb, and practice to develop the playing technique, older children do better with these cymbals than younger ones.

TRIANGLE. This three-sided instrument of metal or steel hangs from a string and is played by striking with a metal or wooden stick. Its bright timbre is useful for sounding accents. Children may find it hard to resist the fast "dinner-bell" sound of the triangle, and its vibration may seem like a tickling sensation to them.

TAMBOURINE. A tambourine features pairs of metal disks attached to a circular wooden rim that make a jingling sound when shaken. Tambourines with a drumhead are similar to a hand drum. Most of the countries bordering the Mediterranean, including Spain, Italy, Greece, Turkey, Israel, and Egypt, feature the tambourine in their songs and dances. Because its multiple jingles are sensitive to slight movement, older children may be more physically adept at playing it with rhythmic accuracy.

JINGLE BELLS. Small bells on a stick or a plastic ring worn around the wrist or ankles, jingle bells can be added to seasonal music and to the sounds of some Native American Indian groups. Children find the instrument particularly joyous in the clustering of sounds that it makes, although their sheer weight may challenge young children to shake it for a great length of time.

GONG. The flat brass gong found in orchestras is also an important percussion instrument in the music of China, and less so in other parts of East Asia. Played with a padded mallet or wooden stick, various sizes of gongs are capable of playing different pitches, providing bright and long sustained sounds. These flat gongs are not to be confused with the mellow-sounding knobbed gongs of Southeast Asia, including Indonesia. The coordination of mallet to gong surface can be challenging to some younger children, but older children have both the concentration and the coordination to play it in ways called for by the music.

COWBELL.   A bell found hung around the necks of cows, the cowbell produces open, lower sounds when struck by a mallet near its opening and closed, higher sounds when struck at the top near its handle. It is an important instrument in much Caribbean and South American dance music. Older children can learn the technique of closing and opening the hand on and off the bell itself, which adds timbral flavor.

DOUBLE IRON AGOGO BELLS.   Found in the West African iron-culture countries of Nigeria, Ghana, Dahomey, and the Ivory Coast, these connected iron bells of two sizes produce a higher- and lower-pitched sound when struck by a mallet. A polyrhythmic layering of patterns played simultaneously adds an authentic timbral color with agogo bells. Children are fascinated by the sound of the two bells, and when it can be worked steadily into its part in a polyrhythm, they cannot help but groove along with it.

These nonpitched percussion instruments provide an array of timbres for children's musical growth. They can develop children's aural awareness and can motivate children to learn to read rhythmic notation. A rhythm band approach (common in the 1930s and 1940s) is to be avoided. Children are capable of far more than merely striking, tapping, rubbing, or shaking instruments without direction or a coherent musical concept in mind. Instead, experiences such as those described in Lesson 8.2 allow children to sample timbral qualities and also to match the durations they hear with how they are symbolized. See the collections of Schmid (1998, 2003, 2012), Sipes (2011), and Solomon (1999) for ways to bring nonpitched percussion instruments, especially the drumming traditions of West Africa and the Caribbean, into a central place in the curriculum.

> *"In learning to drum in West African traditions, only after students grasp the entire musical idea do they play a part on drums. First, we chant mnemonic vocables; next, we play on our legs while vocalizing at the same time; then, we play the part in duet with the time-keeping parts."*
>
> **David Locke, 2004**

LESSON 8.2
Experiences with Nonpitched Percussion Instruments

1. Gather all of the available instruments together. Experiment with the possibilities for sound on each of them. Seek answers to these questions: Which ones produce pitched or nonpitched sounds? How many different sounds can be produced? What are the traditional ways of sound production? Can you invent new ways? Categorize the instruments according to material (gourd, wood, skin, and metal) or sound production (struck, shaken, rubbed).

2. Read a poem together. Ask children to choose instruments that can aid in the expression and interpretation of the poem.

THE DIESEL ENGINE
(P. S. Campbell)

Here,
About half-past eight,
   I like to hear the diesel engine whining.

Once,
It whirred, purred, and clicked,
   ticking track after track in a prearranged pulse.

Now,
It rattles, and coughs,
   spewing smoke in white puffs out its stumpy red stack.

Still,
I like to hear the diesel engine whining,
   about half-past eight.

(Continued)

3. Play a Latin-flavored rhythmic piece with these instruments and their ostinato patterns. First, chant the mnemonic syllables and word-phrases of the rhythms, then play by gradually adding one instrument after another. Play the piece with a recording of salsa music.

(open = strike at bell opening; close = strike at top near handle)

(Strike conga drum with left hand heel or fingertips; strike with right hand either flat or cupped.)

4. Divide children into small groups. Ask them to select a scene (the seashore, a forest, a busy downtown street, the building of a house, the last day of school) and to create the aural image of the scene by making a sound-piece performed by nonpitched instruments. Encourage free rhythms as well as pulsive pieces.

5. Encourage children to invent notation for their rhythmic compositions. Allow their own graphic notations to lead (or return) them to the reading of standard rhythmic notation of the Western staff.

Pitched Instruments

Children can play melodies and accompaniments on many kinds of instruments. Among them are the barred instruments, such as xylophones, metallophones, glockenspiels, and tone or melody bells; wind instruments, such as recorders and the closely related song flutes; chording instruments, such as guitars and Autoharps; and keyboards, such as pianos, lap pianos, synthesizers, and organs. A number of these pitched instruments are likely to be found in schools and in the home. They are described here, along with suggestions for their use in developing children's musical understanding and fundamental performance skills. Instructional resources are available for those who wish to teach or learn these instruments, which also provide children with skills, techniques, and repertoire beyond the beginning levels.

Barred Instruments of the Orff Approach

The barred instruments developed by German composer Carl Orff are widely known for their exceptional tone quality. These are often referred to as "Orff instruments" and consist of larger and smaller wooden or metal bars laid across a frame, which are struck by mallets made of wood, plastic, rubber, felt, wound yarn, or cloth. Other styles of metal xylophones, consisting of colored bars or black-and-white chromatic bars similar to a keyboard, predate the increasingly popular Orff-style instruments. Orff instruments were developed to complement the Orff-Schulwerk approach to teaching music to children. Still, they can be employed by all who wish to offer children instrumental experiences. The sounds are pleasing to the ears and attractive to children, who enjoy playing with sound, developing their playing skills, and expressing themselves through improvised and composed pieces they create. Whether played alone, in ensemble, or as an accompaniment for singing, the Orff instruments greatly enrich children's musical experiences.

Pitched and non-pitched percussion instruments a la Orff

FIGURE 8.1

Melodic Ranges of Barred Instruments

Ranges in pitch for the bass, alto, and soprano xylophone and metallophone, and the alto and soprano glockenspiel.

All barred instruments are notated as

but only alto xylophones and metallophones sound the actual notated pitch

The barred instruments of the Orff-Schulwerk consist of xylophones made of wood as well as metallophones and glockenspiels made of metal. The xylophones and metallophones come in three sizes (soprano, alto, and bass); glockenspiels, in two (soprano and alto). All contain a pitch range of a C to A octave (an octave and a sixth), in various registers (see Figure 8.1). The instruments can be played in combinations of different registers or groups of metals and woods.

Barred instruments are usually placed on the floor in front of the musicians, the larger, lower bars to their left, with the players sitting comfortably on the knees or cross-legged. (Glockenspiels can be elevated on a stack of books for easier access, eliminating the need to bend over.) There should be room for movement of the arms and elbows while playing. The mallets are held as if holding a hammer, hairbrush, or toothbrush. Some experimentation and practice may be necessary before the right spot to strike on the bar is found. Eye-hand coordination is critical for mastery in playing. For the best resonance, children should be encouraged to pull out the sound rather than hammer it in; the mallets should bounce away from the bars rather than rest on them.

The bars are removable, so that only those pitches necessary for a particular melody or accompaniment may be played. For example, if a pentatonic melody is to be played, then two bars per octave are removed, making it easier to play the melody. In the case of a repeated accompaniment pattern, or ostinato, all bars not a part of the pattern are removed, clearing the way for the ostinato. Additional bars provide the chromatic pitches for G major (F#) and F major (B♭); these are provided with the initial purchase. Other accidentals may be purchased, however, as well as fully chromatic instruments.

Barred instruments are most frequently used to supply an accompaniment to a song, using a wide array of musical techniques, from drones to ostinati. Examples of techniques for accompaniment are ordered from simple to more complex in Box 8.1. While not all-inclusive, these examples convey the flavor of the potential for instrumental accompaniment. The Brazilian children's song "Bambu" is an example of a simple orchestration for glockenspiel, xylophones, and nonpitched percussion instruments. These techniques require preparation before playing. Children should

BOX 8.1 Accompaniment Techniques on Xylophones, Metallophones, and Glockenspiels

Several ostinati can be combined to create colorful textures.

pat the patterns on their laps that they will eventually play on the instruments. The success with which these accompaniments are played will depend on children's motor development. Similarly, the extent to which they can be used to accompany folk songs and children's songs will depend on the teacher's musical ear and training. Orff-Schulwerk training offers lessons in orchestration and mastery of the performance techniques and the pedagogical process. A number of sources on Orff-Schulwerk describe and illustrate the various barred instruments, including Frazee (1987, 2007) and Steen (1992).

Barred instruments also function as melody instruments and as means for improvisation. Children can play songs they know on xylophones, either by ear or by reading notation. A host of familiar songs such as "Little Sally Walker," "Suogan," "Hey, Betty Martin," "I've Been to Harlem," "Leila," "Shortnin' Bread," and "Scotland's Burning" are excellent selections to challenge children to play what they already know, while they also master the instrument.

Barred instruments can be their own music-making experience, too, as in the marimba traditions of Guatemala and other coastal regions of Central and South America, and xylophones of the Chopi and Shona peoples of southeastern Africa. Wood and bronze or metal xylophones are found in southeastern Asia, too, as in Java and Bali and in the court music of Cambodia and Thailand. Children can be led to learning styles and structures of these musical experiences through transcriptions (and modified arrangements) of recorded music from these cultures and through collections by Hampton (1996, 1999), Campbell with Frega (2001), Lew and Campbell (2006), and Sam and Campbell (1992). The prospects of a children's full-blown marimba ensemble for public performances for parents and community members are rich, and the musical results can be nothing short of electric.

From imitation to expressive tasks, children can develop creative musical thinking and improvisatory skills through playing these instruments. For example, as children hear a rhythmic pattern of four or eight beats clapped by the teacher, they can play it back on the instruments, choosing pitches as they play. As they hear a short musical question played for them by a leader, children can play back an invented short musical answer. In another task, children can be directed to listen to a simple melody, and to play it back as closely as they can to the way they heard it—without delay. They can experiment with playing the simple melody softer or louder. They can also attempt to play it twice as fast or twice as slow. With partners, children can play musical dialogues, questioning and answering each other every four, six, or eight beats. They can take a known melody and vary it, adding an ostinato pattern. Alternately, they can take a drone and invent a melody for it. The possibilities for building their musicianship through instrumental improvisation are nearly endless, and the rewards are great.

Tone bells, also known as melody bells, belong to the family of barred instruments. They are separate metal bars attached to a resonating box, which are played with a plastic or rubber mallet. Tone bells are kept in a large box and can be played as a xylophone, or they can be distributed to a group of children to play a collaborative melody in a manner similar to that of a handbell choir, with each child contributing separate pitches to the melody. The tone quality is soft and bell-like; thus, tone bells function well as harmonic accompaniment to children's voices. In this function, children can contribute the root, third, and fifth (and seventh) of tonic, dominant, and subdominant chords to accompany a vast selection of folk and popular songs.

"Whether played alone, in ensemble, or as an accompaniment for singing, the Orff instruments greatly enrich children's musical experiences."

Bambu (Brazil)

The Recorder

The recorder was a popular instrument of the European Renaissance period. It is also among the most common melody instruments played by children in the elementary grades today. Various other instruments are related to the recorder, using the same playing techniques and featuring a similar pure, clear tone quality, including song flutes, flutophones, and tonettes. When children have been singing, listening with discrimination and in directed ways, and playing percussion instruments in their early years at home and in school, a logical next step is reading and playing melodies. When they show the physical development that enables them to move their fingers with ease, they are ready for the coordinated tasks of reading, breathing, and finger dexterity that are required to play the recorder. Beginning at about the age of nine, children in the third, fourth, and fifth grades are able and eager for the recorder, a pathway for furthering their musical understanding.

Children often relish the chance to play the recorder. For some, the recorder is an important precursor to the study of band instruments, and it is used to give them the feel of fingering the wind instruments they may later choose to study. The recorder is also an important means of understanding melody—its highs, lows, contours, and intervallic pitch relationships. In typical ensembles of Orff instruments found in elementary classrooms, the recorder is the only nonpercussive instrument (with the exception of the voice). The smooth and sustained melodic flow of the recorder is complementary to the more static and percussive sounds of the barred instruments.

Soprano recorders are best for beginners; alto recorders can be added after fundamental playing techniques are learned and after fingers have grown long and wide enough.

Playing the recorder in proper position

© Karen Howard

FIGURE 8.2

Recorder Fingerings: Baroque System

b   a   g   e   f   f#   d   b♭   c   c'   d'   e'

● Covered hole

○ Open hole

◐ Half-covered hole

Professional recorder musicians play wooden instruments, but those made of plastic are inexpensive and offer a surprisingly mellow tone when played gently. Most beginners' recorders come with a soft or plastic tubular case. The mouthpieces can be sterilized with hot water or with aerosol spray sanitizers. Instructional books are available for playing recorder, although a chart of fingerings, musical exercises, and familiar songs are all that may be needed to introduce children to the instrument.

Children will follow the model of the teacher in finding the correct playing position. The top of the mouthpiece is placed in front of the teeth between the lips. The left hand is placed above the right hand, and its fingers cover the back hole and the top front three holes. The right hand's fingers cover the bottom front four holes (including the bottom two double holes). Children must meet the challenges of (1) feeling the holes that they cannot easily see; (2) balancing the recorder with the thumbs at the back, the fingers at the front, and the mouth at the tip; (3) curving the fingers and placing the fleshy finger pads on the appropriate holes; and (4) blowing gently while forming the sound "doo" with the mouth and tongue. Fingerings are shown for the c–e´´ in Figure 8.2. When the sounds are incorrect or piercingly painful, the most common problems will be resolved by blowing more lightly and covering the (appropriate) holes.

One way to teach the recorder involves singing a familiar song, then singing it with letters, numbers, or solfège syllables while fingering it on the recorder, and finally playing it. Because children know many songs, they may be able to play them quickly, as they have already mentally processed the rise and fall of the melody and the repeated patterns. Songs such as "Mos' Mos!'," "Hop Old Squirrel," "Long-Legged Sailor," "Bow Wow Wow," and "Hey, Betty Martin" feature limited ranges and repeated patterns that children may find more easily transferable to their recorders. The second stage, singing while silently playing, is a critical one, because it links the sound with the kinesthetic feeling. During this stage, which may be repeated numerous times until the fingers move easily, children may hold their recorders at their chin to ensure that no tones are sounded.

The recorder is neither a toy nor an instrument limited to playing simple folk songs and exercises. An exciting repertoire is available for children who learn the fundamental performance techniques, which stem from fourteenth- through seventeenth-century Europe. Further, the music of other cultures, particularly some East Asian and Native American genres, can be played on recorder. Children can continue to play songs they know on recorder, as well as to invent their own. Those children who continue past the introductory lessons can eventually play the sophisticated music of a Renaissance consort or melodies found in Latin American (including Andean) wind ensembles (King, 1998). They can learn to play other sizes of recorders, such as alto, tenor, bass, or sopranino, too. Recorders combined with other timbres can be beautiful and aesthetically pleasing. Also, many songs that students hear on the radio or on compact discs (CDs) are simple enough to play on the recorder. Children can develop high levels of skill on recorder when challenged to learn high-interest songs as extra-credit projects on their own time. There are several recorder books noteworthy for classroom use, including those by Burakoff and Burakoff (1997), and Hall and Kelsey (2005).

Harmony Instruments

While all melody instruments are capable of producing a melody that functions harmonically by playing an ostinato or descant against a melody (such as xylophones, metallophones, and recorders), several instruments are known for their primary function as accompaniments for singing. The Autoharp and the guitar are chordal instruments found at school or at home. Both are social instruments arising from American musical heritages steeped in evening sing-alongs on the back porch, around the campfire, and in the parlor. While the guitar has long been an important part of the American pop and rock music scene, it still remains, along with the Autoharp, an important means of producing chords for any folk, popular, or personal music that children may wish to sing and play.

The Autoharp

Historically, one of the most important instruments for the accompaniment of folksingers in the Appalachian hill-country, the Ozark Mountains, and Anglo-American communities elsewhere was the Autoharp. It became useful to teachers who wanted a portable instrument to provide harmony to songs sung by children in the classroom or outdoors, one that could be easily learned by teachers and children alike. Its sound is soft enough to support children's singing voices without overwhelming them. By following chord markings in songbooks and music series texts, the Autoharp functions as a bona fide musical instrument almost immediately.

The Autoharp is a zither, commonly equipped with twelve, fifteen, or twenty-one chord bars that are depressed by pressing on buttons. When a button on the chord bar is pushed, the felts on the bottom of the bar are pressed against the strings that are not part of the chord, which silences those pitches. The chord names are printed on the buttons. The Autoharp player reads the chord names found above the melody line of notated songs and presses the corresponding chord bars with one hand while strumming the strings with the other. Different strumming patterns can be used to enhance rhythmic characteristics of a variety of songs.

While the Autoharp is generally easy to play, there are two challenges to consider. One is in the player's adjustment to the traditional Appalachian playing position, in which the Autoharp is held upright and somewhat diagonally, with the left hand pressing the buttons and the right hand crossing over the left to strum the strings. Alternative positions for children include laying the instrument flat on the lap, on a tabletop, or on the floor.

The second challenge is tuning the Autoharp, a time-consuming task even for those with a good ear. The instrument is affected by weather conditions, so tuning is necessary almost daily—and sometimes more frequently than that. A metal tuning key is provided for tightening the string to raise the pitch and for loosening it to lower the pitch. By pressing one chord button (for example, G major) and then slowly brushing across each G, B, and D string from highest to lowest, flat and sharp pitches can be heard and adjusted with the tuning key. At the very least, all pitches in chords of the song(s) to be played should be tuned. If the Autoharp is not in good tuning, it should not be played, or it may lead to out-of-tune singing. Electronic tuners greatly simplify this chore.

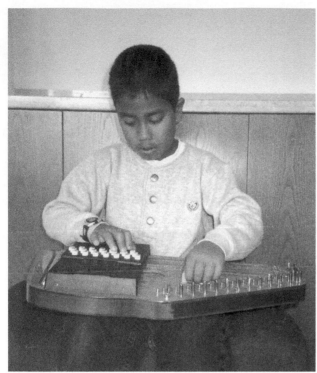

© Patricia Shehan Campbell

The advent of the Omnichord, a type of electronic Autoharp, eliminated the tuning difficulties of the acoustic instrument. The Omnichord has no strings but retains the push-button chord system. In addition, the Omni-chord plays rhythmic ostinati, waltz, and rock-style rhythms, and it can be set at various tempi, volumes, and timbres that include piano, guitar, brass, banjo, and chimes.

The Autoharp and its newer cousin facilitate children's awareness of harmony—major and minor chord qualities, the function of chords in their support of melody, and the relationship of tonic, dominant, subdominant, and mediant chords to one another. For children in the primary grades, the teacher may wish to press the chord buttons while a child strums the strings. Just as children in the intermediate grades are beginning to hear harmonic changes, they can also play the instrument by themselves. Familiar songs with one chord ("Shortnin' Bread," "Little Johnny Brown"), two chords ("Alabama Gal," "Bluebird," "Looby Loo," "I Went to California"), and three chords ("This Train," "Weevily Wheat," "Liza Jane," "Knick-Knack Paddy Whack") can be played by reading chord charts—or by ear, providing children with exercise in hearing harmonic changes as they sing. Further information on the Autoharp is available in Peterson (2002) and McCabe (2004).

The Guitar

Children are eager to learn the guitar long before they are able to play it, motivated by seeing and hearing it in many popular styles of music, from rock to country to folk, on TV, radio, recordings, and films. When their hands are sufficiently large to stretch around the neck to the strings, they are ready to play; for most children, that occurs around fourth grade.

There are many types of guitars, but the nylon-strung folk or classical guitars are easier on the fingers than the steel strings found on larger acoustic instruments. Nonamplified

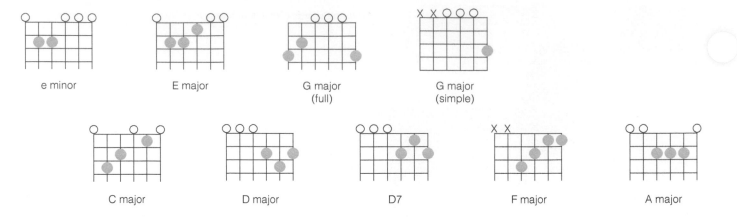

e minor   E major   G major (full)   G major (simple)

C major   D major   D7   F major   A major

FIGURE 8.3

Guitar Tablature for the Left Hand

electric guitars can also be played by children because, despite the steel strings, their necks are narrow and thus easier on the hand and finger expanse.

As a chording instrument, the guitar can accompany songs with as few as one, two (I, V), or three (I, IV, V) chords. The right-hand strums can be as basic as one chord per measure or per pulse, to syncopated rhythms and patterns that combine plucking with strumming. While there are many manuals for playing guitar, children often learn to play through observation and experimentation. Time spent in practice pays off; therefore children who play at home or who come to the music room before or after school can become proficient. The use of a capo, a plastic-covered bar that is clipped across the strings, extends the possibility to play song accompaniments in practically any key.

Children can play guitar accompaniments to songs they know even in their first lesson. Once they find a comfortable way to hold the guitar, imitating the teacher's seated position with the guitar resting on the crossed leg, they are ready to play their first chord: e minor. Figure 8.3 presents tablature, or fretboard diagrams, of chords in e minor, E major, G major (simplified and more sophisticated versions), C major, F major, A major, and D major (and D⁷). When they are played correctly, the left-hand fingers are curved, their tips pressing the designated strings to the fingerboard. Children should be checked and reminded to avoid touching other strings that are not a part of the chord configuration.

Once the fingers of the left hand are comfortable in their chord positions and in changing chords, children can begin to learn strumming patterns. Several common patterns are featured in Figure 8.4. They are best learned by saying "down" and "up" in rhythm before and while playing. Down refers to the downward brushing of the thumb from the lowest string to the highest; up is the thumb's upward brush across the higher to lower strings and toward the player's face. Strumming patterns add distinctive flavors to songs and soon separate beginners from more proficient players.

Children who have mastered a few chords and their strums can play the harmonic accompaniment for a great variety of songs. The e-minor chord alone enables children to play "Shalom Chaverim," "Hey, Ho, Nobody Home," and "Zum Gali Gali." The great majority of children's songs often require no more than three chords and often only the tonic and dominant. Guitar accompaniment is especially appropriate for such Latin American songs as "Tinga Layo," "Las Mañanitas," and "La Raspa." Collections of folk and popular songs are readily available with guitar accompaniment.

Tuning the guitar can present still another challenge, and the parent or teacher often must match the pitches of the six strings (E, A, D, G, B, e) to each other or to a pitch

FIGURE 8.4

Guitar Strums for the Right Hand

pipe, piano, or the guitar's special tuning pipes. Most instructional manuals feature tuning along with a great variety of chord tablatures and strumming and picking patterns. For a sequential handbook on playing folk guitar, including chording and picking patterns, see Schmid and Koch (2002) and Molenda (2007). The logistics of, and sequence for, teaching guitar in a classroom setting, with guitars for every child, are outlined in a manual by Bay and Christiansen (2000).

Keyboards

Either at home or in school, children are bound to have opportunities to play a keyboard; that is, pianos, organs, synthesizers, MIDI instruments, and lap pianos. Keyboards are the most popular type of instrument in American homes. Over half of American families today own acoustic or electronic pianos or organs.

Some electronic keyboards are inexpensive to own individually (for example, Casio models) and come with color-coded notation for playing familiar melodies and their chords. Frequently, children play with these or other types of pianos at home and are likely to have explored the black and white keys to figure out familiar songs. Keyboard instruments are often responsible for children's first chance to play music and may be the source of their growing interest in music. Some children have sampled chords and timbres with the press of a button. They may even have access in their homes to more sophisticated keyboard technology, including MIDI and assorted attachments that allow the sounds of rain forests, windstorms, and outer space to be mixed with violin, guitar, koto, and talking-drum timbres.

Most schools are likely to have available at least one classic grand or upright acoustic piano. The music room, auditorium, and assembly space are the most likely locations for the piano. When in tune and played well, the piano can bring unity to group singing of patriotic and traditional songs as well as add to the artistic quality of a choral performance. Yet it is far more than an accompaniment instrument. It can stimulate eurhythmic movement to music through its percussive quality and its broad spectrum of expressive capacities. It can illustrate musical features, from pitch to duration to dynamic intensity. It can add color and interest to stories and poems. The piano can also underscore and reinforce musical learning for children of every age.

Whether the music is initiated by the teacher to stimulate musical responses in children or whether the music is read and performed or invented by children themselves, keyboards provide an effective avenue of music instruction. Children can learn by observing the teacher play or by exploring on their own the concepts of scale, intervals, register, range, ascending and descending pitches, melodic contour, repetition, and sequence. They can experiment with tone matching (playing and then singing pitch patterns) and can come to terms with the function of the staff, treble and bass clefs, and notation when they take these to the piano. Children enjoy experimenting with the piano's potential as both a melodic and a harmonic instrument. For those who develop basic facility at the piano (or any keyboard), it will become an important channel for personal expression in the original music that they create.

In some schools, pianos are purchased as keyboard laboratories. A music room may thus be equipped with ten, twenty, or more electronic pianos on stands, with student headphones. The student pianos are linked to a teacher's station that includes piano and audio facilities for listening to the performances of individual students, small groups, or the entire class. Beginning in the intermediate grades, children can learn to read notation as well as basic piano technique through instruction manuals that progress from one-hand melodies to song melodies with simple chordal accompaniments, to full-fledged piano pieces from the classical and popular repertoire. Group piano classes in the schools are generally focused on learning about music—its structures and sonorities—through performance. See Chapter 3 for a discussion of the Yamaha Corporation's Music in Education program, and Chapter 17 for descriptions of MIDI and other technologies for making music and aiding music instruction.

Music teachers may be an important link to children's further training and development as pianists and as musicians. Because they have presented children with musical problems and have observed the nature of each child's capacity to solve them, music teachers are in a position to evaluate and recommend further instruction. They have noted the rhythmic capacity, aural acuity, and eye-hand coordination of individual children in group piano lessons or in other musical activities, and they can thus predict with reasonable accuracy the prognosis of children who wish to study piano (or other instruments) privately. For those children who enjoy playing piano, classroom instruction in keyboard laboratories is ideal. For those few who aspire to become pianists, the music teacher may offer a pathway.

Adapting Instruction for Various Needs

SENSORY NEEDS

- *Blind or visually impaired*: In many cultures, the blind and visually impaired are often competent and even highly accomplished musicians. Children may require additional practice time to adjust themselves spatially and kinesthetically to an instrument, and so arrangements should be made for their additional practice time. Children may learn by ear and by kinesthetic feel, even as Braille notation can be made available to them.

(Continued)

- *Deaf or hearing impaired*: Percussion instruments may be especially useful for children who are guided by vibration, and so drums of various sorts may appeal; Evelyn Glennie's amazing talent as a world-class percussionist comes to mind. As well, keyboards with headphones may be effective in transmitting sound.

BEHAVIORAL NEEDS

- *Externalizing behaviors*: Set careful guidelines for the acting-out child, and offer reminders of expectations and consequences for not meeting them. In this way, children can learn to control themselves for when to play and how to show respect for the manner in which instruments are played.

- *Internalizing behaviors*: A teacher can allow time for a withdrawn child to find his/her voice on an instrument, and pairing with a sensitive and sharing child may help to develop musical skill and expressive qualities.

MOBILITY IMPAIRED

- A number of instruments are adaptable with Velcro straps that fit mallets, wood blocks, and bells to the hand. Big knob sets of rhythm instruments are available to allow easier grasping, and thicker and shorter claves may work better than longer sticks.

Accomplishing Multiple Music Standards through Playing

1. *Singing*: Encourage children to sing (or chant, in the case of percussion instruments) the music they play, either preliminary to playing or as a means of reinforcing or underscoring the features of their instrumental music.

2. *Playing*: All of the ideas in this chapter connect to playing.

3. *Improvising*: Children do well to improvise on musical instruments. Some of it can be quite free-wheeling, as when the teacher cues them to take their instruments and simply "play" for 10- or 20-seconds, followed by a cue to stop. At other times, the teacher may offer parameters for improvisation on keyboard, or xylophones, or nonpitched percussion instruments, including definitions of length, prescribed pitch material, and rhythm patterns to feature.

4. *Composing and Arranging*: Challenge children to create (and notate) short pieces on favorite instruments, in small groups, in partners or individually. Such motivations as "seasons," or a poem, or a picture may lead to children's personal and collective expressions.

5. *Reading and Notation*: Offer opportunities to sight-read new music on their instruments, at a tempo that is comfortable for them.

6. *Listening*: Provide opportunities for hearing instrumental music performed by expert players of recorder, xylophone, marimbas, percussion ensembles, piano, guitar, and various other instrument they are learning to play.

7. *Analyzing and Evaluating*: Assess children as to their accuracy and tone on the musical instruments of choice, per rubrics and other teacher-constructed tools. They can also assess and evaluate their own instrumental technique, and that of their peers.

8. *Connecting to Other Arts and Curricular Areas*: Play music on classroom instruments to enliven stories, to accompany scripts created from the stories, and to accompany basic choreography in a movement piece.

9. *Connecting to Culture and History*: Using recorders, pitched and nonpitched percussion instruments, play music of other historical times and places, including "Alle Meine Entchen," "Savalivalah," "Billy Boy," and "Rocky Mountain."

Assessment of Playing Instruments

Children can rattle around on classroom instruments, trapped in an endless and non-progressive first-level exploratory stage. They can rigidly step through a routine of school-music skills that do not bring them personal satisfaction or an understanding of how these skills might be transferred to music making beyond school. Or they can succeed in developing the techniques and the musical intelligence for playing instruments as soloists and ensemble members, from notation or by ear, and with both technical facility and interpretative, improvisatory power. Pitch by pitch, and rhythmic duration by rhythmic phrase, children can progress to a repertoire of songs and musical sounds that give pleasure to them and those who listen. They can be so motivated by their own progress as to want to travel with their recorders, playing the tunes they learned in school and making up new ones, or to play their school keyboard compositions on the old family upright piano. They can be inspired by the rhythmic instruments they have begun to learn to want their own at home to play with their favorite CDs, or they can be driven to transfer the sense of harmony learned on xylophones (and the cooperative spirit of playing together) to a more perceptive ability to listen to harmonic changes, to perform harmonies on other instruments, and to create their own music, with a refined sense of how melodies and chords move.

Formative Evaluations

Children can sense their own progress in learning to play instruments, and they can be assessed (or can learn to self-assess) this progress in numerous ways. The following questions can frame this assessment.

1. Is the tone quality of your instrument, however simple the music, pleasing to your (and others') ears? Why or why not? (Check your playing position, as well as breath control and mouth and tongue actions for wind instruments.)

2. Is the performance of your instrument musically accurate? Are you reading the rhythms and pitches correctly? Are you listening carefully to the musical models, particularly in the case of traditional and popular music from oral traditions?

3. Are you playing with ease? (Check your fingerings, work on transitions between phrases, and play the harder parts repeatedly.)

4. Does the music sound the way you would like it to sound (within the parameters permitted by the musical work or tradition)? Are you able to express yourself as you would like to?

5. Can you play a piece alone, from start to finish, accurately and expressively? Can you play your instrument in tandem with others, listening to them and blending with them in their playing?

The teacher may wish to engage parents, too, in assessing the amount of daily or weekly practice time (particularly on instruments such as the recorder, which all children may be required to learn and to take home to practice). Like all musical activities that occur within the classroom, children's musical skills can be subject to ongoing and regular assessment, with teachers calling out remarks like "Good tone, Jenny," "Watch your rhythm on the second measure, Sean," "Take a bigger breath to float you through the phrase," and "We've got it, the whole piece by the whole class." Still, it is useful to provide individual feedback to children and to pull them into the realm of self-assessment by questioning them in ways that lead them to their own recognition of what it takes to play an instrument well.

Summative Evaluations

Checklists of exercises and specific phrases, scales, and songs learned can be posted to the classroom wall or stapled to the back of the instrumental manuals, to be filled in by the teacher for each individual student at the end of the year, term, or unit (or as he or she meets the requirements). A set of rubrics can be employed that cover the gamut from beginning to emerging, then proficient, and finally exemplary musicianship regarding the performance of repertoire that encompasses accurate pitch, rhythm, style, dynamics, phrasing, expression, and tone. While one imagines such accomplishments in the hands of privately tutored piano or violin students, these qualities are apparent in the performance of children on recorders, guitars, djembe drums, and xylophones, too. An evaluation of skills may include also the ability to play alone as well as together, in ensemble settings that are typical of school music programs everywhere.

The Benefits of Instrumental Study

For some children, making music is equivalent to playing musical instruments. The appeal of tapping, striking, shaking, blowing, and strumming musical instruments is one of the great joys in their lives. Because musical instruments are extensions of the musical self, when children play they are often demonstrating what they know and can express musically. To play a musical instrument is to deliver to others ideas that are not easily expressed verbally.

Musical instruments enhance the development of musical understanding. Why count rhythms when they can be felt and played? Why learn staff notation unless the symbols can be realized musically? Along with the singing voice, classroom instruments are teaching aids for experiencing musical concepts such as high and low, loud and soft, long and short, fast and slow, and choppy and smooth. The practice of playing a minor third, a perfect fourth, a legato phrase, or a chord progression underscores principles of music theory. Until children can be engaged in the practice of music making, they are not likely to fully understand the musical structures behind the sound. The playing of a musical instrument can precede, and later coincide with, the reading and writing of notation.

Teachers and parents who are aware of children's attraction to musical instruments, and of their capacities for playing them, can facilitate their musical growth. Children can develop performance skills quite rapidly when they are developmentally ready; that is, when they have arrived at the motoric and perceptual stages required for successful performance. There is the danger that when instruments and their performance techniques are introduced before children are capable of playing them, they may experience frustration and failure that may result in negative attitudes and demotivation. Teachers should recognize the importance of preparatory experiences that set in motion the physical skills necessary for playing with rhythmic accuracy, and they should allow children repeated opportunities to practice their parts while avoiding possibilities for boredom by delivering a variety of rapid-fire rehearsal strategies.

The old adage "practice makes perfect" should be reinforced for children who hope to develop their performance skills on instruments such as the recorder, piano, or guitar. Daily practice at home will undoubtedly result in marked improvement. At school, the teacher may wish to institute an open-door policy for children to spend time before— or after—school practicing. Where there is interest in the study of a musical instrument, the motivation to become a proficient player may be awaiting general encouragement from the teacher and parent.

Scenario

A COMBINED CLASS, MRS. Barr's second- and third-grade group, has arrived to Miss Hailey's music room for their late-morning class. They settle themselves into places just behind the instruments that have been laid out in sections on the carpeted floor. There are three xylophones and three metallophones (soprano, alto, and bass). Grouped together in each of the four corners of the room are two glockenspiels; two conga drums, a goblet drum, and four hand drums; two woodblocks, two claves, a slit log drum, and a guiro; and one each of the metal instruments (gong, cowbell, triangle, finger cymbals, maracas). Children know the routine, but Miss Hailey reminds them, "Do what I do. Listen to me, watch my cue, then you do it." She picks up claves and plays a four-beat pattern, then extends her arms and nods her head to the children, and they immediately imitate her. That pattern is followed by another and another and another. She increases the length of the patterns to eight beats, and some of the children are unable to produce a completely accurate imitation. The children on the three xylophones are playing on the keys of the pentatonic scale (the Fs and Bs have been removed) with less rhythmic precision than, for example, the children on claves, woodblocks, or conga drums, but Miss Hailey continues to maintain a steady pace to keep the class on-task and motivated.

Miss Hailey switches gears as she begins to chant, "A stitch in time saves nine," accenting the second, fourth, and sixth syllables, and clapping twice at the end of the phrase. The children join in the chant as Miss Hailey plays the claps on her claves, and they are soon following her lead and also playing the claps on their instruments. She moves over to the xylophone group, takes the mallet to the bass xylophone, and alternately plays C and G on every chant syllable as the chanting proceeds. While the children continue to chant and play, she moves to the metal instruments, cues them in on the second and fourth syllables, and then invites the drums to play on the words "time saves nine." This leaves only the woods to play the double clap at the end of a phrase, and so instruments sound across the proverb's eight-beat phrase. Miss Hailey is listening now, asking the children to phase out their chanting to hear the textures. Some children are rushing the tempo, so she waves her arms above her head in an exaggerated fashion to keep them together. Taking it one step further, Miss Hailey reminds the children again to watch her, and with her body stretched high or low, she conducts their dynamic levels. She is pleased with their playing (although the drum players have been playing very hard and very loud, and talking and laughing as they play) and tells them so.

As she has done in the past, Miss Hailey distributes photographs of landscapes (the seashore, mountains, a river, a volcano) and assigns the children on each instrument group the task of creating a soundscape for the scene. "You have five minutes to work together with your group to make up an aural image for your scene." The children set out to work on this open-ended project, and Miss Hailey sets the timer and sits at her desk to thumb through a new instrument catalog. She feels that the din of four groups of children playing at once is vital and a clear indication that the children are productive. At the sound of the timer, each group plays its soundscape, and while it is difficult to distinguish between pieces, Miss Hailey firmly believes that the children have had an opportunity to explore their instruments and to express themselves. There is still time remaining, so directing the children to take their places behind instruments in a different group, she repeats the soundscape exercise. As the class comes to a close, Miss Hailey asks them to describe what they have learned in the class session, and one little girl's answer brings much agreement among the children: "To wear ear-muffs to music!"

Questions

1. Which of Miss Hailey's three musical activities was the most musically valid or pedagogically sound? Explain.

2. If the children were more, or less, skilled, would it influence the success of the lesson? Could Miss Hailey have intervened at any point in developing the children's instrumental skills?

3. Would it have been possible to involve the children in more singing, moving, or listening along with their instrument playing? How? Why?

REVIEW

1. Why are xylophones recommended for use by school-age children instead of by kindergarten and preschool children?

2. What is a corpophone? How many corpophones can you demonstrate?

3. How can classroom instruments be categorized, so that children can understand similarities among instruments regarding their function and the materials from which they are made?

4. What are children's challenges for playing recorder? What direction can the teacher provide to meet these challenges?

5. How is an Autoharp tuned? A guitar?

6. Discuss the contributions of the piano in reinforcing children's musical learning.

CRITICAL THINKING

1. What factors should be taken into consideration in the teaching children to play nonpitched and pitched percussion instruments?

2. Give one example each of a formative and summative evaluation of performance skills on piano, guitar, djembe drum, and tambourine.

PROJECTS

1. Create a body-percussion piece. Begin with a poem or song that can serve as the stimulus for the rhythm and

can then be performed together with or as an alternate to the body-percussion piece.

2. Collect a set of children's songs from various cultures that can be performed with one or two nonpitched percussion instruments. Determine which instruments are representative of the cultural tradition.

3. Experiment with various accompaniment techniques for xylophones, metallophones, and glockenspiels. Arrange or orchestrate one folk song to feature each of the following techniques on Orff xylophones: simple drone, moving simple drone, moving double drone, ostinato, layered ostinato.

4. Practice guitar strums shown in Figure 8.4, and invent three new strums for 4, 4, and 8 meter.

5. Write a letter of appeal to the parents of your students, in which you inform them of the importance of home practice in learning a musical instrument. Choose recorder, guitar, or keyboard. Be persuasive in your support of the educational value of playing a musical instrument—individually and in the class ensemble.

MINDTAP Visit **MindTap** to access classroom videos, audio, and more!

9

The Listening Child

IN THIS CHAPTER

- The Centrality of Listening
- Growth in Listening
  - The Development of Perceptive Listening
  - The Development of Attitudes toward Music
- Active Involvement in Listening
  - Principles in Teaching Music Listening
  - Listening in Early Childhood Settings
  - Building Skills of Aural Perception
  - Deep-Listening
  - Student Construction of Listening Experiences
  - Building an Aural Repertoire
  - Listening Sequence
- Assessment of Listening
  - Formative Evaluations
  - Summative Evaluations
- Keys to Listening

The Centrality of Listening

COURTNEY CONCENTRATES HAPPILY AS her mother sings a new song to her. When her mother stops, she says, "Sing it again, Mommy, sing it again!" Her mother sings it over several times and, finally, Courtney joins in, singing the song accurately. Josh walks down the street, almost dancing, as he listens through his headphones to his latest purchase, a download of his favorite pop group. Ofewe sets a rhythm pattern on his synthesizer, focuses on its flow, then begins to improvise a melody to it. Michiko practices a phrase from her latest piano piece, shakes her head in frustration, tries it again, then smiles with satisfaction.

Each of these children is engaged in the perceptive activity that is at the heart of all that is done with music, whether singing, dancing, creating, or playing. That activity is listening. Music is an aural art that stimulates ears and challenges minds, usually bringing a pleasure and satisfaction that transcends much of what is experienced in life. Most music is received through the ear, not the eye. And most music performed throughout the world is aurally transmitted and will never be written down. Development of the ear is crucial to development of musicianship.

Learning to listen perceptively is a skill that can grow as surely as the gourmet can learn to detect the ingredients in a dish from a single taste. The reward of developing that skill is the same that any person feels at being perceptively sensitive, at being able to notice the subtleties and nuances present in an experience. Of all the musical abilities teachers try to help children develop, the ability to listen with focus and insight is perhaps the most important and long-lasting. Of all the ways people interact with music, the most frequently used lifelong skill is listening.

To help children develop their aural perceptive abilities, teachers and parents need to engage children in what composer R. Murray Schaefer calls "ear cleaning." This is difficult to achieve in a world in which people are constantly bombarded with sounds, and quiet is virtually impossible to find. To counter the effects of noise pollution, children's ears and minds must be opened to events in all aspects of music making:

THINGS TO THINK ABOUT

- What motivates you to listen to music?

- When you listen deeply to a piece of music, what do you listen for?

- How has your ability to notice the subtleties of music changed over the years?

- What role has your education in music played in your ability to listen deeply?

- What role has experience played in your ability to listen deeply?

- What responsibility do you feel educators have to enhance listening skills and the awareness and knowledge of a wide variety of genres and styles of music?

"In this time of global awareness, music is an aural pathway for understanding the world in which we live. It is a means of social and self-definition, and a bridge for young people from the self to others...."

Patricia Shehan Campbell, 2004

singing, playing instruments, moving, conducting, composing, and reading. Children need to learn to reflect on the quality of their own and others' performances.

Increased sophistication in listening can also be developed through listening to recorded music. This does not mean the kind of functional listening most people do when they use music as a background to help them celebrate, relax, clean house, or study. In most of those instances, the music is a kind of tonal bath that surrounds and washes over them but is not seriously attended to. The teacher needs to foster *active listening*, in which the learner focuses on musical events such as patterns that repeat and contrast, the creative use of tone colors, or the shaping of the music through dynamic change. Campbell calls this "deep-listening" (2004). Increased sophistication also comes through exposure to and development of a wide repertoire of music of various styles, cultures, and genres—from Bach to rock or from Indonesian gamelan music to Native American flute music.

Growth in Listening
The Development of Perceptive Listening

Key to the development of listening skills is the ability to perceive sounds and to form thoughts about those sounds. The auditory sense develops early and is remarkably keen in most children. Infants at birth can differentiate between pitches and quickly learn to identify the sound of their mother's voice. All babies go through a babbling stage in their first six months of development, in which they become increasingly sophisticated in matching vocal and mouth sounds that their parents generate. It is through this listening and corresponding vocal play that children form the mental constructs for language production and for the music of their culture.

Children as young as three months, perhaps younger, can vocally match sustained pitches. Children as young as six or seven months appear to have acquired a sense of musical phrase, and by eight months, a sense of what constitutes a good fit melodically in their culture. By the time children are in preschool they are developing vocabulary to describe what they hear. Concepts of tone color, dynamics, tempo, and style seem to emerge early. Concepts of pitch, rhythm, and form emerge later, around the age of four or after. Children continue to grow in their perceptiveness, and can show this in remarkable ways. Older children are able to recognize and apply a wide range of concepts to music listening experiences, provided they have had a strong foundation in music education (for further details on the development of these skills, see Scott-Kassner, 1992; and Haack, 1992).

Everyone can aurally identify hundreds, if not thousands, of pieces of music that he or she has been exposed to through a lifetime, explain details about the music and the context in which particular pieces are known, and attach personal meaning to that music. Music, in many ways, is a thread connecting the different periods of one's life, marking special moments. Our task as music educators is to help build students' skills and understanding in order to help them go deeply enough into the music to be able to glean its many riches.

The Development of Attitudes toward Music

Most music teachers are eager to have their students love music. That often translates into the selection of works for performance and listening that have an immediate

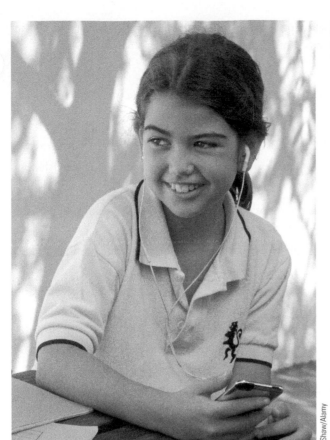

Ian Shaw/Alamy

appeal but may not have lasting value. Many complex factors besides the music itself enter into the development of attitudes toward music. A number of these factors are outside the teacher's control. A child's gender, ethnic background, age, personality, socioeconomic status, and the ensuing beliefs, feelings, and values that emerge all contribute to the formation of attitudes toward music. Teachers, families, peer groups, the media, and other adult authority figures also have an influence.

Young children from preschool through the age of eight are usually remarkably open to all kinds of music. This period of children's lives seems to be a good time to introduce them to a wide range of excellent music of many styles, genres, and cultures. Around the age of nine or ten, children begin to exhibit much more sensitivity to peer culture and the influence of the media, often rejecting, on a surface level, music that is not endorsed by that culture. Tests of preference show that children of this age prefer music that is loud rather than soft, fast rather than slow, and strong in beat rather than less intrusive. They are also drawn to humorous music. Teachers need to encourage children of this age to be receptive toward music that they do not necessarily prefer, so that they can learn about and from that music.

As most people mature, they will once again open themselves to a wider range of music than they were attracted to during their teenage years. At the same time, music they associate with certain times or events may continue to appeal to them throughout a lifetime.

Teachers can take heart in the knowledge that, in spite of children's preferences and tastes in music, they can be helped to understand a wide range of music through active involvement in listening. Because the area of attitude development is so complex, teachers cannot guarantee that experiencing a work of music will cause a student to like that work. However, there is some evidence that humans:

- Are drawn to complexity
- Tend to value what is familiar and feel uncomfortable with the unfamiliar
- Can learn to focus their perception of subtle changes
- Can change their attitudes through learning, in spite of enculturated tastes

These findings should encourage teachers to formulate an approach to active listening in which children:

1. Regularly listen to music that is more complex and challenging than much of the music they are exposed to in their daily environments

2. Listen to pieces of music enough times so that those works become familiar and no longer seem exotic

3. Gain the conceptual tools for discussing and analyzing music and perceive and respond to musical events in increasingly refined fashion

4. Discuss their preferences (a choice between two different events) and attitudes (a more generalized network of beliefs, values, and feelings) without being told that their choices or feelings are incorrect

5. Engage in listening activities that allow them to reflect and document what they have perceived and felt

Once children express an attitude about a piece of music, whether positive or negative, they need to be encouraged to go to the next step and describe what about the music makes them feel that way. A fifth grader, Steve, said he "loved" the classic song "Bridge over Troubled Water," as sung by Simon and Garfunkel. All of the other students agreed. The teacher played the recording again, asking the children to connect their feelings to what was happening musically. At the end, Steve eagerly raised his hand and offered a detailed analysis of the dynamic and melodic shaping of the A section of the piece, which built emotional tension, then released. This was in contrast with the B section, which was all on one level dynamically and melodically. He then went on to discuss the lyrics in each of these sections, and how they fit expressively with what was going on in the music. Steve had clearly connected his affective response with actual musical events.

Active Involvement in Listening

Principles in Teaching Music Listening

The teacher plays a key role not only in selecting what music will be the focus of active listening but in developing appropriate strategies to engage students with increasing depth in what they are listening to. Jarjisian and Kerchner suggest the following principles apply when planning ways to incorporate listening as a key element in a balanced music curriculum.

Listening in Early Childhood Settings

Listening to recorded music is not a passive activity for very young children. The energy of the music translates into physical energy for them, which quite naturally

BOX 9.1 Selected Principles in Teaching Music Listening

- Music listening is a skill that can and should be developed.

- Listening to music requires active and creative engagement.

- Teachers should involve students with musical exemplars from a variety of styles, genres, and cultures.

- The music itself suggests the concepts to receive attention and the activities most appropriate for facilitating development of those concepts. (Not all strategies are equally appropriate for all music.)

- The instructional activities, not the music, suggest age suitability.

- Students should have the opportunity to hear the same music several times, in brief segments, over time. The activities should change and become more involved with each listening opportunity.

- Listening activities should be multisensory, involving the tactile/kinesthetic, visual, and aural senses.

- Movement, like other concrete experiences, facilitates the development of aural memory. For young or preliterate children, movement is often the *only* accurate musical response.

- Only when tasks/questions are presented *before* the music is heard can they serve to focus attention on the features to be noticed.

- Teachers can often design future instruction by taking cues from student responses during a listening experience.

C. Jarjisian and J. Kerchner, unpublished document

Adapting Instruction for Various Needs

SENSORY NEEDS

- *Blind or visually impaired*: Isolate a space for children to move using a mat or hula hoop. Move with a sighted partner. Move upper body only in personal space from a seated or standing position. Make "raised" listening maps gluing string to trace the lines of the map for children to trace. Enlarge notated examples using bold print.

- *Deaf or hearing limited*: Place speakers on a wooden floor and invite children to "feel" the music through their bare feet. Have children hold an inflated balloon against the side of their head, aiding in perception of the sound. Provide visual cues such as listening maps for what is going on in the music. Invite children to trace those. Model patterned movements to fit the melody or rhythm of a listening example. Invite children to imitate those movements.

BEHAVIORAL NEEDS

- Establish clear parameters for movement to music, particularly movement through general space. Review what those rules are in terms of running into objects or other people. Establish a consequence ahead of time for not following those rules. Develop a nonverbal signal to use with children who may need to return to their seat or the edge of the room if they are out-of-control in their moving. Establish clear parameters for the holding and playing of instruments as an accompaniment to listening activities. Verbally or visually reward children for doing well.

flows into movement. The more young children listen and respond freely through movement to recorded music of various styles, the more refined their movements will become (Chen-Hafteck, 2004). These movements are remarkable in indicating young children's sense of the style of the music being played. In fact, movement may be their most accurate response to music. Custodero (2002) likens these untethered movements to being in flow. Children are totally immersed in the music to the point of becoming one with it. It is incumbent upon teachers, therefore, to create time and space for young children to move freely to a wide range of music on a regular basis. A movement space with mirrors to view movements and ribbons or scarves to extend the movements can become a permanent place in the early childhood classroom.

Young children are also capable of more refined responses to music through discrete or guided movements as well as by playing instruments to accompany music. Andress (1998) advocates the use of props and maps that children can manipulate to track events in recorded music.

Sims (1986) found that children pay more attention to music when the teacher also listens attentively, keeping eye contact and modeling movements that correspond to the music. Jarjisian (1998) suggests responding enactively (physically) to music through

---

LESSON ACTIVITIES 9.1 "Berceuse," from *Firebird Suite* by Stravinsky

NONLOCOMOTOR MOVEMENTS	LOCOMOTOR MOVEMENTS	TRANSFER TO PERCUSSION INSTRUMENTS
A Section (changing movement for each 8-beat phrase)	**A section** (changing movement for each 8-beat phrase; use circle formation)	**A section** (changing sound for each 8-beat phrase; groups of children have different sets of instruments; play the beat)
Patsch	Walk forward counterclockwise	Shakers
Tap shoulders	Sway side-to-side	Jingles
Tap head	Walk clockwise	Woods
Patsch	Turn and walk counterclockwise	Shakers
Tap shoulders	Sway side-to-side	Jingles
Tap head	Walk clockwise	Woods
Tap sides	Step around in a small circle	Drums with fingertips
B Section Begin in crouched position and "swoop" up with the music, waving arms. (2x)	**B Section** Holding hands, move to the center of the circle, swooping up with arms. Turn and, holding hands, move to the outer rim of the circle, swooping up with the music.	**B Section** Shake or tap instrument gently, moving it from low to high position. (2x)
A' Section	**A' Section**	**A' Section**
Patsch	Tiptoe forward counterclockwise	Shakers
Cross-handed patsch	Sway side-to-side	Jingles
Tap shoulders	Tiptoe in clockwise direction Sway side-to-side	Woods
Cross-handed shoulders	Tiptoe forward	Shakers
Tap head	Step around in small circle	Jingles
Tap back of head		Drums with fingertips
Coda Begin standing with arms overhead; gently "bump" down with each step of lowering pitch, gradually "melting" onto the floor.	**Coda** Repeat same pattern as column A.	**Coda** Hold instrument in air and shake or tap it gently, bringing it quietly into your lap.

either locomotor (through space) or nonlocomotor movements. Teachers can listen carefully to various pieces of recorded music and develop hand motions or large body movements through space that reflect the phrases, melodies, rhythms, and sectional patterns in the music. Children respond by imitating those movements. The following sequence of movement responses to the "Berceuse" from the *Firebird Suite* by Stravinsky comes from Jarjisian's work with preschool children. The activities in each column should be done more than once on different days, and represent movement to greater complexity as the children move from personal space to general space to instruments. Explore resources by Bennett and Bartholomew (2011, 2012) for ideas of musical play for young children with classical music.

Building Skills of Aural Perception

A program in active listening has several goals:

- Building heightened aural perception and sensitivity to music and musical events (aural skills development)

- Illustrating and reinforcing or expanding concepts of music

- Building an aural repertoire that represents a wide range of styles, cultures, and genres of music and that places music within a context

- Linking children's felt responses to their perceptions and understandings

Although these may seem to be discrete activities, they are interdependent; growth in one area affects another. For example, the greater your ability to perceive musical events, the more likely you are to form concepts about those events, and the richer your experience of listening to all kinds of music becomes. Growth in one or all of these skills should lead to greater aesthetic satisfaction through listening.

"Learning to listen perceptively demands focus and attention."

Learning to listen perceptively demands focus and attention. Teachers can use a variety of techniques to help children from preschool through the elementary years become aware of sounds.

1. Have children close their eyes. Drop a familiar object, such as keys or a pencil, and have children name the object.

2. Have children hide behind a screen and play different rhythm instruments while other children name what they hear.

3. Ask a child to close his or her eyes and then identify the voice of a classmate, after hearing a sung phrase.

4. Have children shape the upward or downward sounds of a slide whistle as they listen with their eyes closed.

Each of these listening activities helps children focus on aural stimuli by eliminating most or all visual cues. This training leads naturally to the more difficult task of listening for specific events in recorded music—a more difficult task because the music is usually more complex, with more things occurring, not just one. To help children focus, teachers need to develop active listening strategies.

Active listening to recorded music means involving more than the ears and the mind. To help children focus on a particular aspect of the music, teachers may use some physical means, such as having students perform, read, or move as they listen. In many instances, only a segment of a recorded work will be played. Sometimes, an entire work or section of a work will be used.

FIGURE 9.1

Listening Map for
Threnody for the
Victims of Hiroshima
by Krzysztof
Penderecki

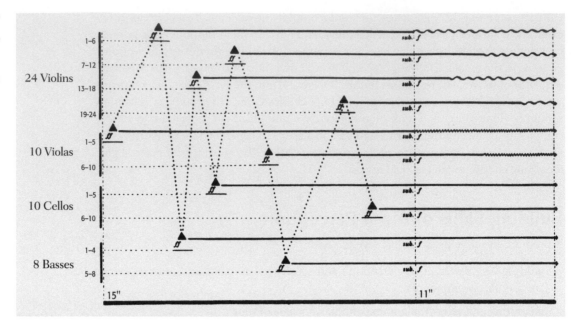

Source: From Music and You, Grade 6 (New York: Macmillan, 1989). Reproduced with permission from The McGraw-Hill Companies, Inc.

Lesson Activities 9.2 through 9.7 suggest a variety of active listening strategies designed to focus attention on different aspects of music: tone color, rhythm, pitch, texture, dynamics, form, and style. These strategies are designed for use with a broad variety of recorded music and with live performances by children, teachers, and guests. Specific concepts appropriate to the early childhood and elementary curriculum are listed on the left, and ideas to focus children's perception by using movement, performing, or reading are listed in their respective columns. Such experiences will provide a variety of opportunities for children to develop National Standard 6—listening to, analyzing, and describing music. (See also Figure 9.1.)

LESSON ACTIVITIES 9.2   Active Listening to Tone Color

CONCEPT	MOVING	PERFORMING	READING
Voices or instruments alone Voices or instruments in groups	Raise your hand when you hear the first trumpet; tap your head when you hear the first trombone. Clap to the pattern the bass drum plays. Pretend to play the violin whenever you hear it. Listen to a movement in a string quartet. In a group of four, assign each person to listen for a different instrument and decide how to move when each hears the sound of his or her instrument.	Sing with the pattern of the two-toned bell. Sing with the female voice only; listen to the male. Identify the pitches of the marimba ostinato and play it on the bass xylophone while listening to the recording. Select a rhythmic percussion instrument that would fit stylistically with a given piece, and improvise a rhythm to accompany the recording.	Circle the names or pictures of the instruments you hear in this piece. List in order of entrance the instruments you hear. Make a simple score of entrances and exits and relationships of the instruments in a work featuring three contrasting timbres. Visually follow a simple score, and cue the instruments or voices as they enter. Follow a call chart like the one shown on the facing page.

A call chart helps students track events by tone color, dynamics, and tempo. Students follow events as they listen to a recording with numbers spoken as events occur.

1. Introduction: full orchestra; *ff*; fast.

2. Low strings, low brass; *f*, then *mf*; slow.

3. English horn, clarinet, strings, tambourine; *mp*; slow.

4. Clarinet and piccolo solos, strings accompany; *mf*; slow.

5. Horns, woodwinds, tambourine; *f*; fast.

6. Strings, tambourine, brass; *ff*; slow.

7. Oboe, clarinet, low strings *pizzicato* (plucked); *mp*; slow.

8. Woodwinds, strings, brass, percussion; *ff*; very fast.

9. Full orchestra, brass section predominates; *f*; fast.

10. Full orchestra to end; bass drum "stinger."

Source: Call chart for "Sailor's Dance" from *The Red Poppy* by Reinhold Glière. From *World of Music, Grade 7* (Parsippany, NJ: Silver Burdett & Ginn, 1992, Pearson Education, Inc. or its affiliates). Used by permission. All Rights Reserved.

LESSON ACTIVITIES 9.3 Active Listening to Rhythm

CONCEPT	MOVING	PERFORMING	READING
Beat Rhythm Meter Tempo Syncopation	Tap the beat, off-beat, or rhythm on various parts of the body. Move around the room to the rhythmic flow of a piece; change directions at the ends of phrases. Create a movement pattern using different body levels (stomp, pat, clap, snap) to accompany patterns in a recording. Pass a ball around a circle to the beat, changing direction when the tempo changes. Work with a partner to show meter through movement; make the downbeat a strong motion. Bounce a ball on the accented beat; catch, roll, or hold on the weak beats.	Select instruments that complement a recording and add an accompaniment that highlights the beat, rhythm, and meter. Create a rhythmic ostinato to accompany the music. Identify a repeated pattern in the music; play along with it whenever it occurs.	Learn to read the rhythm of the main motivic pattern in a piece of music; find that pattern whenever it enters (aurally and visually). Read and notate the rhythm patterns in a work that features layered rhythms. Read and interpret by conducting the various meters in works in single meters and works that change meters. Read and maintain a rhythm pattern as an accompaniment to the music.

LESSON ACTIVITIES 9.4 Active Listening to Pitch

CONCEPT	MOVING	PERFORMING	READING

Horizontal
  Upward and downward
  High and low
  Step, leap, and repeat
  Melodic curve and patterns
  Phrase
	Alone and with a partner, shape the general curve of the melody.
	
	Show the highest and lowest notes of the recorded work by using high and low movements.
		Sing along with the melodic line of a work using words or a neutral syllable.
		
		Play the melodic line with the recording.
			Look at the melodic shape or notation of a motive, pattern, or theme. Notice each time it occurs in the music.

(Continued)

Scale
Tonality
Range and register
Vertical
    Chords
    Cadences
    Clusters

Shape phrases.

Develop discrete movements to show steps, leaps, and repeats in a melody.

Discover the main theme or motives in a work; create a movement to represent each motive; perform the appropriate movement when you hear each theme.

Move through general space, pausing at cadence points; make contrasting motions to show half and full cadences.

Change motions each time a chord changes.

In a group of three, have one person move on the I chord, a second on the IV chord, and the last on the V chord.

Play or sing motives or melodic themes with the recording.

Develop a melodic ostinato to play as an accompaniment to a pentatonic melody.

Play chord progressions on a synthesizer along with a pop or rock piece.

Draw the shape of the melody as it unfolds.

Read through the melody in a score ahead of time. Notice its shape: smooth or angular; its register: high or low; its range: low to high; its use of steps, leaps, and repeats. Imagine what it will sound like, then listen to test your perception.

As you listen, notate the chord changes and number of beats on each chord of a blues or pop song.

Circle the cadence points on a score as you listen. Listen again, and mark them as half or full.

CONCEPT	MOVING	PERFORMING	READING

Texture
  Monophonic
  Homophonic
  Polyphonic
  Mixed
	Move to the line of a single melody, upper body in personal space, then through general space.
	
	In a group of three or four, have each person move to a different line in a polyphonic piece.
	
	Show the layers of a round or canon by moving in concentric circles to the lines as they enter (each circle represents a different part).
	
	While one group moves to a melody, have another show the pattern of the underlying chords.
	
	Create different movements to show that you hear various textures.
		Sing or play in unison with the melody of a monophonic work.
		
		Sing or play with various lines or chords of other works, adding to the texture; fade the volume to listen to students, then increase volume.
		
		Add a countermelody or ostinato to a recording to create a polyphonic texture.
		
		Add chords to a recording of a melody to create a homophonic texture.
		
		Shift textures in your accompaniment to create mixed textures.
			Trace the line on a score of a monophonic melody as you listen.
			
			Draw or notate the line as you listen.
			
			Visually track the entrances and exits of lines in a polyphonic work.
			
			Using different colors, draw the separate lines as you listen.
			
			Follow the notation of a homophonic work, noting the relation between the melody and the chords.
			
			Follow a call chart that outlines the textures in a mixed-texture work.
			
			Invent your own call chart.

Dynamics
  Loud and soft
  Dynamic accent
  Gradual change
  Sudden change
	Show changes from loud to soft through changes in energy and flow.
	
	Show dynamic accents through angular movements.
	
	Develop group crescendo/decrescendo.
		Clap or play a rhythm instrument on selected or all dynamic accents.
		
		Play rhythm instruments to accompany gradual and sudden changes.
			Follow the dynamic markings on a score, gesturing or conducting to show changes.
			
			Draw a score of the dynamic changes while listening.

CONCEPT	MOVING	PERFORMING	READING

Repetition and contrast
  Phrase
  Unitary
  Binary
  Ternary
Rondo theme and variations
Through-composed
Tone poem
Program music
	Make up one motion for initial idea, contrasting motions for other idea(s); perform motions solo or in groups.
	
	Change directions with each new phrase, showing repetition and contrast in phrases with specific motions.
	
	Show a rondo by using different colored scarves and movements; assign each section to different groups.
	
	Have one group pattern the theme through movement while additional groups pattern the variations, incorporating the theme.
	
	Develop creative movements or dramas to tell the story or convey the mood as a piece unfolds.
		Select different instrumental or vocal timbres to accompany various phrases or sections of a work.
		
		Using only hands as a sound source, accompany a recorded rondo; change the playing technique (clap, rub, snap) with each theme.
		
		Learn to perform the theme by playing or singing, then identify it in each of its incarnations.
		
		Play or sing the main themes of the characters or sections before listening, such as in the listening guide for *Carmen*, below.
			Have simple shapes such as triangles, squares, and circles at your desk to show the structure of a piece as you listen (AA, AB, ABA, ABACABA).
			
			Follow the score as you listen; label each section as it occurs.
			
			Read the theme before you hear the music; note the contour and rhythm; discuss ways it might be varied; chart the variations on a piece of paper as you listen.
			
			Follow or draw a storyboard of a piece as you listen.
			
			Follow story in book, with puppets, or illustrate storyline or mood.

A Notated Listening Guide for "Prelude" from *Carmen* by Georges Bizet

Theme 1

Theme 2

Theme 3

"Fate" Theme

Source: Reproduced with permission from *World of Music,* Grade 5 (Parsippany, NJ: Silver Burdett & Ginn, 1992).

CONCEPT	MOVING	PERFORMING	READING

Style is the result of the combination of the elements of music reflecting cultural or personal choices	Change the quality of movement to reflect the style of the music (curved and flowing versus sharp, short, and angular moves).
	
	Learn specific dances or patterns of movement from various times and cultures to show styles of music.
	
	From Greece: grapevine step, arms at shoulders.
	
	From some parts of Africa: knees bent, arms bent slightly, palms down, eyes downward, movement toward ground, feet toward ground, upper body moves in and out.
		Add a clapping or percussive accompaniment that fits the style of the music on the recording. For clave in a calypso piece:
		
		Imitate through singing or playing the vocal or instrumental style used on a recording (blue notes, chest-resonated voice, open sound toward front of facial mask).
			Select from a set of style cards that match the music being played.
			Set 1 (touch)
			  Velvet
			  Gravel
			  Steel wool
			  Lima beans
			  Bubble plastic
			  Plush rug
			  Fake fur
			Set 2 (art)
			  Impressionist
			  Baroque
			  Classical
			  Romantic
			  Abstract
			Set 3 (images)
			  Houses from different periods
			  Costumes from different periods
			Set 4 (cultures)
			  Native American
			  African American
			  Latin American
			  Sub-Saharan African
			  East Asian
			Children should be able to describe why they made a certain style choice for the music.

"When children and youth are led by teachers into deep-listening experiences with music, they can discover gems of artistic and social expression, and sometimes even discover new meanings of the music that has always seemed so familiar to them."

Patricia Shehan Campbell, 2004

Deep-Listening

Many of the activities suggested in Lesson Activities 9.2 through 9.7 would begin to involve students in what Campbell (2004) refers to as deep-listening. This kind of listening demands that teachers use their abilities in analytical listening, conducting, performing, arranging, and communication to engage students in exploring music on more than a superficial level. Students are guided through focused involvement "into an ever more thorough understanding of music's constituent components and meanings" (2004, p. 2). Whatever music is used should be placed in its cultural and historical context for the students to derive the deepest meaning.

The three phases of deep-listening are:

1. *Attentive Listening*, in which the teacher focuses the students on musical structures by use of diagrams that highlight points of musical interest in the piece. Each listening could invite students to note something new, such as themes or motives, melodic shape, dynamic changes, timbral changes, or sectional forms. (See Figure 9.1.)

© Jerry Gay

2. *Engaged Listening*, which occurs when the learner is drawn into fuller participation in the music by tapping the beat, playing an ostinato, singing a melody, or performing a groove. In order to do this effectively, students have to listen to the music carefully to discover patterns to perform. Over many listenings, students can engage in performing various parts: rhythmically, melodically, and/or harmonically. (See ideas in Listening Activities 9.2–9.7)

3. *Enactive Listening*, which involves the learner at even deeper levels, such as learning to perform a piece in style and reflecting the nuances of that work of music, whether from an aural or notated tradition. It takes repeated focused listening and engagement with the music to begin to perform successfully within the style of a given work. Because of the time and sophistication required, enactive listening is most appropriate from middle school into adulthood.

Student Construction of Listening Experiences

Current theories of learning suggest that using strategies in which children solve problems leads to the formation of mental constructs or schemas that are much deeper and better formed than approaches that are completely teacher-directed. Such strategies invite students into the music by having them use one or more modalities—kinesthetic, visual, or verbal—to represent what they notice happening in the music. In these approaches, teachers structure the types of activities and select the music to be explored, but they turn the response to the music over to the students. Children work individually or in small groups and represent the music in some way, such as speaking about it, drawing aspects of it, solving puzzles in which they put themes in order, moving to the music using their own ideas, or creating their own works based on it. Because this process requires multiple hearings of the music, it is advisable to select short works or sections of works lasting under two minutes. If several listening devices are available, students can work at their own pace, determining when they need to relisten. These activities can also be done with the group as a whole.

Many music educators have long advocated having children draw their own maps of music or musical events. The maps may be drawn most successfully after children have physically responded to the music through movement of their hands to shape dynamics or tempo change or melodic and rhythmic ideas or timbral changes. Children could try to represent only one of these elements, or they could represent a combination of elements. Espeland (1987) and a group of teachers from Norway developed a number of ways that children might respond to the music. They call their program "Music in Use." Figure 9.2 suggests a variety of ways to engage children in constructing their response to a piece of recorded music.

Kerchner (1996) views this type of listening as engaging students in creative approaches that demand "cognitive acts including perception, focus of attention, recall, and comparison. The process also includes anticipation or expectation." In mapping, students can draw maps, add to their maps through multiple hearings, and share their maps

FIGURE 9.2

"Music in Use" Activities

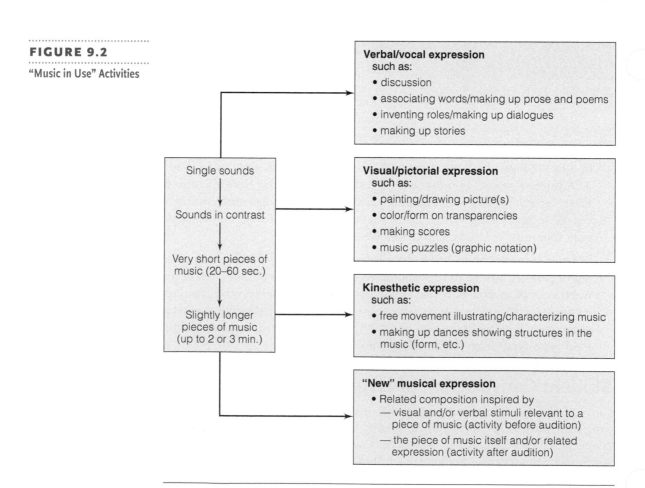

Source: Espeland (1987, p. 288).

with others, asking them to respond to the drawings. Students could use limited movement of their upper bodies to physically map a portion of a piece, then gradually work into whole body movement or plan a group choreography of a piece. It is worthwhile to have several groups visually map or choreograph the same piece of music and then have the students share their ideas, followed by a discussion of similarities and differences and the reasons underlying their choices.

Building an Aural Repertoire

Teachers will often want to play a work of recorded music across a series of lessons or several times throughout a year. This approach helps children take works into long-term memory, so they become internalized references for a lifetime of musical learning and valuing. Repeated hearings help children become friends, not simply acquaintances, with the music that teachers, parents, and the children themselves find significant.

One approach to repertoire building is to utilize techniques of deep-listening or of student construction of listening experiences. These techniques involve students deeply through their own explorations and representation of the music and necessitate listening to the music many times. Another approach to repertoire building is to take a gestalt, or holistic, point of view. This allows the children to hear the entire piece, section, or movement in the initial listening. Subsequent hearings may concentrate on smaller parts for a particular focus. A final listening returns to the whole. This whole-part-whole approach to listening can take advantage of many active-listening techniques already discussed in this chapter. This is often teacher directed.

Ideally, the repertoire should come from a wide range of music of the highest aesthetic quality, well crafted and well performed. This could include masterworks of Western art music, as well as folk, traditional, and popular music from any culture. Teachers may wish to set a goal of building deep knowledge of six works each year. Works could be organized around themes such as composer, artist, or culture of the month. At the elementary school level, children can become acquainted with individual styles within the Western art music tradition but are not yet ready for a strict historical approach to that music. At the same time, placing music in a cultural and historic context helps create deeper meaning for the students. A contextual perspective connects the work to the culture and time in which it was written to help students gain insight into ideas of cultural meaning, style, and performance practice.

Resources for listening are abundant, as close as the nearest record store or music downloads from the Web. Recordings and listening lessons are also incorporated in music series texts. Visuals, such as charts and music maps as well as animated listening maps are included in music series to assist in the development of listening skills. *Music Smart!* by Hotchkiss (1990) provides a rich resource of listening lessons. Other delightful recordings, DVDs and books about the lives of composers are available from Classical Kids Productions in Toronto. Many children's books have been written to tell the stories of recorded works and composers. Such publications, along with music DVDs to enhance listening, can be found in local music stores and in online catalogs that feature materials for teachers. The Metropolitan Opera Guild in New York publishes *The Metropolitan Opera Guild Presents: Growing Up with Music* (Box set). The archive of Smithsonian Institution's Folkways Recordings offers a wide range of educational recordings, including folk and traditional music from throughout the world. In addition, listening lessons can be developed by teachers using any available recorded music. In the pop and jazz fields, it is often advisable to purchase "best of" albums from artists who have demonstrated staying power in constantly changing fields.

Listening Sequence

A listening sequence (adapted from work by Sandra L. Stauffer), whether completed in one day or spread across many class periods, includes several steps. Again, the opportunity to hear a work many times and experience it from many perspectives helps in the process of repertoire building.

Step 1: Prepare. Children need to be prepared to listen. The preparation will depend on the purpose of the listening. They could listen to a story such as "The Nutcracker"; they could be told the background of the culture the music is from and be asked to find the region on a map; they could view a painting or picture that helps establish a mood or sense of style; they could hear a story of the composer, composition, or the lives of the people from whom the music originated; or they could sing a melodic theme or sing and clap a pattern or motive they are to notice (this could be taught by rote or from a score). It is very important to give children something specific to listen for and a way to show that they hear it. These should be quiet responses such as raising hands, pointing, or writing, so that all children can concentrate on the music. (Ideas for directing and monitoring perception appear in Lesson Activities 9.1 through 9.7.)

Step 2: Listen. Play the recording, and check students' perceptions or feelings through class discussion.

Step 3: Activate and Participate. Listen again, while actively involving students in performing or moving in some way to the music. These exercises can be repeated more than once and over time. It is a wonderful way to build a work into children's internal repertoire. For example, young children never seem to tire of moving like dwarves to *In the Hall of the Mountain King* by Grieg.

Step 4: Question and Discuss. Discussion should take place throughout this sequence, and can address the music, portions of the music, the activities the children are doing, or their emotional response to the experiences or the music.

Step 5: Listen Again. Listen to the recording quietly, simply to notice familiar moments, expand insight into the music, and reestablish the work as a whole.

Step 6: Extend the Listening. Use this listening as a stimulus to have the children:

1. Compose music in similar forms or with similar characteristics

2. Listen to other music by the same composer or culture that has similar or contrasting characteristics

3. Listen to other music by other composers or cultures that has similar or contrasting characteristics

The activities shown in Lessons 9.1 through 9.3 illustrate these principles and suggest possible ways to approach repertoire building with selected works. Music teachers who see children only once or twice a week may wish to enlist the help of classroom teachers in reinforcing listening experiences with children. (Remember that dubbing compact discs [CDs] or sharing downloads, distributing copies to others is illegal under the copyright law. However, CDs owned by the school or district may be used in any classroom.) Lesson 9.1 is based on a familiar piece of Western classical music. Lesson 9.2 is adapted from suggestions in the book *Multicultural Perspectives in Music Education* (3rd ed.) by Anderson and Campbell (2010); See the source for access to the recording that accompanies the lesson. Lesson 9.3 is an example of a listening strategy developed from recordings by contemporary artists and integrated with children's literature. Note that each series of activities strives to attain many goals related to musical elements, skills, repertoire, cultural or historical context, or other disciplines.

LESSON 9.1 "Minuet in G" by Ludwig van Beethoven

Grades	Second to fourth.
Repertoire and Context Goals	To internalize Beethoven's "Minuet in G," to gain a sense of musical style typical of his period, and to learn something about Beethoven.
Concept Goal	To understand that ABA form can exist in an orchestral work. To put into words the musical differences between the sections.
Skills Goals	To perceive the differences in the sections. To coordinate movements to the sections.
Day 1	Show a picture of Ludwig van Beethoven. Ask the children if they have ever heard his name. (Discuss what they know about him.) Explain that he wrote many kinds of music, including music to be danced to. A popular dance of his day was called a minuet. Tell them you are going to play a particular minuet called "Minuet in G." Listen to this music and try to imagine the dancers. What kinds of motions might they be making and why? (Play recording. When it is finished, have children demonstrate some motions and discuss their choices.)
Day 2	Put "Minuet in G" on board. Have children tell you what they remember about the piece. Tell the children they are going to help invent a dance to do to the music, but first they need to develop a sense of the way the music is organized. Review AB and ABA form. Ask them to listen to the music and to discover which pattern best fits its structure. Once children have discovered ABA form, show pictures of people dancing the minuet.
	Discuss the style of dress and hair. Discuss the elegance of the posture. Have them suggest stylized motions to do during the A section and contrasting motions during the B. Try those with the music. Note whether they change movements with the change in sections. Have them discuss how effective their choices were in terms of the music.
Day 3	Play "Minuet in G" as a mystery tune on a recording or on the piano. See how long it takes the children to name it and the composer. Put two words on the board: *even* and *uneven*. Tell them you want them to clap the rhythm of the melody of the "Minuet in G" as they listen and decide which word best fits the A section and which best fits the B. Later, help them to discover other ways the two sections contrast.

(Continued)

Extensions

1. Play the audio or videotape of the program *Beethoven Lives Upstairs* by Classical Kids Productions from Toronto. Have the children select other works by Beethoven they want to know.

2. Invite a guest artist to play some Beethoven and discuss why the children are attracted to his music.

3. Learn steps from the minuet and practice dancing them to the Beethoven selection.

4. Compose an ABA-form piece for instruments in which each section is sixteen beats long.

LESSON 9.2 "San Antonio"

Using *In Praise of Oxala and Other Gods: Music from Colombia, South America*, Nonesuch Records

Grades   Fourth to sixth.

Repertoire Goal To internalize the piece "San Antonio," gaining a sense of style represented by African-derived music from Colombia.

Concept Goals To understand that this music is created by the use of layers of various percussion instruments playing ostinati plus voices singing in call-and-response fashion. To understand the context in which the piece is used.

Skills Goals To perceive the layers and specific rhythm patterns of the instruments. To be able to replicate by ear at least one of the patterns. To name the instruments being played. To play and sing the parts with accuracy. To add vocal harmony.

Day 1 Find Colombia on a map of South America. Discuss the fact that a large part of the country is a tropical rain forest and that much of it can be reached only by boat because the vegetation is so thick. Most of the people are very poor and make their money from growing bananas and catching fish. African slaves were brought to this region to work in the gold mines. The people who brought them left, and the blacks stayed. About five thousand blacks live there today. Although Colombia is a Spanish-speaking country, much of the music has been influenced by the music that the African people brought with them.

Tell the students that in the religious music that comes out of the Catholic church, the people often sing songs to saints. The song "San Antonio" is a song to Saint Anthony and is usually sung on Christmas Eve as a lullaby. It is sung in Spanish, but there are some African influences, including the instruments used. (Review some of the traditional African instruments learned in an earlier unit.) Listen to "San Antonio," and notice the instruments used. Be ready to name them. (Discuss the use of marimba, rattles, and drums.) Listen again and notice the relation between the two voices and the instruments. Focus particularly on patterns that repeat.

(Discuss the call-and-response vocal form and the instrumental ostinato.)

Day 2 Show children the notation for the call-and-response section of "San Antonio." Teach them the response pattern. Sing the call and have them respond. Play the recording and have them join in each time they hear the response. (They may be able to sing this in harmony.) Ask for volunteers to learn the call. Take turns using different leaders. Other children may wish to add the rattle or drum part, learning it aurally.

Day 3   Echo clap the rhythms for the call and response in the marimba part for "San Antonio." Have children discover those patterns in the score of the marimba part. How are they similar to the sung line? Teach some children to play those patterns on the marimba or keyboard. Put the whole piece together.

With
Call

With
Response

Extensions   1. Listen to other music on this recording, and compare and contrast the use of elements such as call and response and ostinato.

2. Research and report on other aspects of the importance of music in the Colombian culture.

3. Discover and perform some African American songs based on the call-and-response form. How are they similar or different?

4. Using a pentatonic scale, compose a call-and-response-form piece with a contrasting marimba ostinato.

Accomplishing Multiple Music Standards through Listening

1. *Singing*: Invite children to sing the themes of the music before hand to set them up for the listening. When an orchestral piece is based on an entire song such as "Simple Gifts" in Copland's *Appalachian Spring* or "The Birch Tree" in Tchaikovsky's 4th Symphony, learn to sing the entire song before listening to the music.

2. *Playing*: Teach children to play themes on melodic instruments or rhythmic motives on rhythmic instruments. Have them join the music when those themes or motives enter. Choose appropriate instrumental timbres to accompany various sections of the recorded music—playing the beat, meter, or rhythms to enhance the music.

3. *Improvising*: Once children are familiar with a short piece of recorded music, invite them to work in a large group to improvise a piece in response to that—conveying the same mood and qualities the original piece did. With older children, listen to a master performer such as Gabriela Montero in her improvisations on the music of J. S. Bach. Listen to the original recording first, then to her improvisations, discuss some of the techniques used, and use those ideas in new improvisations. Take a theme from a piece of recorded music of any historical or cultural style, and improvise on that theme.

4. *Composing and Arranging*: Once you are familiar with a piece of recorded music, divide it into sections or units of sixteen bars. Have older children work in small groups to create an appropriate instrumental accompaniment for their section of the music, incorporating tempo and dynamic shadings reflective of the original work.

5. *Reading and Notating*: Sight-read rhythmic or melodic motives from a piece of recorded music. Read a listening map and accurately trace the development of the music. Create your own listening map for a given piece of recorded music.

6. *Listening*: All of the ideas in this chapter connect to listening.

7. *Analyzing and Evaluating*: Analyze and discuss various effects or moods created in recorded music. Analyze the form of recorded music. Compare three different versions of the same work and develop criteria to evaluate which is the most effective and why.

8. *Connect to Other Arts and Curricular Areas*: Study music inspired by specific paintings. View the painting and listen to the music and make the connections. View videos of ballet or other dancing. Discuss the connection between the dancers' movements and the music.

9. *Connect to Culture and History*: Study the lives of composers or artists. Connect them to specific time and place. View a timeline of "classical music." Connect time, history, and style.

Assessment of Listening

Formative Evaluations

Many means exist to understand what children are hearing and feeling as they listen. One tool that is commonly used in music series texts to test for aural perception of discrete elements is "What do you hear?" charts (see Figure 9.3). These focus narrowly on whether or not students have formed a concept or understanding of an element and whether they can identify it in a short segment of recorded music. Lesson Activities 9.1 through 9.7 include many techniques for observing what children are perceiving in the music. Certainly the activities suggested in deep-listening and student-constructed listening give ample evidence through movement, notation, and performance of what the students are hearing.

FIGURE 9.3

"What Do You Hear?"

Source: From *World of Music, Grade 1* (Parsippany, NJ: Silver Burdett & Ginn, 1992, Pearson Education, Inc. or its affiliates). Used by permission. All Rights Reserved.

The ability to identify a musical work studied during the year could be assessed by having children listen to a range of familiar pieces, name them, and share something they remember about each piece.

A much richer understanding of what students are hearing and feeling can be gained by asking them to describe the music in some way—verbally, kinesthetically, or visually. Rodriguez and Webster (1997) found clear age-related differences in the quality of verbal descriptions children offered in response to recorded music. They asked children four questions to get at their cognitive responses, their knowledge of how to create music, their awareness of their feeling response to music, and the musical features that evoked these feelings.

The questions were:

1. What were you thinking when you listened to this music?

2. If you were going to make music like this, how would you start?

3. How does this music make you feel?

4. What in the music makes you feel that way?

LESSON 9.3 "Hush Little Baby"

Using "Hush Little Baby" by Heidi Grant Murphy and Auréole and *Hush* by Yo-Yo Ma and Bobby McFerrin

Grades	Pre-K to second.
Repertoire Goals	To internalize a sense of style that comes from contrasting versions of a familiar song. To understand that one piece can occur in many different arrangements.
Concept Goals	To review the meaning and traditional style of a lullaby. To understand that improvising is a way to be musically playful.
Skills Goals	To physically and vocally respond to the flow and mood of the music. To aurally perceive ways that a familiar work has been altered. To experiment with musically altering other familiar works.
Literature Goals	To become familiar with contrasting styles of illustrating a familiar song and to connect that with similar styles in music. To write and illustrate an arrangement of that song.
Day 1	Read the picture book *Hush Little Baby* as illustrated by Aliki (1968).
	Discuss the sequence and the predictability of the rhymes. Learn to sing the folk song "Hush Little Baby." Sing it as you follow the pictures in the book.
Day 2	Bring in a doll or stuffed animal. Pretend to put it to sleep by rocking it. When it resists falling asleep, suggest that a lullaby might help. Have the children listen carefully to see if they can help rock pretend babies and also sing the lullaby. Begin to sing "Hush Little Baby" on the neutral syllable "loo." Watch to see when children recognize the song and enter in. Have them name the song and then sing it while they pretend to rock their babies and put them to sleep. Gently place the sleeping babies away as you play the recording of "Hush Little Baby" by Heidi Grant Murphy and Auréole. Invite children to stand, find a place in space, and gently move to the flow of the music. Extend their movements by having them used colored scarves or streamers to show the flow. Invite children to share what they noticed about the music and how it made them feel.
Day 3	On the board, put the words *word* and *bird*, *sing* and *ring*, *down* and *town*, and so on. Invite children to help read them. Ask them what song the words are from. Sing the song using soft, soothing voices. Discuss the flow (gentle) and dynamic quality (soft) of the lullaby. Tell them

(Continued)

you are going to play a recording of two men performing "Hush Little Baby." Ask them to listen to decide whether they think it will put the baby to sleep or not. Listen and discuss their responses as to why it would not put the baby to sleep. (It is loud and fast.) Have the children stand, face a partner, and hold hands. Play the recording again while the children rock back and forth to the flow of the music, creating an imaginary cradle.

Day 4

Introduce children to the names of the two musicians who performed "Hush Little Baby." Show them their pictures. Discuss the fact that they are both famous musicians who love to experiment or play with sounds. Listen to their arrangement of "Hush Little Baby" to discover what they did to make it different from the original. Discuss those ideas (faster, louder, different words, higher pitches, sliding, mouth sounds, clapping). Have children join in vocally with the recording, trying some of the techniques. Discuss the delightful character of this style of singing. Read the book *Hush Little Baby* illustrated by Margot Zemach (1976). Does its quality capture more of the original version of the song or the Yo-Yo Ma–McFerrin version? Why or why not?

Teacher with young children and dolls, singing "Hush Little Baby"

© Jerry Gay

Extensions

1. Have the children develop their own vocal improvisations (playing with sounds) using familiar nursery rhymes.

2. Take another lullaby and turn it from a gentle piece to an upbeat piece by improvising.

3. Share the book *Hush Little Baby* by Sylvia Long (1997). Have the children discuss what is different about this book. Encourage them to create their own version of "Hush Little Baby," illustrate it, and then bind it into their own book.

4. Listen to other selections from the album *Hush*, such as "Flight of the Bumblebee" by Rimsky-Korsakov. Discuss how the various effects were created.

5. Find out more about Bobby McFerrin and Yo-Yo Ma (videotapes from PBS, other recordings). Build their names into the children's vocabulary. Compare Yo-Yo Ma's cello style on "Hush Little Baby" with a more traditional style. Discuss the differences.

Summative Evaluations

Generally, as children mature, they are more able to connect feelings with the music, use musical terminology, and understand the need for training, organization, and collaboration in making music. Responses to such questions could become part of a child's portfolio, either in written form or taped form. Kerchner (1999) found that children were more detailed in their descriptions of music when they drew maps or responded kinesthetically than when they tried to describe the music verbally. This research points to the value of including several ways of having children describe music and their responses to the music, and it suggests that different modes will be preferred by different children. Children's musical maps or videos of their movement solutions and reflections on those solutions could become part of a portfolio that is presented in a conference with parents.

Keys to Listening

Opening ears and minds to the sounds and subtleties of music and watching the discoveries children make and the excitement they feel bring great satisfaction to the teaching of music. To do this successfully, teachers need to continue listening themselves—not just to familiar works but also to unfamiliar ones, and to the comfortable and uncomfortable. Teachers need to bring attitudes of openness, curiosity, and discovery to the act of listening. They need to be willing to engage in deep and focused listening themselves in order to become effective guides into the structure and the subtleties of recorded works.

Teachers who actively nurture their own musical growth through listening have greater riches to offer their students. The keys to listening can be developed and, through them, worlds of pleasure unlocked. To paraphrase philosopher Harry Broudy, teachers need to develop their own connoisseurship to help their students engage in a lifetime of enlightened cherishing.

TECHNOLOGY *for* TEACHING *and* LEARNING
MUSIC: THE LISTENING CHILD

Children are keenly interested in the sounds things make and are naturally drawn to music. No video game, movie, or TV show would succeed without the vital component of interesting sounds and music. Many software programs engage children deeply in listening carefully by focusing on musical components of tone color, dynamics, tempo, style, pitch, rhythm, and form. Children's perceptions sharpen, they gain competence in listening skills, become familiar with a wide array of compositions in many styles, and learn to love music even more. Programs often encourage children to listen attentively, actively, and reflect on and express what they have perceived and felt. Using listening software and websites is an easy and elegant way to give students fine music listening experiences beyond the classroom time. To learn more, visit the Technology Resources links in the MindTap.

MINDTAP

Scenario

MRS. DELACORTE HAS BEEN eager to share a recording of the overture to Mozart's opera *The Magic Flute* with her fifth graders. The music is playing as the children enter the room. They move to their assigned seats with their cooperative groups. Mrs. Delacorte has trained the students to be prepared to describe something they notice about the music that is playing when they enter. When the music stops, she gives the groups a short period of time to discuss what they noticed. She has each team captain share ideas, and she lists them on the board. Mostly, the children name the instruments that they heard and their responses to the lively style of the music. Some talk about the tempo and sudden dynamic changes.

Next, Mrs. Delacorte invites the children to listen to the music again and imitate her hands as she moves them upward and downward to the shape of the melody. She adds dynamic emphasis as she moves. Some children have a hard time imitating the movements as the music moves by so quickly. Two or three children start to laugh, but Mrs. Delacorte ignores them and continues to map the music through movement of the arms and hands. Once the music finishes, she asks the students to describe what more they noticed. The children begin to talk about the shape of the melodies and the repetition of some of the patterns.

Mrs. Delacorte asks the team captains to distribute drawing paper and colored pens to each member of their team. The assignment is to...

Questions

1. What approach to active listening is Mrs. Delacorte using?

2. Discuss what might happen next in this lesson. What will the assignment be?

3. How will the children report back to the rest of the class?

4. What else might be valuable for children to understand about this music?

5. How might Mrs. Delacorte approach this music another day to expand student understanding of it?

REVIEW

1. What is the difference between active perceptive listening and passive functional listening? What are three techniques to enhance active listening?

2. At what age or stage are students likely to form strong preferences for particular kinds of music? How might that influence what recordings you use with them?

3. What are useful steps for planning listening lessons designed to build repertoire?

4. What are the benefits to having children construct their own responses to listening experiences?

5. What are the different stages of deep-listening and what happens at each stage?

6. What techniques can be used to assess listening?

7. How can teachers nurture their own ongoing growth as perceptive listeners?

CRITICAL THINKING

1. How would you justify spending class time having children listen to recorded music?

2. How might a teacher respond to older elementary children's requests to bring pop music recordings to music class?

3. Discuss with others in your class the validity of the following statement: "A teacher can make children like music that the teacher likes."

4. Which approach(es) to listening outlined in this chapter seem to hold the most potential for having children own a piece of music and why?

PROJECTS

1. Interview two preschoolers, two kindergartners, two second graders, two fourth graders, and two sixth graders about what kind of music they like and why. Are their stages of preference similar to those outlined in this chapter? Summarize and report your findings to your class.

2. Select a piece of recorded music you find exciting. Determine why you find it exciting. Using the steps outlined for a listening sequence, plan a series of activities to share this music with children.

3. Develop a set of materials and activities that children might use to enter more deeply into a listening experience. These could include ideas from the reading column of Lesson Activities 9.2 through 9.7 or ideas in deep-listening or student-constructed listening.

4. Develop a listening map to help children track events in a recorded work.

5. Find a listening map in a music series text or create one of your own. Cut it into phrases and create a puzzle for children to place in order as they listen to that music. Try it with children of different ages and see whether they are able to solve the puzzle.

6. Closely examine different music series texts to see how they incorporate listening to music. What literature have they chosen? How have they helped get children actively involved? How have they helped to build repertoire, if at all? Teach one of those lessons to your class or to a group of children. Assess what they have learned from this experience.

7. Interview children of different ages using the questions designed by Rodriguez and Webster (1997) in response to a piece of music. Compare the responses you collected to those in their article.

MINDTAP Visit **MindTap** to access classroom videos, audio, and more!

10

The Creating Child

IN THIS CHAPTER

- The Importance of Creativity
- Developmental Sequence
- Creative Thinking
- Creative Processes
  - Exploration and Discovery
  - Improvisation
  - Composition
- Assessment
- Formative Evaluations
- Summative Evaluations
- The Rewards of Nurturing Creativity in Music

"Teaching music without having children compose would be like teaching art without having children draw or paint, or teaching writing by having children copy other people's work."

The Importance of Creativity

TO A GREAT EXTENT, everything the very young child does musically comes out of his or her creative imagination and exploration. Anna engages in the typical vocal sound play of the infant, with her "bahs," "duhs," and "gurgles" throughout her range. Juan rhythmically strikes a wooden spoon against a pan, and Marianne laughs and claps with joy when she discovers she can make sounds on the piano. All of these responses represent a satisfaction of the inherent desire children have to generate and manipulate sounds and, eventually, to place them into meaningful structures.

Campbell (2010) describes these spontaneous responses as "musical utterances." She sees them as ways of thinking aloud and communicating through the language of music. This desire to express ideas musically continues through the elementary years and beyond, as children eagerly invent words and rhythms for a rap, improvise a pentatonic melody on a soprano xylophone, write a song, or work in a group to arrange a favorite musical selection. The creative impulse is alive in children of all ages, and the music classroom is an ideal setting to stimulate the growth of that creativity beyond the initial stages of exploration and discovery.

The arts come into being through the creativity of individuals and groups. To deny children the opportunity to work creatively with the materials and structures of music is to limit their capacity to think artistically and, ultimately, to limit the full exploration of what it means to be musical. Teaching music without having children compose would be like teaching art without having children draw or paint, or teaching writing by having children copy other people's work. Including composition, improvisation, and arranging as important aspects of a general music program provides the third element of a balanced program of listening, performing, and creating.

Developmental Sequence

The development of musical creativity, both conceptual and practical, appears to be the result of the interaction of factors of environment, musical thought or cognition, and individual intellectual and personality traits. Children are exposed to a wide range of music as a result of enculturation and have much to draw from as composers. As children grow in their musical experience and their capacity to physically manipulate or control the sounds of their instruments or voices, they can move to higher levels of creative production. If they are in environments that encourage them to improvise, arrange, and compose music, they will perceive these activities as natural and as part of what one does to express musical ideas. Some children may feel more comfortable with this process than others and express more musically sophisticated ideas. All children, however, can benefit, both musically and cognitively, from active involvement in the creation, not just the re-creation, of music.

Several theories have been proposed about the development of creative thinking and creative production in music. Although these theories need to be tested in classroom settings where children are allowed extended time to craft pieces, they are included in Table 10.1 to suggest the growth of creativity during preschool as well as the elementary years. Critics of these studies suggest that children at the ages of five and six do compose pieces that reflect structural thinking in music. This is most often done when children use their voices or when they are given more time to develop confidence in using instruments than is typically allowed in a research setting. (See a summary of these ideas by Barrett, 1996, 1998. See also Flohr, 2005.)

Creative Thinking

Much of the thinking teachers ask children to do is convergent thinking, the type of thinking that results in a single, correct answer. When children are asked to name things such as signs, symbols, composers, or pieces of music, they are directed to think convergently. In performance, children are asked to conform to the correct pitches and rhythms of a song, although creativity is often encouraged in the area of interpretation.

At the heart of creative thought is a different type of thinking, divergent thinking. This is when teachers ask children for many possible answers. For example, children could be invited to discover how many different sounds a percussion instrument makes or how many techniques might be used in playing it.

Webster (1990) has developed a theory of creative thinking in music. According to that theory, qualities of divergent thinking include:

1. Musical extensiveness—how many ideas are generated

2. Flexibility—the ease of shifting within parameters such as high and low or loud and soft

3. Originality—how unique the musical ideas are

In the area of originality, for example, creative children might generate their own songs and themes instead of using more familiar ones. These qualities interact with others, such as a child's musical understandings and sensitivities, ability to imagine pitches and rhythms, aesthetic sensitivity, and ability to craft a piece to effect the final product of the creative effort. From the standpoint of the teacher, the key is to establish an environment where these various skills and understandings are consciously developed.

THINGS TO THINK ABOUT

- What role does composing, improvising, and/or arranging music occupy in your life?

- How important do you feel learning to compose, improvise, and arrange is to developing full musicianship in children?

- How comfortable do you feel with your ability to guide children to improvise, compose, or arrange music?

- How motivated do you think children are to compose or invent their own music?

- What is your sense of children's ability to compose on their own, with minimal guidance from a teacher?

- As you think about planning a curriculum in music, what do you think the balance should be between activities related to performing (vocally and instrumentally), listening, and creating?

TABLE 10.1 Development of Creative Production

AGE	FLOHR (1985); KRATUS (1985, 1991)	TILLMAN AND SWANICK (1989)	TEACHER ACTION
BIRTH TO FOUR-TO-FIVE YEARS	Driven by motor energy. Highly individualistic in approaches and patterns. Lacking musical syntax.	Mastery of materials and range of sounds through sensing and manipulating.	Provide age-appropriate instruments to explore. Encourage and reinforce discovery and respect individuality.
FOUR-TO-FIVE TO NINE (KINDERGARTEN TO GRADE FOUR)	Predictable rhythmic and tonal patterns, influenced by familiar music. Changing meters and emerging sense of tonality. Lack strong sense of phrase structure and cadence.	Imitation of both personal and vernacular ideas occurs with greater expressive quality. Meter emerges, greater use of dynamic expression, ostinati.	Encourage growth of ideas and craftsmanship. Build musical concepts and awareness of many conventions. Build skills of self-evaluation.
TEN TO TWELVE (GRADES FOUR TO SIX)	Music becomes organized according to cultural rules or structures. Use of melodic and rhythmic motives. Increased use of sounds and patterns of familiar music. Often less original.	Imaginative play in which surprise is an element but using more references to popular music idioms. Concern for form and structure, use of harmony emerges.	Keep expanding the repertoire of conventions for structuring music. Help students to avoid becoming too critical of their or others' works. Encourage self-expression.

Creative Processes

Exploration and Discovery

The first stage in the creative process for all students is to explore and discover possibilities that exist for manipulating sounds. Children need to have the freedom to explore the range of sounds an instrument or voice might make in terms of color (ringing, thunking, raspy, rattling); techniques (scraping, shaking, striking, rubbing, blowing, plucking, strumming); and dynamics (loud or soft), pitch (definite or indefinite, high or low), duration (long, short, or sustained impression), and texture (thin to thick). In early childhood settings, children could have a special location in the room where there is regular access to instruments and a recorder for sound exploration.

In the process of free exploration, children are building a repertoire of sound possibilities and techniques from which they can later draw to make musical or artistic decisions. As a stimulus for exploring sounds, the teacher might give every child a piece of paper and say, "Discover as many different sounds as you can make with this piece of paper in the next two minutes. The signal for you to stop and look at me will be when I flash the lights." When the two minutes have passed, students share their discoveries. During this time, the teacher can guide by asking questions that help the children to compare sounds or group them into categories. "Who has rattling sounds?" "Whose sound was almost like that sound?" The teacher can use this time to build musical vocabulary such as high and low or loud and soft: "Play that sound again, but change from loud to soft." "Make your buzz swoop from low to high." "Repeat the sound of the 'thunk' five times, letting it fade gradually." These same techniques can be used in exploring any sounds.

Stevens (2003) has suggested that the concept of free play be implemented on a regular basis in music classrooms. In such a setting, the teacher structures the room so children can explore musical instruments in a variety of different spaces or centers. Once rules about behavior are established, children are free to experiment, discover, create, and share. Stevens found that this time was very meaningful, as children applied concepts at whole new levels and began to "create music that was meaningful to them" (p. 45).

Over time, children should be encouraged to explore the sound possibilities of a wide range of sources and to use those sounds creatively. Suggestions are found in Box 10.1. Once children have discovered what their instruments or voices can do, they can move into either a mode of improvisation, arranging, or composition.

Children trading improvised patterns on drums

BOX 10.1 Sound Sources

FOUND SOUNDS
Paper
Objects (rulers, cups, pens, keys)
Kitchen implements (egg beater, whisk, grater, spatula)
Garage sounds (hammers, saws, nails, drills, tin cans, wood, springs)

MOUTH SOUNDS
Voiced (hum, shout, sing, sigh, shriek, buzz, animal sounds, machine sounds)
Nonvoiced (pop, click, whistle, slurp, hiss)

ROOM SOUNDS
Pencils, notebooks, rulers, grates, shades, doors, music stands

BODY SOUNDS
Hands, fingers, feet, arms, chest, head

TOY SOUNDS
Whistles, hummers, drums, xylophones, music boxes, rattles, doll, kazoos, Zube Tube

ENVIRONMENTAL SOUNDS
Birds, animals, machines, vehicles, water, wind, waves

INSTRUMENTAL SOUNDS
Classroom (nonpitched percussion, xylophones and metallophones, Autoharps, recorders, pianos, guitars)
Electronic (keyboards, synthesizers, recorders)
Ethnic (membranophones, chorophones, idiophones, aerophones)
Band or orchestra (brass, strings, woodwind, percussion)

STUDENT-INVENTED OR -CONSTRUCTED INSTRUMENTS
Give students simple materials (canisters, string, wood, beans, paper, tape, nails, metal, glass) and have them invent an instrument.

Improvisation

An improvised piece or section of a piece is invented spontaneously. It is not formalized, refined, or repeated. It is performed by the composer/improviser. Improvisation at a beginning level allows children to play with sounds and with musical syntax (or putting those sounds together). Improvisation at the highest level—in jazz or certain world traditions such as Indian sitar and tabla duos, Nigerian drum ensembles, or Chopi (Mozambique) xylophone ensembles—involves advanced performance technique combined with deep knowledge of the idiom being used (Campbell, 1991). Regardless of the age or musical sophistication of the improvisers, this process is essential to developing an ease and flexibility in manipulating the language of music. Opportunities to improvise should occur throughout children's development, stimulating them to converse in music in the same way they converse using words—freely and spontaneously, with meaning. National Standard 3 is dedicated to improvisation. Ideally, children should be invited to improvise during portions of each class.

Students can engage in free or structured improvisations. Free improvisations occur when children of all ages are encouraged to experiment with possibilities on an instrument or vocally and to literally "play with" the sounds and structures. This

"Opportunities to improvise should occur throughout children's development, stimulating them to converse in music in the same way they converse using words—freely and spontaneously, with meaning."

moves beyond exploration, as children are actually improvising pieces that have a beginning and end. Depending on their age, they may be more driven by motoric energy than by musical possibilities, but they are clearly improvising music, not just exploring sounds.

There are numerous possibilities to use in structuring improvisation with children. A whole-class improvisation with the paper sounds that the children have discovered could include the following activities:

1. Ask each person to select three paper sounds he or she found the most interesting.

2. Perform each sound once over one minute and distribute the sounds across the time.

3. Conduct the work—either student or teacher—and mark the passage of time visibly with an arm acting as the second hand of a clock.

4. Record the piece, listen to the results, and discuss them in terms of musical interest and success.

In early childhood settings, simple forms can be used to stimulate improvisation. Teachers could have a musical conversation with one or more students in which the teacher generates a musical idea and the child responds with another idea. Children could be invited to finish a phrase of music in a question-and-answer form. Children could also improvise various ideas to create characters in a familiar story or to create mood, such as angry or excited or happy. (See additional suggestions in Flohr, 2005, and Sims, 1995.)

Lesson Activities 10.1 offers many ideas to stimulate individual improvisation. Although individual children would be inventing ideas, many of these could be done simultaneously by the whole group vocally or using body percussion. As children gain skills and confidence, individuals can share their improvisations as solos. Many of these can also be done on instruments. Children can also be called on to improvise

LESSON ACTIVITIES 10.1 Improvisation Starts

Rhythm	Improvise over a steady beat using body or mouth sounds.
	Use an eight-beat cycle and have different children enter on different beats.
	Improvise over a rhythm pattern or ostinato.
	Improvise over a recording, fitting rhythms into the musical ideas.
	Improvise over a metric pattern.
	With older children, have one group in threes and another in fours.
Melody	Improvise on a neutral syllable over a drone or an ostinato.
	Improvise on a familiar melody over the top of a chord sequence.
	Improvise a melody using scat syllables such as do-be-do, do-wop, shu.
	Improvise in a particular style using pitches from a known scale.
	Improvise based on a melodic theme, embellishing it. Improvise a short song or instrumental piece or an accompaniment.

accompaniments to songs using body rhythms or classroom instruments, movements to music, and music for dramatizations and storytelling. The possibilities for improvisation are endless.

Each of the European approaches to elementary music teaching includes improvisation as a deep part of developing children's musical vocabulary and imagination. An improvisation characteristic of Orff-Schulwerk might feature children's invention of the B section of an ABA or ternary-form piece, where A is a composed or known section. The children, using soprano xylophones, would be directed to invent a melody on a C pentatonic scale, fitting it into an eight-beat frame. Rondo form (ABACA, ABACADA) would allow multiple sections for solo or group improvisation. Children might also improvise a section of a piece using vocal syllables or creative movements.

In a Kodály setting, children might be asked to generate four-beat rhythm patterns for echo clapping or pitch patterns using sol, mi, and la for echo singing. Once children have built an internal collection of rhythm and pitch patterns, they might be asked to improvise a longer melody or rhythm, a melody with additional pitches, or, perhaps, the "answer" to a "question."

The Dalcroze tradition also uses improvisation as an important component in its pedagogy. Children may listen to their teacher's improvisation at the piano and then be expected to complete or continue the piece, retaining the same style in the extension. They could perform melodically using the piano or voice, or rhythmically on a hand drum or through movement. Through this process, they learn to improvise within an established musical quality.

Jazz is a quintessential form for improvisation. Children can be encouraged to improvise vocally or instrumentally over a blues progression. Fitzgerald, McCord, and Berg (2003) developed an approach to helping children from third through sixth grades get a feeling for the rhythms, scales, techniques, and chords of jazz. Using their voices and/or Orff instruments, children learn to scat and to swing in their improvisations. Children who develop these skills at the elementary level will be prepared to explore more advanced approaches to jazz improvisation in middle and high school.

Another context for improvisation exists within the framework of an African drumming ensemble. Once children learn the basic rhythms in a drumming complex and are able to hold their parts against each other, the person in the master drummer role is free to improvise over the top of the rhythm complex. (See Chapter 7, "Rhythm and the Child," for examples of a drumming complex.)

Improvisation can play several valuable roles in the creative process. It can help to develop and expand musical ideas that may be used in compositions; it can help children attain a sense of structure, form, and style; it can be used to introduce and reinforce concepts and technical skills; and, at the highest level, it provides an opportunity for the synthesis of these concepts and skills.

Although not always included as a part of the improvisational process, children can be asked to reflect and comment on the musical effectiveness of the improvisation. Questions could focus on whether it met the requirements of the limits imposed and what was inventive or interesting about the ideas. These reflections should not focus on mistakes, as improvisation by its nature requires risk taking.

Further ideas for improvising in classroom settings can be found in Dadson and McGlashan (1995); Mead (1994); Steen (1992); Fitzgerald, McCord, and Berg (2003); Brophy (2001); and Higgins and Campbell (2010) on group improvisation.

Composition

A more planned realization of the creative process is the act of composition. It differs from improvisation in that it involves the opportunity for crafting a piece, for reflection and revision. It is not instantaneous. Arranging also requires this kind of thinking. National Standard 4: Composing and Arranging speaks to some of the processes and outcomes that might result from having children engage in composing and arranging.

STRUCTURE AND CONTEXT. Even though composing is highly regarded for what it contributes to children's musical and cognitive growth, few teachers choose to spend the time it takes to have children compose. Ideally, each teacher will plan a minimum of three or four composition units per year, lasting two to three weeks or longer. Some teachers choose to build their entire curriculum around composition and listening, with performance skills emerging from the creative work children do.

The teacher has several roles in setting the climate and parameters for composing:

1. Create spaces in the room or adjoining rooms for groups and/or individuals to work.

2. Decide what sound sources will be available and how these will be distributed.

3. Decide whether students will work individually or in small groups. Small groups can be randomly selected, or students can have the freedom to select those they want to collaborate with. An ideal size is four to five. (Both approaches work, but Wiggins [2003] has found that students are often more successful when they are free to work with people they know well.)

4. Decide the amount of time students will have to work on their assignments. It is rare that the entire process can occur in one class period; of necessity, it may have to extend over several days to allow students to truly engage with all dimensions of composing.

5. Decide what the limits of the composition will be, and give the composition a problem or problems to be solved (see ideas in Box 10.2). Sometimes teachers will want all students to solve the same problem so that students can compare the solutions. Other times, it is possible to give different groups different assignments, or to give them the freedom to structure their own work. Usually, that freedom comes after students have gained a lot of confidence as composers.

6. Establish a means of quickly getting the attention of all of the students. Turning off the lights and asking students to "freeze and stay frozen as the lights come on" is a good way to get them to focus.

7. Communicate to students that you will be present to answer questions and help with resources, but that you will not interfere in their composition process. Remember, your role is to be a guide on the side or facilitator, not someone who imposes your musical ideas on the children. You will help them to evaluate their work.

> "As the creative act is at the centre of all artistic activity, so we place creative activity firmly at the centre of musical education, from which all other, more traditional activities radiate, fed by the work of creation and in turn feeding back into it...."
>
> **Christopher Small, 1977**

Adapting Instruction for Various Needs

BEHAVIOR DISORDERS
- *Externalizing behaviors*: For a child who acts out on a regular basis, establish guidelines for working in small groups and with instruments. Place such a child in a group with a strong positive leader. Working with that child on a behavior contract ahead of time is often helpful. This may include an agreement to remove the child from the group if behavior is disturbing to others. Monitor the small group's progress. Reward the child for effective behaviors.

(Continued)

- *Internalizing behaviors*: Often groups will be selected by random. For a child who is withdrawn, you may wish to assign that child to a group with a leader that he or she trusts.

AUTISM SPECTRUM DISORDERS

- The ability of a child to participate effectively in a small group will depend on where he or she is on the autism spectrum. High functioning students will usually participate well and often have wonderful ideas to contribute although too much noise may be challenging. Low functioning students may be very sensitive to touch or to too much noise or may not be able to contribute ideas verbally. As children experiment with sounds, it may be overwhelming. Find a quiet space where groups that include a child with autism can work. Getting to play the instruments freely and be inventive can be motivating for all children. At the same time children with autism can struggle with anything out of the ordinary or unpredictable. Clear structures will need to be established for them in order to be able to participate without being overwhelmed.

MOBILITY IMPAIRMENTS

- Pair children with mobility impairments with a child who will get them the instruments they desire. Work with the aide to adapt instruments so the child can fully participate. Make sure that the group leader is someone who will listen to the ideas of all children.

GIFTED CHILDREN

- Often highly gifted children want to simply take off with composition assignments, leaving other children in the dust. Encourage them to learn to listen to various ideas and to be willing to relinquish their ideas if the group consensus is in another direction. Older gifted children may be stimulated to compose on their own, both in and out of class. Try to provide equipment for performing and recording their work(s).

BOX 10.2 Motivations for Compositions

Themes: "Life and Death of a Mosquito," "Clouds," "A Day in a Factory"

Emotions or moods: angry, happy, sad, excited, proud, regal, frustrated, mysterious

Pictures or images: photographs from magazines, paintings, designs, maps, scores

Stories: wordless books, children's own stories, fairy tales

Poetry: sound or a melodic setting of children's own or other's poetry

Sounds: families of sounds, individual sounds, contrasting sounds

Patterns or cycles: "The Seasons," "A Day," "A Storm," "The Butterfly," "The Water Cycle," "The Life Cycle of a Salmon"

Musical elements: melody, rhythm, harmony, tone color, tempo, dynamics

Aesthetic ideas: density, texture, tension and release, repetition and contrast

Musical structures: ostinato, phrase, motive, AB, ABA, rondo, layered, theme and variations, blues, free form

Recorded Music: any music has the potential to evoke creative responses; works need to be carefully selected for various age levels based on complexity.

With very young children, the teacher may participate throughout the compositional process, pulling ideas from the group and helping the students refine their thinking. At the same time, young children are capable of creating their own compositions (see Gromko, 2003). From late first grade on, children are usually socially mature enough to work in groups of four to five to solve a composition problem, especially if they work regularly in cooperative groups (see Lessons 10.1 and 10.2). Once older children are familiar with the compositional process, they can work quite independently.

LESSON 10.1
A Group Composition Built on a Trip to the Zoo

Teacher Role	Student Role
Ask children to notice the qualities of movements of various animals during their field trip to the zoo.	Carefully observe movements such as smooth or jerky, fast or slow, even or uneven, continuous or random, upward or downward.
Review with the children what they noticed about the movement qualities of the animals. Help them generate sample rhythms that might illustrate those qualities.	Share what they noticed. Generate various rhythmic responses.
Divide children into groups based on the animal they wish to represent, and provide instruments for them to play.	Develop a short piece that conveys the sense of movement of an animal. Practice and refine it.
Select a child to conduct by walking to a temple block from animal to animal. Record the results.	Perform rhythm pattern as long as the conductor is standing in front of the group.
Play the recording and lead children in a discussion of the results. What animal did each group represent? How could one tell? What could be done differently?	Listen to recording. Respond to questions. Evaluate your performance. Suggest ideas for revision.

LESSON 10.2
Group Composition of Layers of Long and Short Sounds

Teacher Role	Student Role
Assign composition limits: Compose a piece for contrasting patterns of long and short sounds in which the texture is never thicker than three sounds. Group students and provide instruments. Serve as resource person to groups if necessary.	Select instruments that will play long and short sounds (xylophones, sticks, metallophones, drums, woodblocks, temple blocks, triangles, and so on). Experiment with various patterns. Select the most interesting ones. Structure the piece, deciding when the various patterns will sound and what creates a sense of completeness. Refine it so it is ready to share.

(Continued)

Teacher Role

Make either audio or visual recordings of the pieces.

Guide children in assessment of their own work and the work of others. Expand thinking and vocabulary as the opportunity arises.

Encourage students to expand or refine compositions. Help expand their thinking by bringing in recorded works that use the same principles. (*Daphne of the Dunes* by Harry Partch is a good example.)

Student Role

Perform own piece and listen to others.

Access the work of your own group and individual roles in it. Assess the composition and suggest ideas for refinement. Help assess the compositions of other groups.

Refine own work to make it more satisfying. Listen to other works, including recorded works that illustrate the same principles.

As children work together, Wiggins (2003) observed that individuals in the group will all be going through a similar process. It is a circular process that can occur many times, until the students are satisfied with their work. Initially, they gather and discuss ideas, select sound sources, invent musical materials, create a text if one is required, and decide which student will play the roles of performer and conductor. Next, students set the material into the context of the assignment; organize, evaluate, revise, and refine; rehearse; and perform. Once the performance occurs and is recorded, there is a chance for feedback. At that point, the composition may be complete or students may go through the entire process again. Across time, the group develops a shared meaning of the work in progress as well as of the compositional process. Children become quite adept at this process in a short period of time. Wiggins (1994) found that working in groups facilitates musical thinking as children challenge each other's ideas. They often start with a large picture of what they want, work on details, and then return to large ideas, completing their compositions.

Once the compositions have been performed and recorded, the teacher helps guide the students in evaluating their work. Building skills of critiquing or reflective evaluation is crucial to the compositional process. Evaluative skills are covered in National Standard 7, and a number of ideas are suggested at the end of this chapter. Finally, the teacher can help students transfer what they have learned to other pieces of music by bringing in recordings that incorporate ideas or techniques the children have developed.

For more ideas to inspire student compositions, see Haines (1996); Katz and Thomas (2004); McNicol (1992); Upitis (1990, 1992); Wiggins (1990); Winters and Northfield (1992); and various issues of the *Music Educators Journal*, listed in the references.

AURAL PLANS. The first stage in the formal compositional process is to help children structure aural plans for their pieces. This simply means that they will work together to refine a piece, trying many different ideas, selecting and rejecting, and finally reaching consensus on the end product through an aural plan. No graphing or notation

© Billie Judy/Reel Life Productions

will be used to record their work. To a certain extent, aural plans are improvisational because, even though the children may rehearse their piece several times, surprises usually occur.

An example of a whole-group composition for primary children with teacher guidance is given in Lesson 10.1. Extensions of this composition would be to use the music as a basis for creative movement. Another day, listen to "Carnival of the Animals" by Saint-Saëns and discuss the ways the composer conveys a sense of the various animals. Identify and discuss similarities, if any, to the students' compositions. Discuss differences, such as the use of animal sounds. You could then add creative movements to sections of the Saint-Saëns work.

The same assignment can be given to each group if the goal is to discover or reinforce a particular concept or theme via composition. It is exciting for children to discover the variety of solutions that can be generated by a single idea. Different assignments can be given to various groups if the goal is a multimovement composition with each group contributing a part (for example, types of clouds), or if the goal has more to do with the process of composing than with a particular outcome. Lesson 10.2 gives an example of an aural plan that might be developed by children from the age of eight or beyond.

This particular strategy could expand into a unit in which children invent and construct their own instruments out of unusual and found materials, then tune them in unique scales in the style of American composer Harry Partch. Ideas could also be developed on a synthesizer or MIDI (Musical Instrument Digital Interface) keyboard, where children have a rich opportunity to invent their own sounds.

NOTATIONAL SYSTEMS. Children grow gradually in their ability to utilize aspects of music notation. Research on children's self-constructed notational systems suggests that they move from pictorial or iconic means of representing their music to more symbolic means of notating rhythm and pitch, in which they use numbers or letters (Upitis, 1990, 1992). At the next stage, they begin to use actual or discrete notation. Gromko

FIGURE 10.1

Invented Notation Using Abstract Symbols

This piece is notated with teardrops to show that it is in a minor key. Other symbols are used as well, but it is not possible to reproduce the piece from the notation itself.

Reproduced with permission from Upitis (1990, p. 66).

(2003) found children as young as three who had begun to represent their music visually. Figures 10.1 and 10.2 show two examples of children's invented notations.

Once children have a sense of the compositional process through creating aural plans, the use of notation can be introduced. Children should be free to devise their own systems. Ideally, the initial system should be a representation of a piece they have already crafted with an aural plan. For example, second graders are each asked to compose a "one-tone tune," lasting as long as one breath. They experiment with varying the tone color, dynamics, pattern, and vowel and consonant sounds. Once the piece is refined and shared, each child devises a means of notating the ideas in a way another person could understand. They then share their notation with another child and ask that child to interpret it. Dialogues between composer and performer about notation as a means of communication result in interesting insights. A sample notation of a "one-tone tune" is:

Buh ———————————— Zz z z z z z *te te te te m___ ah-t*

As children experience standard notation through the use of music texts and training in reading, they will want to incorporate it in notating all or part of their compositions. They might start by notating rhythm patterns using stick notation or pitch patterns on a three-note staff. Compositions using notation can also tie into skills children are acquiring. For example, once children have learned to play B, A, and G on a soprano recorder, they could be asked to compose and notate a four-measure melody in $\frac{4}{4}$ time using B, A, and G, ♩ ♫ 𝄽 rhythmic values, and ending on G.

Children of all ages will be stimulated to use notation programs available on computer. (See Chapter 17 for a list of programs suitable for children from preschool through the elementary years. See also Reese, 2001.) Regardless of age, children need to remain free to create aural plans, invent devised systems, or use discrete notation, or a combination thereof. Exposure to performing contemporary works that use devised systems will help children understand that notation is malleable and must convey what the composer intends.

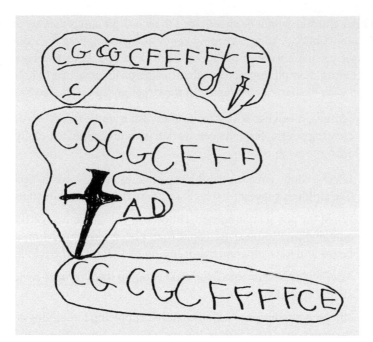

FIGURE 10.2

Invented Notation Using Letter Names of Pitches

The backwards 2 [upper left] means "with two hands and two times." The knife next to the F indicates the note F# ("It is a pirate's knife, and a pirate's knife is very sharp").

Reproduced with permission from Upitis (1990, p. 63).

INVENTING SONGS. Children are natural inventors of song. Any preschool teacher can testify to the fact that young children are constantly singing self-made songs as they play. Campbell's 2010 ethnography, *Songs in Their Heads*, is a profound testament to the rich role that song invention and elaboration play in the lives of both individual children and groups of children. Often, teachers do not leave a place for children to share these songs in their music classes. Wise teachers can continue to encourage the singing of spontaneous, self-made songs by providing both a context and encouragement for children to share their ideas. Children from preschool through grade one could have a song circle where a child in the center sings a spontaneous song about a pet, about something he or she has been doing, or perhaps about a story in a picture book. This is improvisational in nature.

Older children might be encouraged to record the songs they've created, keeping them in a portfolio. A song recording center using computer recording technology could be set up in a corner of the room. Each child could create a cover for his/her CD by including their photograph or other images on an envelope to hold their CD. Children who wish to share their songs with the larger group could also be encouraged to do so.

Sometimes, a teacher will want to establish a more formal structure and procedure for creating songs. Teachers can work with young children to create a song using the following procedures:

1. Select a topic. Create a word bank of descriptive words generated by the children. The children suggest phrases for a poem that the teacher transcribes on the board.

2. When the poem is completed, children chant it together, getting a feel for its rhyme and rhythm. The teacher could then play a tonic chord on an Autoharp or keyboard and have different children sing melodies for the first line of the poem.

3. After trying several ideas, the class votes on their favorite melody, and it is sung by all and recorded.

4. The process continues with the teacher supplying underlying chords, which support the harmonic structure of the melody. (An alternative is to provide a harmonic structure in which children create the melodies.)

5. Children listen to the entire song and suggest changes. The song is sung and recorded in its entirety. The teacher can notate it at a later time and share it with the class in that form.

The song "Freckles" (see Box 10.3) was composed by a group of second graders in collaboration with their teacher, Jackie Wiggins (1990, p. 45). She suggests the following

BOX 10.3 "Freckles" by Jackie Wiggins's Second-Grade Class

Wiggins (1990, p. 45).

Sixth grader playing her notated composition on Taiko drum

procedure for writing a song with elementary children. This procedure reflects one of the many ways professional song-writers work, beginning with lyrics and moving to an accompaniment and melody. It is also possible to begin with a melody, chord sequence, or rhythm and have the lyrics emerge.

Day 1

1. Invite students to suggest a topic and a title.

2. Ask students for a good first line to introduce the topic. Write it on the board.

3. Develop that into a poem. (Younger children may need more guidance in finding rhyming words and structure.)

4. Guide children into writing a short refrain around the topic, usually four lines with some repetition.

Day 2

1. Write the poem on the board.

2. Play two or three possible accompaniments, contrasting style such as rock and roll, blues, or lullaby and tonality—major or minor.

3. Have students vote on the accompaniment style they think is most appropriate.

4. Play the accompaniment and speak the words over the top, making them fit a metric pattern.

5. Have the class improvise a melody over the accompaniment. Experiment with various melodies, shaping them until students come to a consensus about which

melodies they want to use. Move back and forth between the chanting and the singing until children are satisfied.

Day 3

1. Distribute a notated copy of the song to the children with their class name at the top.

2. Decide to leave it as is or invite children to arrange the piece, adding introductions, interludes, and codas to be played on various instruments.

3. Rehearse it and either record it or perform it for others.

Older children can use a similar process but can work more independently. They might be given a poem with the rhythm notated and encouraged to experiment with different melodic shapes on a keyboard, staying within a single tonal center. They could experiment using stepwise motion, small leaps, and repeated tones. Later, build in concepts of repetition and contrast and melodic sequence. As children grow in their abilities, use ideas of tone painting and have students compose their own words and melodies.

When children are ready to start notating their own rhythms, the teacher can show them how the lyrics suggest rhythms and how the rhythms suggest a meter, paying special attention to heavy beats and lighter beats. (They might need to practice this first with familiar nursery rhymes, then advance to notating the rhythms of unfamiliar poems or song lyrics.)

INDIVIDUALIZED PLAN. As children mature, many prefer to work on their own or in small groups with their friends. Teachers can structure the classroom with learning stations where children develop skills by working on their own with keyboards, guitars, synthesizers, and recorders, as well as areas dedicated to listening and composition. In each learning center, folders are provided that tell students the requirements for that center. The teacher structures the environment, then serves as an observer or as someone to answer questions as they arise.

Folders for a composition center could be color-coded and numbered for type of assignment and level of complexity. Instruments and recordering equipment are made available for the students. File folders have the title on the outside; the left inside pocket contains pictures, scores, maps, or other images; and the right pocket contains the chart shown in Lesson 10.3.

LESSON 10.3 Format for Independent Compositions

Problem State the limits of the composition.

Compose a sixteen-beat piece in duple meter for Autoharp or Omnichord and nonpitched rhythm instruments.

Materials State the size of the group, and the materials and equipment needed.

1. Four students
2. One Autoharp and pick
3. Various rhythm instruments
4. Recording equipment

(Continued)

Procedures	State the steps to be followed in a logical order.

1. Experiment with various chord progressions until you find one you like.

2. Write the progression down, indicating each of the sixteen beats and the chord changes. Make sure the final chord is one that gives a sense of resolution.

3. Select rhythmic percussion instruments that will enhance your piece, and add the rhythmic accompaniment.

4. Use an interesting strum to create a rhythm on the Autoharp.

5. Practice your piece, refining as necessary.

6. When you are satisfied, record the piece, label the recording with your group name and the folder name, and place the recording in the box on the composition table.

Assessment	List questions the students need to answer as part of the process of reflecting on their composition and the process. Each group member answers the following questions separately and submits them with the recording.

1. How satisfied are you with your composition and why?

2. Did you change anything? Is there anything else you would like to change? How might you change it?

3. What contributions did you make to the process of composing this piece?

Challenge	Ideas for further compositional work, reflection, or transfer into listening.

Listen to the recording in the composition folder. These ideas represent other people's solutions to this problem. Compare them with your own. Discuss your responses with other members of your group.

Accomplishing Multiple Music Standards through Creating

1. *Singing*: Have children sing songs they created—individually or as a class. Work to develop correct intonation and phrasing skills. Encourage children to try a variety of vocal techniques such as the use of neutral syllables or scat syllables when improvising vocally. Use improvisatory techniques to expand their range.

2. *Playing*: After children have crafted instrumental compositions, work with them on their playing techniques as needed to perform their compositions well. Encourage a variety of playing techniques to create various effects.

3. *Improvising*: See activities in this chapter for improvising.

4. *Composing and Arranging*: See activities in this chapter for composing and arranging.

5. *Reading and Notating*: See activities in this chapter for reading and notating.

6. *Listening*: Once children have composed a piece, find a recorded work to reinforce and extend their ideas. For example, if their piece uses layered nonpitched percussion

(Continued)

sounds, play drumming music from Ghana or Nigeria. Have them compare their work to that work. Find examples of interesting recording that might stimulate children's creativity such as the music of Harry Partch or Henry Cowell. Play that music for children, discuss the sounds and techniques and invite them to compose a work that reflects some of those ideas.

7. *Analyzing and Evaluating*: See ideas in this chapter for having children analyze and critique their compositions and those of others.

8. *Connect to Other Arts and Curricular Areas*: Throughout this chapter you will see ideas for using content of other curricular areas as a stimulus for improvisations or compositions. Various works of art can be used as a stimulus for composing. See ideas in Chapter 14, "Integrated Curriculum." As appropriate, children could be invited to choreograph some of their compositions. Children can set simple stories to music, inventing themes for the characters. They can use nature as a stimulus for composition including many of the patterns in nature. If they are studying rain or weather or the planets in science, they could create compositions to represent the essence of types of rain; different weather systems; or the various planets. The possibilities are unlimited.

9. *Connect to Culture and History*: Students can listen to the music of various cultures, learn the instruments and discuss the scales, harmonies, rhythms and structures of the music. Then they could compose music in the style of a given culture.

Assessment

Any creative individual learns to critique his or her own work using objective as well as intuitive standards. Building skills in self-assessment and evaluating the work of others is crucial to the compositional process. This can be done verbally, with the teacher guiding the entire class, individually, or within peer or small group settings. Students can share comments about what they liked about a composition. All students can engage in a guided critique of their own work using the questions below. Assessment sheets could be kept by individual students as a part of a portfolio project, along with selected recorded compositions. Teachers or students could also develop rubrics to use in assessing compositions. (See Chapter 13 for suggestions for creating rubrics.)

Formative Evaluations

Webster (2003) suggests that there may be three stages to the revision and extension process. The first stage is a formative stage, where children are discovering how to work with musical ideas. Here the teacher needs to take care not to be too directive, but still make suggestions for improvement. Questions like "What can you do to make it more interesting?" would be helpful in moving students along. If children are searching for ideas, the teacher could suggest several possibilities. The second stage he calls craftsmanship. In this stage, students are quite familiar with the process of critiquing and revision, and the teacher serves more as a coach or consultant. Here the students will ask for specific ideas and will be able to respond on a more sophisticated level musically. The third stage is called the expert stage, in which the teacher becomes a mentor. This stage would probably not occur until the student is quite advanced, such as in high school or college.

The following questions are useful in guiding an evaluation of the composition as well as the process. They represent teacher engagement at the formative level. Reese (2003) has also developed extensive ideas for ways teachers might respond to student compositions.

1. How well did the composition meet the requirements of the assignment?

2. Did you revise? What did you change? How did you change it?

3. Did you hear music inside your head? When and how did this happen?

4. What worked or was interesting musically about the composition?

5. If you had more time to spend on the composition, is there anything you would change?

6. How successful was the process? Does anything in it need to change?

Summative Evaluations

Should the teacher wish to keep a written record of student progress in composition, it is useful to consider how compositions can be assessed on qualities of musical features, general style and effectiveness, originality, and performance directions. Assessment can also record student growth in attitudes, commitment, interpretation, confidence, and discretion. Other ideas for student and teacher assessment of compositions and the compositional process can be found in Winner, Davidson, and Scripp (1992),.

Any of these ideas could be adapted to fit the teacher's criteria for creativity, commitment, and skill development. Formal evaluation would not need to be used each time a student composed but could be used several times a year to keep track of the quality of a given student's work. Along with recordings of various compositions, the assessments, including rubrics, could become a part of documentation included in student portfolios.

The Rewards of Nurturing Creativity in Music

A challenge in teaching music is to implement a curriculum that balances performing, listening, and creating. Teachers are naturally drawn to teach those things with which they are the most familiar. Because so much of their own musical training required the development of sophisticated performance skills, teachers are drawn to emphasize performance with children. Yet, teachers who are willing to develop the processes of listening and creating with children will find the rewards gratifying.

Quality programs in composition and improvisation will foster many important skills. Children will develop a sense of control over the materials of music as they engage in aesthetic decision making. The result is a feeling of pride and of ownership of their ideas. They will develop a musical vocabulary of sounds, patterns, and concepts with which to create musical syntax, assisting them in thinking musically. They will learn to apply critical and creative thinking skills to the process of making musical decisions. These skills will transfer from composing to listening and performing. Children will learn to work cooperatively with others in the composition process. They will learn to assess their own work and the work of others. They will discover that effective composition involves craft, not just inspiration. Children will grow creatively, critically, musically, and aesthetically. As Pablo Picasso remarked, "Every child is an artist. The problem is how to remain an artist once she grows up."

Scenario

THE SIXTH GRADERS IN Mr. Jensen's music class love to compose and have been doing so for two years. They are familiar with the group problem-solving process. Today they are working on the beginning stages of writing a two-part song in their groups. Each group has a synthesizer station at which to work. The details of the assignment are written on the board. Mr. Jensen uses his familiar technique of counting students off by fives and having them go to a station with other students who have the same number. The students have thirty minutes to work that day and are expected to come up with lyrics around a theme that they choose in their groups. Subsequent class periods will be devoted to writing their tunes.

All of the groups go to their stations and seem to be working. One boy, Jared, comes up quietly to Mr. Jensen and says that he prefers to work alone and wants to compose a piece by himself. Mr. Jensen knows that Jared will probably succeed at that task, so he sends him over to work at the piano, once Jared excuses himself from his group. Out of the corner of his eye, Mr. Jensen notices that one group of four girls and one of the more popular boys is not focused on the assignment. The girls seem uncomfortable and shy. He applies his cardinal rule not to interfere with the dynamics of a group and simply stays at the side of the room, watching and listening to the exchanges in the various groups. Jared works away happily by himself.

When the twenty minutes are up, Mr. Jensen flicks the lights on and off, which is the signal to the children to stop what they are doing and share their progress with the whole group. Jared quickly volunteers that he was writing a song about the adventures of Harry Potter, one of his favorite storybook characters. Four of the groups share their ideas. When Mr. Jensen turns to the fifth group, the students just stare at him and look embarrassed. They do not have anything to share, and they try to shrug it off by looking cool.

Questions

1. Why do you think students in the fifth group failed to meet the assignment?

2. What could Mr. Jensen have done to avoid such potential problems?

3. Do you think that it was appropriate or inappropriate for Jared to work alone? Why?

4. How appropriate was the compositional assignment for sixth graders?

5. What did you use as the basis for your decision?

REVIEW

1. What is the difference between composing and improvising? What is the difference between convergent and divergent thinking?

2. How is the type of thinking developed during creative activities different from the type of thinking in most of the rest of schooling?

3. What are the benefits to children of improvising? Of composing? Why or why not?

4. What role(s) does the teacher play in the composition process? What role(s) does the student play?

5. List several ways you and your students could keep track of their growth as composers.

6. Which methods in general music include improvisational strategies as a regular part of their instruction? How do strategies vary between those approaches?

7. What motivates young children to invent their own songs? How could you build on that as teachers?

CRITICAL THINKING

1. Is it important to build skills in evaluative or critical thinking as part of the composition process? Why or why not?

2. Why might teachers be reluctant to include compositional assignments in their classrooms?

3. How could teachers overcome those blocks?

PROJECTS

1. Find some nonconventional sound sources and work with a group of children to help them explore and discover the sound possibilities. Help guide them through a simple improvisation using those sound sources.

2. Find a composition assignment from one of the books or articles listed in the references and implement it with a group of children or with college classmates. Try to include all of the elements of the compositional process listed in this chapter. Discuss your response to this process and the response of the participants.

3. Write three composition assignments for older elementary children using the format explained in the section "Individualized Plan." Share your assignments with a classmate to check for clarity and logic. Try your ideas with students. Refine the plans if necessary.

4. Develop a two-paragraph rationale to be used with parents for having composition as a significant part of the general music program.

5. Read and review one book on composition or improvisation from the References. Note a minimum of five ideas you would want to use with your students.

6. Find a picture from a magazine that might be a good start for a composition. Write a composition assignment to go with it.

7. Review a text with activities oriented toward Orff-Schulwerk, Dalcroze, or Kodály methods. Discover strategies that promote improvisation and those that promote composition.

8. Examine through experimentation any of the computer programs designed to encourage children to develop song-writing skills. Decide which would be most appropriate for your setting and develop a plan for its use.

9. Interview three teachers to find out whether or not they have their students improvise and compose. If they do not, find out why. If they do, find out what procedures they use and what benefits they see for their students. Report your findings to your class.

10. Get permission to visit an early childhood center to observe and record instances of spontaneous singing during a forty-minute period. Document who sang, what the nature of the singing was, and what the children were doing as they sang. Summarize your findings and reflect on what this means to you regarding children's inherent musicality, as well as what this might mean for your teaching.

MINDTAP Visit **MindTap** to access classroom videos, audio, and more!

PART 2

The Facilitating Teacher

IN PART ONE OF *Music in Childhood*, we invited you to look at the world of music education largely through the eyes of the developing child and the musical world surrounding the child. In Part Two, The Facilitating Teacher, we ask you to consider many of the other dimensions that will influence your work as a teacher: managing children and materials in the music classroom; working with diverse materials from various cultural traditions; collaborating with classroom teachers to integrate the arts across the curriculum; planning and implementing your curriculum; and assessing the growth of students. In the fourth edition, we've suggested ideas throughout the book for adapting instruction to meet the needs of all children. Part Two also includes an entire chapter on exceptionality, to give you greater depth of understanding as to the source and nature of many of the needs you will be asked to meet, the legal requirements for teachers in meeting those needs, and further strategies you can utilize to make your classroom a welcoming place for all children.

Each of the chapters in Part Two challenges you to enter the profession of teaching aware of specific factors and trends that directly affect your decision making as an educator. Ultimately, your ability to work effectively with these many dimensions of teaching will help increase your confidence and competence in the exciting work of bringing music to children. We hope you find these ideas helpful.

11

Motivation and Management

IN THIS CHAPTER

- What Is Motivation and Where Does It Come From? A Short Review of Educational Psychology
  - Three Sources of Motivation
  - Drive Reduction Theory of Motivation
  - Behaviorism: Operant Conditioning
  - Competition as a Motivator
- Foundations of Understanding and Managing Student Behaviors
  - Understanding the Role of Personal Traits and the Educational Environment
  - Understanding Self and Others through Enneagrams
  - Understanding Self and Others through Transactional Analysis
  - Logical Consequences
- Setting Up Your Classroom to Nurture Positive Social and Academic Learning
- Organizing Classes into Cooperative Learning Groups
- Organizing the Classroom and Record Keeping
- Learning and Remembering Students' Names
- Guidelines for Motivating and Managing Students
- Token Prizes
- Special Person
- Other External Motivators
- Strategies for Confronting Inappropriate Behavior
  - Establishing Expectations and Procedures
  - Judicious Discipline
  - Discipline with Love and Logic
  - Behavior Expectation Forms
  - Behavior Contracts
  - The Intervention Thermometer

KIM BEGAN HER TEACHING internship after several years of college preparation. She was excited about getting to teach, and she projected high enthusiasm that the students recognized and enjoyed. Most of Kim's lessons went well, but sometimes glitches arose that left her wondering how she could have managed the situation better. In one lesson, a student was knocked down and hurt in a stampede to get instruments. (Kim quickly realized she needed to organize a system for sending a few students at a time to get instruments.) In another class, three students chose to talk with each other most of the period rather than attend to the lesson. In yet another class, two students traded insults and got into a fistfight.

Kim was frustrated that her lessons had not gone perfectly, and she wanted her cooperating teacher, Mr. Chen, to tell her what to do. But Mr. Chen wisely explained that each teacher needs to develop a leadership presence and an array of interventions that are uniquely successful for herself, her particular philosophy, and the situation. He reminded Kim that the ultimate goal of any motivational or management technique is to help students learn responsibility for motivating and managing themselves.

Kim experimented with several ideas and found some that worked most of the time, but nothing that worked all the time. Mr. Chen reassured Kim, reminding her to be gentle with herself, relax, and not expect to be perfect. "Everyone has setbacks—even long-time teachers," he said. He even shared a poem he kept on his wall: "Ring the bells that still can ring. Forget your perfect offering. There's a crack in everything: That's how the light gets in" (Cohen, 1994). As the term progressed, Kim realized that understanding human nature and building a repertoire of skills for motivating and managing students takes a long time.

The ability to motivate and manage students is one of the most necessary skills of good teachers. Every interview for teaching positions, every job description, and every annual evaluation form includes references to motivation and management. Clearly, school districts, principals, parents, and students expect teachers to manage and motivate. Society as a whole expects teachers to guide students to learn and abide by the values underlying the society and the cognitive and social skills necessary for lifelong productive contributions to society. Motivation and management are so intricately bound up with each other that they will be discussed as an integrated unit in this chapter. To reach a level of high-quality music achievement, students must be motivated. Highly motivated students display four characteristics: (1) they choose musical activities over nonmusical of their own free will, (2) they are intensely involved in musical activities, (3) they are highly persistent in staying with musical activities over time, and (4) they engage in musical activities with a high quality of strategic approaches (see Maehr, Pintrich, and Linnenbrink, 2002).

So many competing personal theories, philosophies, and approaches exist regarding this subject that teachers can become confused and wonder what to do. Ideas run the gamut from iron-fist teacher-controlled manipulation and rule enforcement to child-centered, "as-we-go-along" meaning-construction. The many discipline consultants and plans on the market tout the merits of their particular approaches, but no gimmicks or plans work for every teacher with every student at every grade level in every school in every community at every time of the year. Each teacher needs to become aware of many techniques, then develop his or her own unique philosophy and set of interventions. Motivation and management are challenging for any teacher, but more so for music teachers, because they see so many children coming from so many different class structures each day, and they have limited time options for dealing with problems. Music is also equipment- and materials-intensive. There is a lot to think about managing, apart from the students themselves.

THINGS TO THINK ABOUT

- What motivates you to get things done, and why do you think this motivates you?

- How do you feel when involved in something you really enjoy?

- What do you do to motivate yourself when you have to do something you don't enjoy?

"No gimmicks or plans work for every teacher with every student at every grade level in every school in every community at every time of the year."

What Is Motivation and Where Does It Come From? A Short Review of Education Psychology

Three Sources of Motivation

Motivation is any factor that increases the vigor of an individual's activity. Some tasks, such as doing a hobby, are enjoyable in themselves and are said to be intrinsically motivating. *Intrinsic* motivation is a property of the task itself. Csikszentmihalyi (1990, p. 49) identifies eight major properties of intrinsically motivating tasks:

1. We feel we have a chance to complete the task

2. We are able to concentrate all attention on the task

3. The task has clear goals

4. The task provides immediate feedback

5. We are able to act with deep but effortless involvement that blocks out mundane worries

6. We feel a sense of control when involved in the task

7. Concern for the self disappears

8. The sense of time is altered while involved in the task

He also refers to an intrinsically motivated experience as an *autotelic* experience (auto = self + telos = goal), that is, doing a task not for some outside benefit, but because doing the task is itself the reward. "When the experience is autotelic, the person is paying attention to the activity for its own sake; when it is not, the attention is focused on its consequences" (p. 67). Music teachers should keep these principles in mind and strive to hook students' interest when designing lesson tasks.

Tasks do not have the same intrinsic motivating value, however, for all people. A task that is immensely intrinsically motivating for some students may not be enjoyable at all for others, so teachers also need to rely on other types of motivation. Another source of motivation focuses not on the task, but on the person. Some people are motivated internally; that is, their own inner goals, values, or beliefs override the nonmotivating nature of an unpleasant task or add to the intrinsic motivation of an enjoyable task. *Internal* motivation comes from within the person. When a person is internally motivated, whether the task itself is motivating makes little difference, provided the task is perceived as helping to reach the overall goal and the cost of doing the task, in terms of time and effort, is not too great. Music teachers can help stimulate internal motivation by pointing out how a particular lesson or task will help students understand themselves better, relate better to others, understand history and different cultures and beliefs systems, and so on.

The third source of motivation, *external* motivation, comprises any kind of reward, feedback, or punishment from others, such as grades, money, points, awards, tokens, compliments, criticism, and so on. If students are not intrinsically or internally motivated to perform a task, external motivation can be very effective in stimulating students to do the task anyway, especially when beginning a new or unfamiliar area of learning. External motivating techniques can help bridge the gap of engagement until intrinsic motivation builds and takes over. Music teachers need to develop a wide array of these techniques, but use them only as backup devices, keeping in mind that the

TABLE 11.1 Four Factors of Motivation

	PERSON IS MOTIVATED	PERSON IS NOT MOTIVATED
TASK IS MOTIVATING	Best of all worlds. Person believes the task will help achieve one of his or her goals (internal motivation) and the task is fun (intrinsic motivation). Few, if any, external rewards will be necessary.	Person does not see the relevance of the task (no internal motivation) but does the task anyway because it is fun (intrinsic motivation).
TASK IS NOT MOTIVATING	Person understands the task is necessary to reach a higher goal (internal motivation) and does the task, even though it is boring (no intrinsic motivation).	Worst-case scenario. Person does not see the relevance of the task, and the task is unpleasant. External rewards will probably be necessary to get the task completed.

ultimate goal is to guide students to feeling that learning itself is fun (extending mastery over their environment) and that building a full and rich life for themselves is important and fulfilling work. Table 11.1 illustrates the differences and relationships between intrinsic, internal, and external motivation.

In summary, teachers need to think carefully about the intrinsic motivational qualities of the tasks they pose to students. Dynamic interactive tasks that most students consider enjoyable will be more motivating than dull drills and repetitive exercises. Teachers also need to present lessons in such a way that students understand the relevance of the tasks to their continued musical and personal growth. Students are most highly motivated when they love what they are doing and know that doing it is helping them become better people. Humans are naturally curious, so the act of learning is itself usually motivational.

"Motivation is any factor that increases the vigor of an individual's activity."

Motivation comes naturally from intrinsic and internal sources

FIGURE 11.1

Maslow's Hierarchy of Human Needs

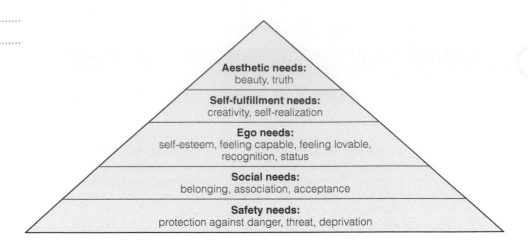

Drive Reduction Theory of Motivation

Some psychologists believe that motivation comes from drive reduction. This theory recognizes that human beings have drives that need satisfaction: oxygen, water, food, shelter, sensory stimulation, acceptance, belonging—the list could go on and on. Each drive motivates behaviors in predictable and unpredictable ways. One sign of a good teacher is the ability to capitalize on students' internal drives and put them to good use. For example, a student may be continually seeking attention in class through inappropriate behaviors (getting off-task, hitting other children, tattling, and so on). If the behavior is caused by a need for attention, a good teacher finds an alternative, acceptable way of satisfying the need, such as greeting the student when he enters the room, engaging him in a short conversation about something he is interested in, asking him to babysit a stuffed animal during class, or noticing even small appropriate productive behaviors. Maslow (1971) classifies human needs into a tiered hierarchy (see Figure 11.1).

A satisfied need is no longer motivating, but if a lower need is unmet, the person will generally stop working at the higher level and take care of the lower need. There is less consistency of importance in the higher categories. For example, a person may forgo social needs to concentrate on creative or aesthetic needs. Sometimes our efforts as teachers to motivate students in music are undercut by more basic needs (hunger, family problems, social problems, inadequate sleep), and we will probably not be effective in motivating for music until these more basic needs are met.

Figure 11.2, Many Kinds of Fun, is based on Maslow's hierarchy and is particularly helpful in motivating students (with internal motivation) to use lessons and rehearsals to strive for the highest fun (which is akin to making beautiful music) rather than settling for lower fun (which is equivalent to talking with friends—or making noise). As in Maslow's hierarchy, achieving the highest levels of fun is difficult when some members of the group focus on satisfying their lower needs.

Behaviorism: Operant Conditioning

Advocates of behaviorism believe that people can be motivated to increase or decrease particular behaviors by four types of operant conditioning: positive reinforcement, negative reinforcement, punishment, and extinction. Positive and negative reinforcement strengthen the likelihood that a particular behavior will continue, while punishment and extinction weaken the likelihood.

FIGURE 11.2

Many Kinds of Fun—from Noise to Music

Many Kinds of Fun
—from Noise to Music
==

Super Fun
achieving high expectations
making something beautiful

}}}} Big Fun {{{{
participating in enjoyable
activities with friends

++++ Medium Fun ++++
talking or interacting with friends

//// Little Fun \\\\
being a couch potato, being bored, putting others down

—— No Fun ——
being put down, getting beat up, being with jerks

**All people control the kinds of fun they will have by the ways they choose to
behave and the words they choose to say.**

1. *Positive reinforcement* increases motivation by giving students desirable rewards for sought-after behaviors, such as receiving a point for their team by answering a question correctly or singing a phrase accurately.

2. *Negative reinforcement* increases motivation by removing a condition that students do not like, such as allowing students to return to their groups after being required to go to a time-out area.

3. *Punishment* weakens students' desires to do particular behaviors by connecting the behaviors with negative consequences, such as taking a point away from his group when a student hits someone.

4. *Extinction* of a behavior is more likely to occur when neither positive nor negative reinforcement occurs, such as the teacher redirecting a question without comment after receiving a silly answer from a student.

Operant conditioning does not always change the behavior in the way a teacher wants, because the teacher may not accurately understand what is positive or negative for a particular student, or may not understand other effects on students' motivation. Teachers must remind themselves that the meaning they intend for a reinforcement, positive or negative, may not have the same meaning for their students. "Conveying reward and punishment is often done in terms of the conveyer's biases....it is not the reward (or punishment) given per se, but the *meaning* [emphasis original] of the reward and punishment that determines reactions" (Maehr, Pintrich, and Linnenbrink, 2002, p. 352). For example, punishing a student for repeated interruptions to a lesson will not succeed when the student is motivated by simply getting some attention of any kind. The teacher would be more successful by providing this student with extra attention, such as having him serve as a special helper.

Punishment can easily backfire, if students perceive it as too harsh or unjustified. Preceding punishment with a statement of empathy helps students feel the teacher is on their side, even while they receive the punishment. For example, if one student hits another, the teacher can say "I'm sorry you made that choice. Now I will have to do something. Let's talk about your consequence after class." Skillfully administered punishment and extinction at just the right level can be highly effective in producing dramatic, permanent cessation of unwanted behaviors. These techniques, however, must be immediately followed by positive reinforcement of substituted desired behaviors. Knowing what *not to do* is not the same as knowing what *to do*.

Competition as a Motivator

Competition can sometimes be a source of motivation, but it can also backfire. Students who enjoy challenge and risk may be motivated by competition, but students who are anxious and have low levels of expectancy may not enjoy competition at all. Some teachers advocate abolishing competition altogether. Kohn (1996) considers competition the number one community destroyer. He believes that any activity that rewards students for doing better than others (spelling bees, awards assemblies, segregating special needs children or gifted students) reduces their sense of interdependence with, responsibility for, and caring about each other. Building on Kohn's work, Bennett and Bartholomew (1997) suggest alternatives to competition, rewards, and praise. Teachers whose personal theories agree with these ideas would eschew competition in favor of other forms of motivation.

Some teachers, on the other hand, find competition a useful motivator, reflective of and preparation for life in society. In U.S. society, children are frequently exposed to competition in sporting events, card games, board games, politics, and advertising and other business promotions. Csikszentmihalyi (1990) asserts, "What each person seeks is to actualize her potential, and this task is made easier when others force us to our best" (p. 73). Johnson and Johnson (1987) advocate using intergroup competition through team tournaments. Many children find competition in teams exciting and fun, even those who prefer not to compete individually. Competition between groups can achieve the same benefits as individual competition, but is less risky, especially when groups are well balanced regarding varying levels of student competence. Competition through cooperative groups can promote acceptance of diversity, sharing of effort, sharing of responsibility, orderliness, and productivity. Competition between groups in a friendly atmosphere can foster cooperation within groups, communication, a sense of belonging, and self-esteem. Low-self-esteem students, who may have little chance of winning individually, enjoy feeling successful when they belong to a group that wins. Group competition must not, however, be allowed to produce hostility to people outside one's group.

"Competition through cooperative groups can promote acceptance of diversity, sharing of effort, sharing of responsibility, orderliness, and productivity."

Foundations of Understanding and Managing Student Behaviors

Understanding the Role of Personal Traits and the Educational Environment

Dynamic teachers lessen the possibilities for inappropriate student behaviors with generally positive personalities that show plenty of enthusiasm, energy, self-assurance, good senses of humor, sensitivity, self-control, and sincerity. Chances for good behavior are even more assured when teachers are well organized, knowledgeable, affirming, observant, fair, flexible, punctual, and generally effective in helping students learn. Students tend to focus on good learning behaviors when the teacher challenges them with intriguing musical tasks suitable for their level of development, monitors and adjusts instruction, and varies the pace so that students do not get bored, lost, frustrated, or defeated. When students behave inappropriately, Bennett and Bartholomew (1997) suggest that teachers first consider aspects of their own behavior: "the energy level you are demonstrating[,] . . . the clarity of behavior expectations for the activity[,] . . . the level of fascination that the activity holds for the students [, and] . . . the potential for success that students see in the activity" (p. 210).

> *"Students tend to focus on good learning behaviors when the teacher challenges them with intriguing musical tasks suitable for their level of development, monitors and adjusts instruction, and varies the pace so that students do not get bored, lost, frustrated, or defeated."*

Understanding Self and Others through Enneagrams

One powerful frame for understanding one's own and one's students' behaviors is the Enneagram, as described in the book *The Essential Enneagram* (Daniels and Price, 2000). All people have traits of personality that group into nine basic types. No one type is superior or inferior to another, as each has its strengths and weaknesses. By learning the characteristics of the nine types, teachers can understand their own and their students' motivations for a multitude of behaviors. For example, if you discover that you are a Type 1 "Perfectionist" on the Enneagram, you know your strengths are integrity, concern for improvement, putting forth a lot of effort, idealism, self-reliance, industriousness, having high standards, self-restraint, and being highly responsible. You also learn that the drawbacks of Type 1 are not being able to quiet the internal critic and the associated anxiety and worry, feeling overburdened by a sense of personal responsibility and conscientiousness, and letting go of resentments and associated tension. Type 1 personalities can also become frustrated with those who do not share their hard-work ethic. A Type 1 teacher, for example, may have difficulties working with a Type 7 student: the Epicure. Type 7 personality strengths are enjoying and experiencing life to its fullest, keeping options open and life upbeat, an active imagination, playfulness, inventiveness, high energy, optimism, love of life, vision, enthusiasm, and helpfulness. Wise teachers will take time to understand their own personality types (including how to deal with their weaknesses) and the personality types of their students (and how to work with each type successfully).

Understanding Self and Others through Transactional Analysis

Thomas A. Harris (1969) explained a wonderful way of understanding and managing student behavior in his popular book, *I'm OK—You're OK*. Teachers can educate their older students in the basics of Transactional Analysis (TA) and ask them to use it to understand their own and others' behavior. Harris explained that all humans

FIGURE 11.3

Transactional Analysis Diagram

Parent   Hooks   Parent

Adult   Best   Adult

Child   Hooks   Child

Teacher   Student

can interact in three modes: the Parent, Child, and Adult. The Parent mode comes from those memories and feelings from childhood that informed the child to do or not to do something because the big, powerful authority said so in an authoritative voice, for example, "DON'T TOUCH THAT KNIFE!" The Child mode comes from impulsive feelings of wanting to have fun right now and ignoring the consequences. The Adult mode is the reasoning, thoughtful mediator. Harris envisions a social interchange as arrows going forth and back between two circle clusters or snowmen (see Figure 11.3). The best transactions are conducted between both people's Adult modes, as in Teacher: "It seems to be getting too noisy in here. Billy, we need to use our inside voices." Billy may respond in his Adult mode with a softer voice, "Sorry! I guess that song got me too excited."

If the teacher sends out a message in Parent mode, it may sound like, "Billy I've told you over and over that you are making too much noise. You should be quiet right now, or else!" Parent voices often state or imply the word *should* in the tone of voice that would accompany shaking the index finger at someone. Unfortunately, the Parent from one person tends to hook the Child in the other (and vice versa), and Billy may respond in his Child, "I feel like talking loud and I can if I want to." Sometimes students respond in their Parent, "I'm not talking loud. You're talking louder than me! You be quiet!" In either case, the stage is set for an escalation, causing wasted class time and interpersonal tensions that affect the entire class. Students can make statements in their Parent that hook the teacher's Child as in this scenario: Student: "This song is dumb. We shouldn't be singing it." Teacher: "I'm the teacher and we sing what I want." The teacher could instead respond in his or her Adult: "What one person may think is dumb others may find very interesting. Tell us, what is it about this song that doesn't appeal to you—the lyrics, the harmony?" Or better yet, the teacher can explain Transactional Analysis (to older students), then ask, "Was that statement in the voice of your Parent or Child?" Could you express the same idea in the Adult?"

When the teacher analyzes interactions with TA, he or she has a good chance of responding to any challenging statement in Adult mode. Few students will stay in Parent or Child long if the teacher skillfully stays in Adult. Some students, however, habitually operate in the Parent or Child (probably modeled in home interactions), which the teacher can help change. In a private conference, review the three modes and ask the student to write a short list of statements he or she has made recently in Parent or Child modes (provide examples, if the student can't or won't). Ask the student to restate each in Adult mode. When it is clear the student understands the different modes, make a snowman chart with rows labeled P, A, C. Explain that this chart will be posted on the wall (without the student's name so no one else in the class need know what is happening) and that the teacher will write a tally mark in the appropriate row after every statement the student makes. Student and teacher will review the tallies briefly after class or in another private conference. This can continue in subsequent classes, until the student fully understands the system and/or begins making most statements in the Adult. If necessary, the student can keep his or her own tally chart to discuss with the teacher after class. Simply being aware of the three modes can often help students modify their behaviors with very little teacher intervention. Operating from the Parent or Child is often deeply ingrained from many past interactions, so don't be alarmed when people slip back into them once in a while. Try not to get hooked by staying in your Adult.

Adapting Instruction for Various Needs

Music teachers need to be aware that there will probably be at least one, if not several, children with special needs of different kinds in each class they teach, requiring some adaptation of strategies and interventions for motivation and management.

Mobility impairments:

- Students with muscle control problems or using crutches or wheelchairs, for example, can be encouraged to participate in class movement activities by adapting the activity in such a way that they can be successful.
- Standing dances can be modified for them to chair-dancing, where all the movements are in the upper body.

Auditory impairments:

- Students with severe hearing loss may need the teacher to wear a microphone to send a radio signal to special hearing aids in their ears.

Behavioral needs:

- Children diagnosed with ADHD need special accommodation of management techniques. Sometimes special coaching and frequent reminders are needed to keep their faces pointed at the teacher so their eyes and ears have a better chance to maintain attention. Breaking down instructions into smaller chunks and asking them to repeat the instruction or write it down is also helpful.
- Children with severe behavior problems will usually already have a written plan for behavior modification, which the music teacher must read and follow. Although time-consuming, it is very important for music teachers to attend building screening meetings, where all those dealing with a special needs student (all his or her teachers, principal, school counselor, parents, psychologists, nurse, aide, et al.) get together to examine the particular special needs, diagnose the problem(s) in detail, and devise a consistent plan for dealing with the problem(s) throughout the student's day. In such meetings, music teachers often gain valuable insights into the student's motivations and specific useful techniques for managing the student in music class. Music teachers also get a chance to give their input as to how the special needs student functions in a musical environment and make suggestions about the overall management plan adopted by the building screening committee.

Logical Consequences

Rudolph Dreikurs (1968) advocates managing inappropriate behaviors with natural and logical consequences. A natural consequence is something that would happen without a teacher intervention, because it is following a law of nature. For example, if a child leans back in his chair far enough, the law of gravity will eventually pull him over, possibly resulting in being hurt or embarrassed. We often cannot wait for natural consequences to occur, nor do we want them to occur, so teachers devise logical consequences: something imposed between the behavior and the natural consequence that extinguishes the behavior before the natural consequence occurs. For example, when observing a child leaning back in his chair after being warned already, the teacher can have him sit on the floor for five minutes to help him remember to "drive" his chair more safely in school. Good logical consequences have five characteristics. They:

1. Are closely related to the behavior

2. Use little teacher time or energy

3. Do not disrupt the learning process

4. Are not punishment, but show respect and concern for the student

5. Employ humor when possible

Logical consequences are good ways to manage behavior by changing the rules of the game so that the student no longer gets reinforcement from the behavior.

Dreikurs also explains four levels of behavior that help teachers deal with inappropriate student behaviors. Children sometimes use Attention-Getting Mechanisms (AGMs) to bolster their self-worth; that is, they exhibit any behavior (often inappropriate) that gets the teacher's attention. If the teacher suspects the child is using an AGM, he or she can help the child find more appropriate ways of satisfying needs for attention (by helping the teacher or other students, doing better work, and so on). Sometimes children go past the AGM to Power Struggle—behaviors that challenge the teacher's authority or attempt to take over the classroom. The teacher must not get into power struggles. If the child loses, he or she may be humiliated and go into stage three (Revenge) or stage four (Assumed Disability). In addition, even though the child does not win a power struggle, he or she does win self-esteem and the esteem of other students for standing up to the powerful teacher, or at least for having the power to derail the lesson and frustrate the teacher. When a teacher suspects that a student is behaving in Power-Struggle mode, he or she can immediately cut off the exchange and discuss the situation privately with the student during recess or after school. In the private conference, the teacher can ask questions about what is bothering the student and what he or she can do to help. The teacher may also need to use the conference to clarify roles and expectations, and possibly draft a student-learning contract that spells out student expectations and consequences for failing to meet them. In rare incidences and usually after prolonged severe mistreatment, some students turn their rage outward to Revenge (behaviors that get even with people they believe have wronged them) or inward to Disability (refusal to even try any task). Teachers need additional help to deal with students in Revenge and Disability modes and should talk to the school counselor, principal, or parents. The situation may require a behavior contract that clearly defines Revenge and Power Struggle behaviors and lists step-by-step warnings and consequences. The student can be asked to sign and abide by the contract as a condition of returning to and staying in class.

> *"Logical consequences are good ways to manage behavior by changing the rules of the game so that the student no longer gets reinforcement from the behavior."*

Setting Up Your Classroom to Nurture Positive Social and Academic Learning

Organizing Classes into Cooperative Learning Groups

Cooperative Learning (CL) is a system developed by David W. Johnson, Roger T. Johnson, E. J. Holubec, and P. Roy (1984) to improve student learning of subject matter and help students become more interdependent, better self-managers, and more effective problem solvers.

Music making requires many qualities that are inherent in Cooperative Learning: positive interdependence, individual accountability, emphasis on task, direct teaching of social skills (as they relate to music making), frequent teacher observation and intervention, and group processing of musical effectiveness.

Forming Cooperative Learning groups can be easy or difficult depending on the makeup of classes, their experience with CL, and the number of individuals who bring with them difficulties relating to others or low interpersonal intelligence. Four or five students in a group is best. Fewer create a group too small to consider divergent points of view, and more can prevent group cohesion and cause some students to retreat to wallflower status. Ideally, students of different abilities will be equally distributed in each group. Give each person in the group a specific function: The captain provides overall leadership and speaks for the group, the assistant captain substitutes for the captain when absent, and others can be encouragers, timekeepers, paper handlers, and so on. Inform students that groups will be changed every six to seven weeks, so that everyone will have the opportunity to function in each role.

There are many ways to divide the class into groups. Some teachers prefer to form groups through chance by having students draw colored pieces of paper out of a hat or count off by sixes (or however many groups are desired). The technique for group

> *"Forming Cooperative Learning groups can be easy or difficult depending on the makeup of classes, their experience with CL, and the number of individuals who bring with them difficulties relating to others or low interpersonal intelligence."*

Learning music in cooperative groups

formation that most students prefer is to be allowed to choose their own groups. Although problems placing unpopular children may arise, these problems can usually be solved by thoughtful teacher interventions. Furthermore, these groups cohere better than randomly chosen groups.

Require those who want to be captain to find two others willing to be in their group. This eliminates the problematic waste of time when would-be captains cannot attract enough others to form a group. It also identifies and empowers the natural leaders, who help the teacher keep the others directed toward meaningful musical goals. After each embryonic group of three is established, captains choose the remaining unattached students, one at a time, until all students belong to a group.

When allowing students to form their own groups, the teacher may have to intervene at several points in the process. If past problems have shown that some students do not do well when sitting next to each other, the teacher lists their names on the board and announces that they cannot be in the same group. If one or more students are not chosen at the end of the selection process and no captain comes forward to invite, the teacher can assign students either to the groups he or she thinks best or by using a chance system (drawing straws, lottery, coin-flip). The teacher could also take this time to talk with students about why some students are not being chosen. This must be done with care and compassion to help students learn to modify behavior without lowering their self-esteem. Skillful teachers can take this problem and turn it into a valuable learning experience in interpersonal skills (Kassner, 2001).

Once groups are established, teachers can reward groups for individual team members' work. For example, when a team member answers a question or performs a musical task, the member's team is rewarded with one or more points. All the National Standards for music can be taught through CL groups. (For more details about organizing through cooperative groups, see Kassner, 2001).

Organizing the Classroom and Record Keeping

Once groups are established, write student names on a seating chart. This works well if the music teacher uses chairs or benches consistently arranged in the same pattern. Some teachers also make this work without seating furniture, by assigning students to specific places in the room marked by some easily identified method: carpet squares, poster signs on the wall, lines drawn on the floor with permanent marker, or banners hung from the ceiling (made from cloth or paper and differently colored or decorated). The use of tape of any kind to mark lines on the floor is not recommended, as it quickly comes loose or is picked off by students (either absentmindedly or on purpose to make tape balls to throw at others). Seating charts work well to help teachers learn student names as long as students are in their assigned spots. Until the teacher has had a chance to learn everyone's name, it is best to do lessons in which students stay in their spots or leave only for short intervals (to get instruments, for example). Seating charts also make it easier to take roll, keep track of student absences, and organize comments to help report academic and effort grades at end of term. Many teachers write lesson plan codes and codes for assessments of student skills right on the seating chart. A seating chart for each class can be placed in a loose-leaf three-ring binder and organized in a way that the teacher can retrieve most easily. For example, charts can be arranged by day of the week if the teacher sees each class only once per week, or arranged by grade level, or in alphabetic order by classroom teachers' names. This system keeps everything in one place and reduces the need for a separate grade book and lesson plan book. Full lesson plans can be written on computer, printed out, and kept in or behind the seating chart book.

"Seating charts work well to help teachers learn student names as long as students are in their assigned spots... [and] also make it easier to take roll, keep track of student absences, and organize comments to help report academic and effort grades at end of term."

FIGURE 11.4

Sample Seating Chart Reflecting the Room Arrangement

Figure 11.4 illustrates an effective organization of a music room. Chairs are arranged in a parabola with the open end facing the whiteboard. This gives every student a clear view of instructional material. Spaces are left between groups of chairs to delineate the groups and provide passage for walking between groups. Students are far enough away from others when sitting on chairs to discourage kicking chairs, unwanted touching, and so on. There is enough space in the center of the room for students to play instruments or to gather on the floor to observe music-related books and charts. There is enough space around the outside of the chairs to perform circle movements to music and enough space between chairs to perform snake or train movements winding between chair groups.

Learning and Remembering Students' Names

After setting expectations and procedures, the teacher needs to take the next most important step for good student behavior: learn students' names. Being able to call on each student by name helps the teacher establish a personal rapport that conveys the message, "You're unique and important." A teacher who knows each student's name is more likely to personalize instruction and less likely to teach lessons to "the class." Learning names can be a daunting task, especially if the teacher is new to the building and there are hundreds of children. Many classroom teachers have younger students wear name tags for the first few days until they can associate the students' names with their faces. When students come to music classes wearing their name tags, it is much easier for the music teacher. Some music teachers make name tags for students to wear just in music class. The tags can be grouped together and put into envelopes for quick storage and distribution. This is effective, but it takes time and materials to make and keep organized.

Another aid to learning students' names is to take pictures of small groups of students and write names under faces. Pictures can be studied between classes or arranged on a poster for easy reference during music class. Students also love to see their pictures posted on the wall. This technique works better in schools with stable populations and less well in schools with high turnover.

> *"A teacher who knows each student's name is more likely to personalize instruction and less likely to teach lessons to 'the class.'"*

McDaniel (1985) believes that students will be well motivated if teachers follow ten commandments:

1. Build an interesting curriculum
2. Set clear goals
3. Communicate high expectations
4. Employ positive reinforcement
5. Invite success
6. Teach cooperation
7. Demonstrate enthusiasm
8. Personalize instruction
9. Induce readiness to learn
10. Encourage student responses

"Teachers need to know their own motivations, and they must employ only humane, respectful, concerned ways of motivating students."

Some people try to motivate others through threats, intimidation, coercion, shame, rejection, belittling, sarcasm, and other power ploys. These tactics may appear to produce submission for a short time, but ultimately they lower self-esteem, foster resentment, destroy person-to-person bonds, kill initiative, and fail to build a basis for cooperation and positive self-discipline. Unfortunately, some people were raised by parents or had teachers who used these behaviors to control them. When people who are thus abused grow up, they may repeat the abuses on their own children or students. These tactics are common in totalitarian regimes of third-world countries but are decidedly undemocratic and out of place in America. Teachers need to know their own motivations, and they must employ only humane, respectful, concerned ways of motivating students. There is no latitude for choice on this issue: America's judicial system has consistently upheld students' rights.

Token Prizes

"There are endless possibilities for music-related rewards that build self-esteem."

Most elementary students enjoy a small amount of friendly group competition, especially if it involves some kind of token prize. Some suitable inexpensive prizes they enjoy receiving include having music-related imprints made from rubber stamps (on paper, on the back of their hands, on their book bags, as temporary tattoos on their arm muscles, and so on), eating their lunches with the teacher in the music room, having their names printed in the school newspaper as winners in music class, being first in line to leave music class, getting first choice of instruments to play in subsequent lessons, having their names entered on a Hall of Fame poster in the music room, or getting special mention at a music program. Some music teachers find good results with giving classes a star on a chart as they leave the music room, if everyone has been cooperative and productive. When a certain number of stars are earned, students get a special music day during which they can choose their favorite songs to sing, play instruments, play music learning games, play computer music programs, and so on. There are endless possibilities for music-related rewards that build self-esteem. Almost all children (and adults, for that matter) want to appear successful, smart, skilled, and with-it (Kassner, 1996). Be careful, however, not to base motivation on tokens. Token rewards should only be insignificant manifestations of the greater inner motivation that comes from increased self-esteem (Stephens and Cooper, 1987).

Special Person

Another technique to motivate appropriate student behaviors is designating a "Special Person." In each music class, a Special Person is elected every two weeks. The Special Person sits in a special chair, takes care of the music room mascot (stuffed animal), has first choice of instruments, assists the teacher in many tasks, and receives many other privileges. The Special Person is selected in the following procedure.

1. Captains of each Cooperative Learning group nominate and send to the front of the room a group member they believe to have shown the character trait of the week (rotating list of kind, helpful, caring, and sharing).

2. Nominees turn around and hide their eyes, then the other students vote on the person they think is best at the character trait by raising their hands when the teacher points to each contestant. (Students are reminded never to tell the nominees who voted for them or how many votes they received, so no one's feelings get hurt.)

3. Nominees open their eyes and turn around, and the teacher gives the mascot to the winner and also fills out a certificate of award for the Special Person to take home.

The Special Person designation is a highly coveted award, because students' peers elect them, not the teacher. During the election process, the teacher has several opportunities to reinforce ideas about why the characteristics of kind, helpful, caring, and sharing are important to each individual and to the smooth functioning of the entire class. After the system is established and the character traits are well ingrained, the teacher can have students evaluate inappropriate behaviors in terms of the four traits. For example, if a student intentionally sticks his foot out to trip another student, the teacher can poll the class's opinion: "Which of our Special Person characteristics does this behavior demonstrate? Kindness? Helping? Caring? Sharing?" The class usually answers "no" to each one, and the teacher concludes, "If it isn't kind, helpful, caring, or sharing, it keeps us from working well together and you should not do it." The music teacher is in a unique position to affect the climate of the entire school, and it is amazing to hear students on the playground rebuke an affront with "That wasn't very kind, helpful, caring, or sharing! You won't get to be Special Person if you keep that up."

The music teacher is in a unique position to affect the climate of the entire school.

Children receiving a token award after class

© Carol Scott-Kassner

© Carol Scott-Kassner

Other External Motivators

Older students are often motivated by being caught at their best and receiving edible rewards in addition to public recognition. Whenever students answer questions correctly, perform a passage of music well, help another student, and so on, the teacher writes their names on the board. The second time students are caught doing good, the teacher writes check marks next to their names. The student with the most check marks at the end of class gets a "pizza lottery" ticket to sign and put in a drawing basket. At the end of each term, lottery tickets are drawn and the winners attend a "pizza lunch with the teacher." (Pizzas can be delivered to schools for reasonable prices, or teachers could bake frozen pizzas themselves.) This is popular with students, especially if their names are written in the school bulletin or if morning announcements read the name of those who have won and need to be excused to attend. It is also a great recruitment and public relations vehicle for the music program and a tremendous motivational tool to foster positive and productive behaviors (Kassner, 1996).

Strategies for Confronting Inappropriate Behavior

A variety of motivational methods is the best way to manage normal student behaviors. "I" statements usually work better than "you" statements, and noticing good behavior usually gets better results than attacking poor behavior. For example, when a group of students is talking instead of paying attention, the teacher can remark, "Thank you, [another group]. I can teach easily, because you are quiet and attentive! I appreciate your attentiveness." Occasionally, student behavior requires the teacher to use intervention techniques that are more direct, focused, and powerful.

The foundations for student behavior management discussed above are extremely important. In a perfect world, teachers would not need anything more. Some students, however, are naturally mischievous, have quirky senses of humor, or just do not like following rules. Many students' brains function differently, resulting in problems

"'I' statements usually work better than 'you' statements, and noticing good behavior usually gets better results than attacking poor behavior."

with learning, attention, self-management, and social awareness. Sadly, some students do not live in loving, stimulating, peaceful, and supportive homes, nor in safe, quiet neighborhoods where they can be assured of walking home without assault or getting a full night's sleep. Some students arrive in our classrooms carrying unhealthy models of behavior, deep anger, hate, resentment, and hostility. Teachers need a wide variety of techniques for dealing with the different kinds and levels of class disruptions that these problems spawn. Three of the most difficult tasks new teachers face are:

1. Discerning the causes of behavior problems

2. Developing a large repertoire of management techniques

3. Knowing when and how to use the most effective technique for each problem.

Richard Kindsvatter and Mary Ann Levine (1987) discuss twelve myths of discipline that are sometimes recommended to new teachers but are not best practice for classroom management. Among the myths they urge teachers to eradicate are:

- The best teachers are those whose students do not dare misbehave

- Good control depends on finding the right gimmick

- Punishment is educational

- Students do not know how to behave

- Teachers should not look at students' records so as not to get prejudicial information

- Being consistent should take precedent over all other considerations

Many good reasons exist for not doing what these myths suggest, as will become apparent as you proceed through this chapter.

Establishing Expectations and Procedures

Most school districts and individual schools have adopted student rights and responsibilities handbooks, which all students and parents must read and sign. Teachers need to be familiar with those handbooks and make sure their classroom regulations are consistent with the district's or school's master plan. Within individual classrooms, teachers need to set clear expectations and procedures, discuss them, and model them. These are the beginnings of successful student behavior management. (The terms *expectations* and *procedures* sound more collaborative, less top-down, than the term *rules*, which is often used instead.) Teachers can post the expectations on a chart or include them in an information packet that parents and students read and sign. During the first class or two, the teacher might model several procedures and do a T-chart activity on some of the expectations. For example, if one of the expectations is that everyone be respectful of each other, the teacher draws a large T on butcher paper or chart board and writes "Respect" on top of the T, then "Sounds Like" on the left side and "Looks Like" on the right side. Students contribute examples of what respect sounds and looks like, and the teacher writes them down. (The teacher may need to have several ideas ready to get the discussion rolling, for example, respect sounds like "waiting for your turn to talk.") Post the chart on a wall and bring it down now and then to review and add examples to it—especially if students exhibit disrespectful behavior.

Clear expectations can also be communicated through posters. For example, students respond well to a Peanuts© panel in which Peppermint Patty says in the first frame, "Yes Mamm, I'm back from the principal's office." Second frame: "He said I should try

© Billie Judy/Reel Life Productions

harder at paying attention." Third frame: "How's this?" (Peppermint Patty is sitting at her desk, head straining forward, and eyes staring straight at the teacher.) The teacher reads the panel to the students, then states the expectation that every student will keep his or her head and eyes facing the teacher when the teacher is instructing. Posters with many positive messages can be purchased at learning stores, through catalogs, and through the Internet. Stories are also great ways to convey expectations that students do not forget. Some teachers start each year telling the story of the man who wanted wisdom (see Box 11.1). After telling the story, the teacher can bring the moral home to the classroom: "Whenever I'm standing right here in my teaching station and giving instruction, I expect you to give me the attention of your eyes, ears, and brains." If some students allow their eyes to wander, the teacher could ask someone to review the three attentions verbally or ask the wandering students to write or draw pictures of the three attentions. The teacher could also teach students an Asian sign of respect (palms together, fingers pointing up, and a short bow). The teacher can then inform students that with this gesture he or she is asking for the three attentions and would like to see students give the sign back to acknowledge that they will give three attentions.

BOX 11.1 Attention, Attention, Attention

A man went to a wise old guru and asked what he needed to do to become wise. The guru wrote *Attention* on a piece of paper and gave it to the man. The man was puzzled and said, "Surely there is more to wisdom than 'Attention.'" The guru smiled and said, "Yes, there is more." He took the paper back and again wrote *Attention*. The man was getting a little upset and said, "Oh, great guru, I'm sure there is more to wisdom than 'Attention, Attention.'" The guru laughed and said, "Ah yes, there is indeed one more thing!" and he again wrote *Attention* on the paper. The man sputtered angrily, "I don't get it. I ask what to do to become wise and all you say is 'Attention, Attention, Attention.' What is attention anyway?" The guru said, "Ah, you have asked exactly the right question! Now I will tell you the whole truth and you will be wise! Attention…is…Attention!" With that the guru resumed the lotus position and would say no more. The man walked toward home mumbling and complaining, until he suddenly realized what the guru meant: If you want to be wise you must pay keen attention *with* something—attention with your eyes, attention with your ears, and attention with your brain. From that day on he paid careful attention to everything and became very wise.

Judicious Discipline

Another approach to established expectations and procedures is called Judicious Discipline. This system, developed by Gathercoal (1993), is discussed in detail by Nimmo (1997). Instead of being based on teacher power and dispensing of justice, Judicious Discipline is based on principles established in the Bill of Rights of the US Constitution, with the central belief that individuals have the right to maximum personal freedom as long as they do not diminish the rights of others. Expectations are developed to ensure maximum responsible freedom for the maximum number of people, and fall into four large categories:

1. Safeguarding property from loss or damage
2. Promoting legitimate educational purpose
3. Protecting health and maintaining safety
4. Avoiding serious disruption of the educational process

Student behavior is discussed as it relates to time, place, and manner. When a student behaves inappropriately, the teacher's first response is to gain more information by asking questions instead of taking immediate action based on what he or she thinks is going on. For example, "Is this the right time and place to be doing this? Is what you are doing being done in an appropriate manner?"

There are several sample questions teachers can ask students to help them understand inappropriate behavior and take responsibility for improving it:

1. Can you tell me which of our classroom expectations that action violates?
2. What were you trying to accomplish with that? Did you achieve your goal?
3. Why do you think we have a class rule about doing that?
4. What could I do to persuade you to stop that?
5. How could you do that differently next time?
6. On a scale of one to ten, how helpful to the group would you rate that action?
7. Would you recommend that everyone do that, and, if so, how would it affect our music making?
8. Would it help to clarify your values if you wrote a description, analysis, and evaluation of this behavior?
9. That seems so unlike you—has something happened to upset you?
10. Have we reached the point where the only choice left is a parent conference/referral to principal/finding another class for you/(and so on)?

Questioning in this way asks for more information and deeper thinking without casting blame and shame, or undermining students' self-esteem. It clearly informs students that a behavior is inappropriate and conveys faith in students' abilities to rethink the situation and come up with a better plan for the future. The focus is on education, not blame. Questions can convey possibilities for future action without the weight and force of threats, and do not have to be backed down from or apologized for, as a statement might have to be, if new information proves a teacher's initial assessment is incorrect. (Kassner, 1998c).

Judicious Discipline develops a healthy educational community by sharing power between teacher and students. "When power is shared, students tend to feel more valued and respected. Moreover, they tend to be more interested in the endeavor at hand, more goal-oriented, more inspired, more integrally involved, more fulfilled, and more complete" (Nimmo, 1997, p. 32).

> "Judicious Discipline is based on principles established in the Bill of Rights of the U.S. Constitution, with the central belief that individuals have the right to maximum personal freedom as long as they do not diminish the rights of others."

> "[In Judicious Discipline] the focus is on education, not blame."

Discipline with Love and Logic

"The most important thing a teacher can do to motivate and manage students is to establish meaningful relationships built on mutual respect and caring empathy."

The preceding system is quite similar to Discipline with Love and Logic, developed by Jim Fay and David Funk (1995). Love and Logic is a very practical and powerful approach to classroom management, because it is grounded in mutual respect, building strong positive relationships between teacher and students, enhancing student self-concept, sharing control with students within limits, administering consequences with empathy and compassion, and sharing the burden of thinking through appropriate questioning. Especially helpful for new teachers are explanations of their suggested interventions, including the evil eye, proximity, enforceable statements, providing choices, and removing students to time out. Also extremely helpful are the eighteen Love and Logic tips scattered throughout the book, which provide advice in a nutshell for implementing various techniques. Especially important are Tip #3: Rules for Giving Choices; Tip #4: Consequences with Empathy; Tip #8: Thinking Words and Fighting Words; Tip #10: Possible Choices in the Classroom; Tip #13: Styles of Teaching (Helicopter, Drill Sergeant, Consultant); and Tip #18: Better Ways to Say "No." Love and Logic has been very successful in many schools across the country and works best when an entire building adopts it as its main discipline plan. Many of the principles will still work well in music classes, even if the rest of the building is not using them. More information about Discipline with Love and Logic can be found at www.loveandlogic. com and in their publications. I have had the privilege of working with many fine teachers over three-and-a-half decades, who all had one value in common: the most important thing a teacher can do to motivate and manage students is to establish meaningful relationships built on mutual respect and caring empathy. When students feel accepted and valued as human beings by the teacher, they are far more likely to contribute to a positive classroom environment. This value is the core of Love and Logic, and new teachers would be well advised to investigate this approach at their earliest opportunity.

Behavior Expectation Forms

If a child repeatedly disrupts class, destroys property, or endangers his or her own or others' health and safety, the teacher can send the student to a time-out chair to read, sign, and date a behavior expectation form while the rest of the class goes on with the lesson (see Box 11.2). The teacher then files the form and forgets about it unless the student behaves inappropriately again, in which case the exercise is repeated. Having two separate copies signed on separate days establishes evidence of a pattern. On the second or third infraction, the student can be required to write out the expectations in his or her own handwriting, on the grounds that writing is a more kinesthetic way of learning than reading (which does not seem to have worked so far). The teacher might conjecture out loud, "If writing it out once doesn't work, maybe the student needs to write it five or ten times to learn the message." Most students will assert that they do not need to write it multiple times and that they have learned the expectations and have decided it is in their best interest to follow them.

Behavior Contracts

Behavior contracts are more individualized and specific versions of the general behavior expectation form, and they are negotiated with a misbehaving student, not imposed on him or her. These contracts may be preprinted forms, with several clauses followed by blank spaces for the student to write specifics, including (1) a description of the inappropriate behavior, (2) a substitute behavior that is appropriate, (3) a plan for changing the behavior, (4) a reward for changing or a punishment for not changing,

BOX 11.2 **Behavior Expectation Form**

BEHAVIOR EXPECTATIONS

This classroom is a place for learning. All students have a right to learn and the teacher has a right to teach. If some students behave inappropriately, other students cannot learn and the teacher cannot teach. Students are expected to respect others' rights and behave in a manner that (1) safeguards property from loss or damage, (2) protects everyone's health and safety, and (3) avoids serious disruption of the educational process.

There are many ways to disrupt a class: talking, telling other students what to do, arguing, making other sounds, making faces, threatening others, acting silly, moving to attract attention, touching others or their chairs, taking other people's property, to name just a few.

To have a peaceful, happy, and productive classroom all students must be responsible for following the behavior expectations and for paying attention.

I have read and I understand the expectations above. I want to remain in the class and I promise to behave as expected.

Student signature _____

Date _____

(5) a method of monitoring and evaluating progress, (6) the length of time the contract will be in effect, and (7) the student's and teacher's signature. Usually, the contract works well to extinguish the behavior problem, but if it does not, the teacher and student can discuss why the contract did not work and make a new, adjusted contract. If a student refuses to negotiate a contract, the teacher can include the refusal in a discussion with those at the next level (counselor, parents, vice principal, and so on). Refusal to cooperate is usually grounds for more severe consequences administered by those above the teacher. More details about behavior contracts are available in Rossman (1989).

Some problem behaviors may be so ingrained that even behavior contracts are not strong enough to effect the changes needed. More often than not, problem behaviors overlay and cover up fears of inadequacy. We need to guard against any illusions that we are trained psychologists, but music teachers can help educate students about

Children volunteering answers

© Billie Judy/Reel Life Productions

interpersonal issues by having them write an essay about events taking place in our classrooms. Teachers could give students a paper printed with some or all of the following specifications to be included in the essay:

1. Describe the behavior that resulted in your needing to write this essay (in a complete, detailed description of the event, with exact quotes when possible).

2. Write out and complete this statement: "The name of the only person in the world who can control my behavior is _____."

3. Write a detailed description of the event or events that led to this behavior. (What triggered this behavior?)

4. Describe how your behavior affected the class. (Was the learning of other students disrupted? Were other students upset? Did anyone get hurt?)

5. Describe your feelings about your behavior. (Are you feeling proud? Sorry? Angry? Sad? Happy?)

6. Describe how you think other students feel about your behavior.

7. What steps can you take to undo or lessen any bad feelings. (Apologize, promise not to repeat, give something?)

8. If you could turn back the clock and replay the events, what would you do differently?

9. If you behaved as you describe in #8, would you feel better about yourself?

10. If you behaved as you describe in #8, do you think others would feel more happy to be around you?

Completing these thought prompts helps some students do a reality check, in which they examine and evaluate their beliefs and feelings. The teacher reads and keeps all essays for future reference. If the responses seem truthful and sincere, the teacher can congratulate the student on growth in emotional intelligence. If the responses seem untruthful, defensive, evasive, blaming, and so on, the teacher can talk to the student about perceptions, beliefs, honesty, and such, and make notes on the essay. If the student behavior improves, no follow-up is necessary. But if the same inappropriate behavior continues, one or two more essays could be required. If this does not help, the teacher could call a conference with the parents and student to discuss the responses in the essays, or could append the essays (and any other documentation, such as dated behavior expectation forms) to a report to the counselor, vice principal, principal, or whoever handles inappropriate behavior at the next level. This approach provides documentation, mostly on the student's time, of the interventions the teacher has used to resolve the problem and any progress or lack of progress. Such documentation helps those at the next level of power deal more quickly and effectively with the problem.

> "This approach provides documentation, mostly on the student's time, of the interventions the teacher has used to resolve the problem and any progress or lack of progress. Such documentation helps those at the next level of power deal more quickly and effectively with the problem."

The Intervention Thermometer

Teachers may find it difficult to remember so many choices of ways to deal with student motivation and management and to know the proper time to use each. If we envision some of the many options a teacher has to change student behavior as degrees on a thermometer, we could group interventions into six distinct temperature zones (see Figure 11.5). It is best to stay in the lowest level whenever possible. Good teachers try to stay cool at least 95 percent of the time. Knowing which levels to use and when to use them comes only with experience. Generally it is best to start at the bottom and work up, unless a student has shown a pattern of poor behavior in the past that responded to a higher level or unless the misbehavior is egregious.

FIGURE 11.5

The Intervention Thermometer

Red-Hot & Referring. Course of last resort. Referral to principal for disciplinary action, include documentation of previous interventions tried and their results.

(*Warning:* If you get to this temperature too often, the principal will start wondering about your ability to perform the job, and your evaluations may suffer. Once or twice a year in an average community is plenty at this level.)

Sizzling & Serious. Involve people with more perspectives, training, or power than the teacher. Request conference with parents, counselor, building screening committee. If appropriate, have counselor urge medical tests, unless your district has a policy of not suggesting medical tests due to court cases requiring the district to pay for the tests.

Hot & Handling It. Student suffers minor consequences for his or her behavior. Natural consequences, logical consequences, behavior contract, special essay assignments to improve interpersonal understandings, time out to think of more productive behavior options, time out to read and sign behavior expectation form, time out to copy behavior expectation form.

Tepid & Talkative. Get complete information about the problem. Discuss problems with student outside class, insist on sticking to the point, being honest, and taking personal responsibility for his or her actions. Ask probing questions that force students to think at higher levels and accept responsibility. Check with other teachers and cumulative file to see if problem is particular to your class or broad-based and long-lasting. Discuss problem with counselor or principal to get their recommendations and insights.

Warm & Wondering. Question for greater understanding and give student limited choices. Is the room too hot/cold/dark/bright? Are you uncomfortable? Is this task too difficult/easy for you? What can we do to make it just right? Was that statement/question in the Parent, Adult, or Child mode? Do you understand our behavior expectations? Is there any part of our behavior expectations that you are not sure about? What is it you really want? I do not think that way is working for you. Is this the appropriate time and place to do that? Is this the appropriate manner of doing that? Can you think of another way? If you had a chance to do that over again, what would you do? Would you prefer to apologize or…(some consequence)? You seem to be needing a lot of attention today. Could you suggest a way we could provide the attention you need, yet still go on with the lesson?

Cool & Calm. Catch kids in the act of doing good. Ask students to review classroom expectations. Encourage students with constructive information about their behavior. Give token prizes and public recognition. Teacher moves into close proximity to student with inappropriate behavior and continues with lesson uninterrupted (teacher notices student).

TECHNOLOGY *for* **TEACHING** *and* **LEARNING MUSIC:**
MOTIVATION *and* **MANAGEMENT**

Many software programs are available for helping teachers motivate students and manage their classrooms. To learn more, visit the Technology Resources links in the MindTap.

MINDTAP

Scenario

PAUL TAUGHT HIMSELF TO play guitar in seventh grade and, though painfully shy, performed in a few garage bands through high school for pocket money. Making music was a pleasant pastime for him, so when he heard about the shortage of teachers, he thought he might give school teaching a try. Paul had earned a college degree in liberal arts, so he was able to get an emergency teaching certificate without further college classes in music or education. He was quickly hired to teach band, violin, and general music in a small rural elementary school desperate to fill the position.

Paul's first class was a fourth-grade general music class. Remembering how cool he thought guitars were when he was young, he planned to start the year off with an impressive lesson about the guitar. As the students entered, Paul was writing guitar chords on the whiteboard and hollered over his shoulder, "I'll be with you in a minute. I'm almost done." He finally got the class started about eight minutes later by picking up his guitar, turning around to face the students, and saying, "This is a guitar. I can do some really cool stuff on it." Paul sat down and played some chords, then pointed to the board at various places and said, "Here's how you write the C chord in root position. Here's how you write the B7 chord. You have to be careful not to play the big E string on this chord." After about ten minutes of pointing to the tablatures and showing how to play and write several chords, he said, "Now I'll put the chords in a song." He then began playing "House of the Rising Sun"—all twenty-six verses.

The children's bottoms were getting a little fatigued and cold sitting on the cement floor while he lectured and played. Billy started squirming and accidentally bumped into the class bully, Mack. Mack screamed, "Get away from me, you jerk!" and pushed Billy, who fell backward, bumping his head into Stephanie's face. When Stephanie's sobs reached earsplitting level, Paul stopped playing his guitar and looked out at the students.

"This class should learn some manners. You! The kid who knocked into that girl. Get to the principal's office. The rest of you sit still and listen to this song again."

Paul started to play "House of the Rising Sun" again, but the bell rang just as he fingered the first A-minor chord. The students jumped up and ran, pushing each other, to the door. Stephanie continued to sob while looking at the bloody tooth in her hand.

Questions

1. Get into groups of three or four and reflect on Paul's lesson in terms of his motivational style, lesson appropriateness, and his student management techniques. Discuss what did and did not work in terms of principles discussed in this chapter. Share your observations and suggestions with the class as a whole. (There are at least fifteen major problems with this lesson. How many did your group find?)

2. Imagine teaching your first lesson as a school music teacher. Specify the type of class (general music, band, chorus, orchestra) and the grade level you imagine it to be. Write a detailed lesson plan for your first class that reflects better pedagogy than Paul's lesson. (Hint: Much or all of the lesson should involve principles of motivation and class management. [As the twig is bent, so grows the tree.])

REVIEW

1. Discuss the three types of motivation (intrinsic, internal, external).

2. Discuss why negative reinforcement should never be used alone.

3. "Competition is motivational." Argue the pros and cons of this statement.

4. List several ways you plan to establish meaningful relationships built on mutual respect and caring empathy.

CRITICAL THINKING

1. Choose four personal traits of effective teachers (enthusiasm, energy, self-assurance, good sense of humor, sensitivity, self-control, sincerity, well organized, knowledgeable, affirming, observant, fair, flexible) that you feel are most characteristic of yourself and briefly describe an instance where you demonstrated each trait.

2. You are a new music teacher preparing for the first day of classes. What are the three most important expectations or procedures that you want to establish and how do you plan to convey these to the students?

3. You are a teacher. Describe the type of class you are teaching and the system that you have employed to be able to call on your students by name.

4. In a small group, brainstorm some statements that students might make in Parent mode or Child mode of Transactional Analysis. Brainstorm teacher replies in the Adult.

5. Good logical consequences have five characteristics. List all five, then choose the one you think is most important and explain why. Compare your answer with other prospective teachers.

6. A large sixth-grade girl has disrupted your music classes for several days in a row by making faces at smaller girls and, when catching their eyes, shouting insults and threats at them, such as, "Stop looking at me, you little creep!" Describe your plan of action to deal with this problem. Discuss and compare it with other students' plans.

7. A fifth-grade boy seems to have some strong negative power to control most of the other students in your music class. It is barely perceptible, but you notice he seems to give silent gestures that warn others not to raise their hands to answer questions or otherwise participate in your lesson. Describe your plan of action to deal with this problem. Discuss and compare it with other students' plans.

PROJECTS

1. Customize the wording of the behavior expectation form in this chapter to reflect your own values, personality, and style.

2. Using a word-processing program, design and print a behavior contract form based on the suggestions in this chapter.

3. Using a word-processing program, design and print an intervention thermometer that you could post in your classroom to remind you of the options you plan to use to respond to inappropriate behaviors.

4. Using a word-processing program, design and print a sample list of essay thought-starters.

5. Interview a practicing music teacher to find out how he or she would respond to Critical Thinking items 1, 2, 3, and 4 or pose the ideas on an Internet bulletin board or chat room for music teachers. Explain how and why the answers you receive compare or contrast with your own answers.

6. Find an Enneagram self-discovery test on the Internet, take the test to discover your own personality type, and read about its pros and cons. Reflect on how this type will affect your work with students, colleagues, administrators, and parents of the same or different types.

MINDTAP   Visit **MindTap** to access classroom videos, audio, and more!

12

Curriculum Design

IN THIS CHAPTER

- Program Vignettes
- The Nature of Curriculum
- Types and Sources of Curriculum
  - National Standards
  - State and Local Standards
  - Other Sources of Curriculum
- Planning a Curriculum
  - General Curriculum Content
  - Early Childhood Planning
  - K–6 planning
- Implementing a Curriculum
  - Lesson Planning
  - Thematic and Unit Planning
- Distilling the Essence of Curriculum

Program Vignettes

IN EARLY MAY, Ms. Santiago finished a production of the Broadway musical *Cats* with her fourth through sixth grade children. Her principal and the parents of the children were thrilled to see the children in lights. Ms. Santiago was pleased with their reactions because the entire school year had been spent preparing for this event. Each year she has done a different musical, and her reputation for high-quality productions has spread throughout the region. Some talented children have become stars, although all children are involved in some way, many behind the scenes.

In a neighboring school, Mr. Congdon also just completed his annual spring concert to the acclaim of parents, other teachers, and administrators. During April, the children voted to share with parents two or three things they had done in music class during the year. The choices were wide-ranging. First graders sang and dramatized some songs they had learned during their unit on bears; second graders sang and shared a dance they had invented to go with a folk song; third graders played their soprano recorders, accompanied by orchestrations on Orff xylophones and metallophones; fourth graders performed some partner songs that they accompanied on various instruments; fifth graders sang a medley of songs related to American history, and small groups performed their own compositions; and sixth graders sang a song in three-part harmony and shared a short video they had made, with a soundtrack of electronic music they had composed. Students from each grade level introduced their selections and explained why they had chosen those pieces and what they had learned from involvement in music.

In a third elementary school in the same district, Ms. Solecki's students presented a theme concert called "Our Musical World." Students from each grade level performed music and dances from cultures they had studied during the year. Children dressed in simple, but representative, costumes from each culture. Some classes created instruments that they incorporated into the performance. Children's artwork, reflecting representative styles and techniques from the various cultures, decorated the gymnasium. A PowerPoint of specific artworks was projected during the performances. During the final number, all of the children joined hands and voices to sing a song about world peace. The entire audience sang with them on the last chorus.

- How do you define curriculum?

- What role do you think teachers have in planning their own curriculum?

- What outside factors might influence that planning?

- When within the school year do you think a curriculum should be determined and why?

"Curriculum can be thought of as the activities that occur in the classroom. Curriculum should never be static, but should be in constant change as the conditions that surround it change."

Children signing a song in preparation for a concert

The Nature of Curriculum

These spring concert vignettes illustrate the wide differences among music programs and the freedom individual teachers have in determining the content of their own curriculum. Curriculum can be thought of as the activities that occur in the classroom. It is usually hoped that those activities promote significant musical learning. Although spring concerts rarely represent an entire year's work, they do reflect what teachers value and what they have emphasized out of the myriad of possibilities existing in music education.

These examples clearly indicate that the *operational curriculum*, or that which is implemented, is dynamic rather than static and is subject to such variables as teacher attitudes and training; parental and administrative expectations; and current trends in education. They also show that the *experiential curriculum*, or that which the students receive, can differ remarkably, even within the same school district.

The curricular goals for Ms. Santiago appear to revolve around achieving a quality and entertaining performance, with certain students receiving a high level of recognition. Any skills and understandings in music emerge from the activities that are contained in the musical. Mr. Congdon's curriculum reflects an emphasis on student leadership and clear development of a range of musical performance skills in singing, dancing, and instrument playing, as well as composition. In addition, children are encouraged both to think about what they are learning in music and to make values choices about what they have produced. Ms. Solecki's curriculum appears to be stimulated in part by its connection to the rest of the school program, particularly social studies. It also reflects attention to issues of multiculturalism and societal values. Students learn to express ideas through several art forms and experience an integration of these art forms within and across cultures.

None of the preceding choices is inherently right or wrong. Each curriculum could be justified based on differing philosophies and circumstances. However, some reflect more closely than others what the profession of music education has come to value as a comprehensive and balanced approach to the early childhood and elementary curricula. This is called the *ideal curriculum* (Abeles, Hoffer, and Klotman, 1993).

Types and Sources of Curriculum

Curriculum plans exist in many forms at many levels and are available from a range of sources (see Table 12.1). Most are highly structured and suggest a logical sequence of concepts, skills, and attitudes to be achieved through the scope of an entire music program. A *formal curriculum* helps to provide all the teachers in a school or district a frame for their plans and helps to assure that some consistency exists within a program. It helps provide articulation as students move from one level to another, such as elementary to middle school. Most important, a formal curriculum helps establish clear goals or outcomes and becomes a structure for directing teacher and student activity and for measuring musical learning.

Types of Curricula

- *Ideal*: That which professionals have come to value as a comprehensive and sequential approach to the subject matter content of a particular field.
- *Formal*: A general frame of goals or outcomes that ensures that some consistency occurs in a program from pre-K to grade twelve.
- *Instructional*: The specific plans, reflecting the formal curriculum that teachers make for their lessons, including use of materials. This also indicates how individual student progress will be assessed.
- *Operational*: The curriculum that is actually implemented. It is dynamic and subject to many influences.
- *Experiential*: The curriculum that the students actually receive, and parents and administrators perceive.

A quality formal curriculum establishes large goals, competencies, and outcomes, leaving teachers free to develop an *instructional curriculum* for their own classroom and a personal method for attaining the goals. Such a curriculum reflects the nature and content of music; is balanced, comprehensive, and sequential; and reflects what is known through research about musical development in children. It has built-in measures for assessing student growth toward musically significant ends.

National Standards

Since 1994, music educators in the United States have had access to the National Standards in Music Education. These standards are voluntary, not mandatory. They represent an effort by the Music Educators National Conference (MENC, now known as NAfME – the National Association for Music Education) to articulate age-appropriate, sequential, and measurable standards in music from prekindergarten through grade twelve as a part of the general standards movement that was taking place at that time. Similar standards were developed and implemented in Britain at about the same time. The National Standards movement came out of efforts by governments to pressure educational systems to produce students capable of competing in a global economy. These standards have become a kind of benchmark for music educators to use in their planning. Virtually every state in the United States has adopted state standards that reflect the National Standards in significant ways.

State and Local Standards

The 2014 Music Standards focus on Music Literacy, particularly conceptual understandings about the artistic processes of creating, performing, and responding. Support for applying these standards to planning are available on the NAfME website.

A music curriculum may be established for teachers by a state or a local school district. Teachers may be held accountable for achieving state standards through formal, statewide testing at particular grade levels such as grades four, eight, and twelve. Such documents are usually created by committees of music teachers and music administrators. Usually these curricula are revised every seven to ten years to reflect current trends in education, research in learning, and changing National Standards in music education. They may or may not be followed by every teacher in a school district, but they can often be very helpful in planning instruction. Successful implementation of standards is usually dependent on training teachers in how to use the curriculum.

In private schools, teachers often create their own curricula. These tend to be much more idiosyncratic, reflecting the values and training of the teacher(s) and the values of the school. They are more likely to be followed because they are determined locally. They may or may not be formally assessed. Many sources are available for individual teachers and committees to consider in determining their own curriculum. These sources, ranging from formal to informal, are highlighted in Table 12.1.

Other Sources of Curriculum

Current music series textbooks and/or interactive digital resources can be of tremendous help to both the music specialist and classroom teacher in planning and implementing a core curriculum in music, as well as in integrating music across the curriculum. The most frequently adopted series are based on diverse musical materials woven carefully into a scope and sequence of significant musical skills and understandings and placed within a cultural, historic, and artistic context. These series also incorporate the National Standards in their lesson goals. In addition to print materials, texts are accompanied by recordings, ancillary materials such as activities booklets, piano accompaniments, and technology connections. Materials can be used in a sequential fashion, or teachers can select and implement lessons or units they find compelling for their children in their unique setting.

Textbook companies are known for providing extensive materials and ideas that would be very difficult and expensive for any teacher to gather in one place. These are wonderful curricular resources for learning how to teach general music. Silver Burdett (2012, 2017) and Macmillan/McGraw-Hill (2016) publish the most extensive materials. State or local districts normally take the leadership in adopting music texts and recordings although individual schools can also do so

TABLE 12.1 Type and Sources of Curricula

IDEAL	FORMAL	INSTRUCTIONAL	OPERATIONAL	EXPERIENTIAL
National Standards of the Music Educators National Conference; Kodály; Orff; Dalcroze	Individual states, school districts, and schools; consultants and other outside experts	District or school guides; music series texts; technology; individual teachers; outside experts; school curriculum	Music; teacher and methodology chosen; students; other teachers; school administrator; music administrator; parents	Students; parents; other teachers; administrators; school boards
Highly formal	←		→	Less formal

independently of district resources. These companies can be contacted through their websites, which can be linked to through the online technology resources. Advantages to using such materials include the size and diversity of resources and the fact that teachers do not have to take time, energy, and expense complying with copyright laws, which have already been taken care of by the publishers.

A collection of lessons for a variety of music education settings, based on the National Standards, is available from the National Association for Music Education (NAfME). It is called the *Strategies for Teaching* series, developed and coordinated by Carolyn Lindeman. Books in this series are inexpensive and can be ordered from the NAfME website. (See Stauffer and Davidson, 1996.) In addition, pedagogies such as Orff-Schulwerk, Dalcroze, and Kodály often provide detailed sequences of concepts and skills, along with materials and processes for achieving those goals. Some even suggest specific lesson plans based on curriculum in addition to process. Books by Choksy, Abramson, Gillespie, Woods, and York (2000), Choksy (1999a, 1999b, Mead (1994), Steen (1992), and Frazee (1987) provide useful models for incorporating some of these pedagogies within the framework of a sequential curriculum.

Woods and Gordon (1985) designed a series called *Jump Right In*, which implements learning principles espoused by Edwin Gordon. The key to thoughtful use of these or other pedagogies is to reflect on whether they constitute a comprehensive and balanced approach that engages students actively in music and musical thinking that stimulates musical growth.

Planning a Curriculum

General Curriculum Content

Teachers need to think through what they want to accomplish each year in their instructional curriculum. If a formal curriculum for music has been established where they are working, they should follow its guidelines when developing their operational curriculum. If no formal curriculum exists locally, teachers may wish to use State or National Standards in music education as a guide. Those standards represent an ideal. It is up to teachers to make them real. Tables 12.2 and 12.3 show how a general

TABLE 12.2 Relationships between Levels of Outcome and Music Elements

STATE LEVEL	DISTRICT OR SCHOOL LEVEL	SPECIFIC GRADE LEVEL
Students will use the conceptual language of music to organize musical concepts, ideas, and sounds.	Students will develop and apply musical concepts of rhythm, melody, harmony, tone color, expression, form, and style through listening, performing, and creating.	First graders will understand the concept of beat as an organizing device, be able to recognize it in a variety of settings, and use beat as a basis for composition and improvisation.
General ←		→ Specific

TABLE 12.3   Relationships between Levels of Outcome and Skills Development

NATIONAL OR STATE LEVEL	DISTRICT LEVEL	SPECIFIC GRADE LEVEL
Students sing expressively, with appropriate dynamics, phrasing, and interpretation.	Students sing a wide range of songs demonstrating vocal control and expressiveness.	Fourth graders will sing the song "Wings of a Dove," using breath support, correct phrasing, and soft dynamics.
General ←		→ Specific

Discussion point:

Failure to plan and teach within a formal curriculum framework results in a string of activities, rather than systematic growth in musical skills and concepts.

program outcome on the state or national level becomes increasingly specific as it is realized in the classroom.

A curriculum needs to be balanced, appropriately sequenced, and comprehensive. It needs to reflect what musicians do with music; needs to help children discover the nature of music; and needs to show how music is put together and situate it in both a cultural and historical context. It needs to challenge children to grow artistically, creatively, and aesthetically, and it needs to give them a wide repertoire of vocal and aural literature that they can enjoy through a lifetime. Such a thoughtful program will accomplish the ultimate goal of individual musical independence for each child.

When planning a curriculum, teachers need to have a big picture and a specific picture in mind. The big-picture view is to think of where the children should be musically by the time they complete fifth or sixth grade. This can be gained by looking at formal curricula such as National or State Standards. The more specific view is to look separately at each grade level. One possibility for planning would be to establish age-appropriate goals and/or procedures for attaining the following components of music engagement and learning. The teacher could create a series of outcomes for each grade level for the various components they hope to address in that particular year.

1. *Skills* of singing, moving, listening, playing, reading, creating (composing, improvising, and arranging), and evaluative or critical thinking

2. *Concepts*, including elements (melody, harmony, rhythm, tone color, and expression), form (how the elements are put together), style and genre (what emerges from structure and culture), and context (the relationship of music to culture, history, and the other arts)

3. *Attitudes* about music, as well as children's preferences for various kinds of music and commitment to involvement in music

4. *Repertoire* of vocal music, including cultural heritage and folk songs from the country in which the children live, composed songs, and songs from various parts of the world, often accompanied by children on various instruments or with dance; and a listening repertoire of a wide range of quality works that students can identify, discuss, and evaluate

These four curriculum elements are implemented differently depending on how they are developed in the learner. *Skills* must be developed gradually, moving from simple to complex tasks. For example, the skill of singing expressively and confidently across a wide range needs to be developed in small steps (see Chapter 4). Skills must also be practiced regularly to be retained. Reasonable goals can be established for children's vocal growth during a given year, and attainment of each step measured throughout that year. Chapters 4–10 will help in formulating developmentally appropriate skill sequences in each of the major processes of music. The National Standards also establish benchmarks, or standards, for levels of attainment for fourth grade and eighth grade in skills development and provide a guide for stages of development in reaching those benchmarks from prekindergarten to grade four. (See *Performance Standards for Music: Grades Pre K–12* [(MENC, 1996].) Table 12.3 shows how skills might move from the general level of National and State Standards to the specific behaviors found in a classroom. See also the 2014 NAfME standards that focus on developing music literacy through creating, performing, and responding.

Concepts, once learned, do not need to be practiced. A person either does or does not understand a concept. Once a concept is attained, it does need to be applied to new situations or used in new ways. For example, a teacher might implement a short unit that introduces the concept of beat, go on to teach several other concepts, then return to beat, applying that concept to new pieces of music at a more sophisticated level. Once the concept of beat is understood, children have the basis for understanding concepts of rhythmic durations and metric organization. Chapter 5 on pitch, Chapter 7 on rhythm, and Chapter 9 on listening are sources for specific concepts about elements typically taught at the elementary level. Children also form concepts or understandings of processes, such as singing well or playing barred percussion instruments. Concepts, or generalized understandings, are modified constantly as children have new experiences with music.

All music should be placed in a cultural and stylistic context when taught, and children should be helped to perform in the appropriate style as they learn new pieces. (See Chapters 4, 8, and 15 for examples.) From a developmental perspective, very young children are not ready to understand the history of music, but they can learn about individual composers, and they are highly sensitive to style. Older elementary children can begin to gain a conscious understanding of the attributes of music that come together to create specific musical styles, periods, and genres.

Attitudes do not need to be taught, but emerge in response to musical experiences. The kinds of questions the teacher asks the students throughout the year will help them to grow in their valuing of and sensitivity to music. Asking questions such as these will help children make musical decisions consciously and will build patterns of aesthetic thinking: "What did you find interesting about that piece of music and why?" "If you had money to go to a concert or buy an album, what would you choose to listen to, and why?"

Repertoire develops from engaging children in quality music through singing, playing, moving, and listening. Repertoire building is having children internalize key works to gain a sense of mastery and ownership. Such internalization results from many experiences with a work of music. Excellent literature is available in music series texts with recordings that use authentic instruments from various cultures, played in a style true to that culture. Many separate song collections of contemporary music are available through music stores and online services. Numerous Kodály-inspired books provide collections of American folk music. The Orff-Schulwerk American-edition books include many songs, chants, and instrumental works (see Chapter 4 for names of resources). Various published collections of songs and listening experiences from throughout the world are available (see Chapter 15). Other ideas for building a listening repertoire can be found in Chapter 9.

Early Childhood Planning

The early childhood years are usually defined as encompassing prebirth to age eight. Music educators working in schools are usually not asked to teach children below the age of three. If public schools are serving children as young as three, they may be there as part of a Head Start program or to meet the requirement under PL 99-457, which mandates school-based services for exceptional children beginning at the age of three.

The formal content of the early childhood music curriculum focuses mainly on singing, playing instruments, creating, and listening. (See Pre-K Standards in National Standards.) It highlights the need to use developmentally appropriate practice in working with very young children. NAEYC (National Association for the Education of Young Children) has long emphasized that programs for young children need to:

- Be child centered, rather than teacher centered
- Be based on play and exploration as well as active involvement in making and responding to music, rather than on being told about music
- Be sequential, but respect that each child develops at his or her own rate
- Be within the context of a community where children feel safe and valued
- Challenge children to grow by engaging in activities that are just beyond their reach developmentally
- Respect young children's need for repetition in order to attain mastery of a skill, but variety in order to continue to stimulate and interest them in learning
- Respect the whole child: physical, social, emotional, and cognitive

It is suggested that music educators untrained in early childhood education spend time in early childhood classrooms to see how these principles are implemented in such settings. Take ideas for ways to work with children and adapt those ideas for music instruction. See specific ideas for working with young children in Chapters 4–10. Also consider possibilities in the MENC publication *Strategies for Teaching Prekindergarten Music* (Sims, 1995) and *The Musical Lives of Young Children* (Flohr, 2005).

K–6 Planning

A sample framework for a year's plan for second grade appears in Box 12.1. It is based on the idea of a spiral approach to curriculum planning, in which concepts and skills are presented gradually in a logical order, each being built upon again and again, spiraling upward to more advanced skills and understandings. To make this model useful, teachers need to adapt it to their own setting and include specifics for each grade level. Units of study can be superimposed on the framework, as in the example of the unit on Asian music.

BOX 12.1 A Planning Map for a Year's Curriculum (Grade Level: Second Grade)

MUSIC CONTENT	AUGUST OR SEPTEMBER TO OCTOBER	NOVEMBER TO DECEMBER	JANUARY TO MARCH	APRIL TO MAY OR JUNE	OUTCOMES
Concepts Melody	Specific patterns of melodic movement— high/low, step, leap, repeat	Melodic phrases	Pentatonic melodies	Tonality and tonal center	Demonstrate *understanding* of each of these concepts
	Sol, Mi, La	Do	Re	High and low Do	
Harmony or texture	Thick/thin Accompanied and unaccompanied	Layered, using ostinati	Experience heterophonic and polyphonic structures of much of Asian music	Bourdon	Give concrete examples of each of these concepts
Rhythm	Beat Quarter note and rest, double eighth	Beat/rhythm Duple meter Half note	Free rhythm	Triple meter Sixteenth notes	Understand and apply each of these concepts
Expression	Loud/soft Fast/slow Smooth/detached	Dynamic Shaping Articulation	Gradual change in dynamics and tempo Accents	Synthesize concepts of expression	Apply concepts to performance
Tone color or timbre	Percussion sounds from many regions	Choral sound Solo—female/male	Sounds from Asia—vocal/ instrumental	String sounds, bowed and plucked	Aurally identify each of the instruments and instrument types studied
Form	Same/different Call and response Solo/chorus	AB, ABA *d.c. al fine*	Through composed	Cumulative songs Rondo	Aurally identify each form studied
Style or genre	Percussion ensemble Blues	Holiday songs from various traditions— compare styles	Chinese, Japanese, Indonesian music styles	Folk style Country style	Identify music studied by style, using correct terminology
Cultural context	Background on roles percussion instruments play in various cultures Songs in context	Contexts of songs from various cultures—what meaning and role they have in celebrations	Background on each of the three cultures studied	Background on folk and country music styles	Talk about various pieces from perspective of culture
History	Brief history of blues	History of "Silent Night"	Some history of travel of musical sounds and styles through Asia	Short history of the banjo	Recount some of the historical facts that have been gained
Relation to other arts and subjects	View the use of repeated patterns in paintings by Kandinsky and Klee, and decorative cloth from Ghana		Chinese brush painting Japanese haiku Wayang Kulit puppets		Understand that there is a connection between the ways music, art, and poetry is created within and across cultures
Skills Singing	Sing comfortably in range of 5th	Expanding range to octave, C4–C5 Sing melodic ostinati	Sing in head voice Sustain tones Sing with expression	Sing with style and expression songs in various keys, following a conductor	Sing a familiar song from memory accurately and with expression, using a good tone

(Continued)

BOX 12.1 (*Continued*)

MUSIC CONTENT	AUGUST OR SEPTEMBER TO OCTOBER	NOVEMBER TO DECEMBER	JANUARY TO MARCH	APRIL TO MAY OR JUNE	OUTCOMES
Moving	Move creatively in response to beat Invent own hand jive	Learn a simple Israeli circle dance Feel patterns in 2s	Learn two folk dances from Asia	Feel patterns in 3s Learn a play party game	Show increased repertoire of creative movements and coordination within dances
Listening	Percussion montage Traditional Blues singer Listen perceptively and describe using music vocabulary	Develop a listening map in a group	Chinese Dragon music Japanese koto Indonesian gamelan	String montage Folk music Country music	Identify and describe various works; listen perceptively enough to map a recorded work
Playing	Basic mallet techniques Hand percussion techniques Layered percussion	Melodic ostinati Melodic patterns	Pentatonic songs by ear	Bourdon Moving bourdon, cross-over bourdon Ensemble playing	Demonstrate ability to hold part against other parts within rhythmic and melodic context
Reading	Read all durations and pitches listed in rhythm and melody above				Sight read a simple song in Do pentatonic
Creating	Improvise own part in layered hand percussion piece Improvise vocally in blues piece	Improvise an ostinato on keyed percussion Improvise B section of ABA	Set a haiku to music, using the pentatonic scale	Arrange instrumental accompaniment to folk tune using hand percussion	Show increased ability to improvise, compose, and arrange musical ideas
Critiquing/ evaluating	Reflect on the quality of own improvisations and those of others	Reflect on the quality of own improvisations and those of others	Critique and refine own composition and critique composition of others using established criteria	Begin to develop own criteria for critiquing creative efforts	Demonstrate increased ability to use objective criteria to critique own performances and compositions
Attitudes Musical judgments and preferences	Emerges throughout year Monitor through questioning				Justify preferences for music using musical vocabulary
Repertoire Vocal	"America" "Star Spangled Banner" "Good Mornin', Blues"	"Silent Night" "O Hannukah" "Song of Peace"	Five songs from Asia: three with accompaniment, two instrumental pieces	"Boysie" "Old Brass Wagon" "She'll Be Comin' Round the Mountain"	Sing any of the repertoire songs from memory

BOX 12.1 *(Continued)*

MUSIC CONTENT	AUGUST OR SEPTEMBER TO OCTOBER	NOVEMBER TO DECEMBER	JANUARY TO MARCH	APRIL TO MAY OR JUNE	OUTCOMES
Listening	"Rainy Day Blues" "Oya" from *Primitive Fire*	"Sleigh Ride" by Anderson	Gamelan— "Silver Rain" "Chinese Dragon Dance" "Sakura" on Koto	"Buckaroo Holiday" from *Rodeo* "Lazy John" by Ritchie	Identify works or ensembles by name and give descriptions of each piece
Programs			Second- and third-grade program on Music of Asia		

Additional considerations in planning a yearly curriculum are:

1. The number and length of contacts per year with each group of children

2. The number and types of programs or concerts to be given each year

3. The structure of the school and goals for the integration of the music program with the rest of the curriculum

4. Expectations of administrators and other members of the community

5. The number of music teachers at a particular school

How much can realistically be accomplished will depend on the contact time the teacher has with the children. An ideal would be thirty minutes daily with each class. Much more common is two to three times a week for thirty to forty minutes each. An inadequate program is thirty minutes per week or less.

Other factors that often influence the successful implementation of the curriculum include:

• Teacher attitudes, priorities, and training

• Facilities and equipment

• Socioeconomic status of the community

• Stability or transience of the student population

Of these, the most important factor is teacher attitude. It is discouraging for a teacher to spend more time disciplining than teaching, to adjust to a yearly turnover of one-third in student population, or to teach by going from room to room with equipment on a rolling cart. However, if a teacher truly cares about connecting children with music, a great deal can be taught, even under adverse conditions. With dedication and innovation, most challenges can be met.

Implementing a Curriculum

Lesson Planning

Once the yearly curriculum has been established, individual lessons can be planned. Lessons weave together the strands of the yearly plan. Skills, concepts, and attitudes merge as the imaginative teacher decides how to achieve the goals established. Key con-

TABLE 12.4 The Three-Legged Model of Lesson Planning

National or State Standards _____

OBJECTIVES	STRATEGIES	MONITOR AND EVALUATE
Concepts, skills, and attitudes specific to the curriculum. Most music lessons have multiple objectives, not just one.	All of the materials and activities, in logical order, that will help children to achieve the lesson's objectives. Questions can be listed. Processes from specific approaches to music education as well as technology can be incorporated.	Monitor whether students understand the task to be done and where they are in their understanding or skills at the end of a lesson. Evaluate whether objectives were realistic and whether strategies were effective.

siderations in effective lesson planning and implementation are (1) the unique learning needs of each group of children and individuals within those groups, (2) the yearly curriculum, (3) methods and materials (how to reach curriculum goals), and (4) assessment strategies. (See Chapter 13 for ideas regarding assessment.) The process of lesson planning and implementation usually provides teachers with great satisfaction, because it taps into their creativity and musicianship as well as their insights into what children need.

THE THREE-LEGGED MODEL. Effective lessons can be thought of in three parts: (1) *objectives*, or what this lesson is trying to achieve in terms of student growth in music (these come directly from the curriculum goals and outcomes); (2) *strategies*, or what procedures and materials will be used to achieve the objectives (this is where personal method and technology enter); and (3) *evaluation*, or reflecting on whether the objectives were achieved and whether the strategies were effective (what did each child learn?).

In addition to these core ideas, teachers need to think of what prerequisite understandings or skills children need to be successful in achieving the goals of a particular lesson and what follow-up activities might be done to extend the ideas from that lesson over time. This model is shown more specifically in Table 12.4. Movement, as shown by the arrows, is from left to right, then back again.

Lesson 12.1 takes this planning model and illustrates how it can be used for a music lesson in the first or second grade. Note the relationship between the columns and the variety and flow of the activities through the lesson. The activities are linked to specific National Standards for children at this age.

Prerequisite understandings: knowledge of the syllables sol, mi, do and their hand signs; familiarity with tracking a melody on a staff; and knowledge of a range of repertoire songs as well as experience in shaping music expressively.

Follow-up activities: transfer the sol, mi, do awareness to another song; understand the cultural context of "Jubilee!" and learn the traditional dance for that song, relating it back to the AB form; and select an interpretation of a repertoire song and internalize it to prepare for an upcoming concert.

Mouse, Mousie

Jubilee!

2. Hardest work I've ever done.
   Workin' on the farm.
   Easiest work I've ever done.
   Swingin' my true love's arm! *Refrain*

3. If I had a needle and thread,
   Fine as I could sew,
   Sew my true love to my side,
   And down this creek I'd go. *Refrain*

4. If I had no horse to ride,
   I'd be found a-crawlin',
   Up and down this rocky road,
   Looking for my darlin'. *Refrain*

5. All out on the old railroad.
   All out on the sea;
   All out on the old railroad.
   Far as eye can see. *Refrain*

OBJECTIVES

1. To develop skills of pitch matching, sight singing, interval awareness, and inner hearing.

   (National Standard 5)

STRATEGIES

Warm up with sight singing exercise, drawing patterns of sol, mi, do from the song "Mouse, Mousie."

Use hand signs. Work on internal hearing of pattern.

MONITOR AND EVALUATE

Listen for intonation and accuracy. Correct as necessary.

Note whether children are maintaining hand signs while moving from inner singing to singing out loud.

(Continued)

2. To discover sol, mi, do pattern in a song and to add a bourdon accompaniment.

(National Standards 4 and 5)

Put fingers on sol, mi, do pattern in "Mouse, Mousie." Sing the song.

Sing again while patting an F, C bourdon on laps to the beat. Select children to play the bourdon on xylophones.

Watch to see that everyone is pointing to the pattern in the book, tracing it as they sing.

Monitor accuracy of playing.

Note on file cards who performed and how well they did.

3. To begin focus on the concept of binary, or AB, form.

(National Standard 6)

Sing the song "Jubilee!"

Clap hands on the A section, pat laps on the B section.

Once children get a sense of where to switch, have them suggest other contrasting movements. Invite children to discuss why the movements changed.

Observe whether children switch movements at the B section.

Monitor responses to the question.

4. To review one or two repertoire songs and refine a sense of style in singing them.

(National Standards 1 and 7)

Have children vote for the songs they want to refine using a thumbs up or thumbs down procedure.

Experiment with various interpretations using suggestions from the class.

Observe where individual children still need help with words or melody.

Guide children in reflecting on the success of the various interpretations.

Source: "Mouse, Mousie" and "Jubilee!" reproduced with permission from *World of Music,* Grade 1 (Parsippany, NJ: Silver Burdett & Ginn, 1992).

While planning individual lessons, ask yourself the following questions:

- *What are my objectives in teaching this lesson?* Are they significant and musical?

- *How am I going to get there, and what materials do I need?* Do these processes engage students actively in music making and in thinking about and responding to music?

- *How will I know I've been successful?* How am I going to assess student learning? How will I assess the quality of what I've done and determine needed changes to the lesson?

THE PROBLEM-SOLVING APPROACH. Another approach to lesson planning is to establish a problem for students to solve. Lesson components of setting goals or objectives, planning strategies, and assessing will still be present, but the structure will be slightly different. Students will be more involved in constructing their own learning through their problem solving. This approach is particularly useful for composition and listening assignments but can also be used for performance. It is more child directed and moves the teacher to the side to become a facilitator or guide, rather than the only expert or the total director of learning. Lesson 12.2 is an example of a lesson based on problem solving. Other examples of this type of lesson can be found in Chapter 9, on listening, and Chapter 10, on creating.

National Standards:

4b. Create and arrange short instrumental pieces within specified guidelines.
4c. Use a variety of sound sources when composing.

Level	Grades two to six
Objective	To have students demonstrate their understanding of ternary form through composition.
Materials	An array of classroom instruments and synthesizers
Problem	Work in a small group to compose a piece in ABA form, showing clear contrast of ideas between sections.
Process	Children choose groups and brainstorm initial ideas about how they want to demonstrate their knowledge of a simple structure involving repetition and contrast. They will select the instruments they want to use and experiment with developing the contrasting themes. Through experimentation and dialogue they will refine their themes and rehearse their piece until ready to share.
Assessment	After each piece is performed, invite students to reflect on whether the piece met the requirements of the problem; what in the piece was particularly satisfying; what they might want to change if they had more time; and what decisions they made in the process of refining their pieces. It is also valuable to compare solutions to the problem among the different groups—how were they similar and different?

Learning Style Types

Divergers: need concrete experiences and time for reflection; look at whole rather than parts; enjoy people and are influenced by peers.

Assimilators: are abstract thinkers and reflective observers; interested in theories, not the practical; set goals and plan systematically.

Convergers: are abstract thinkers and active experimenters; deduce ideas from experience and like to apply them to practical things; are goal setting; like right answers; enjoy things more than people.

Accommodators: need concrete experiences and active experimentation; are flexible and adaptive; intuitive; use trial and error; at ease with others but sometimes pushy; are influenced by peers.

THE QUADRANT APPROACH. Yet another approach to lesson planning is to apply a model developed by Bernice McCarthy (1987)—called the 4-Mat System®— that incorporates in its structure the principles of research into learning styles. She created a strategy for presenting lessons that teach to all four cognitive styles identified by David Kolb's research: divergers, assimilators, convergers, and accommodators.

McCarthy's elaborate system visualizes a lesson as a circle divided into quadrants—one for each type of learner. She goes on to subdivide each quadrant into right- and left-brain stimulation and other factors. The model becomes complicated. The main point of structuring lessons in quadrants is to remind the teacher constantly that he or she is dealing with many kinds of learners and must teach with different emphases to build on the strengths of each learner and to encourage development in weaker methods of processing.

Quadrant 1: Why? This part of a lesson answers the students' questions (either asked or unasked), "Why are we doing this?" "What is the significance to me, to now, to the future, to other ideas, to meaning?" This quadrant usually takes very little time and can be in the form of words of introduction or relationship, cues for focusing on specific musical events, provocative questions to stimulate thinking, or any other activity that hooks students' interest.

Quadrant 2: What? This part of a lesson answers the students' question (either asked or unasked), "What is it we are supposed to be learning?" The teacher explicitly informs students exactly what the skill or concept to be learned is, checks for understanding, and reteaches as necessary until all students are clear about what they need to learn.

Quadrant 3: How? This part of a lesson answers the students' questions (either asked or unasked), "How exactly do I do this?" "How do I relate it to other learning?" "How do I do the skill?" This section usually consists of some kind of practice, repetition, or activities to reinforce and internalize the concept or skill.

Quadrant 4: What if? This part of a lesson answers the students' question (either asked or unasked), "If I have learned this concept or skill, what else can I do with it?" This section helps students see the bigger picture, stimulates their creativity, and encourages divergent thinking and personal meaning making. Students are often asked to apply their new knowledge or skill to a new situation and to evaluate the success of their learning. Lesson 12.3 illustrates this model in a series of activities designed to explore popular music with older elementary children. (See also Box 12.2 on page 332.)

LESSON 12.3 The 4-Mat® Model of Lesson Planning

Lesson Objective	Develop skills in evaluating popular music using musical criteria.
Grades	Five, six.
National Standards	6a. Identify simple music forms when presented aurally.
	6b. Demonstrate perceptual skills by answering questions about, and by describing aural examples of, music of various styles representing diverse cultures.
	6c. Use appropriate terminology in explaining music, music notation, music instruments and voices, and music performances.
	6d. Identify the sounds of a variety of instruments, including many orchestra and band instruments and instruments from various cultures, as well as children's voices and male and female adult voices.
	7a. Devise criteria for evaluating performances and compositions.
	7b. Explain, using appropriate music terminology, their personal preferences for specific musical works and styles.
Materials	Recording of "La Bamba" or other popular music, music description forms, T-chart for each class, and recorded popular music brought in by students.

Procedure

Quadrant 1. Why?

1. Listen to "La Bamba," then ask group to whisper the meter to the captain; captains stand when they are ready to answer. Award points for correct answer (4).

2. Ask students to discuss with their group as many things as they perceive in the music: what the instruments are (jarana [eight-string chord guitar], requinto [small guitar], harp); how many vocal parts there are (2); who is singing (men); what language (Spanish); how to clap the rhythmic ostinato that runs through the whole song (titi ta titi ta titi ta ta); whether the melody in the vocal part moves mainly by step or leap (step); whether the tempo is fast, medium, or slow; where the music is from.

3. In a round robin answering format, give one point for each new description item the captains can name. Use incorrect answers for teachable moments.

Quadrant 2. What?

4. On a scale of zero to ten, predict whether this music is very popular (ten) or not at all popular (zero) in the country from which it comes. Groups discuss with captain, who gives answer.

5. What makes music popular? Think of some music you know that you and many people like. What are its characteristics? Pass out the form and have groups work on writing responses in each category. Have each group report to the whole class. Award points for thoughtful, meaningful, accurate responses.

6. If you and your friends like a piece of music, do you think everyone in the world likes it the same as you? Why or why not? What do you think causes differences? Should there be just one popular music? Why or why not? What would we gain or what would we lose?

Quadrant 3. How?

7. To practice identifying things we like and why we like them, you are encouraged to bring in one of your favorite songs on compact disc (CD) or tape. By listening to each others' favorites and discussing why music is popular, we will gain a greater understanding of ourselves, our musical preferences, and what makes music interesting. There are some guidelines we will follow, listed on your information form. (Review guidelines.)

8. Listen to several examples brought in by students. When discussing musical preferences in class, comments may be made only about the music. No comments about the person who brought the music or that person's musical taste will be made. Our goal is to understand what makes music popular, not whose or what music is popular.

Quadrant 4. What if?

9. What if we were writing a book on popular music? What would we write about the characteristics of popular music? Make a T-chart to agglomerate ideas. Have each group work together to create a summation that arranges these ideas in a logical, coherent, paragraph form. Award twenty points for each thoughtful, meaningful, and accurate summation that exhibits higher-level thinking skills and includes all the ideas generated by the class.

Method of Evaluation   Teacher continuously observes students' working together, answers to questions, music contributed, and written summations.

THE IMMERSED APPROACH. Often music teachers feel pressured to "try to do everything" or to "cover the curriculum." The result of trying to do a little bit of everything can be that children receive a superficial experience, rather than an in-depth experience, leaving them mentally impoverished. Some critics of this approach have suggested that teachers need to do less, but do a few things in more depth. Such an approach immerses children in the learning over a period of time.

BOX 12.2 Guidelines for Exploring Popular Music in the Classroom

Throughout history, music has always had a lighter side that appealed to many people. Much of it is popular for a short time, then discarded when new music catches people's attention. People's taste in music changes over time just as their taste in clothing or hair style changes. Different groups of people have different preferences in their music.

What is popular right now among students at this elementary school? Does everyone like the same kind of music, or do differences occur between different people? Why is some music well liked and other music less liked? What characteristics in the music are most appealing?

Students are urged to bring their favorite recorded music to school to share with others in music class. By listening to each other's favorites and discussing why music is popular, students will gain a greater understanding of themselves, their musical preferences, and what makes music interesting. Here are some guidelines to follow:

- Write your name and homeroom teacher's name on the compact disc (CD) or cassette tape case so the teacher can return it to you.

- Recordings brought to school may not contain (1) profane language, (2) glorification of violence, (3) advocacy of drug use, (4) advocacy of intolerance toward any individual or group of people, or (5) promotion of a specific religious doctrine.

- When discussing musical preferences in class, comment only on the music. No comments will be allowed about the person who brought the music or that person's musical taste.

- For each music title you want the class to hear, fill out an information form (see form on the reverse side) and tape it to the CD or cassette tape case.

- Give the music and attached form(s) to the teacher at least one day before it is shared with the class. Cue your tape to the starting place of the music you want the class to hear.

Name of music _____ by _____

Name of student _____ Homeroom teacher _____

Cooperative group name _____

Write below at least one specific characteristic in the music that appeals to you and why. General statements, such as "I like it," "It's cool," "It's got a good beat," "The melody goes up and down," do not qualify.

Melody _____

Harmony _____

Rhythm or meter _____

Form _____

Expression _____

Lyrics _____

Other (specify): _____

You will earn five points for every category containing a thoughtful and accurate comment about the music. (Attach another sheet of paper if you need more space.)

Courtesy of Dr. Kirk Kassner.

The National Standards Web in Figure 12.1 could be used for planning a series of lessons around a song or listening activity in which the musical event is approached from many different perspectives, much like a rich tapestry or the changing view of images in a kaleidoscope. To use this in planning, place the name of the song or listening

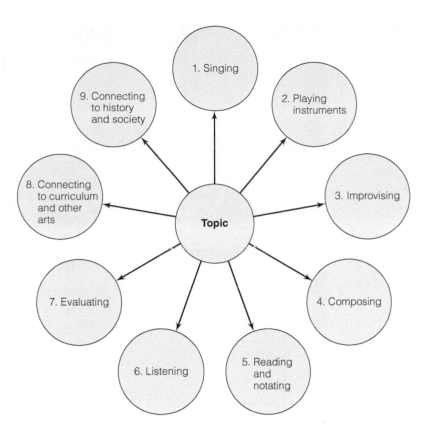

FIGURE 12.1

National Standards Web for Planning
Unit of Study

experience in the middle, then determine how many ways you could approach it through each area of the nine standards. Movement activities could also be planned, even though they are not a part of the standards. Over a period of several lessons, students would be immersed in experiences that deepen and enlarge their engagement with and understanding of that particular piece of music. Many important learning objectives, including some that are unanticipated, could be accomplished in the process of this deep exploration.

Other models of lesson planning that show the flow through a lesson can be found throughout this book. There is not one right way to plan a lesson. In fact, sticking to a formula can prove to be boring for both teachers and students. Regardless of the model selected, it is important that teachers develop clear goals and objectives that are supported by classroom activities. Some teachers get so caught up in selecting appealing materials or in following a method that they lose sight of the larger reasons for what they are doing. It is as if they have entered the process of planning, as noted in the middle column of Table 12.4. When asked to state their goals, such teachers often reply, "to learn the song" or "to have fun," instead of to build a foundation of musical skills and concepts children can carry through their lives. Remember, the highest form of fun is to gain a feeling of competence, because confidence emerges from knowing you have achieved something and can use it in the rest of your life.

Thematic and Unit Planning

One way to visualize an entire school year is to think in terms of large themes that can encompass many, if not all, aspects of the music curriculum. An example of such a theme might be to dedicate a year to creativity in music. Children could compose, improvise, and arrange music. They could learn the craft of songwriting and compose and perform their own songs. Children could build musical instruments and learn to play them,

© Jerry Gay

accompanying pieces they have learned. They could study the lives, music, and creative processes of renowned composers of music, both living and dead. Teachers who elect to plan their year in this way need to make sure the themes are large enough to allow room for many different ways of approaching a topic. Selecting too specific a topic, for example, Wolfgang Amadeus Mozart, could quickly become boring to children.

Some teachers prefer to divide their year into units around specific ideas rather than using a spiral approach. Early childhood programs frequently use a unit plan because young children do not yet separate life into subject areas to be covered; they learn more holistically. Units can be of different lengths but usually last at least three class periods at a minimum. Some units may extend across several weeks, depending on the reason for the unit. Units can also be interjected into a more traditional spiral curriculum.

Units have the advantage of allowing students to become deeply immersed in a topic over a period of time. They are often rich and stimulating for children because an idea can be approached from so many perspectives. Units can focus on many different topics and take many different forms. A range of possible subjects for units follows. This list is by no means comprehensive.

CURRICULUM CONNECTIONS (National Standards 8 and 9)

1. A culture or subculture, including music, dance, visual arts, stories, and other aspects of that culture

2. A topic that relates to an area of the classroom curriculum such as the Westward Movement, families, nature, journeys, the planets, and so on (see Chapter 14)

3. Children's literature

4. A composer or musician

5. Connecting music with an artwork, style, or artist (see Chapter 14)

TOPICS WITHIN MUSIC (National Standards 1 through 8)

1. Instruments of the orchestra

2. Opera

3. Folk dance

4. Patriotic music

5. Holiday music, including such holidays as Martin Luther King Jr. Day, Chinese New Year, Cinco de Mayo

6. The process of composing (see Chapter 10)

7. A skill, such as playing the recorder

8. A particular work of recorded music explored from many perspectives (see Chapter 9 and Lesson 12.4)

Regardless of the focus, units still need to address key concepts and skills in music to be valid as part of a music education program. See Barrett, McCoy, and Veblen (1997) for excellent suggestions on developing series of lessons that view music from many perspectives. Figure 12.1 suggests another model for planning a unit, using a web based on the National Standards. Teachers will be more likely to achieve important musical skills and understandings if they make sure they approach a topic from as many of the standards as are valid. They should not force an activity if it makes no sense.

Units can be accomplished in collaboration with classroom teachers or other school personnel. Parents can also become involved in sharing expertise. For example, in a unit that focuses on a cultural study, the teacher may include individuals in the school from a particular tradition, who can help to teach songs and dances and share in-depth understandings about their culture of origin. Other specialists such as the librarian, art teacher, or physical education teacher may wish to collaborate on a unit so that their combined expertise will benefit the children. Artists-in-residence can also add their expertise. Artists and funds for residencies are available through local, regional, or state arts commissions, and Parent Teacher Student Associations (PTSAs) are often willing to provide matching grants from the school.

Lesson 12.4 is an example of a unit that could be accomplished with the collaboration of classroom teachers and an art specialist. The process involves "spinning a thread through the arts." Appropriate in grades two through four, the lesson can stand on its own or connect with a unit on sea life for greater richness.

LESSON 12.4 Unit Plan Connecting Music with Other Arts

Day 1	Children's literature
Classroom Teacher	• Read the book *The Rainbow Fish* to the children. • Have them discuss the plot and the characters. • Invite children to suggest the moral of the story. • Ask them to think about what kinds of sounds they would use if they were going to compose music to tell this story.

(Continued)

Day 2	Visual art
Art Teacher	• View photographs of tropical fish.
	• Discuss the range of sizes, shapes, colors, and designs.
	• Using colored paper, oil pastels, and glitter glue or foil, have each child create a rainbow fish, applying some of the designs they have seen in real fish. Use the initial shape as a template to create the opposite side. Fasten both sides together, leaving some room to stuff the fish.
	• Add a dowel to turn it into a stick puppet.
Day 3	Music
Music Teacher	• Review the images in *The Rainbow Fish* with the children. Ask them to recall what sounds they imagined using to tell the story.
	• Tell them that a French composer named Camille Saint-Saëns wrote a piece called "The Aquarium," in which he tried to suggest the movement of fish.
	• Listen to the music and describe the sounds.
	• Listen again and ask the children to follow the shape of the melody and map it in the air with their fish puppets.
	• Have them draw musical maps of the melody.
Days 4 and 5	Music and nature
Music Teacher	• View the video of "The Aquarium" by Saint-Saëns on *Tropical Sweets* © by William Patterson (2015).
	• Discuss how the videographer and editor were able to realize the music through images of tropical fish.
	• Ask the children to use their music maps to compose their own music on a synthesizer, bells, or metallophones or tell the story of *The Rainbow Fish* musically.
	• Consider having the children experiment with using a whole-tone scale.
	• Ask the children to refine their pieces, share them with others, and evaluate them.
Days 6 and 7	Creative movement
Music Teacher	• Discuss the ways that fish move through the water. Discuss what happens when they move individually and in schools.
	• Ask the children to experiment moving their bodies and using that flow and awareness of space.
	• Work in groups to choreograph either the music of "The Aquarium" or some of the student compositions. Share those works. Digitally record them and evaluate them. (These could become part of children's portfolios.)

Distilling the Essence of Curriculum

Because the role of the arts in education is constantly being questioned, music educators must be clear about the importance and value of music. One of the best ways to convey this is by having a clearly stated curriculum with a sense of direction, in which students are growing through active involvement in listening to music, creating music, and performing music. Many excellent sources are available to provide that structure. There are numerous ways to achieve these goals. Thoughtful and creative instruction by dedicated teacher-musicians will help to ensure that the journey is meaningful and the destination worthwhile.

TECHNOLOGY *for* TEACHING *and* LEARNING MUSIC: CURRICULUM DESIGN

Not long after several dozens of computer programs were developed in the 1970s and 1980s and music educators began experimenting with their use with children in classrooms, thoughtful educators started to think about building curricula supplemented with technology and, in some cases, curricula completely driven by technology. Many schools adopted music curricula heavily dependent on technology. Music educators continue to develop curricula and strategies for using music technology. To learn more, visit the Technology Resources links in the MindTap.

MINDTAP

Scenario

MS. RAMIREZ LOVES HER job as a music teacher and also loves to gain new ideas to infuse into her curriculum. She regularly attends music education workshops offered in her city.

She finds activities that she thinks her children will love and brings them in the next week after attending a workshop. Indeed the children enjoy the activities. Some of these are retained by Ms. Ramirez into her internal repertoire of "things that work" and some of them she discards over time.

Twice a year, the children perform in concerts for the parents as well as for the school. Ms. Ramirez usually backs up her teaching to six weeks before each concert and begins to teach children the materials for those events. Her concerts are usually very entertaining.

Questions

1. What seem to be the main drivers for Ms. Ramirez's decisions about the content of her music curriculum?

2. What might be the advantages of this curriculum for her? For her students?

3. What might be the disadvantages of this curriculum for her? For her students?

4. How does her curriculum represent the principles on curriculum development outlined in this chapter?

5. How could this curriculum engender musical growth from year to year?

6. What bases might Ms. Ramirez use for assessing the success of this curriculum and the success of individual students?

7. What bases might others such as parents and the administrator use for assessing the success of this curriculum?

REVIEW

1. What is a curriculum, and why is it important to have one?

2. Describe the differences between an ideal curriculum, a formal curriculum, an instructional curriculum, an operational curriculum, and an experiential curriculum. Give sources for each type.

3. What constitutes a balanced and effective curriculum in music?

4. What considerations are important when establishing a curriculum? What factors might influence its successful implementation?

5. What are the elements of a three-legged lesson plan, and how do they relate to each other?

6. How do these elements relate to any effective lesson plan format?

7. Where do specific lessons belong in the curriculum, and how do they connect back to the curriculum framework?

8. How are unit plans different from a sequential curriculum based on musical skills and concepts?

CRITICAL THINKING

1. What role(s) does the individual teacher play in regard to the curriculum? Where does personal method fit in?

2. What are the benefits of using the 1994 National Standards or the 2014 Common Core Standards as a basis for your curriculum, and what might be the limitations?

3. Critique the following idea. "I see the children only once a week, which is totally inadequate, so I choose materials and activities that I think are fun. I want them to have a good time. It's impossible for me to follow a sequential curriculum."

4. What might be the limitations of basing your whole curriculum on a series of units? What might be the benefits?

5. Critique the following statement. "Good lesson planning is a formula, and once you learn that formula, you are set for success."

PROJECTS

1. With another person, review and discuss at least two music curricula, preferably from different levels such as national and local. Notice their similarities and differences. Determine how comprehensive they are in light of the standards set forth in this chapter. Discuss how useful they would be as a frame for your teaching. Would they help in assessing student growth?

2. Review an instructional curriculum, whether it be in a music series text or from a specific pedagogy. Determine what goals and outcomes are being emphasized in skills development, conceptual development, attitudes and values in music, and listening and vocal repertoire. How are these being developed? How are they being assessed in the lessons provided?

3. Observe a model music lesson based on a three-legged model. Follow the lesson and assess how effective it was and how the parts related to each other. Observe another model music lesson without knowing the goals and objectives. See if you can determine what the teacher was trying to accomplish. Discuss this with a partner and with the teacher.

4. Find two different goals or outcomes from a formal music curriculum. Write specific goals for an operational curriculum that would come out of the general goals. Develop a lesson plan using one of the models in this chapter to achieve those goals.

5. Plan and implement lessons based on the three different models provided in this chapter. Compare the level of student engagement and thinking involved in each type of lesson. Discuss the results with others in your class.

6. View Box 12.1, A Planning Map for a Year's Curriculum. Analyze it to determine how ideas move sequentially in rows but are interrelated vertically in the columns. Choose one column and plan two lessons in which you accomplish several of the musical learnings and/or activities listed in that grid.

7. Select a topic you believe is worthy of a unit focus. Identify the materials you will use to teach that unit and the key ideas that will hold that unit together. Sequence those ideas and the accompanying activities across the days you think it will require to implement the unit.

MINDTAP Visit **MindTap** to access classroom videos, audio, and more!

13

Assessment and Evaluation

IN THIS CHAPTER

- Evaluation
  - Formative and Summative Evaluation
  - Teacher Evaluation
- Testing and Measurement
- Assessment
  - Teacher Assessment of Children
  - Student Self-Assessment
  - Peer Assessment
  - Teacher Self-Assessment
- Tracking Student Growth
  - Record Keeping
  - Portfolios
- Reporting to Parents
- Distilling the Essence of Assessment and Evaluation

IN MRS. BOURNE'S CLASS the children eagerly raise their hands to share their ideas as to specific ways the student conductor might work with them to interpret the music they are learning in elementary chorus. Children in Mr. Yin's class are quietly circling ideas on a rubric they have developed to evaluate their compositions on form. Later, they will share and discuss the results of their thinking with the rest of the class. Mrs. Taylor is writing in her professional journal about what she observed today in working with a child who is having particular problems paying attention. She writes a description of the child's behavior, her responses to that behavior, and then reflects on what she learned and other techniques she might use in the future. The principal, Mr. Abbott, is preparing for his semiannual evaluation of the music specialist, Ms. Shadduck. This evaluation is required by law, and the school district has a standard procedure that he must follow. Before he goes in to watch her teach and to conference with her, he reviews the professional development plan that she submitted before the beginning of the school year so that he can discuss her progress in meeting her goals.

Each of these snapshots is a way of looking at some aspect of assessment or evaluation that occurs daily in the lives of teachers and children. Some of these are informal and happen automatically as a part of thorough lesson planning and implementation. Others are more formal and are a part of teaching in an educational environment that requires assessment and evaluation. All are deliberate, meaning that they have been consciously planned and have not happened by accident.

Evaluation

ONE OF THE MOST IMPORTANT and often challenging tasks educators engage in is evaluation. *Evaluation* is often used as an umbrella term to describe taking stock of a program or the people in it. Other terms such as *assessment*, *measurement*, and *testing* may be used to describe specific tools in the evaluation process. Each of these tools can help to increase the base of objective information to use in making evaluative decisions.

Evaluation involves making a value judgment about something or someone. According to law, principals must formally evaluate teachers each year. Teachers constantly evaluate their students, sometimes formally, sometimes informally. Teachers also evaluate their administrators, often based on how supportive they are, how well they communicate, and how well they lead. Parents evaluate the success of the music program based on the attitudes of their children toward the music classes and on the musical quality of the concerts. Ideally, teachers evaluate their own curriculum on a regular basis and reshape it as necessary. Table 13.1 illustrates a variety of ways, both formal and informal, that evaluation of curriculum and of teachers occurs.

As can be seen from these illustrations, evaluation is often subjective or highly personal, lacking in objective or measurable standards. A complete lack of objective standards could be troublesome. For instance, teachers would find it distressing to have their music curriculum evaluated solely on how well the students performed in a spring concert or to have their abilities evaluated on impressions the principal received about them and their program from faculty-room discussions over coffee.

Effective evaluation involves collecting a combination of objective and subjective data as well as affective, or feeling responses, using many different perspectives or sources of information. Lehman (1992) suggests that evaluation should be a part of every music program and should be built in from the start of the program, not added afterward. It is best done if the goals of the program have been clearly stated from the beginning.

Formative and Summative Evaluation

Current literature differentiates between two main types of evaluation, formative and summative. There are many ideas throughout this chapter for both formative and summative techniques to use in evaluating students. Additional ideas appear in the assessment sections throughout this book.

Evaluation strategies that occur throughout the year that involve giving individuals specific feedback as to their performance, what needs improvement, and how to improve it is called formative evaluation. This is constructive evaluation that helps students and teachers improve the quality of their performance. This can be done informally, such as giving students verbal feedback regarding technique or phrasing during a rehearsal, or formally, such as inviting students to critique the effectiveness of their compositions by using rubrics. This type of evaluation helps those being evaluated improve what they are doing because it is specific to the tasks they are performing. It helps to "form" more effective performances.

THINGS TO THINK ABOUT

- Think of a grade you received in music. How aware were you of what the grade was based on?

- What were your feelings associated with that grade?

- What bases should be used for grades in music?

- What roles do you think elementary general music educators should take in assessing student progress in music?

"Evaluation is often used as an umbrella term to describe taking stock of a program or the people in it.... Evaluation involves making a value judgment about something or someone.... Ultimately, the best evaluation is constructive, helping the learner, administrator, teacher, or program grow."

TABLE 13.1 Evaluation of the Curriculum

IDEAL	FORMAL	INSTRUCTIONAL	OPERATIONAL	EXPERIENTIAL
National testing of student achievement Accreditation of teachers and programs	Statewide or district-level testing School or program accreditation	District testing Individual teacher testing Tracking of students Ongoing assessment of curriculum	Individual teacher testing Tracking of students Ongoing assessment of goals and procedures Student self-assessment and peer assessment Evaluation of program and teacher by administrators	Student attitudes and growth Teacher reflections and comments Parent observation of student achievement and attitudes
Highly formal ←				→ Less formal

Evaluations conducted at the end of a unit of study or the end of a term or school year, are called summative evaluations. These can take the form of examinations, papers, ratings of performances, or portfolios that are assessed. These are all formal in nature and often result in a grade or rating.

Teacher Evaluation

Music teachers who anticipate a formal (summative) evaluation of their program and teaching need to be proactive in communicating their vision and clear goals to their administrator early in the school year. The administrator would then conduct a formative evaluation involving an ongoing series of interactions with the teacher about the program, including their teaching, to help them progress. Ultimately, the best evaluation is constructive, helping the learner, administrator, teacher, and program grow.

Research published by the Gates Foundation regarding the evaluation of teachers shows that most systems are inadequate and ineffective. The once every year observation by the principal rarely helps a teacher improve. This research that looked at 13,000 lessons taught by teachers in eight school districts across America found that "good teacher evaluations require multiple nuanced observations by trained evaluators. Those results should be combined with other measures, such as student test scores and classroom surveys, to gather enough information to both evaluate teachers and help them improve" (Blankinship, 2012).

Regardless of whether a formal evaluation of a teacher's program is done by an administrator, the teacher needs to engage in regular evaluation of his or her program and teaching. That begins by establishing what the teacher hopes to accomplish during the year through the curriculum. It continues by monitoring student progress toward those goals on a regular basis and also by assessing how well the teacher has achieved other goals set for the program such as public performances, acquisition of music and instruments, and projects with other teachers. The teacher will also need to evaluate his or her own progress in achieving goals for professional growth. Ideas in this chapter should be of help.

Testing and Measurement

"To be valid, a test needs to be specific to the behavior is it measuring, and it must be constructed to be consistent across different sets of students."

Testing involves systematically observing a person's behavior, and then quantifying that behavior in a numerical scale or by placement in a category. A teacher might test children's knowledge of basic musical terminology through a written test or their understanding of a concept through a test of aural perception, such as a "What do you hear?" test, which is often included in music series texts. Attitudes could be formally sampled via a rating scale using a like-to-dislike continuum or an interest inventory. Skills might be tested by rating performance accuracy. To be *valid*, a test needs to be specific to the behavior it is measuring, and it must be constructed to be consistent across different sets of students. Tests can be constructed by the teacher, or a standardized test such as those available to test musical achievement could be used. Most music software that is trying to teach children some fact or skill tests them constantly and gives them feedback as to the accuracy of their answers, sometimes using funny sounds to make the learning seem more like a game. (See online technology resources for software.) Often such software will compile the scores of all of the students in a class so that the teacher can monitor their progress, both individually and as a group.

Measurement also involves assigning a range of numbers to individuals or events but is less specific to a particular behavior than a test. It allows the comparison of individuals or groups, and it often involves statistical treatment of the data collected. Teachers could measure individual student progress across time by using rating scales or rubrics or student self-assessments. Once ratings are collected, teachers could compare the data with each other or compile it for a final grade. Also, teachers might measure all the students in a class and compare the results with those of another class.

Assessment

Assessment is often used synonymously with *evaluation*. However, it can also mean a more deliberate collection of information for specific purposes. It does not necessarily involve numbers. Through it, students receive and participate in continuous feedback on both process and product. It may be subjective within the framework of standards. For example, children might be asked to assess the quality of their own performance (self-assessment) or that of others (peer assessment). Criteria related to expression, tone, phrasing, and rhythmic and pitch accuracy could be used. Teachers could assess a child's progress in playing the Autoharp or xylophone. Children could assess their own musical growth by writing about their progress in a music journal.

Assessment has become a hot-button issue in education. This is partly due to the public demand for accountability and partly due to the standards and high-stakes testing movement. Parents, business leaders, administrators, and politicians want to know that students are learning what teachers claim they are teaching. Are they meeting the standards? In addition, learning theorists have raised the issue of assessment in their critique of the narrowness of traditional ways of conducting assessment. They have called for alternatives to traditional paper-and-pencil tests for measuring student achievement. The cry throughout the education community is for *authentic assessments*, or assessments that reflect tasks that people perform in the real world.

In many ways, music educators have always used authentic assessments, particularly of performance. They measure performance by having children perform, not by having them take paper-and-pencil tests. Performing is a real-world skill in music. At the same time, music educators have often been led to believe that to grade children, they had to administer written tests. They have resorted, therefore, to giving children written tests on such things as the names of the notes and other musical signs and symbols in order to fit into a system that saw these measures as objective evidence of learning. Happily, many other and more effective alternatives now exist for assessing children as well as for having them assess each other and themselves.

> "Assessment means a deliberate collection of information for a specific purpose. It is often subjective. Through it students can obtain continuous feedback. Authentic assessments reflect the tasks that people perform in the real world such as playing an instrument or singing."

Teacher Assessment of Children

Teacher assessment of children should be continuous. Teachers are constantly monitoring many dimensions of the learning process as well as the learners. Much of this is done almost intuitively as they note which children are paying attention and which are not; which children seem to understand the task and which need more instruction; and how well each child is performing or answering questions. Effective teachers process this information and adjust their teaching to meet the needs of the situation and of individual learners. This is part of the art of teaching.

OVERT AND COVERT BEHAVIORS. One of the more provocative questions in assessing music learning is how to get at what is happening inside a student's head. Success in music, a performance art, is most often measured by performance. That is something tangible that can be seen and heard. However, the comprehensive elementary general music program is not based solely on musical performance, but also attempts to help children attain a variety of concepts and skills.

Musical behaviors can be *overt* (observable to others) or *covert* (internalized and private). Overt behaviors most commonly developed at the elementary level are singing, moving, playing, reading, identifying, critiquing, and creating. (Specific ideas for assessing those behaviors have been included throughout this textbook.) Covert behaviors are such things as listening, conceptualizing, perceiving, discriminating, recognizing, imagining, feeling, and valuing.

Developing techniques for measuring overt behaviors is relatively simple. All teachers have to do is observe what children produce and use musical standards to evaluate their performance. Developing techniques for measuring covert behaviors is more challenging and needs to reflect as much as possible what is happening mentally and emotionally. Box 13.1 suggests ways that teachers can help make internal responses observable.

BOX 13.1 Measuring Covert Behaviors

COVERT RESPONSE	OVERT RESPONSES
Listening—a complex aural response to music that depends on attention and perception and is influenced by attitudes and past experience.	Ideas presented in Chapter 9 suggest how to focus perception and how to assess what children perceive. Some options are describing, diagramming, pointing, sequencing, circling, listing, moving, singing, and playing.
Perceiving—the act of noticing something through one or more of the senses. Auditory perception is the most important in music, but reading music and following a conductor demand visual perception, and performing music demands muscular and touch perception.	Children could identify, discuss, shape, draw, diagram, notate, point to, circle, order, sing, play, conduct, or move to what they perceive.
Discriminating—the ability to tell the difference between two things, people, or events.	Present children with two musical events and have them tell you verbally or through thumbs up (same) or thumbs down (different) whether those events are the same or different from each other. It could be two pitches, two rhythm patterns, two phrases, two melodies, or two chord sequences.
Recognizing—the knowledge that something is familiar.	Children could point to, circle, or talk about what they recognize. At the next level, have them identify or name what they recognize, such as a song or a recorded work, a composer, a style, or a country from which a work comes.
Conceptualizing—the formulation of a generalized understanding based on grouping similar but different objects or events into a category based on their commonalities; this depends on skills of discrimination and perception.	Children can group sounds based on commonalities, such as all high sounds or all ringing sounds. They can group patterns such as similar melodic shapes or styles of music such as rock or folk. Once they attain a concept, they can (1) define it in their own terms, (2) bring in examples that illustrate that concept, (3) perceive it in unfamiliar music, and (4) compose using that concept. *Note:* People can understand a musical concept without being able to demonstrate it through accurate performance. Performing a chromatic scale vocally is a high-level skill, different from understanding what a chromatic scale is.
Imagining—the ability to internally image musical ideas or to image other ideas that are stimulated by music.	Aural imagination can be examined through sight-reading or sight singing; strategies using internal or external responses within a piece; improvising; and composing. Other images could be shared through describing, writing, drawing, or moving.

(Continued)

Feeling—the emotional or affective response to music. This is influenced not only by the music itself, but also by the experiences the listener may associate with that music. Feelings are not right or wrong, they just are.	Have children discuss or write down their feeling responses to music. They could also dance, move, or draw their responses or write poetry to describe their feelings.
Valuing—the worth people attribute to a piece or style of music or to musical experiences. Values cannot be imposed, as in "You will like this music," but must emerge from active involvement with music. Values can be influenced by other factors, including families, peers, live concerts, and the media. Values can change.	Observe students' responses to a variety of music, and have them discuss or write down their responses. After they state a value response, such as "I really like that music" or "I hate that music," encourage them to discuss why in terms of the music. Observe what recordings they purchase, what concerts they attend, or what pieces they want to sing or perform over and over. Encourage them to discuss their musical preferences.

QUESTIONING. Questioning is also a powerful way to assess student thinking as well as to challenge them to think in new ways. Pautz (1989, p. 68) says, "To be an [effective] teacher is to be a facilitator, a guide, a nurturer of curiosity, a cognitive referee rather than a teller, an expert, a disseminator of knowledge." To be a facilitator and guide, teachers need to know how to ask questions at a variety of levels. Kassner (1998c) lists a series of do's and don'ts that are helpful in developing effective questions. They are shown in Box 13.2.

Teachers often fall into the trap of asking questions that measure knowledge-level thinking only, such as "Can you name this note?" or "Who wrote that piece?" Asking some questions of this nature is fine, but they do not challenge children to think at higher levels. More sophisticated questioning engages children in such behaviors as summarizing and describing; demonstrating and classifying; analyzing and contrasting; inventing and predicting; and justifying and critiquing. (See Kassner, 1998b.)

BOX 13.2 **Effective Questioning**

QUESTIONING "DO'S"	QUESTIONING "DON'TS"
Ask stimulating questions	Ask questions that can be answered with a "yes" or "no"
Ask personal and relevant questions	
Vary the length and difficulty of the questions	Ask vague questions
Keep questions clear	Ask multiple questions before students can answer
Move around the classroom when asking questions	Ask questions that require a long answer
Ask questions that allow students to demonstrate what they know, understand, believe, or value	Call the name of a student unless a particular reason exists for seeking information from that person only
Stretch students' thinking, but ask questions easy enough to answer	Ask questions only of students who volunteer to answer
Use humor whenever appropriate	Trap, trick, or punish with questions
Wait a minimum of three to five seconds before soliciting an answer to give all children time to think	Use sarcasm
Use a variety of techniques to engage all students in answering a question—everyone who agrees, show thumbs up; disagree, thumbs down; not sure, thumbs sideways. (Student responses can be varied.)	

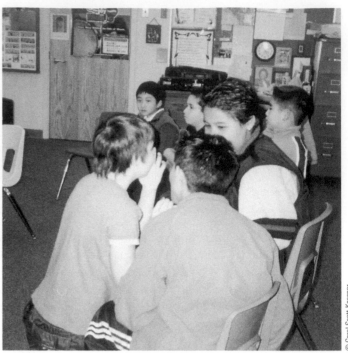

© Carol Scott-Kassner

Questions and challenges that help children to stretch could be phrased in the following ways:

- What ideas do you have for interpreting this piece, reflecting the essence of what it is about?

- What key ideas do you need to think of when composing your next piece?

- Can you show your learning partner how to finger this pattern on your recorder?

- Compare these two arrangements of *Beauty and the Beast* and be prepared to explain how they are the same and how they are different.

- Justify your choice of music to serve as an accompaniment to a video based on the qualities in the music and the qualities in the video.

- Devise criteria for evaluating your performance in the spring concert.

Effective questioning takes time to develop, and it is helpful for beginning teachers to write the questions they are going to ask into their lesson plans to assure that they are encouraging children to think about music, their own performance, and ideas in challenging ways.

RUBRICS. A popular form of assessment used by many teachers is the rubric. Rubrics provide a set of scoring criteria that can help to determine the value of a student's performance on a task such as singing, playing, reading, improvising, or composing. The rubric can be specific to a limited task, or it can be stated in terms of benchmarks that measure student progress toward a specific national, district, or program standard, or might be developed from the enduring understandings and essential questions of the 2014 standards. They can also be used to evaluate children's thinking, such as their ability to analyze or critique their work using musical criteria. A well-designed rubric will not only help to establish performance standards for students; it can also help provide feedback as to what must be done in the future to improve their performance. Students can even be involved in helping to designate those standards, and they can

TABLE 13.2 **Rubric Scoring the Skill of Singing "America"**

ADVANCED LEVEL	PROFICIENT LEVEL	BASIC LEVEL	NEEDS IMPROVEMENT
Maintains accurate pitch throughout	Pitch is good, with some minor discrepancies	Pitch is generally accurate but there are mistakes	Difficulty in maintaining pitch or showing contour of melody
Rhythm is excellent and beat is steady	Rhythm is generally good and the beat is maintained	Rhythm is generally good but lacking in precision, beat is unsteady	Rhythm is uncertain and beat is unsteady
Tone, resonance, and articulation are excellent	Tone, resonance, and diction are good	Tone and diction are generally good, but there is breathiness and some words are hard to hear	Tone is harsh and there is little evidence of support, words are unclear
Posture and support are excellent, mouth is open	Posture and support are good, mouth is open	Difficulty supporting tone, and posture is marginal	Poor posture and breath support, head is often down and mouth closed

use rubrics in self-assessment. Table 13.2 shows a rubric for assessing the skill of singing based on the National Standards (MENC, 1996).

To be effective, rubrics must clearly state what students should be able to do as a result of instruction. They need to be multilevel and rich in detail, helping to motivate students. They need to relate to real-life situations students are likely to face outside of school. Rubrics can be used to quickly score students, and points could be assigned if necessary for awarding grades. Remember that a single measure of a child on any skill would be unfair or invalid. A single measure only reflects that particular time and can be influenced by many factors. These rubrics could be used throughout a year to track a student's growth in his or her skills and understandings. Details in the rubric would need to change depending on the nature of the individual tasks or materials to be performed.

Hickey (1999) advocates the use of rubrics in assessing compositions. She has developed a rubric using general criteria for assessing any composition, as well as rubrics using criteria tailored to specific compositional assignments. In a modification of ideas suggested by Hickey, Table 13.3 shows a rubric that could be used to assess a composition in ABA form.

Other, more elaborate forms of teacher assessment of students are valuable when teachers need to gather detailed information on an individual student for purposes of getting a better understanding of what is happening with that child. Teachers could write a descriptive narrative of a child's behavior, reflect on that, try other techniques of working with the child, write another narrative, and reflect on the impact those changes made. Often this process helps a teacher to stand back and view other possibilities.

TABLE 13.3 Assessment Rubric for Composition in ABA Form

COMPONENTS	NEEDS WORK ⟵		⟶ TERRIFIC	
ABA FORM	No form is evident	Clear A idea but B section is not developed	In ABA form; sections need a more clear delineation	In clear ABA form with distinct contrasts between sections
MELODY	Does not feel complete or coherent	Seems complete but not intriguing	Musically complete and has some interesting qualities	Musically coherent and aesthetically satisfying—it makes sense
RHYTHM	Erratic and does not make musical sense	Stable but predictable	Makes musical sense and helps create the form	Clearly helps to delineate the form, coherent and satisfying
TIMBRAL CHOICES	Choice of instruments and combination seems erratic	Tone color choices blend and are used to help create contrast	Tone color choices are interesting and are clearly used to highlight differences	Uses timbral change to create musical interest and define sections in ways that are satisfying and imaginative

Student Self-Assessment

One of the goals of assessment is to help children develop ownership of their own growth. Instead of always being assessed by the teacher, in a top-down fashion, students are encouraged to make decisions about their own performance. This can happen informally through questioning. It can also happen more formally through student journals, either audio or written, and reflections on their own growth. If teachers use a portfolio system to collect student work from throughout the year, each child needs to reflect on the contents of his or her portfolio. Students can also help develop rubrics to use in assessing performance or for the culmination of a project. Ideas can be stated in simple terms for young children or in more detail for older children. National Standard 7 encourages teachers to help students develop and apply criteria for evaluating music as well as their own work. Ideas for self-assessment of students' improvisations and compositions can be found in Chapter 10, and for listening in Chapter 9. Teachers will need to assess the quality of thinking students use in their self-assessments. See ideas in Wells (1998) and in *Arts PROPEL: A Handbook for Music* by Winner, Davidson, and Scripp (1992).

Peer Assessment

Another way to involve students in real-world assessment in music is to have them critique the work of their peers. Teachers are often afraid to open to this possibility because they do not want children to be negative. They can keep critiques positive by inviting children to answer questions such as "What did you like about that performance?" Or they can ask the children to make at least one positive comment, followed by a suggestion for refinement. Children can also use rubrics to assess peer work, or they can use other forms such as those suggested in *Arts PROPEL: A Handbook for Music* (Winner, Davidson, and Scripp, 1992) or in Freed-Garrod (1999). An efficient way to get everyone involved in peer rating is to have them play the role of Olympic judge. Every child holds up from one to ten fingers to rate a performance, with ten being Olympic quality. A discussion of the ratings can follow. Finally, students can conduct peer interviews about involvement in music activities and likes and dislikes in music (Smith, 1995) and reflect on what they have learned from that experience.

Teacher Self-Assessment

Many resources are available to help teachers become more self-aware. Teachers can maintain a journal of reflections about their work, highlighting areas in which they need to grow or ways they have made progress. Teachers who want the input of a colleague in music education to help them grow could invite someone to be their mentor. That person could talk with them on the phone, via e-mail, or over coffee. He or she could come to see the teacher in the classroom or view a video recording of a class meeting and provide feedback.

Teachers can also challenge themselves to grow in their use of different levels of reflective practice. Griffiths and Tann (1996, pp. 45–47) suggest that teachers frequently stay on the first level of reflection (see Box 13.3) but need to work across all of these levels over time to change. Typically, teachers go through periods of growth and plateau, with the first five years representing rapid growth. The key is to continue growing after that. Reflective practice should help in that process.

Many school districts require teachers who are on continuing contract to construct an annual professional development plan that establishes their program goals for the year as well as their professional goals for growth. These are reviewed by the principal and discussed with the teacher at the end of the year, providing a wonderful opportunity for the teacher to assess his or her progress. All states require continuing credit for teachers to maintain their certificates. Some require advanced degrees. These opportunities for further study are meant to enlarge the frameworks of thinking that teachers bring to their work and enhance their practice and feelings of success.

BOX 13.3 Levels of Reflection for Teachers

Rapid reflection	This is immediate and automatic as you teach. It is part of a teacher's thinking as he or she notices how students respond to material. Teachers instinctively answer a question or help a student who asks. It is private. It is called reflection-on-action.
Repair	This is thoughtful reflection-on-action. The teacher may notice a student behavior, think about it briefly, and change his or her actions to fit the student's needs. It may mean ignoring a student's behavior based on previous experience with the student's response to feedback. This is also private.
Review	This takes place after the incident and can happen at any time during a teacher's workday. It may involve a dialogue with a colleague and gathering perspective. It could involve collaborating with others and changing direction. This is reflection-on-action at a particular time.
Research	This may happen over weeks or months as a teacher reflects on an idea or a needed change and gathers information from colleagues, professional journals, or through staff development. This is more systematic reflection-on-action.
Research and retheorizing	This results from advanced academic study and learning current theories. It could occur in the process of obtaining a master's degree or fifth year of study. It happens gradually over a long period of time and much reflection. When teachers receive new information, they change many of the ways they think and, therefore, change the ways they work with children.

Tracking Student Growth

To both document how each child is growing in music and measure the effectiveness of instruction, it is valuable and important to develop a system for tracking student growth. Often preschool or elementary teachers rely solely on informally gathered impressions of children, and they fail to take the time to establish a system that will provide a more objective basis for evaluation.

Record Keeping

> "We teach in groups, but individuals learn. It is necessary, therefore, to develop systems for tracking the growth of each individual student."
>
> **Carol Scott-Kassner, 2005**

Systems for gathering and recording data may vary from simple to elaborate, depending on the teacher's preference, how many students are in each class, student contact time per week, what reporting system(s) are used, and how much technical and physical support the teacher gets in accomplishing this important task. For instance, it would be virtually impossible for a teacher assigned to two schools, seeing 1,200 students one time each week, to do much more than instruct. However, a teacher assigned to one school with 350 students, seeing them two or three times a week, should be able to establish a more formal system.

One method is to identify key behaviors or markers to follow, consistently measure, and record. This might include skills such as singing accurately, expanding vocal range, performing a bourdon on the beat, or playing an ostinato using a crossover pattern. It might also include recording attitudinal responses or age-appropriate understandings. A separate file card for each child in a class could be made, listing key behaviors. File cards could be color-coded for different classes or grade levels. The file cards should be randomly ordered and selected from the top of the pile as those students are asked to demonstrate skills or understandings in the context of a lesson. Notes could be made

Child	Singing	Playing	Improvising	Composing	Reading and Notating	Listening	Evaluating	Music and Other Arts	History and Society
Beth									
Chet									
Dena									
José									
↓									

Class _____ Grade Level _____

Note: o = minimal; + = beginning competence; ++ = proficient; +++ = outstanding.

immediately about level of understanding or skill, and the card placed on the bottom of the pile. This system ensures that, over time, every child in the class gets to play instruments or lead a game or a song, and in turn to be carefully observed by the teacher. Grades on tests could be entered on the card, in a grade book, or on a computer database, where all of the data are finally compiled.

Another system might be to keep a file folder for each class. Duplicate charts with student names, listed alphabetically, could be pasted inside both halves of the folder. On one chart, the teacher could track student behaviors regarding attitude, attendance, and participation. On the other chart, skill and concept goals for various segments of the year could be listed, and individual student growth toward or attainment of those goals could be marked using a rating or checkoff system. A system based on the National Standards might look like Box 13.4.

Scott (1999) suggests that it may be too much to try to assess the progress of every child on all of the standards each year. She proposes as a workable alternative implementing four assessment units during the year that relate to different combinations of the standards. The first and last might focus on assessing singing and performing with a group. The other two could focus on composition and evaluation. Each year thereafter, teachers could assess some basic skills and focus on some other standards. Students could be assessed in groups and also engage in self-assessment.

Teachers can record information about children's musical behaviors directly onto a computer database. Advantages of this system include the ability to (1) sort in each category, (2) group information for measurement, and (3) generate detailed personalized reports for parents.

Portfolios

Some models focus less on outcomes and more on the ongoing process of assessment. This process includes what students are able to learn from assessing themselves and their own and others' products. In these models, each child is given a portfolio in which to record evidence of their work, including drafts. Portfolios must reflect the domain in which the child is working. Because music is a discipline that involves

TABLE 13.4 **Portfolio Contents in Music**

MUSICAL BEHAVIOR	EVIDENCE	CONTEXT
Performance	Video and/or audio recordings	Individual and group performances
Perception and cognition (including listening)	Tests, journal entries, charts, grids, interviews, discussion, rubrics, poetry, and videos	Individual growth and reflection
Composing and improvising	Drafts of ideas in journals, scores, and recordings of compositions and improvisations	Individual and group efforts

performance, perception and cognition, and creativity, evidence that reflects those dimensions must be included. Table 13.4 indicates the various means of collecting and recording data in music classes.

Also key to portfolios is students' reflection on their own artistic growth and the growth of the groups in which they participate. Through reflection they become active in the learning process and learn to apply musical standards to production, be more inventive, and generate ideas for new work. Reflection can be done in journals or on forms developed for that purpose. Projects are long-term and portfolio work ongoing. Portfolios can be assessed by teachers, students, and parents. Sources for portfolio assessment ideas in music come from Winner (1991) and Winner, Davidson, and Scripp (1992). Additional ideas for alternative assessment, including how to structure a system, can be found in Herman, Aschbacher, and Winters (1992).

Reporting to Parents

School systems, whether public or private, usually establish standards or procedures for reporting to parents both about the curriculum and about student progress. A variety of methods for reporting about curriculum are typical at early childhood and elementary levels. They include:

1. Autumn open house or curriculum night at which teachers describe the program to parents

2. Informal programs at the end of units to which parents, other classes, and administrators are invited

3. Descriptions about the program that go out in brochures or in school or music newsletters

4. Parent Teacher Student Association (PTSA) meetings that feature the music program and can include teachers and children discussing the curriculum and modeling lessons

5. Music in Our Schools Week (MIOSW), an international celebration with children, teachers, and community, with supporting materials available annually from the Music Educators National Conference

6. Parent observation in the classroom during MIOSW or throughout the year

There are also many methods for reporting to parents about student progress and achievement. With the exception of concerts, these are specific to each child and usually involve a dialogue that helps educate parents not only about their child or children but also about the music curriculum. The following ideas reflect practices that exist in many different settings. In some settings, however, parents may only have the opportunity to gain a sense of the music program through concerts and discussions with their children.

- **Parent/Teacher Conferences.** These are usually with the classroom teacher and rarely involve the music teacher. In schools where the arts are central to learning, arts specialists may also hold conferences with parents, or the music specialist may be required to be in the building during conferences in case parents want to come and ask questions.

- **Concerts for the Community.** These are important vehicles for recognizing student achievement in music. They are most useful when they feature all students, although individuals may be recognized. Performances can be turned into "informances" by including program notes or student presentations that help parents understand how these activities emerged from the music curriculum and what was learned by the students.

- **Student Contracts.** These are signed by students and parents, outlining what the student hopes to achieve in music. See article by Kassner (1996) to see a model of a student contract.

- **Student Projects.** These result in a culminating event and in sharing of student portfolios.

- **Individual Conferences.** These take place any time during the year as requested by the parent or the teacher. They could include individualized education program (IEP) conferences about children with special needs.

- **Report Cards.** These might include any of the following, depending on the school district:

  1. Letter grades or marks of satisfactory or unsatisfactory in music, assigned by music teacher or the classroom teacher

  2. Comments about each child's performance in music, written by the music teacher

  3. Checklist in music that shows progress in specific skills areas, attainment of understandings, and attitude toward music assigned by the music teacher

  4. No acknowledgment of the music program on report cards

Music teachers need to consider how to make these communications as effective as possible so that parents understand that the purpose of the music program is to educate children, not simply to entertain them. Grades and comments, if required by a system, need to be based on systematically collected and broadly based data about musical growth, not just on attitudes or behavior in the music classroom. Teachers who rely only on a big show to impress parents or who grade strictly on whether a child is cooperative in music limit the purposes of music education.

"Grades and comments, if required by a system, need to be based on systematically collected and broadly based data about musical growth, not just on attitudes or behavior in a music class."

Distilling the Essence of Assessment and Evaluation

Effective evaluation, whether of individual students, groups of students, teachers, or programs, can be accomplished with greater ease if it is based on a clearly articulated curriculum and substantive data. Information that has been gathered regarding student learning and teacher effectiveness should be drawn from a range of sources, both formal and informal, and subjective and objective. Parents, administrators, and the broader community will be more likely to support programs that offer both substance and results.

Teachers also need to challenge themselves to reflect not only on the growth of their students and the effectiveness of their program, but also on their own growth as a professional. Teachers can gain tremendous satisfaction from helping children grow as well as from growing themselves—and turning what could merely be the job of teaching into a profession.

Scenario

MS. JONG IS A highly effective music teacher in a suburban school district. She is known for her enthusiasm, her excellent musicianship, and the quality of her concerts. Children are thrilled when it is time for her music classes. She teaches private piano lessons after school to students in the broader community and she sings in her church choir.

Her school district is now requiring regular assessment in music in response to state standards. Ms. Jong is frustrated, because having to keep track of student growth for 436 students in her elementary school adds a lot to her already busy schedule. Besides she knows that children are learning because she can see and hear the results of her teaching. She is finding herself resisting the requirement to implement regular assessment procedures and is sharing her frustration quite vocally with the other music teachers. It all seems exhausting and not worth it.

Questions

1. What might be the source(s) of resistance to grading coming from Ms. Jong?

2. What are some techniques she might use to begin gathering effective data on student growth that wouldn't overwhelm her?

3. What strategies could Ms. Jong use in conjunction with other music colleagues to help her move to a place of more assurance and competence in implementing evaluation strategies in her program?

4. What might be the benefits of those efforts?

REVIEW

1. What are the differences and similarities between assessment, evaluation, testing, and measurement?

2. What are the reasons for the call for alternatives to traditional forms of assessment?

3. What are four different ways teachers can assess children in music?

4. What does authentic assessment mean, and why is it important?

5. What is the difference between overt and covert behaviors?

6. What are five ways teachers can understand what is going on inside children's heads?

7. What are ways that teachers can grow in their ability to reflect and to self-assess?

CRITICAL THINKING

1. Why might teachers struggle with asking higher-order questions of children?

2. What are the potential challenges to assessing elementary general music students, and how could those challenges be overcome?

3. What kinds of goals might you want to state on a professional development plan and why?

4. Critique the four different types of report cards that you might find in the schools. Which one of the four would be the most ideal and why? What might be the challenges in completing such a report card?

PROJECTS

1. Interview music teachers from three different school systems about how they evaluate their children in music and how they are expected to report to parents. Discuss with them their perceptions of that process.

2. Observe a music teacher in action and note all of the ways children are assessed—from asking questions to monitoring and adjusting his or her teaching. Interview the teacher afterward about what he or she was thinking while teaching and how he or she changed depending on student behavior. Ask what caused the change. Ask how his or her thinking grows.

3. Keep a journal of your emerging vision of yourself as an elementary music teacher. What are possibilities that you find exciting? What are areas in which you feel you need to grow? What are some goals you might set for your growth?

4. Collaborate with others in your class to collect examples of report cards from elementary schools in your area. Compare them to find what systems are in place for reporting on musical growth.

5. Develop a rubric to assess student performance of a song on the soprano recorder. What would you look for at different levels of attainment?

6. Read and report on two articles on assessment in music from recent issues of the *Music Educators Journal* or *Teaching Music*. Include implications of these ideas for your own teaching in your report.

MINDTAP Visit **MindTap** to access classroom videos, audio, and more!

14

Music in an Integrated Curriculum

IN THIS CHAPTER

- Vignettes of Artistically Rich Music Classrooms
- The Invitation to Arts Integration
- The Challenges of Arts Integration
- Integrating Other Arts into the Music Curriculum
  - Interdisciplinary Curriculum in the Arts
  - Shared Curriculum in the Arts
- Models of Integration
  - The Thematic Web Design
  - The Threaded Curriculum
  - The Immersed Curriculum
- Creating Valid Connections
  - Integrating the Arts Process
  - The Arts in Social Studies
  - The Arts in Science and Math
  - The Arts and Language Arts
- Assessment
- Reflections on the Integrated Curriculum

Vignettes of Artistically Rich Music Classrooms

MS. LUEBKE'S GENERAL MUSIC class is alive, not only with sounds but with colors and designs, creative movement and dance, poetry and stories, and creative drama. Children often work in small groups to solve problems involving several art forms. Ms. Luebke is committed to integrating other arts into her music classroom. She believes that her role is to help children understand the nature of the arts, interpret and express ideas through them, and develop their aesthetic sensitivity. She is motivated to do this because she has seen what engagement in the arts has done for her and her own children, and she is distressed that the arts seem to be less and less a part of the elementary curriculum. She hopes that the children will leave her program with heightened artistic literacy, as she sees this as crucial to being able to function critically and creatively in such a highly mediated society.

Mr. Parker's music classes are busy practicing sub-Saharan African songs and dances. With each new song or dance, the children learn something about the culture from which it came and the meaning it has for the people of that culture. The older children have just finished constructing African-style drums, two-toned bells, and rattles with the help of parents and a visiting artist from Nigeria. The artist will teach them some traditional drumming patterns. Mr. Parker works in a school where everyone is immersed in the study of Africa for nine weeks. At the end of that time, the children, teachers, and parents will come together for an evening of sub-Saharan African food, culture, and festivities, at which the children will share what they have learned and guest artists from West Africa will perform with them. Mr. Parker was able to get a grant from the local arts commission to pay the musicians from Africa. He sees music as an integral part of the curriculum and is eager to contribute to this schoolwide focus in ways that help children not only grow musically, but also grow in their awareness of the central role of music in other cultures.

At the beginning of the school year, Ms. Steinhurst met with the primary teachers in her school to determine what the children will learn in science during their study of insects. She decided that there were creative things the children could do in music that would reinforce their science curriculum and still meet standards in her music curriculum. The children created chants, movement patterns, and instrumental accompaniments in music class to describe various insects. Each class selected one insect to highlight in a program for their parents at the end of this unit. Ms. Steinhurst helped them create original songs with accompanying movements about the insect they had chosen. Insect sounds, habits, and motions were carefully observed and reflected in the music. Children created a story line that placed the insects in a larger ecosystem and held their "insect musical" together.

Ms. Steinhurst has a double degree in art and music. In her role as art teacher, she used simple materials such as paper sacks, construction paper, cardboard tubes, and tinfoil to help the children design and create their costumes. They looked through books of insects for design details, which were reflected in their costumes. Ms. Steinhurst went to this extra effort because she believes that the arts function as symbol systems that both reflect and affect society. She believes that encouraging students to synthesize their understandings in science through the arts by creating their own symbols engages them in the highest levels of thinking possible, is good for their brains, and makes learning much more memorable.

Each of these teachers was hired to teach music, and each has gone beyond the boundaries of what has traditionally been taught in the elementary general music curriculum. Yet, in every instance, children are developing important musical understandings and

THINGS TO THINK ABOUT

- What role or roles do you feel the arts play in the lives of people?

- How important do you think the arts are to people living in the twenty-first century?

- How might gaining artistic literacy help people to sort out the myriad of commercial stimuli bombarding them every day?

- What role do the schools have in preparing people to engage in the arts in meaningful ways?

- In what ways do you think learning about and through the arts might enhance the ability of children to learn?

- What role or roles might the music educator have in bringing more than just musical arts to children?

skills. Ms. Luebke and Mr. Parker are committed to helping to integrate music across various areas of the curriculum. They know that they cannot do this with every aspect of the school curriculum throughout the school year. At the same time, they realize that it is very important to incorporate music into a broader whole. It helps to weave music into the fabric of all school life, rather than isolating it from other subjects to periods of once or twice a week.

Ms. Steinhurst teaches in a school where the entire curriculum is integrated and the arts are at the core. The classroom teachers, most of whom lack deep training in the arts, work in collaboration with the music/art teacher to plan meaningful arts activities to enhance whatever curricular content they are studying. The fact that Ms. Steinhurst has training in both music and art helps to ensure that significant artistic growth will occur in the students.

The Invitation to Arts Integration

IN MOST CULTURES, MUSIC and the other arts are not separate from daily living. People sing to accompany their work, participate in rituals in which the arts are central, and surround themselves with decorative images on clothing and in their homes. In Western cultures, the arts are often removed from daily living, relegated to the role of entertainment, and turned over to the talented few who are the designated artists. Many people are even afraid to decorate their own homes, leaving that task to a hired interior decorator. Messages that people in Western educational systems often receive from schooling are that they are not creative, musical, or artistic, and that the arts are not important. Children are frequently told not to sing or dance and to be sure to draw inside the lines. It is no wonder that people grow into adults who are afraid to express themselves creatively in the arts or in the rest of their lives, including their workplaces.

During the early childhood years, children do not separate the arts from life. They sing and dance spontaneously, eagerly experiment with crayons and paper without fear of judgment, and often create highly imaginative metaphors to verbally describe their world. The Reggio Emilia approach from Italy, used in the United States, is a powerful curricular model that builds on these natural tendencies in young children (Hendrick, 1997). Jalongo and Stamp (1997) have developed extensive ways to put arts at the center of the early childhood curriculum, again respecting the power of the arts to enhance young children's learning. Trends to use the languages of the arts across the curriculum throughout the elementary years hold much promise for returning children to a sense of a holistic culture, informed by expressive possibilities and alive with imagination. (See the work of Gallas, 1994).

National Standards 8 and 9 encourage music educators to consciously connect music with the other arts and disciplines in the curriculum as well as with culture and history.

Roles of Music Educator in Curriculum Integration

- Plan and teach arts-integrated lessons
- Serve as a resource person to classroom teachers
- Collaborate with classroom teachers and community artists
- Serve as a visionary leader in the school and community for arts in education

Billie Judy/Reel Life Productions

The specialist can take a direct role in planning and implementing instruction that accomplishes those standards. The role of the music specialist in schools committed to arts integration, however, is often expanded beyond that of direct instruction with children. In such settings, the specialist assumes the role of collaborator with other teachers and community-based artists and art organizations to help create an artistically rich environment. This role demands time for careful planning and sensitivity to the uniqueness of the individual arts and to the roles they can play. An effective integrated project takes about twenty hours for a team to plan.

The specialist may also become a resource person, directing teachers and students to key musical, library, and community resources, including visiting artists. Classroom teachers and administrators need to recognize that the music specialist also has a music curriculum with its own scope and sequence to teach. Support needs to be given for planning time and thoughtful communication to occur. Finally, the specialist can become a visionary leader, encouraging teachers to obtain grants from local, regional, or state arts commissions to connect their children to artist-in-residence programs and community arts organizations.

The Challenges of Arts Integration

Trends that call for the integration of the arts across the entire curriculum have sometimes caught music teachers by surprise and left them defensive. Music teachers become understandably distressed when a classroom teacher suddenly wants them to suspend the music curriculum to teach frog songs, because her class has begun a frog unit in science. It is important that music specialists and classroom teachers communicate early in the school year about issues of curriculum coordination and integration, so that mutually beneficial goals can be established.

Models for integrating the curriculum vary, but key to all of them is that true integration respects the integrity and uniqueness of each of the disciplines to be combined. The integrated curriculum seeks to relate fragmented learning experiences through planning that combines the significant curricular goals in music and the arts with other curricular areas. This might be conceived of as cocurricular education. (For resources on planning, see the References and Resources section at the end of the book.)

Roles of Classroom Teacher in Arts Integration

- Plan and implement arts-integrated lessons
- Seek resources from specialists
- Collaborate with teams of teachers, specialists, and community artists
- Pursue grants for artists-in-residence

Singing a song about frogs is not music education, even though it may be a delightful way to enhance learning about frogs. If the classroom teacher wants frog songs, the music specialist can provide those resources for the teacher, who can incorporate them as he or she wishes. However, without prior planning, the music specialist should not be expected to interrupt his or her planned curriculum in music.

Given the opportunity for prior planning, the music specialist may find that the first-grade frog unit coincides with work she is doing on pitch motion, including melodic leaps. She also sees ways that working with poetry about frogs would help her further develop planned rhythm work, as well as reinforce the concepts of ostinato and motive. As the classroom teacher communicates some of the vocabulary and concepts the children will be learning about frogs, including the life cycle of the frog, the music specialist sees that she could use the stages of the life cycle as a basis for creative movement and composition, further expanding children's awareness of form. Careful planning and communication among teachers can enhance and integrate the curriculum and bring greater meaning to all that the children do. Books by Drake (1993) and Jacobs (1989a, 1989b) help to give insight into principles and structures for planning the integrated curriculum.

"... true integration respects the integrity and uniqueness of each of the disciplines to be combined."

Goldberg (2006) notes that, in spite of the challenges, efforts to provide artistically rich environments for children have many benefits. In a multicultural society where many children do not speak English as a first language, the arts provide other forms of literacy that are accessible to all. Such classrooms focus on the development of multi-literacies. Children learn *with* music by studying and performing existing works and connecting them to other curricular areas, and through music by using creative processes in music to demonstrate learning across the curriculum. Table 14.1 provides a sample of effective arts resources.

Integrating Other Arts into the Music Curriculum

Music specialists are frequently the only arts specialists hired at the elementary level. In that role, they are often called on to be an advocate for all the arts and to bring a broader awareness of the arts to the children with whom they work. Many teachers have responded with excitement to the opportunity to help create aesthetic literacy through their program. However, this can be a challenge to specialists who may have

TABLE 14.1 A Sample of Arts Resources for Teachers and Children

NAME OF ORGANIZATION	WHAT IT OFFERS	HOW TO ACCESS IT
PARENT TEACHER ASSOCIATION (PTA, PTSA, PTO)	"Reflections" program for children's creativity in the arts	http://www.pta.org/2032.asp
NATIONAL ENDOWMENT FOR THE ARTS (NEA)	Grants for schools and districts to develop arts in education programs; publications to support arts in education	http://arts.endow.gov/pub/pubArtsed.php
METROPOLITAN OPERA EDUCATIONAL PROGRAMS (MET IN SCHOOLS)	Teacher training in how to create operas with children. Collaboration between classroom teachers and music specialists.	http://www.metoperafamily.org/metopera /Then click on "Met in Schools."
WASHINGTON NATIONAL OPERA	Teacher training and programs and materials for schools	http://www.dc-opera.org/educationtraining /educationcommunity.asp
NATIONAL SYMPHONY ORCHESTRA	Teacher training and lessons as well as programs in schools.	http://www.kennedy-center.org/nso /nsoed/
METROPOLITAN MUSEUM OF ART	Online resources for teachers and children. Summer teacher training.	http://www.metmuseum.org/events /teachers
SMITHSONIAN INSTITUTION	Scholars in residence, traveling exhibits, teaching training, grants, publications	http://www.metmuseum.org/events /teachers
ARTSTARTS	Additional listings of resources for teachers	http://www.artstarts.com/resources /aielinks.html
CHILDREN'S MUSIC FOUNDATION	Online resource to help teachers, music, children	http://cmfinc.org/
ARTS HORIZONS	Arts programs for all grades for NY area schools	www.artshorizons.org

had strong training as musicians but minimal training in the other arts. Numerous workshops in creative movement, visual arts, literary arts, and creative dramatics, available for all teachers, can help expand skills and understandings about those forms. Orff-Schulwerk training can be especially helpful in developing skills for using language and movement in the music curriculum. University courses in aesthetics and interrelated arts are rich sources, as are programs for teachers through museums and other community arts organizations.

Every art form is unique. Visual arts, dance, theater, music, literature, and media arts each have their own language, expressive medium, set of symbols, and technical demands. Yet the arts are deeply connected, because they all (1) challenge people to grow aesthetically; (2) are languages of the emotions, mind, and spirit; and (3) embody meaning far beyond what humans can express with words or numbers. In working with multiple arts, teachers need to be sensitive both to the commonalities between the arts and to the things that make each unique or different.

Interdisciplinary Curriculum in the Arts

Common links among the arts can be found in numerous aesthetic principles highlighted in the following box. Teachers can enhance children's awareness of how these principles work in various arts by bringing in illustrative examples from different art forms and comparing them. Although the generative impulse may be music, this could be thought of as an interdisciplinary curriculum that focuses on the understanding of broad aesthetic principles. Many disciplines are viewed in terms of a broader set of ideas.

Some Common Aesthetic Principles in the Arts

- tension and release
- repetition and contrast
- pattern, motive, theme and variation
- density
- balance, symmetry
- foreground and background

To teach the principle of repetition, the teacher could help children notice it as a forming device in nature, a song or instrumental work, a poem, a painting, and a dance. Discuss the impact of the use of repetition. (It creates a sense of rhythm; fulfills expectations; creates unity; and, taken to an extreme, could be boring.) Have the children create their own short compositions that use repetition as the main structural device. Follow up a review and critique of their compositions by listening to some music from minimalist composers such as John Adams, Steve Reich, or Philip Glass. Determine how they use repetition as a forming device and reflect on the effect of that on the listener. These activities not only teach music, but also expand children's awareness of a concept that permeates all the arts as well as life.

National Standard 8 asks that music teachers help children understand relationships among music, the other arts, and disciplines outside the arts. The publication

What Every Young American Should Know and Be Able to Do in the Arts (MENC, 1994) provides a guide for standards in all of the arts. This can be particularly helpful in finding ways to integrate significant content from each of the art forms. (See also, Cornett, 2003.)

Shared Curriculum in the Arts

Another means by which teachers can stimulate the development of children's broader understanding and skills in the arts is to find ways in which aspects of other arts intersect with music. The intersected or shared curriculum attempts to find areas in which two content areas overlap (see Figure 14.1). There are many ways in which an individual teacher can plan lessons and activities that readily accomplish multiple objectives in the arts. The following ideas may help to stimulate thinking about some of those possibilities.

CREATIVE MOVEMENT AND DANCE. The art form that is probably the most analogous to music is dance. They are both arts that unfold through time and occupy space, either acoustic or physical. Music educators frequently use creative movement and dance to get children physically involved with the music. Box 14.1 outlines the elements of dance. Dance is a language, similar to that of music, but different because the expressive medium is the body, not sound. Through capturing the language of dance and incorporating it in the music curriculum, teachers can do a great deal to build and reinforce dance concepts, helping children express themselves more creatively through movement.

BOX 14.1 **Elements of Dance**

TIME
- Tempo: fast, medium, slow, gradual change, stillness
- Duration: long, short
- Beat: steady, even, can change speed
- Accent: stressing a beat
- Rhythm: patterns with notes of different durations

FLOW
- Sustained: smooth, flowing, connected
- Percussive: jerky, segmented
- Vibratory: shaking, swinging

SPACE
Personal
- Size: large, small, wide, narrow
- Nonlocomotor movements: stretch, shake, twist, curl, bend
- Force field: protective bubble that surrounds you so that you do not bump other things or people

General Space
- Directions: up or down, front or back, right or left, diagonal
- Pathways: curved, straight, angular
- Locomotor: walk, run, leap, skip, hop, jump, slide, crawl, scoot

(Continued)

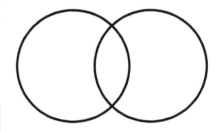

FIGURE 14.1

The Shared Curriculum Design

Two subjects come together and common understandings are developed.

BOX 14.1 (*Continued*)

FORCE

Strong or gentle

SHAPE

Individual: curved, straight, twisted, balanced, symmetrical, asymmetrical

Group: lines, clumps, touching, not touching, balanced

Thematic: animal, sports, emotions

This can often be done by asking open-ended questions using music as the stimulus:

1. "How many ways can you show me a high motion? A low motion? Switch from one to another as you hear the pitches on the bells change from high to low."

2. "When you hear the drum, move across the room in a curved pathway to the rhythm I play. Change levels as you move."

3. "Work in personal space to shape the phrases of this music. Start with one body part and gradually add others until your whole body is involved."

4. "Listen to the suspended cymbal as I strike it once. Be ready to describe the sound." (Model and discuss.) "Show with your body the energy at the beginning of that sound, and keep your body moving until you can no longer hear the sound. Think of how you will move as the sound dies out." (Repeat the same process with various instruments of contrasting timbre. Play them in a series and have children shift movements in response to the sounds.)

5. "Work with a partner to interpret the contrasting sections of an AB form piece. Decide which of you is A and which is B. Face each other and act as a mirror of your partner. During the A section, partner A gets to lead while B imitates. Try to stay within the style of the music. When the B section occurs, switch leaders."

6. "Work in a group of three to show meter in threes. Plan your movements so that the accented beat is a strong, sharp motion."

7. "Move around the room to the beat, showing the accent in different parts of your body." (Play strong-beat music where the accent is on four. Have them show that accent in their head, shoulders, elbows, hips, knees, and so on.)

1	2	3	4	1	2	3	4
			>				>

Each of these movement strategies helps children extend a musical concept, gain coordination skills with music, and apply various movement concepts.

The possibilities are endless. If these ways of thinking and moving are instilled in young children, they will be eager to choreograph music in the intermediate grades, showing great ability to connect what is happening in the music with what their bodies can do. Many superb resources connect dance and creative movement with music.

VISUAL ARTS. The visual arts are more removed from music in terms of analogous concepts. Although some of the terms are the same, their meaning is very different, because the visual arts function in space, not time. Box 14.2 highlights the basic elements.

BOX 14.2 Elements of the Visual Arts

SHAPE

Square, rectangle, triangle, circle. Created by line and color. Can form pattern creating rhythm and design.

COLOR

Red, green, yellow, and so on. It creates intensity and contrast. It gives light.

TEXTURE

Smooth, rough, soft, hard. It is the feel of the work when touched. It can be created by building up layers, carving into, or weaving.

LINE

Straight, curvy, zigzag, thin, thick, broken, connected, soft, loud, echoing, parallel. Lines make patterns, designs, shapes, objects.

SPACE

Negative, positive. Created by placement of shapes.

The visual arts can be combined authentically with music in a variety of ways. The following suggestions may serve as a stimulus for further possibilities.

1. Give each child a long, narrow strip of paper. Discuss various types of lines (straight, broken, curved, angular, thick, thin, and so on). Have children draw a line composition moving from left to right across the strip. Each person must use at least three different types of line. Have them interpret the lines vocally, using pitched sounds, or instrumentally on pitched percussion instruments. Extend this project by having the children work in groups, combining patterns vertically or horizontally and interpreting them through movement as well as through sound. View works by artists such as Mondrian or Klee and discuss their use of line.

2. Use lines, shapes, colors, and patterns to illustrate different musical events as they occur in absolute, or nonreferential, music. For example, listen to a Bach two-part invention. Use different colored lines to show the shape of melodies in the two lines in the invention. Use the same patterns to show where imitation occurs. View art prints based on interwoven patterns. Discuss similarities and differences between those and what the students have drawn.

3. Use art prints from various periods and cultures (often available through school art docent programs or art specialists) to introduce children to stylistic characteristics that are reflected in both art and music. Discuss the commonalities. For example, compare Monet's *Water Lilies* to Debussy's *La Mer*. Discuss the blurring of lines, muted colors, and reflected light of the Monet and the shimmering, dreamy, blurred quality of the Debussy. Experiment with making an impressionist-style painting using various water color techniques.

4. From a range of art prints, have children select the style that most closely matches the style of a piece of music they are listening to. Have them justify their choices.

5. Play works of music that have been stimulated by artworks, such as the various movements of *Pictures at an Exhibition* by Mussorgsky or *The Twittering Machine* by Gunther Schuller. Bring in prints of the works that inspired the compositions, such as *The Hut of Baba Yaga* by Victor Hartmann from *Pictures* or *The Twittering Machine* by Paul Klee. Discuss the connections among the works. Have children create their own musical compositions using an artwork as a stimulus. (See Kuzniar, 1999.)

6. Use program music as a stimulus for painting, drawing, or puppetry. Have children develop their own puppets to dramatize works that tell stories, such as *William Tell* or *The Nutcracker*. Help children demonstrate a sense of style in their work. Build art concepts of balance, design, color, and line into the creation of the works. Art skills and techniques can also be incorporated and reinforced. Try to avoid nebulous assignments connecting visual arts and music such as "draw the music." The results of such experiences are rarely artistic in any sense, although they may be useful in helping children represent musical events, as suggested in Chapter 9 on listening.

LITERATURE AND POETRY. As with movement and music, a close relation exists between the literary arts and music. When performed, both are arts of time and sound. Words have many musical elements such as rhythm, pitch, and accent. Onomatopoeic words (splash, rickety-rackety, and so on) suggest sounds that can be interpreted musically. Both music and language can be used to create imagery. Music can be used to tell stories in an abstract sense, such as *The Little Train of the Capiera* by Villa Lobos, or, combined with words, tell an actual story, such as *Peter and the Wolf* by Prokofiev. The combination of poetry with music often results in song. Sensitivity to the elements of the literary arts—phanopoeia, or imagery; melopoeia, or music; and logopoeia, or content, story, and meaning—can be developed within the music classroom, often more readily than in other settings. Children should be encouraged to notice how words and music connect, and be stimulated to combine them through their own creative explorations.

1. Use fine, already existing, children's literature to connect students with music. Many beautiful books exist that (1) illustrate folk, patriotic, and children's songs; (2) tell the stories behind works of program music, ballets, or operas; (3) tell the stories of various composers and musicians; and (4) set the cultural context for various songs or listening experiences. School librarians are eager to assist in finding children's literature that can enhance their musical experience. Such books can become the stimulus for children's own creative writing or for further research and understanding (Lamme, 1990).

2. Books, stories, and poetry can be used as a stimulus for musical composition. Wordless books and familiar fairy tales can be told through sounds instead of words or through a combination of sounds and words. For example, "Goldilocks and the Three Bears" can easily be transformed to themes in various registers of the keyboard for the characters. Maurice Sendak's *Where the Wild Things Are* lends itself to orchestration, movement, and drama. Literature from various cultures can be set to music using the instrumental sounds, rhythms, and scales of those cultures.

3. Children can generate banks of descriptive words in response to recorded music, then use them to write stories or poetry in various forms to describe the music. The poems might include the title of the music and the name of the composer.

4. Children can write poetry, then set it to music, with or without melodies. Poetic forms that emerge from a specific culture should be written to respect the tradition. For example, haiku from Japan is always about nature; is set in a particular season; describes where, what, and when; is mysterious; and has a syllabic structure of 5–7–5. A musical setting for a haiku can also reflect classical Japanese music: pentatonic; flowing; bent pitches; no beat; rhythms that punctuate; no harmony; and use of flute, drums, sticks, and plucked strings.

5. Children can listen to music designed to tell a story and write their own imagined story based on the music.

6. Children can set existing poetry or literature that uses onomatopoeic sounds or particularly strong imagery to music. (Encourage them to move beyond sound effects by creating a musical setting for the words.) Work with expressive use of the voice in speaking the poem; try single and combined voices for different effects.

Katz and Thomas (2004) suggest a range of ideas for combining literature and poetry with music and movement. Gallas (1994), Mantione and Smead (2003), and Hanson, Bernstorf, and Stuber (2004) have all developed wonderful ideas for combining literature and the various arts including many ideas for creative writing that might appeal to classroom teachers. The specialists could then coordinate with the classroom teachers to add in a music element.

CREATIVE DRAMA AND THEATER. Elements of creative drama and theater can readily be developed and incorporated into the music classroom. Skills such as the development of focus, concentration, facial and body movements, and respect for space can be incorporated into any music lesson involving characterization. Many of these skills are common to those developed in creative movement. Teachers can also help children become sensitive to other elements of a drama or story line.

1. Setting: where the drama takes place and the mood of the place

2. Characters: who is involved and how they relate to each other

3. Action: what is happening, including plot and tension, and why the events are happening; the motivation of the characters

4. Theme: what is the main idea being communicated

5. Dialogue: what are the verbal and gestural communications

6. Spectacle: what is needed in terms of costumes, props, lights, music, sounds, or scenery

Many of these ideas can be incorporated into any dramatization. Elements of dialogue and spectacle will not be needed as frequently, and they need only be used if a formal production is developed.

1. Sing songs that describe characters or tell stories, including story songs from various cultures. Discuss the characters, their motivations, and actions. Experiment with various ways of creating character and conveying the dramatic action of the song. Work with concentration and focus. Try to avoid stereotypical responses. Encourage all children to experiment with each character. (Avoid assigning roles too early and creating a star system.)

2. Learn the stories of various programmatic works or operas. Listen to the music and discuss how it helps heighten the experience of the drama or tell the story. What musical devices are used? Experiment with ways to tell the story with action using

mime or dialogue, characterization, and, perhaps, simple props. Puppetry could be used instead of people. There are many excellent children's books about famous operas that can provide a basis for this work.

3. Using a familiar children's story, create an opera, singing the dialogue, and adding other music to be created as necessary, as well as dramatic action, to tell the story. Music teachers may want to collaborate with classroom teachers to have a class write their own opera, creating the script in class and working with the music teacher on the musical aspects.

4. Create a musical around a theme such as U.S. history. Incorporate traditional folk songs and dances learned throughout the year. Ask children to write a story line to tie together the different aspects. Incorporate all the elements of drama in realizing the musical. Share it with others.

Walker's 1993 publication helps to generate more ideas for dramatics, story-telling and art combined.

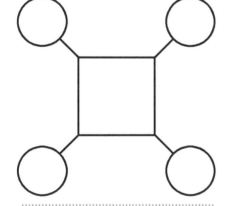

FIGURE 14.2

Webbed Curriculum Design

An examination of the web shows that children are involved in significant content in each area of the curriculum. The individual subjects keep their boundaries, but the webbed relationships feed a metaunderstanding.

Models of Integration

The Thematic Web Design

Many models exist for integrating the curriculum. The most commonly used at the elementary level is the thematic web design (see Figure 14.2). It strives to build important understandings and skills in all areas of the curriculum. The arts activities help to reinforce learning in other areas of the curriculum but also help children to develop or reinforce important skills and understandings in each of the arts disciplines. The arts are approached with depth or integrity, not superficially. This multidisciplinary approach could be taught by one teacher or by several teachers (see Lesson 14.1).

MUSIC

Experiment with rain sounds, using body or instruments as sources. Attempt to convey different kinds of rain. Create a storm. Learn songs about rain. Discuss different qualities. Add rain sounds to accompany. Listen to recorded works about rain. What images are created and how?

VISUAL ARTS

Learn to use various watercolor techniques, including wash, to create a rain scene. Discuss the way rain mutes the colors of other objects and obscures things outside. Try to reflect that feeling in the painting. Look at the ways other artists create a sense of rain.

CREATIVE DRAMA

Dramatize settings in which rain, or lack thereof, plays an important role.

- A young child in a mud puddle
- A couple, caught in a downpour in the park
- The first rain after a drought
- A flood that threatens your property
- A dog coming in after the rain

Dramatize stories about rain.

DANCE

How would you move if you were:

- a raindrop
- a storm
- lightning
- water down a drain
- dripping

Discuss using dance terms.

Learn or create a rain dance.

RAIN

SCIENCE

Learn about the water cycle. Create one in the classroom. Study what causes rain to fall and which kinds of clouds generate which kinds of rain. Watch a weather report. Interview a reporter. How do they predict?

MATHEMATICS

Construct a rain gauge. Collect and measure rainfall over a period of several weeks. Chart the daily and weekly totals.

Compare with monthly report in paper. Research and chart average annual rainfall in your community for the past ten years.

LANGUAGE ARTS

Read various poems about rain. How do the poets create a sense of rain? Do they use onomatopoeia or alliteration? Write your own rain poem using at least five words to describe rain. Read books about rain. How does rain affect people, animals, the environment? Write a story about how rain affects a family.

SOCIAL STUDIES

Look at a map that shows weather patterns.

Learn about the lives of people who live with heavy rains, no rains.

Learn traditions for asking for rain. Learn the importance of rain to various people.

The Threaded Curriculum

The threaded curriculum is similar to the webbed curriculum (see Figure 14.3). In this curriculum, children may start with a particular theme or idea and then explore it in a sequential, or linear, fashion through several disciplines or through multiple intelligences as proposed by Gardner (1983/2004). (See Chapter 2 for a list of the multiple intelligences.)

In this approach, the teacher might introduce a topic such as geologic eras. The children receive input from a variety of sources, then proceed through stations in which they do further research as well as synthesis activities using the various intelligences. The thread is the large theme or concept; each station allows children to experience through a different intelligence (Campbell, Campbell, and Dickinson, 1992; and Lazear, 1991).

FIGURE 14.3

Threaded Curriculum Design

The thread is the large theme or concept. Each station allows the child to experience the concept through a different intelligence.

Sometimes the arts experiences in this model are merely that—experiences. For example, in a unit on geology, a strategy calling only for the creation of a geologic rap in the music station may result in a demonstration of some of the understandings of geology but may not help the children grow musically. Teachers wishing to stimulate musical growth need to help children understand that a rap is more than a rhythmic chant. It commonly uses (1) forced rhyme and punctuated words, chanted in rhythm by a single voice; (2) a synthesized pulse and layered rhythmic framework as an accompaniment; (3) two-part form with other voices entering on the chorus; and (4) scratched segments from other music that are layered in to reinforce the theme, usually focused on social protest. Some raps are more effective than others; for example, they have better lyrics and rhymes and offer more congruence between chant and accompaniment. Students need to develop a sense of what those qualities are and learn to assess their own raps in aesthetic terms.

The Immersed Curriculum

Perhaps the most difficult curriculum to create is the truly integrated one, because it is largely motivated by a child's interests. This is a curriculum in which children immerse themselves completely in a topic of study or area of interest that they examine from all points of view. Ideas and resources are networked, and the boundaries between subjects are blurred or eliminated. This experience is analogous to living in another culture and having an opportunity to learn the language, understand the history and contemporary culture, interpret the arts, communicate with indigenous people, and experience the geography and ecology. There is no separation among subjects; they all are part of a larger whole. Networks are established among people interested in the same things, and ideas are shared (see Figure 14.4). The Reggio Emilia approach, used in preschools, is a wonderful example of an immersed curriculum (Hendrick, 1997).

The truly integrated curriculum helps children perceive new relationships among subjects through problem solving and identify life problems, social issues, and individual concerns they wish to address through a kind of metacurriculum. In this curriculum, both affective and cognitive growth are enhanced, and a synthesis occurs in individuals and the group as they derive personal and shared meaning from their experiences.

An example of this curriculum would be when young children explore a curiosity about insects by observing their behavior, counting them, drawing them in ways to reflect their patterns and designs, studying insect biology and habitat, and sharing discoveries with others. Gallas (1994) describes a classroom where children are watching a butterfly trying to emerge from its chrysalis. While one child sketches the process, another says, "I'll sing him out." Teachers in this setting become facilitators and sources of ideas and information. Depending on the topic, the arts may or may not be directly linked. Teachers in such settings are dedicated, however, to finding ways to help children pursue their ideas through one or more art forms. Such settings respect children's innate capacity for representing their worlds through images, poetry, dance, drama, and music (see Gallas, 1994).

Creating Valid Connections

Perhaps the biggest challenge to using the arts with integrity throughout the curriculum is teachers' surface understanding of the nature of the arts. Yet, thoughtful integration by people who are relatively inexperienced in the arts can happen, provided they are willing to ask the question, "How are children growing artistically by doing this activity?" Music and arts specialists, other teachers, and artists-in-residence can

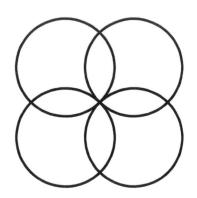

FIGURE 14.4

Immersed and Networked Curriculum

Children immerse themselves completely in a topic of study or area of interest and examine it from all points of view. The boundaries between subjects blur or disappear through a networking of ideas, and resources are networked.

"[In the immersed] curriculum, both affective and cognitive growth are enhanced, and a synthesis occurs in individuals and the group as they derive personal and shared meaning from their experiences."

often be a source of answers for the teacher new to arts integration. Regretfully, many, if not most, of the commercially available materials on the integrated curriculum fail to reflect understanding of the arts as disciplines.

A remarkable exception can be found in *Sound Ways of Knowing* by Barrett, McCoy, and Veblen (1997). In this book, the authors develop a model of viewing the arts in the interdisciplinary curriculum as if looking through facets in a jewel. In the center of the model is the name of the artwork. In each facet of viewing the artwork, teachers ask one of the following questions.

1. Who created it?

2. When and where was it created?

3. Why and for whom was it created?

4. What does it sound or look like?

5. What kind of structure or form does it have?

6. What is its subject?

7. What is being expressed?

8. What techniques did its creator use to help people understand what is being expressed? (p. 77)

The answers to these questions lead naturally to the integration of history, culture, other arts, and other disciplines.

The following ideas may serve as models for setting goals to achieve artistic growth in combination with goals in other curricular areas. Most of the ideas are examples of integration with subjects coequal, but some represent infusion, in which an arts activity is used to get at a learning in another area of the curriculum. See Wood (1997) for further ideas on interdisciplinary instruction.

Integrating the Arts Process

Regardless of the context in which the arts are integrated, it is helpful to use the arts process as a reminder of ways they can be incorporated without violating their integrity as unique disciplines. Any one mode or a combination of modes from the arts process can be consciously integrated with other aspects of the curriculum. The following modes are central to every art form.

- *Perceiving* (noticing and thinking)—to listen perceptively to music or poetry; to notice patterns of repetition and contrast; to visually discover the use of line in a painting

- *Responding* (discussing, feeling, and producing)—to identify, describe, and discuss what one notices in an artwork; to express how an artwork affects personal mood and thought and connect that with aspects of the work itself; to perform an already existing work in an expressive and stylistically authentic manner

- *Skills Development* (learning to manipulate the materials and processes of the various arts disciplines)—to learn to sing in tune, then with expression, then in harmony; to learn various techniques of working with clay, such as coil technique, building, throwing; to develop a range of skills in creative movement involving control of the body in time and space with force and flow

- *Evaluating* (assessing and critiquing)—to grow in the ability to assess one's own and others' works based on their technical, formal, aesthetic, and expressive qualities

- *Understanding* (forming concepts of elements, structures, history, and culture)—to understand pitch, rhythm, melody, harmony, tone color, and expression in music; to understand how patterns in music are used to create form; to understand the relationship between a piece of music and the culture and time in which it was created

- *Creating* (generating original ideas and products)—to improvise an eight-beat rhythm pattern; to draw a picture that incorporates three different kinds of line; to compose a work in ABA form; to arrange a setting for a folk song; to choreograph a dance to a favorite piece of music

---

Key Elements of the Arts Process

- Perceiving
- Responding
- Skills development
- Evaluating
- Understanding
- Creating

The Arts in Social Studies

Combining the arts with social studies creates natural connections, because so much of what is known and understood about culture comes through the arts. Studying the arts of a culture can help people understand:

1. What that culture values

2. What makes that culture unique

3. What resources were (are) available to that culture

4. How that culture has changed

5. How that culture is like other cultures

6. What expressive forms and symbols typify that time, culture, and region

In addition, the arts can help people understand individuals within cultures. As a person's stories, poems, diaries, songs, performances, and arts or crafts are examined, others come to know that person in a way that would not be possible if they relied only on others' memories. As the curriculum moves toward an emphasis on helping children understand and document their own stories and the stories of others, the arts can serve as rich resources for study and expression. National Standard 9 addresses the importance of understanding music in relation to history and culture.

Box 14.3 lists some of the art forms that might be (1) enjoyed and examined for their artistic qualities; (2) performed or replicated with sensitivity to style and technique; (3) studied in terms of their cultural purpose, practice, and value; or (4) studied within their historical context.

Lesson 14.2 presents a series of ideas for integrating the arts into the study of Northwest Coastal Indian Cultures. The left-hand column shows the use of the arts as activities. Ideas in the right-hand column represent a more holistic approach, placing the arts within the cultural context and having children create arts with sensitivity to artistic style and processes from that culture.

BOX 14.3 Forms and Resources of the Arts

VISUAL ARTS
- Painting
- Sculpture
- Drawing
- Weaving and textiles
- Carving
- Printing
- Calligraphy
- Jewelry
- Costumes and clothing
- Puppets
- Masks
- Pottery
- Decorative arts
- Architecture
- Landscape design
- Interior design

MUSIC
- Folk music
- Art music
- Popular music
- Sacred and ritual music
- Instruments

DRAMA
- Theater
- Puppetry
- Mime

LITERATURE
- Stories and folktales
- Poetry
- Plays
- Graffiti

DANCE
- Folk dance
- Ceremonial dance and drama
- Dance as pure art form

MEDIA
- Photography
- Video and film
- Laser art
- Digital art
- Mixed media

Salmon mask in the style of NW Coastal Indians

Billie Judy/Reel Life Productions

Paddling Song (Lummi Indians)

for water sound:
swish hands together

ARTS AS ACTIVITIES APPROACH

Sing Lummi "Paddling Song" and pretend to paddle the canoe while you sing.

Read and discuss the legend of how Mt. Rainier came to be.

INTEGRATED ARTS APPROACH

Learn the "Paddling Song," singing with a vocal style typical of the Lummi culture (as illustrated in listening examples). Decide the purpose of your journey by canoe. Map out your route on a map of Puget Sound. With a group, form the shape of a Lummi canoe. How can you create the height and shape of its bow? Pretend to paddle through the waters of Puget Sound, singing your song as you go. Is the weather calm or stormy? How do you know? (It is calm because the song glides along smoothly.) Keep your paddles synchronized to the beat. When you get to your destination, show through movement or drama where you were going and what your purpose was.

Discuss the purpose of legends. How does this legend differ from scientific knowledge of how Mt. Rainier came to be? Research the meaning Mt. Rainier holds for the native peoples. Learn to tell the legend in a dramatic style that conveys some of that sacred meaning. Accompany the telling with motions and the sounds of drums and rattles. Later, write your own legend about how a landmark in your community came to be.

Color in the images on a predrawn totem. Cut out the totem and paste it onto a milk carton.

Study various totems and the images on them. Learn what each figure means. Learn why each totem is unique. Notice common aspects of each image: bold, symmetrical, curved lines; shapes are outlined; uses dyes of red, black, and white. Why was cedar used to make the totems? Design a totem for your family or school, selecting images that have symbolic meaning for them. Use images in the style of traditional totems. Carve your totem out of foam, adding colors when you finish. Or, for a school totem, hire a native carver to instruct the children and all design and carve a totem for your school.

Learn a salmon dance and accompany it with drums and shakers.

Research different kinds of dances used and occasions on which they were used. View videos of the dances and ceremonies attached. Note the style of the dancing and the instruments used to accompany them. What makes a salmon dance different from other dances? Construct some of the instruments, decorate them, and play them to accompany dancing.

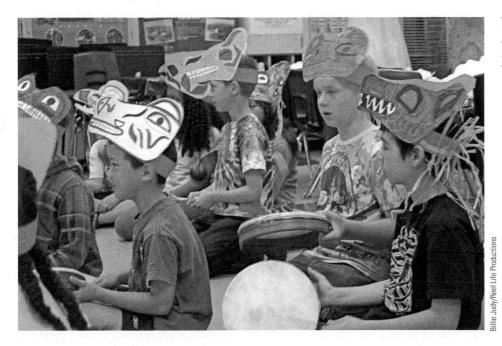

Fourth grade arts immersed study of NW Coastal Indians—drumming and masks

Billie Judy/Reel Life Productions

The Arts in Science and Math

Science and math are more remote than social studies for integration of the arts, but some topics provide common ground.

1. Music is made up of scales that are tuned according to frequencies, which are expressed in cents and measurable by electronic tuners. Children can experiment with using a synthesizer or tuner to tune intervals to scales found in various cultures.

2. Children of all ages can discover various principles of the science of sounds such as vibration, amplification, and the relationship of the length of the vibrating surface to the pitch of the sound. Children can experiment with creating their own instruments or use standard instruments to illustrate some of these principles.

3. Equations in math represent symmetrical balance, a principle found in the visual arts.

4. Persian rugs are created with symmetrical patterns based on numerical principles. Students can create their own visual artworks using numbers represented by colors and shapes to create designs.

5. Basic geometric shapes underlie math as well as the visual arts. Children can work to combine shapes to create art. Those shapes can also be represented by individuals or groups in dance movements. Shapes can be used to represent musical forms (AB, ABA, ABACA).

6. Students can number each tone of the scale (twelve-tone or diatonic) and then play with random orders of those numbers in lines, playing them forward, backward (retrograde), upside down (inversion), and any combination thereof. They can also stretch the length of the sounds by doubling them (augmentation) or cut them in half (diminution).

7. Nature consists of patterns. Mathematics describes those in one way, science in another. Use various patterns in nature as a stimulus for composition (see Chapter 10 for suggestions).

8. As with any thematic approach to the integrated curriculum, the arts and arts processes can be integrated in authentic ways with topics that arise from science or math. An example would be a focus on the topic of whales. Children could create their own whales with cloth or paper, showing sensitivity to size, shape, and design. They could listen to any number of recorded works inspired by whales and note how the composers responded musically to whale sounds. They could learn how whales use sounds or songs to communicate, and they could create their own whale-inspired composition. They could move like whales as they migrate or feed. They could sing whaling songs and research their origin, the routes the whaling ships took, and the lives of the sailors. They could learn the hornpipe and other dances and learn to carve scrimshaw out of soap after learning how these activities reflected the life, interests, and culture of the sailors.

The Arts and Language Arts

Although the word *arts* is included in the term *language arts*, much of language arts teaching has focused on the learning of the low-level skills of reading, grammar, punctuation, printing and writing, and spelling.

Approaches to language arts instruction, such as whole language, focus on a generative approach to language learning, where the desire to learn grows out of an experiential base. The arts can provide rich experiences to stimulate language usage and to motivate children to want to read, spell, write, and speak. Many ideas have already been suggested earlier in this chapter under the topics of literary and dramatic arts. The following ideas offer other possibilities.

1. Have kindergarten and first-grade children learn to read books that contain the words and illustrations of songs they already know. Share such books with preschool children.

2. Have preschool and primary-age children create books, including shape books of their favorite songs, with their own illustrations. (A shape book for "Twinkle, Twinkle, Little Star" would be in the shape of a star.) Have older elementary children create illustrated books featuring familiar songs to share with a young child.

3. Have children practice spelling in rhythm, adding body percussion for accompaniment. Make chants or ostinati out of spelling words. Layer them or group them according to themes. Chant words in relation to the beat and determine how many sounds occur for each word. Notate rhythm patterns to fit the syllables of various words. Chant them and play them on instruments.

4. Punctuate sentences using different vocal sounds for each type of punctuation mark. (Victor Borge was a master at this.)

5. Learn to spell words that are introduced in music or other arts classes. Use them in writing.

6. Listen to recorded music and develop a word bank with young children, or a personal web of words with older children, that is stimulated by the music. Use those words to write a poem or story about the music. Play the music as many times as necessary to stimulate the writing. Play the music as you read the poem or story to others.

7. Read books about the lives of famous composers or musicians. Listen to some of their music. Develop a story or illustrated book about some of that music. Or, write a play about the composer's life, incorporating some of the music performed by classmates or played on recordings.

8. Write the lyrics for a song or work with the class to write the lyrics for a class song. Invite a music teacher or composer-in-residence to help with the melody or encourage children to compose their own melody. (See ideas for song writing in Chapter 10.)

Again, the possibilities are endless. All that is required is a teacher who is willing to think and act creatively.

Accomplishing Multiple Music Standards

1. *Singing*: Sing in response to lines or colors in a painting, using the voice in a variety of expressive ways to suggest the intensity of the color or the shape of the lines. Sing songs as a part of a musical that children create to culminate and synthesize a unit of study.

2. *Playing*: Compose an instrumental piece and have children choreograph movements to it. Play instruments to accompany stories in children's books. Play instruments to set poetry to music.

3. *Improvising*: Improvise an instrumental piece to accompany movement patterns other children are doing.

4. *Composing and Arranging*: Compose a piece in response to an art work. Depending on the art work, use instrument color, line, texture, pattern, and so forth, to convey a sense of space, design, and/or mood of the piece.

5. *Reading and Notating*: Plan a piece to accompany a poem that you have written. Notate that piece so that it can be replicated by others. Use notation software if possible. Share your notation with others to see if they can interpret it the way you intended the piece to sound. Make changes as necessary.

6. *Listening*: Listen to and analyze music you think might be appropriate to choreograph. Decide what movements should be used to represent the music in physical space. Refine your movements as you deepen your acquaintance with the music.

7. *Analyzing and Evaluating*: Use critiquing techniques suggested in Chapter 10, Creating, to evaluate the works you've created in response to the various arts.

(Continued)

8. *Connect to Other Arts and Curricular Areas*: Throughout this chapter you will see ideas for connecting music to all of the arts as well as other curricular areas.

9. *Connect to Culture and History*: When studying another culture, delve into all of the arts that reflect that culture. Try to recreate many of those arts. Learn what the various arts symbolize for people of that culture, who performs or creates them, and how they are used in the culture.

Assessing

Because the ideas in this chapter are all focused on creating within the various arts in response to music, techniques of assessment are the same as in Chapter 10, Creating. The difference will be that children need to critique the effectiveness of their expressions in whatever areas of the arts that are created in response to music as well as the combination of the two areas.

Responding to evaluative questions throughout the creative process will help children to refine their work. Using rubrics and collecting works in a portfolio along with reflections on what they've done and how they've grown would be appropriate for summative evaluations.

Reflections on the Integrated Curriculum

An array of models exists for achieving curriculum integration. In selecting the most useful for a particular situation, teachers need to consider (1) time, (2) focus, (3) expertise, (4) support materials, (5) cooperation, and (6) assessment. If the model chosen relies on several people, including arts specialists, can all of them be counted on to help? If team teaching is required, will those people work well together? Will schedules be flexible enough to accommodate the sharing of classes and the needed planning time? If an artist-in-residence is to be part of the team, are funds available to hire that person?

In planning the curriculum, are the goals clear, and are they articulated in written form? Is the curriculum balanced and truly integrated? Is the content, including that in the arts, meaningful and valuable instead of a waste of time for the children? Are ideas and activities sequenced in a way to provide a logical order, if necessary? Or, if the model is one of immersion and networking, are the materials and resources available for a rich experience? Will the ideas chosen be generative? Is flexibility built in so children can explore many different directions? How much time will be spent with a theme or topic (one year, several weeks, a month, a week)? Finally, what plans are there for assessment that is authentic to the goals and processes of the curriculum? What sort of documentation of growth will be used (videos, journals, performance portfolios, creative writing, or other possibilities)?

Integrating the arts throughout the curriculum has the potential to enrich the lives of children and of teachers. To be surrounded by and immersed in the arts is to live more fully and more beautifully. If more classrooms and schools did this well, they might become like the country of Bali, where they say, "We have no art; we do everything as well as we can."

Scenario

MR. YEE IS PART of a group of four fifth-grade teachers who enjoy sharing ideas for enhancing their instruction. They are collaborating to plan a big unit on the science of ecology but are struggling to figure out how to incorporate the arts. They know that they have a wonderful resource person in Mrs. Bloomquist, the music specialist, but aren't sure whether or not she has the time to help them out. They are planning to meet after school for three days a week for awhile and also during the times their students are with the specialists in their building. That poses a problem for Mrs. Bloomquist as she has to rush home two of those days after school to teach her private students and she is teaching during their other planning time. She would be willing to meet with them one day a week after school.

The other limit is that Mrs. Bloomquist feels inadequate to give them ideas in the other arts and there are no other arts specialists in their building. Finally, Mrs. Bloomquist is planning her final schoolwide performance of the year at about the time the fifth-grade unit will be in full swing. She is reluctant to take time from preparation for the concert with those students to also teach them music content for the ecology unit. But, she has some great ideas for some compositions the students could write using her music instruments that would fit right in and she'd love to help guide them through that process.

Questions

1. What ideas could Mrs. Bloomquist suggest in music that would fit with a unit on the science of ecology?

2. What other resources in the various arts could she suggest to Mr. Yee's team to help them have an arts enriched unit?

3. What would you do if you were Mrs. Bloomquist in response to the choice of whether or not to work with the students to prepare for the spring concert or integrate music into their science unit? Why?

4. Would it be appropriate for the fifth graders to share some of their compositions in the spring concert instead of singing the songs she had planned for them? Why or why not?

REVIEW

1. What are some of the challenges to integrating the arts across the curriculum?

2. What is necessary for true integration to occur?

3. List, define, and give examples of four different models for integrating the curriculum.

CRITICAL THINKING

1. Determine which aspects of the arts process, as well as which arts, have been integrated into the short series of ideas on Northwest Coastal Indian Culture.

2. What role(s) might an arts specialist play in integration of the curriculum? A classroom teacher? Parents? Administrators? Artists-in-residence?

3. What factors should be considered in selecting and implementing an integrated curriculum?

4. How could National Standards 8 and 9 be accomplished through ideas suggested in this chapter? Find a specific standard and highlight two or three ways that standard might be accomplished in a way authentic to the various disciplines.

PROJECTS

1. Plan a social studies unit, focusing on a particular culture or subculture, in which the arts of that culture play a major role. Do research on the authentic forms, styles, uses, and meanings of the arts in that culture. Incorporate a series of arts-integrated lessons into your unit. Use the arts processes to make sure you have approached this with integrity.

2. Work with a librarian to discover children's books that relate directly to music. (Some ideas are suggested in the references.) Develop at least three different ways to creatively extend the book using music and one other art form.

3. Identify two works of program music that might appeal to children. Develop a series of arts activities that help develop children's knowledge of the music as well as engage them creatively and significantly in another art form.

4. In a team of four people, select a theme that would be appealing to children; develop and collect ideas for integrating the arts into that focus. Use a multidisciplinary approach with a thematic web design similar to the model in Lesson 14.1.

5. Find and visit a school or classroom in which curriculum integration is taking place. What is the atmosphere in the room? The level of involvement of the children? The role of the teacher(s)? The subjects being integrated? The use of the arts, if any?

6. Plan a series of music lessons in which other arts are integrated in artistically significant ways. State at least two objectives for each lesson: one in music and one in the other art form. Make sure your lesson strategies achieve those goals. Use the 1994 National Standards in the arts as a basis for forming your objectives.

MINDTAP Visit **MindTap** to access classroom videos, audio, and more!

15

Music, Children, and Cultural Diversity

IN THIS CHAPTER

- Definitions
- Uncertainties in Teaching New Musical Styles
- The Musically Competent Teacher
- New Repertoire for Familiar Pedagogies
- The Aural-Oral Transmission Process
- Curricular Redesign
- Many Musical Worlds
- Scenario

CHILDREN COME IN MANY sizes, shapes, hues, and views. The music they know well and can perform derives from the rich cultural traditions of their homes and ethnic communities. Mikael hums the songs of his grandmother's Russian childhood. Maisa sings the way she does with her Norwegian relatives, adding harmonies in parallel fourths and fifths to the melodies she hears. Ramon comes to school with the tunes of his uncle's Mexican mariachi band in his ears, and the Spanish words at the tip of his tongue. Luis claps and pats the sophisticated syncopations of Puerto Rican claves and congas easily, never missing a moment in time. Shirelle sways as she sings, because "that's the way it's done" in the gospel choir in which she performs on Sundays. Bisi sings a duple-metered melody while clapping in three, performing with ease the typical cross-rhythm of a Nigerian game song. With encouragement, Charoen performs the graceful ramvong dance of Laos, Li-Chen demonstrates the ribbon dance of China, Joseph steps the circle dance of the Sioux, and Saroda communicates through the gestural language of the Bharata Natyam, a South Indian classical dance. A gathering of children such as these is an occasion for a microcosmic classroom experience, a reflection of the cultural diversity that comprises the world in which they live.

Diversity is apparent in the faces of children in schools, on playgrounds, and in neighborhoods. It is apparent in the various perceptions of the world they share; in their languages, dialects, and variations of English; in the holidays they celebrate; and in the customs they choose to share with their friends and schoolmates. The cultural traditions of so many varieties of children do not melt into some all-American "people-pot."

Recent trends in immigration and birthrates in the United States have resulted in a population spread of 16 percent Hispanic-Latin Americans, 13 percent African Americans, about 5 percent Asian Americans, and 1 percent Native Americans, with a little less than two-thirds of European heritage. These are broad demographic categories, such that there is diversity within diversity: A Latin American may be of an

- What does cultural diversity mean to you, and how do you see it manifested in your daily doings—in your home/ neighborhood, classes, school observations?

- Are you musically competent in any of the styles and traditions beyond your training in Western European art music?

- What does a teacher need to know to be able to facilitate children's learning of a musical culture?

- How do you go about selecting the music of another culture to teach? What resources are there, and how credible are they?

- Do you think it is possible to teach musical skills while also teaching cultural understanding through music?

elite class of Argentinians who trace their roots to Spain, Italy, or Israel; a fourth-generation Caribbean American whose family has kept alive the language and cultural traditions of Puerto Rico; a Syrian or Somali whose family has recently sought and found asylum from the daily violence of war and terrorism; or a Chicano whose family has known border crossings, migrant work, and barrio neighborhoods in any of dozens of American cities. By the mid-twenty-first century, the average American will trace his or her roots to multiple regions and cultures in Africa, Asia, the Hispanic world, the Pacific Islands, and the Middle East—almost anywhere but Caucasian Europe. Americans are living in a fast-changing society, with the statistical charts on race and ethnicity turning upside down and inside out.

Alongside the cultural diversity of communities and classrooms, there is a rich musical diversity with which to contend in developing the lessons and sessions that comprise the education of children. Regardless of the ethnic-cultural composite of children within classrooms, the music itself calls for inclusion within programs of instruction. It is compelling music, too, some of it exquisite in its subtle delicacies of timbres and tunings, and some driving people to their feet to dance the dynamic rhythms that are as much felt as heard. With the explosion of global sounds that has developed in recent years, the prospects of teaching children the features and meanings of diverse musical expressions are strong. In classrooms of preschool, primary-level, and preadolescent children, there are tremendous opportunities to open young ears and minds to the breadth of soundscapes that emanate from around the globe. Music in the education of children can be selected from a diversity of traditions, and experiences in these traditions can develop children's skills in performance, listening, and creative expression. Importantly, the presence of musical diversity in a program of instruction can bring an understanding of its cross-cultural meanings in the lives of people of every nation and culture.

Definitions

IF SCHOOLS ARE THE vehicles through which children are presented with the knowledge and values of a given nation, then the music program should offer children (1) opportunities to experience a broad sampling of the world's musical traditions, (2) more thorough-going journeys into selected musical cultures, and (3) multiple approaches to musical skills and understandings that appeal to their varied modes of learning. While it is certainly a logical stance, the prospects of teaching music from a multicultural perspective may sometimes seem overwhelming. One reason for this is the all-encompassing definition of multicultural education, which technically includes the study not only of the music of groups distinguished by race or ethnic origin, but also of the music of people of different ages, social classes, genders, religions, lifestyles, and exceptionalities (Banks and Banks, 2012, 2004). Within this framework, the tasks of cultural diversity in music education are enormously broad, and perhaps too comprehensive to be applied to the curricular changes that are occurring.

"Multiethnic" is a label applied to curricular developments that focus exclusively on the study of a diversity of groups distinguished by ethnic origin. Music programs that focus in depth on musical styles of a group of people united by national or ethnic origin, such as the music of the Chinese, Filipinos, the Yoruba of Nigeria, or Brazilians, are referred to by the rubric "multiethnic music education." While *multicultural* is the term featured prominently in curriculum and instruction materials in North America as a recognition of multiple cultural groups; *multiethnic* refers more directly to ethnicity rather than age, social class, gender, or other issues; *intercultural* is sometimes preferred as it describes communities in which there is a deep understanding and respect between and among cultures.

© Jerry Bav

Curricular plans may be designed to feature an intensive study of music, per-haps run-ning four or more sessions, from more than one ethnic-cultural group. Fourth-grade children who are learning to sing Japanese and Chinese songs, to listen analytically to the music of the Japanese koto and the Chinese zheng (zithers), and to play Japanese shakuhachi and Chinese di (flute) melodies on recorders are reaping the benefits of a multiethnic curriculum. First-grade children who are learning the melodies, move-ments, and functions of singing games from Zimbabwe and Venezuela are also being served a multiethnic-flavored music curriculum. Even an intensive study of one new and less familiar musical culture begins to approach the mission of multiethnic music education, because children are already making subconscious comparisons of the mother-tongue music acquired in their homes with the music of the teacher's choice. The intent of multiethnic music education is, in addition to the provision of a variety of musical experiences (singing, listening, moving, playing instruments, and creating), to offer children an understanding of how music reflects people's lifestyles and ways of thinking across a diversity of cultural boundaries.

Yet it must also be said that in teaching music—or any subject—to children, *multiethnic* refers to the varied instructional approaches that need to be provided to children from different cultural perspectives so that they can develop skills and understandings that are as complete as those developed by children from the mainstream majority. In the past, children who have fared best from instruction have tended to be those whose cultural understanding and learning styles have matched the teacher's own experience and training. Teacher education programs, curricular materials, and even instructional delivery systems have been oriented toward the white middle-class teacher and her children. In a multiethnic approach to music education, children's own ethnic-cultural heritage(s) must be kept in mind not so much in the selection of repertoire (although that can be a way to develop meaningful learning) but in the design of processes by which children's individual interests, learning modes, and special linguistic, social, and religious needs can be considered with the utmost sensitivity. All music, from Mozart canons to folk tunes from Mozambique, must be taught with the knowledge of who the children are and how their cultural heritage may season their learning.

Another curricular concept in music education programs for children is "world music education" (also called "world musics in education" or "global musics in education"). As distinguished from multiethnic music education, world music education features the study of musical components as they are treated in various musical styles across the world. For example, preschool children may learn to clap or step the steady pulse to the music of an African American blues song, a Chinese luogu (percussion ensemble), an Indonesian gamelan piece, and a Puerto Rican salsa number. Third-grade children may learn about timbre by listening to fiddles and musical bows from Ireland, Pakistan, Malawi, Cambodia, and Mexico. Sixth-grade children may come to understand syncopation as a prominent characteristic in the music of Ghana, Cuba, China, and African American gospel music. Like the term *multiethnic*, world music education suggests another type of comparative approach to music. Unlike multiethnic music education, world music education is concerned with cross-cultural comparisons that span a great many musical styles across the globe, instead of concentrating more narrowly and more deeply on a smaller selection of ethnic groups. World music education may also allow less contextualization of musical experiences, as the emphasis is placed on more extensive (instead of intensive) sonic musical (instead of cultural) experiences. Still, this approach does not preclude the study of music's cultural meaning and value, which is seen as deepening one's understanding of the music.

The discipline of ethnomusicology, which has long been about the study of music as culture and music in culture, is influential in providing musical expressions and ideas about music that are relevant to music education practice. Somewhere between the scholarly discipline of ethnomusicology and the practice of musically educating students is the newly emergent phenomenon known as *world music pedagogy* (Campbell, 2004). This concerns the careful selection of music of the world's cultures for ever increasing levels of participatory listening and performance as well as attention to the process by which music is taught/transmitted and received/learned within cultures, and how best the processes can be preserved or at least partially retained in classrooms (Campbell and Bannerman, 2010). World music pedagogy features opportunities to create music in the style of a given musical selection, and to learn how the integration of musical study with all the arts, as well as language arts and social studies, deepens both musical and cultural knowledge and values. An understanding of music's transmission processes in various cultures is useful, too, and parallels the need to know the sonic structures and social meanings of music, such that experiences in the music of Brazilian samba, or Balinese gamelan, or Russian polyphonic song are best if facilitated in accordance with the manner in which it is taught and learned in the culture of origin (Schippers, 2010).

Which is better: to teach a small selection of musical traditions thoroughly, as in the case of multiethnic music education, or to teach music conceptually through cross-cultural examples, as in the case of world music education? There may be room for both within the design of musical experiences for children. In the scope of a year's plan, children can learn aspects of melody, rhythm, timbre, texture, and form by engaging in active listening to many samples of the world's musical styles and genres. Just as the examples of a musical concept can be historically broad—from the music of Monteverdi through Messiaen—they can also be culturally broad and globally varied, chosen from Bulgaria, Bali, and Brazil, for example. Within the same year, a series of lessons on one musical tradition or genre (for example, dance music of the Pueblo Indians of New Mexico or the Macedonians of southeastern Europe) can lead children into a knowledge of people and their musical ways of thinking. Side by side in a single school year, children can experience the best of both musical and cultural understanding. There is no limit to the ways in which many musical styles can be brought to children to develop their understanding of music.

One thing is certain: as products of a culturally diverse society, children must be led to listen and to respond to the aesthetic components and cultural meanings of more than a single musical tradition (Anderson and Campbell, 2010). They are living in a less-homogenized world than any earlier generation, one that demands their understanding of many people. Ideally, through their musical experiences, sensing its ebbs

"Understanding of a foreign musical style is assisted by a willingness to view the world from an unfamiliar perspective."

Peter Fletcher, 2001

and flows, learning its logical structures, and feeling its power, children may come to understand not only the music, but also the music makers. They may learn to take note of not only the differences among people and their musical expressions, but also the similarities that transcend all people.

Uncertainties in Teaching New Musical Styles

There are misgivings, uncertainties, and well-founded questions to consider in offering a broader palette of musical colors and styles. Consider the often-quoted statements both for and against offering children the music of many cultures.

"My kids are not ethnic; they are white." In fact, everyone is ethnic, including European Americans. All music is ethnic, too, including the master-works of Mozart and Mahler, of Charles Ives, Ruth Crawford Seeger, Nusrat Fateh Ali Khan, Cesoria Evora, Ali Farka Toure, Paddy Maloney, and Paul Simon. Each song and instrumental piece manifests the characteristic musical components of the culture from which it derives. Even those rare teachers who still teach homogeneous groups of children whose ancestors arrived from Europe generations ago know that those children will venture beyond their neighborhoods. They will have the opportunity to associate with people in diverse ethnic communities in an increasingly pluralistic society. It may be that by knowing about other ethnic groups' values, their traditions, and their artistic and musical expressions, children will also come to know the world's people better.

"My schedule is too packed to include music of so many diverse cultures." According to the manner in which multiethnic and world music education are defined, it is unnecessary to offer additional classes to explore a diversity of music traditions. Teachers can inject new or less-familiar music into their lessons to illustrate the cross-cultural similarities, and yet vast diversity, of musical thought and expression. Comparative approaches to the study of music is a much-valued (and effective) means of deepening and understanding of music, and it takes little time to work in experiences in s-m-r-d, or 6/8 meter, across a diversity of musical styles.

Musical experiences intended to bring about cultural understanding may also require new ways of teaching across the curriculum. Teachers of music, art, and classroom subjects can team together to develop monthly and quarterly units on a given country, cultural region, or ethnic group. Colloquial expressions can be spoken; customs can be practiced; stories can be told, read, and reenacted; visual arts and crafts can be viewed and copied; songs can be sung; and traditional instrumental pieces and dances can be performed. Children and their families may be tapped as experts, too, with firsthand knowledge of their culture's music. In a collaborative and thorough way, music teachers can join together with others to enlighten children about the worlds of people and their cultural expressions.

"I don't know the languages of the foreign songs." Although foreign language songs challenge teachers and children, the cultural experience can be very powerful. There is an added dimension when the original language of a song intermingles with the song's rhythm and melody, rather than an English translation. Music teachers, whose ears are fine-tuned to discriminate fractional sound variations, can often easily learn the phonemes of new languages as well. A foreign-language song is best learned by listening—at home, in the car, and at school—with the ears perceiving the music and language as one. Once it is aurally channeled and internalized, there is a growing confidence in transmitting the song to children. The song becomes a part of the listener's and singer's repertoire.

Children can also be initiated to a musical culture through music listening experiences, movement, and opportunities to play instruments of the culture and by teachers with a commitment to cultural diversity in music education. Listening can be active, engaging children to gesture the rise and fall of a Japanese shakuhachi (flute) melody or to snap, clap, pat, and stamp the ostinato of a Cuban bomba drum. Basic circle and line dances of the Middle East, Eastern Europe, and Native American cultures can be performed by young children as early as first or second grade. Children can play West African polyrhythms on various nonpitched percussion instruments and selected melodies from many cultures on recorders. They can play the melodies and polyphonic textures of selected Southeast Asian and sub-Saharan African music on xylophones, if in a somewhat modified manner. Occasionally, listening, movement, and instrumental performance can be combined with songs, a four-dimensional experience for children.

The Musically Competent Teacher

Increasingly, courses within collegiate music and teacher education programs expose students to musical styles beyond Western European art music. Prospective teachers can gain initial acquaintance with musical cultures through one or more broad-based world music survey courses, followed with specialized seminars for the in-depth study of the music of African, Asian, European, Latin American, Native American, Australian, and Pacific Island cultures. Although these may be offered only as elective or optional courses in collegiate music programs, they are nonetheless invaluable for teaching music as a culturally diverse set of practices.

In addition to full-fledged courses, workshops are also occasions for learning the music of other cultures. These workshops are commonly offered through summer school programs by musicians from various traditions, by ethnomusicologists with considerable study of one or more musical cultures, and by music educators with a commitment to world music pedagogy. For those who cannot squeeze additional courses into their undergraduate program, these workshops can be taken during the summer interim period soon after teaching certification is completed. In addition to courses and workshops, musicians in the community may offer lessons on traditional instruments and singing styles for a moderate fee.

Many teachers have chosen to learn to play or sing music other than Western European art music. Those who are competent in a musical tradition or style are best able to teach it accurately and easily. The musical competence they achieve through specialized training includes aural competence, or the ability to listen to and understand the structural components of a musical style. Ideally, musically competent teachers also attain a measure of performance proficiency, vocally or on an instrument. Children are fascinated with the music that is performed live for them and are eager for opportunities to play instruments or sing in the style of a confident performer. When fundamental instrumental techniques and pieces can be demonstrated by the performing teacher, and when songs can be sung using their original language and appropriate vocal timbre and inflections, the music becomes more appealing to children. The performing teacher also gains credibility in the children's eyes.

Gaining proficiency within a musical tradition requires time and effort. Just as aural and performance competence in Western European art music requires many years of listening, reading, and practice, it is also the case in knowing well the music of the Zulu of South Africa, the Han Chinese, the Sephardic Jews of Spain, or African Americans. Those who take the time to sing or study an instrument of a favorite other culture, and then build a school or personal library of recordings, writings, and videotapes on the music and culture, are well on their way to gaining proficiency within that tradition. Listening long and hard pays off, too, and the Internet provides access to a treasury of music in audio- and video-packaging. See, for example, the vast collections at Smithsonian Folkways (www.folkways.si.edu/) and the Association for Cultural Equity (<culturalequity.org/>). By becoming musically competent in a style, they have the skills, knowledge, enthusiasm, and confidence to present it to children.

Teachers of music usually become competent in Western European art music through their training, but they can also progress to the study of another musical culture. Those

Andrew playing West African shekere

with aural and performance competence in more than one music are said to be bimusical; it is this quality that approaches the goals of cultural diversity in music education. A modified bimusicality is a goal to be achieved in children as well, so that they can listen to and perform the music of more than one culture. Becoming musically competent in more than one tradition may develop an appreciation for the complexities of other music, as well as recognition of their validity and logic. Performance proficiency is not necessary for selecting examples of a pentatonic piece, a triple-metered song, or a polyrhythmic texture from a variety of musical traditions (a curricular tactic featured in world music education). Still, any attempt to know musical traditions more than superficially will excite both teachers and their children.

New Repertoire for Familiar Pedagogies

Teaching music from the perspectives of multiethnic or world music education does not mean negating or discarding the old or the well-established pedagogical approaches. Techniques such as speech rhythms, rhythmic syllables, movable do, stem notation, melodic mapping, instrumental performance, listening grids and call charts, part-singing, eurhythmic movement, and improvisation may be readily used in teaching nearly all music traditions. In fact, three of the classic methods associated with teaching music to children may find new freedom in the repertoire that is introduced (see Lesson 15.1).

LESSON 15.1 "Haere, Haere," "Uncle Jessie," "Ala De'lona," "Hashewie"

Scan these songs for musical features that might be emphasized in lessons for children. Consider the application of Orff, Kodály, and Dalcroze techniques in developing these songs for inclusion in the curriculum. Design an Orff-style accompaniment, a Kodály-inspired ear-training sequence, and a Dalcroze eurhythmics movement experience in a pedagogically appropriate manner. Consider the integration of speech-chant, body percussion, steps and stages of aural skill building, and means of listening and visual elaboration of these songs. Explore traditional ways of making music, too.

Haere, Haere (Maori farewell song; New Zealand/Aotearoa)

nu - a i te ta - ha   o te to -

nga   e   wha - ka - ria   nei. _____

Hae - re   hae - re   ha - e - re - ra.

Translation
Farewell, go with strength and courage
To that chosen direction (south)
Illuminated for you.

Note: "wh" is pronounced as "f."

Source: Traditional Songs of Singing Cultures, by Patricia Shehan Campbell, Sue Williamson, and Pierre Perron (Miami, FL: Warner Bros. Publications, 1996).

Uncle Jessie (African American song; Georgia Sea Islands/United States)

1. Now, here comes Un - cle Jes - sie,   Com - ing through the
2. Now, here comes Un - cle Jes - sie,   He's   look - ing ve - ry

field,   With his horse and   bug - gy and   I
sad.   He's   lost his cot - ton   and his corn and

Clap: x   ⅹ   x   ⅹ   x

know just how he feels. Walk, walk, ___ Un - cle Jes - sie,
eve - ry - thing he had.

ⅹ x ⅹ x ⅹ x ⅹ x ⅹ x

walk,   walk,   walk, ___ Un - cle Jes - sie walk, walk, Step,

(Continued)

_ Un - cle Jes - sie, step, step, step, __ Un - cle Jes - sie, step.

Source: Roots and Branches, by Patricia Shehan Campbell, Ellen McCullough-Brabson, and Judith Cook Tucker (Danbury, CT: World Music Press, 1994).

Ala De'lona (Jordan, Lebanon, and Syria)

A - la De' - lo - na, A - la De' - lo - na, Hi - war shi - ma -

li gha - yar ih - lo - na. *Fine* Ma - ba - di i - mi ma - ba - di

D.C. al Fine ba - yi; Ba - di ha - bi - bi as - mar ih - lo - na.

Translation

Fair De'lona with dark skin, Chilled by the wind;
I would leave my mother and father to visit my fair De'lona.

Source: Tunes and Grooves in Music Education, by Patricia Shehan Campbell (Upper Saddle River, NJ: Pearson, 2008).

Hashewie (Eritrea, As sung by Hidaat Ephrem)

Solo Ha - shew - i - e __ *Chorus* Shew - i - e *Solo* Ha - shew - i - e __ *Chorus* Shew - i - e *Solo* Ha -

shew - i - e __ *Chorus* Shew - i - e *Solo* Bi - ha - de ha - bir - na *Chorus* Shew - i - e - *Solo* Hashew - ie'e - na - bel -

na Shew - i - e.   A - lem kit - fel - to Shew - i - e   Ku - lu - me - nin - et - na Shew i -

e   Ha - shew - i - e ni - bel Shew - i - e   Ne - fa - lit - a - di - na Shew - i -

e   Bi - ha - de ha - bir - na Shew - i - e Ha - Shew - i - e____ Shew - i - e Ha -

Shew - i - e____ Shew - i - e Ha - Shew - i - e____ Shew - i - e.

Translation

Going round, all together, enjoying one another.

Source: Tunes and Grooves in Music Education, by Patricia Shehan Campbell (Upper Saddle River, NJ: Pearson, 2008).

Orff-Schulwerk provides children with experiences that are as social as they are musical. Many of the world's music traditions beautifully suit its components. The music of West African cultures such as the Akan, the Ewe, the Ibo, and the Yoruba offer call-and-response songs, layered polyrhythmic compositions on nonpitched percussion instruments, stories replete with music in choral response, and movement created to follow the repeating and contrasting phrases. The xylophone cultures of Bali, Guatemala, Java, and Zimbabwe are natural repositories of music that can be performed on Orff's familiar xylophones and metallophones. Hampton's volumes (1996, 1999) are exemplars of how an ensemble of Orff-styled instruments can launch children's exploration of a musical culture (the Shona of Zimbabwe) in an active, engaging manner that is not unlike the Orff process itself.

Proponents of the Hungarian approach that Kodály inspired consider folk and traditional music to be at the heart of music instruction. Unadulterated folk music is alive and well in every culture and applicable to children's learning of both music and their national heritage. The child-centered Kodály sequence for teaching melodic and rhythmic concepts can extend to many of the world's musics. Transfer of the tools of the method—movable do, rhythmic syllables, hand signs, and the shorthand notation of stems and solfège initials—from Hungarian to Anglo-American and African American songs occurred as early as the 1960s. Given the goal of the Kodály approach to foster musical and cultural understanding, such tools could transfer to the traditional and art music of Asian, African, Latin, and Native American cultures as well. The musical vocabulary used by a culture in its children's songs, folk and folk dance music, and instrumental and choral works may be better understood through the application of Kodály techniques.

If rhythm is the primary element of almost all music, and the source for musical rhythms is contained within the natural movements of the body, then the techniques of the Dalcroze approach should be suited to the development of a thorough understanding of music from many cultures. The eurhythmics techniques of follow, quick reaction, and canon can apply aptly to styles as diverse as the rhythmically dynamic Jamaican soca (soul calypso) style and the rhythmically subtle Japanese koto concert repertoire.

Walking the pulse, conducting the meter, and changing directions as each new phrase appears are Dalcrozian responses for music of any style, period, or form. When an unfamiliar selection from a little-known tradition becomes the stimulus for movement, the challenge to respond correctly to a different but equally logical musical structure is considerable. The reward, however, is greater intimacy through natural body movements that express musical understanding. The Dalcroze approach may provide the difference between simple exposure to, and integral, intensive experience of, the world's music.

The Aural-Oral Transmission Process

One of the marks of Western thinking is the tendency to emphasize the end, or product, not the ways and means, or process, by which the product is achieved. Children can be guided to bring music they study to concert-level perfection in their performance, but product-oriented instruction without attention to process is only half the musical and cultural experience. The emphasis on how music and music learning evolves is central to valid experiences for children in the various musical styles the world can offer them.

An emphasis on process also distinguishes many of the world's great music traditions: the classical music of India; the African American gospel song; the gamelan music of Java; the Chopi (Mozambican) xylophone and drum ensemble; the Bulgarian polyphonic song; the rock, reggae, and rap music of North America; and the siku (panpipe) music of the Bolivian Andes. While musicians strive for a finished musical work in any tradition, their interaction with each other and with the musical components in the process of learning and rehearsing together is critical in defining both the music and the musical culture.

If authenticity is to be taken seriously, the transmission of much of the world's popular, traditional, and even art music can only be delivered orally—as it can only be received aurally. Notation, a marvelous technological invention, is not pervasive, and it cannot replace direct contact with the musical sound. Teachers and children can best become acquainted with unfamiliar music through listening, the most direct route.

Children performing in an African drumming ensemble

© Jerry Gay

How then should the teaching of the world's music proceed? The transmission process, by which the teacher can facilitate both musical and cultural understanding, involves familiar teaching and learning practices. The use of teacher modeling, student imitation, and exploration and improvisation are important components of the transmission of music in many cultures, just as they are often integral to any well-planned lesson. Central to the process, however, is listening, at ever-deepening levels. Three listen-to-learn world music pedagogy phases are linked to instructional processes for knowing music from any of the world's cultures: (1) Attentive Listening, directed and focused on musical elements and structures, and guided by specified points of attention; (2) Engaged Listening, the active participation by a listener in some extent of music-making (by singing a melody, patting a rhythm, playing a percussion part, moving to a dance pattern); and (3) Enactive Listening, the performance of a work in which, through intensive listening to every musical nuance, the music is re-created in as stylistically accurate a way as possible (Campbell, 2004). While these listening phases may sit as separate entities within a class session, Lesson 15.2 presents a sequence by which all three may be woven into children's learning of a song or instrumental selection.

LESSON 15.2 Deep-Listening to the World's Musical Expressions

1. Choose a favorite listening selection: Puerto Rican salsa, English hornpipe, Navajo social song, Trinidadian soca, Japanese gagaku, Brazilian samba, African American blues, Balinese ketjak, or North Indian khyal.

2. Attentive Listening: Play the recording (or a one- to two-minute selection) three times, with a directed question preceding each listening. Questions may include "How many instruments do you hear?" "Which instrument (or word) sounds the highest pitch?" "Are there any repeated phrases?" Allow time for discussion of the answers following each listening.

(Continued)

3. Engaged Listening: Play the recording (or a one- to two-minute selection), with the invitation to participate in the music as it sounds, by singing the melody, patting or playing a percussion part, or moving in lines or circles to the pulse (and even changing directions on the phrase changes). Multiple listenings are necessary to practice and develop participatory engagement.

4. Enactive Listening: Learn by listening to the whole song or selection (or a segment), with emphasis on the sonic features that can be performed vocally or on available instruments, repeating a cycle of listen-perform-listen checks and comparisons until the music can be performed in a reasonably close approximation of its recorded sound.

5. Before, during, and/or following the listening sequence, provide information on context and function: Who performs it? Why? When? Where? How? What do the words mean?

"All over the world, people make music meaningful and useful in their lives."

Bonnie C. Wade, 2013

When a traditional song or instrumental piece is transferred from an attentive listening mode into the realm of engaged listening (participation) or enactive listening (performance), an aural or oral delivery system can be easily applied. The teacher as transmitter of a musical piece owes it to the tradition to consider ways to maintain the authenticity not only of the finished product but also of listening as integral element of the transmission process. Notational literacy is an important goal of music instruction, and may be treated as an ancillary and effective technique. But for achieving the goals of cultural literacy and understanding, the oral or aural process by which music is taught and learned may temporarily override more traditional curricular objectives. See Campbell (1991 [2001]) for further discussion of classroom teaching in light of world music transmission systems, and Goetze (2002) for choral songs that can be taught and learned without the need for notational support.

Curricular Redesign

Many established curricular programs are undergoing revitalization to meet the needs of children growing up in a changing American society. Education in social studies, language arts, math, sciences, and the arts is becoming more inclusive of African American, Asian American, Latin American, and Native American cultures. Music is no exception. A study of textbooks over the past few decades underscores the tremendous leap the profession has taken to teach a broader variety of musical styles that are more fairly represented as well as more authentically presented. Curricular change comes slowly, however, and both the revision of pedagogical materials and the infusion of a more comprehensive perspective on music and music making into classes for children take the time, effort, and creativity of the teacher.

In the pioneering efforts to achieve the curricular goals of cultural diversity in music education, several important determinants should be considered.

1. Because many of the instructional materials, and the longer-range curricular plans, are not written down, they must be invented through the teacher's own cultural immersion, musicality, and knowledge of how children learn.

2. An understanding of children's learning styles and attitudes can guide the teacher in designing a curriculum that provides active participation in music-making experiences along with initial exposure to selections of a culture's music.

3. Arrangements with members of particular ethnic-cultural communities to sing their traditional songs, play folk instruments, and tell traditional tales can provide children with the human interaction so vital in understanding music and culture.

These considerations can be supported, although not replaced, by the recorded, filmed, and printed materials that are becoming available, so that children become more broadly experienced in the music of many cultures. Where authenticity was once of grave concern to teachers, such that considerable energy was expended to determine just what the earliest or original source of a song might be, many teachers are carefully selecting out various renditions of a song as testimony to the travels of a song and the creative reinvention of it by musicians. Songs such as the South African "Mbube," for example, or "Little Sally Walker," or "Sakura" have been performed in various musical renderings. While it is useful to hear source recordings of a song, and respectful to attribute these songs to earlier (if not original) singers, it is not altogether honest to perpetuate a belief that music should be static, unchanging, and hands-off for anyone but the originators. There are exceptions, of course, within particular cultures where songs are guarded as personal property, and it is generally informative for young people to hear more than their own classroom renderings of music, it should not be necessary to construct roadblocks to musical traditions based on the position that the classroom musical arrangements are not "authentic." Musical authenticity occurs with every effort by performers, including children, to express themselves in ways that are musically sincere. Often, the very best learning derives from a comparative experience in which children listen to exemplar recorded versions of a song, listens to their own rendering, and makes comparisons between "them" and "us" in the way of melodic, rhythmic, and timbral qualities. In this way, historic recordings and newly invented renditions are honored in the recognition that they all fall in alignment as "variations on a theme."

The design of an all-inclusive music curriculum can take several directions. Music education that is culturally conscious and globally diverse is likely to be packaged within a curricular unit of several weeks, a month, two months, or longer, and it will feature a variety of experiences in the music of a selected culture or country. In the larger realm of year-long curriculum design, the multiethnic-styled intensive study of one musical culture can lead to the study of further cultures (including the music of the teacher's training, or the mother-tongue music of the teacher or of the majority of the children within the classroom or school). More than a single musical culture can conceivably be explored in shorter or longer periods of time, and comparisons can be made among several musical cultures.

In a study of China's music, for example, a unit may begin with samples of instrumental sounds, followed by exposure to the appearance and sound production capacities of the huqin (fiddle), pipa (lute), zheng (zither), di (flute), and luogu (drum and gong ensemble) through live demonstration or videotapes. The unit may unfold to include vocal music, with opportunities to perform several traditional children's songs and chants, and to view videotapes of the premiere Chinese performing art, Beijing Opera. Maps, slides, transparencies, posters, and photographs of China and its people, places, and paintings can provide a cultural context for the music, along with occasions for reading Chinese traditional poetry and folktales. With ample experiences in listening analytically to Chinese music, children can be guided to create music in the Chinese style, using recorders, cymbals, gongs, and drums to render pentatonic melodies with syncopated rhythms in duple meter. Lesson 15.3 presents a calendar of events in a study unit on Chinese music for children in the intermediate grades, to provide one of several pathways to realizing the goals of multiethnic music education.

LESSON 15.3 Seven Sequential Lessons on Chinese Musical Culture for Fourth-Grade Children

Lak Gei Moli (Jasmine Flowers of the Sixth Moon)

Lak gei___ mo li___ jin jian___ shui.   Long gun___ si(n) zui___
Lahk gay___ moh lee___ jin john___ shwee.   Long gun___ see(n) zwee___

jin___ go zhui.   Ho hui lan_____ die___ xien___ xiang___
jin___ goh zhwee.   Hoh hwee lan_____ dee___ zhehn___ zhahng___

dui___ Xin bin(n) mou_____ gun xiung_____ ka_____ kui.
dwee___ zhin bihn moo_____ gun zhung_____ kah_____ kwee.

Weekly Class Meetings	Two at thirty minutes each
	(Note that suggestions are oriented toward student rather than teacher behaviors)
Lesson One	Enter class while listening to Chinese music*
	Listen to recording of Chinese instrumental music selections
	1. How do you play these instruments? (Pretend/show)
	2. What do these instruments look like?
	See illustrations (photos, slides) of instruments
	Find China on a map; discuss geography
	Depart class while listening to Chinese music*
Lesson Two	Match listening samples to illustrations of instruments (huqin, pipa, zheng, di)
	Play "Jasmine Flowers of the Sixth Moon" (Lak Gei Moli) on recorder
	Read and discuss text of "Jasmine Flowers"
	Sing "Jasmine Flowers"
	Share Internet samplings of Chinese culture, the arts, and music
	Host Chinese "culture-bearer"
Lesson Three	Review by identifying instruments by sight and sound
	Review "Jasmine Flowers" on recorder
	Add woodblock and bells on "Jasmine Flowers"

*All classes can begin and end with sounds of Chinese traditional music.

Feng Yang (The Flower Drum Song)

Verse

Zuo __ sho __ luo   you __ sho __ gu   shou na __ luo __ gu
Zoh __ shoh __ loh   yoh __ shoh __ guh   shoh na __ loh __ guh

lai __ chang   ge   Bie de __ ge   er __   wo   ye   bu   hui   chang
la __ ee chang   geh   Bee deh __ geh   ehr __   wo   yay boo hwee chang

Zhi hui __ chang   ge   Feng - Yang   ge   Feng feng - yang   ge __
zee hwee __ chang   geh   Feng - Yang   geh   Feng feng - yang   geh

Refrain

yi __ yo __ ya.   Drr ling dang piao e piao   Drr ling dang piao e piao
yee __ yoh __ yah   Drr ling dang pe ow eh pe ow   Drr ling dang pe ow eh pe ow

Drr piao Drr piao   Drr piao drr piao   piao you drr ling dang piao e piao
drr pe ow Drr pe ow   Drr pe ow drr pe ow   pe ow yoh drr ling dang pe ow eh pe ow

Match listening samples of illustrations of instruments (luogu ensemble of gongs, cymbals, drums)

Play luogu parts for "The Flower Drum Song" (Feng Yang) See videotape clip of Chinese instruments

Lesson Four   Review luogu parts for "The Flower Drum Song"

Sing (or play on recorders) "The Flower Drum Song"

Sing and add luogu parts for "The Flower Drum Song"

See Internet for examples of Chinese festivals

Host Chinese "culture-bearer"

Review "Jasmine Flowers" for recorder, woodblock, bells

Lesson Five   Listen to recording of Chinese instrumental musical selections (presented in first lesson)

1. Can you tap the steady pulse?
2. What is the meter? [duple]
3. Can you hum the melody?
4. How many pitches are there? [five]

Sing "Jasmine Flowers" and "The Flower Drum Song"

Repeat questions 1–4; summarize meter/melody concepts

(Continued)

	Tell the Chinese folktale "Money Makes Cares" and/or
	Read "The Musical Journey "
Lesson Six	Watch clips of Beijing (or other) Opera
	Review "The Flower Drum Song" with luogu
	Review "Jasmine Flowers" for recorder, woodblock, bells

    1. Do you hear uneven syncopated rhythms?

    2. Can you clap them as you sing the songs?

	Discuss syncopated rhythms, pentatonic melodies, and duple meter as characteristic of Chinese music
	Review/retell the Chinese folktale "Money Makes Cares" and/or
	Read "The Musical Journey"
Lesson Seven	Review characteristics of Chinese music
	Review tale of "Money Makes Cares"
	Assign children to groups to prepare

    1. narration of tale

    2. dramatization of tale

    3. creation of incidental instrumental music for tale (on recorders, gongs, drums, woodblock, bells)

    4. performance of "Jasmine Flowers" and "The Flower Drum Song" for inclusion in tale

Lesson Eight	Rehearse performance project in individual groups
Lesson Nine	Continue rehearsal
	Integrate groups into performance/production of tale
Lesson Ten	Perform tale
	Teacher-directed evaluation to determine children's understanding of Chinese music/culture

Sources: Anderson and Campbell (2010), "Jasmine Flowers of the Sixth Moon"; Cole (1982), "Money Makes Cares"; Han and Campbell (1992), "The Flower Drum Song" and "Jasmine Flowers"; Liow Kah Joon's *A Musical Journey: From the Great Wall of China to the Water Towns of Jiagnan* (2003).

In designing lessons that incorporate the goals of cultural diversity in music education, the teacher may choose from among several pathways. The musical components avenue was highlighted in the earlier definition of world music as a curricular concept, where cross-cultural comparisons are made regarding specific aspects of melody, rhythm, timbre, texture, and form. The music material approach features a study of similar musical instruments across cultures, for example, the incidence of lutes in Europe, Asia, and the Middle East, or the spread of bamboo and bronze instruments in Southeast Asia. Still another approach is parallel genres, the study of theater, dance, orchestral, wedding, or opera music (to give a few examples) in a variety of cultures. Lesson 15.4 presents examples of these directions in world music education for children of various ages and grade levels. Note that Western European art music is not abandoned in these approaches, because it is one of the important world music traditions.

Grade	Any
Musical Concepts	Triple Meter
Suggested Listening or Song Experience	Korea: "Ahrirang." (Internet selections)
	Austria: Mozart, Symphony 40, K440, Movement 3.
	Sweden: "Vals" (See Vasen or other Internet selections)

Mos'! Mos'! (Hopi, Native American)

Tritonic Melody

(d, m, s)

Mos', mos', nai - ti - la Mos', mos', nai - ti - la
[neh - tee - lah]

Ka - nel per - kye nai - ti - la Ka - nel per - kye nai - ti - la
[Ka - nel pehr-kyay]

Mo - - sa Mo - - sa nya-nya-ya-ya etc.

Sorida (Zimbabwe)

(d, m, s)

So - ri - da So - ri - da ri - da ri - da So - ri - da
[Soh - ree-dah]

So - ri - da ri - da ri - da da da da da da da ri

da ri - da da da da da da da ri - da ri - da

(Continued)

Yuyake (Japan)

(s, l, t)

Yu - ya - ke   ko - ya - ke   A - shi - ta ten - ki - ni   na ___ re!
[Yoo - yah - keh koh - yah - keh Ah - shee-tah ten - ke - ne   nah ___ reh]

Leak Kanseng (Cambodia)

(s, l, t)

Leak   kan - seng   chma kaim   keng   oh   long   oh   long
[Lee ahk kahn - sahng chmah kahm kehng oh   long   oh   long]

Syncopation	Ghana: "Chalala Eh" and "Wateh Eh." *Mustapha Tetty Addy: Master Drummer from Ghana.* Lyrichord 7250 (or YouTube, Internet)
	China: "The Hero's Defeat." *China's Classical Masterpieces.* Lyrichord 7182 (or YouTube, Internet)
	Cuba: "A Los Rumberos de Belen." *Sabroso! Havana Hits.* Virgin/Earthworks 91312 (or YouTube, Internet)
Lutes	'Ud (Egypt, the Middle East). *Music in the World of Islam.* Tangent 131-136 (or YouTube, Internet)
	Sitar (India). *The Sounds of India: Ravi Shankar.* Columbia 9296 (or YouTube, Internet)
	Shamisen (Japan). *Japan: Kabuki and Other Traditional Music.* Nonesuch 72084 (or YouTube, Internet)
	Pipa (China). *Floating Petals, Wild Geese, The Moon on High: Music of the Chinese Pipa.* Nonesuch 72085 (or YouTube, Internet)
Bronzes in Southeast Asia	Balinese metallophones/gongs. *Music from the Morning of the World.* Nonesuch 72015 (or YouTube, Internet)
	Javanese metallophones/gongs. *Javanese Court Gamelan, Vols. 1–3.* Nonesuch 72044, 72074, 72083 (or YouTube, Internet)
	Cambodian metallophones. *Silent Temples, Songful Hearts.* World Music Press (or YouTube, internet)
	Vietnamese coin clappers. *Music of Vietnam.* Lyrichord 7337 (or YouTube, Internet)
	Filipino gongs (kulintang). *Philippine Gong Music.* Lyrichord 7322 (or YouTube, Internet)
Theater Music	Italy: Puccini, *Gianni Schicchi* (YouTube, Internet)
	China: Beijing Opera, "Hu Hung-yen: Aspects of Peking/Beijing Opera) (YouTube, Internet)
	Japan: Kabuki. "Martial Arts of Kabuki from the National Theater Institute of Japan" (YouTube, Internet)

Suite	Peru: Suite of dances. *Music of the Incas* by Ayllu Sulca. Lyrichord 7348 (or YouTube, Internet)
	Iran: Suite in Dastgah Mahour. *A Persian Heritage.* Nonesuch 72060 (or YouTube, Internet)
	Bach: *French Suite* (YouTube, Internet)

Many resources are available for use in teaching the world's musical traditions. Community resources, including traditional performing artists, are rich and waiting to be tapped for assembly programs, long-term residencies, and contractual teaching. Readers may wish to collect a set of ethnomusicology and world music references, including books by Miller and Shahriari (2017); Nettl, Capwell, Bohlman, Wong, and Turino (2011); Titon (2009); and Wade (2013), all with associated recordings and websites. Selected world musical traditions are available as books with recordings and instructor's manuals, such as *Music in Bulgaria* (Rice, 2004), *Music in Brazil* (Murphy, 2008), *Mariachi Music in America* (Sheehy, 2006), *Music in Korea* (Kwon, 2012), *Music in the Hispanic Caribbean* (Moore, 2009), and *Music in West Africa* (Stone, 2005). Experiences for children are found in books by Anderson and Campbell (2010), and in a collection of lessons by Campbell (2004) on attentive listening, engaged participation, and enactive performance suggests ways of teaching music globally. Books accompanied by recordings of children's songs from various world cultures include collections by Campbell, McCullough-Brabson, and Tucker (1994); Campbell (2008); and Vanaver (1990). Audio and video-recordings are easily accessible on the Internet, and "Tools for Teaching" on the Smithsonian Folkways site and "For Teachers" on the Association for Cultural Equity site contain lessons that are ready-to-go into classrooms for teaching children more of the world's musical cultures.

Many Musical Worlds

Cultural diversity in music education is a well-considered phrase and a broad concept, but certainly the objectives of the movements in multiethnic and world music education can be at least partially met through children's exposure, experience, and education in music. The world of music offers a comprehensive view of the sounds, functions, and meanings of music globally and within the many ethnic groups of a single nation. The musical expressions of groups of people are the focus of multiethnic music education, in which children are offered intensive study of one and then another musical culture. Likewise, world music education provides children with knowledge of how groups of people organize the elements of music in unique modes of musical expression.

Formal as well as informal experience in listening to and (ideally) performing the music of another culture increases children's understanding and thus appreciation of unfamiliar musical styles and music makers. Carefully planned experiences in the music of many cultures can bring about improved musicianship, increased preference for new (to the children) musical styles, and a deeper understanding of people and their music. Through the intermediate grades, children are open to changing their values and attitudes, so the palette of music offered to children in their early years can be a powerfully awakening and broadening experience.

> *"We should try to keep up with the world in our teaching, because it is in the world that our students will have to apply what they have learned—not only when their education is complete, but every day.*
>
> **Anthony Seeger, 2002**

TECHNOLOGY *for* TEACHING *and* LEARNING MUSIC: CHILDREN *and* CULTURAL DIVERSITY

Technology offers many, many resources for teaching and learning cultural diversity. Videos of singing, dancing, and playing instruments abound from almost every country and ethnic group in the world. To learn more, visit the Technology Resources links in the MindTap.

MINDTAP

Scenario

MS. JOHNSON IS TEACHING at Baker Elementary, a school that she describes as "mildly diverse," with 20 percent African American children; 10 percent Hispanic children (mostly Puerto Rican, Dominican, and Cuban); another 10 percent children whose parents or grandparents arrived from Vietnam or the Philippines; 5 percent Jewish children; a few children from Somalia, Eritrea, and Ethiopia; and all the rest of the children from one or another European heritage. She is becoming aware of diversity in the array of languages spoken by the children, the many religious and seasonal holidays they celebrate, the variety of foods brought in brown bags for lunch, the varied manner of dress and hairstyles sported, and most relevant to her, the songs and records that children bring to share with her at music time. Times have changed since her own elementary school experience out in a suburban school, and she is adamant in her goal to allow her music program to reflect the diversity of the school community.

It is just a few weeks before the winter program, and Ms. Johnson has been rehearsing the fifth graders (a microcosmic composite of the larger school population) on music that will comprise a "Festival of Lights" concert. There is a carol for Christmas, a xylophone arrangement of a song for Divali (India), a Hanukkah song with countermelody for recorders, a dance with recorded music to commemorate St. Lucia's Day (Swedish), music for Kwanzaa to sing and drum, an a cappella song for Loy Kratong with partner-game (Thailand), and a circle dance with recorder-and-drum accompaniment for Solstice. As she is distributing the recorders and drums for the Solstice song, Jamal murmurs something about "honky music." Several other boys join in while chanting, "We won't play that h-o-n-k-y music," rhythmically waving their arms while their fingers take on contortionist positions. They are rhythmic, but they are loud, and Ms. Johnson worries that the message they are sending to the other children is offensive—by way of both word and gestures. She orders them to stop. Jamal (an African American boy) protests, "That song is lame. It's so white." And Ms. Johnson nervously replies in a sweet tone, "But we've already done your music, so you can do ours." The hip-hop boys hold their recorders to their mouths, but they do not play.

The class is invited next to review the song for Divali. The children take their places by the wood and metal xylophones, and Ms. Johnson conducts the singers and players through several repetitions of the unison song. Shanta, who arrived two years ago from India, raises her hand to inform the class, "We really don't have xylophones in India." Ms. Johnson grimaces, several children look at each other and roll their eyes (why? she wonders), and although she carries on with the song's arrangement as planned, she is feeling uneasy inside.

"Okay, let's see what we remember of the Loy Kratong. Partner up so we can sing and perform the actions." Ms. Johnson walks up to Isaias and Kaleta and pairs them up.

They are not pleased with the arrangement and will not join hands in the opening position. While others sing and play the partner game, the two boys stand stiffly facing each other, silently glowering. (Later, Ms. Johnson learns that Isaias is from Ethiopia and Kaleta is from Eritrea, two warring nations with deep-seated feelings of animosity toward one another that spreads from adults to children.)

"Why aren't we doing 'Feliz Navidad'?" asks Marisol. Ms. Johnson realizes that she has committed another faux pas in her selection of repertoire, having assumed that the Hispanic children knew "The First Noel" in English (because it is a Catholic hymn, and they are Catholic). There is not enough time for the entire class to learn another song, so she invites Marisol, Maria, and Ramona to sing it in the winter program by themselves. The girls look shy yet pleased at the prospect of being featured, until Katerina and Anna complain, "What about us? Can we play one of our Ukrainian songs on our accordions?" As their classroom teacher arrives at the door to pick up her class, Ms. Johnson realizes that the class has disintegrated into cultural enclaves and animosities that she never would have predicted. She is beginning to think that an "all-American" program might be safer next time around.

Questions

1. How did Ms. Johnson's best intentions to celebrate cultural diversity go sour? Could any of these circumstances have been averted through more careful planning?

2. Is Ms. Johnson approaching the design of the winter concert in a manner akin to multiethnic music education or world music education or both? Explain.

3. Would the outcome have been any different had Ms. Johnson been teaching children in a less diverse setting than this one at Baker Elementary? In what ways?

REVIEW

1. Consider definitions of multicultural, intercultural, multiethnic, and world music as they inform music education approaches. How are they distinguished from one another? In what ways are they similar?

2. What uncertainties may have slowed the curricular advances in the teaching of world music?

3. Describe ways in which classic methods of music for children can be used in teaching world music traditions.

CRITICAL THINKING

1. What are some of the important issues to consider regarding authenticity and representativeness in the selection of music for children?

2. How might a teacher go about teaching a unit of study on African American gospel music (a) to a group of African American children, (b) to non-African American children, (c) if she were African American, and (d) if she were not African American? Or would it make a difference?

PROJECTS

1. Launch a demographic study of the city or district in which you may teach. Study the recent changes in the ethnic composite of the school population, as well as projections for the future.

2. Choose a favorite culture. Develop an annotated list of books, recordings, and videocassettes useful in teaching the music of this culture.

3. Develop a month-long curricular plan in teaching children the music of a favorite culture.

4. Choose one avenue of guiding children into experiences with the world's musical cultures (musical components, music material, parallel genres), and collect songs and listening experiences from various musical traditions to illustrate selected features within that category.

5. By listening to a recording, prepare to teach a song or instrumental performance from an oral tradition, with careful attention to rendering an authentic sound.

MINDTAP Visit **MindTap** to access classroom videos, audio, and more!

16

Music for Exceptional Children

IN THIS CHAPTER

- Who Are Exceptional Children?
  - Public Laws
  - Person-First Language
  - Children At-Risk
- Educating Exceptional Children
- Inclusion and the Music Classroom
- IEP in Music
- Inclusion in Music Instruction
- The Music Classroom and Exceptional Children
  - Intellectual and Developmental Disabilities
  - Specific Learning Disabilities
  - Attention Deficit Hyperactivity Disorder (ADHD)
  - Emotional or Behavioral Disorders
  - Autism Spectrum Disorders
  - Sensory Disorders
  - Physical Disabilities
  - ELL—English Language Learners
  - Gifted and Talented
- The Joys of Reaching All Children

MALINKA, AGE EIGHT, LOVES to sing; she does so with great enthusiasm but has a difficult time controlling her voice and her impulse to sing constantly. Trebon, age ten, is an active composer; he can replicate, by ear, challenging piano pieces he has heard two or three times. Jessica, age eleven, is withdrawn; she comes to music class but sits there, looking downward. James, age six, seems to need constant attention; he moves all the time, hits the children next to him, talks out of turn, and rarely sings without shouting, but he loves to play the African drums.

Each one of these children has unique needs and abilities, some of which are being met through special education, and some through regular education. All attend music classes with children their own age in a regular education setting as a part of their school's goal to place them in an environment where they can achieve their maximum growth. This is called the least restrictive environment (LRE). Although these children have been labeled exceptional, they are more like other children than they are different. Musically, they are frequently similar in their interests and abilities to other children in regular classrooms (Jellison and Flowers, 1991).

The music teacher who works with these children is part of a child study team that helps to determine how to accommodate each child with special needs. As a team member, the music teacher is able to communicate with the others the goals of the music program to make sure each child can be successful. Everyone learns from each other how to help meet the unique needs of the children and what support can be expected in the process. The music teacher helps decide how inclusion in music can help achieve goals set forth in each child's annual Individualized Educational Plan (IEP). The following descriptions outline the factors that the child study team considered in placing Malinka, Trebon, Jessica, and James in a music setting.

Malinka has Down syndrome, with a moderate intellectual disability and a gift for relating with joy to the people around her. Although she has some problems inhibiting her responses, she is developing increased self-control. Her performance in school suggests she should be able to live in a group setting as an adult and hold a job, provided there are some supports for her. The committee decided that she would benefit from the structure of the music setting, the challenge of learning to match her voice to those of the children around her, and the intellectual and physical stimulation of being with a range of students. Although she will largely learn music by rote, her participation is immediate and feeling of success immense.

Trebon has many gifts, particularly in music, although he is also a part of his school's pull-out gifted program, where he receives additional instruction. When the music specialist recognized Trebon's exceptional gifts in music, she encouraged his parents to get him private lessons. Although they wanted that for him, they could not afford the cost. The music specialist contacted the district music supervisor, who had begun a program, funded through a combination of school funds, Parent Teacher Student Association (PTSA) grants, and community corporate grants, to give private music lessons to economically disadvantaged children. Members of a local private music teachers association agreed to come to the schools to offer lessons at reduced rates as part of their dedication to public service. In her music class, the specialist offers Trebon opportunities for leadership as an accompanist and a teaching assistant, helping her when she divides the class into smaller groups for guitar instruction and for composition assignments.

Jessica is a child who has been emotionally and physically abused by her parents. She is now living in a foster home and is receiving counseling. She has coped with her abuse by withdrawing, and her self-esteem is at a very low level. She has normal intelligence but poor social skills. Her teachers are eager to help her learn to express herself and to trust and interact with others in group settings. Because the music classroom is based on group expression of musical ideas, the team decided to place Jessica with a class of fifth graders. Although Jessica withdraws during group singing, she is willing to play accompaniments on Orff xylophones. She is also starting to express some ideas, both verbally and musically, in the small-group composition sessions. (The music specialist has elected to form cooperative groups that retain a stable membership for three months.) As a result, Jessica is beginning to trust the other students in her group and is making some friends. Her teachers report that she is increasingly eager to go to music class.

James has been diagnosed as having attention deficit hyperactivity disorder (ADHD) and some learning disabilities. His parents have decided not to control his behavior with Ritalin because they are concerned about the negative effects of continued medication. James comes to music from a resource room, where teachers are working with him on specific academic and social skills. The resource-room teachers have worked with the music specialist to implement a behavior-management procedure that is consistent with the one they are using with James. Some of the musical goals for the year include reducing the amount of energy James uses in singing, building accuracy in reproduction of patterns through techniques of echoing, and having James notate and then read and perform his own patterns.

Who Are Exceptional Children?

ALTHOUGH IT COULD BE said that on some level every child is exceptional, with unique abilities and needs, current practice defines exceptional children as "individuals whose physical, mental, or behavioral performance deviates so substantially from the average (higher or lower) that additional support is required to meet the individual's

THINGS TO THINK ABOUT

- In what ways can you or people you know well be defined as "exceptional"?

- How have those exceptionalities required schools to adjust to meet various needs?

- What roles and responsibilities do you think music teachers have to accommodate the needs of children with disabilities?

needs" (Hardman, Drew, and Egan, 2011, p. 11). The challenge has been to determine the nature of programs to support the varied and unique needs of these children and to fund such programs.

Public Laws

In 1975, a landmark federal law was passed called the Education for Handicapped Children Act, or Public Law 94-142. This law did much to revolutionize the ways schools served exceptional children. Practices such as mainstreaming and writing an Individualized Educational Plan, or IEP, came out of that law. (See descriptions of those terms later in this chapter.) In 1990, P.L. 94-142 was amended to redefine handicapped children as *children with disabilities*. The new law, P.L. 101-476 (Individuals with Disabilities Education Act, or IDEA), addressed a number of issues to help students receive needed services and assistance, including children with attention deficit disorders, or ADD.

The legislation in IDEA replaced P.L. 94-142. It, along with P.L. 99-457, which focuses on intervention in early childhood, mandates that a free and appropriate public education be provided for children and young people between the ages of three and twenty-one regardless of the nature or extent of their disability. To qualify for services, the disability must affect student performance. Currently under federal law disabilities are listed as:

- Intellectual disabilities
- Developmental delay
- Specific learning disabilities
- Behavior disorders (serious emotional disturbance)
- Communication (speech and language) impairments
- Hearing impairments, including deafness
- Visual impairments, including blindness
- Orthopedic impairments
- Autism spectrum disorders
- Multiple disabilities
- Traumatic brain injury
- Other health impairments

An amendment to the law was passed in 1997 and became P.L. 105-17. It further strengthened the rights of students with disabilities. It extended the idea of the LRE or least restrictive environment to assure that all students would have access to the general education curriculum. It required consideration of the addition of assistive technology devices and services as a part of the IEP for students. And it requires that orientation services be given for students with vision or mobility impairments who may have trouble getting around a school. Each of these laws has helped to raise the consciousness of the schools as to how best to serve the wide range of student needs.

Person First Language

The language used to describe a child's disability is frequently open to misinterpretation and confusion. A national movement called People First Language works to sensitize us all as to how language can often hurt or limit rather than free. The basic premise is to avoid labeling anyone as being defined by their unique need such as saying, "He is autistic." It is preferable to say, "He has autism." There are many organizations and resources available to help to understand this movement.

It is useful to think of children with various needs as "differently abled" instead of "disabled." For example, exceptional children may or may not have a disability, or "the reduced function or loss of a particular body part or organ" (Heward and Orlansky, 1992, p. 27). Children who cannot perform tasks involving seeing, hearing, or moving the way others can may be said to be disabled. Persons with disabilities may or may not be handicapped, referring to the "problems a person with a disability or impairment encounters when interacting with the environment" (Heward and Orlansky, 1992, p. 28). A person using a wheelchair may be handicapped when trying to go to the second floor of a building without elevators, but not handicapped intellectually in the school classroom. PL 101-336, the Americans with Disabilities Act (ADA), passed Congress in 1990. This sweeping law created a national mandate for the elimination of any discrimination against people with disabilities and named the federal government as the enforcer of these laws. Title III of this law applies to schools, ensuring equal access and services.

Children at Risk

A category of at-risk children is often described in the literature (Gargiulo and Metcalf, 2013). Although these children are not currently identified as disabled, they run a greater-than-usual chance of developing a problem. They are often preschoolers whose conditions of birth (such as premature birth or fetal drug or alcohol syndrome) or home environment (such as abuse or economic deprivation) suggest that they may be at risk for developmental problems and may need special help. At-risk children are those in the primary or intermediate grades who demonstrate learning problems in the regular classroom and are at risk for placement in special programs or, if older, for school dropout. These children are not currently classified as exceptional but their needs are real, and early intervention by schools and social agencies is common.

Educating Exceptional Children

Several factors go into structuring programs to meet the educational needs of all children. In addition to requiring free public education for children with disabilities, IDEA requires that individuals and families of individuals with disabilities have a say in their education and that an annual IEP, or Individualized Educational Plan, be developed for each individual, helping to place him or her in the least restrictive environment (LRE) for growth. In music, that would mean that children with identified disabilities be provided with a situation in which they feel included psychologically as well as physically and that the tasks be adapted to meet their needs. Gifted children are the only group of exceptional children not covered in this act, but they may be included in corresponding state laws for the education of children with special needs.

> "The student is educated in the least restrictive environment consistent with his or her educational needs and, insofar as possible, with students without disabilities."
>
> Hallahan and Kauffman, 2000, p. 29

Since 1975, schools have responded in various ways to this legislation. Thankfully, schools have moved away from isolating to including them into different parts of the school program with support from resource rooms, aides, and teachers trained in special education. Historically, mainstreaming has usually occurred in areas typically taught by specialists, such as music, physical education, and art, but since the late 1990s—with the shift from mainstreaming to inclusion—it is common practice to include children of various needs in all subjects in the curriculum.

Since the late 1980s, many schools have integrated children with disabilities into the regular classroom throughout the entire day using a model called inclusion. In such schools, children and faculty not certified in special education are taught to assist these children as needed, and support is usually provided to meet their additional physical and educational needs. Paraprofessionals or teacher aides are frequently assigned to assist individual children to help assure success.

The federal government encourages but does not require states to create and fund special programs for gifted and talented students. Forty-eight states have such programs, but the relative amount spent on them is minimal compared with that spent on children with disabilities. Many models exist for serving gifted and talented children; one of the most common is to pull them out of their regular classroom for enrichment classes. Entrance into these classes is usually based on a measured IQ (intelligence quotient) of 130 to 135. Some schools teach the most intellectually gifted children (the top 1 percent) in completely separate programs. Other schools, particularly at the secondary level, screen students based on specific gifts in math and science, humanities, or the arts. Selected students are placed in magnet schools that stimulate them to achieve advanced levels of performance in the area(s) of their gifts.

Of the children in special education (about 10 percent of the total school population), 44.6 percent are diagnosed with specific learning disabilities, 19 percent with speech and language impairments, 10 percent with other health impairments, 8.6 percent with intellectual disabilities, 7.6 percent with emotional disturbance, 3.7 percent with autism spectrum disorders. Smaller percentages exist in the remaining categories of special education (IDEA Data Accountability Center, 2006–2007. As of 2008, 95 percent of these children received at least part if not all of their education in a regular classroom with the support of a resource room. Three percent are served in special schools for students with disabilities Ninety percent of children receiving special education are mildly affected by their disability (U.S. Department of Education, National Center for Education Statistics [2011], *Digest of Education Statistics, 2010* [NCES 2011-015], Chapter 2.)

Inclusion and the Music Classroom

The decision to include a child with disabilities in music is justified for a variety of positive reasons that relate directly to the nature of music and music learning.

1. Music taps into nonverbal ways of knowing and allows children to express ideas regardless of verbal abilities. At the same time, singing can help children to develop vocabulary and understanding of language as well as breath support and expression.

2. Music is multimodal in nature, stimulating the eyes, ears, and muscles along with the mind. Children who have a disability in one sensory area may still participate in music via other senses. The joy of producing sounds and movements draws children actively into the process of music making instead of requiring them to be passive receptors of new ideas.

3. Music can be performed at very sophisticated levels by rote. It is not necessary to be able to read music to perform it well. Although an important outcome of a quality music program is the skill of reading music, children who have difficulties with abstract symbols, such as reading words or translating numbers, can still enjoy success in music.

4. Music making is generally a collaborative endeavor. Music is usually made and learned in groups, not alone. This is particularly true of preschool and elementary

"Inclusive education *means students with disabilities receive the services and supports appropriate to their individual needs within the general education setting. This concept may be described as 'push-in services.' Whereas the traditional model for special education 'pulls the students out of the general education class to receive support.'"*

Hardman, Drew, and Egan, 2011, p. 54

general music programs. Therefore, children can gain a sense of belonging and commitment to a group, which is important to social development.

5. Music, as a performing art, allows for the expression of a wide range of emotions, and it can communicate on very deep levels without the use of words. It stimulates and challenges people to grow aesthetically.

6. A single activity in a music classroom can be adapted to a wide range of ability levels.

7. Music, as a temporal art, challenges the mind to recognize patterns across time, a skill that often needs to be developed in children with patterning and memory deficits.

Yet, in spite of the many potential benefits of including children in music, such decisions need to be weighed carefully for each child in terms of (1) his or her unique needs and abilities and (2) the demands of the music classroom. The purpose of the LRE is to place children in a situation in which they can succeed and grow, not where they will be ignored or fail. Part B section 612(a)(5) of the 2004 Individual with Disabilities Education Act, defines the "the least restrictive environment" in which children must be taught. It is the legal obligation of the teacher to consider how they will adapt the context of the classroom to least restrict the child's ability to succeed. Throughout this chapter and book there are many ideas for adapting the music classroom to help children with various needs to succeed.

Although it is tempting to focus on the possible therapeutic values of musical involvement for exceptional children, general music teachers are rarely trained as music therapists. Therefore, they do not have the background or credentials to plan for placement of children in music classes for therapeutic reasons or to systematically implement therapeutic uses of music. Every music teacher can, however, determine effective ways to adapt their instruction and materials to meet the needs of all children.

The most effective plan to include a child in music will result from clear communication and cooperation among the members of the team involved. One of those members should, by law, be the music specialist if he or she is being asked to receive a child. The music specialist needs to attend the meetings and help determine a myriad of ways that child can succeed in the music classroom. He or she needs to gain insight from the team members about how best to work with each child.

Regrettably, many schools ignore this requirement and simply send the children to music classes for "social experiences" without any warning, a practice known as "dumping." Results of such decisions sometimes lead to anger and confusion on the part of music teachers, lack of acceptance of the child by the other children, and, ultimately, a more, rather than less, restrictive environment.

Inclusion done well has the potential to benefit all children and is the ideal to which all schools and teachers should strive. Music classes are wonderful places where children with diverse backgrounds and abilities can thrive.

IEP in Music

As part of a successful placement in music, the music teacher will need to join other members of the child study team to make sure that the IEP for that child reflects realistic goals for musical attainment. By law, a child study team must include at least (1) the child's teacher(s), (2) a representative of the local school district other than the child's teacher, (3) the child's parents or guardian, and (4), whenever appropriate, the child herself or himself. Other specialists, including music specialists, can be added as necessary.

Each IEP is required to contain basic information about and goals for the child, and it must be established at the beginning of the school year and reviewed once during the year. Local school districts have usually developed their own forms. Ideally these plans should help identify the student's level of functioning at the beginning of the year, long- and short-term goals, how these goals will be achieved, and how the student's progress will be evaluated. In addition, the services and kinds of assistance needed should be identified. Box 16.1 shows an example of an IEP in music.

BOX 16.1 Individualized Education Plan (IEP)

1. Student

Name: Heidi Strom

School: Mirror Lake Elementary

Grade: 2

Current placement: Resource Room

Date of birth: 11/22/96

Age: 8

2. Committee

NAME	POSITION	INITIAL DATE
Mr. Webb	Music teacher	
Ms. Santiago	Resource teacher	
Ms. Turrin	School counselor	

3. Present Level of Functioning	**4. Annual Goal**	**5. Instructional Objective**	**6. Assessment Procedure**
Strengths: Works well in cooperative group. Sings accurately from C to c. Maintains a beat through clapping.	To expand vocal range upward to e.	Work on head voice and lightness.	Sing a song across a wide range using head voice.
Needs: To expand voice upward. To learn to visually decode simple rhythmic and pitch patterns with fluency. To gain eye-hand coordination.	To decode patterns involving quarter and eighth notes and songs using three pitches (s,m,l), and to perform those patterns through clapping and signing.	Practice clapping, tapping, and playing simple patterns. Use manipulatives for pitch and rhythm.	Read a simple song with three pitches, isolating pitch and rhythm, then combining them.

7. Educational Service to Be Provided

a. Services Required	**b. Date Initiated**	**c. Duration**	**d. Individual Response**
The use of various manipulatives designed for children with disabilities to develop multimodal perception.	11/13/04	8 weeks	Sally Fine

e. Extent of Time in Regular Educational Program

Placed in regular second-grade music class, two 30-minute periods each week.

f. Justification for Placement

Based on assessment of progress in music classroom.

8. I have had the Opportunity to Participate in the Development of this Individualized Education Program.

Parent's Signature _____

Although involvement in this process clearly takes time, music specialists need to understand that their right to participate is protected under the law and that doing so can help create a more positive environment for the mainstreamed child. Specialists also need to know that schools should be committed to educating all students in music whether they are mainstreamed or not.

Inclusion in Music Instruction

Because of the shift in schools from mainstreaming to inclusion, the music teacher may not have been formally involved on a child study team, deciding whether music would be the best placement for a particular child. Regardless of whether a child with disabilities enters the music classroom through mainstreaming or inclusion, an IEP will have been written. Knowledge of that information will be helpful in integrating the child successfully. The more awareness the teacher has of each child's unique needs and abilities, the more effectively that teacher can tailor learning strategies to meet that child's needs. The music specialist needs to engage in collaborative consultation with special education teachers to learn as much as possible about how to meet each child's needs.

Successful integration means providing an environment where each child participates to the highest level possible, has experiences that all children are having, learns to interact with other children, and receives respect for his or her unique needs (Adamek, 2001). To accomplish this, the music teacher may wish to request a Summary Sheet of Information on the Special Needs Children in Class (Adamek, 2001, p. 24). Such a sheet should include the following information:

Name

Grade

Teacher

Date

Strengths, Skills, and Talent

Weaknesses and Limitations

IEP Objectives

Strategies for Success

"Successful integration means providing an environment where each child participates to the highest level possible, has experiences that all children are having, learns to interact with other children, and receives respect for his or her unique needs."

The Music Classroom and Exceptional Children

Whether teachers work with exceptional children in a mainstreamed classroom, through inclusion, or in a self-contained setting, the key to success is the willingness of the teachers to adapt instruction to meet the needs of those children. Each category of exceptionality has unique characteristics, as does each child within a category.

For some students, teachers need to *adapt the pace and clarity of instructions*, slowing down what they do, repeating directions, and modeling tasks. For some children, teachers will need to *adapt the complexity* either of the task, the music, or the level of thought required, sometimes simplifying it and other times making it more challenging. For other students, teachers will need to *adapt the materials and instruments*, making print larger, using sequencing cards, using assistive technology to teach or to

"... the key to success is the willingness of the teachers to adapt instruction to meet the needs of ... children [classified as exceptional]."

understand children's responses, or adding Velcro fasteners to gloves so children can hold bell mallets. And for others, teachers will need to *adapt the processes and support* they provide, using student buddies and cooperative groups, allowing students to experience instruction (seeing, hearing, moving) and demonstrate knowing (telling, singing, playing, writing, moving) through multiple instead of single modalities. Learning to adapt will actually help the teacher improve instruction for all students.

Ultimately, deciding how to adapt instruction can be an exciting and challenging process that will increase a teacher's repertoire of strategies designed to meet the needs of all children. The following ideas should provide an initial base. Other resources include the special education teachers and specialists (hearing, speech, and psychologists) assigned to work with exceptional children, the parents, the children themselves, print resources, and classes in working with disabilities.

Intellectual and Developmental Disabilities

Children who are classified as intellectually disabled are significantly below average in general *intellectual functioning* (average IQ is 100), which either results in or is associated with deficits in *adaptive behavior*. Some children with low IQs are able to function well in school and society. Those children would not be classified as intellectually disabled. However, if a child has a low IQ and does not meet age-level standards of personal independence and social responsibility, then he or she will be labeled as having intellectual disabilities or developmental delays. A small percentage of the overall student population falls into this category.

The American Association on Intellectual and Developmental Disabilities has suggested strongly that a single measure of IQ is inadequate to describe the kinds of support an individual might need to function effectively. They proposed a system in 1992 based on classifying people according to the level of support they need to function: intermittent, limited, extensive, or pervasive. There is some evidence that schools are now taking social, practical, and conceptual intelligence into consideration when placing students in the appropriate level of services. (See Hardman, Drew, and Egan, 2011, Chapter 9.)

There are typically four levels of intellectual disability or delay that are defined in terms of levels of IQ. These should be used along with other measures of adaptive behavior and/or level of identified need for support in placing a child.

- *Mild Disability or Delay (IQ of 50–55 to approximately 70–75)* Children in this category are the most likely to be mainstreamed into music classes, with the assistance of a resource-room teacher to meet individual needs. Often these children are not identified until they begin schooling. The largest percentage of intellectually disabled children in school settings falls in this group. With excellent support, many grow significantly in their cognitive, social, and practical skills and live independently as adults. They would fall into the category of intermittent or limited support.

- *Moderate Disability or Delay (IQ of 35–40 to 50–55)* Children in this category have usually been identified at an early age and often have other handicapping conditions and physical abnormalities. Music educators may begin working with them in early childhood classes beginning at the age of three. Normally they are accompanied by an aide to assist them in music. These children are usually taught in a self-contained classroom where focus on daily living and functional skills generally outweighs academics. Many of these children have Down syndrome or are brain damaged. They continue to need support as adults. They may need limited or extensive support, depending on their level of functioning.

- *Severe Disability (IQ of 20–25 to 35–40)* and *Profound Delay (IQ below 20–25)* Most children in these two categories are identified at birth and have significant central nervous system damage. They usually have not been taught in schools, although that is beginning to change. New technologies are helping to reach children who are profoundly delayed. Most of these people will need pervasive care, some twenty-four hours a day, throughout life. However, some may be able to function semi-independently as adults, requiring extensive support.

Music teachers are most likely to be asked to work with children who have mild and moderate intellectual disabilities either through inclusion, mainstreaming, or in self-contained settings. Box 16.2 provides a breakdown of characteristics of children with mild disabilities and specific teaching strategies to meet their special needs.

BOX 16.2 A Breakdown of Intellectually Disabled Characteristics and Specific Teaching Strategies

1. Children with intellectual disabilities may have problems with focusing attention or distinguishing the important from the unimportant. They may also be unable to generalize learning to new settings.
   - Use color highlighting of notated melodic and rhythmic patterns.
   - Notate their part (such as an ostinato) separately; use color highlighting.
   - Teach songs without recordings or other accompaniment.
   - State lesson goals clearly, and repeat during the lesson.
   - Speak in short simple sentences without talking down.
   - Ask children to perform only one musical task—for example, chant or sing, or maintain a steady beat or ostinato—not multiple tasks.

2. Children with intellectual disabilities may have problems with memory from one lesson to another and also short-term memory of patterns within a lesson.
   - Repeat materials, skills, and concepts across several lessons.
   - Keep musical patterns for echo clapping or singing short, simple, and slow; repeat them if necessary.
   - Break tasks down into small units and teach with simple directions; use hand movements to practice dance patterns ahead of time or patschen (patting the lap) to practice instrument patterns.
   - Use visual cues such as pictures or movements to help them remember the order of events in a song; for example, "I Know an Old Lady Who Swallowed a Fly."
   - In learning a new song, have children perform only the part that repeats; for example, "Sandy Land."
   - Use assistive devices to help with building memory.

3. Children with intellectual disabilities may have trouble with cognitive organization of ideas and abstractions.
   - Use iconic notation to represent patterns.
   - Teach ideas by rote instead of note.
   - Let them develop their own way of writing down music.
   - Help them chunk or group information using visual, verbal, or movement cues; for example, music charts that come with music series or bulletin boards that highlight or review concepts.

4. Children with intellectual disabilities may have trouble singing in tune across a wide range or may sing with too much energy
   - Work to expand their tessitura upward (often it is low, from B to g).
   - Have them sit next to an effective singer and encourage them to match that singer's voice.

(Continued)

BOX 16.2 (*Continued*)

5. The mental age (MA) of children with intellectual disabilities is usually behind their chronological age (CA), yet they often identify with same-age peers.

- If mainstreamed based on CA, adapt instruction per suggestions above; have them work with a partner who can monitor and assist but not solve or take over for them.
- Respect their CA when selecting song and listening materials; do not treat older students like little children.
- Discover something they do well in music, and let them offer leadership, or have them lead a cooperative group with a sensitive buddy as their assistant.

Specific Learning Disabilities

The area of learning disabilities is perhaps the most difficult to define of all of the areas of exceptionality. Generally children identified as having learning disabilities (LD) are of normal and sometimes advanced intelligence but have "significant difficulties in the acquisition and use of language, listening, speaking, reading, writing, reasoning, or mathematical abilities" (Heward and Orlansky, 1992, p. 137). It is assumed that these limits are intrinsic and stem from a *dysfunction* in the central nervous system (CNS), and are not a result of other handicapping conditions or extrinsic influences such as environment or lack of education.

By far, the largest number, approximately 50 percent, of exceptional children served in schools today are identified as learning disabled, although the form(s) that the disability takes varies greatly. The majority are males (a three-to-one ratio), are identified in the elementary grades, are more deficient in spelling and reading than in mathematics, and have increased difficulty in learning with increased age.

Trevor playing the drum

© Jerry Gay

Because learning disabled is an umbrella term covering a wide range of behaviors, it is difficult to state principles that will apply in every case. A child may have perceptual disabilities, brain injury, minimal brain dysfunction, dyslexia, or developmental aphasia. A careful dialogue with the resource-room teacher and a review of each mainstreamed child's folder should help the music teacher better meet individual needs. Box 16.3 provides some general characteristics and specific teaching strategies to address student needs.

BOX 16.3 General Characteristics of Children with Learning Disabilities and Specific Teaching Strategies

1. In general, develop strategies that allow children with learning disabilities (LD) to hear, see, move, or touch either simultaneously or sequentially. Children with learning disabilities have difficulty receiving and translating input from one or more of the senses used for learning.

   VISUAL (VERBAL AND NONVERBAL)

   - Highlight visuals using large print, color, frames that isolate patterns on overheads, PowerPoints, or in their books.
   - Use assistive technology as appropriate to enlarge and/or highlight materials that are confusing

   AUDITORY (VERBAL AND NONVERBAL)

   - Slow down verbal input and recordings; teach difficult parts separately.
   - Separate the reading of rhythms from pitch.
   - Learn songs by rote, then add the tracking of words; print one line of words under a song, not multiple verses.

   TACTILE (TOUCH) OR KINESTHETIC (MUSCLE MOVEMENT) (VERBAL AND NONVERBAL)

   - Use concrete manipulatives to reinforce musical ideas such as notation: magnet boards or hand staffs for pitch work; Popsicle sticks for rhythm work; and also felt or sandpaper notes.
   - Practice instrument parts kinesthetically away from the instrument first.

2. Children with learning disabilities may have problems cognitively integrating all of the different information they receive during a music lesson. Depending on the complexity of the task, they have to move from paying attention to what it is the teacher is emphasizing, to perceiving the place in the music, to forming an image of what that is, to interpreting a symbol of how it is represented, to conceptualizing it in terms of other similar musical events or in terms of the task. This is particularly challenging in music because even a simple folk song printed in a music book is full of information. Most of the musical tasks children are asked to perform involve complex coordination of the mind and the body.

   - Perform a task analysis of the skills or concepts children are expected to do or understand.
   - Teach children to perform something in a series of smaller steps:
     - How to hold a mallet and how to strike it
     - Later, how to coordinate with complex patterns
     - Later, how to read
     - Later, to understand an ostinato
   - Know that motor coordination may be a problem and simplify motor tasks.

3. Children with learning disabilities may have difficulty showing what they know through writing or reading.
   - Provide alternative means of showing what they know: pointing, circling icons such as arrows or lines, matching, manipulating, singing, moving, and telling.

Attention Deficit Hyperactivity Disorder (ADHD)

In 1999 the USDOE amended the definition of "other health impairments" (§ 300.7(c) (9)) to include ADD/ADHD rendering diagnosed children eligible for special education services under this definition. The phenomenon of children diagnosed as having ADHD is quite real and can often affect the smooth functioning of any classroom. Some children with ADHD have difficulty paying attention in class, while others are mainly hyperactive and impulsive. Some exhibit a combination of those behaviors. Children with ADHD are primarily known to lack the ability to inhibit behaviors and to use executive functions of the brain in planning. Current theories suggest it is a neurological dysfunction that will continue into adulthood.

The following represent the three types of ADHD:

- Combined ADHD (the most common type), which involves all of the symptoms

- Inattentive ADHD (previously known as ADD), which is marked by impaired attention and concentration

- Hyperactive-impulsive ADHD, which is marked by hyperactivity without inattentiveness

As with learning disabilities, many children with ADHD have normal intelligence. Similarly, this condition is more prevalent in males than in females. There is some evidence that it is hereditary and that relatives of many of these children had other problems, such as depression or tics. It is suggested that from 3 to 7 percent of the school population has ADHD although some researchers suggest that percentage is too low. (Hardman, Drew, Egan, 2011, p. 183.) There is often overlap between other conditions and ADHD, including the following: learning disabilities, emotional or behavior disorders, Tourette's syndrome (children burst out with inappropriate language at inappropriate times), and substance abuse as adults.

Children with ADHD may evidence any one or combination of the following symptoms:

- Difficulty paying attention to details and making careless mistakes

- Easily distracted by irrelevant stimuli, paying attention to irrelevant noises or events

- Inability to sustain focus on activities

- Difficulty finishing tasks such as homework or performance tasks that require concentration

- Shifting frequently from one task to another or shifting in conversation, not listening to others, not following details or rules

- Procrastinating

- Disorganized work habits

- Forgetfulness in daily activities such as bringing homework or instrument to school

Hyperactivity symptoms are usually present before the age of seven and look like the following:

- Getting up frequently to walk or run around

- Fidgeting and squirming while seated

- Having difficultly playing quietly

- Talking excessively

Some parents elect to use a category of drugs called psychostimulants, such as Ritalin, to help with behavioral inhibitions and executive functioning in children with ADHD.

Behavioral treatment is also available. Some parents do not elect treatment for their children. Regardless, it is the responsibility of teachers to take initiative in working with children with this disability. Many of the strategies suggested in Table 16.1 will be helpful to students with ADHD. The ideas in Box 16.4 are also directed to the specific needs of these children. Happily, music classes are places where children are encouraged to sing and move and play instruments and there are many opportunities to engage in a variety of tasks.

TABLE 16.1 Classroom Management Procedures

CLASSROOM PROCEDURE	POSSIBLE ADAPTATION
Entering and leaving classroom and finding place to sit.	Lines with leaders, single file, no talking, assigned seats or carpet squares—make it more musical by moving children to a drum, piano, or recorded signal. See also Chapter 11, on Cooperative Groups.
Distributing, holding, and collecting books.	Include children with emotional or behavior disorders or ADHD as leaders for the day or week to distribute and collect books—one book per child so there are no difficulties with sharing. Establish attitude of respect for the books. Model this process at beginning of year.
Distributing and playing instruments.	Model the correct way to hold mallets or other instruments and correct playing technique. Have children imitate teacher's model. Move around, not over, Orff-barred percussion instruments, leaving mallets in holders or on top of instruments.
	Distribute instruments one at a time to add color to a piece instead of taking a rhythm-band approach. Place hand percussion instruments under chair when finished, or collect immediately by instrument type, for example, placing all tambourines on the front table. Develop silent freeze signal if noise gets out of hand, for example, hand on chin or lights out. Immediately remove instrument from possession of student who is not respecting it.
Selecting a partner for a dance or giving an instrument to another person.	Avoid saying, "choose a partner." Use colored tags, shapes, numbering off, or letters signifying individuals. "Everyone with a red tag stand with someone with a blue tag. Move to the drumbeat for eight beats." "Pass your instrument to the person on your right."
Forming a circle or other formation for a dance.	Place Xs on floor with tape or white (washable) shoe polish in the proper formation. Stand on the X with no touching until given the signal.
Working in small groups for composition or other projects.	Establish cooperative groups of four to five with a balance of different types of children in them. Keep the groups consistent for at least three months. Let them select a group name. Always have them work in the same area of the room. Send group leader to collect and distribute instruments. (See Chapter 11 on Cooperative Groups.)
Establishing and reinforcing behavior standards	Have students generate a list of class rules (or teacher does so if necessary). Keep the list short and clear. Post it in front of room. Discuss the rules to make sure children understand what their responsibilities are. Refer to them regularly. Have children understand consequences of not following the rules, such as warnings, time-outs, or discussion with the teacher or parents.
	Try to use praise and positive reinforcement as much as possible. Be patient and calm. If a child is on a behavior modification plan, follow its guidelines in teaching music.
	Use nonverbal signals such as a gesture or a bell to signal the need for paying attention.

BOX 16.4 Teaching Strategies to Assist Students with ADHD

(These ideas will also help other students.)

1. Keep classroom well-organized and structured.
2. Have rules posted clearly in front of room.
3. Use nonverbal signals to suggest appropriate behaviors. (See Chapter 11 for ideas.)
4. Approach learning tasks through different modalities: auditory, visual, and tactile/ kinesthetic.
5. Intersperse low-interest tasks with high-interest tasks.
6. Limit the complexity of tasks. (See ideas for those with intellectual and learning disabilities in this chapter.)
7. Keep attention by keeping instruction high energy but focused on tasks, involving the children.
8. Reduce the length of written assignments.
9. Help individual students set goals for themselves in music learning, then help them monitor how and when they achieve those goals.
10. Reward students when they achieve goals.
11. Check for understanding of both content and process on a regular basis.

Emotional or Behavioral Disorders

The term *emotional or behavior disordered* is increasingly used to apply to children who might have previously been labeled emotionally disturbed, socially maladjusted, or psychotic. Children with schizophrenia or autism and those with affective disorder and anxiety disorder are also included in this category. The behaviors may have either a biological or a psychological cause.

Children identified as having emotional or behavior disorders are usually either very aggressive and act out (externalizers) or shy, anxious, and withdrawn (internalizers). Generally these children manifest behavior that is extreme, chronic, and unacceptable in terms of social or cultural norms. As a result of their behavior, they are often socially isolated and in trouble academically. Included in this category are also students who have bipolar disorder and those who have schizophrenia.

Because the range and variety of behaviors in these children is so broad and potentially disruptive, it is essential that the music specialist communicate with the special education teachers and school psychologists to know how best to adapt their teaching for successful mainstreaming or inclusion of these children. This planning needs to be done ahead of time because children with emotional or behavior disorders need (1) consistency in expectations, (2) clarity in the communication of those expectations, (3) options or choices, not mandates, (4) extrinsic guidelines and support for behavior modification, and (5) provision for practice of new skills. Writing a plan for behavior expectations into the IEP for these children helps to create clarity for the teacher, the student, and the parents. Happily, most of these children have normal intelligence and can be helped to gain needed social skills in the regular classroom and at home.

Music teachers need to anticipate places in their lessons that might be difficult for children with emotional or behavior disorders and implement procedures that will result in appropriate behaviors. The classroom procedures and adaptations highlighted in Table 16.1 are relevant to the teaching of all children. Many of the techniques in Chapter 11 will also be useful with these children.

In establishing an IEP for children with behavior disorders, the team needs to establish clear standards for children who may be disruptive and create agreements within the IEP for how their behavior is to be handled. Ideally, an aide will be sent with children who have those needs so that the child will be helped to focus during the music class.

Autism Spectrum Disorders

Even though autism is classified under emotional and behavioral disorders, it is worth focusing separately on this disorder. The Centers for Disease Control (CDC) estimates that approximately one in every one hundred people are affected by ASD (Kirk, Gallagher, Coleman, Anastasiow, 2012, p. 142).

Autism is a developmental disorder that occurs within the first three years of life. It affects the normal development of the brain in terms of social and communication skills. There are many theories about the cause of autism, but no clearly identified cause at this point. Brain chemistry and abnormal biology seem to be factors contributing to this disorder. As with learning disabilities and ADHD, boys are more commonly impacted by autism than girls.

Autism occurs across a wide spectrum from mild to severe. There are also related disabilities such as Asperger's syndrome, which is a mild form of autism. Children with Asperger's syndrome usually have normal intelligence and language development (although the rhythm, pitch, and emphasis are irregular), age-appropriate self-reliance, and interest in the world around them. They are often very bright and can have strong abilities in one or more areas of interest. Sometimes, they will be so verbal, they dominate conversations.

Children with autism spectrum disorders may exhibit the following behaviors:

- Perform repeated body movements
- Show unusual attachments to objects
- Show unusual distress when routines are changed
- Are highly sensitive in sight, hearing, touch, smell, or taste

As a result, they may:

- Get stuck on a single topic or task (perseveration)
- Have a short attention span and narrow interests
- Act up with intense tantrums
- Show aggression to self or others

Often children with autism struggle to relate to others and exhibit withdrawal symptoms instead. Eye contact and social interaction are difficult. Making friends and showing empathy are also challenges. Children with autism are often slow to develop language and what they do develop can be limited. Communication, therefore, is also limited. Sometimes gestures will be used but not pointing to direct attention to someone or something else. Rhymes or phrases from commercials or films are often repeated in rote fashion.

Sometimes there is heightened sensitivity to noise or loud sounds, which could be a negative factor in music classes. There may be withdrawal from physical contact.

Key for music teachers in working with children with autism is to accept the fact that a given child may be withdrawn, subject to distress with changes in routines, unable to communicate verbally, and may become upset at loud noises. At the same time, these children are often very bright and certainly capable of learning and of participating in class. In an IEP or team meeting, try to discover where the child is on the autism spectrum and what techniques will work with him or her. Sometimes pictures to suggest directions or tasks can be helpful. Keep the sequences of the events in the music classes similar from day to day. Inform the children as to when there is going to be a change. Simple games such as sitting in a circle and rolling a ball to individual children, asking them to sing a response, will allow the child with autism to be in the group but to respond individually. Always call the child by name. Be clear about expected behaviors using simple instructions. Do not force or punish a child for failing to do exactly what you want. Do not touch the child unless you know that is safe to do so.

If there are problems with a child in the music setting, check to find out what is happening with a child with autism in his/her other classes. Sharing ideas of what works and doesn't work can be helpful for all teachers involved in successfully meeting the needs of every child including those with autism.

Sensory Disorders

HEARING IMPAIRMENTS. Students with hearing impairments are often assumed to be incapable of perceiving sounds or of learning to make music, but nothing could be further from the truth. The term *hearing impairment* refers to a wide range of hearing losses. Most students who have hearing impairments are capable of hearing some musical sounds and responding to and performing music. Even children who are deaf can perceive vibration and pitch changes through their sense of touch, and they can learn to play various percussion and wind instruments as well as dance in time to music.

A person who is deaf may perceive some sounds, but not clearly enough to understand speech either with or without a hearing aid. It is very hard for children who are deaf to communicate aurally. They rely on vision. A child who has hearing loss can perceive enough sounds to be able to understand speech and communicate similarly to the normal hearing child. Most children with hearing impairments do not require special services. Most children who are deaf are now being served in regular schools, not in special schools for the deaf.

In working effectively with children with hearing impairments in music, the music specialist would benefit from knowing answers to the following questions:

1. What is the degree of the hearing loss?
   a. Mild (20–55 decibels): can understand conversation from three to five feet, gets confused in groups, may speech-read (read the movements of the mouth of a speaker)
   b. Moderate (55–70 decibels): can understand loud conversation only, may have impaired speech and language comprehension
   c. Severe (70–90 decibels): may hear loud sounds about one foot from ear, may identify some environmental sounds, probably has difficulties with speech (consonants) and language, uses vision to understand
   d. Profound (90–110 decibels): may hear some loud sounds but mostly senses vibrations, difficulty with speech and language, relies on vision rather than sound for communication
2. How are they receiving information?
   a. Through auditory learning (learning to listen to actual sounds)
   b. Through amplification instruments: hearing aid, microphone and hearing aid, or cochlear implant (find out what frequencies they can hear)

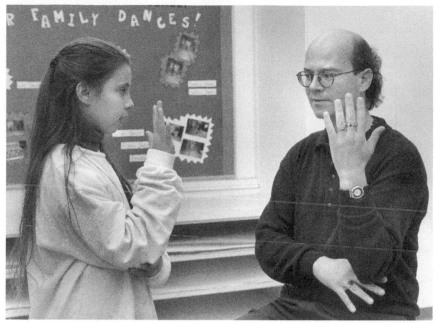

Teacher signing with a hearing-impaired child

  c. Through speech-reading (trying to understand through careful attention to a speaker's face)

  d. Through assistive technology that turns the spoken word into print.

 3. What methods are being used to teach them? (See Box 16.5.)

  a. Oral approaches: emphasis is placed on auditory, visual, and tactile means of reaching children; speech-reading; amplification; and talking (will need to sit where they can read speech)

  b. Total communication: use of speech-reading, signing, and finger spelling (may need an interpreter or a note taker and must sit where they can read speech)

  c. Various assistive technologies

BOX 16.5 Strategies for Working with Children with Hearing Impairments

Adapting for the child with hearing impairments may involve some or all of the following suggestions.

- Seat the child at the front of the room and make sure light falls on your face.

- Face the child and speak directly to him or her.

- Speak clearly but not too fast.

- Do not shout or raise the level of your voice.

- Cue children if you are going to ask them a question.

- Assign a note taker for older children.

- Use visual communication such as pictures, icons, charts, overheads, chalkboards, written notes. For example, for songs and words representing key concepts, place the page numbers in order on the chalkboard. Various assistive technologies can provide visual reinforcement of ideas for the children.

- If you are wearing a microphone, be sensitive to the potential of distortion from ambient noise and instruments. Have students adjust hearing aids accordingly.

(Continued)

BOX 16.5 (*Continued*)

- Model fingerings and mallet techniques for playing instruments.

- Have children touch instruments to feel vibrations: piano sounding board, body of the guitar, frame of a drum, the body of Orff bass bars (good for pitch discrimination).

- Give children instruments that have low frequencies or can be felt through the hand, such as rhythm sticks. Avoid instruments that have bright, piercing sounds.

- Do not expect that children in the moderate- to profound-loss categories can hear recorded music clearly.

- Use instruments such as alto recorders or Melodicas (with or without extensions) to work on pitch motion, articulation, breathing, and rhythm.

- Tap patterns on desks or other sound-conducting surfaces to help children feel meter and rhythm.

- When possible, teach music in rooms with wooden floors so that vibrations can be felt; a wooden platform increases the resonance potential of sounds from instruments such as pianos and xylophones.

- Place stereo speakers on the floor of a gymnasium, select music with a strong beat, such as popular dance music, and encourage hearing-impaired children to dance with their shoes off, feeling the music through vibrations in the floor.

- Help all children learn to sing some songs by signing; all children need to understand that there are many ways to communicate.

VISION IMPAIRED. Children with vision impairments constitute a very small percentage (0.4 percent) of the school-age population (US Department of Education, National Center for Education Statistics [2011]. *Digest of Education Statistics, 2010*). The causes of vision impairment and the degrees of loss of sight vary greatly. Children may have blurred vision or poor peripheral vision, be very nearsighted, see light and shadows, or see nothing. Many (about 30 percent) have other handicaps. Most attend regular classes with peers.

Again, the key for the music teacher is to understand the type of vision impairment a child has and to learn how to maximize use of any residual sight that might exist. Children who are legally blind (20/200 vision in best eye with correction) will probably be learning through a Braille system. Other students with vision impairments may use technological devices, such as the Optacon, that enlarge and raise regular print for easier reading. Other assistive technologies are available using computers to enlarge images and words for easier visual perception.

Music, an aural art, is readily accessible to the blind child through listening and imitation (see Box 16.6). Even if reading notation is involved, children can learn through a variety of concrete manipulatives (such as tongue depressors for rhythm patterns or magnet boards with raised staff for melody work) or through Braille notation. The ideas in Box 16.6 may help in adapting for the vision-impaired child.

Physical Disabilities

Children who are physically disabled may have an orthopedic impairment (involving the skeletal system and muscles), a neurologic impairment (involving the nervous system), or both. Cerebral palsy (CP) is a major cause of physical disabilities. In addition to CP, a whole range of accidents and diseases can result in physical handicaps. Some

BOX 16.6 Strategies for Working with Children Who Have Vision Impairments

1. Develop manipulatives to use for sensing through touch: sandpaper or felt notes, notes outlined in string, individual staffs to use at seats with staff raised up with layers of Elmer's glue or tape, tongue depressors for rhythm work, listening maps with raised patterns using glue or string, Braille notation or labels if necessary.

2. Enlarge notation through: patterns notated with black pen on tagboard, blowing a song up to a larger size through magnification on a copy machine, large notation on chalkboards or overheads, chart books available with music series, using an Optacon. Or adapt using assistive technology.

3. Use the auditory sense by: recording lessons or song materials on tape, explaining unusual noises, training auditory perception of sounds in foreground and background, verbally cuing when they are to play instruments or change chords, using playground balls with bells for activities using balls in music, identifying persons who are speaking by name.

4. Increase confidence in movement by: placing chairs and instruments in room consistently; using sighted partners for dancing or hula hoops, ropes tied in circles, parachutes for circle dances; talking students through patterned movements for dances or instrument playing; guiding individual movement in personal space in time, flowing with music; helping children move by walking next to them while supporting with a hand under their elbow (do not push or pull).

of these result in limited physical functioning because they affect breathing (asthma) or energy (diabetes or AIDS). Usually, treatment and schooling focus on what parts of the body are involved (one or more limbs) and whether the motor and perceptual-motor handicaps are mild, moderate, or severe.

Children with mild disabilities are usually able to improve motor and perceptual functioning with intervention, and they are able to keep up with peers in academic work. Children with moderate and severe disabilities may have some academic delays as well as motor-coordination problems that keep them from achieving age-level expectations. Physical and occupational therapists can help the music specialist understand how to best serve these children. For example, output for children who cannot verbally express their ideas can be through a communication board attached to their wheelchair or an assistive device using computer technology. These can often be operated using the breath or facial gesture.

Because there are so many different types of physical disabilities, it is important that the music teacher know the specific needs of each child in order to adapt instruction for them. The goal for all of these children is physical independence, participation, and control.

ADAPTING FOR MOVEMENT

- Create space for activities and sight lines that is accessible for wheelchairs (do not isolate nonambulatory children in back of music room or concert hall)

- If doing creative movement, have children move a part of their body they can still move: "Open and close your mouth to the beat"; "Click the rhythm pattern with your tongue"; "Stand and rock to show the beat"; "Lift your legs up and down"

- Use a standing table or walker for support for movement activities

- Do patterned dances in a space large and open enough that nonambulatory students can dance in their chairs; use music with a tempo they can manage

- Assign a sensitive ambulatory partner to dance with a nonambulatory student

© Carol Scott-Kassner

ADAPTING INSTRUMENTS AND MATERIALS

- Insert mallets, strikers, or small handles through a foam ball or small rubber ball for easier gripping

- Attach mallets or small instruments to hands or gloves with Velcro

- Use baby teething rings or rubber doorstops to strum Autoharps if child lacks pincer grasp

- Restring guitars or ukeleles if necessary for child to strum with left hand and chord with right

- Tape holes on soprano recorders closed to allow children with missing fingers to play

- Tape or clamp small instruments to desks or music stands for children to strike

- Use magnetic tape to attach lightweight bells or other small instruments to metal surfaces

© Carol Scott-Kassner

- Have one child hold an instrument while a partner with limited mobility strikes it
- Clip and tape paper to a clipboard for easier writing or drawing

English Language Learners (ELL)

The number of English Language Learners in the public schools of the United States increased by 2.3 million in the ten years from 1997 to 2007. Learning to function in English is crucial to adapting successfully in American society. Failure to speak English fluently is not a disability but it may mean that children struggle to succeed across the academic spectrum. Children who are learning English as a second or third or fourth language may come from a family where no English is spoken. Some may come from families where only English is spoken. Some may be second generation in America. Regardless, it is a paramount duty of the school system to help such children develop fluency in English so that they can learn and succeed in school and beyond.

There are several models in schools for teaching children to speak English.

1. **English immersion:** Instruction is entirely in English. Teachers strive to deliver lessons in simplified English so that students learn English and academic subjects.

2. **English as a second language:** May be the same as immersion but also may include some support to individuals in their native tongue. Typically, classes comprise students who speak many different languages but are not fluent in English. They may attend classes for only a period a day, to work strictly on English skills, or attend for a full day and focus both on academics and English.

3. **Transitional bilingual education:** Instruction for some subjects is in the students' native language but a certain amount of each day is spent on developing English skills. Classes are made up of students who share the same native language.

4. **Two-way bilingual or dual-language education:** Instruction is given in two languages to students, usually in the same classroom, who may be dominant in one language or the other, with the goal of the students' becoming proficient in both languages. Teachers usually team teach, with each one responsible to teach in only one of the languages. This approach is also sometimes called dual-immersion or dual-language.

It is overwhelming to realize that there may be as many as 82 different languages spoken in a single school district. Meeting such diverse needs is both a challenge and an invitation. Even though there may be ELL teachers in an elementary school, generally ELL students attend music and physical education classes for socialization purposes. Music is an ideal place to teach ELL students. Teachers should welcome each child and assign a student mentor to help him or her feel welcome and to coach them in the music classes. Having a world map posted in the room will allow all children to learn where the new child is from and locate that country on the map—a celebration of diversity. If you have a globe, show the location on a flat map, then spin the globe and have children find it on the globe.

When possible, it is helpful to teach songs in the languages of the ELL students. This allows them to become the experts and help to teach the others their native language. It also brings delight for them to hear a song from their country. This also helps the English-speaking students to understand the challenges of learning to sing in a language other than their own. Singing the same song in both languages helps everyone to feel connected in spite of differences in native language.

Learning to sing songs in English is a wonderful way to help ELL students succeed in English. The songs are repeated; they require fluency of production; they are often associated with stories, games, gestures, or images; children are not isolated and therefore are not embarrassed to be singled out; they hear English being modeled by English speakers; and they feel included and successful. Playing instruments, adding gestures to songs, and performing dances are all nonverbal activities common to music classes—leading to ease of participation and ready success for the ELL students. Adding visual images to story songs will also help ELL children learn to associate meaning with the words being sung. Parents of ELL students can often be wonderful resources of cultural knowledge, artifacts, and the arts if you ever plan to do an assembly focusing on their culture. Find ways to welcome and involve them.

Gifted and Talented

Children who are gifted (who show advanced, natural abilities, usually in the preschool years) or talented (who have a disposition toward something that they work hard to develop) are most likely to come to a music classroom without being previously identified for the music teacher as exceptional. Although some schools have separate self-contained classes for gifted and talented students, the music teacher will probably work with such children in the context of a heterogeneous group and will have to discover the gifts a child brings. It is rare that a program for gifted students will have screened for or recognized musical giftedness.

Generally, schools have used high IQ scores or achievement test scores as the single measure of giftedness. However, the federal definition of giftedness moves beyond intellectual giftedness to recognize advanced abilities in creativity, leadership, academics, and visual or performing arts. A focus on a broader view of intelligence has been supported by the theories of Guilford (1967) and Gardner (1983). Teachers who are aware of these more encompassing theories of intelligence are better prepared to recognize and build on the gifts each child may bring.

Because there is a range of ways of being gifted, it is difficult to create a single list that would apply to all children. However, children who are gifted are usually quick to relate ideas to each other (they are good at conceptualizing); can acquire and manipulate symbol systems easily, including those used in the arts; make good judgments; and can see broader implications of ideas than most of the general population. Furthermore, creatively gifted children often suggest unusual solutions to questions, use their intuitive sense, and have a sense of humor.

Although not all gifted students are musically gifted or talented, and not all elect to perform musically, much can be done to recognize the capacity of gifted children for accelerated learning.

If children show musical gifts or talents:

- Encourage private lessons with competent teachers
- Introduce notation to them so they can use it as a tool for musical independence
- Give them opportunities for musical leadership in class: teaching other children, conducting
- Have computer programs available so they can advance on their own in music theory and composition
- Have synthesizer or Musical Instrument Digital Interface (MIDI) hookups available so they can compose independently and print out their own music

> "It is rare that a program for gifted students will have screened for or recognized musical giftedness."

- Encourage them to use Internet and other resources to learn more about different kinds of music, learn to play various instruments, and learn about favorite artists and composers
- Make sure that school instrumental teachers are aware of their gifts, and help develop plans for careful articulation between the general music program and the instrumental program

If children are gifted in other ways:

- Provide activities that will allow them to expand their study of various musical ideas, such as the study of a composer, performing artist, or a kind of music that interests them; encourage independent research activities resulting in reports
- Challenge them with small group and individual composition assignments such as those suggested in Chapter 10; have a range of instruments available for their use
- Create a classroom with learning centers where gifted children can work independently on a range of projects such as music listening and research, learning to play the electronic keyboard or the guitar, composing, playing musical games, using music software on the computer, and exploring the Web.
- Bring in artists-in-residence or guests from the community to challenge children musically

The Joys of Reaching All Children

Working with exceptional children can be a rewarding experience for the music teacher. The keys to success are a willingness to learn, curiosity about how to be effective, clarity of communication with people who understand the needs and abilities of the children involved, and flexibility to change when something is not working.

Many resources are available to help teachers or parents who need more information on music therapy and music for children with special needs. Other resources, including classes in mainstreaming or inclusion, will connect you with the knowledge of a range of people who are committed to helping children learn. Through collaboration and cooperation, both teachers and children will be enriched and challenged to grow.

TECHNOLOGY LINKS *for* TEACHING *and* LEARNING *with* EXCEPTIONAL CHILDREN

With many recent developments of adaptive devices and software to drive them, technology is making huge strides to assist learning of exceptional children. Check out amazing technology available for exceptional learners. To learn more, visit the Technology Resources links in the MindTap.

MINDTAP

Scenario

MS. SMELTZER IS AN enthusiastic teacher who enjoys having a lot of activity in her music class. It is time for Mr. Mayes's third-grade class to come to music. Ms. Smeltzer stands next to the door and greets each child as they move to their assigned seats in the rows she has created. She happily greets the five children in wheelchairs who are mainstreamed into this class from their resource room. Those children take their place in their own row at the back of the class.

The class begins by singing a familiar song and discussing the patterns in the melody. Children sing those patterns in isolation and shape them in the air with their hands and then with their heads. They go on to learn to play two different melodic ostinatos and a bourdon on the barred percussion instruments. She uses adaptive techniques to allow the children with limited mobility to play the bourdon. Those children are assisted by the teacher aides who accompanied them to the class.

At the end of the class, the children from Mr. Mayes's class beg to play their favorite note-name game, in which groups identify names of patterns of notes that Ms. Smeltzer reveals, and team captains race to the front to be the first to write the word those notes spell on the board. The children in wheelchairs observe from their row.

Questions

1. What did Ms. Smeltzer do that showed sensitivity to the needs of the mainstreamed children?

2. What teaching strategies did not take the needs of those children into consideration?

3. Based on what you have learned in this chapter, how would you change any or all of the following to make this classroom more inclusive?

   - Seating
   - Relation to other students
   - Adaptation of materials
   - Adaptation of procedures
   - Adaptation of support
   - Classroom atmosphere

REVIEW

1. Define the following terms: child study team, LRE, IEP, mainstreaming, at-risk, and inclusion.

2. Describe the role the music specialist should play in making decisions concerning mainstreaming in music.

3. What is the difference between a disability and a handicap?

4. The key to effective integration of exceptional children in music is adapting. List several dimensions of the learning situation that the music teacher needs to consider adapting.

5. What levels of intellectual disability is the music specialist likely to work with? What are some key ideas in adapting for the child with such disabilities?

CRITICAL THINKING

1. What would you say to the parents of a child with hearing impairments who ask to have their child excused from music because of his or her hearing loss?

2. How would you respond to the request of a special education teacher that your select elementary chorus include her children with developmental delays?

3. Work with a partner to create an example of a potentially handicapping condition in an elementary general music class. Describe a way to change that situation so it would not be handicapping.

4. What could you do to establish an environment in which all students are responsive to the needs of exceptional students?

PROJECTS

1. Interview two elementary music specialists to determine how they work to integrate children with various needs. Find how they learn about the unique talents and needs of those children.

2. Visit a music classroom where children with various needs participate either through mainstreaming or inclusion. Note ways in which the teacher is adapting for the children. Note how the children respond.

3. Visit a music classroom in which the teacher is working with children in a self-contained setting. Describe the children and their responses to music. Describe ways the teacher is working to meet the needs of the children.

4. Review one or more references in music therapy, mainstreaming, or inclusion in music. List additional suggestions for adapting for children in a category of exceptionality of particular interest to you.

5. Create music materials to use with children who have vision impairments.

6. Do some one-on-one teaching with a child in one of the categories of exceptionality discussed in this chapter. Experiment with different musical tasks to discover how to best reach this child. Describe in a written report what the child was and was not able to do. Describe how you adapted instruction to meet the needs of the child.

7. Begin to build a collection of songs in various languages you might use in working with children designated as ELL as well as children who speak English already.

MINDTAP Visit **MindTap** to access classroom videos, audio, and more!

APPENDIX

The School Music Program: A New Vision

PREKINDERGARTEN (AGE 2–4)

The years before children enter kindergarten are critical for their musical development. Young children need a rich musical environment in which to grow. The increasing number of day-care centers, nursery schools, and early-intervention programs for children with disabilities and children at risk suggests that information should be available about the musical needs of infants and young children and that standards for music should be established for these learning environments as well as for K–12 settings.[1]

The standards outlined in this section reflect the following beliefs concerning the musical learning of young children:

1. All children have musical potential.

2. Children bring their own unique interests and abilities to the music learning environment.

3. Very young children are capable of developing critical thinking skills through musical ideas.

4. Children come to early-childhood music experiences from diverse backgrounds.

5. Children should experience exemplary musical sounds, activities, and materials.

6. Children should not be encumbered with the need to meet performance goals.

7. Children's play is their work.

8. Children learn best in pleasant physical and social environments.

9. Diverse learning environments are needed to serve the developmental needs of many individual children.

10. Children need effective adult models.

Curriculum Guidelines

A music curriculum for young children should include many opportunities to explore sound through singing, moving, listening, and playing instruments, as well as introductory experiences with verbalization and visualization of musical ideas. The music literature included in the curriculum should be of high quality and lasting value, including traditional children's songs, folk songs, classical music, and music from a variety of cultures, styles, and time periods.[2]

Play is the primary vehicle for young children's growth, and developmentally appropriate early music experiences should occur in child-initiated, child-directed, teacher-supported play environments. In prekindergarten, the teacher's role is to create a musically stimulating environment and then to facilitate children's engagement with music materials and activities by asking questions or making suggestions that stimulate children's thinking and further exploration.

Children also need group music time to experience the important social and musical aspects of sharing music and making music together. Ideally this should be delivered by either early-childhood arts specialists employed as staff members in child-care centers and preschools or by visiting music specialists with training in child development, in order to provide musicality and creativity and to serve as models and consultants for the child-care staff.

Effective music teaching in the prekindergarten should:
1. Support the child's total development—physical, emotional, social, and cognitive.

2. Recognize the wide range of normal development in prekindergartners and the need to differentiate instruction.

3. Facilitate learning through active interaction with adults and other children as well as with music materials.

4. Consist of learning activities and materials that are real, concrete, and relevant to the lives of young children.

5. Provide opportunities for children to choose from among a variety of music activities, materials, and equipment of varying degrees of difficulty.

6. Allow children time to explore music through active involvement.

Assessment

The assessment of prekindergarten children provides special challenges. A substantial body of music education research has determined that young children know and understand much more about music than they can verbalize. Also, young children have not yet developed the ability to respond in a paper-and-pencil testing format. Another factor that affects their assessment is the very wide range of individual developmental differences displayed by young children.

Because of these characteristics, methods of assessment that are most appropriate to assess young children's music knowledge, skills, and attitudes include: (1) checklists or anecdotal reports completed by teachers, parents, or aides to record and describe verbal and nonverbal behavior; (2) systematic observation documenting such behavior as time on task, number of instances of an event or behavior, and participation tendencies over time; and (3) rating scales to provide data related to quality of responses, such as degrees of accuracy, originality, or involvement. Finished products and correct solutions are not the only criteria for judging whether learning has occurred. Audio and video recording are recommended methods of gathering samples of children's musical behavior for assessment and of examining growth and development over time. In order to develop a profile of each child's musical responses, representative samples of assessment materials should be placed in a music portfolio that is maintained for each child, beginning with the child's entrance into an educational/child-care setting and culminating with entrance into kindergarten.

Music Experiences for Infants and Toddlers

Infants and very young children experience music by hearing it, by feeling it, and by experimenting with pitch and timbre in their vocalizations. Children should experience music daily while receiving caring, physical contact. Adults can encourage the musical development of infants by:

1. Singing and chanting to them, using songs and rhymes representing a variety of meters and tonalities

2. Imitating the sounds infants make

3. Exposing them to a wide variety of vocal, body, instrumental, and environmental sounds

4. Providing exposure to selected live and recorded music

5. Rocking, patting, touching, and moving with children to the beat, rhythm patterns, and melodic direction of music they hear

6. Providing safe toys that make musical sounds the children can control

7. Talking about music and its relationship to expression and feeling

Musical Experiences for Two-, Three-, and Four-Year-Old Children

Two-, three-, and four-year-old children need an environment that includes a variety of sound sources, selected recorded music, and opportunities for free improvised singing and the building of a repertoire of songs. An exploratory approach, using a wide range of appropriate materials, provides a rich base from which conceptual understanding can evolve in later years. A variety of individual musical experiences is important for children at this age, with little emphasis on activities that require children to perform together as a unit. As a result of their experiences with music, four-year-olds should initiate both independent and collaborative play with musical materials, and they should demonstrate curiosity about music.

The standards in this section are intended for age four. The skills of young children develop along a continuum, and developmentally appropriate activities should be used at earlier levels. Age five is included in the K–4 section.

1. Content Standard: Singing and playing instruments
   Achievement Standard: Children

   a. Use their voices expressively as they speak, chant, and sing

   b. Sing a variety of simple songs in various keys, meters, and genres,[3] alone and with a group, becoming increasingly accurate in rhythm and pitch

   c. Experiment with a variety of instruments and other sound sources

   d. Play simple melodies and accompaniments on instruments

2. Content Standard: Creating music
   Achievement Standard: Children

   a. Improvise songs to accompany their play activities

   b. Improvise instrumental accompaniments to songs, recorded selections, stories, and poems

c. Create short pieces of music, using voices, instruments, and other sound sources

d. Invent and use original graphic or symbolic systems to represent vocal and instrumental sounds and musical ideas

3. Content Standard: Responding to music
Achievement Standard: Children

a. Identify the sources of a wide variety of sounds[4]

b. Respond through movement to music of various tempos, meters, dynamics, modes, genres, and styles to express what they hear and feel in works of music[5]

c. Participate freely in music activities

4. Content Standard: Understanding music
Achievement Standard: Children

a. Use their own vocabulary and standard music vocabulary to describe voices, instruments, music notation, and music of various genres, styles, and periods from diverse cultures

b. Sing, play instruments, move, or verbalize to demonstrate awareness of the elements of music and changes in their usage[6]

c. Demonstrate an awareness of music as a part of daily life

NOTES

1. "MENC Position Statement on Early Childhood Education," *MENC Soundpost* 8, no. 2 (winter 1992): 21–22.

2. "MENC Position Statement on Early Childhood Education," 21.

3. E.g., opera, chamber music, hip hop, Japanese gagaku, South African mbube

4. E.g., crying baby, piano, guitar, car horn, bursting balloon

5. E.g., folk songs, ethnic songs, singing games

6. E.g., changes in rhythm, dynamics, tempo

From *National Standards for Arts Education.* Copyright © 1994 by Music Educators National Conference (MENC). Used by permission. The complete National Arts Standards and additional materials relating to the Standards are available from MENC—The National Association for Music Education, 1806 Robert Fulton Drive, Reston, VA 20191.

GRADES K–4

Performing, creating, and responding to music are the fundamental music processes in which humans engage. Students, particularly in grades K–4, learn by doing. Singing, playing instruments, moving to music, and creating music enable them to acquire musical skills and knowledge that can be developed in no other way. Learning to read and notate music gives them a skill with which to explore music independently and with others. Listening to, analyzing, and evaluating music are important building blocks of musical learning. Further, to participate fully in a diverse, global society, students must understand their own historical and cultural heritage and those of others within their communities and beyond. Because music is a basic expression of human culture, every student should have access to a balanced, comprehensive, and sequential program of study in music.

The standards in this section describe the cumulative skills and knowledge expected of all students upon exiting grade 4. Students in the earlier grades should engage in developmentally appropriate learning experiences designed to prepare them to achieve these standards at grade 4. Determining the curriculum and the specific instructional activities necessary to achieve the standards is the responsibility of states, local school districts, and individual teachers.

1. Content Standard: Singing, alone and with others, a varied repertoire of music
Achievement Standard: Students

a. Sing independently, on pitch and in rhythm, with appropriate timbre, diction, and posture, and maintain a steady tempo

b. Sing expressively, with appropriate dynamics, phrasing, and interpretation

c. Sing from memory a varied repertoire of songs representing genres and styles from diverse cultures

d. Sing ostinati, partner songs, and rounds

e. Sing in groups, blending vocal timbres, matching dynamic levels, and responding to the cues of a conductor

2. Content Standard: Performing on instruments, alone and with others, a varied repertoire of music
Achievement Standard: Students

a. Perform on pitch, in rhythm, with appropriate dynamics and timbre, and maintain a steady tempo

b. Perform easy rhythmic, melodic, and chordal patterns accurately and independently on rhythmic, melodic, and harmonic classroom instruments

c. Perform expressively a varied repertoire of music representing diverse genres and styles

d. Echo short rhythms and melodic patterns

e. Perform in groups, blending instrumental timbres, matching dynamic levels, and responding to the cues of a conductor

f. Perform independent instrumental parts[1] while other students sing or play contrasting parts

3. Content Standard: Improvising melodies, variations, and accompaniments

Achievement Standard: Students

a. Improvise "answers" in the same style to given rhythmic and melodic phrases

b. Improvise simple rhythmic and melodic ostinato accompaniments

c. Improvise simple rhythmic variations and simple melodic embellishments on familiar melodies

d. Improvise short songs and instrumental pieces, using a variety of sound sources, including traditional sounds, nontraditional sounds available in the classroom, body sounds, and sounds produced by electronic means[2]

4. Content Standard: Composing and arranging music within specified guidelines

Achievement Standard: Students

a. Create and arrange music to accompany readings or dramatizations

b. Create and arrange short songs and instrumental pieces within specified guidelines[3]

c. Use a variety of sound sources when composing

5. Content Standard: Reading and notating music

Achievement Standard: Students

a. Read whole, half, dotted half, quarter, and eighth notes and rests in +, T, and Y meter signatures

b. Use a system (that is, syllables, numbers, or letters) to read simple pitch notation in the treble clef in major keys

c. Identify symbols and traditional terms referring to dynamics, tempo, and articulation and interpret them correctly when performing

d. Use standard symbols to notate meter, rhythm, pitch, and dynamics in simple patterns presented by the teacher

6. Content Standard: Listening to, analyzing, and describing music

Achievement Standard: Students

a. Identify simple music forms when presented aurally

b. Demonstrate perceptual skills by moving, by answering questions about, and by describing aural examples of music of various styles representing diverse cultures

c. Use appropriate terminology in explaining music, music notation, music instruments and voices, and music performances

d. Identify the sounds of a variety of instruments, including many orchestra and band instruments, and instruments from various cultures, as well as children's voices and male and female adult voices

e. Respond through purposeful movement[4] to selected prominent music characteristics[5] or to specific music events[6] while listening to music

7. Content Standard: Evaluating music and music performances

Achievement Standard: Students

a. Devise criteria for evaluating performances and compositions

b. Explain, using appropriate music terminology, their personal preferences for specific musical works and styles

8. Content Standard: Understanding relationships between music, the other arts, and disciplines outside the arts

Achievement Standard: Students

a. Identify similarities and differences in the meanings of common terms[7] used in the various arts

b. Identify ways in which the principles and subject matter of other disciplines taught in the school are interrelated with those of music[8].

9. Content Standard: Understanding music in relation to history and culture

Achievement Standard: Students

a. Identify by genre or style aural examples of music from various historical periods and cultures

b. Describe in simple terms how elements of music are used in music examples from various cultures of the world[9]

c. Identify various uses of music in their daily experiences[10] and describe characteristics that make certain music suitable for each use

d. Identify and describe roles of musicians[11] in various music settings and cultures

e. Demonstrate audience behavior appropriate for the context and style of music performed

NOTES

1. E.g., simple rhythmic or melodic ostinati, contrasting rhythmic lines, harmonic progressions and chords

434

2. E.g., traditional sounds: voices, instruments; nontraditional sounds: paper tearing, pencil tapping; body sounds: hands clapping, fingers snapping; sounds produced by electronic means: personal computers and basic MIDI devices, including keyboards, sequencers, synthesizers, and drum machines

3. E.g., a particular style, form, instrumentation, compositional technique

4. E.g., swaying, skipping, dramatic play

5. E.g., meter, dynamics, tempo

6. E.g., meter changes, dynamic changes, same/different sections

7. E.g., form, line, contrast

8. E.g., foreign languages: singing songs in various languages; language arts: using the expressive elements of music in interpretive readings; mathematics: mathematical basis of values of notes, rests, and meter signatures; science: vibration of strings, drum heads, or air columns generating sounds used in music; geography: songs associated with various countries or regions

9. E.g., Navajo, Arabic, Latin American

10. E.g., celebration of special occasions, background music for television, worship

11. E.g., orchestra conductor, folksinger, church organist

From *National Standards for Arts Education*. Copyright © 1994 by Music Educators National Conference (MENC). Used by permission. The complete National Arts Standards and additional materials relating to the Standards are available from MENC—The National Association for Music Education, 1806 Robert Fulton Drive, Reston, VA 20191.

GRADES 5–8

The period represented by grades 5–8 is especially critical in students' musical development. The music they perform or study often becomes an integral part of their personal musical repertoire. Composing and improvising provide students with unique insight into the form and structure of music and at the same time help them to develop their creativity. Broad experience with a variety of music is necessary if students are to make informed musical judgments. Similarly, this breadth of background enables them to begin to understand the connections and relationships between music and other disciplines. By understanding the cultural and historical forces that shape social attitudes and behaviors, students are better prepared to live and work in communities that are increasingly multicultural. The role that music will play in students' lives depends in large measure on the level of skills they achieve in creating, performing, and listening to music.

Except as noted, the standards in this section describe the cumulative skills and knowledge expected of all students upon exiting grade 8. Students in grades 5–7 should engage in developmentally appropriate learning experiences to prepare them to achieve these standards at grade 8. These standards presume that the students have achieved the standards specified for grades K–4; they assume that the students will demonstrate higher levels of the expected skills and knowledge, will deal with increasingly complex music, and will provide more sophisticated responses to works of music. Every course in music, including performance courses, should provide instruction in creating, performing, listening to, and analyzing music, in addition to focusing on its specific subject matter. Determining the curriculum and the specific instructional activities necessary to achieve the standards is the responsibility of states, local school districts, and individual teachers.

1. Content Standard: Singing, alone and with others, a varied repertoire of music
   Achievement Standard: Students

   a. Sing accurately and with good breath control throughout their singing ranges, alone and in small and large ensembles

   b. Sing with expression and technical accuracy a repertoire of vocal literature with a level of difficulty of 2, on a scale of 1 to 6, including some songs performed from memory

   c. Sing music representing diverse genres and cultures, with expression appropriate for the work being performed

   d. Sing music written in two and three parts

   Students who participate in a choral ensemble

   e. Sing with expression and technical accuracy a varied repertoire of vocal literature with a level of difficulty of 3, on a scale of 1 to 6, including some songs performed from memory

2. Content Standard: Performing on instruments, alone and with others, a varied repertoire of music
   Achievement Standard: Students

   a. Perform on at least one instrument[1] accurately and independently, alone and in small and large ensembles, with good posture, good playing position, and good breath, bow, or stick control

   b. Perform with expression and technical accuracy on at least one string, wind, percussion, or classroom instrument a repertoire of instrumental literature with a level of difficulty of 2, on a scale of 1 to 6

c. Perform music representing diverse genres and cultures, with expression appropriate for the work being performed

d. Play by ear simple melodies on a melodic instrument and simple accompaniments on a harmonic instrument

Students who participate in an instrumental ensemble or class

e. Perform with expression and technical accuracy a varied repertoire of instrumental literature with a level of difficulty of 3, on a scale of 1 to 6, including some solos performed from memory

3. Content Standard: Improvising melodies, variations, and accompaniments
Achievement Standard: Students

a. Improvise simple harmonic accompaniments

b. Improvise melodic embellishments and simple rhythmic and melodic variations on given pentatonic melodies and melodies in major keys

c. Improvise short melodies, unaccompanied and over given rhythmic accompaniments, each in a consistent style, meter, and tonality

4. Content Standard: Composing and arranging music within specified guidelines
Achievement Standard: Students

a. Compose short pieces within specified guidelines,[2] demonstrating how the elements of music are used to achieve unity and variety, tension and release, and balance

b. Arrange simple pieces for voices or instruments other than those for which the pieces were written

c. Use a variety of traditional and nontraditional sound sources and electronic media when composing and arranging

5. Content Standard: Reading and notating music
Achievement Standard: Students

a. Read whole, half, quarter, eighth, sixteenth, and dotted notes and rests in +, T, Y, Z, K, and alla breve meter signatures

b. Read at sight simple melodies in both the treble and bass clefs

c. Identify and define standard notation symbols for pitch, rhythm, dynamics, tempo, articulation, and expression

d. Use standard notation to record their musical ideas and the musical ideas of others

Students who participate in a choral or instrumental ensemble or class

e. Sight-read, accurately and expressively, music with a level of difficulty of 2, on a scale of 1 to 6

6. Content Standard: Listening to, analyzing, and describing music
Achievement Standard: Students

a. Describe specific music events[3] in a given aural example, using appropriate terminology

b. Analyze the uses of elements of music in aural examples representing diverse genres and cultures

c. Demonstrate knowledge of the basic principles of meter, rhythm, tonality, intervals, chords, and harmonic progressions in their analyses of music

7. Content Standard: Evaluating music and music performances
Achievement Standard: Students

a. Develop criteria for evaluating the quality and effectiveness of music performances and compositions and apply the criteria in their personal listening and performing

b. Evaluate the quality and effectiveness of their own and others' performances, compositions, arrangements, and improvisations by applying specific criteria appropriate for the style of the music and offer constructive suggestions for improvement

8. Content Standard: Understanding relationships between music, the other arts, and disciplines outside the arts
Achievement Standard: Students

a. Compare in two or more arts how the characteristic materials of each art[4] can be used to transform similar events, scenes, emotions, or ideas into works of art

b. Describe ways in which the principles and subject matter of other disciplines taught in the school are interrelated with those of music[5]

9. Content Standard: Understanding music in relation to history and culture
Achievement Standard: Students

a. Describe distinguishing characteristics of representative music genres and styles from a variety of cultures[6]

b. Classify by genre and style (and, if applicable, by historical period, composer, and title) a varied body of exemplary (that is, high-quality and characteristic) musical works and explain the characteristics that cause each work to be considered exemplary

c. Compare, in several cultures of the world, functions music serves, roles of musicians,[7] and conditions under which music is typically performed

NOTES

1. E.g., band or orchestra instrument, keyboard instrument, fretted instrument, electronic instrument

2. E.g., a particular style, form, instrumentation, compositional technique

3. E.g., entry of oboe, change of meter, return of refrain

4. I.e., sound in music, visual stimuli in visual arts, movement in dance, human interrelationships in theater

5. E.g., language arts: issues to be considered in setting texts to music; mathematics: frequency ratios of intervals; sciences: the human hearing process and hazards to hearing; social studies: historical and social events and movements chronicled in or influenced by musical works

6. E.g., jazz, mariachi, gamelan

7. E.g., lead guitarist in a rock band, composer of jingles for commercials, singer in Beijing Opera

REFERENCES *and* RESOURCES

Abeles, H. F., and L. A. Custodero, eds. (2009). *Critical issues in music education*. New York: Oxford University Press.

Abeles, H. F., C. Hoffer, and R. H. Klotman (1993). *Foundations of music education* (2nd ed.). New York: Schirmer Books.

Abrahams, R. D. (2005). *Everyday life: A poetics of the vernacular*. Philadelphia: University of Pennsylvania Press.

Abramson, R. (1973). *Rhythm games*. New York: Movement Press.

___ (2003). *Feel it! Rhythm games for all* (Book/CDs). Miami, FL: Warner Bros..

Adamek, M. S. (2001). Meeting special needs in music class. *Music Educators Journal*, 87(4), January, 23–26.

Adzinyah, D. M., D. Maraire, and J. C. Tucker (1996). *Let your voice be heard*. Danbury, CT: World Music Press.

Aliki (1968). *Hush little baby: A folk lullaby*. New York: Simon & Schuster Books for Young Children.

Alvin, J., and A. Warwick (1991). *Music therapy for the autistic child* (2nd ed.). Oxford, England: Oxford University Press.

Anderson, W. M., and P. S. Campbell, eds. (2010). *Multicultural perspectives in music education* (3rd ed.). Reston, VA: Rowman & Littlefield.

Andress, B. (1998). *Music for young children*. Fort Worth, TX: Harcourt Brace College Publishers.

Appadurai, A (1996). *Modernity at large*. Minneapolis: University of Minnesota Press.

___ (2001). *Globalization*. Durham, NC: Duke University Press.

Atterbury, B. W. (1990). *Mainstreaming exceptional learners in music*. Englewood Cliffs, NJ: Prentice Hall.

Ausubel, D. P. (1968). *Educational psychology*. New York: Holt, Rinehart & Winston.

___ (2000). *The acquisition and retention of knowledge: A cognitive view*. Dordrecht, Netherlands: Kluwer Academic.

Bandura, A. (1977). *Social learning theory*. Englewood Cliffs, NJ: Prentice Hall.

___(1986). *Social foundations of thought and action*. Englewood Cliffs, NJ: Prentice Hall.

___(1997). *Self-efficacy: The exercise of control*. New York: W. H. Freeman.

Banks, J. A. (2012). *Encyclopedia of Diversity in Education*. Thousand Oaks, CA: Sage.

Banks, J. A., and C. M. Banks (2004). *Handbook of research in multicultural education*. New York: Macmillan.

___ (2007). *Multicultural education: Issues and perspectives*. New York: Wiley.

Barbe, W. B., and R. S. Swassing (1979). *Teaching through modality strengths: Concepts and practices*. Columbus, OH: Zaner Bloser.

Bartle, J. A. (2003). *Sound advice: Becoming a better children's choir director*. New York: Oxford University Press.

Barrett, J. R., C. W. McCoy, and K. K. Veblen (1997). *Sound ways of knowing: Music in the interdisciplinary curriculum*. New York: Schirmer.

Barrett, M. (1996). Children's aesthetic decision making: An analysis of children's musical discourse as composers. *International Journal of Music Education*, 28, 37–62.

___(1998). Researching children's compositional processes and products: Connections to music education? In B. Sundin, G. E. McPherson, and G. Folkestad, eds., *Children composing* (chapter 1). Malmö, Sweden: Lund University, Malmö Academy of Music.

Bateson, G. (1978). *Steps to an ecology of mind*. New York: Ballantine Books.

Bateson, G., and R. Donaldson (1991). *A sacred unity: Further steps to an ecology of mind*. New York: Harper Collins.

Bay, W., and M. Christiansen (2000). *Mastering the guitar class method*. Pacific, MO: Mel Bay.

Bennett, P., and D. Bartholomew (1997). *SongWorks I and SongWorks II*. Belmont, CA: Thomson.

Bennett, P. (2010). *Rhyme play: Playing with children and Mother Goose*. Van Nuys, CA: Alfred Music.

___ (2011). *Playing with the classics: Music masterworks for children*. Van Nuys, CA: Alfred Music.

___ (2012). *Playing with the classics: Music masterworks for children*. Van Nuys, CA: Alfred Music.

Berger, D. S. (2002). *Music therapy, sensory integration, and the autistic child*. London: Jessica Kingsley.

Blacking, J. (1985). Quote from unpublished lecture.

___ (1995). *Venda children's song*. Chicago: University of Chicago Press.

Blankinship, D. G. (2012). Study: Once-a-year teacher evaluations not enough. *Seattle Times*, January 6, 2012.

Bloom, K., and R. Shreeves (1998). *Moves: A sourcebook of ideas for body awareness*. London: Routledge.

Boardman, E., ed. (1989). *Dimensions of musical thinking*. Reston, VA: Music Educators National Conference.

Boyle, J. D., and R. E. Radocy (1987). *Measurement and evaluation of musical experiences*. New York: Schirmer Books.

Bronfenbrenner, U. (1979). *The ecology of human development*. Cambridge MA: Harvard University Press.

___ (1996). *The state of Americans: This generation and the next*. New York: Free Press.

___ (2004). *Making human beings human: Bioecological perspectives on human development*. Thousand Oaks, CA: Sage.

Brophy, T. S. (2001). Developing improvisation in general music classes. *Music Educators Journal* 88(1), 34–41, 53.

Bruner, J. (1960). *The process of education*. New York: McGraw-Hill.

___ (1966). *Toward a theory of instruction*. Cambridge, MA: Harvard University.

___ (1996). *The culture of education*. Cambridge, MA: Harvard University Press.

Brunk, B. K. (2004). *Music therapy: Another path to learning and communication for children in the autism spectrum*. Paddyfield UK: Future Horizons.

Burakoff, G., and S. Burakoff (1997). *Hands on recorder*. Ft. Worth, TX: Sweet Pipes.

Campbell, B., L. Campbell, and D. Dickinson (1992). *Teaching and learning through multiple intelligences*. Stanwood, WA: New Horizons for Learning.

Campbell, P. S. (1991). *Lessons from the world*. New York: Schirmer Books.

___ (2004). *Teaching music globally*. New York: Oxford University Press.

___ (2008). *Tunes and grooves in music education*. Upper Saddle River, NJ: Pearson.

___ (2010). *Songs in their heads: Music and its meaning in children's lives* (2nd ed.). New York: Oxford University Press.

Campbell, P. S., and J. Bannerman (2010). Anatomy of Mused 452: A course called ethnomusicology in the schools. *Diskussion Musikpedagogik*, 48, 10.

Campbell, P. S., with A. L. Frega (2001). *Canciones de America Latina: De su origen a la escuela*. Miami, FL: Warner Bros.

Campbell, P. S., E. McCullough-Brabson, and J. C. Tucker (1994). *Roots and branches*. Danbury, CT: World Music Press.

Campbell, P. S., and T. Wiggins (2013). *Oxford handbook of children's musical cultures*. New York: Oxford University Press.

Campbell, P. S., S. Williamson, and P. Perron (1996). *Traditional songs of singing cultures*. Miami, FL: Warner Bros.

Chen-Haftek, L. (2004). Music and movement from zero to three: A window to children's musicality. *Proceedings of the 11th International Conference of the ISME Early Childhood Commission*. Barcelona, Spain: Escola Superior de Musica de Catalunya.

Chiesa, M. (2004). *Radical behaviorism: The philosophy and the science*. Cambridge, MA: Authors Cooperative.

Choksy, L. (1999a). *The Kodály method I: Comprehensive music education* (3rd ed.). Upper Saddle River, NJ: Prentice Hall.

___ (1999b). *The Kodály method II: Folksong to masterwork*. Upper Saddle River, NJ: Prentice Hall.

Choksy, L., R. M. Abramson, A. E. Gillespie, D. Woods, and F. York (2000). *Teaching music in the twenty-first century*. Upper Saddle River, NJ: Prentice Hall.

Cohen, L. (1994). Anthem. In D. Schiller, ed., *The little Zen companion*. New York: Workman.

Cole, J. (1982). *Best-loved folk tales*. Garden City, NY: Anchor Press/Doubleday.

Colwell, R., ed. (1992). Section D: Perception and cognition. In *Handbook of research on music teaching and learning*. New York: Schirmer Books.

Cornett, C. E. (2003). *Creating meaning through literature and the arts: An integration resource for classroom teachers* (2nd ed.). Upper Saddle-River, NJ: Merrill Prentice-Hall.

Csikszentmihalyi, M. (1990). *Flow: The psychology of optimal experience*. New York: Harper & Row.

Custodero, L. (2002). Connecting with the musical moment: Observations of flow experience in pre-school-aged children. *Proceedings of the 10th International Conference of the ISME Early Childhood Commission* (pp. 68–74). Copenhagen, Denmark: Danish University of Education.

Dadson, P., and D. McGlashan (1995). *The from scratch rhythm workbook.* Portsmouth, NH: Heinemann.

Daniels, D., and V. Price (2000). *The essential enneagram: The definitive personality test and self-discovery guide.* New York: HarperCollins. Originally published as *The Stanford enneagram discovery inventory and guide.*

Daniels, H., M. Cole, and J. V. Wertsch, eds. (2007). *The Cambridge companion to Vygotsky.* New York: Cambridge University Press.

Deliege, I., and J. Sloboda (1996). *Musical beginnings.* New York: Oxford University Press.

Dissanayake, E. (2001). Aesthetic incunabula. *Philosophy and Literature,* 25(2), 3335–3346.

Drake, S. M. (1993). *Planning the integrated curriculum: The call to adventure.* Alexandria, VA: Association for Supervision and Curriculum Development.

Dreikurs, R. (1968). *Psychology in the classroom.* New York: Harper & Row.

Dunbar-Hall, P., and G. Hodge (1991). *A guide to music around the world.* Marrickville, NSW, Australia: Science Press.

Duncan, A. (2010). *The National Endowment for the Arts. Strategic Plan FY 2012–2016.* <www.nea.gov/about/Budget/NEAStrategic Plan 2012-2016.pdf>

Dunn, R., and K. Dunn (1992). *Teaching elementary students through individual learning styles.* New York: Allyn & Bacon.

East, H. (1989). *The singing sack: 28 song-stories from around the world.* London, England: A & C Black.

Edelstein, S., L. Choksy, P. Lehman, N. Sigurdsson, and D. Woods (1980). *Creating curriculum in music.* Menlo Park, CA: Addison-Wesley.

Eisner, E. W. (2002) *Arts and the creation of mind.* New Haven, CT: Yale University Press.

Ellis, C. J. (1986). *Aboriginal music, education for living: Cross-cultural experiences.* St. Lucia, Queensland: University of Queensland.

Erdei, P., and K. Komlos (1974). *150 American folk songs for children to sing and play.* New York: Boosey & Hawkes.

Ericsson, A. K., N. Charness, P. Feltovich, and R. R. Hoffman (2006). *Cambridge handbook on expertise and expert performance.* Cambridge, UK: Cambridge University Press.

Espeland, M. (1987). Music in use: Responsive music listening in the primary school. *British Journal of Music Education,* 4(3), 283–297.

Evans, D. (1978). *Sharing sounds.* London: Longman.

Fay, J., and D. Funk (1995). *Teaching with love and logic: Taking control of the classroom.* Golden, CO: The Love and Logic Press.

Feierabend, J. (1999). *First steps in music.* Simsbury, CT: GIA.

___ (2002a). *The book of simple songs and circles* (2nd ed.). Simsbury, CT: GIA.

___ (2002b). *The book of bounces* (2nd ed.). Simsbury, CT: GIA.

Finckel, E. A. (1993). *Now we'll make the rafters ring: 100 traditional and contemporary rounds for everyone.* Pennington, NJ: A Cappella Books.

Fitzgerald, M., K. McCord, and S. Berg, (2003). *Chop-Monster Jr.: Jazz language tutor for general music education.* Van Nuys, CA: Alfred.

Fletcher, P. (2001). *World musics in context.* New York: Oxford University Press.

Flohr, J. (1985). Young children's improvisations: Emerging creative thought. *The Creative Child and Adult Quarterly,* 10(2), 79–85.

___ (2005). *The musical lives of young children.* Upper Saddle River, N.J.: Prentice Hall Music Education Series.

Forrai, K. (1988). *Music in preschool* (J. Sinor, Trans.). Budapest, Hungary: Corvina Press.

Fowke, E. (1969). *Sally go round the sun.* Garden City, NY: Doubleday.

___ (1977). *Ring around the moon.* Englewood Cliffs, NJ: Prentice Hall.

Fowler, C. (1974). *The arts process.* Harrisburg: Pennsylvania Department of Education.

___ (1994). *Music! Its role and importance in our lives.* New York: Glencoe.

Fraser, D. L. (2000). *Danceplay.* Lincoln NE: iUniverse.com.

Frazee, J. (1987). *Discovering Orff: A curriculum for music teachers.* New York: Schott.

___ (1999). *Discovering Keetman.* New York: Schott.

___ (2007). *Orff Schulwerk today.* New York: Schott.

Freed-Garrod, J. (1999). Assessment in the arts: Elementary-aged students as qualitative assessors of their own and peers musical compositions. *Bulletin of the Council for Research in Music Education,* 139, Winter, 50–63.

Gagné, R. M. (1993). *The conditions of learning* (4th ed.). New York: Holt, Rinehart & Winston.

Gagné, R. M., W. W. Wager, K. Golas, J. Keller. (2004). *Principles of instructional design* (5th ed.). Fort Worth, TX: HBJ College Publishers.

Gallas, K. (1994). *The languages of learning: How children talk, write, dance, draw, and sing their understanding of the world.* New York: Teacher's College Press.

Gardner, H. (1983/2004). *Frames of mind: A theory of multiple intelligences.* New York: Basic Books.

___ (1991). *The unschooled mind.* New York: Basic Books.

___ (2000). *The disciplined mind.* New York: Penguin Putnam.

___ (2007). *Five minds for the future.* Boston: Harvard Business School.

Garfias, R. (2004). *Music: The cultural context.* Senri Ethnological Reports No. 47. Osaka, Japan: National Museum of Ethnology.

Gargiulo, R. M., and D. Metcalf (2013). *Teaching in today's inclusive classrooms: A universal design for learning approach* (2nd ed.). Belmont, CA: Wadsworth.

Gathercoal, F. (1993). *Judicious discipline* (3rd ed.). San Francisco, CA: Caddo Gap Press.

Geschwind, N., and A. N. Galaburda, (1988). *Cerebral dominance: The biological foundations.* Cambridge MA: Harvard University Press.

Gilbert, A. G. (1992). *Creative dance for all ages.* Reston, VA: National Dance Association.

Goetze, M. (2002). *Global voices in song: An interactive multicultural experience.* New Palestine, IN: Mj & Associates.

Goldberg, M. (2006). *Integrating the arts: An approach to teaching and learning in multicultural and multilingual settings* (3rd ed.). New York: Longman/Addison Wesley.

Goodkin, D. (1998). *A rhyme in time.* Miami, FL: Warner Bros.

___ (1999). *Name games.* Miami, FL: Warner Bros.

___ (2002). *Play, sing and dance: An introduction to Orff-Schulwerk.* London: Schott.

Goodlad, J. (1984). *A place called school.* New York: McGraw-Hill.

___ (2004). *Romances with schools: A life of education.* New York: McGraw-Hill.

Gordon, E. E. (2005a). *Primary measures of music audiation* (CD-Rom). Iowa City; Chicago: GIA.

___ (2005b). *Intermediate measures of music audiation* (CD Rom). Chicago: GIA.

___ (2012). *Learning sequences in music: Skill, content, and patterns.* Chicago: GIA.

Gordon, E. E., et al (2003). *Jump right in! The music curriculum.* Chicago: GIA.

Griffiths, M., and S. Tann (1996). Cited in K. M. Zeichner and D. P. Liston, eds., *Reflective teaching: An introduction.* Mahwah, NJ: Erlbaum.

Gromko, J. (2003). Children composing: Inviting the artful narrative. In M. Hickey, ed., *Why and how to teach music composition* (pp. 69–90). Reston, VA: Music Educators National Conference.

Guilford, J. P. (1967). *The nature of human intelligence.* New York: McGraw-Hill.

Guskey, T. R., and S. L. Gates (1986). Synthesis of research on the effects of mastery learning in elementary and secondary classrooms. *Educational Leadership*, 43(8), 73–80.

Haack, P. (1992). The acquisition of music listening skills. In D. Colwell, ed., *Handbook of research on music teaching and learning* (chapter 29). New York: Schirmer Books.

Haines, N. (1996). *Composing at the electronic keyboard.* Oxford, England: Oxford University Press.

Hall, D. (1956). *Music for children.* Mainz, Germany: B. Schott's Söhne.

Hall, M., and N. Kelsey (2005). *Teaching kids recorder.* Lincoln NB: iUniverse.

Hallahan, D. P., and J. M. Kauffman. (2000). *Exceptional learners: Introduction to special education.* Boston, MA: Allyn & Bacon.

Hamann, D. L., ed. (1992). *Creativity in the music classroom: The best of MEJ.* Reston, VA: Music Educators National Conference.

Hampton, W. (1996). *Hot marimbas!* Danbury, CT: World Music Press.

___ (1999). *Mojo marimbas.* Danbury, CT: World Music Press.

Han, K.-H., and P. S. Campbell (1992). *The lion's roar: Chinese luogu percussion ensembles.* Danbury, CT: World Music Press.

Hanson, D., E. Bernstorf, and G. M. Stuber (2004). *The music and literacy connection.* Reston, VA: Music Educators National Conference.

Hardman, M. L., C. J. Drew, and M. W. Egan (2011). *Human exceptionality: School, community, and family* (10th ed.). Belmont, CA: Wadsworth.

Hargreaves, D. J. (1986). *The developmental psychology of music.* Cambridge, England: Cambridge University Press.

Harris, R. and E. Hawksley (1989). *Composing in the classroom.* Cambridge, England: Cambridge University Press.

Harris, T. A. (1969). *I'm ok—you're ok.* New York: Harper & Row.

Hendrick, J., ed. (1997). *First steps toward teaching the Reggio way.* Upper Saddle River, NJ: Prentice Hall.

Herman, J. L., P. R. Aschbacher, and L. Winters (1992). *A practical guide to alternative assessment.* Alexandria, VA: Association for Supervision and Curriculum Development.

Heward, W., and M. Orlansky (1992). *Exceptional children.* New York: Macmillan.

Hickey, M. (1999). Assessment rubrics for music composition. *Music Educators Journal*, 85(4), 26–33.

Higgins, L., and P. S. Campbell (2010). *Free to be musical: Group improvisation in music*. Lanham MD: Rowman & Littlefield.

Holtfreter, L. (1996). *Flowing waters: The Javanese gamelan*. Danbury, CT: World Music Press.

Hooper, S., and M. J. Hannafin (1988). *Cooperative learning at the computer: Ability-based strategies for implementation*. ERIC Document Reproduction Service No. ED 295-647. New Orleans, LA: Association for Educational Communications and Technology.

Hope, S. (2000). Why study music? In C. K. Madsen, Ed., *Vision 2020*. Reston, VA: Music Educators National Conference.

Hotchkiss, G. (1990). *Music smart!* Reston, VA: Music in Motion.

Houlahan, M., and P. Tacka (2008). *Kodaly today: A cognitive approach to elementary music education*. New York: Oxford University Press.

Jacobs, H. H. (1989a). *Interdisciplinary curriculum: Design and implementation*. Alexandria, VA: Association for Supervision and Curriculum Development.

___ (1989b). Interdisciplinary options: A case for multiple configurations. *Educational Horizons*, 68(1), 25–27.

Jalongo, M. R., and L. N. Stamp (1997). *The arts in children's lives: Aesthetic education in early childhood*. Boston: Allyn & Bacon.

Jaques-Dalcroze, É. (1921). *Rhythm, music, and education*. (H. F. Rubenstein, Trans.). London: The Dalcroze Society.

Jarjisian, C. (1998). Can we get students to listen? *Music Educators Journal*, 84(6), May, 26–29.

Jarjisian, C., and J. L. Kerchner (unpublished). *Teaching music listening: Selected principles*.

Jellison, J. A., and P. J. Flowers (1991). Talking about music: Interviews with disabled and nondisabled children. *Journal of Research in Music Education*, 39(4), 322–333.

Jessup, L. (1992). *World music: A source book for teaching*. Danbury, CT: World Music Press.

Johnson, D. W., and R. T. Johnson (1987). *Learning together and alone* (2nd ed.). Englewood Cliffs, NJ: Prentice Hall.

Johnson, D. W., R. T. Johnson, E. J. Holubec, and P. Roy (1984). *Circles of learning*. Washington, DC: Association for Supervision and Curriculum Development.

Jonassen, D. H. (1991). Evaluating constructivist learning. *Educational Technology*, 36(9), 28–33.

___ (2011). *Learning to solve problems: A handbook for designing problem-solving learning environments*. New York: Routledge.

Jonassen, D. H., and S. L. Land, eds. (2000). *Theoretical foundations of learning environments*. Mahwah NJ: Erlbaum.

Joon, L. K. (2003). *A musical journey: From the Great Wall of China to the water towns of Jiangnan*. Quebec, Canada: SilkRoad Networks.

Jorgensen, E. (1997). *In search of music education*. Urbana: University of Illinois Press.

___ (2003). *Transforming music education*. Bloomington: Indiana University Press.

JVC video anthology of world music and dance. (1989). Washington, DC: Smithsonian/Folkways.

Kassner, K. (1992). *Effects of computer-assisted instruction in a mastery learning/cooperative learning setting on the playing abilities and attitudes of beginning band students*. Doctoral dissertation, University of Oregon, 1992.

___ (1996). Management systems for music teachers. *Music Educators Journal*, 82(5), 34–41.

___ (1998a). Funding music technology. *Music Educators Journal*, 84(6), 30–35.

___ (1998b). Improving your IQ—Intelligent questioning. *Music Educators Journal*, 84(5), March, 33–36.

___ (1998c). Would better questions enhance music learning? *Music Educators Journal*, 84(4), January, 29–36.

___ (2001). Cooperative learning revisited: Music learning and more. *Music Educators Journal*, 88(4), 17–23.

Katz, S. A., and J. A. Thomas (2004). *The word in play: Language, music, and movement in the classroom* (2nd ed.). Baltimore: Brookes.

Keetman, G. (1970). *Elementaria: First acquaintance with Orff-Schulwerk*. London: Schott.

___ (1974). *Elementaria: First acquaintance with Orff-Schulwerk*. (M. Murray, Trans.). London: Schott.

Keil, C., and P. S. Campbell (2017). *Born to groove*. <borntogroove.org>

Keil, C., and S. Feld (1994). *Music grooves*. Chicago: University of Chicago Press.

Kerchner, J. L. (1996). Creative music listening. *General Music Today*, 10(1), Fall, 28–30.

___ (1999). Children's verbal, visual, and kinesthetic responses: Insight into their music listening experience. *Bulletin of the Council for Research in Music Education*, 142, Fall, 84–85.

Kindsvatter, R., and M. A. Levine (1987). The myths of discipline. Reprinted in F. Linder and J. H. McMillan, eds. *Annual editions: Educational psychology 87/88* (pp. 170–174). Guilford, CT: Dushkin.

King, C. (1998). *World winds: Pan-American pipes*. Memphis, TN: Musicraft.

Kirk, S., J. Gallagher, M. R. Coleman, and N. Anastasiow (2012). *Educating exceptional children* (13th ed.). Belmont, CA: Wadsworth.

Kirton, J. J. (2003). *Adaptation and innovation in the context of diversity and change*. London: Routledge.

Kleiner, L. (1996). *Kids make music, babies make music, too*. Miami, FL: Warner Bros.

Kodály, Z. (1974). *The selected writings of Zoltán Kodály*. (F. Bonis, Ed.; L. Halapy and F. Macnicol, Trans.). London: Boosey & Hawkes.

Kohn, A. (1996). *Beyond discipline: From compliance to community*. Alexandria VA: Association for Supervision and Curriculum Development.

Kratus, J. (1985). The use of melodic and rhythmic motives in the original songs of children aged 5 to 13. *Contributions to Music Education*, 12, 1–8.

___ (1991). Growing with improvisation. *Music Educators Journal*, 78(4), 35–40.

Kuzniar, M. (1999). Finding music in art. *Teaching Music*, 7(3), 44–47.

Kwami, R. M. (1998). *African songs for school and community*. New York: Schott.

Kwon, D. (2012). *Music in Korea*. New York: Oxford University Press.

Lamme, L. L. (1990). Exploring the world of music through picture books. *The Reading Teacher*, 44(4), 294–300.

Langstaff, J., P. Swanson, and G. Emlen (1999). *Celebrate the spring: Celebrations for schools and communities*. Watertown, MA: Revels.

Lavendar, C. (1998). *Songs of the rainbow children*. Milwaukee, WI: Hal Leonard.

Lazear, D. (1991). *Seven ways of knowing*. Tucson, AZ: Zephyr.

___ (1992). *Seven ways of teaching*. Tucson, AZ: Zephyr.

Lehman, P. (1992). Curriculum and program evaluation. In R. Colwell, ed., *Handbook of research on music teaching and learning* (chapter 18). New York: Schirmer.

Levitin, D. (2006). *This is your brain on music*. New York: Dutton.

Lew, J. C.-T., and P. S. Campbell (2006). *Games children sing…Malaysia*. Van Nuys, CA: Alfred.

Lindeman, C. (2003). *Benchmarks in action: A guide to standards-based assessment*. Reston, VA: Music Educators National Conference.

Locke, D. (2004). The African ensemble in America. In T. E. Solis, ed., *Performing ethnomusicology*. Berkeley: University of California Press.

Lomax, A. (1960). *The folk songs of North America*. Garden City, NY: Doubleday.

Long, S. (1997). *Hush little baby*. New York: Scholastic.

Longden, S. H., M. Longden, and C. Derfler (2006). *Dances of the seven continents*. Evanston IL: FolkStyle Productions.

Longden, S. H., and P. S. Weikert (2003). *Cultures and styling in folk dance*. Ypsilanti, MI: High/ Scope Press.

Ma, Y., and B. McFerrin (1992). *Hush*. Sony Master-works SK 48177.

MacGregor, H. (1995). *Listening to music: Elements age 5+*. London: A & C Black.

Macmillan/McGraw (2016) *Spotlight on music*. http://www.mheducation.com/prek-12/program/music-studio-spotlight-music-2016/MKTSP-AKL01M0.html

Madsen, C. H., Jr., and C. K. Madsen (1981). *Teaching/discipline* (3rd ed.). Boston: Allyn & Bacon.

Madsen, C. K., and T. L. Kuhn (1994), *Contemporary music education* (2nd ed.). Raleigh, NC: Contemporary Publishing Company.

Maehr, M. L., P. R. Pintrich, and E. A. Linnenbrink (2002). Motivation and achievement. In R. Colwell and C. Richardson, eds., *The new handbook of research on music teaching and learning* (pp. 348–372). New York: Oxford University Press.

Mantione, R. D., and S. Smead (2003). *Weaving through words: Using the arts to teach reading comprehension strategies*. Newark, DE: International Reading Association.

Mark, M., and C. Gary (2007). *A history of American music education* (3rd ed.). Blue Ridge Summit, PA: Rowman & Littlefield Education.

Maslow, A. H. (1971). *The farther reaches of human nature*. New York: Viking Press.

McCabe, L. (2004). *How to play Autoharp*. Danvers, MA: Santorella Mel Bay.

McCarthy, B. (1987). *The 4-Mat System: Teaching to learning styles with right/left mode techniques*. Barrington, IL: EXCEL.

McDaniel, T. R. (1985). The ten commandments of motivation. Reprinted in F. Linder and J. H. McMillan, eds. (1987). *Annual editions: Educational psychology 87/88* (pp. 159–163). Guilford, CT: Dushkin.

McNicol, R. (1992). *Sound inventions: 32 creative music projects for the junior classroom*. Oxford, England: Oxford University Press.

McRae, S. W. (1991). *Directing the children's choir*. New York: Schirmer Books.

Mead, V. (1994). *Dalcroze eurhythmics in today's classroom*. New York: Schott.

MENC (1991). *Teaching General Music*. Reston, VA: Music Educators National Conference.

___ (1994). *What every young American should know and be able to do in the arts: National standards for arts education*. Reston, VA: Music Educators National Conference.

___ (1996). *Performance standards for music: Grades preK–12*. Reston, VA: Music Educators National Conference. Issues of the *Music Educators Journal* and *Teaching Music* from 1992 on include numerous articles on assessment in music.

Merriam, A. P. (1964). *The anthropology of music*. Evanston, IL: Northwestern University.

Miller, T. M., and A. Shahriari (2017). *World music: A global journey*. New York: Routledge.

Moore, R. (2009). *Music in the Hispanic Caribbean*. New York: Oxford University Press.

Molenda, M. (2007). *The guitar player book*. New York: Backbeat Books.

Murphy, J. (2008). *Music in Brazil*. New York: Oxford University Press.

Murphy, H. G., and Auréole (1999). *Dreamscape: Lullabies from around the world*. Koch 3-7433-2HI.

Music Educators Journal. Issues dedicated to special learners: April 1972; April 1982; February 1985; April 1990; January 2001.

Music Educators Journal. September 1993; January 1995; November 1996; November 1997; November 1999; July 2001.

Music in Education. (1989a). *Program components*. Buena Park, CA: Yamaha Corporation.

___ (1989b). *Scope and sequence*. Buena Park, CA: Yamaha Corporation.

Myers, I., P. Briggs, M. H. McCaulley, and R. Most (1985). *Manual: A guide to the development and use of the Myers-Briggs Type indicator*. Palo Alto, CA: Consulting Psychologists Press.

NAfME (2014) Standards for music education - http://www.nafme.org/my-classroom/standards/

Nattiez, J. J. (1990). *Music and discourse* (C. Abbate, Trans.). Princeton, NJ: Princeton University Press.

Nettl, B., C. Capwell, P. V. Bohlman, I. K. F. Wong, and T. Turino (2011). *Excursions in world music* (6th ed.). Englewood Cliffs, NJ: Prentice Hall.

Nguyen, P., and P. S. Campbell (1992). *From rice paddies and temple yards: Traditional music of Vietnam*. Danbury, CT: World Music Press.

Nimmo, D. (1997). Judicious discipline in the music classroom. *Music Educators Journal*, 83(4), 27–32.

Noad, F. M. (1994). *Solo guitar playing, Book I* (3rd ed.). New York: Schirmer Books.

Patterson, W. (2015). Classical sweets: Classical music video adventure. Available on iTunes and YouTube as well as on DVD.

Pautz, M. P. (1989). Musical thinking in the general music classroom. In E. Boardman, ed., *Dimensions of musical thinking*. Reston, VA: Music Educators National Conference.

Paynter, J. (1992). *Sound and structure*. Cambridge, England: Cambridge University Press.

Peery, J. C., I. W. Peery, and T. W. Draper, eds. (1987). *Music and child development*. New York: Springer-Verlag.

Peterson, M. (2002). *Mel Bay's complete method for Autoharp or chromaharp*. Pacific, MO: Mel Bay.

Phillips, K. (1992). *Teaching kids to sing*. New York: Wadsworth.

Piaget, J. (1952). *The psychology of intelligence* (M. Percy and D. E. Berlyne, Trans.) London: Routledge & Kegan Paul.

Piaget, J., and B. Inhelder (1969). *The psychology of the child*. New York: Basic Books.

Pouthas, V. (1996). The perception of time and temporal regulation of action. In I. Deliege and J. Sloboda, eds., *Musical beginnings, 88-112*. New York: Oxford University Press.

Quay, H. C., and D. R. Peterson. (1987). *Manual for the revised behavior problem checklist*. Coral Gables, FL: Author.

Reese, S. (2001). Tools for thinking in sound. *Music Educators Journal*, 88(1), 42–46, 53.

___ (2003). Responding to student compositions. In M. Hickey, ed., *Why and how to teach music composition* (pp. 211–232). Reston, VA: Music Educators National Conference.

Reimer, B. (2000). *Performing with understanding: The challenge of the national standards for music education*. Reston, VA: Music Educators National Conference.

Restak, R. M. (1979). *The brain: The last frontier*. Garden City, NY: Doubleday.

Rice, T. (2004). *Music in Bulgaria*. New York: Oxford University Press.

Rodriguez, C. X., and P. R. Webster (1997). Development of children's verbal interpretive responses to music listening. *Bulletin of the Council for Research in Music Education*, 134, Fall, 9–30.

Rogers, C. (1969). *Freedom to learn*. Columbus, OH: Merrill/Macmillan.

Rohner, J. M. (1994). Fundraising for fun and very large profits. *The Instrumentalist*, 49(5), December, 12–17.

Rossman, R. L. (1989). *Tips: Discipline in the music classroom*. Reston, VA: Music Educators National Conference.

Ryan, C., 2009. *Building strong music programs*. Lanham, MD: Rowman & Littlefield.

Sadler, M. E. (2007). *The eurhythmics of Jacques-Dalcroze*. New York: BiblioLife.

Sam, S. A., and P. S. Campbell (1992). *Silent temples, songful hearts: Traditional music of Cambodia*. Danbury, CT: World Music Press.

Schippers, H. (2010). *Facing the music: Shaping music education from a global perspective*. New York: Oxford University Press.

Schmid, W. (1998). *World drumming curriculum*. Milwaukee, WI: Hal Leonard.

___ (2003). *World music drumming: New ensembles and songs*. Milwaukee, WI: Hal Leonard.

___ (2012). *More world music drumming: New ensembles and songs*. Milwaukee, WI: Hal Leonard.

Schmid, W., and G. Koch (2002). *Hal Leonard guitar method beginner's pac*. Milwaukee, WI: Hal Leonard.

Schnebly-Black, J., and S. F. Moore (2003). *The rhythm inside: Connecting body, mind and spirit through music*. Van Nuys, CA: Alfred.

___ (2004). *Rhythm: One on one*. Van Nuys, CA: Alfred.

Scott, S. J. (1999). Assessing student learning across the national standards for music education. *General Music Today*, 13(1), 3–7.

Scott-Kassner, C. (1992). Research on music in early childhood. In D. Colwell, ed., *Handbook of research on music teaching and learning* (chapter 45). New York: Schirmer Books.

Seeger, A. (2002). Catching up with the rest of the world: Music education and musical experience. In B. Reimer, ed., *World music and music education: Facing the issues*. Reston, VA: Music Educators National Conference.

Seeger, R. C. (1948). *American folk songs for children*. New York: Doubleday.

Serafine, M. L. (1988). *Music as cognition*. New York: Columbia University.

Shaw, G. (2000). *Keeping Mozart in mind*. San Diego, CA: Academic Press.

Sheehy, D. (2006). *Mariachi music in America*. New York: Oxford University Press.

Shehan, P. K. (1984). Teaching music through Balkan folk dance. *Music Educators Journal*, 71(3), 44–49.

Silver Burdett. (2008). *Making music*. http://www. sbgmusic.com.

Silver Burdett. (2017). *Interactive Music Exchange*. www .pearsonschool.com/index.cfm?locator=PS1dIe.

Sims, W. L. (1986). The effect of high versus low teacher affect and passive versus active student activity during music listening on preschool children's attention, piece preference, time spent listening, and piece recognition. *Journal of Research in Music Education*, 34, 173–191.

Sims, W. L., ed. (1995). *Strategies for teaching prekindergarten music*. Reston, VA: Music Educators National Conference.

Sipes, C. (2011). *Getting in the groove: Drumming in the classroom*. Van Nuys, CA: Alfred.

Skinner, B. F. (1953). *Science and human behavior*. New York: The Free Press.

___ (1968). *The technology of teaching*. New York: Appleton-Century-Crofts.

___ (1971). *Beyond freedom and dignity*. New York: Knopf.

___ (1987). *Upon further reflection*. Englewood Cliffs, NJ: Prentice Hall.

Small, C. (1977). *Music-society-education*. New York: Schirmer Books.

___ (1998). *Musicking*. Hanover, NH: University Press of New England.

Smith, J. (1995). Using portfolio assessment in general music. *General Music Today*, 9(1), 8–12.

Solomon, J. (1998). *D.R.U.M.* Miami, FL: Warner Bros.

Sosniak, L. (1985). Three phases of learning. In B. S. Bloom, ed., *Developing talent in young people*. New York: Ballantine Books.

Stauffer, S. L., and J. Davidson, eds. (1996). *Strategies for teaching K–4 general music*. Reston, VA: Music Educators National Conference.

Steen, A. (1992). *Exploring Orff: A teacher's guide*. New York: Schott.

Stephens, T. M., and J. O. Cooper (1987). The token economy: An affirmative perspective. Reprinted in F. Linder and J. H. McMillan, eds. *Annual editions: Educational psychology 87/88* (pp. 92–94). Guilford, CT: Dushkin.

Stevens, S. (2003). Creative experiences in free play. *Music Educators Journal*, 89(5), 44–47.

Stone, R. (2005). *Music in West Africa*. New York: Oxford University Press.

Subotnick, M. (1995). *Making music*. Irvington, NY: Voyager. (CD-ROM dual platform [Macintosh and-Windows], http://www.voyagerco.com, ISBN 1-55940-662-3).

Suzuki, S. (1983). *Nurtured by love: The class approach to talent*. (W. Suzuki, Trans.). Smithtown, NY: Exposition Park Press.

Swanwick, K. (1999). *Teaching musically*. London: Routledge.

Szönyi, E. (1974–1979). *Musical reading and writing* (3 vols.). New York: Boosey & Hawkes.

Tillman, J., and K. Swanick (1989). Towards a model of development of children's musical creativity. *Canadian Music Educator*, 30(2), 169–174.

Titon, J. T., et al., eds. (2009). *Worlds of music*. Belmont, CA: Schirmer Cengage.

Toga, A. W., and J. C. Mazziotta (2002). *Brain mapping: The methods* (2nd ed.). San Diego, CA: Academic Press/Elsevier Science.

Tracey, A., and J. Uzoigwe (2003). *Ensemble: Musical arts in Africa*. Pretoria: University of South Africa.

Trehub, S. E. (2005). Foundations: Music perception in infancy. In J. W. Flohr, ed., *The musical lives of young children*. Upper Saddle River, NJ: Prentice Hall.

___ (2006). Infants as musical connoisseurs. In G. McPherson, ed., *The child as musician*. New York: Oxford University Press.

Tyler, R. W. (1949). *Basic principles of curriculum and instruction*. Chicago: University of Chicago Press.

Upitis, R. (1990). *This too is music*. Portsmouth, NH: Heinemann.

___ (1992). *Can I play you my song*? Portsmouth, NH: Heinemann.

U.S. Department of Education, *IDEA* data (2011), retrieved from https:www.ideadata.org/PartBReport.asp

U.S. Department of Education, *Digest of Education Statistics,* (2011), retrieved from http://nces.ed.gov/programs/digest/2010menu.tables.asp.

Vanaver, B. (1990). *Sheaves of grain: Songs of the seasons from around the world*. Danbury, CT: World Music Press.

Vygotsky, L. S. (1978). *Mind in society: The development of higher psychological processes*. Cambridge, MA: Harvard University.

Wade, B. C. (2014). *Thinking musically*. New York: Oxford University Press.

Warner, B. (1991). *Orff-Schulwerk: Adaptations for the classroom*. Englewood Cliffs, NJ: Prentice Hall.

Warner Brothers (2003). *Music expressions*. http://music expressions.com

Webster, P. R. (1990). Creativity as creative thinking. *Music Educators Journal*, 76(9), 22–28.

___ (2003). What do you mean, "Make my music different?" Encouraging revision and extension in children' music composition. In M. Hickey, ed., *Why and how to teach music composition* (pp. 55–65). Reston, VA: Music Educators National Conference.

Weikert, P. S. (2003). *Teaching movement and dance* (2 vols.). Ypsilanti, MI: High Scope.

Wells, R. (1998). The student's role in the assessment process. *Teaching Music*, 6(2), October, 32–33.

Wiggins, J. (1990). *Composition in the classroom: A tool for teaching*. Reston, VA: Music Educators National Conference.

___ (1994). Children's strategies for solving compositional problems with peers. *Journal of Research in Music Education*, 42(3), 232–252.

___ (2003). A frame for understanding children's compositional processes. In M. Hickey, Ed., *Why and how to teach music composition* (pp. 141–165). Reston, VA: Music Educators National Conference.

Winner, E. (1991). *Arts propel: An introductory handbook*. Cambridge, MA: Harvard Project Zero and Educational Testing Service.

Winner, E., L. Davidson, and L. Scripp, eds. (1992). *Arts propel: A handbook for music*. Boston: Harvard Project Zero and Educational Testing Service. Find current work of the Arts in Education Program at Harvard online at http://www.gse.harvard. edu/~aie-web or on Harvard Project Zero at http://www.pz.harvard.edu.

Winters, G., and J. Northfield (1992). *Starter composing packet*. Essex, England: Longman Group.

Witkin, H. (1977). Field dependent and field independent cognitive styles and their educational implications. *Review of Educational Research*, 47, 1–64.

Wood, K. E. (1997) *Interdisciplinary instruction: A practical guide for elementary and middle school teachers*. Upper Saddle-River, NJ: Merrill Prentice-Hall.

Woods, D.G. and E. E. Gordon (1985). *Jump right in*. Chicago: GIA.

Zemach, M. (1976). *Hush, little baby*. New York: E. P. Dutton.

Zentner, M., and T. Eerola (2010). Rhythmic engagement with music in infancy. *Proceedings of the National Academy of Sciences*, 10, 1073.

Organizations

The Dalcroze Society of America.

Education through Music. Richards Institute of Music Education and Research.

Institut Jaques-Dalcroze. www.dalcroze.ch/

Organization of American Kodály Educators. <www.oake.org/conferences/>

International Kodály Society.

American Orff-Schulwerk Association.

Gordon Institute for Music Learning <www.giml.org/gordon.php>

INDEX

A

Academic learning, setting up classroom to nurture, 299–304
Accompaniment
  barred instruments of Orff approach and, 223
  for singing child, 88
Accurate singing, 81–86
  pitch and, 81–82, 84–85
Action songs
  "Johnny Works with One Hammer," 137
  movement and, 130–131
  music-and-movement experiences, 136–139
  "Pleeng Chaang," 138–139
  "Rig-a-jig-jig," 137–138
  "Suogan," 136
  "Teddy Bear," 137
Active listening
  enactive listening, 251
  to form, 249
  involvement in, 242–257
  to pitch, 247–248
  to rhythm, 247
  to style, 250
  to texture and dynamics, 248
  to tone color, 246–247
Activities
  arts as, 374–375
  harmony, 123
  "Music in Use," 252
  phrase, 120–121
  pitch, 123–124
  rhythmicking, 43
  scale, 120–121
  sequence, 120–121
  texture, 123
  tonality, 120–121
Adapting instruction for various needs. *See also specific needs*
  composition, 271–272
  integrated curriculum, 362
  listening, 243
  management, 297
  motivation, 297
  movement, 159

  pitch, 116
  playing child, 232–233
  rhythm, 196
  teaching, 98
ADHD. *See* Attention deficit hyperactivity disorder
Adolescence, child vocal development, 75
Aesthetic enjoyment, 6
Aesthetic principles in arts, 362
Age
  child vocal development and, 73–75
  harmony and texture activities, 123
  melodic development and, 113
  movement development, 131
  music experiences for two-, three-, and four-year-olds, 432–433
  pitch discrimination and contour activities, 115
  pitch register, motion, and interval size activities, 118
  rhythmic development and, 167
  tonality, phrase, scale, and sequence activities, 120–121
AGMs. *See* Attention-Getting Mechanisms
"Ah, Poor Bird," 100
  pitch set, 85
"Alabama Gal," 5
"Ala De'Iona," 390
"All Around the Kitchen," 182–183
"Alle Meine Entchen," 119
"All Round the Brickyard," 184
APD. *See* Auditory Processing Disorder
Appadurai, Arjun, 23
Artistically rich classroom, vignettes of, 356–358
Arts
  as activities, 374–375
  aesthetic principles in, 362
  forms and resources, 373
  language and, 376–377
  process, integrating, 371–372
  resources, 361, 373
  in science and math, 375–376
  in social studies, 372
Arts curriculum. *See also* Curriculum
  creative drama in shared, 367–368
  creative movement in shared, 363–364

  dance in shared, 363–364
  interdisciplinary, 362–363
  literature in shared, 366–367
  poetry in shared, 366–367
  shared, 363–368
  theater in shared, 367–368
  visual arts in shared, 364–366
Arts integration. *See also* Integrated curriculum
  arts as activities *versus*, 374–375
  challenges of, 359–360
  invitation to, 358–359
Assessment
  of children, teacher, 343–348
  creating child, 282–283
  distilling essence of, 353–354
  listening, 258–261
  moving, 159–161
  peer, 348–349
  pitch, 124–125
  playing child, 234–235
  prekindergarten music program, 432
  rhythm, 204
  scenario, 354
  singing child, 107–108
  student self-assessment, 348
  teacher self-assessment, 349–350
  technology links for, 354
Attention, 306
Attention deficit hyperactivity disorder (ADHD)
  music classroom and children with, 416–417
  teaching strategies to assist students with, 418
Attention-Getting Mechanisms (AGMs), 298
Attitudes
  curriculum and, 321
  listening and music, 241–242
Audiation, 61
Auditions, children's choir, 106–107
Auditory impairments
  motivation and management instruction adapted to, 297
  music classroom and children with, 420–422
  pitch instruction for, 116
Auditory Processing Disorder (APD), 116
Aural approach, to present song, 95–96

449

Aural learning, 42. *See also* Listening
Aural-oral transmission process, 392–394
Aural perception, building skills in, 245–246
Aural plans, composition, 274–275
Aural repertoire, listening and building, 253
Ausubel, David, 20
Autism spectrum disorders
    composition instruction adapted to, 272
    instruction for, 98
    movement instruction adapted to, 159
    music classroom and children with, 419–420
    rhythm instruction adapted to, 196
Autoharp, 228–229
"Autumn's Here," 101

B

"Bambu," 225
Bandura, Albert, 19, 26
Barbe, Walter, 20, 30–31
Barred instruments of Orff approach
    accompaniment techniques on, 223
    "Bambu," 225
    glockenspiels, accompaniment
        techniques on, 223
    melodic ranges of, 222
    melody bells, 224
    metallophones, accompaniment
        techniques on, 223
    pitched instruments, 221
    recorder, 226–228
    tone bells, 224
    xylophones, accompaniment techniques on, 223
Bateson, Gregory, 19, 21–22
Beat. *See* Pulse
Beethoven, Ludwig van, 255–256
Behavior, student
    behavior contracts and, 308–310
    behavior expectation forms, 308, 309
    Discipline with Love and Logic, 308
    in educational environment, 295
    enneagrams and, 295
    establishing expectations and procedures,
        305–306
    inappropriate, 304–311
    intervention thermometer, 310–311
    Judicious Discipline and, 307
    logical consequences of, 298
    managing, 294–298
    teacher assessment and overt/covert, 344–345
    transactional analysis and, 295–296
Behavioral disorders, music classroom and
        children with, 418–419
Behavioral needs
    composition instruction adapted to, 271–272
    instruction for, 98
    listening instruction adapted to, 243
    motivation and management instruction
        adapted to, 297
    movement instruction adapted to, 159

playing child instruction adapted to, 233
    rhythm instruction adapted to, 196
Behavior contracts, 308–310
Behavior expectation forms, 308, 309
Behaviorism: operant conditioning, 292–294
Behaviors, covert/overt, 344–345
Bells
    cowbell, 219
    double iron agogo, 219
    jingle, 218
    melody, 224
    tone, 224
Bennett, Peggy, 64
"Berceuse," from Firebird Suite (Stravinsky), 244
Bill of Rights of United States Constitution, 307
"Billy Boy," 192
"Bluebird," 74, 88
Body as percussion instrument, 211–212
    experiences in, 212–214
Bongo drums, 217
"Bounce High," 180
"Bow, Wow, Wow," 142
Breath control, vocal exercises for, 78–80
Breathing
    exercises, 78
    for singing, 77–78
Briggs, Peter B., 20, 34
Bronfenbrenner, Uri, 22–23
Bruner, Jerome, 19, 21
    instructional theories, 20
"Bucket of Water," 200
    pitch set, 85

C

Chants
    melodic direction, 83
    rhythmic, 169–170
    rhythmic duration through name, 169
"Charlie Over the Ocean," 32–33
"Charlie's Neat," 191
Chevé system of rhythmic mnemonics, 53
Child-centered curriculum, 38–39
Child development, 209–210
    age and developmental activity in vocal, 73–74
    creativity and, 265
    developmental sequence of playing child,
        209–210
    movement and, 130–132
    Piaget's theories on, 18–20
    of playing child, 209–210
    rhythm and, 166–168
Children
    at risk, 407
    in changing society, 12–13
    creating, 264–286
    exceptional, music for, 404–429
    joys of reaching all, 427
    learning theories, 17–18

listening, 239–263
listening skills, 9
movement and, 128–164
multiple meanings of music for, 2–16
music, and cultural diversity, 381–403
musical capabilities, 8–10
musical future of, 13–14
musical learning to engage, 3–5
music experiences for two-, three-,
    and four-year-olds, 432–433
pitch and, 111–127
play and, 208–238
response to music, 9
rhythm and, 165–207
singing, 71–110
teacher assessment of, 343–348
teaching music to, 17–46
thinking musically, 125
Children's choirs, 105–107
    auditions, 106–107
    rehearsals, 107
Child vocal development, 72–75
    adolescence and, 75
    age and, 73–75
    developmental activity, 73
    males and, 75
    methodological suggestions for early
        childhood and, 76
    tessitura and, 74–75
Child voice, physical training for, 76–78
Classroom
    exploring popular music in, 332
    organizing, and record keeping, 300–301
    setting up, to nurture positive social and aca-
        demic learning, 299–304
    vignettes of artistically rich, 356–358
Claves, 216
CL groups. *See* Cooperative Learning groups
CMP. *See* Contemporary Music Project
Cognitive development, 18–20
"Come, Let's Dance," 101
    pitch set, 85
Common elements approach to music, 61
Communication, 6
Competition (as motivator), 294
Composition
    adapting instruction for various
        needs, 271–272
    aural plans, 274–275
    creative processes and, 271–281
    group, 273–274
    independent, format for, 280–281
    individualized plan, 280
    inventing songs, 277–280
    motivations for, 272
    notational systems, 275–277
    structure and context of, 274
    teacher's roles in, 271–272

Comprehensive Musicianship, 47
    common elements approach to music and, 61
    music learning and, 60–61
    Orff approach and, 57
Concepts, 112
    curriculum and, 321
    pitch, 119–121
Concerts for the community, 353
Conducting meter, 176–177
Conga drum, 217
Constructivist theory, 19, 24–25
Contemporary Music Project (CMP), 60–61
Contours
    melody, 81
    pitch and awareness of, 113–115
Contribution to continuity and stability of culture, 6
Contribution to integration of society, 6
The Cool "OO" (vocal exercise), 79
Cooperative Learning (CL) groups, 299–300
Counter-melody, 100
Covert behaviors, 344–345
Cowbell, 219
Creating
    accomplishing multiple music standards
        through, 281–282
    polyrhythms, 202–203
    valid connections in integrated curriculum,
        370–378
Creating child, 264–286
    accomplishing multiple music standards
        through, 281–282
    assessment, 282–283
    creative processes and, 266–282
    developmental sequence, 265
    formative evaluations of, 282–283
    rewards of nurturing creativity in
        music and, 283
    scenario, 284–285
    summative evaluations of, 283
    technology for teaching and learning, 284
Creative drama, in shared arts
    curriculum, 367–368
Creative movement, 132, 149–152
    experiences in, 150–152
    inspiring, 150
    in shared arts curriculum, 363–364
Creative processes
    composition and, 271–281
    exploration and discovery, 266–267
    improvisation and, 268–270
Creative production, development of, 266
Creative thinking, 265
Creativity
    importance of, 264
    in music, rewards of nurturing, 283
Cultural diversity
    aural-oral transmission process, 392–394
    curricular redesign, 394–401
    definitions, 382–385

early childhood and, methodological
    suggestions for, 386
ethnomusicology, 384
many musical worlds, 401
multicultural (term), 382
multiethnic (term), 382–384
music, children and, 381–403
scenario, 402–403
seven sequential lessons on Chinese
    musical culture for fourth-grade
    children, 396–398
technology for teaching and learning, 402
world music education, directions
    in, 399–401
Culture
    contribution to continuity and stability of, 6
    musical, 53, 103
Curricular redesign, cultural diversity and, 394–401
Curriculum
    attitudes and, 321
    child-centered, 38–39
    concepts and, 321
    content, general, 319–322
    design, 315–339
    distilling essence of, 337
    early childhood planning, 322
    elements, 320–321
    evaluation of, 341
    formal, 317
    guidelines, for prekindergarten music
        program, 431–432
    immersed, 370
    implementing, 325–335
    instructional, 317
    interdisciplinary, in arts, 362–363
    K-6 planning, 322–325
    lesson planning, 326–333
    levels of outcome and, 319–320
    music in, 7–8
    music's historical role in, 10–12
    national standards, 317
    nature of, 316
    other arts integrated into music, 360–368
    planning, 319–325
    program vignettes, 315
    relationships between levels of outcome and
        skills development, 320
    repertoire and, 321–322
    scenario, 337–338
    shared arts, 363–368
    sources of, 317–319
    state and local standards, 318
    technology for teaching and learning, 337
    thematic and unit planning, 333–336
    threaded, 369–370
    types of, 317–319
Curriculum Connections, 334
Curwen, John, 81
Cymbals, 218

D

Jacques-Dalcroze, Émile, 48
Dalcroze approach, 48–49
    eurhythmics and, 50, 145–149, 173–174
    "Galloping Horses" and, 51–52
    improvisation and, 50–51
    musical experience inspired by, 51–52
    rhythmic movement and, 173
    sampling, 50–52
    solfège and, 50
    "Trotting Horses" and, 51–52
Dance, 153–159
    folk, 153–158
    movement development and, 132
    in shared arts curriculum, 363–364
"Dance Josey," 188–189
"Dance the Kolo," 155
Deep-listening, 250–251
    to world's musical expressions, 393–394
Descant, 100
Developmental disabilities, music classroom and
    children with, 412–414
Developmental sequence of playing child, 209–210
Disabilities
    developmental, 412–414
    intellectual, 362, 412–414
    learning, 414–415
    physical, 422–425
Discipline
    Discipline with Love and Logic, 308
    Judicious Discipline, 307
    myths, 305
    punishment and, 293–294
Discipline with Love and Logic, 308
Discovery, creative processes and, 266–267
Discrimination learning, 61–62
Diversity. See Cultural diversity
Djembe drum, 218
"Doctor Foster," 173
Double iron agogo bells, 219
Dreikurs, Rudolph, 298
Drive reduction theory, 292
Drums. See Skins (drums)
Duncan, Arne, 7
Dunn, Kenneth, 20, 31
Dunn, Rita, 20, 31
Durations, 61
    rhythm, 169, 178–193
Dynamics, 248

E

Early childhood, methodological suggestions for
    child vocal development and, 76
    cultural diversity and, 386
    curriculum planning and, 322
    eurhythmics, 149
    playing instruments, 214

Early childhood, methodological (*Continued*)
  rhythm and, 178
  teacher as transmitter and, 40
  teaching methods and, 60
Early childhood settings, listening in, 243–245
The Echo (vocal exercise), 80
Education
  of exceptional children, 407–408
  MIE, 63–64
  music at curricular core of, 7–8
  world music, 383–384, 399–401
Education environment
  music classroom, 37–38
  personal traits in, 295
  student behavior in, 295
Education through Music (ETM), 64–65
ELL. *See* English Language Learners
Ellis, Catherine, 19, 21–22
Emotional disorders, music classroom and
    children with, 418–419
Emotional expression, 6
Enactive listening, 251
Enforcement of conformity to social norms, 6
Engaged listening, 251
English Language Learners (ELL), 425–426
Enneagrams, 295
Entertainment, 6
Environment
  education, 37–38, 295
  music classroom, 37–38
Ericsson, Anders, 19
Ethnomusicology, 384
ETM. *See* Education through Music
Eurhythmics, 48, 50, 173–174
  Dalcroze, 145–149
  methodological suggestions for early
    childhood, 149
  movement development and, 132
  sample experiences in, 146–147
  sample piano pieces and, 148
Evaluation, 340–342
  of curriculum, 341
  distilling essence of, 353–354
  formative, 341–342
  scenario, 354
  summative, 341–342
  teacher, 342
  technology links for, 354
Exceptional children
  ADHD, 416–417
  autism spectrum disorders, 419–420
  behavioral disorders, 418–419
  children at risk, 407
  developmental disabilities, 412–414
  educating, 407–408
  ELL, 425–426
  emotional disorders, 418–419
  gifted, 426–427

IEP in music and, 409–411
inclusion and music classroom, 408–409
inclusion in music instruction, 411
intellectual disabilities, 412–414
learning disabilities, 414–415
music classroom and, 411–427
music classroom management
    procedures for, 417
music for, 404–429
People First Language, 406–407
physical disabilities, 422–425
public laws, 406
scenario, 428
sensory disorders, 420–422
talented, 426–427
technology links for teaching and learning, 428
who are, 405–407
Expectations, establishing, 305–306
  behavior expectation forms and, 308, 309
Exploration
  creative processes, 266–267
  Orff approach and, 58
Exploratory movement with/without music, 135
Expression
  emotional, 6
  world's musical, deep-listening to, 393–394
External motivation, 290–291
External motivators, 302–304
  Special Person, 303
  Token prizes as, 302
Extinction, 293

F
Fay, Jim, 308
Feld, Steven, 10
"Feng Yang," 397–398
  pitch set, 85
Field dependence, 31–34
Finger cymbals, 218
Folk dances, 153
  "Dance the Kolo," 155
  "Gerakina," 158
  "La Raspa," 156–157
  "Sakura," 156
  "Schottische," 157–158
  "Skip to My Lou," 155
  teaching, 154
  "Tinikling," 157
Folk music, Kodály and, 53
Form
  active listening to, 249
  musical form: rondo, 171–172
Formative evaluations, 341–342. *See also*
    Evaluation
  creating child, 282–283
  listening, 258–259
  moving, 160–161
  playing child, 234

rhythm, 204
singing child, 107–108
4-Mat Model of lesson planning, 329–331
Four-year-olds, music experiences for, 432–433
Frequency, 61
Freud, Sigmund, 23
Funk, David, 308

G
Gagné, Robert, 20
  "events of instruction," 35–36
"Galloping Horses," 51–52
Gardner, Howard, 20, 29–30
Gathercoal, 307
"Gerakina," 158
  pitch set, 85
Gifted children
  composition instruction adapted to, 272
  instruction for, 98
  music classroom and, 426–427
Global music, 11
Glockenspiels, accompaniment techniques on, 223
Glover, Sarah, 81
Goblet drum, 218
"Going on the Bus," 54–55
Gong, 218–219
Goodland, John, 7
Gordon, Edwin, 20, 35, 61
  Music Learning Theory, 61–62
  rhythm mnemonics and, 194
The Gordon Institute for Music Learning, 62
Gourds, 215
Grade level song I instructional
    strategies, 42–43
Grade level song 2 instructional strategies, 43
Grades K-4 music program, 433–435
Grades K-6 curriculum planning, 322–325
Grades 5-8 music program, 435–437
Guiro, 217
Guitar, 229–231
  strums, 231
  tuning, 230–231
Guntherschule, 56
"Guru Ndiani," 142

H
"Haere, Haere," 388–389
The Ha-Ha (vocal exercise), 78–79
Hall, G. Stanley, 19, 23
Hand drum, 217
Harmonic development, 122
Harmony activities, 123
Harmony instruments
  autoharp, 228–229
  guitar, 229–231
  keyboards, 231–232
Harris, Thomas A., 295
"Hashewie," 390–391

"Hava Nashira," 102
  pitch set, 85
Hearing, inner, 52–55
Hearing impairments, music classroom
    and children with, 420–422
"Hey, Betty Martin," 86, 181
  pitch set, 85
"Hey, Ho, Nobody Home," 100
Hierarchy of musical skill-building, 61–62
"Hill an' Gully Rider," 89
Hope, Samuel, 7
"Hop Old Squirrel," 90
"How Many Miles to Babylon?", 142–143
"Hush Little Baby," 259–260

I
IDEA. See Individuals with Disabilities
    Education Act
IEP. See Individualized Education Plan
"I Got a Letter This Morning," 184
  pitch set, 85
Imitation, Orff approach and, 58
Immersed approach to lesson planning, 331–334
Immersed curriculum, 370
Improvisation
  creative processes and, 268–270
  Dalcroze approach and, 49, 50–51
  Kodály approach and, 270
  Orff approach and, 57, 58
  starts, 269
Inappropriate behavior, 304–311
  behavior contracts and, 308–310
  behavior expectation forms, 308, 309
  Discipline with Love and Logic, 308
  establishing expectations and procedures,
    305–306
  intervention thermometer, 310–311
  Judicious Discipline and, 307
Individual conferences, 353
Individualized Education Plan (IEP),
    353, 409–411
Individuals with Disabilities Education
    Act (IDEA), 406
Infants, music experiences for, 432. See also
    Children
Informed teaching, 44
Inner hearing, 52–55
  sampling Kodály approach and, 54
Instructional strategies, 41–44
  choice activity, 43
  in full-fledged lesson, 42–43
  grade level song 1, 42–43
  grade level song 2, 43
  rhythmicking activity, 43
Instructional theories, 20
Instruction theories, music, 34–35
  child-centered curriculum, 38–39
  in classroom environment, 37–38
  components of, 18

constructivist theory, 19, 24–25
  instructional strategies, 41–44
  learning style theories, 20, 29–34
  musical play and socialization theories, 19, 23–24
  neuroscience and musical learning,
    19, 28–29
  relating theory to practice, 36–44
  social learning theories, 19, 26–28
  social systems and scapes, 19, 22–23
  stage and phase, 18–22
  teacher as transmitter, 39–40
Instrumental study, benefits of, 235
Instruments. See also specific instruments
  barred instruments of Orff approach, 221–228
  harmony, 228–232
  nonpitched percussion, 215–220
  percussion, 211–212, 215–220
  pitched, 221
  playing, developmental sequence for, 210–211
Integrated curriculum
  accomplishing multiple music standards,
    377–378
  adapting instruction for various needs, 362
  assessing, 378
  challenges of arts integration and, 359–360
  creating valid connections, 370–378
  immersed curriculum, 370
  invitation to arts integration and, 358–359
  models of integration, 368–370
  music in, 356–380
  other arts in, 360–368
  reflections on, 378
  scenario, 379
  shared arts, 363–368
  technology links for, 379
  thematic web design, 368–369
  threaded curriculum, 369–370
Integration
  arts, 358–360, 374–375
  models of, 368–370
  of society, 6
Intellectual disabilities
  characteristics, 413–414
  integrated curriculum adapted for, 362
  music classroom and children with, 412–414
Intensity, 61
Interdisciplinary curriculum in arts, 362–363
Interference learning, 62
Intervention thermometer, 310–311
Inventing songs, 277–280
"I Went to California," 93
  pitch set, 85

J
Jazz, 270
Jingle bells, 218
"Johnny Works with One Hammer," 137
Jonassen, David, 19, 24

Jorgensen, Estelle, 8
"Jubilee!", 327
Judicious Discipline, 307
"Just from the Kitchen," 90

K
"Kaeru No Uta," 101
  pitch set, 85
Keetman, Gunild, 56
Keil, Charles, 10
Keyboards, 231–232
"Knick-Knack Paddy Whack," 181
  pitch set, 85
Kodály, Zoltán, 52
  folk music and, 53
  rhythmic movement and, 174
  Richards and, 64–65
Kodály approach, 52–55
  improvisation and, 270
  musical experience inspired by, 54–55
  rhythmic notation, 197
  rhythmic patterns and, 178–179
  rhythm mnemonics, 194
  sampling, 54
  for singing, 83
  solfège, 53
Kodály-Curwen hand signs, 81–82
"Kookaburra," 96–98
  pitch set, 85
  rhythmic patterns, 187
"Kye Kye Kule," 200
  pitch set, 85

L
"Lak Gei Moli," 396
  pitch set, 85
Language, 169
  arts and, 376–377
  ELL in music classroom, 425–426
  People First Language, 406–407
"Leak Kanseng," 141, 400–401
Learning
  aural, 42
  CL groups, 299–300
  creating child, 284
  cultural diversity, 402
  curriculum, 337
  dimensions of, 21–22
  discrimination, 61–62
  exceptional children, 428
  interference, 62
  listening, 261
  modalities, 31
  motivation and management, 312
  movement, 125
  musical, 3–5, 19, 28–29
  music playing, 236

Learning (*Continued*)
    personality factors and, 34
    personality factors informing, 34
    phases of, 21
    pitch, 125
    rhythm, 204
    setting up classroom to nurture social and academic, 299–304
    students' names, 301
    style theories, 20, 29–34
    style tips, 329
    theories, 17–18
Learning disabilities
    auditory, 415
    characteristics of, 415
    music classroom and children with, 414–415
    tactile, 415
    teaching strategies, 415
    visual, 415
Learning sequence, rhythm, 168
"Leila," 187
Lesson planning, 326–333
    application of, 327–328
    4-Mat Model of, 329–331
    immersed approach, 331–334
    problem-solving approach, 328–329
    quadrant approach, 329–331
    Three-Legged Model of, 326
Lessons
    instructional strategies in full-fledged, 42–43
    seven sequential lessons on Chinese musical culture for fourth-grade children, 396–398
"Let Us Chase the Squirrel," 90
Levels of outcome
    curriculum and, 319–320
    music elements and, 319
    skills development and, 320
Levitin, Daniel, 19
Linear pitch structures, 112–113
Listening, 9
    accomplishing multiple music standards through, 203, 257
    active, to form, 249
    active, to pitch, 247–248
    active, to rhythm, 247
    active, to style, 250
    active, to texture and dynamics, 248
    active, to tone color, 246–247
    active involvement in, 242–257
    adapting instruction for various needs, 243
    assessment, 258–261
    attentive, 250–251
    building an aural repertoire and, 253
    centrality of, 239–240
    child, 239–263
    deep-, 250–251, 393–394
    in early childhood settings, 243–245
    enactive, 251

    engaged, 251
    experiences, student construction of, 251–253
    formative evaluations of, 258–259
    growth in, 240–242
    "Hush Little Baby," 259–260
    keys to, 261
    music attitudes and, 241–242
    perceptive, development of, 240
    principles in teaching music, 242–243
    resources, 253
    scenario, 262
    sequence, 254
    summative evaluations of, 261
    technology for teaching and learning, 261
Listening Map, 246
Listening skills
    aural perception and, 245–246
    children, 9
Literature in shared arts curriculum, 366–367
"Little David," 91
"Little Johnny Brown," 185–186
"Little Sally Walker," 74, 181
"Liza Jane," 186
Logical consequences of behavior, 298
"London Bridge Is Falling Down," 140
    pitch set, 85
"Long-Legged Sailor," 94
"Looby Loo," 89
"Loop de Loo," 92
Loudness, common elements approach to music and, 61
Love and Logic, Discipline with, 308

M

Madsen, Clifford K., 28
Major modes, 120
Males, child vocal development and, 75
Management
    adapting instruction for various needs, 297
    of exceptional children in music classroom, 417
    guidelines for student, 302
    of inappropriate behavior, 304–311
    learning, 312
    mobility impairments, 297
    scenario, 312–313
    setting up classroom to nurture positive social and academic learning, 299–304
    student behavior, 294–298
    teacher and, 288–314
    teaching, 312
    technology for teaching and learning, 312
"Las Mañanitas," 190
    pitch set, 85
Manhattanville Music Curriculum Project (MMCP), 35, 62–63
    types of experiences, 63
Many Kinds of Fun, 292–293
Maslow's Hierarchy of Human Needs, 292

Mason, Lowell, 10–11
"Mbube," 105
McCarthy, Bernice, 329–330
Measurement, 342–343
Melodic development, 112–113
Melodic direction chants, 83
Melodic motion, pitch and, 117–119
Melodic ranges of barred instruments, 222
Melodic sequence, 120
Melody, 111
    contours, 81
    pitch-related aspects of, 112
Melody bells, 224
MENC. *See* Music Educators National Conference Now called NAfME
Metallophones, accompaniment techniques on, 223
Metals (nonpitched percussion instruments)
    cowbell, 219
    cymbals, 218
    djembe drum, 218
    double iron agogo bells, 219
    finger cymbals, 218
    goblet drum, 218
    gong, 218–219
    jingle bells, 218
    tambourine, 218
    timpani, 218
    triangle, 218
Meter
    conducting, 176–177
    rhythm and, 175–176
    sensing and understanding, 176–177
Methodological suggestions for early childhood. *See* Early childhood, methodological suggestions for
"Michael Finnigan," 188
MIDI. *See* Musical Instrument Digital Interface
MIE. *See* Music in education
"Mighty Pretty Motion," 182
Minor modes, 120
"Minuet in G" (Beethoven), 255–256
MIOSW. *See* Music in Our Schools Week
MMCP. *See* Manhattanville Music Curriculum Project
The "Mmmmm" on the Vowels (vocal exercise), 80
Mobility impairments
    composition instruction adapted to, 272
    instruction for, 98
    motivation and management instruction adapted to, 297
    movement instruction adapted to, 159
    pitch instruction for, 116
    playing child instruction adapted to, 233
    rhythm instruction adapted to, 196
Modes, 120
"Mos'! Mos'!", 399
Motivation
    adapting instruction for various needs, 297
    autotelic experience of, 290

behaviorism: operant conditioning and, 292–294
competition as motivator, 294
for composition, 272
drive reduction theory of, 292
external, 290–291
external motivators, 302–304
factors of, 291
guidelines for student, 302
internal, 290
intrinsic, 290
learning, 312
Many Kinds of Fun, 292–293
Maslow's Hierarchy of Human Needs and, 292
scenario, 312–313
setting up classroom to nurture positive social and academic learning, 299–304
sources of, 290–291
teacher and, 288–314
teaching, 312
technology for teaching and learning, 312
Motivational tool
Special Person as, 303
Token prizes as, 302
"Mountain Climbing," 193
"Mouse, Mousie," 327
Movement
action songs and, 130–131
adapting instruction for various needs, 159
child development and, 130–132
children and, 128–164
children's natural, 129
creative, 132, 149–152
Dalcroze eurhythmics, 145–149
dance and, 132, 153–159
eurhythmics, 132
exploratory, with/without music, 135
for musical development, 161
music-and-movement experiences, 134–144
physical disabilities and adapting for, 423
precepts and principles of, 133–134
responses, 129
rhythm in, 172–174
scenario, 162–164
sequence, 65
singing games and, 130–131
technology for teaching and learning, 162
Movement development
age and, 131
dance and, 132
Moving
accomplishing multiple music standards through, 160
assessment, 159–161
formative evaluation of, 160–161
summative evaluation of, 161
Multicultural (term), 382
Multiethnic (term), 382–384
Music

children's response to, 9
creativity in, rewards of nurturing, 283
and cultural diversity, 381–403
at curricular core, 7–8
in curriculum, 7–8, 10–12
ETM, 64–65
for exceptional children, 404–429
exploratory movement with/without, 135
functions of, 3–7
IEP in, 409–411
in integrated curriculum, 356–380
listening, principles in teaching, 242–243
listening and attitudes towards, 242–243
National standards for, 129
reading and writing, 198
Topics Within Music, 335
transmission, 13
Musical capabilities, children's, 8–10
Musical culture, 53, 103
Musical development, movement for, 161
Musical form: rondo, 171–172
Musical Instrument Digital Interface (MIDI), 208
The Musical Lives of Young Children (MENC), 322
Musically competent teacher, 386–388
"Music Alone Shall Live," 102
pitch set, 85
Musical play
child-centered curriculum and, 38–39
theory, 19, 23–24
Musical styles, uncertainties in teaching new, 385–386
Musical theories, 17
Musical thinking, 125
Musical traditions, 103
Musical training
formal, 10
in schools, 10–11, 14–15
summer courses, 68
teacher, 67–68
Music-and-movement experiences
action songs, 136–139
arranging for, 134
prelude to, 135–139
preparation for, 134
singing games, 136–144
Music appreciation, 11
Music classroom. See also Classroom
environment, 37–38
exceptional child inclusion in, 408–409
exceptional children and, 411–427
exceptional children and management procedures in, 417
Music Educators National Conference (MENC), 317
The Musical Lives of Young Children, 322
Strategies for Teaching Prekindergarten Music, 322
What Every Young American Should Know and Be Able to Do in the Arts: Standards for Arts Education, 7, 363

Music elements, levels of outcome and, 319
Music experiences
for infants and toddlers, 432
for two-, three-, and four-year-olds, 432–433
Music for children
in changing society, 12–13
multiple meanings of, 2–16
singing and, 71–110
teaching, 17–46
Music in education (MIE), 63–64
Music in Our Schools Week (MIOSW), 352
Music instruction, exceptional children and inclusion in, 411
Music instruction theories, 34–35
child-centered curriculum, 38–39
in classroom environment, 37–38
components of, 18
constructivist theory, 19, 24–25
instructional strategies, 41–44
learning style theories, 20, 29–34
musical play and socialization theories, 19, 23–24
neuroscience and musical learning, 19, 28–29
relating theory to practice, 36–44
social learning theories, 19, 26–28
social systems and scapes, 19, 22–23
stage and phase, 18–22
teacher as transmitter, 39–40
"Music in Use" activities, 252
"Musicking," 8
Music learning. See also Learning
to engage children, 3–5
Music Learning Theory, 61–62
neuroscience and, 19, 28–29
Music learning, approaches to
Comprehensive Musicianship as, 60–61
ETM and, 64–65
MIE and, 63–64
MMCP, 62–63
Music Learning Theory, 61–62
Weikert's Movement Sequence, 65
Music Learning Theory, 61–62
Music literacy, 52–55
Orff approach and, 58
sampling Kodály approach and, 54
Music program, school
grades K-4, 433–435
grades 5-8, 435–437
prekindergarten, 431–433
Music standards, accomplishing multiple
through creating, 281–282
through integrated curriculum, 377–378
through listening, 203, 257
through movement, 160
through playing, 233
through singing, 106
Myers, Isabel, 20, 34

N

National Association for Music Educators (NAfME), 317
National Association of Schools and Music, 7
National standards
    use in curriculum development, 317
    for music, 129
National Standard Web for Planning Unit of Study, 332–333
Negative reinforcement, 293
Neuroscience and musical learning, 19, 28–29
The "No-ah's Ark" (vocal exercise), 79
"The Noble Duke of York," 144
Nonpitched percussion instruments, 215–220
    bongo drums, 217
    claves, 216
    conga drum, 217
    cymbals, 218
    djembe drum, 218
    experiences with, 219–220
    finger cymbals, 218
    goblet drum, 218
    gong, 218–219
    gourds, 215
    guiro, 217
    hand drum, 217
    jingle bells, 218
    metals, 218–219
    sandblocks, 216
    skins (drums), 217–218
    slit log drum, 216–217
    sticks, 216
    tambourine, 218
    temple blocks, 216
    timpani, 218
    triangle, 218
    woodblock, 216
    woods, 216–217
Notation
    for reading, 96, 196–199
    rhythmic, 197
    for writing, 196–199
Notational systems, composition, 275–277
Note approach
    example of, 96–98
    to present song, 96

O

"Oh, How Lovely Is the Evening," 192
    pitch set, 85
"Old Joe Clarke," 183–184
    pitch set, 85
"Old John the Rabbit," 114
"Old Texas," 99
Omnichord, 229
Operant conditioning, 292–294
    drive reduction theory of, 292
    Many Kinds of Fun, 292–293

Maslow's Hierarchy of Human Needs, 292
Oral approach to present song, 95–96
Orff, Carl, 56
Orff approach
    barred instruments of, 221–228
    Comprehensive Musicianship and, 57
    exploration and, 58
    imitation and, 58
    improvisation and, 57, 58
    incorporating, 58
    literacy and, 58
    musical experience inspired by, 59–60
    "A Pocket of Miracles and, 59–60
    process, 57–58
    rhythmic movement and, 173
    rhythm in speech and, 168–169
    rhythm mnemonics, 194
Orff-Schulwerk approach, 56
Overt behaviors, 344–345

P

"Paddling Song," 374
Parents, reporting to, 352–353
Parent/teacher conferences, 353
Parent Teacher Student Association (PTSA), 352
Pedagogies, new repertoire for familiar, 388–392
Peer assessment, 348–349
People First Language, 406–407
Percept, 112
Percussion instruments
    body as, 211–212
    nonpitched, 215–220
Perfect singing posture (PSP), 76–77
Personality factors, learning informed by, 34
Personal traits in educational environment, 295
Pestalozzi, Heinrich, 10
Phrase, 81
    activities, 120–121
Physical disabilities
    adapting for movement, 423
    adapting instruments and materials, 424–425
    music classroom and children with, 422–425
Physical response, 6
Physical training for child voice, 76–78
Piaget, Jean, 18–20
Piano, 88
Pitch
    active listening to, 247–248
    activities, 123–124
    adapting instruction for various needs, 116
    advanced concepts of, 119–121
    assessment, 124–125
    children and, 111–127
    common elements approach to music and, 61
    contour awareness, 113–115
    Dalcroze approach and, 49
    discrimination, 113–115
    interval size, 118

melodic motion and, 117–119
    register, 118
    relations, 117–119
    scenario, 126
    singing accuracy and, 81–82, 84–85
    technology for teaching and learning, 125
Pitched instruments, 221. See also Nonpitched percussion instruments
Pitch-matching
    exercises, 86
    sampling, 82
Pitch patterns, songful sequence of, 84–85
Pitch-related aspects of melody, 112
Pitch structures
    growth in understanding linear, 112–113
    growth in understanding vertical, 122–124
Play, musical
    child-centered curriculum and, 38–39
    theory, 19, 23–24
Playing child, 208–238
    accomplishing multiple music standards through, 233
    adapting instruction for various needs, 232–233
    assessment of, 234–235
    barred instruments of Orff approach, 221–228
    developmental sequence, 209–210
    formative evaluations of, 234
    harmony instruments, 227–232
    instrumental study and, benefits of, 235
    methodological suggestions for early childhood and, 214
    nonpitched percussion instruments, 215–220
    pitched instruments, 221
    scenario, 236–237
    summative evaluations of, 235
    technology for teaching and learning, 236
Playing instruments, developmental sequence for, 210–211
"Pleeng Chaang," 138–139
"A Pocket of Miracles," Orff approach and, 59–60
Poetry in shared arts curriculum, 366–367
Polyrhythms
    accomplishing multiple music standards through listening, 203
    creating, 202–203
    eight-count, 201–202
    four-part, 202
Popular music in classroom, guidelines for exploring, 332
Portfolios tracking student growth, 351–352
Positive reinforcement, 293
Prekindergarten music program
    assessment, 432
    curriculum guidelines, 431–432
    music experiences for infants and toddlers, 432
    music experiences for two-, three-, and four-year-olds, 432–433
Presenting song
    aural approach to, 95–96

note approach to, 96
oral approach to, 95–96
rote approach to, 95–96
Problem-solving approach to lesson planning, 328–329
Procedures, establishing, 305–306
PSP. *See* Perfect singing posture
Psychomotor skills, 130
PTSA. *See* Parent Teacher Student Association
Pulse
establishing sensitivity to, 174
rhythm and, 174
"Punchinella," 141
pitch set, 85
Punishment, 293–294

Q

Quadrant approach to lesson planning, 329–331
"¿Quien es ese pajarito?", 190

R

"Rain, Rain, Go Away," 74, 180
Range, voice
in children, 74
extending, 86
"La Raspa," 156–157
pitch set, 85
Reading music, 198
Reading notation, 96
for rhythm, 196–199
Recorder, 226–228
Record keeping
organizing classroom and, 300–301
tracking student growth and, 350–351
Rehearsal, 42
children's choir, 107
Reinforcement
negative, 293
positive, 293
theories, 19, 26–28
Religious rituals, validation of, 6
Repertoire
aural, listening and building, 253
curriculum and, 321–322
for pedagogies, 388–392
Repetition, 42
Report cards, 353
Reporting to parents, 352–353
Resources
arts, 361, 373
listening, 253
Restak, Richard, 19
Rhythm
active listening to, 247
adapting instruction for various needs, 196
child and, 165–207
child development and, 166–168

common elements approach to music and, 61
durations, 169, 178–193
formative assessment, 204
full phrase of, 171
half phrase of, 170–171
learning sequence, 168
meter and, 175–176
methodological suggestions for early childhood and, 178
in movement, 172–174
musical form: rondo, 171–172
from natural rhythm to rhythmic training, 203–204
notation for writing and reading, 196–199
Orff approach and, 168–169
polyrhythms, 201–203
pulse in, 174
rhythmic chants: animals, 170
rhythmic chants: colors, 169
rhythmic chants: fruits, 170
rhythmic duration through name chants, 169
scenario, 205–206
in speech, 168–169
summative assessment, 204
syncopations, 199–200
technology for teaching and learning, 204
two layers of, 173
Rhythmic chants
animals, 170
colors, 169
fruits, 170
Rhythmicking activity, 43
Rhythmic patterns, 178–193
"All Around the Kitchen," 182–183
"All Round the Brickyard," 184
"Billy Boy," 192
"Bounce High," 180
"Charlie's Neat," 191
"Dance Josey," 188–189
"Hey, Betty Martin," 181
"I Got a Letter This Morning," 184
"Knick-Knack Paddy Whack," 181
Kodály approach and, 178–179
"Kookaburra," 187
"Leila," 187
"Little Johnny Brown," 185–186
"Little Sally Walker," 181
"Liza Jane," 186
"Las Mañanitas," 190
"Michael Finnigan," 188
"Mighty Pretty Motion," 182
"Mountain Climbing," 193
"Oh, How Lovely Is the Evening," 192
"Old Joe Clarke," 183–184
"¿Quien es ese pajarito?", 190
"Rain, Rain, Go Away," 180
"A la Rueda de San Miguel," 189
sequence of, 179–180

"The Ship's Carpenteer," 193
"Singabahambayo," 187
"Sing Together," 191–192
"Skip to My Lou," 189
"Tideo," 189
"Tinga Layo," 182
"Weevily Wheat," 184–185
"Zum Gali Gali," 189
Rhythmic training, 203–204
Rhythm mnemonics, 193–195
Chevé system of, 53
Gordon and, 194
Kodály approach, 194
Orff approach, 194
Richards, Mary Helen, 64–65
"Rig-a-jig-jig," 137–138
pitch set, 85
"Ring around the Rosy," 140
"Rise Up, O Flame," 103
pitch set, 85
"Rocky Mountain," 90
Rondo (musical form), 171–172
Rote approach
example of, 96–98
to present song, 95–96
Rubrics, teacher assessment of children and, 346–348
"A la Rueda de San Miguel," 189

S

"Sakura," 156
"San Antonio," 256–257
Sandblocks, 216
"Sansa Kroma," 200
pitch set, 85
"San Serení," 143–144
pitch set, 85
"Savalivalah," 104–105
Scale
activities, 120–121
pitch and, 119
School
musical training in, 10–11, 14–15
music at curricular core of, 7–8
School music program, 431–437
grades K-4, 433–435
grades 5-8, 435–437
prekindergarten, 431–433
"Schottische," 157–158
Science and math, arts in, 375–376
"Scotland's Burning," 101
Self-assessment
student, 348
teacher, 349–350
Sensory disorders
hearing impairments, 420–422
music classroom and children with, 420–422
vision impaired, 422

Sensory needs
    listening instruction adapted to, 243
    movement instruction adapted to, 159
    playing child instruction adapted to, 232–233
    rhythm instruction adapted to, 196
Sequence
    activities, 120–121
    developmental, of playing child, 209–210
    learning, rhythm, 168
    listening, 254
    melodic, 120
    movement, 65
    pitch patterns and songful, 84–85
    of rhythmic patterns, 179–180
    rhythm learning, 168
    Weikert's Movement Sequence, 65
Shaw, Gordon, 19
"The Ship's Carpenteer," 193
"Shortnin' Bread," 91–92
"Singabahambayo," 187
Singing
    accurate, 81–86
    breathing for, 77–78
    Kodály approach to, 83
    music for children and, 71–110
    in parts, teaching, 99–105
    PSP, 76–77
Singing child, 71–110
    accompaniment for, 88
    accomplishing multiple music standards
        through, 106
    accurate, 81–86
    assessment of, 107–108
    breathing and, 77–78
    children's choirs, 105–106
    child vocal development and, 72–75
    formative evaluation of, 107–108
    physical training for child voice and, 76–78
    reasons to sing, 108
    recordings and, 88
    sampling of songs, 88–94
    scenario, 109–110
    summative evaluation of, 108
    teacher and, 87
    vocal model, 87–88
Singing games
    "Bow, Wow, Wow," 142
    "Guru Ndiani," 142
    "How Many Miles to Babylon?", 142–143
    "Leak Kanseng," 141
    "London Bridge Is Falling Down," 140
    movement and, 130–131
    music-and-movement experiences, 136–144
    "The Noble Duke of York," 144
    "Punchinella," 141
    "Ring around the Rosy," 140
    "San Serení," 143–144
"Sing Together," 191–192

Skill-building
    aural perception, 245–246
    hierarchy of musical, 61–62
Skills development, levels of outcome and, 320
Skinner, B. F., 19, 27
Skins (drums)
    bongo drums, 217
    conga drum, 217
    djembe drum, 218
    goblet drum, 218
    hand drum, 217
    slit log drum, 216–217
"Skip to My Lou," 155
    rhythmic patterns, 189
"Skye Boat Song," 103–104
Slit log drum, 216–217
Social institutions, validation of, 6
Socialization theories, 19, 23–24
Social learning, setting up classroom to nurture,
    299–304
Social learning theories, 19, 26–28
    applications of, to music instruction, 27
Social norms, enforcement of conformity to, 6
Social studies, arts in, 372
Social systems and scapes, 19, 22–23
Society
    contribution to integration of, 6
    music for children is changing, 12–13
Socratic method, 149
Solfège
    Dalcroze approach, 50
    Kodály approach, 53
Songs
    action, 136–137
    "Ah, Poor Bird," 100
    "Alabama Gal," 5
    "Ala De'lona," 390
    "All Around the Kitchen," 182–183
    "Alle Meine Entchen," 119
    "All Round the Brickyard," 184
    approaches for presenting, 95–96
    "Autumn's Here," 101
    "Bambu," 225
    "Berceuse," 244
    "Billy Boy," 192
    "Bluebird," 74, 88
    "Bounce High," 180
    "Bow, Wow, Wow," 142
    "Bucket of Water," 200
    "Charlie over the Ocean," 32–33
    "Charlie's Neat," 191
    "Come, Let's Dance," 101
    "Dance Josey," 188–189
    "Dance the Kolo," 155
    "Doctro Foster," 173
    "Feng Yang," 397–398
    "Galloping Horses," 51–52
    "Gerakina," 158

    "Going on the Bus," 54–55
    grade level song 1 instructional strategies, 42–43
    grade level song 2 instructional strategies, 43
    "Guru Ndiani," 142
    "Haere, Haere," 388–389
    "Hashewie," 390–391
    "Hava Nashira," 102
    "Hey, Betty Martin," 86, 181
    "Hey, Ho, Nobody Home," 100
    "Hill an' Gully Rider," 89
    "Hop Old Squirrel," 90
    "How Many Miles to Babylon?", 142–143
    "Hush Little Baby," 259–260
    "I Got a Letter This Morning," 184
    inventing, 277–280
    "I Went to California," 93
    "Johnny Works with One Hammer," 137
    "Jubilee!", 327
    "Just from the Kitchen," 90
    "Kaeru No Uta," 101
    "Knick-Knack Paddy Whack," 181
    "Kookaburra," 96–98, 187
    "Kye Kye Kule," 200
    "Lak Gei Moli," 396
    "Leak Kanseng," 141, 400–401
    "Leila," 187
    "Let Us Chase the Squirrel," 90
    "Little David," 91
    "Little Johnny Brown," 185–186
    "Little Sally Walker," 74, 181
    "Liza Jane," 186
    "London Bridge Is Falling Down," 140
    "Long-Legged Sailor," 94
    "Looby Loo," 89
    "Loop de Loo," 92
    "Las Mañanitas," 190
    "Mbube," 105
    "Michael Finnigan," 188
    "Mighty Pretty Motion," 182
    "Minuet in G," 255–256
    "Mos,' Mos'!", 399
    "Mountain Climbing," 193
    "Mouse, Mousie," 327
    "Music Alone Shall Live," 102
    "The Noble Duke of York," 144
    "Oh, How Lovely Is the Evening," 192
    "Old Joe Clarke," 183–184
    "Old John the Rabbit," 114
    "Old Texas," 99
    "Paddling Song," 374
    "Pleeng Chaang," 138–139
    "A Pocket of Miracles," 59–60
    "Punchinella," 141
    "¿Quien es ese pajarito?", 190
    "Rain, Rain, Go Away," 74, 180
    "La Raspa," 156–157
    "Rig-a-jig-jig," 137–138
    "Ring around the Rosy," 140

"Rise Up, O Flame," 103
"Rocky Mountain," 90
"A la Rueda de San Miguel," 189
"Sakura," 156
"San Antonio," 256–257
"Sansa Kroma," 200
"San Serení," 143–144
"Savalivalah," 104–105
"Schottische," 157–158
"Scotland's Burning," 101
selecting and teaching, 94–99
"The Ship's Carpenteer," 193
"Shortnin' Bread," 91–92
"Singabahambayo," 187
"Sing Together," 191–192
"Skip to My Lou," 155, 189
"Skye Boat Song," 103–104
"Sorida," 399
starting, 86
"Suogan," 136
teaching, 94–99
"Teddy Bear," 137
"This Train," 92–93
"Tideo," 189
"Tinga Layo," 86, 182
"Tinikling," 157
"Trotting Horses," 51–52
"Uncle Jessie," 389
"Vista," 88
"Viva la Musica," 102
"Weevily Wheat," 184–185
"What Do You Hear?", 258
"With Laughter and Singing," 4
"World music education," 383–384
"Yo Mamana, Yo!", 104
"Yuyake," 400
"Zum Gali Gali," 189
"Sorida," 399
Sosniak, Lauren, 19, 21
Sound sources, 268
Special Person, motivational tool, 303
Speech, rhythm in, 168–169
    full phrase of rhythm, 171
    half phrase of rhythm, 170–171
    musical form: rondo, 171–172
    rhythmic chants: animals, 170
    rhythmic chants: colors, 169
    rhythmic chants: fruits, 170
    rhythmic duration through name chants, 169
Stage and phase theories, 18–22
Stage-dependent theory, 18
Sticks, 216
Strategies for Teaching Prekindergarten Music
    (MENC), 322
Stravinsky, Igor, 244
Student behavior
    behavior contracts and, 308–310
    behavior expectation forms, 308, 309

Discipline with Love and Logic, 308
in educational environment, 295
enneagrams and, 295
establishing expectations and procedures,
    305–306
inappropriate, 304–311
intervention thermometer, 310–311
Judicious Discipline and, 307
logical consequences of, 298
managing, 294–298
teacher assessment and overt/covert, 344–345
transactional analysis and, 295–296
Student contracts, 353
Student growth
    portfolios and, 351–352
    record keeping and, 350–351
    reporting to parents, 352–353
    tracking, 350–352
Student projects, 353
Student self-assessment, 348
Students' names, learning and remembering, 301
Styles
    active listening to, 250
    musical, uncertainties in teaching new, 385–386
    tips, learning, 329
Style theories, learning, 20, 29–40
Summative evaluations, 341–342. See also Evaluation
    creating child, 283
    listening, 261
    moving, 161
    playing child, 235
    rhythm, 204
    singing child, 108
"Suogan," 136
Suzuki approach, 210
Swassing, Raymond, 20, 30–31
Symbolic representation, 6
Syncopations
    "Bucket of Water," 200
    experiences, 199–200
    "Kye Kye Kule," 200
    "Sansa Kroma," 200

T

Talented children, music classroom and, 426–427.
    See also Gifted children
Tambourine, 218
Taxonomy, 112
Teacher assessment of children, 343–348
    overt and covert behavior, 344–345
    questioning and, 345–346
    rubrics and, 346–348
Teachers and teaching
    adapting instruction for various needs, 98
    ADHD and strategies for, 418
    children with learning disabilities, 415
    composition and roles of, 271–272
    creating child, 284

cultural diversity, 402
curriculum, 337
evaluation, 342
exceptional children, 428
folk dance, 154
harmonic development and, 122
informed, 44
instructional strategies, 41–44
listening, 261
melodic development and, 112–113
methods, 47–70
motivation and management, 288–314, 312
movement, 162
musically competent, 386–388
music playing, 236
new musical styles, uncertainties in, 385–386
personal teaching methods of, 66–68
pitch, 125
rhythm, 204
scenario, 45–46
self-assessment, 349–350
singing child and, 87
singing in parts, 99–105
songs, 94–99
technology, 44
training, 67–68
as transmitter, 39–40
Teaching methods, 47–70
    comparison of, 66
    Comprehensive Musicianship, 60–61
    Dalcroze approach, 48–49
    ETM, 64–65
    Kodály approach, 52–55
    methodological suggestions for early childhood
        and, 60
    MIE, 63–64
    MMCP, 62–63
    Music Learning Theory, 61–62
    Orff approach, 56–60
    other approaches to music learning, 60–66
    personal, 66–68
    scenario, 68–69
    Weikert's movement sequence, 65
Technology for teaching and learning, 44
    creating child, 284
    cultural diversity, 402
    curriculum, 337
    exceptional children, 428
    listening, 261
    management, 312
    motivation, 312
    movement, 162
    pitch, 125
    playing child, 236
    rhythm, 204
Technology links
    for assessment/evaluation, 354
    for integrated curriculum, 379

"Teddy Bear," 137
Temple blocks, 216
Tempo, 85
Tessitura, children's voices and, 74–75
Testing, 342–343
Texture
    active listening to, 248
    activities, 123
Theater in shared arts curriculum, 367–368
Thematic planning, 333–336
Thematic web design, integrated curriculum, 368–369
Theories. *See also* Music instruction theories
    instructional, 20
    learning, 17–18
    learning style, 20, 29–34
    musical, 17
    musical play, 19, 23–24
    Music Learning Theory, 61–62
    reinforcement, 19, 26–28
    socialization, 19, 23–24
    social learning, 19, 26–28
    stage and phase, 18–22
    stage-dependent, 18
"This Train," 92–93
Thorndike, Robert, 19
Threaded curriculum, 369–370
Three-Legged Model of lesson planning, 326
Three-year-olds, music experiences for, 432–433
"Tideo," 189
Timpani, 218
"Tinga Layo," 86, 182
    pitch set, 85
"Tinikling," 157
Toddlers, music experiences for, 432. *See also* Children
Token prizes, motivational tool, 302
Tonality activities, 120–121
Tonal memory, 83
Tone bells, 224
Tone color, active listening to, 246–247

Topics Within Music, 335
Tracking student growth, 350–352
Training
    musical, 10–11, 14–15, 67–68
    physical, for child voice, 76–78
    rhythmic, 203–204
    teacher, 67–68
Transactional analysis, 295–296
Triangle, 218
"Trotting Horses," Dalcroze-inspired musical experience and, 51–52
TST, 41–42
Two-year olds, music experiences for, 432–433

U
"Uncle Jessie," 389
Unit planning, 333–336
    connecting music with other arts, 335–336

V
Validation of social institutions and religious rituals, 6
Vertical pitch structures, 122–124
Vision impairments, music classroom and children with, 422–423
"Vista," 88
Visual arts in shared arts curriculum, 364–366
"Viva la Musica," 102
    pitch set, 85
Vocal development, child, 72–75
    adolescence and, 75
    age and, 73–75
    developmental activity, 73
    males and, 75
    methodological suggestions for early childhood and, 76
    tessitura and, 74–75
Vocal exercises
    for breath control, 78–80
    The Cool "OO," 79
    The Echo, 80

The Ha-Ha, 78–79
The "Mmmmm" on the Vowels, 80
The "No-ah's Ark," 79
Vocal model, 87–88
Vygotsky, Lev, 19, 24

W
"Weevily Wheat," 184–185
Weikert, Phyllis, 65
"What Do You Hear?", 258
What Every Young American Should Know and Be Able to Do in the Arts: Standards for Arts Education (MENC), 7, 363
"With Laughter and Singing," 4
    pitch set, 85
Witkin, Harold, 20, 31
Woodblock, 216
Woods (nonpitched percussion instruments), 216–217
    claves, 216
    sandblocks, 216
    sticks, 216
    temple blocks, 216
    woodblock, 216
World music education, 383–384
    directions in, 399–401
World's musical expressions, deep-listening to, 393–394
Writing music, 198

X
Xylophones, accompaniment techniques on, 223

Y
Yamaha Corporation, 63–64
"Yo Mamana, Yo!", 104
"Yuyake," 400

Z
"Zum Gali Gali," 189

Music in Childhood

FROM PRESCHOOL THROUGH THE ELEMENTARY GRADES • Enhanced Fourth Edition

by Patricia Shehan Campbell and Carol Scott-Kassner

SONG	CITED ON BOOK PAGE	SONG	CITED ON BOOK PAGE	SONG	CITED ON BOOK PAGE
A la Rueda de San Miguel	189	Just from the Kitchen	90	Rain, Rain, Go Away	180
Ah, Poor Bird	100	Kaeru No Uta	101	Rig-a-Jig-Jig	137
Ala De'lona	390	Knick-Knack Paddy Whack	181	Ring around the Rosy	140
Alabama Gal	5	Kookaburra	96, 187	Rise Up O Flame	103
All Around the Kitchen	182	Kye Kye Kule	200	Rocky Mountain	90
All Round the Brickyard	183	La Raspa	156	Sakura	156
Alle Meine Entchen	119	Lak Gei Moli	396	San Serení	143
Autumn's Here	101	Las Mañanitas	190	Sansa Kroma	200
Bambu	225	Leak Kanseng	141, 400	Savalivalah	104
Billy Boy	192	Leila	186	Schottische	157
Bluebird	88	Let Us Chase the Squirrel	90	Scotland's Burning	101
Bounce High	180	Little David	91	Shortnin' Bread	91
Bow, Wow, Wow	142	Little Johnny Brown	185	Sing Together	191
Bucket of Water	200	Little Sally Walker	181	Singabahambayo	186
Charlie over the Ocean	32	Liza Jane	186	Skip to My Lou	155, 189
Charlie's Neat	191	London Bridge Is Falling Down	140	Skye Boat Song	103
Come, Let's Dance	101	Long-Legged Sailor	94	Sorida	399
Dance Josey	188	Looby Loo	89	Suogan	136
Dance the Kolo	155	Loop de Loo	92	Teddy Bear	137
Feng Yang	397	Mbube	105	The Noble Duke of York	144
Gerakina	158	Michael Finnigan	187	The Ship's Carpenteer	193
Guru Ndiani	142	Mighty Pretty Motion	182	This Train	92
Haere Haere	388	Mos'!, Mos'!	399	Tideo	188
Hashewie	390	Mountain Climbing	193	Tinga Layo	182
Hava Nashira	102	Mouse, Mousie	327	Tinikling	157
Hey, Betty Martin	181	Music Alone Shall Live	102	Uncle Jessie	389
Hey, Ho, Nobody Home	100	Oh, How Lovely Is the Evening	192	Vista	88
Hill an' Gully Rider	89	Old Joe Clarke	183	Viva la Musica	102
Hop Old Squirrel	90	Old John the Rabbit	114	Weevily Wheat	184
How Many Miles to Babylon?	142	Old Texas	99	With Laughter and Singing	4
I Got a Letter This Morning	184	Paddling Song	374	Yo Mamana, Yo!	104
I Went to California	93	Pleeng Chaang	138	Yuyake	400
Johnny Works with One Hammer	137	Punchinella	141	Zum Gali Gali	189
Jubilee!	327	¿Quien es ese pajarito?	190		